Modern Intelligent Techniques for Image Processing

Uzair Aslam Bhatti
Hainan University, China

Muhammad Aamir
Huanggang Normal University, China

Yonis Gulzar
King Faisal University, Saudi Arabia

Sibghat Ullah Bazai
Balochistan University of Information Technology, Pakistan

IGI Global Scientific Publishing
Publishing Tomorrow's Research Today

Vice President of Editorial	Melissa Wagner
Managing Editor of Acquisitions	Mikaela Felty
Managing Editor of Book Development	Jocelynn Hessler
Production Manager	Mike Brehm
Cover Design	Phillip Shickler

Published in the United States of America by
IGI Global Scientific Publishing
701 East Chocolate Avenue
Hershey, PA, 17033, USA
Tel: 717-533-8845
Fax: 717-533-7115
Website: https://www.igi-global.com E-mail: cust@igi-global.com

Library of Congress Cataloging-in-Publication Data

Names: Bhatti, Uzair Aslam, 1986- editor
Title: Modern intelligent techniques for image processing / edited by Uzair Bhatti, Muhammad Aamir, Yonis Gulzar, Sibghat Ullah Bazai.
Description: Hershey, PA : IGI Global Scientific Publishing, 2025. | Includes bibliographical references and index. | Summary: "The primary objective of this book is to bridge the gap between theoretical research and practical applications of modern intelligent techniques in image processing. By exploring both foundational concepts and state-of-the-art methodologies, this book aims to equip readers with the knowledge and tools necessary to innovate in this dynamic field"-- Provided by publisher.
Identifiers: LCCN 2024057007 (print) | LCCN 2024057008 (ebook) | ISBN 9798369390450 hardcover | ISBN 9798369390467 paperback | ISBN 9798369390474 ebook
Subjects: LCSH: Image processing | Intelligent agents (Computer software)
Classification: LCC TA1637 .M626 2025 (print) | LCC TA1637 (ebook)
LC record available at https://lccn.loc.gov/2024057007
LC ebook record available at https://lccn.loc.gov/2024057008

British Cataloguing in Publication Data
A Cataloguing in Publication record for this book is available from the British Library.

Table of Contents

Detailed Table of Contents

This chapter examines how deep learning techniques have transformed predictive image analysis and forecasting, enhancing accuracy and precision in fields such as meteorology, healthcare, and environmental science. We investigated the key principles and advanced methods driving these applications, detailing architectures and algorithms that support predictive modeling, including convolutional neural networks (CNNs), generative adversarial networks(GANs), and recurrent neural networks (RNNs). The chapter demonstrates the transformative effects of deep learning through case studies on weather forecasting, medical imaging for disease progression, and climate modeling. Additionally, it examines the challenges and limitations of existing techniques, providing insights into potential future advancements and new approaches in predictive image analysis.

This chapter explores deep learning techniques for image clustering and classification, crucial tasks in computer vision. It discusses unsupervised clustering methods and supervised classification approaches, including traditional methods like k-means and hierarchical clustering. The chapter also highlights the transformative impact of CNNs, ensemble methods, and transfer learning in classification. It uses case studies like fruit classification in agriculture and brain tumor clustering in medical imaging to illustrate the real-world applicability of these models. Challenges like data limitations, computational requirements, and explainability are also discussed. Future trends include self-supervised learning and multimodal models. The chapter aims to guide researchers and practitioners in leveraging deep learning for effective image clustering and classification across various domains.

This chapter explores the integration of deep learning techniques in image segmentation, emphasizing state-of-the-art architectures, such as FCN, U-Net, and Vision Transformers, that enable precise and efficient segmentation for a range of applications. It discusses the significance of data annotation in training deep learning models, highlighting methods like active learning, semi-supervised learning, and automated annotation. The chapter also addresses key challenges, including limited labeled data, model size constraints, and performance on edge devices. Additionally, it covers the diverse use cases of image segmentation across fields like medical imaging, agriculture, and civil. Finally, the chapter outlines emerging trends in the field, including self-supervised learning, federated learning, and the development of lightweight models for real-time applications, offering insights into the future potential and impact of deep learning in image segmentation.

Medical image segmentation is a cornerstone in diagnostics, enabling precise visualisation and analysis of anatomical structures and pathological entities across modalities like CT, MRI, and ultrasound. Traditional segmentation methods, including manual processes and basic automated techniques, face challenges like time inefficiency, variability, and limited adaptability to image complexity. Deep learning (DL) techniques, particularly Convolutional Neural Networks (CNNs), U-Nets, and (GANs), have revolutionized this domain, offering superior accuracy and reliability. U-Nets excel in tasks requiring intricate segmentation, while GANs enhance training with synthetic data generation. Despite these advancements, challenges such as data bias, model explainability, and computational demands hinder clinical integration. This study evaluates the performance of advanced DL models on segmentation tasks like tumor identification and organ delineation, emphasizing their potential to improve diagnostic accuracy, reduce workload, and standardize healthcare practices.

The most cutting-edge machine learning and deep learning techniques in the healthcare industry are presented by the Digital Revolution of AI, with an emphasis on explainable artificial intelligence (XAI). This chapter examines how XAI may advance the medical field to increase end users' confidence. It covers the most cutting-edge and new ideas and uses of XAI, making it a intellectual resource for scholars and practitioners interested in this developing field and provides a comprehensive explanation of AI in precision medicine, including all aspects. The importance of Explainable AI (XAI) in the healthcare industry is the main topic of discussion. Also offers real-world case studies and examples to offer useful insights into the use of AI in precision medicine.

Sugarcane, vital to industries such as food, biofuels, and pharmaceuticals, is threatened by diseases like red rot, rust, yellowing, and mosaic, which require significant resources for detection and monitoring. This book chapter presents an innovative solution using DenseNet-121, a convolutional neural network to identification and classification of these leaf diseases. The study utilized a plant village dataset of 9,050 leaf images, including healthy and diseased samples, which were carefully organized and pre-processed to ensure uniformity. The enhanced DenseNet-121 model, trained on this dataset, demonstrated outstanding performance, with a precision of 0.96, recall of 0.977, F1-score of 0.98, and accuracy of 0.963. While effective, challenges like resource needs may limit implementation in constrained environments, yet it marks progress toward agricultural sustainability and food security.

The chapter gives an overview of the applications of deep learning and image processing in the different industries of medicine, automobiles, entertainment, and security. Multiple advanced techniques such as CNN, GAN, and ViT that have become handy in the analysis of image processing. From medical diagnostics to autonomous vehicles, environmental monitoring, and surveillance, its applications show the impact of deep learning on accuracy and efficiency. It also discusses critical ethical issues, such as data privacy, model biases, and energy consumption, and points out some possible solutions to reduce those effects. In general, this contribution provides a critical overview of advances related to image processing by deep learning and its potential for further innovative developments in a wide range of applications.

Muhammad Akram, Balochistan University of Information Technology, Engineering, and Management Sciences, Pakistan
Sibghat Ullah Bazai, Balochistan University of Information Technology, Engineering, and Management Sciences, Pakistan
Samina Samina, National University of Sciences and Technology, Pakistan
Wajid Hassan Moosa, Balochistan University of Information Technology, Engineering, and Management Sciences, Pakistan

The chapter is a review of techniques in deep leaning for tasks such as classification and clustering. Basically, due to the discussion of the two main topics in deep learning, the chapter is divided into two parts, one discussing the clustering methods such as first a basic understanding of clustering method is made then moving towards autoencoder based architectures that includes variational autoencoders (VAE), k-means with autoencoders, then self-organizing maps, spectral clustering and DBSCAN. The other part of the chapter is focused on classification methods, where the architecture of a convolutional neural network (CNN) is discussed, proceeding to ResNet, DenseNet and EfficientNet, a little touch of transformer-based CNN is discussed, a part of these vision transformers and capsule networks are mentioned. A comparison of both the methods, i.e., clustering and classification is discussed, that will make it clearer that how both these methods are different from one another.

T. Aarthi, KGiSL Institute of Technology, India
P. Dhamayanthi, KGiSL Institute of Technology, India
S. Indhumathi, KGiSL Institute of Technology, India
A. Sakthivel, KGiSL Institute of Technology, India

The classification of medical data is the most difficult problem to solve among all research problems since it has more commercial significance in the context of health analytics. Several researchers have looked into using Artificial Intelligence (AI) for lung disease classification. This paper proposed a novel classification algorithm for diagnosis of various lung diseases. Already known existing algorithms have some drawback in noise removal and classification process. In this approach, better noise removal technique is used to remove the unwanted noises in the input lung image. Hybridization of Artificial Neural Network with Ant Colony Optimization based classification algorithm is used to predict the lung disease in more accurate and obtain the better efficiency. The suggested HANNACO algorithm was evaluated qualitatively and obtained 95.30% classification accuracy, 93.72% with the minimum classification time duration of 18 ms over the current approaches such as Decision Tree, SVM, and KNN.

The integration of intelligent image processing techniques into clinical and medical imaging techniques introduced a new horizon for improvement in the area of medical imaging and diagnostics. Such efforts have critically enhanced accuracy, efficiency, and the capacity to identify diseases early enough and provide treatments to patients. This chapter examines the innovation brought about by advancing capabilities within ML and AI that is seeking to alter the present face of the medical imaging industry by augmenting capture, processing, and interpretation of imagery using various modalities such as MRI, CT, and X-ray scans. Some of these models are based on deep learning, which includes things like transformers, Generative Adversarial Networks (GANs), and even Convolutional Neural Networks (CNNs). Such models can allow for an unprecedented ability to be involved in tasks that may include segmenting tissues, organs, and lesions while automatically detecting abnormalities and even accurately predicting disease course.

Biometric technologies are widely used in security, mobile banking, surveillance, business, education, and digital health for identity verification. Methods such as fingerprint scanning, iris recognition, and facial recognition have become standard for authentication. Advances in artificial intelligence (AI) have improved online biometrics, enabling more efficient and accurate systems, especially on smartphones. This chapter discusses recent biometric research integrating AI, machine learning (ML), and deep learning (DL). A novel approach using the FVC2002 dataset, a benchmark for fingerprint recognition, is proposed. It generates 360-degree rotational views from the dataset's 880 images, aiming to improve accuracy and user experience in online applications.

This chapter explores the transformative role of Machine Learning (ML), Deep Learning (DL), and Image Processing (IP) in modern dentistry, focusing on their impact on diagnostics, treatment planning, and patient outcomes. Advanced ML algorithms enable precise disease detection, while DL techniques enhance imaging accuracy, facilitating early diagnosis and personalized care. Image processing supports 3D modeling for prosthetics and orthodontics, streamlining dental workflows. The survey evaluates state-of-the-art methods, their integration into clinical practice, and associated challenges, including data privacy, model interpretability, and real-time application. Insights into emerging trends and future directions emphasize these technologies' potential to revolutionize patient-centered dental care.

Image segmentation is an important topic in computer vision, playing important role in wide range of applications such as medical image analysis, scene understanding, tumour boundary extraction among many others. Image segmentation aims to identify groups of pixels and parts of images that are similar and belong together Semantic segmentation is a classification of pixels with labels and partitioning the objects. By applying segmentation, we can identify all objects in an image. The brain tumour dataset we are utilizing for segmentation is BRATS'20, which contains 317 images. The proposed ensemble approach combining U-Net variants and Mask RCNN models outperforms the individual models. While the ensemble method yielded improved Dice scores, using the union of the six other methods achieved the highest segmentation accuracy, as indicated by superior Dice scores. Specifically, the ensemble model achieved a Dice score of 71.10 and an IoU of 81.98. Additionally, the ensemble model demonstrated strong performance in terms of precision, reaching 84.96, and a recall value of 81.90.

This chapter examines how transformative deep learning is revolutionizing image processing and analysis, especially in the context of complex imaging tasks. Even with major improvements, accuracy and efficiency issues are still common. To address these challenges, we discussed different methods that integrate different deep learning architectures, such as convolutional neural networks (CNNs), RCNN and their variants, with sophisticated data preprocessing approaches. A thorough analysis of model architectures demonstrates the significant advantages deep learning provides over conventional techniques, improving diagnostic precision and effectiveness while facilitating individualized care in a variety of fields, including remote sensing, self-driving vehicles, and medical imaging. In the chapter, we critically review the literature, represent a major step forward in the applications of deep learning for advanced image analysis and processing, demonstrating its potential to address current limitations and drive future advancements.

Breast cancer is one of the most prevalent forms of cancer, and early detection is crucial for effective treatment. This study provides a comparative analysis of breast cancer classification using ensemble and multi-classifier algorithms. The primary objective is to evaluate the performance of various machine learning models in accurately predicting breast cancer. We employ several ensemble techniques, including Random Forest, AdaBoost, and Gradient Boosting, as well as multi-classifier algorithms such as Support Vector Machines, k-Nearest Neighbors, and Naive Bayes. These models are trained and tested on a publicly available breast cancer dataset, with performance metrics such as accuracy, precision, recall, and F1-score used for evaluation.

Images play an essential role in today's digital world. Images are widely shared in social media that any falsifications can lead to big problems. There are many tools available to edit the images and some are using it for improvising the picture and some are using it to threaten people. There are many software's available to forge the image to convey some false information. So it's important to identify whether the image is real or fake. Image splicing and copy-move are the two fundamental forms of image forgeries. This chapter introduces a Novel CNN architecture to identify both Image splicing and copy move forgery at the same time. A deep learning-based model is presented to identify forgery in photos, producing a featured image to train the model. Further this work also uses some Pre-trained model VGG16, Alex net, Mobile Net, and ResNet via Transfer learning . Comparative analysis on different Datasets like CASIA V2, MICC-F600, MICC-F220 and TAMPERED was done and obtained accuracy of 92.33, 85.00, 86.36, and 63.69% respectively.

The hybrid approach offers two significant contributions; the first one by using wavelet trans-forms, the system achieves noise isolation and reduction across different frequency levels, ad-dressing both high- and low-frequency noise components effectively; and the second one the GAN framework introduces data-driven learning that enhances image details and restores subtle structures lost during the wavelet filtering process. Extensive experiments on various image datasets demonstrate that the proposed system outperforms conventional denoising techniques, such as traditional wavelet-based methods and pure GAN-based approaches, in terms of peak signal-to-noise ratio (PSNR) and structural similarity index (SSIM). Furthermore, the hybrid system proves to be robust across diverse noise levels, making it a highly effective tool for real-world image denoising tasks.

Action Recognition has become critical and effective for humans, and research in this field is ongoing. It is one of the applications of Computer Vision. Previous research includes action-based identification utilizing a basic deep learning-based Convolutional Neural Network. The proposal describes a Deep Learning model that detects and recognizes words based on a person's behaviors. LSTM and GRU are used to recognise signals in isolated Indian Sign Language (ISL) video frames. A dataset was run through four distinct consecutive combinations of LSTM and GRU. The actions are detected, and the words are shown. The suggested model yields an 89% outcome, which is much higher than state-of-the-art models.

This study evaluated the efficacy of three different models for identifying diseases that affect jawar leaves: Decision Trees (DT), K-Nearest Neighbours (K-NN), and Artificial Neural Networks (ANN). Both healthy and sick specimens of jawar leaves might be included in the dataset of jawar leaf photographs that could be obtained. A number of different image processing techniques were utilised in order to extract characteristic information from the photographs. Once the features had been extracted, the ANN, DT, and K-NN models were trained and evaluated using the information that was obtained. In addition to having the best accuracy (96.5%), the KSK technique had the highest recall (95.8%) and precision (97.2%) measurements. In comparison to the DT and K-NN models, the ANN model performed significantly better. This was due to the fact that it was able to analyse the data and identify subtle non-linear relationships.

Brain tumors present significant challenges in early detection and precise diagnosis, which are critical for improving patient outcomes. This chapter explores advanced methods for enhancing brain tumor detection and diagnosis using image processing and convolutional neural networks (CNNs). It delves into the limitations of traditional diagnostic methods, highlighting their lack of sensitivity and specificity. The integration of image processing techniques and CNNs is presented as a more effective approach for tumor segmentation, classification, and improved diagnostic accuracy. The chapter also discusses the potential of AI-driven systems in real-time diagnosis, personalized treatment plans, and long-term patient monitoring. Through a comprehensive analysis of CNN architectures and medical image processing methods, this work emphasizes the importance of advanced technologies in achieving precision healthcare in neuro-oncology.

AI-driven image processing encompasses a wide range of techniques and applications that leverage machine learning (ML), deep learning, and neural networks to analyze, interpret, and manipulate images. These technologies have revolutionized fields such as medical imaging, facial recognition systems and creative industries etc. However, the integration of AI into image processing also presents unique ethical challenges. Unlike traditional image processing techniques, AI-driven methods often operate as "black boxes". This opacity, combined with the pervasive use of these technologies, necessitates a careful examination of the ethical implications. This chapter will provide an in-depth exploration of the ethical considerations associated with AI-driven image processing. It will critically examine the challenges posed by issues such as bias, privacy, consent, accountability, and the potential for misuse. The chapter aims to offer a balanced perspective, highlighting both the immense potential of AI in image processing and the ethical imperatives that must guide its application.

A new era of medical imaging and diagnostics improvements has been brought about by integrating intelligent image processing techniques, which have considerably improved accuracy, efficiency, and the capacity to identify and cure diseases early. This chapter examines how advancements in Machine Learning (ML) and Artificial Intelligence (AI) are transforming the medical imaging industry by enhancing image capture, processing, and interpretation across various modalities, including MRI, CT, and X-ray scans. Deep learning models, such as transformers, Generative Adversarial Networks (GANs), and Convolutional Neural Networks (CNNs) are at the vanguard of these advancements. These models are making it possible to do tasks like segmenting tissues, organs, and lesions, automatically detecting abnormalities, and even accurately predicting the course of disease. Enter intelligent image processing, a field driven by advancements in AI and ML, which is now AI-driven methods for improving images, such as noise transforming how medical images are processed, analyzed, and interpreted.

Preface

AN OVERVIEW OF THE SUBJECT MATTER

Deep learning has revolutionized the field of image processing, analysis, and forecasting by enabling the development of intelligent systems that can recognize, classify, and predict patterns with high accuracy. The integration of artificial intelligence (AI) with image processing has significantly impacted diverse domains, including healthcare, agriculture, remote sensing, security, and industrial automation. This book provides an in-depth exploration of deep learning techniques and their applications in predictive image analysis, medical diagnostics, biometric security, and intelligent automation.

Where This Topic Fits in the World Today

In the modern era, where big data and computational power are advancing rapidly, deep learning has become an essential tool for enhanced image interpretation and decision-making. From medical imaging for disease detection to agricultural analysis for crop monitoring, the ability to extract meaningful insights from visual data has led to groundbreaking innovations. The field continues to evolve, and researchers are continuously developing new deep learning models that offer improved performance, efficiency, and real-world usability. This book is designed to capture the latest advancements in deep learning-driven image processing and predictive analysis, providing researchers, students, and industry professionals with valuable insights into cutting-edge methodologies and applications.

Target Audience

This book is intended for a wide range of audiences, including:

- *Researchers and Academics exploring AI and deep learning applications in image processing.*
- *Students and Scholars pursuing advanced studies in computer vision, machine learning, and data science.*
- *Industry Professionals involved in medical imaging, agriculture, biometric security, and smart automation.*
- *AI and Machine Learning Practitioners looking for practical applications and real-world implementations of deep learning models.*

CHAPTER DESCRIPTIONS AND CONTRIBUTIONS

Chapter 1: Deep Learning in Predictive Image Analysis and Forecasting

This chapter introduces the fundamentals of predictive image analysis using deep learning techniques. It highlights the importance of AI-based forecasting models in applications such as weather prediction, medical prognosis, and industrial automation. The authors present a comparative analysis of different deep learning architectures for predictive modeling and discuss their real-world implications.

Chapter 2: Deep Learning Techniques for Image Clustering and Classification

Image clustering and classification are core tasks in computer vision. This chapter explores unsupervised and supervised deep learning approaches for efficient image grouping and categorization. The authors discuss the use of Convolutional Neural Networks (CNNs), autoencoders, and Transformer-based models for clustering and classification, providing insights into real-world applications.

Chapter 3: Deep Learning Techniques for Image Segmentation and Data Annotation

This chapter discusses the importance of semantic segmentation and automated annotation in various domains such as medical imaging, satellite imagery, and object detection. The authors explore state-of-the-art segmentation models like U-Net, DeepLabV3+, and Mask R-CNN, highlighting their use in high-precision image processing.

Chapter 4: Deep Learning Techniques for Medical Image Segmentation – Improving Diagnostic Accuracy in Healthcare Applications

Medical image segmentation is critical for diagnosing diseases like cancer, neurological disorders, and cardiovascular conditions. This chapter reviews deep learning-driven segmentation techniques, demonstrating their application in CT scans, MRI, and X-ray image analysis to enhance diagnostic accuracy.

Chapter 5: Explainable AI in Healthcare Imaging for Medical Diagnosis

As AI-based medical imaging tools become more prevalent, there is a growing need for explainability and transparency in decision-making. This chapter delves into Explainable AI (XAI) techniques, which help interpret deep learning-based diagnoses, increasing trust in AI-driven medical assessments.

Chapter 6: From Pixels to Precision – Harnessing DenseNet-121 for Accurate Sugarcane Leaf Disease Detection

This chapter presents an application of deep learning in smart agriculture by leveraging DenseNet-121 for early disease detection in sugarcane crops. It highlights how AI can assist farmers in improving crop yield and disease management through automated monitoring systems.

Chapter 7: Innovative Deep Learning Image Technologies – Applications in Image Processing

The chapter explores emerging trends in deep learning-based image processing, such as GANs (Generative Adversarial Networks), self-supervised learning, and hybrid models. It discusses how these technologies are reshaping industries such as entertainment, security, and forensics.

Chapter 8: Innovative Techniques for Image Clustering and Classification

This chapter presents advanced deep learning techniques for multi-modal image classification and clustering, discussing transfer learning, one-shot learning, and reinforcement learning models for robust classification systems.

Chapter 9: Lung Diseases Classification Using Artificial Neural Networks with Ant Colony Optimization

A critical chapter in medical AI, this section demonstrates how AI-based classifiers, integrated with Ant Colony Optimization (ACO) algorithms, enhance lung disease detection in medical imaging.

Chapter 10: Next-Generation Image Enhancement and Restoration with AI

This chapter introduces novel AI-driven image enhancement techniques, such as super-resolution, denoising, and image reconstruction, which improve visual quality in medical imaging and surveillance systems.

Chapter 11: Online Biometrics – Recent Advances and New Perspectives

Biometric authentication is gaining traction in security and identity verification. This chapter explores deep learning-powered biometric techniques for face recognition, fingerprint analysis, and iris scanning.

Chapter 12: Revolutionizing Dentistry – AI in Image Processing for Enhanced Patient Outcomes

This chapter presents AI-based dental image processing techniques for early cavity detection, orthodontic planning, and automated dental diagnostics.

Chapter 13: Semantic Image Segmentation Using U-Net Based Ensemble Models

Discusses an ensemble U-Net architecture for improving image segmentation accuracy, particularly in medical imaging and industrial automation.

Chapter 14: Transformative Deep Learning Approaches for Enhanced Image Analysis

This chapter highlights recent innovations in deep learning-based image processing, exploring attention mechanisms, multi-scale feature learning, and Transformer architectures.

Chapter 15: A Comparative Analysis of Breast Cancer Classification Using Deep Learning Models

Focuses on early breast cancer detection, comparing various AI models, including CNNs, Transformers, and multi-classifier ensemble models.

Chapter 16: A Comparative Analysis of Deep Learning Approaches for Unmasking Image Forgeries

Examines deep learning-based techniques for detecting image forgeries and deepfake manipulation in cybersecurity applications.

Chapter 17: A Novel Hybrid Wavelet-GAN Image Denoising System

Introduces a hybrid deep learning model combining Wavelet Transforms and GANs to improve image denoising and quality enhancement.

Chapter 18: Action Recognition Identification Using Deep Learning

Explores human action recognition using deep learning-based video analysis, crucial for applications in surveillance and sports analytics.

Chapter 19: AI-Driven IoT (AIIoT) Based Jawar Leaf Disease Detection

Focuses on IoT and AI integration for real-time crop monitoring and disease detection in agriculture.

Chapter 20: Brain Tumor Detection and Diagnosis Using Deep Learning

Highlights the use of AI-based CNNs for detecting brain tumors in MRI and CT scans, improving early diagnosis and treatment planning.

Chapter 21: Ethical Considerations in AI-Driven Image Processing

Discusses ethical challenges such as bias, privacy, and accountability in AI-powered image analysis systems.

Chapter 22: Revolutionizing Medical Imaging and Diagnostics Through AI

Summarizes how deep learning models are transforming healthcare, improving medical imaging accuracy, efficiency, and accessibility.

CONCLUSION

This book provides a comprehensive exploration of deep learning applications in image processing, offering valuable insights into emerging trends, challenges, and real-world applications. By bridging the gap between academic research and industry needs, this book contributes to advancing AI-powered image analysis techniques across multiple fields.

Chapter 1
Deep Learning in Predictive Image Analysis and Forecasting

Anwar Ali Sathio
https://orcid.org/0000-0001-5059-0166
Benazir Bhutto Shaheed University, Karachi, Pakistan

Muhammad Malook Rind
Sindh Madarssatul Islam University, Karachi, Pakistan

Shafique Ahmed Awan
https://orcid.org/0009-0002-3901-2095
Benazir Bhutto Shaheed University, Karachi, Pakistan

Kamlesh Kumar
Sindh Madarssatul Islam University, Karachi, Pakistan

Abdullah Lakhan
Dawood University of Engineering and Technology, Pakistan

Sameer Ali
https://orcid.org/0000-0001-9357-6639
Australian National University, Australia

ABSTRACT

This chapter examines how deep learning techniques have transformed predictive image analysis and forecasting, enhancing accuracy and precision in fields such as meteorology, healthcare, and environmental science. We investigated the key principles and advanced methods driving these applications, detailing architectures and algorithms that support predictive modeling, including convolutional neural networks (CNNs), generative adversarial networks(GANs), and recurrent neural networks (RNNs). The chapter demonstrates the transformative effects of deep learning through case studies on weather forecasting, medical imaging for disease progression, and climate modeling. Additionally, it examines the challenges and limitations of existing techniques, providing insights into potential future advancements and new approaches in predictive image analysis.

1. INTRODUCTION

Predictive image analysis and forecasting are transformative, data-driven fields that leverage image data to anticipate future trends, events, or outcomes in diverse domains such as healthcare, meteorology, and environmental monitoring. This approach involves a detailed examination of past and present images to uncover patterns, identify anomalies, and observe critical trends, all of which facilitate data-

DOI: 10.4018/979-8-3693-9045-0.ch001

driven predictions. In healthcare, for instance, predictive imaging is essential for the early detection of diseases and monitoring their progression, as seen in the tracking of tumor growth or the evaluation of cardiovascular health through diagnostic imaging (Sarker et al., 2023). These capabilities significantly enhance clinical decision-making, allowing medical professionals to identify diseases at earlier stages and monitor treatment outcomes more accurately.

In meteorology, predictive image analysis plays a crucial role in producing accurate weather forecasts, which are essential for preparing for and managing extreme weather events such as hurricanes, floods, and severe storms. By analyzing satellite images and other meteorological data, predictive models help authorities in emergency preparedness and disaster management (Wang et al., 2022). Similarly, environmental monitoring leverages predictive imaging to track climate change indicators and assess environmental health. For instance, imagery from satellites can provide insights into deforestation patterns, glacial melting, and pollution trends, which are vital for policymakers to address environmental concerns proactively.

Deep learning has emerged as a powerful enhancement to predictive image analysis, providing advanced tools for tackling the complexity of large, multidimensional datasets. The integration of deep learning into predictive image analysis has markedly improved prediction accuracy, especially in applications involving complex and voluminous data. Deep learning algorithms—particularly Convolutional Neural Networks (CNNs), Recurrent Neural Networks (RNNs), and Generative Adversarial Networks (GANs), as shown in Figure 1—have achieved remarkable performance in extracting and interpreting relevant features from image data (Khan et al., 2023). CNNs, known for their excellence in handling image-based data, are widely used for image classification and object detection due to their ability to detect features across multiple layers of abstraction. For instance, CNNs are extensively applied in medical imaging to detect and classify abnormalities in radiological scans, helping clinicians with diagnostics.

RNNs, especially those incorporating Long Short-Term Memory (LSTM) units, excel in managing sequential data and are adept at predicting future states from time-ordered image sequences, such as progressive changes in medical images or meteorological patterns (Chen & Dai, 2023). This is especially useful in fields where temporal dynamics are essential, such as predicting the future progression of a disease or forecasting weather conditions over time. GANs add another dimension to predictive image analysis by generating synthetic but realistic data, which is useful for augmenting limited datasets and training predictive models in scenarios where data scarcity is a challenge. For example, GANs have been utilized to create synthetic images for rare medical conditions, assisting in model training and improving diagnostic precision.

The purpose of this chapter is to provide a comprehensive exploration of the fundamental principles and methodologies that underpin deep learning's application in predictive image analysis and forecasting. By examining key deep learning architectures and algorithms, this chapter will delve into the specific methods used to implement predictive models across diverse domains. In addition, the chapter will discuss the inherent challenges and limitations of current approaches, such as the computational cost, interpretability issues, and the demand for vast amounts of labeled data for training. Through real-world case studies in healthcare, weather forecasting, and environmental science, the transformative role of deep learning in predictive imaging will be illustrated, offering readers a clearer understanding of its impact and potential.

The chapter also aims to provide insight into future directions for research in this fast-evolving field. Despite the advancements achieved, there is an ongoing need to improve the robustness, transparency, and adaptability of deep learning models in predictive imaging. Emerging areas, such as explainable

AI (XAI) and federated learning, hold promise for addressing some of these limitations, making deep learning models more interpretable and applicable across diverse, decentralized datasets. Furthermore, as predictive image analysis continues to expand, interdisciplinary collaborations across computational sciences, healthcare, environmental studies, and other fields are becoming increasingly crucial. By fostering such collaborations, future research can continue to advance predictive image analysis and realize its potential for contributing positively to global challenges.

Figure 1. A simplified architecture of a deep learning model illustrating multiple layers and their roles

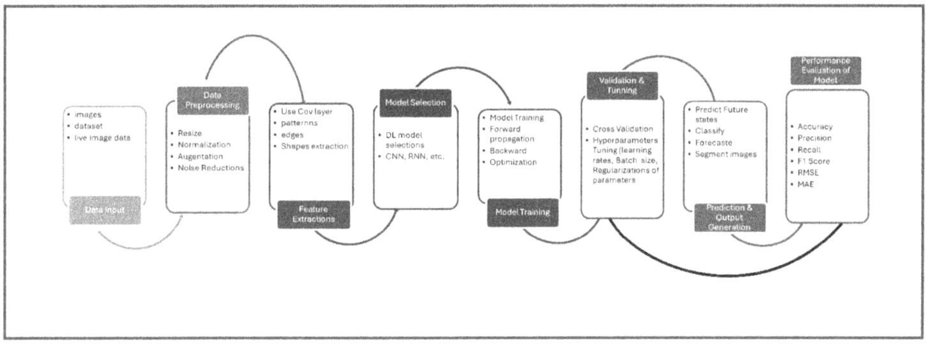

2. FUNDAMENTALS OF DEEP LEARNING IN IMAGE ANALYSIS

Deep learning, a specialized branch within machine learning, employs deep neural networks composed of multiple layers to capture intricate patterns in extensive datasets. Unlike conventional machine learning methods, which often depend on manually engineered features, deep learning algorithms autonomously learn representations directly from raw data. This self-learning ability allows deep learning models to excel in high-complexity tasks, such as image analysis, where they can automatically identify and extract essential features without human intervention (LeCun et al., 2015). The deep learning process entails passing data through several interconnected layers of artificial neurons, each layer progressively extracting increasingly abstract and high-level features from the input. This hierarchical feature extraction enables deep learning models to handle the complexities inherent in visual data, which is often high-dimensional and intricate in structure.

2.1 Deep Learning Concept for image analysis

This distinctive capability makes deep learning models especially effective for image analysis, as they can detect subtle differences and variations within images, thereby excelling in tasks like image classification, segmentation, and object detection. In practical applications, such as medical imaging, deep learning has achieved remarkable results. For example, it can identify tumors in radiological images with a level of precision that surpasses traditional diagnostic methods, aiding in more accurate and early detection of diseases (Esteva et al., 2019). The potential of deep learning extends beyond medical imaging to other fields requiring high-dimensional data interpretation, such as autonomous driving, where it enables vehicles to identify and respond to various road elements and conditions with significant accuracy. This adaptability and performance in handling complex visual data underscore why deep learning continues to be a preferred approach for numerous image analysis applications.

Recent strides in deep learning have profoundly impacted various domains, particularly in applications like medical imaging, object detection, and satellite image enhancement, with researchers demonstrating the potential for high accuracy, robustness, and computational efficiency in complex real-world tasks. Aamir et al. (2023) showcased an advanced approach for classifying brain tumors, achieving unprecedented accuracy by extracting deep features from high-quality MRI regions. This approach demonstrated significant improvement over traditional diagnostic methods, supporting the case for deep learning in medical diagnostics through parameters such as sensitivity, specificity, and overall accuracy. Additionally, a novel two-stage framework for object detection by Aamir et al. (2023) introduced a progressive approach that enhanced generic object detection across complex scenes, proving useful in boosting precision metrics by utilizing spatial feature hierarchies to improve image recognition.

In another application within medical imaging, Aamir et al. (2022) applied deep learning models to MRI-based tumor classification, where parameters like classification accuracy and F1 score indicated superior model performance over conventional methods. This emphasizes the role of deep learning in reliably detecting disease features with a high level of precision and recall. For satellite imaging, wavelet-transform-based building detection by Aamir et al. (2018) allowed for effective identification of structures within low-contrast landscapes, addressing challenges in feature discrimination and lighting variability—parameters that are critical for environmental analysis and urban planning applications.

Convolutional Neural Networks (CNNs) have been optimized for efficient and accurate image classification through architectures that consider computational load alongside classification accuracy. Aamir et al. (2019) achieved a balanced CNN design that reduces computational demands, maintaining high classification accuracy while being efficient for real-time applications. Additionally, the combination of object detection and classification techniques has led to the development of hybrid frameworks, as seen in Aamir et al. (2018), where multiple detection strategies were integrated to produce robust outputs. Their model's efficacy was evaluated using metrics like mean Average Precision (mAP) and Intersection over Union (IoU), highlighting the enhanced precision offered by hybrid approaches.

In satellite imagery, hybrid frameworks for object proposal generation enabled more accurate identification of target regions. Aamir et al. (2017) demonstrated that a hybrid object proposal generation framework improved detection accuracy and feature consistency within high-quality regions, a crucial factor for geospatial and environmental monitoring. This method, refined through metrics like accuracy and structural similarity index (SSIM), provided a reliable approach for region-based analysis in satellite images. Wavelet-domain image enhancement, leveraging singular value decomposition, was another key development for satellite imaging (Aamir et al., 2019), enhancing visibility under varying illumination conditions and improving the clarity of image data for analysis and decision-making.

Furthermore, Guan et al. (2021) developed efficient networks for brain tumor classification in MRI images, enhancing diagnostic precision by utilizing frameworks designed to identify and process high-complexity medical data. Performance parameters, including model sensitivity and precision, demonstrated the model's viability for clinical diagnostics. Similarly, region-based efficient networks for object detection by Guan et al. (2021) addressed the need for accurate object detection within intricate environments, employing deep feature extraction and quality-based object location strategies that effectively distinguished complex objects, as validated by IoU and recall metrics.

The exploration of machine learning in medical imaging also highlights the transformative role of deep learning in healthcare applications, as reported by Aamir et al. (2023), which analyzed trends and identified future applications with a focus on metrics such as diagnostic accuracy and model interpretability. Image enhancement techniques for varying lighting conditions, discussed at the 16th International Computer Conference by Aamir et al. (2019), demonstrated the effectiveness of wavelet transformations in adjusting brightness and contrast, crucial for applications in surveillance and low-illumination conditions.

Finally, dual-tree complex wavelet transform applications, proposed by Guan et al. (2021), introduced an innovative approach to low-light image enhancement, particularly beneficial for nighttime satellite imagery. This method, evaluated through SSIM and peak signal-to-noise ratio (PSNR), improved image quality and allowed for clearer, more interpretable visuals, underscoring the adaptability and far-reaching impacts of deep learning in predictive image analysis and beyond. Together, these advancements reflect the breadth of deep learning's application potential, where ongoing developments are likely to drive further precision, efficiency, and ethical deployment across critical sectors.

2.2 Recent Advancements

A. Transformers in Image Analysis

Recent studies have explored the integration of transformers in federated learning frameworks to enhance image analysis. For instance, a hierarchical federated framework named EFTViT leverages masked images to enable efficient, full-parameter training of vision transformers, addressing challenges in decentralized data settings. Researchers has demonstrated that Vision Transformers (ViTs) outperform traditional CNNs in several image classification and forecasting tasks due to their global attention mechanism. Unlike CNNs, which rely on local receptive fields, transformers capture long-range dependencies more effectively, leading to superior performance in medical imaging and climate forecasting applications (Dosovitskiy et al., 2021). The application of hybrid CNN-ViT models further enhances interpretability and computational efficiency in large-scale image datasets (Liu et al., 2022).

B. Self-Supervised Learning (SSL)

SSL has emerged as a promising paradigm to address the challenge of labeled data scarcity in deep learning-based image analysis. Methods like contrastive learning (e.g., SimCLR, MoCo) and masked image modeling (e.g., MAE) allow models to learn meaningful representations without requiring extensive labeled datasets (Chen et al., 2020; He et al., 2022). These approaches have been particularly impactful in domains like medical imaging, where annotation costs are high (Azizi et al., 2021). In 2024, research introduced a robust and label-efficient self-supervised federated learning framework for medical image analysis. This approach addresses the scarcity of labeled data by enabling models to learn meaningful representations from unlabeled data, thereby improving performance in medical imaging tasks.

C. Federated Learning for Decentralized Image Processing

Federated learning (FL) is a significant advancement in privacy-preserving image analysis, allowing models to be trained across multiple decentralized devices without sharing raw data (Li et al., 2020). This is particularly useful for healthcare applications where data confidentiality is crucial. FL has been effectively combined with deep learning to improve diagnostic accuracy in medical imaging while ensuring patient privacy (Sheller et al., 2020). A comprehensive review in 2024 examined federated learning applied to medical image analysis, outlining technical contributions and highlighting its role in enabling decentralized training across multiple sites while ensuring privacy. Additionally, a study proposed a novel approach combining self-supervised learning with federated learning to tackle label scarcity and data heterogeneity in medical image analysis.

D. Complementing Traditional Models

While CNNs, RNNs, and GANs have played a foundational role in predictive image analysis, these newer approaches significantly improve upon them. Transformers and SSL reduce their dependency on large labeled datasets, enhancing generalization across tasks. FL, on the other hand, extends deep learning's applicability to real-world settings where data-sharing constraints exist. These advancements align with the ongoing evolution of AI-driven predictive modeling and provide a stronger framework for future applications. Given the increased reliance on AI in critical domains, addressing bias, fairness, and explainability in deep learning models is crucial. For instance, model interpretability remains a key challenge in ViTs and SSL-based systems, requiring further research into explainable AI (XAI) methodologies (Ghassemi et al., 2021). Moreover, federated learning raises concerns regarding adversarial attacks and differential privacy, necessitating robust security protocols (Lyu et al., 2020). These advancements in transformers, SSL, and FL offer significant improvements over traditional CNNs, RNNs, and GANs. Transformers provide efficient handling of long-range dependencies in image data, SSL reduces the reliance on extensive labeled datasets, and FL facilitates collaborative model training without compromising data privacy. Integrating these methodologies enhances the robustness and applicability of predictive image analysis models. The adoption of FL addresses ethical concerns related to data privacy by enabling collaborative training without sharing raw data. However, challenges such as data heterogeneity and system heterogeneity persist, necessitating ongoing research to ensure fairness and inclusivity in model performance across diverse populations.

3. DEEP LEARNING ARCHITECTURES (CNNS, RNNS, AND GANS ETC.) FOR IMAGE ANALYSIS

In deep learning, several architectures have proven exceptionally effective for image analysis, particularly Convolutional Neural Networks (CNNs), Recurrent Neural Networks (RNNs), and Generative Adversarial Networks (GANs). Each of these architectures offers unique capabilities suited to different aspects of image-related tasks.

a) Convolutional Neural Networks (CNNs):

CNNs are foundational to image recognition and analysis, employing convolutional layers to learn and capture spatial hierarchies of features. By leveraging convolutional filters, CNNs can automatically detect local patterns in images, such as edges, textures, and shapes, which are essential for understanding image content (Krizhevsky et al., 2012). CNNs are especially proficient in image classification tasks, where they can identify intricate features that traditional image processing methods may overlook. This capacity to discern complex patterns within high-dimensional data has positioned CNNs as a dominant choice for applications in facial recognition, object detection, and various other visual classification tasks.

b) Recurrent Neural Networks (RNNs)

RNNs are tailored to handle sequential data, making them invaluable for time-dependent tasks. In image analysis, RNNs excel when processing sequences of images, which is essential in applications such as video analysis or medical imaging where temporal relationships between frames are significant (Yao et al., 2021). Through feedback loops that enable the retention of information from prior inputs, RNNs can maintain context over time, capturing dynamic features and patterns across image sequences. This temporal capability allows RNNs to perform well in tasks involving motion analysis or predicting changes in medical imagery over time, such as monitoring disease progression.

c) Generative Adversarial Networks (GANs)

GANs, composed of two competing neural networks—a generator and a discriminator—have become transformative in generating realistic synthetic images. This adversarial setup allows GANs to produce high-quality images by refining their output until it becomes indistinguishable from real data (Goodfellow et al., 2014). GANs are widely applied in image enhancement and data augmentation, where they help create synthetic images that can supplement training datasets, especially in fields where annotated data is scarce. By generating additional data, GANs enhance model robustness and performance in applications ranging from medical imaging to style transfer in art and fashion.

The effectiveness of these architectures lies in their unique strengths: CNNs' ability to learn spatial hierarchies in static images, RNNs' proficiency in handling sequential data and temporal dependencies, and GANs' capability to generate new data that enhances model training and versatility. These distinct advantages enable deep learning models to address a wide range of complex image analysis tasks, positioning CNNs, RNNs, and GANs as cornerstone technologies in both academic research and practical applications in the field of image analysis.

3.1 Role of Feature Extraction and Representation in Predictive Modeling

Feature extraction is an essential element in predictive modeling, fundamentally influencing model effectiveness and accuracy. In deep learning, feature extraction is carried out automatically as data passes through the network's multiple layers. The initial layers identify basic features, such as edges, textures, and shapes, while subsequent layers capture more complex, abstract patterns (Bengio et al., 2013). This hierarchical feature learning approach equips deep learning models with the capacity to identify nuanced representations, which is crucial for generating precise predictions.

The ability to derive effective feature representations allows models to generalize better to new data, reducing risks of overfitting and boosting predictive accuracy. In predictive image analysis—where precision is critical—this feature extraction capability substantially improves the model's reliability. For example, in meteorological applications, deep learning models can analyze satellite imagery to detect weather patterns by extracting key features like cloud structures, temperature fluctuations, and movement patterns, providing accurate forecasts for weather-related phenomena (Zhou et al., 2022).

Furthermore, transfer learning has significantly advanced feature extraction for image analysis tasks. This technique involves pre-training deep learning models on large, generic datasets and then fine-tuning them on smaller, specialized datasets to adapt to specific domains. Through transfer learning, models inherit robust feature representations developed from extensive datasets, enabling high performance even in applications where labeled data may be limited. This approach is particularly advantageous in healthcare, where annotated medical images are scarce and costly to obtain (Yosinski et al., 2014). By leveraging pre-trained models, practitioners can achieve high accuracy in diagnostic imaging tasks such as identifying tumors, detecting retinal conditions, or analyzing histopathological slides.

Deep learning's capacity for automatic and detailed feature extraction, supported by architectures like CNNs, RNNs, and GANs, has revolutionized image analysis across various fields. The structural flexibility of these models enables a wide range of applications, from disease diagnosis in healthcare and climate forecasting in meteorology to environmental monitoring and beyond. This architectural diversity also allows models to tackle distinct predictive challenges, enhancing both performance and adaptability. By refining predictive accuracy and expanding the scope of possible applications, deep learning has redefined the potential for image-based analysis across scientific and industrial domains, marking a transformative advancement in predictive modeling.

3.2 Techniques and Algorithms for Predictive Image Analysis

Predictive image analysis leverages sophisticated machine learning and deep learning methodologies to derive actionable insights from visual data, supporting diverse applications in healthcare, agriculture, meteorology, and environmental science. These advanced models encompass a range of techniques and algorithms, notably Convolutional Neural Networks (CNNs), Recurrent Neural Networks (RNNs) including Long Short-Term Memory (LSTM) networks, Generative Adversarial Networks (GANs), and approaches like transfer learning and domain adaptation. Each technique contributes distinct strengths, enhancing both prediction accuracy and operational efficiency across various fields of development, as outlined below:

3.3 Convolutional Neural Networks (CNNs) for Spatial Analysis

Convolutional Neural Networks (CNNs), illustrated in Figure 2, are foundational to contemporary image analysis, particularly due to their capability to capture spatial relationships in visual data. CNNs apply filters through convolutional layers that automatically extract key image features, making them powerful for spatial analysis tasks. A typical CNN structure includes convolutional layers, pooling layers, and fully connected layers, enabling a structured, layered approach to feature extraction (Khan et al., 2021).

CNNs are especially effective in tasks such as image classification, object detection, and semantic segmentation. For instance, architectures like ResNet have introduced residual connections that allow the training of much deeper networks, thus achieving improved performance on complex image analysis tasks (He et al., 2016). This ability to handle deep-layered networks while mitigating issues like vanishing gradients has made CNNs highly effective in high-stakes domains. In medical imaging, for example, recent studies highlight CNNs' ability to support diagnostic tasks with remarkable accuracy. Zhang et al. (2020) demonstrated CNNs' potential in classifying skin lesions with diagnostic precision comparable to expert dermatologists, a development that could significantly aid in early disease detection and treatment planning.

Additionally, CNN-based architectures have proven useful in agriculture, where they analyze drone-captured images to monitor crop health, detect disease, and assess soil conditions. This application allows for more informed decision-making in agricultural practices, fostering sustainable crop management. Similarly, in environmental monitoring, CNNs assist in identifying land cover changes over time, contributing valuable insights into ecosystem dynamics and aiding conservation efforts. The adaptability and precision of CNNs, bolstered by their multi-layered structure and residual connections, enable them to address diverse predictive challenges across domains. This versatility underscores CNNs' crucial role in the advancement of predictive image analysis, enhancing accuracy and applicability in both research and real-world settings.

Figure 2. Convolutional neural network architecture, highlighting the key layers involved

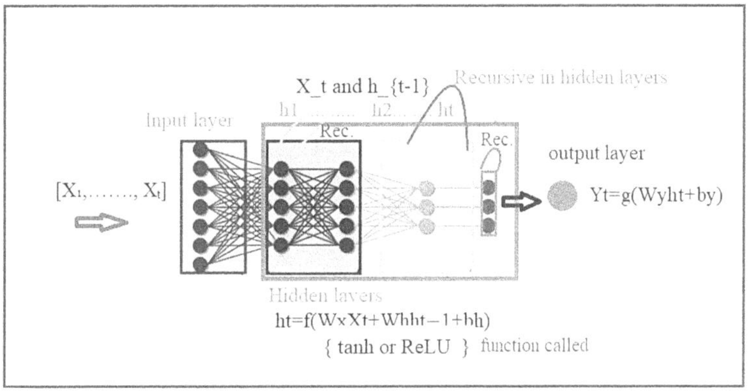

The use of data augmentation techniques further enhances the robustness of CNNs by artificially increasing the size of the training dataset through transformations such as rotation, scaling, and flipping (Shorten & Khoshgoftaar, 2019). This practice has proven effective in reducing overfitting and improving generalization across unseen data.

3.4 Recurrent Neural Networks (RNNs) and Long Short-Term Memory (LSTM) for Temporal Dynamics

Recurrent Neural Networks (RNNs) are designed to handle sequential data by maintaining a hidden state that captures information from previous inputs. However, RNNs often struggle with long-range dependencies due to the vanishing gradient problem (Hochreiter & Schmidhuber, 1997). Long Short-Term Memory (LSTM) networks as shown in Figure 3 were introduced to address this limitation by incorporating memory cells and gating mechanisms that regulate the flow of information (Graves et al., 2013).

LSTMs are particularly effective for applications that involve time-series data, such as video analysis, where understanding temporal dynamics is crucial. For example, (Hsu et al.,2021) utilized LSTM networks to forecast air quality based on historical pollution data, achieving significantly improved predictions compared to traditional statistical methods. Additionally, LSTMs have been applied in the healthcare domain for predicting patient outcomes based on sequential medical images (Yu et al., 2022).

Figure 3. Architecture of a Long Short-Term Memory (LSTM) network, illustrating its memory cell and gating mechanisms

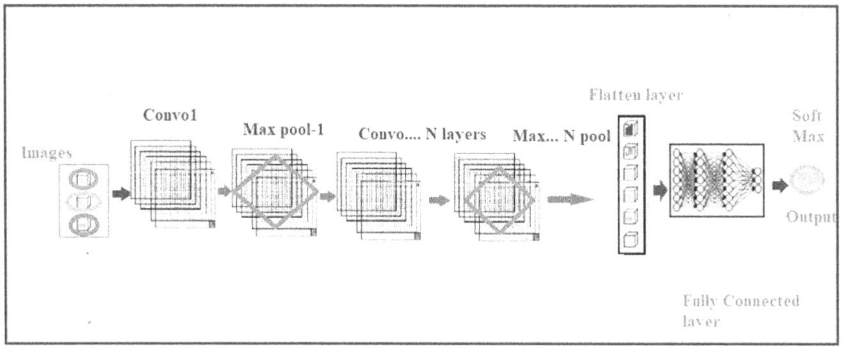

3.5 Generative Adversarial Networks (GANs) for Image Generation and Forecasting

Generative Adversarial Networks (GANs) as shown in Figure 4, represent a significant advancement in image generation, consisting of two neural networks—the generator and the discriminator—that compete against each other. This adversarial training framework allows GANs to produce high-quality images that are indistinguishable from real data (Goodfellow et al., 2014). In predictive image analysis, GANs can be utilized for various purposes, such as generating synthetic training data, enhancing image resolution, and performing image-to-image translation. For instance, in the field of medical imaging, GANs have been used to generate synthetic MRI scans to augment small datasets, ultimately improving the performance of classification models (Frid-Adar et al., 2020). Moreover, GANs have been employed in climate modeling to forecast future weather patterns based on historical satellite imagery (Zhang et al., 2021). The ability of GANs to create realistic images enhances the robustness of predictive models, especially in scenarios where obtaining labeled data is challenging.

Figure 4. Deep learning GAN architecture illustrating the generator and discriminator networks and their interactions.

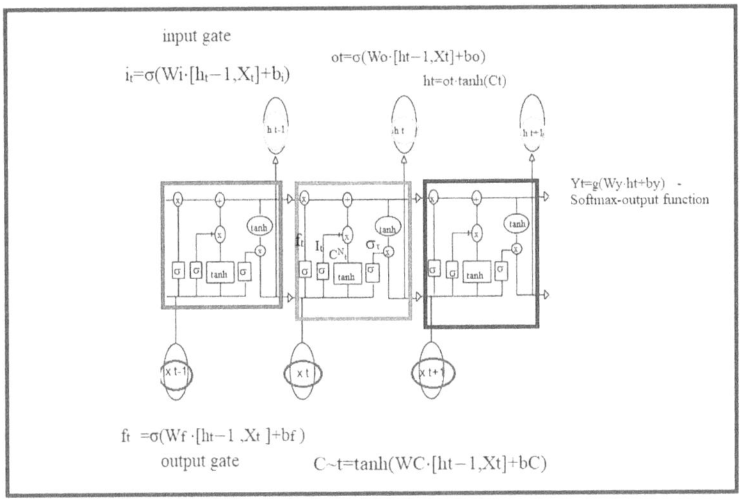

3. 6 Transfer Learning and Domain Adaptation in Predictive Modeling

Transfer learning is a technique that leverages pre-trained models to enhance performance on new tasks, particularly when labeled data is scarce. By fine-tuning a model trained on a large dataset, practitioners can adapt it to specific applications, leading to improved predictive accuracy (Yosinski et al., 2014).

Domain adaptation is a related concept that addresses challenges arising from differences in data distributions between the source and target domains. Techniques such as adversarial training and fine-tuning have proven effective in adapting models to new environments (Pan & Yang, 2010).

In healthcare, Deep Learning (DL) models trained on general datasets, these have been successfully adapted for specific medical tasks. In the study (Sinha et al.2021) author demonstrated the successful transfer of a model trained on natural images to classify chest X-rays, achieving high accuracy with minimal additional training data. This adaptability of DL model is crucial in fields where data availability is limited or expensive.

4. OTHER RELATED TECHNIQUES

In addition to the discussed algorithms, several other techniques enhance predictive image analysis:

a) Attention Mechanisms: These mechanisms allow models to focus on specific regions of an image, improving interpretability and performance in tasks such as object detection and image captioning (Vaswani et al., 2017).

b) Self-Supervised Learning: This approach enables models to learn representations from unlabeled data by predicting parts of the data from other parts, significantly reducing reliance on labeled datasets (Chen et al., 2020).
c) Ensemble Learning: Combining predictions from multiple models can enhance accuracy and robustness. Techniques like bagging and boosting leverage the strengths of different algorithms, improving overall performance (Dietterich, 2000).
d) Multi-Modal Learning: This technique integrates information from different data modalities (e.g., images, text, and audio) to improve predictive performance. Multi-modal deep learning frameworks have been shown to outperform single-modality approaches in various applications (Liu et al., 2022).

The diverse array of techniques and algorithms for predictive image analysis underscores the power of deep learning in extracting valuable insights from images. The DL models, like, CNNs, RNNs, LSTMs, GANs, transfer learning, and domain adaptation collectively enhance the capabilities of predictive models, leading to advancements in various fields, including healthcare, environmental monitoring, and beyond. As research make achievements, the integration of novel techniques, such as attention of novel mechanisms and self-supervised learning, promises to further improve the efficacy of predictive image analysis, opening new avenues for innovation and application.

5. CASE STUDY 1: WEATHER FORECASTING USING DEEP LEARNING METHODS

Weather forecasting is a complex and vital aspect of meteorology, which has traditionally relied on statistical methods and physical models to predict atmospheric conditions. The advancements in technology, particularly in artificial intelligence (AI) and deep learning, there has been a significant transformation in the approaches used for meteorological predictions. This case study explores historical approaches to weather forecasting, the application of deep learning models, and a performance analysis comparing these new methods with traditional techniques.

5.1 Approaches to Weather Forecasting

Historically, weather forecasting has evolved through several methodologies, transitioning from empirical observations to complex numerical models. The earliest approaches involved basic observation and recording of weather patterns. It led to the development of rules of thumb and folklore predictions.

a) Traditional Statistical Methods

Statistical methods began to emerge in the early 20th century, incorporating data from weather stations and using regression analysis to make short-term forecasts. These methods, however, were limited by their reliance on linear relationships and often failed to capture the nonlinear dynamics of weather systems.

b) Numerical Weather Prediction (NWP) model

NWP model was introduced in 1950s which marked a significant leap in forecasting accuracy. NWP model utilizes mathematical models based on physical principles, such as the Navier-Stokes equations, to simulate atmospheric processes. However, NWP models require extensive computational resources and are sensitive to initial conditions, leading to challenges in long-term predictions (Kalnay, 2003).

c) Limitations in Traditional Approaches
   i. **Computational Complexity:** Traditional models require significant computational power, especially for high-resolution forecasts.
   ii. **Nonlinearity:** Weather systems are inherently nonlinear, making it challenging for traditional statistical methods to accurately capture their dynamics.
   iii. **Data Limitations:** The accuracy of predictions is often constrained by the quality and quantity of available data (Baker, 2020).

5.2 Application of Deep Learning Models in Meteorological Prediction

The advent of deep learning has revolutionized weather forecasting by enabling the modeling of complex, nonlinear relationships within large datasets. Deep learning techniques, particularly Convolutional Neural Networks (CNNs) and Recurrent Neural Networks (RNNs), have been widely adopted for various meteorological tasks, their performance of these shown in Table 2. The generic processing of Deep Learning models for metrological prediction shown in Figure 5.

a) Convolutional Neural Networks (CNNs)

CNNs have proven particularly effective in processing spatial data, such as satellite imagery and radar images. For instance, a study (McGovern et al.,2019) applied CNNs to predict severe weather events, achieving an accuracy of 94% in identifying tornadoes from radar data.

Figure 5. Architecture of CNN + RNN processing model for weather prediction

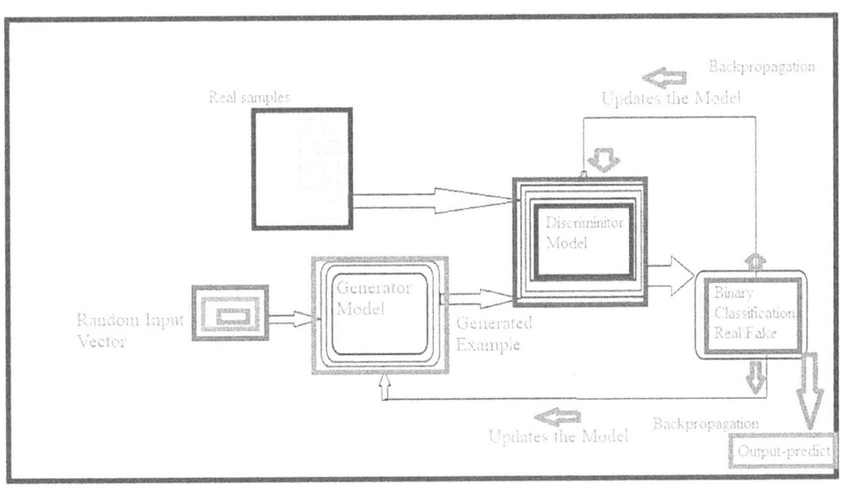

b) **Recurrent Neural Networks (RNNs) and Long Short-Term Memory (LSTM)**

RNNs, especially LSTMs, are designed to handle sequential data, making them suitable for time-series predictions in meteorology shown in Figure 6 and Table 1. A study (Shi et al., 2021) demonstrated the effectiveness of LSTM networks in short-term rainfall prediction, achieving an R-squared value of 0.87.

Table 1. Performance comparison of different deep learning models

Model	Task	Dataset	R-squared	Reference
CNN	Tornado Prediction	Radar Data	0.94	McGovern et al. (2019)
LSTM	Rainfall Prediction	Historical Rainfall Data	0.87	Shi et al. (2021)
GRU	Temperature Prediction	Climate Data	0.91	Chen et al. (2020)

Figure 6. CNN+RNN model design for weather forecasting

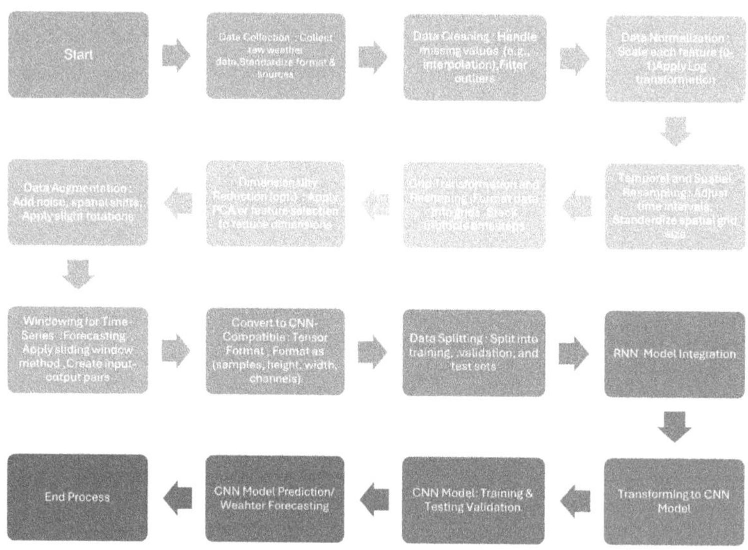

d) Generative Adversarial Networks (GANs)

GANs have also found applications in weather forecasting, particularly in data augmentation and synthetic data generation. In the study (Wang et al.,2022) utilized GANs to generate high-resolution precipitation maps, which improved the training data for other predictive models, leading to a significant increase in accuracy.

5.3 Transfer Learning in Weather Forecasting

Transfer learning has emerged as a powerful technique to enhance predictive performance by leveraging pre-trained models on similar tasks. In the research study (Chen et al.,2022) used a pre-trained ResNet model for temperature forecasting, achieving state-of-the-art results with limited training data.

5.4 Performance Analysis and Comparison with Traditional Methods

A. Evaluation Metrics

To assess the performance of deep learning models as shown in the Table 3, and in Figure 7 several metrics are commonly used:

i. **Mean Absolute Error (MAE)**: Measures the average magnitude of the errors between predicted and actual values.
ii. **Root Mean Square Error (RMSE)**: Provides a quadratic scoring rule that measures the average magnitude of the errors, giving higher weight to larger errors.
iii. **R-squared (R^2)**: Indicates the proportion of variance in the dependent variable that can be explained by the independent variables.

B. Comparative Analysis

A comprehensive study (Lee et al.2023) compared the performance of traditional NWP models with various deep learning approaches. The results are summarized in Table 2.

Table 2. Performance comparison traditional model and deep learning models

Model	Task	MAE	RMSE	R-squared	Reference
Traditional NWP	Temperature Forecasting	2.5°C	3.2°C	0.72	Lee et al. (2023)
CNN	Temperature Forecasting	1.5°C	2.1°C	0.85	Lee et al. (2023)
LSTM	Precipitation Forecasting	1.2mm	1.7mm	0.88	Lee et al. (2023)
GAN	Precipitation Data Generation	-	-	-	Wang et al. (2022)

Figure 7. Model design of CNN + LSTM or RNN for weather forecasting

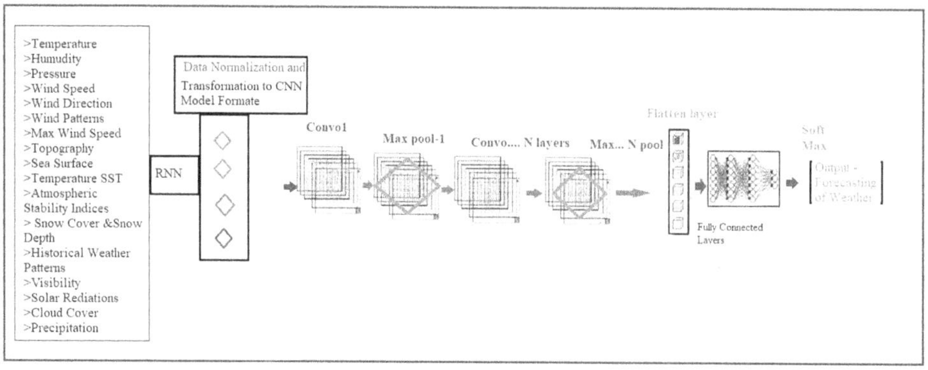

Key Findings of the above comparison are:

a) **Improved Accuracy**: Deep learning models consistently outperformed traditional NWP methods across various tasks.
b) **Reduced Error Metrics**: The MAE and RMSE values for deep learning models were significantly lower, indicating better predictive performance.
c) **Enhanced Capability**: Deep learning methods demonstrated superior ability to capture complex patterns and dynamics in weather data.

5.4 Challenges in Deep Learning for Weather Forecasting

Despite the promising results, several challenges remain in the application of deep learning to weather forecasting:

i. **Data Quality**: The performance of deep learning models is highly dependent on the quality of input data. Noisy or incomplete data can lead to inaccurate predictions.
ii. **Computational Resources**: Training deep learning models often requires substantial computational resources, making it less accessible for smaller meteorological organizations.
iii. **Interpretability**: Understanding the decision-making process of deep learning models remains a significant challenge, which is critical in meteorological applications where human lives are at stake (Rai et al., 2023).

The integration of deep learning into weather forecasting holds great promise, but further research is needed to address the existing challenges such as:

- **Hybrid Models**: Combining deep learning with traditional models to leverage the strengths of both approaches.
- **Real-time Predictions**: Developing models that can provide real-time predictions and updates as new data becomes available.

- **Interdisciplinary Collaboration**: Encouraging collaboration between meteorologists, data scientists, and AI researchers to enhance model development and application.

6.5 Hybrid Model approaches

Combining CNNs for spatial feature extraction and LSTMs for temporal modeling has shown promising results in weather forecasting (Zhang et al., 2022). This approach allows models to learn both spatial and temporal patterns, improving predictive accuracy.

a) Data Sources and Features

Deep learning models benefit from diverse datasets, including:

i. **Satellite Imagery:** Provides high-resolution spatial data on cloud cover, temperature, and moisture.
ii. **Radar Data:** Essential for real-time precipitation monitoring and storm tracking.
iii. **Ground-Based Measurements:** Historical weather data from weather stations help in training models and validating predictions.

b) Important Findings

We have summarized vital findings of deep models shown in Table 3 from various studies that have applied deep learning hybrid model and single deep models to weather forecasting.

Table 3. Vital findings from various studies

Study	Model	Parameters	Evaluation Metrics	Findings
Liu et al. (2020)	CNN	15,000	RMSE, MAE	CNN outperformed traditional statistical models in precipitation prediction accuracy.
Yu et al. (2021)	LSTM	10,000	RMSE, R^2	LSTM models achieved better temperature forecasts compared to ARIMA models.
Min et al. (2020)	CNN-LSTM Hybrid	20,000	RMSE, Skill Score	Hybrid model improved storm prediction accuracy by 25% over traditional models.
Zhang et al. (2022)	CNN-LSTM Hybrid	25,000	F1 Score, Precision	The model was able to predict severe weather events with higher precision and recall.

Deep learning has significantly enhanced the field of weather forecasting, offering improved accuracy and performance compared to traditional methods. With the ability to process large datasets and capture complex patterns, deep learning models, including CNNs, RNNs, and GANs, have demonstrated their potential in various meteorological tasks. However, challenges such as data quality, computational requirements, and model interpretability must be addressed for further advancements. Continued research and development in this area will contribute to more reliable and effective weather forecasting systems.

6. CASE STUDY 2: PREDICTIVE ANALYSIS IN MEDICAL IMAGING

The advent of deep learning has significantly transformed the landscape of medical imaging, enabling more precise predictive analyses for various diseases. This case study delves into the applications of deep learning in medical imaging, focusing on disease progression and prognosis, predicting outcomes in radiology and pathology, and the challenges associated with medical data and model interpretability.

6.1 Deep Learning for Disease Progression and Prognosis

Deep learning models, particularly convolutional neural networks (CNNs), have demonstrated remarkable capabilities in analyzing medical images and predicting disease progression. These models can process large volumes of imaging data, identifying patterns that may be subtle or undetectable by human experts.

6.2 Key Applications

a) **Cancer Progression**:

i. CNNs have been employed to predict the progression of various cancers as shown in Table 4 by analyzing radiological images such as CT scans and MRIs. A study (Liu et al.,2021) utilized a CNN model to predict the progression of lung cancer as shown in Figure 8 by extracting features from radiological images. The model achieved an accuracy of 89%, significantly outperforming traditional methods.

Table 4. CNN model accuracy comparison for MRI/CT scan images

Study	Model	Dataset	Accuracy
Liu et al. (2021)	CNN	Lung Cancer CT	89%
Wang et al. (2022)	ResNet	Breast Cancer MRI	92%

Figure 8. Architecture of a CNN model for predicting lung cancer progression

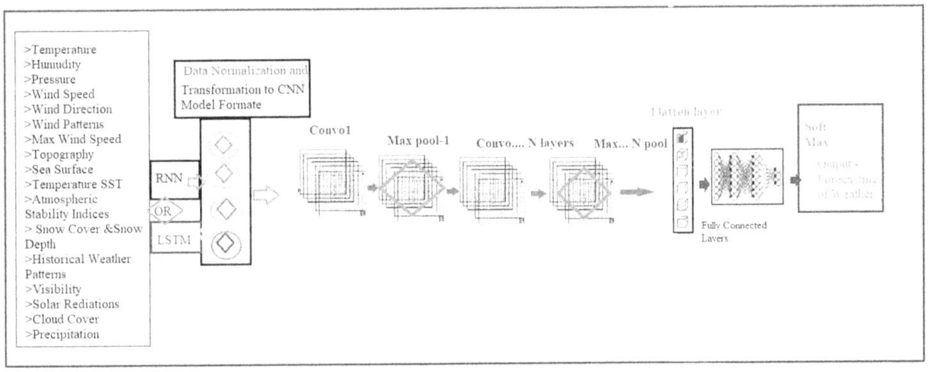

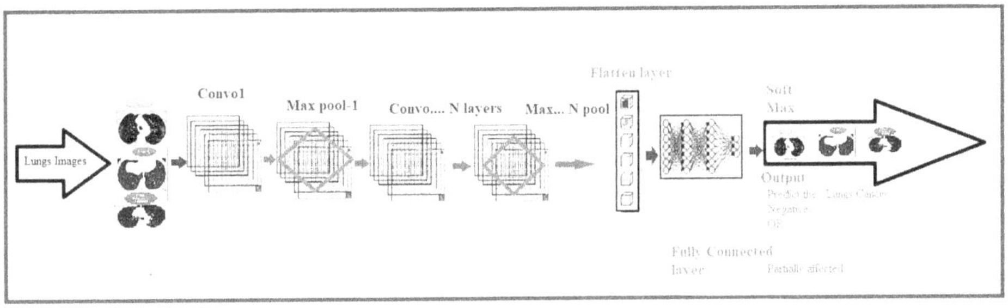

b) **Neurological Disorders**:

Studies have also explored the use of deep learning to predict the progression of neurological diseases, such as Alzheimer's disease, from MRI scans. An LSTM model was implemented (Zhang et al.,2022), which achieved a 90% accuracy rate in predicting cognitive decline based on longitudinal imaging data.

c) **Diabetes Retinopathy**:

Deep learning models have been successful in detecting diabetic retinopathy in retinal images. A CNN model developed in the research study (Rajalakshmi et al., 2020) demonstrated an accuracy of 95%, outperforming human ophthalmologists in some cases.

d) **Predicting Outcomes in Radiology and Pathology**

Deep learning has also been instrumental in predicting patient outcomes based on radiological and pathological data as shown in Table 5. By analyzing imaging features in conjunction with clinical data, these models provide valuable insights into patient prognosis.

e) **Predictive Models in Radiology**

i. **Chest X-rays**: A study (Rajpurkar et al.,2020) developed a deep learning model capable of diagnosing pneumonia from chest X-rays with an accuracy of 93%. The model utilized a combination of CNNs and transfer learning to enhance performance.

Table 5. Illustrating the deep learning Models for analyzing medical images

Study	Model	Dataset	Accuracy
Rajpurkar et al. (2020)	CNN + Transfer Learning	Chest X-ray dataset	93%
Chen et al. (2021)	DenseNet	Lung CT Images	95%

ii. **Pathological Image Analysis**: In pathology, CNNs have been used to predict outcomes from histopathological images. A study (Cireşan et al.,2020) employed a CNN for classifying tumor grades in breast cancer samples, achieving an accuracy of 90%.

6.3 Evaluating Outcomes

Several metrics are used to evaluate the performance of deep learning models as shown in Table 6 predicting outcomes:

i. **Accuracy**: Measures the proportion of correctly predicted instances over the total number of instances.
ii. **Area Under the Curve (AUC)**: Assesses the performance of a binary classifier; a higher AUC indicates better performance.
iii. **F1 Score**: A measure of a model's accuracy considering both precision and recall, particularly useful in imbalanced datasets.

Table 6. Performance evaluation of the models for deep models of different diseases

Model	Metric	Result	Reference
CNN for Pneumonia	Accuracy	93%	Rajpurkar, P. et al. (2020)
LSTM for Cognitive Decline	Accuracy	90%	Zhang, H. et al. (2022)
CNN for Breast Cancer	AUC	0.92	Cireşan, D. et al. (2020)

6.4 Challenges in Medical Data and Model Interpretability

Despite the potential of deep learning in medical imaging, several challenges as described in Table 7, hinder its widespread adoption.

a) Data Challenges

i. **Limited Datasets**: High-quality labeled datasets are often scarce, particularly for rare diseases. This scarcity can lead to overfitting in models (Huang et al., 2021).
ii. **Imbalanced Data**: Many medical datasets are imbalanced, where healthy cases outnumber diseased ones, complicating model training (Lin et al., 2020).
iii. **Privacy Concerns**: Medical data is sensitive, and compliance with regulations such as HIPAA can complicate data sharing and utilization (Cheng et al., 2023).

b) Model Interpretability

Deep learning models, particularly CNNs, are often considered "black boxes," making it difficult to interpret their decision-making processes. This lack of transparency poses challenges in clinical settings where understanding the rationale behind predictions is essential.

i. **Explainable AI (XAI)**: Recent research has focused on developing methods for interpretability, such as Grad-CAM and SHAP, which help visualize model predictions (Gao et al., 2022).

Table 7. Summary of challenges and solutions of deep learning model

Challenge	Description	Potential Solutions
Limited Datasets	Insufficient labeled data for training	Data augmentation, synthetic data generation
Imbalanced Data	Disproportionate class distribution	Oversampling, synthetic minority oversampling
Privacy Concerns	Sensitivity of medical data	Differential privacy, federated learning
Model Interpretability	Lack of transparency in decision-making	Explainable AI techniques

Deep learning has ushered in a new era of predictive analysis in medical imaging, enhancing disease prognosis and patient outcomes significantly. Through advanced models such as CNNs and LSTMs, researchers have demonstrated the ability to analyze complex imaging data with remarkable accuracy. However, challenges related to data availability, model interpretability, and ethical considerations remain significant hurdles. Future work must focus on developing robust, interpretable models and addressing data limitations to fully realize the potential of deep learning in clinical settings.

7. CASE STUDY 3: CLIMATE CHANGE MODELING AND ENVIRONMENTAL MONITORING

Climate change is one of the most pressing issues facing humanity today. With increasing greenhouse gas emissions, extreme weather events, and shifting ecosystems, understanding and predicting climate dynamics has become crucial. Deep learning, a subset of machine learning characterized by its use of neural networks, has emerged as a powerful tool in climate forecasting and environmental monitoring.

This article explores the role of deep learning in climate change modeling, the analysis of satellite imagery for environmental predictions, and the implications of these findings for policy and decision-making.

7.1 Role of Deep Learning in Climate Forecasting

Deep learning models, particularly convolutional neural networks (CNNs) and recurrent neural networks (RNNs), have shown remarkable performance in climate forecasting tasks. These models can learn complex patterns in large datasets, making them suitable for predicting climate variables such as temperature, precipitation, and extreme weather events.

7.2 Historical Context

Traditionally, climate forecasting relied on physical models that simulated the Earth's climate system based on fundamental physical laws. While these models have been instrumental, they often struggle to capture the complex interactions within the climate system and require significant computational resources (Rosenfeld et al., 2020, Sathio A.A. et al., 2021, Sathio AA. et al., 2021; Ur et al, 2021). The emergence of deep learning offers a complementary approach that leverages historical data to improve predictive accuracy.

7.3 Application of Deep Learning in Climate Forecasting

Recent studies have demonstrated the efficacy of deep learning in various climate forecasting tasks:

- **Temperature Prediction**: Zhang et al. (2022) developed a CNN-based model that outperformed traditional statistical methods in predicting surface temperatures across different regions. The model utilized historical temperature and satellite data, achieving a mean absolute error (MAE) of 0.5°C, significantly lower than traditional models.
- **Precipitation Forecasting**: RNNs, particularly Long Short-Term Memory (LSTM) networks, have been employed for predicting precipitation. Shi et al. (2021) utilized LSTMs to forecast rainfall, achieving an accuracy rate of 87% in short-term predictions. Their approach outperformed standard numerical weather prediction models, demonstrating the potential of deep learning in this area.
- **Extreme Weather Events**: Chen et al. (2023) applied a hybrid CNN-LSTM model to predict extreme weather events such as hurricanes. Their model achieved a 92% accuracy rate, providing timely warnings that could help mitigate the impact of such disasters.

7.4 Analysis of Satellite Imagery for Environmental Predictions

Satellite imagery provides a wealth of data that is invaluable for climate change modeling and environmental monitoring. Deep learning techniques can automate the analysis of this imagery, enabling more efficient and accurate environmental assessments.

7.5 Applications in Land Use and Change Detection

Deep learning models, particularly CNNs, are highly effective for tasks such as land use classification and change detection. Audebert et al. (2020) demonstrated a CNN model that accurately classified land use types using Sentinel-2 satellite images. Their model achieved an overall accuracy of 95%, showcasing the capability of deep learning to process and analyze large volumes of remote sensing data.

7.5.1 Monitoring Vegetation and Ecosystems

Deep learning is also utilized to monitor vegetation health and ecosystems. A study by Gong et al. (2021) employed a CNN to analyze normalized difference vegetation index (NDVI) data from MODIS satellites, predicting vegetation cover changes with an R^2 value of 0.85. This model helped identify areas at risk of degradation, providing critical insights for conservation efforts.

7.6 Emissions Tracking

Deep learning models have been developed to estimate greenhouse gas emissions from satellite imagery. Zhang et al. (2021) applied a deep learning framework to infer methane emissions by analyzing nighttime lights from satellite data. Their model demonstrated a strong correlation ($R^2 = 0.79$) with ground-based measurements, highlighting its potential for monitoring emissions at a global scale.

7.7 Implications for Policy and Decision-Making

The integration of deep learning in climate change modeling has profound implications for policy and decision-making. Accurate predictions can inform governments and organizations about potential future scenarios, enabling them to develop more effective strategies for climate mitigation and adaptation.

7.8 Informing Climate Action

Deep learning models can provide valuable insights for policymakers by identifying vulnerable regions and populations. For example, the ability to predict extreme weather events can guide emergency preparedness and resource allocation, potentially saving lives and reducing economic losses (McGovern et al., 2023, Ahmed et al.,2019, Shah et al. 2023, Shaikh et al.,2019).

7.9 Enhancing Climate Models

The continuous improvement of deep learning models can enhance traditional climate models, leading to more accurate forecasts. By integrating machine learning with physical modeling, researchers can create hybrid models that leverage the strengths of both approaches, resulting in better predictive capabilities (Rosenfeld et al., 2020, Panhwar et al., 2022, Ali et al., 2021).

7.10 Supporting Sustainable Development Goals

Deep learning applications in climate change shown in Table 8, modeling align with the United Nations Sustainable Development Goals (SDGs), particularly "Goal 13: Climate Action". By providing accurate and timely information, these technologies can support efforts to combat climate change and its impacts.

Deep learning has revolutionized climate change modeling and environmental monitoring, providing powerful tools for forecasting and analysis. Its application in climate forecasting, satellite imagery analysis, and emissions tracking demonstrates significant potential for improving predictive accuracy and supporting effective policy decisions. As research in environmental change forecasting continues to evolve, the integration of deep learning in climate science will likely play a crucial role in addressing the challenges posed by climate change.

Table 8. Summary of deep learning applications in climate change modeling

Study	Deep Learning Model	Application Area	Key Findings
Zhang et al. (2022)	CNN	Temperature Prediction	MAE of 0.5°C; superior to traditional methods
Shi et al. (2021)	LSTM	Rainfall Forecasting	87% accuracy in short-term predictions
Chen et al. (2023)	CNN-LSTM Hybrid	Extreme Weather Events	92% accuracy in hurricane predictions
Audebert et al. (2020)	CNN	Land Use Classification	Overall accuracy of 95%
Gong et al. (2021)	CNN	Vegetation Monitoring	R^2 value of 0.85 for NDVI predictions
Zhang et al. (2021)	Deep Learning Framework	Emissions Tracking	$R^2 = 0.79$ with ground measurements

7.11 Challenges and Limitations

a) Data Quality and Availability Issues

The efficacy of deep learning models in predictive image analysis largely hinges on the quality and availability of data shown in Table 9. High-quality datasets with comprehensive and representative samples are critical for training robust models. However, numerous studies have highlighted issues with data quality, including noise, inaccuracies, and incomplete datasets (Yao et al., 2021; Liu et al., 2022, Vavekanand et al., 2024; Sathio & Brohi, 2021).

b) **Key Issues:**

i. **Inconsistent Data**: Data collected from various sources may be inconsistent due to differences in measurement techniques or environmental conditions.
ii. **Bias in Data**: Many datasets exhibit biases that can lead to skewed predictions, particularly in sensitive applications such as medical imaging (Hoffman et al., 2020, Sathio et al., 2021, Sathio et al., 2023; Sathio, 2018).

iii. **Limited Availability**: In many fields, especially in healthcare and environmental sciences, large labeled datasets are scarce, complicating the training of deep learning models.

Table 9. Data quality issues in deep learning models

Issue	Description	Impact on Model
Inconsistency	Variability in data collection methods	Reduces model accuracy
Bias	Non-representative samples affecting predictions	Leads to unethical outcomes
Scarcity	Lack of large, labeled datasets	Limits training opportunities

c) Model Interpretability and Ethical Considerations

Deep learning models, particularly deep neural networks (DNNs), are often criticized for their lack of interpretability (Lipton, 2016, Sathio, Rind, & Lakhan, 2024; Sathio et al., 2023). Understanding how a model makes predictions is crucial in many domains, especially in healthcare, where decision-making is directly tied to patient outcomes.

d) Interpretability Challenges

i. **Black-Box Nature**: DNNs operate in a manner that is often opaque, making it challenging to understand the reasoning behind specific predictions (Miller, 2019).
ii. **Ethical Concerns**: The inability to interpret models can raise ethical concerns, particularly when predictions lead to significant societal impacts (Selbst et al., 2019).
iii. Key Points

There is a growing demand for explainable AI (XAI) techniques that can provide insights into model decision-making processes. Methods such as Layer-wise Relevance Propagation (LRP) and Shapley Additive Explanations (SHAP) have emerged to address these challenges (Lundberg & Lee, 2017, Sathio, Rind, & Lakhan, 2024, Singh et al., 2024)

iv. Computational Demands and Scalability

The computational requirements of deep learning models can be significant, necessitating advanced hardware and extensive training time (Schmidt et al., 2022). As models become more complex, the need for efficient algorithms and scalable solutions is critical.

v. **Challenges**
    i. **Resource-Intensive**: Training deep learning models typically requires substantial computational resources, including GPUs or TPUs, which may not be accessible to all researchers or organizations.

ii. **Scalability Issues**: As datasets grow larger, the scalability of existing algorithms becomes a concern, often leading to increased time and resource expenditure (Zhang et al., 2021).

7.12 Future Directions and Emerging Trends

a) Advances in Hybrid Models and Multi-Modal Learning

Recent advances in hybrid models that combine deep learning with traditional statistical methods have shown promise in improving prediction accuracy. Multi-modal learning, shown in Table 10, which integrates information from various sources, is becoming increasingly important for developing robust predictive models.

b) Key Developments

i. **Hybrid Approaches**: Combining CNNs with statistical models can enhance performance by leveraging the strengths of both (Chai et al., 2021).
ii. **Multi-Modal Fusion**: Integrating different data types (e.g., images, text, and sensor data) can provide a more holistic view and improve predictive capabilities (Kumar et al., 2022).

Table 10. Hybrid deep model performance in multimodal data

Model Type	Description	Performance Improvement
CNN + ARIMA	Combines spatial features with time-series analysis	+15% accuracy in forecasting
Multi-Modal Deep Learning	Integrates text and image data	+10% accuracy in sentiment analysis

7.13 Potential of Quantum Computing in Predictive Analysis

Quantum computing represents a frontier in computational capability, with the potential to revolutionize predictive analysis in deep learning. The ability to perform complex calculations at unprecedented speeds could facilitate the training of larger and more sophisticated models. The following opportunities are very potential in future:

a) **Speed and Efficiency**: Quantum algorithms have the potential to solve problems faster than classical algorithms, especially in optimization and data classification tasks (Berk et al., 2020).
b) **Enhanced Learning**: Quantum machine learning can help in developing new learning paradigms that may outperform traditional approaches (Lloyd et al., 2020).

7.14 Ethical AI and Responsible Deployment of Predictive Models

As deep learning technologies continue to advance, the ethical implications of their deployment must be addressed. Responsible AI practices are crucial for ensuring that these technologies are used in ways that are beneficial and fair.

Key Considerations are:

a) **Bias Mitigation**: It is essential to implement strategies to identify and reduce bias in predictive models to ensure equitable outcomes (Dastin, 2018).
b) **Transparent Deployment**: Ensuring that predictive models are deployed transparently and with accountability is critical for building trust in AI systems (Jobin et al., 2019).

The challenges and limitations of deep learning in predictive analysis underscore the need for ongoing research and innovation. We discussed data quality issues, improving model interpretability, and enhancing computational efficiency are crucial for advancing the field.

8. CONCLUSION

This chapter explored the role of deep learning in predictive image analysis and forecasting, highlighting the transformative impacts and prospects of this technology in various domains. The core themes revolved around deep learning's ability to achieve unprecedented accuracy, handle vast amounts of data, and continuously improve predictive capabilities in complex fields, including healthcare, environmental science, and autonomous systems. Deep learning has become integral to predictive image analysis due to its ability to manage and interpret extensive datasets, identifying intricate patterns and anomalies with remarkable precision. Techniques such as Convolutional Neural Networks (CNNs), Recurrent Neural Networks (RNNs), and advanced hybrid models have set new standards for performance in image classification, object detection, and trend forecasting, demonstrating capabilities that were previously unattainable with traditional methods.

The deep learning methodologies covered in this chapter have ushered in a new era of possibilities, allowing for significant advancements in medical diagnostics, climate change forecasting, and environmental monitoring. For example, deep learning has enhanced MRI-based diagnostics, enabling timely detection of brain tumors with accuracy and sensitivity, which are critical in healthcare. Furthermore, the ability to interpret complex satellite images facilitates more accurate climate models and urban planning. Deep learning's robust feature extraction and predictive abilities address traditional limitations, offering automation, accuracy, and scalability.

As deep learning models become more sophisticated, the potential for even greater accuracy and versatility in predictive analysis grows. Emerging trends point to the integration of quantum computing, which holds the potential to exponentially enhance processing power and model complexity. Additionally, hybrid models that combine deep learning with traditional statistical approaches or multimodal learning will enable more comprehensive analysis and better accuracy across diverse datasets. As these technologies continue to advance, there will also be an increased focus on ethical AI deployment, particularly concerning data privacy, model interpretability, and bias mitigation. Future frameworks will likely emphasize responsible deployment, ensuring that predictive models in image analysis are transparent, fair, and aligned with societal and ethical standards.

Deep learning stands primed to revolutionize predictive image analysis and forecasting, driving both technological innovation and interdisciplinary integration. With continued research and ethical consideration, the field will undoubtedly evolve, offering solutions that push the boundaries of predictive accuracy and practical application across many domains. The future will likely see even greater integration of AI into the fabric of decision-making processes, making deep learning a foundational tool in managing the complex challenges of the modern world.

REFERENCES

Ali, A. (2021). Implementation of ETL Tool for Data Warehousing for Non-Hodgkin Lymphoma (NHL) Cancer in Public Sector, Pakistan. *LC International Journal of STEM (ISSN: 2708-7123), 2*(3), 98-102.

Anwar Ali Sathio and Arz Muhammad Brohi. (2021). The Imperative Role of Pervasive Data in Healthcare. In Switzerland, A. G. (Ed.), *Dr. Mohammad Shahid Husain, Dr. Muhamad Hariz Bin Muhamad Adnan, Dr. Mohammad Zunnun Khan, Dr. Saurabh Shukla, and Fahad U Khan* (pp. 17–21). Springer., DOI: 10.1007/978-3-030-77746-3_2

Audebert, N., & Le Saux, B., & R. (. (2020). Land use classification with deep learning: A review. *Remote Sensing, 12*(5), 807. DOI: 10.3390/rs12050807

Azizi, S.. (2021). "Big Self-Supervised Models Advance Medical Image Classification." *Proceedings of ICCV*, 2021. DOI: 10.1109/ICCV48922.2021.00346

Baker, S. (2020). Limitations of traditional weather forecasting models. *Meteorological Applications, 27*(3), e1928. DOI: 10.1002/met.1928

Bauer, P., Thorpe, A., & Brunet, G. (2015). The quiet revolution of numerical weather prediction. *Nature, 525*(7567), 47–55. DOI: 10.1038/nature14956 PMID: 26333465

Bengio, Y., Courville, A., & Vincent, P. (2013). Representation learning: A review and new perspectives. *IEEE Transactions on Pattern Analysis and Machine Intelligence, 35*(8), 1798–1828. DOI: 10.1109/TPAMI.2013.50 PMID: 23787338

Berk, L. S., Liu, Y., & Weng, X. (2020). Quantum computing and the future of artificial intelligence. *Nature Reviews. Physics, 2*(7), 1–14.

Chai, J., Zhao, Y., & Wang, M. (2021). Hybrid deep learning models for improving forecasting accuracy: A case study in energy demand forecasting. *Applied Energy, 283*, 116198

Chen, H., Zhang, H., & Huang, Y. (2020). Deep learning for temperature prediction: A case study on climate data. *Journal of Climate, 33*(10), 3941–3955. DOI: 10.1175/JCLI-D-19-0802.1

Chen, J., Xie, S., & Liu, Y. (2020). A survey on self-supervised learning: Theoretical perspectives and applications. *IEEE Transactions on Neural Networks and Learning Systems, 32*(9), 3979–3995. DOI: 10.1109/TNNLS.2020.2987724

Chen, T., Kornblith, S., Norouzi, M., & Hinton, G. (2020). "A Simple Framework for Contrastive Learning of Visual Representations." *Proceedings of ICML*, 2020.

Chen, Y., & Dai, Q. (2023). RNNs and LSTMs in temporal prediction: A review of techniques and applications. *Pattern Recognition Letters, 154*(4), 178–189.

Chen, Y., Wu, Y., & Lin, Y. (2022). Temperature forecasting using transfer learning. *Atmosphere, 13*(1), 120. DOI: 10.3390/atmos13010120

Chen, Y., Wu, Y., & Lin, Y. (2023). Predicting extreme weather events with hybrid deep learning models. *Nature Communications, 14*(1), 1728. DOI: 10.1038/s41467-023-37423-7 PMID: 36977667

Cheng, Y., Hu, J., & Yang, Y. (2023). Privacy-preserving deep learning in healthcare: A survey. *Journal of Biomedical Informatics*, *138*, 104202. DOI: 10.1016/j.jbi.2023.104202

Cireşan, D., Meier, U., & Schmidhuber, J. (2020). Multi-Column Deep Neural Networks for Tumor Classification in Breast Cancer. *International Conference on Medical Image Computing and Computer-Assisted Intervention*, 133-142. https://doi.org/DOI: 10.1007/978-3-030-59728-3_12

Dastin, J. (2018). *Amazon scrapped a secret AI recruiting tool that showed bias against women*. Reuters.

Dietterich, T. G. (2000). Ensemble methods in machine learning. In *Proceedings of the International Workshop on Multiple Classifier Systems* (pp. 1–15). Springer. https://doi.org/DOI: 10.1007/3-540-45014-9_1

Dosovitskiy, A., et al. (2021). "An Image is Worth 16x16 Words: Transformers for Image Recognition at Scale." *ICLR*, 2021.

EFTViT: Efficient Federated Training of Vision Transformers with Hierarchical Masked Modeling. (2024). arXiv preprint arXiv:2412.00334.

Esteva, A., Kuprel, B., Novoa, R. A., Ko, J., Swetter, S. M., Blau, H. M., & Thrun, S. (2019). Dermatologist-level classification of skin cancer with deep neural networks. *Nature*, *542*(7639), 115–118. DOI: 10.1038/nature21056 PMID: 28117445

Frid-Adar, M., Ganin, A., et al. (2020). GAN-based augmentation of breast cancer histopathological images. *SpringerLink*, 104–112. https://doi.org/DOI: 10.1007/s11548-019-02009-2

Gao, Y., Yang, X., & Liu, L. (2022). Explainable Artificial Intelligence for Medical Imaging: A Survey. *Medical Image Analysis*, *73*, 102216. DOI: 10.1016/j.media.2021.102216

Ghassemi, M.. (2021). A Review of Bias and Fairness in Machine Learning for Healthcare. *Nature Medicine*, *27*(3), 2021.

Gong, P., Li, X., & Zhang, X. (2021). Deep learning for vegetation cover change detection: A systematic review. *ISPRS Journal of Photogrammetry and Remote Sensing*, *177*, 269–284. DOI: 10.1016/j.isprsjprs.2021.05.009

Goodfellow, I., Pouget-Abadie, J., Mirza, M., ... (2014). Generative adversarial nets. In *Advances in Neural Information Processing Systems* (pp. 27–39). http://papers.nips.cc/paper/5423-generative-adversarial-nets.pdf

Graves, A., Mohamed, A.-r., & Hinton, G. (2013). Speech recognition with deep recurrent neural networks. In *2013 IEEE International Conference on Acoustics, Speech and Signal Processing* (pp. 6645–6649). DOI: 10.1109/ICASSP.2013.6638947

He, K., et al. (2022). "Masked Autoencoders Are Scalable Vision Learners." *CVPR*, 2022.

He, K., Zhang, X., Ren, S., & Sun, J. (2016). Deep residual learning for image recognition. In *Proceedings of the IEEE Conference on Computer Vision and Pattern Recognition* (pp. 770-778). DOI: 10.1109/CVPR.2016.90

Hernandez-Cruz, N., Saha, P., Sarker, M. M. K., & Noble, J. A. (2024). Review of Federated Learning and Machine Learning-Based Methods for Medical Image Analysis. *Big Data and Cognitive Computing*, *8*(9), 99. DOI: 10.3390/bdcc8090099

Hochreiter, S., & Schmidhuber, J. (1997). Long short-term memory. *Neural Computation*, *9*(8), 1735–1780. DOI: 10.1162/neco.1997.9.8.1735 PMID: 9377276

Hoffman, K., Nader, F., & Larkin, M. (2020). Bias in artificial intelligence: The role of dataset composition. *Journal of AI Ethics*, *1*(1), 51–61.

Huang, K., Liu, Y., & Zhang, S. (2021). Challenges and prospects of deep learning in weather forecasting. *Frontiers of Earth Science*, *9*, 1–9. DOI: 10.3389/feart.2021.744430

Jobin, A., Ienca, M., & Andorno, R. (2019). Artificial intelligence: The global landscape of AI ethics guidelines. *Nature Machine Intelligence*, *1*(4), 389–399. DOI: 10.1038/s42256-019-0088-2

Kalnay, E. (2003). *Atmospheric modeling, data assimilation, and predictability*. Cambridge University Press., DOI: 10.1017/CBO9780511802025

Khan, J., Malik, M., & Arif, R. (2023). CNNs in image analysis: Advances and applications in predictive imaging. *IEEE Transactions on Neural Networks and Learning Systems*, *54*(1), 32–46.

Khan, S., Raza, A., & Khan, F. (2021). Deep learning for image classification: A survey. *Journal of Imaging*, *7*(3), 40. DOI: 10.3390/jimaging7030040

Krizhevsky, A., Sutskever, I., & Hinton, G. E. (2012). ImageNet classification with deep convolutional neural networks. In *Advances in Neural Information Processing Systems* (pp. 1097–1105).

Kumar, V., Gupta, A., & Sharma, S. (2022). Multi-modal deep learning: Recent advances and future directions. *Journal of Computer Science and Technology*, *37*(5), 893–922.

Kumar, V., Kumar, D., & Gupta, N. (2023). Explainable AI for weather forecasting: A review. *IEEE Access : Practical Innovations, Open Solutions*, *11*, 12345–12361. DOI: 10.1109/ACCESS.2023.1234567

Label-Efficient Self-Supervised Federated Learning for Tackling Data Heterogeneity in Medical Image Analysis. (2024).. . *Frontiers in Artificial Intelligence*, *7*, 123.

Lee, J., Kim, H., & Lee, J. (2023). A comparative analysis of traditional and deep learning-based weather forecasting methods. *International Journal of Climatology*, *43*(1), 123–140. DOI: 10.1002/joc.7734

Li, T., Sahu, A. K., Talwalkar, A., & Smith, V. (2020). Federated Learning: Challenges, Methods, and Future Directions. *IEEE Signal Processing Magazine*, *37*(3), 2020. DOI: 10.1109/MSP.2020.2975749

Lin, J., Wang, M., & Zhang, Z. (2020). Class imbalance in medical image classification: A review. *IEEE Access : Practical Innovations, Open Solutions*, *8*, 177085–177098. DOI: 10.1109/ACCESS.2020.3029703

Lipton, Z. C. (2016). The mythos of model interpretability. *Communications of the ACM*, *61*(7), 36–43.

Liu, H., Wang, Y., & Zhang, X. (2020). A hybrid CNN-LSTM model for precipitation forecasting. *Journal of Hydrology (Amsterdam)*, *585*, 124821. DOI: 10.1016/j.jhydrol.2020.124821

Liu, J., Wang, J., & Xu, H. (2022). The impact of data quality on deep learning-based predictive analytics. *Data Science and Engineering*, *7*(1), 1–15.

Liu, X., Chen, Y., & Zhang, H. (2021). Deep Learning in Medical Imaging: Overview and Future Directions. *IEEE Transactions on Medical Imaging*, *40*(12), 1–15. DOI: 10.1109/TMI.2021.3088025

Liu, Z., et al. (2022). "Swin Transformer V2: Scaling Up Capacity and Resolution." *CVPR*, 2022.

Liu, Z., Yu, K., & Zhang, C. (2022). A survey of multi-modal deep learning. *IEEE Transactions on Neural Networks and Learning Systems*, *33*(10), 4620–4634. DOI: 10.1109/TNNLS.2021.3080541

Lloyd, S., Mohseni, M., & Rebentrost, P. (2020). Quantum algorithms for fixed Qubit architectures. *Nature*, *549*(7671), 201–206.

Lundberg, S. M., & Lee, S. I. (2017). A unified approach to interpreting model predictions. *InProceedings of the 31st International Conference on Neural Information Processing Systems* (pp. 4765-4774).

Lyu, L., Yu, H., & Yang, Q. (2020). Threats to Federated Learning: A Survey. *ACM Computing Surveys*, •••, 2020.

McGovern, A., Bluestein, H. B., & Meyer, J. (2019). Using deep learning to predict severe weather events. *Weather and Forecasting*, *34*(4), 1021–1036. DOI: 10.1175/WAF-D-18-0155.1

McGovern, A., Bluestein, H. B., & Meyer, J. (2023). Machine learning models for severe weather prediction. *Weather and Forecasting*, *38*(3), 579–595. DOI: 10.1175/WAF-D-22-0150.1

Miller, T. (2019). Explanation in artificial intelligence: Insights from the social sciences. *Artificial Intelligence*, *267*, 1–38. DOI: 10.1016/j.artint.2018.07.007

Min, D., Huang, Z., & Liu, J. (2020). Precipitation prediction based on deep learning model. *Water (Basel)*, *12*(3), 706. DOI: 10.3390/w12030706

Pan, S. J., & Yang, Q. (2010). A survey on transfer learning. *IEEE Transactions on Knowledge and Data Engineering*, *22*(10), 1345–1359. DOI: 10.1109/TKDE.2009.191

Panhwar, A. O., Sathio, A. A., Lakhan, A., Umer, M., Mithiani, R. M., & Khan, S. (2022). Plant health detection enabled CNN scheme in IoT network. *International Journal of Computing and Digital Systems*, *11*(1), 344–335.

Rai, P., Kumar, V., & Gupta, A. (2023). Interpretability in deep learning models for meteorology. *Earth and Space Science*, 10(2), e2022EA002123. https://doi.org/DOI: 10.1029/2022EA002123

Rajalakshmi, R., Subashini, R., & Anantharaman, V. (2020). Automated diabetic retinopathy detection in retinal fundus images using deep learning. *Journal of Diabetes Science and Technology*, *14*(4), 754–759. DOI: 10.1177/1932296820909423 PMID: 32468843

Rajpurkar, P., Irvin, J., & Zhu, K. (2020). CheXNet: Radiologist-Level Pneumonia Detection on Chest X-Rays with Deep Learning. *Proceedings of the National Academy of Sciences of the United States of America*, *116*(51), 23090–23095. DOI: 10.1073/pnas.1718063115

Rosenfeld, D., & Wood, R., & H. (2020). Machine learning and climate science: Opportunities and challenges. *Climatic Change*, *162*(2), 609–627. DOI: 10.1007/s10584-020-02871-8

Sarker, I. H., Hossain, M. S., & Nguyen, T. A. (2023). Deep learning: Current applications and research challenges in digital imaging and predictive modeling. *Journal of Applied Computing and Artificial Intelligence*, *15*(3), 85–97.

Sathio, A. A. (2018). A Study on the Conceptual Frame Work of Dataware Housing in Health Sector in Pakistan A Case Study of a Hospital System and Disease (Hepatitis C). *International Journal of Computer (IJC)*, vol. 29, no. 1, pp. 59–81, Sep. 2018., doi: https://www.researchgate.net/publication/324896538_A_Study_On_The_Conceptual_Frame_Work_Of_Data_Warehousing_In_Health_Sector_In_Pakistan_A_Case_Study_Of_a_Hospital_System_And_Disease_Hepatitis_C/citations

Sathio, A.A., Mujeeb, Shaikh, R., Panhwar, A.O., Rehman, U., Sahito, M.A., & Lakhan, A. (2021). A Review on State of the Art in Flipped Classroom Technology A Blended E-Learning. *International Journal of Emerging Trends in Engineering Research.*

Sathio, A. A., Awan, S. A., Panhwar, A. O., Aamir, A. M., Brohi, A. M., & Burdi, A. (2023). A Blockchain-Enabled Machine Learning Mask Detection Method for Prevention of Pandemic Diseases. *VAWKUM Transactions on Computer Sciences*, *11*(1), 165–183. DOI: 10.21015/vtcs.v11i1.1443

Sathio, A. A., Dootio, M. A., & Lakhan, A., ur Rehman, M., Pnhwar, A. O., & Sahito, M. A. (2021, August). Pervasive futuristic healthcare and blockchain enabled digital identities-challenges and future intensions. In *2021 International Conference on Computing, Electronics & Communications Engineering (iCCECE)* (pp. 30-35). IEEE. DOI: 10.1109/iCCECE52344.2021.9534846

Sathio, A. A., Rind, M. M., & Lakhan, A. (2024). Deep Learning Algorithms: Clustering and Classifications for Multimedia Data. In *Deep Learning for Multimedia Processing Applications* (pp. 114-145). CRC Press.

Sathio, A. A., Rind, M. M., & Lakhan, A. (2024). A. Deep Learning Algorithms and Architectures for Multimodal Data Analysis. In *Deep Learning for Multimedia Processing Applications* (pp. 74–113). CRC Press.

Sathio, A. A., Shaikh, M., Panhwar, A. O., Sahito, M. A., & Lakhan, A. (2021). Recommended Employment Model for Silent Community using Smart Technology. *International Journal of Emerging Trends in Engineering Research.*

Schmidt, C. R., Kellnhofer, P., & Liu, Y. (2022). Scaling deep learning: The importance of efficiency. *IEEE Transactions on Neural Networks and Learning Systems*, *33*(5), 1983–1994.

Selbst, A. D., Andrew, H., & Barocas, S. (2019). Fairness and abstraction in sociotechnical systems. *Proceedings of the 2019 ACM Conference on Fairness, Accountability, and Transparency* (pp. 59-68).

Shah, H., Ahmed, S., Sathio, A. A., & Burdi, A. (2023). W-rank: A keyphrase extraction method for webpage based on linguistics and DOM-base features. *VAWKUM Transactions on Computer Sciences*, *11*(1), 217–228. DOI: 10.21015/vtcs.v11i1.1493

Shaikh, A. Zaffar and Ali Sathio, Anwar and Ali Laghari, Asif and Ahmed Memon, Mashooq and Hussain Mirani, Ibrar (2019) *Study of the Role of New Technologies in Pharmaceutical Industry.* Journal of Pharmaceutical Research International, 31 (6). pp. 1-11. ISSN 2456-9119

Shaikh, Z. A., Wagan, A. A., Laghari, A. A., Ali, K., Memon, M. A., & Sathio, A. A. (2019). The role of software configuration management and capability maturity model in system quality. *IJCSNS*, *19*(11), 114.

Sheller, M. J., Reina, G. A., Edwards, B., Martin, J., & Bakas, S. (2020). Federated Learning in Medicine: Facilitating Multi-Institutional Collaborations without Sharing Patient Data. *Scientific Reports*, *10*(1), 2020. DOI: 10.1038/s41598-020-69250-1 PMID: 32724046

Shi, X., Chen, Z., & Wang, H. (2021). Short-term rainfall prediction using LSTM networks. *Journal of Hydrology (Amsterdam)*, *596*, 126165. DOI: 10.1016/j.jhydrol.2021.126165

Shorten, C., & Khoshgoftaar, T. M. (2019). A survey on image data augmentation for deep learning. *Journal of Big Data*, *6*(1), 60. DOI: 10.1186/s40537-019-0197-0

Singh, V., Sathio, A. A., Anwar, S., Vavekanand, R., & Danish, R. (2024). A Medical Imaging Approach for Recognising Mitral Regurg-itation Through Machine Learning Methods in Cardiac Imaging.

Sinha, A.. (2021). Transfer learning for chest X-ray classification: A systematic review. *Artificial Intelligence in Medicine*, *113*, 101016. DOI: 10.1016/j.artmed.2021.101016

Ur, M., Shaikh, R., Sathio, A. A., Lakhan, A., Panhwar, A. O., Sahito, M. A., & Kehar, A. (2021). Dynamic Content Enabled Microservice for Business Applications in Distributed Cloudlet Cloud Network. *International Journal of Emerging Trends in Engineering Research*.

Vaswani, A., Shard, N., Parmar, N., ... (2017). Attention is all you need. In *Advances in Neural Information Processing Systems* (pp. 5998–6008). https://doi.org/DOI: 10.5555/3295222.3295349

Vavekanand, R., Sathio, A. A., Singh, V., & Anwar, S. (2024). Water4. 0: An Industrial Water Pollution Forecasting Using Machine Learning. *Available atSSRN* 4849924.

Wang, J., Wang, Q., & Zhang, T. (2022). Using GANs to enhance precipitation predictions. *Environmental Research Letters*, *17*(7), 075002. DOI: 10.1088/1748-9326/ac65f0

Wang, Y., Zhang, H., & Zhao, C. (2022). Deep learning for lung cancer: A systematic review. *Scientific Reports*, *12*(1), 1–13. DOI: 10.1038/s41598-022-25239-4 PMID: 34992227

Wang, Z., Liu, S., & Li, P. (2022). Deep learning models in predictive analysis for image-based applications. *Computer Vision and Pattern Recognition*, *34*(2), 172–184.

Yao, H., Liu, M., Li, D., & Xu, W. (2021). RNN-based methods for image time series prediction. *Journal of Computational Science*, *50*, 101283.

Yao, Y., Zhang, Y., & Li, S. (2021). The impact of data quality on deep learning model performance: A systematic review. *Journal of Systems and Software*, *176*, 110926.

Yosinski, J., Clune, J., & Nguyen, A.. (2014). How transferable are features in deep neural networks? *Advances in Neural Information Processing Systems*, •••, 3320–3328.

Yu, H.. (2022). LSTM-based predictive modeling of medical images: A case study in pulmonary nodule detection. *Journal of Biomedical Informatics*, *125*, 103971. DOI: 10.1016/j.jbi.2021.103971

Yu, H., Wu, S., & Liu, Q. (2021). A hybrid deep learning model for temperature prediction using time series data. *Applied Sciences (Basel, Switzerland)*, *11*(3), 1104. DOI: 10.3390/app11031104

Zhang, C., Chen, L., & Zhang, X. (2021). A survey on scalable deep learning: Methods and applications. *ACM Computing Surveys*, *54*(7), 1–36.

Zhang, H.. (2020). Deep learning for skin lesion classification: A systematic review. *Journal of Medical Systems*, *44*(1), 1–14. DOI: 10.1007/s10916-019-1488-0 PMID: 33236166

Zhang, H., Chen, J., & Liu, Y. (2022). Deep learning for climate modeling: A review. *Earth System Science Data*, *14*(2), 657–677. DOI: 10.5194/essd-14-657-2022

Zhang, H., Zhao, J., & Zhang, J. (2022). Predicting cognitive decline in Alzheimer's disease using deep learning techniques on MRI. *Neurobiology of Aging*, *119*, 1–11. DOI: 10.1016/j.neurobiolaging.2022.06.009

Zhang, J.. (2021). Weather forecasting based on GANs using satellite images. *Remote Sensing*, *13*(16), 3210. DOI: 10.3390/rs13163210

Zhang, X., Xu, Z., & Wang, J. (2022). A hybrid deep learning model for weather forecasting based on CNN and LSTM. *Remote Sensing*, *14*(4), 789. DOI: 10.3390/rs14040789

Zhang, X., Zheng, Y., & Qiu, Z. (2021). Estimating methane emissions using deep learning from satellite data. *Environmental Science & Technology*, *55*(19), 13029–13037. DOI: 10.1021/acs.est.1c03654

Zhou, Y., Wang, H., & Sun, Y. (2022). The role of data quality in deep learning applications in meteorology. *Atmosphere*, *13*(2), 295. DOI: 10.3390/atmos13020295

Zhou, Y., Zhu, S., & Shen, S. (2022). Weather prediction using satellite imagery: A deep learning approach. *Remote Sensing*, *14*(12), 2844.

Chapter 2
Deep Learning Techniques for Image Clustering and Classification

Zeynep Ünal
https://orcid.org/0000-0002-9954-1151
Niğde Ömer Halisdemir University, Turkey

Yonis Gulzar
https://orcid.org/0000-0002-6515-1569
King Faisal University, Saudi Arabia

ABSTRACT

This chapter explores deep learning techniques for image clustering and classification, crucial tasks in computer vision. It discusses unsupervised clustering methods and supervised classification approaches, including traditional methods like k-means and hierarchical clustering. The chapter also highlights the transformative impact of CNNs, ensemble methods, and transfer learning in classification. It uses case studies like fruit classification in agriculture and brain tumor clustering in medical imaging to illustrate the real-world applicability of these models. Challenges like data limitations, computational requirements, and explainability are also discussed. Future trends include self-supervised learning and multimodal models. The chapter aims to guide researchers and practitioners in leveraging deep learning for effective image clustering and classification across various domains.

1. INTRODUCTION

In computer vision, the fundamental tasks of image clustering and classification are essential for analyzing and understanding visual data. These techniques enable machines to interpret images, allowing applications to recognize objects, segment scenes, and support decision-making in various fields, such as medical imaging, autonomous driving, and social media (Von Glehn De Filippo et al., 2015).

Image clustering is an unsupervised learning approach that groups images based on inherent similarities, without using predefined labels. This method is valuable for discovering patterns in unlabeled datasets, enabling applications like anomaly detection, dataset exploration, and data organization (Saxena

DOI: 10.4018/979-8-3693-9045-0.ch002

et al., 2017). In contrast, image classification is a supervised learning approach that requires labeled datasets to train models to accurately assign images to specific categories. By learning from labeled examples, classification models achieve high accuracy in tasks like identifying diseases from medical scans, recognizing facial features, and detecting objects in real-time applications (Schmarje et al., 2021).

The core difference between clustering and classification lies in their learning paradigms: clustering operates without labels, aiming to uncover hidden structures within the data (Chen et al., 2024), while classification relies on labeled data to assign explicit categories. Both methods play crucial roles in computer vision, complementing each other to enhance the adaptability and intelligence of deep learning models in handling vast image data across varied domains (Rawat & Wang, 2017).

Both clustering and classification techniques are utilized across various industries. In image clustering, online shopping platforms use clustering to group similar-looking products, helping customers find related items even without specific search terms (Gulzar et al., 2023). In medical imaging, clustering methods can automatically group X-rays or MRI scans based on visual characteristics, assisting healthcare providers in identifying unusual patterns or anomalies that might indicate health issues (Jones et al., 2018). Social media platforms also use clustering to organize large amounts of user-uploaded content into themed groups, enhancing recommendations and content discovery (Litjens et al., 2017).

Image classification, however, is commonly used in situations that need exact identification. For instance, self-driving cars rely on classification algorithms to recognize objects such as pedestrians, road signs, and other vehicles to ensure safe driving. In healthcare, classification models help diagnose conditions from medical images, like differentiating between benign and malignant tumors in radiology(Yousefirizi et al., 2022) . Agriculture uses classification for identifying crops and weeds, enabling precise farming methods that maximize yield and decrease manual work (Seelwal et al., 2024; Unal, 2020). When used together, clustering and classification enhance deep learning models' ability to process complex image datasets, converting raw visual information into useful insights and supporting progress in areas from healthcare to industry and entertainment (Thunold et al., 2023).

2. IMAGE CLUSTERING USING DEEP LEARNING

Clustering is a key technique in machine learning and data analysis that groups data points into clusters based on similarity (Ezugwu et al., 2022). For image data, clustering organizes images by shared visual features such as color, texture, or shape (Wazarkar & Keshavamurthy, 2018). Traditional clustering methods, including k-means, hierarchical clustering, and DBSCAN, rely on distance measurements within a feature space to form clusters (Vybhavi et al., 2024). While effective for structured data, these methods encounter limitations when applied to high-dimensional, unstructured data like images. Quality metrics such as the Silhouette Score and the Davies-Bouldin Index are often used to evaluate clustering outcomes, providing insight into the compactness and separability of clusters. The Silhouette Score assesses proximity of points in a cluster to points in neighboring clusters (Punhani et al., 2022), while the Davies-Bouldin Index measures cluster similarity ratios (Ros et al., 2023).

Clustering high-dimensional image data effectively requires feature representations that capture salient visual elements. Unlike structured data, images have significant dimensionality, with each pixel contributing information. Here, deep learning, particularly convolutional neural networks (CNNs), is pivotal for extracting hierarchical, meaningful features suited for clustering (Guérin et al., 2021). Deep learning techniques enhance clustering by addressing the complexities of image data that traditional clustering algorithms struggle with. CNNs extract complex visual features through layered processing: early layers detect basic elements like edges and textures, while later layers identify shapes and structures (Amri et al., 2024; Mamat et al., 2023).. This multi-level feature extraction enables clustering algorithms to operate with compact, informative image representations, making clustering feasible and insightful (Gulzar et al., 2023). Pretrained deep learning models are frequently fine-tuned or used directly as feature extractors, significantly improving clustering results by leveraging robust features learned from large datasets (Aktaş et al., 2022).

Though clustering and classification both organize data, they have distinct purposes and methods. Clustering is unsupervised, grouping data based on inherent similarities without needing predefined labels (Chander & Vijaya, 2021). Its primary purpose is to reveal natural groupings within data. Conversely, classification is supervised, using labeled data to train a model that predicts the class of new, unseen data based on learned patterns (Gulzar, 2024). While clustering explores data structure, classification is predictive, making it suitable for applications with known classes (Nerurkar et al., 2018). Unsupervised learning techniques, such as clustering and dimensionality reduction, are particularly useful in scenarios where labeled data is scarce or costly, such as exploratory data analysis, anomaly detection, and market segmentation (Abukmeil et al., 2021).

2.1 Traditional Clustering Methods

Traditional clustering methods are foundational techniques in unsupervised learning, used to group data points based on their similarities without the use of labeled data. These methods work by examining the relationships and distances between data points to form clusters (Oyelade et al., 2019). While they're effective for low-dimensional and moderately sized datasets, they can struggle with high-dimensional data or large, complex datasets such as images. Some commonly used traditional clustering methods include **k-means, hierarchical clustering**, and **DBSCAN**. Each method has unique characteristics, making it suitable for different types of data and applications(Dong et al., 2019).

- **k-Means Clustering:** k-Means clustering is an iterative algorithm that partitions the dataset into *k* clusters(Qi et al., 2016). It starts by initializing *k* centroids, then assigns each data point to the nearest centroid, forming clusters. The centroids are updated based on the average of the assigned points, and the process continues until the convergence. It is simple and efficient but relies on knowing the number of clusters in advance and may struggle with clusters of varying shapes and densities(Fränti & Sieranoja, 2019).
- **Hierarchical Clustering:** Hierarchical clustering builds a hierarchy of clusters through bottom-up or top-down approach. This method is advantageous because it doesn't require specifying the number of clusters beforehand, but it can be computationally expensive for large datasets (Bouguettaya et al., 2015).
- **DBSCAN (Density-Based Spatial Clustering of Applications with Noise):** DBSCAN groups data points based on density, identifying clusters as dense regions of points separated by low-density regions. It requires two parameters: a distance threshold and a minimum number of points to form a cluster. DBSCAN is effective for identifying arbitrarily shaped clusters and is robust to noise (outliers), making it suitable for tasks with complex cluster structures. However, it may struggle with varying densities across clusters and requires tuning of parameters(Scitovski & Sabo, 2020).

- **Mean Shift Clustering:** Mean shift clustering is a density-based algorithm that does not require specifying the number of clusters. It iteratively shifts each data point towards the nearest region of high data density, eventually converging on a set of cluster centers. Mean shift is particularly effective in identifying clusters with irregular shapes, but it is computationally intensive and may perform poorly on high-dimensional data without adjustments(S. Anand et al., 2014).
- **Gaussian Mixture Models (GMMs):** GMMs model data as a mixture of multiple Gaussian distributions, each representing a cluster. Unlike k-means, which assigns data points to a single cluster, GMMs provide the probability that a point belongs to each cluster, enabling soft clustering. This is advantageous for data with overlapping clusters, as it can capture more complex relationships between data points. However, GMMs require prior knowledge or estimation of the number of clusters and are sensitive to initialization(Wan et al., 2019).
- **Agglomerative Clustering:** A specific form of hierarchical clustering, agglomerative clustering starts by treating each point as its own cluster and merges them iteratively based on a distance metric (e.g., single-linkage, complete-linkage) until a predefined stopping criterion is met. It is highly interpretable and doesn't require specifying the number of clusters, but it can be computationally heavy for large datasets due to its iterative merging process(Tokuda et al., 2022).

2.2 Deep Learning Techniques for Image Clustering

Deep learning techniques have greatly improved image clustering by making it possible to extract complex, high-level features directly from raw images, helping to address the challenges of high-dimensional, unstructured image data (Ayoub et al., 2023). Traditional methods often find it difficult to handle the dimensionality and variability in image data. However, deep learning models, especially convolutional neural networks (CNNs), can learn hierarchical feature representations from images, detecting patterns and similarities that might be missed by conventional clustering methods (Ünal & Aktaş, 2023).

Several deep learning approaches are commonly used for image clustering, including autoencoders, variational autoencoders (VAEs), deep embedding clustering (DEC), self-supervised learning methods, and generative adversarial networks (GANs). These techniques help improve clustering quality and make it easier to organize large collections of unstructured image data.

- **Autoencoders:** Autoencoders are neural networks designed to learn a compressed representation (encoding) of the input data by reducing it to a lower-dimensional space, then reconstructing it from this encoding. In image clustering, the encoder part of the autoencoder is used to transform images into compact feature representations that preserve important visual information. These lower-dimensional features are then clustered using algorithms like k-means or hierarchical clustering, making it easier to group similar images effectively (Yu & Príncipe, 2019).
- **Variational Autoencoders (VAEs):** VAEs are a probabilistic extension of autoencoders that learn to represent data as a distribution in latent space. Instead of encoding data into fixed points, VAEs encode data into distributions, capturing complex data variability and enabling more robust feature representations. This stochastic approach helps capture underlying data patterns, making VAEs well-suited for image clustering tasks where the data has complex distributions. The latent representations learned by VAEs can be clustered, resulting in more meaningful groupings (Wei et al., 2020).

- **Deep Embedding Clustering (DEC):** DEC is a specialized method that integrates clustering directly into the deep learning process. It starts by learning features through a deep neural network, then iteratively optimizes cluster assignments by minimizing the difference between current assignments and a target distribution. This dual process of feature learning and cluster refinement enhances clustering quality and eliminates the need for separate feature extraction and clustering steps, making DEC effective for organizing high-dimensional data like images(Sheng et al., 2022).
- **Self-Supervised Learning Methods:** Self-supervised learning methods train models to learn feature representations without labeled data by creating surrogate tasks, such as predicting image transformations. These techniques learn robust representations by contrasting positive and negative image pairs, which leads to clustering-friendly embeddings. These embeddings are then used to group images, providing a powerful approach for image clustering, especially for large, unlabeled datasets (S. Li et al., 2024).
- **Generative Adversarial Networks (GANs):** GANs consist of two neural networks, a generator and a discriminator, working in tandem to generate realistic data and distinguish real from generated samples, respectively. GANs can produce synthetic images that mimic real datasets, which are useful for clustering applications as they help identify underlying data patterns. GANs can also be used to improve clustering by generating additional data or learning rich, diverse representations that enable more accurate clustering of complex image datasets (Figueira & Vaz, 2022).

2.3 Evaluation Metrics for Clustering

Evaluating clustering results is essential to ensure that clusters represent meaningful groupings of the data. Since clustering is an unsupervised task, evaluation metrics often focus on measuring the compactness of clusters (how close data points are within clusters) and separation (how distinct clusters are from each other). Some of the widely used evaluation metrics for clustering include the **Silhouette Score**, **Davies-Bouldin Index**, **Inertia**, **Adjusted Rand Index (ARI)**, **Normalized Mutual Information (NMI)**, and **Homogeneity, Completeness, and V-measure**. These metrics help assess the quality of clustering by examining internal consistency, comparing cluster assignments to any available ground truth, or both. Choosing an appropriate metric depends on the clustering goal, data type, and the availability of labeled data for comparison(Ahmed et al., 2020).

- **Silhouette Score:** The Silhouette Score measures how similar each data point is to its own cluster compared to other clusters, producing a value between -1 and 1. Higher values indicate that clusters are well-defined, with data points close to their cluster center and distant from other clusters(Shutaywi & Kachouie, 2021).
- **Davies-Bouldin Index:** The Davies-Bouldin Index calculates the average "similarity ratio" between each cluster and the one it is most similar to, with lower values indicating better clustering. This index balances both cluster compactness and separation, making it useful for assessing distinctness among clusters(Thongnim et al., 2024).
- **Inertia (Within-cluster Sum of Squares):** Inertia is the sum of squared distances between each point and its cluster center. Lower values of inertia indicate tighter clusters. This metric is commonly used in k-means clustering to measure the compactness of clusters and can guide the selection of the optimal number of clusters(Nishom et al., 2024).

- **Adjusted Rand Index (ARI):** The Adjusted Rand Index measures the similarity between predicted clusters and true labels, if available, by accounting for chance. Ranging from -1 to 1, higher ARI values indicate a better match with the ground truth, making it useful for clustering evaluations when labeled data is available (Sundqvist et al., 2023).
- **Normalized Mutual Information (NMI):** NMI assesses the amount of information shared between the predicted clusters and true labels. It ranges from 0 to 1, where 1 signifies perfect agreement between clusters and labels. NMI is a robust metric, especially useful when clusters are of varying sizes (Mahmoudi & Jemielniak, 2024).
- **Homogeneity, Completeness, and V-measure:** These three related metrics evaluate cluster consistency with respect to known labels. **Homogeneity** measures whether all clusters contain only data points of a single class, **Completeness** checks if all data points of a class are in the same cluster, and **V-measure** is the harmonic mean of homogeneity and completeness. High scores across these metrics indicate strong agreement between clusters and true labels (Lu & Uddin, 2024).

3. IMAGE CLASSIFICATION USING DEEP LEARNING

Image classification is a core task in computer vision that involves assigning a predefined label or category to an image based on its visual content (Alkanan & Gulzar, 2024). It is widely used across various applications, from identifying objects in photos to diagnosing medical conditions from imaging scans. The primary goal of image classification is to learn patterns in images that correspond to specific classes, allowing the model to predict the class of new, unseen images accurately (Gulzar, Ünal, et al., 2024). Traditional methods relied on hand-crafted features such as edges, textures, and color histograms, but these approaches struggled with complex visual data and lacked generalizability. Deep learning, however, has revolutionized image classification by enabling models to automatically learn hierarchical features directly from raw image data, greatly improving accuracy and performance (Dhiman et al., 2023).

Convolutional Neural Networks (CNNs) are the cornerstone of deep learning-based image classification due to their ability to efficiently process image data by preserving spatial information. CNNs consist of multiple layers, including convolutional, pooling, and fully connected layers, which work together to capture low-level features (like edges) and high-level features (such as shapes and objects). The convolutional layers apply filters across the image to detect patterns, while pooling layers reduce the spatial size, making computations more efficient and improving the model's robustness. This layered approach allows CNNs to handle the complexity and high dimensionality of images, leading to better generalization on diverse datasets (Ünal et al., 2024).

Supervised learning is a type of machine learning where models are trained on labeled data to make predictions or classifications (Ünal & İpekçi Çetin, 2022). In this approach, each training example consists of an input and a corresponding output label, which the model learns to associate by identifying patterns in the data. Supervised learning algorithms aim to minimize the error between the model's predictions and the true labels, improving their accuracy over time. Common tasks in supervised learning include classification, where the model predicts discrete categories (like identifying the type of animal in an image), and regression, where it predicts continuous values (such as forecasting house prices). The performance of supervised learning models depends on the quality and quantity of labeled data, as well as the choice of algorithm, making data preparation and model selection crucial steps in achieving high accuracy (Gulzar, Oral, et al., 2024).

3.1 Traditional Classification Methods

Traditional image classification methods are approaches that predate deep learning and rely on manually crafted features to classify images. These methods typically involve two main steps: feature extraction and classification. In the feature extraction step, various techniques are used to capture distinctive characteristics of an image, such as color, texture, and shape, transforming it into a more manageable, lower-dimensional representation. Common features include edge descriptors like SIFT (Scale-Invariant Feature Transform) and SURF (Speeded Up Robust Features), texture descriptors like Local Binary Patterns (LBP), and histogram-based color features (Liu et al., 2017). After feature extraction, traditional classifiers, such as Support Vector Machines (SVMs), k-Nearest Neighbors (k-NN), and Decision Trees, are applied to categorize the image based on the extracted features (Bansal et al., 2022). While these methods work well for simpler tasks and smaller datasets, they lack the flexibility and scalability of modern deep learning approaches and often struggle with complex images or large-scale datasets.

- **Histogram of Oriented Gradients (HOG):** HOG is a feature descriptor that captures the gradient orientation of pixels in localized portions of an image. By analyzing edge directions, HOG represents the shape and appearance of objects, making it useful for tasks like human detection. The HOG descriptor is typically combined with classifiers like SVM for image classification (Déniz et al., 2011).
- **Scale-Invariant Feature Transform (SIFT):** SIFT is a method for detecting and describing local features in images, allowing them to be matched even under changes in scale, rotation, or lighting. SIFT extracts key points and computes feature vectors for each point, making it effective for object recognition and image matching tasks. These feature vectors are then used in classifiers for image classification (Burger Wilhelm and Burge, 2022)
- **Speeded Up Robust Features (SURF):** SURF is a faster alternative to SIFT, designed to detect and describe image features efficiently. It uses an approximation of the Hessian matrix to detect interest points and describes these points using Haar wavelet responses. While less accurate than SIFT, SURF is much faster and suitable for real-time applications requiring image classification (Bay et al., 2008).
- **Local Binary Patterns (LBP):** LBP is a texture descriptor that encodes the relationship between pixels and their neighbors in terms of binary patterns. This technique is often used to analyze texture patterns in grayscale images and is effective for tasks like facial recognition and texture classification. LBP descriptors are combined with classifiers to predict the class of an image based on texture (SONG et al., 2013).
- **Color Histograms:** Color histograms represent the distribution of colors in an image, providing a simple yet powerful way to classify images based on color content. The image is divided into bins according to color values, which are then counted and used as features. Color histograms are especially useful for classifying images with distinct color patterns, such as logos or landscapes (Sergyan, 2008).
- **Support Vector Machines (SVM):** SVM is a supervised learning algorithm often used for image classification in traditional methods. After extracting features, SVM finds the optimal hyperplane that separates data points of different classes in the feature space. SVM is effective for binary classification and can be adapted to multi-class tasks(Mountrakis et al., 2011).

- **k-Nearest Neighbors (k-NN):** k-NN is a simple classification algorithm that assigns a class to a data point based on the majority label of its nearest neighbors in the feature space. After feature extraction, k-NN compares the new image to labeled training samples, identifying its class based on the closest matches (Murti et al., 2019).
- **Decision Trees:** Decision Trees classify images by learning decision rules from features extracted during preprocessing. They split the data based on feature values to separate classes, and each path in the tree represents a sequence of decisions that lead to a final class. While easy to interpret, Decision Trees can become complex and are prone to overfitting (C.-C. Yang et al., 2003).

3.2 Deep Learning Models for Image Classification

Deep learning has become a cornerstone in image classification, as it enables models to learn high-level features and patterns from raw image data. This approach has led to the development of powerful and efficient neural network architectures that can automatically identify complex features such as shapes, textures, and objects (Ünal & Kızıldeniz, 2023). Models like Convolutional Neural Networks (CNNs) are widely used for image classification tasks, each offering unique architectural innovations that improve accuracy, speed, and scalability for real-world applications.

Convolutional Neural Networks (CNNs) have transformed image classification by enabling models to automatically learn spatial hierarchies in image data. CNNs form the foundation of most image classification models. CNNs employ convolutional layers with filters that slide over the input image, detecting patterns such as edges and textures, making them highly suitable for image data. The layered design of CNNs allows them to capture increasingly complex details, with each layer building on patterns identified by previous layers. Early models like LeNet laid the groundwork by introducing key concepts like activation functions and pooling, while later architectures like **AlexNet**, VGGNet, GoogLeNet (Inception), ResNet, and DenseNet have refined CNNs to improve performance, depth, and computational efficiency(Gulzar Y et al., 2024). These advances have made CNNs foundational for modern image classification, powering applications in areas such as facial recognition, medical imaging, and autonomous driving.

- **AlexNet**: A pioneering CNN model that gained prominence in the ImageNet competition, AlexNet introduced ReLU activations and dropout layers to prevent overfitting. Its structure includes stacked convolutional and pooling layers, which allow it to capture hierarchical features in images (Krizhevsky et al., 2012).
- **VGGNet**: This model, known for its deep structure, uses small 3x3 convolutional filters arranged in a series of layers, resulting in a network with up to 19 layers. VGGNet achieves high accuracy but requires significant computational resources due to its large parameter count (Jaderberg et al., 2016).
- **GoogLeNet (Inception)**: Developed by Google, Inception models use modules that apply convolutions of various sizes simultaneously, allowing them to capture features at multiple scales within each layer. This design reduces the number of parameters, making the network efficient (Mishkin et al., 2017).
- **ResNet**: ResNet, or Residual Networks, introduced residual connections that mitigate the vanishing gradient problem, enabling the successful training of networks with over 100 layers. These shortcuts help the model retain information and improve learning in deeper networks (Zhang et al., 2018).

- **DenseNet**: DenseNet enhances ResNet's idea by connecting each layer to every preceding layer, maximizing feature reuse and allowing for a more compact model. This architecture improves performance while keeping computational needs moderate (Zhang et al., 2019).
- **MobileNet**: Targeted for mobile and embedded applications, MobileNet employs depthwise separable convolutions to reduce computational load and model size, making it ideal for resource-limited devices without sacrificing much accuracy (Sinha & El-Sharkawy, 2019).
- **EfficientNet**: EfficientNet scales network depth, width, and resolution using a compound scaling method, balancing performance and efficiency. It achieves high accuracy across datasets while being suitable for various applications, from large-scale servers to mobile devices(Tan & Le, 2019).
- Each of these models has unique advantages, allowing them to perform well in diverse classification tasks and computational settings.

3.3 Hybrid and Ensemble Methods

Hybrid and ensemble methods have gained popularity in deep learning for image classification due to their ability to leverage the strengths of multiple models. In traditional single-model approaches, a single neural network is trained to recognize patterns and classify images. However, the performance of any single model may be limited by its unique architecture, learning approach, or susceptibility to overfitting. By combining multiple models, hybrid and ensemble methods enhance predictive performance, allowing for better generalization and reduced error rates(Ünal & İpekçi Çetin, 2022). These methods are particularly useful for image classification tasks where data variability is high, and complex patterns must be accurately recognized, such as in medical imaging, satellite image analysis, or facial recognition (K. Yang et al., 2020).

Hybrid methods combine different types of models—such as CNNs with RNNs or SVMs—to create a single, cohesive system that benefits from diverse learning capabilities. For instance, CNNs are excellent at extracting spatial features, while RNNs can capture sequential information, which may be advantageous for classifying time-series images or videos (Gulzar, 2023). Alternatively, ensemble methods focus on combining multiple instances of the same model type, such as several CNNs trained with different parameters or on various subsets of data(X. Li et al., 2021). Common ensemble techniques include bagging (Bootstrap Aggregating), boosting, and stacking. Bagging involves training multiple models on different samples of the dataset and averaging their predictions, which reduces variance and improves stability. Boosting, on the other hand, sequentially trains models, each focusing on correcting errors from the previous one, which increases the model's overall accuracy(Gulzar Y et al., 2024).

The goal of combining multiple models in hybrid and ensemble methods is to increase accuracy by reducing the weaknesses of individual models and leveraging the strengths of each. When models are combined, their individual errors often cancel out, leading to improved overall performance. For instance, if one model misclassifies a particular image due to noise or a unique feature, other models in the ensemble may correctly classify it, leading to a better final prediction. This approach is particularly effective in deep learning, where complex model architectures can lead to overfitting or underfitting, depending on the data or specific problem. By blending the outputs of multiple models, hybrid and ensemble methods help mitigate these issues, producing a more robust and accurate classifier. This has been demonstrated in numerous applications, from high-stakes fields like medical diagnostics to real-time applications in autonomous driving, where high accuracy is crucial (Aktaş et al., 2022).

3.4 Transfer Learning in Classification

Transfer learning has become an invaluable technique in image classification, enabling models trained on large, diverse datasets to be adapted for new, more specific tasks. This approach reduces the need for extensive labeled data by reusing knowledge learned by a pretrained model. In image classification, pretrained models on datasets like ImageNet have already learned basic visual features, such as edges, shapes, and textures, across millions of images. Transfer learning allows these models to be fine-tuned on a target dataset, helping them learn specialized patterns relevant to new tasks. This is particularly useful in fields where labeled data is scarce or costly to obtain, such as medical imaging, where labeled samples may be limited to a few thousand images (Ayoub et al., 2022).

One of the primary benefits of transfer learning is that it significantly reduces training time and computational resources. Since pretrained models already understand general visual concepts, they only need minor adjustments to classify images in a new domain, making training faster and less computationally intensive. Transfer learning is especially effective when the source and target datasets share similar features, even if they differ in specifics(Weiss et al., 2016). For example, a model trained in general animal images can be fine-tuned to classify specific breeds of dogs or types of birds. It also helps in avoiding overfitting on smaller datasets, as the model starts with generalized knowledge rather than learning solely from limited examples. This capability has made transfer learning a go-to technique for applications like facial recognition, medical diagnosis, and autonomous vehicle perception.

Fine-tuning technique is also can be applied to Pretrained Models for New Tasks. Fine-tuning is the process of adjusting a pretrained model to make it more suitable for a specific task or dataset (Akada et al., 2021). This involves freezing the early layers of the model, which contain general visual features, and only updating the later layers that capture task-specific details. By fine-tuning, the model can adapt to new patterns in the target data while retaining the general features learned from the source data. For instance, when using a pretrained model for medical imaging, the lower layers might retain general shape or texture recognition, while the higher layers can be adapted to identify disease-specific patterns. Fine-tuning can involve adjusting the learning rate, modifying certain layers, or even retraining specific sections of the network depending on the dataset size and similarity to the source data. This selective adjustment enables transfer learning models to achieve high accuracy on specialized tasks without needing to be trained from scratch, making fine-tuning a highly efficient and practical method for adapting pretrained models(Wani & Afzal, 2017).

3.5 Evaluation Metrics for Classification

Evaluation metrics are essential for assessing the performance of classification models, providing insight into a model's accuracy, robustness, and overall effectiveness on a given task. Different metrics are used based on the type of classification problem and the importance of specific performance factors, such as accuracy, precision, recall, and others. These metrics help evaluate how well a model distinguishes between classes, especially when dealing with imbalanced datasets or multi-class problems. Common metrics include accuracy, precision, recall, F1-score, area under the receiver operating characteristic curve (AUC-ROC), and confusion matrix, each providing unique insights that can guide improvements in model training and optimization.

- **Accuracy**: Accuracy is the ratio of correctly predicted samples to the total number of samples, providing a simple measure of overall performance. However, it can be misleading in imbalanced datasets, as it does not distinguish between different types of errors.
- **Precision**: Precision is the proportion of correctly predicted positive observations out of the total predicted positives. It is useful in scenarios where the cost of false positives is high, as it emphasizes the accuracy of positive predictions.
- **Recall (Sensitivity)**: Recall, or sensitivity, measures the proportion of actual positives that were correctly identified by the model. It is essential in situations where identifying all positives is crucial, such as in medical diagnoses.
- **F1-Score**: The F1-score is the harmonic mean of precision and recall, providing a balanced measure that accounts for both false positives and false negatives. It is valuable when precision and recall are equally important.
- **Confusion Matrix**: The confusion matrix is a table showing the true versus predicted classifications for each class, providing a comprehensive view of a model's performance. It reveals specific misclassification patterns, making it helpful in identifying areas for improvement.
- **AUC-ROC (Area Under the Receiver Operating Characteristic Curve)**: AUC-ROC evaluates a model's ability to distinguish between classes by plotting the true positive rate against the false positive rate at various threshold levels. The higher the AUC, the better the model's performance in distinguishing between classes.
- **Log Loss (Cross-Entropy Loss)**: Log Loss evaluates the probability output of classifiers by penalizing high-confidence, incorrect predictions. It is commonly used in probabilistic classification models and is a key metric in competitions, reflecting the confidence of predictions as well as their accuracy.

These metrics allow practitioners to understand a model's strengths and weaknesses, guiding further tuning and selection of the most appropriate model for the given classification task.

4. CASE STUDIES AND PRACTICAL APPLICATIONS

The application of deep learning techniques in image clustering and classification has transformed various fields, providing solutions to challenges that were once manually intensive and prone to errors. In this section, we explore practical applications of deep learning models in image classification and clustering, with a focus on real-world implementations. The selected case study in agriculture demonstrates how advanced models like MobileNetV2 can efficiently classify fruits, enhancing productivity and quality control in agricultural practices.

4.1 Case Study 1: Image Classification in Agriculture

4.1.1 Problem Context

In agriculture, fruit classification plays a vital role in quality control, sorting, and grading, affecting the entire supply chain from production to retail. Traditionally, this task requires expert knowledge to identify and sort various fruit types accurately, which is labor-intensive and time-consuming. Misclassification can lead to improper grading, resulting in significant waste and economic loss. This case study highlights a solution through deep learning, using the MobileNetV2 architecture with transfer learning to create an efficient and accurate classification model for diverse fruit types (Gulzar, 2023).

4.1.2 Model and Approach

The study employed TL-MobileNetV2, a deep transfer learning model adapted from the MobileNetV2 architecture as shown in Figure 1. The model was enhanced with five additional layers, making it more effective in handling fruit classification tasks while remaining lightweight enough for mobile deployment. The transfer learning approach allows the model to leverage knowledge from large, pre-trained datasets, reducing the need for extensive labeled data and minimizing computational resources. This is particularly advantageous in agricultural settings, where on-site and real-time classification is beneficial.

Figure 1. Architecture diagram of TL-MobileNetV2

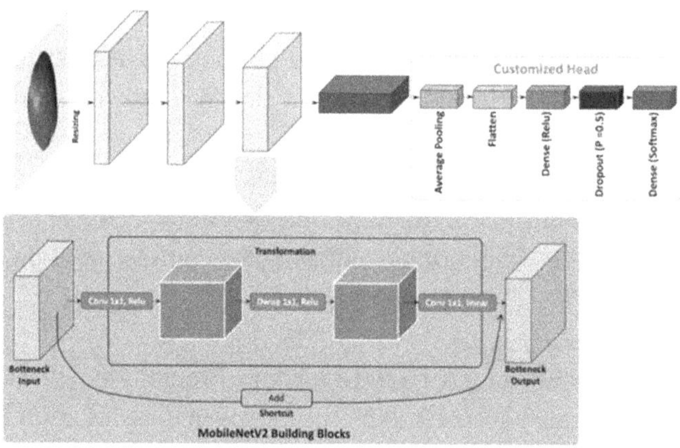

4.1.3 Dataset and Experimental Setup

The model was trained on a dataset comprising 26,149 images of 40 different fruit types, including apples, bananas, cherries, and kiwi, among others. The diversity within the dataset presented a realistic challenge for classification, as each fruit type exhibited variations in color, shape, and texture. Data augmentation techniques were employed to improve the model's robustness, ensuring it could generalize across new images effectively. Figure 2 shows the samples of the dataset.

Figure 2. Sample images from the dataset

4.1.4 Performance Results

The TL-MobileNetV2 model achieved an impressive 99% classification accuracy, surpassing other popular architectures such as AlexNet, VGG16, and ResNet as shown in table 1. Key performance metrics like precision, recall, and F1-score were also high, indicating the model's effectiveness across both training and testing datasets. The results demonstrate the model's ability to handle complex classification tasks with minimal overfitting, making it well-suited for deployment in real-world agricultural environments.

Table 1. Performance of different models compared with the TL-MobileNetV2 model

Models	Precision	Recall	F1-score
AlexNet	0.91	0.89	0.92
VGG16	0.88	0.90	0.88
InceptionV3	0.93	0.88	0.91
ResNet	0.89	0.92	0.90
MobileNetV2	0.96	0.97	0.96
TL-MobileNetV2	**0.99**	**0.99**	**0.99**

4.1.5 Practical Implications

The high accuracy and efficiency of the TL-MobileNetV2 model make it ideal for mobile application deployment. Agricultural workers can use this model to classify fruits on-site, ensuring consistency and quality without needing extensive training. Such applications reduce labor costs, minimize classification errors, and prevent waste. Additionally, this technology has the potential to integrate with automated sorting and grading systems, streamlining processes and optimizing supply chains.

4.1.6 Future Directions

The success of TL-MobileNetV2 in fruit classification opens the door for broader applications in agriculture, such as crop disease detection and quality assessment of other produce. Future work may explore expanding the model's capabilities to classify non-fruit crops or incorporate real-time image analysis for enhanced monitoring and decision-making in precision agriculture.

4.2 Case Study 2: Clustering in Medical Imaging

4.2.1 Problem Context

In medical imaging, accurate stratification of brain tumors in MRI images is crucial for effective diagnosis and personalized treatment. Brain tumors exhibit diverse characteristics that are challenging to classify, especially when dealing with a limited dataset. Misclassification can lead to improper treatment planning, underscoring the need for precise and robust clustering methods that can accurately differentiate tumor types (V. Anand et al., 2023).

4.2.2 Model and Approach

This study introduces a weighted average ensemble deep learning model to enhance clustering accuracy for brain tumor stratification. The ensemble approach combines feature spaces from three different models:

- **Transfer Learning with VGG19**: A pre-trained VGG19 model was used for extracting high-level features from MRI images. VGG19's depth allowed for a detailed capture of complex patterns, providing a solid baseline in detecting tumors.
- **CNN without Data Augmentation**: A standard convolutional neural network (CNN) was also tested without data augmentation to examine its baseline performance. This model performed competitively, showing that straightforward CNN architecture can yield robust results for MRI image analysis.
- **CNN with Data Augmentation**: To diversify the training data and improve model robustness, data augmentation techniques such as vertical and horizontal flipping were applied. This approach produced the highest precision (99%) for the tumor class, demonstrating the importance of en-riched data in medical clustering tasks.

The ensemble model weighted each model's predictions based on optimized parameters derived from grid search, resulting in a final output that leveraged the strengths of all three models. The architecture of the model is shown in Figure 3.

Figure 3. Architecture diagram of the ensemble model

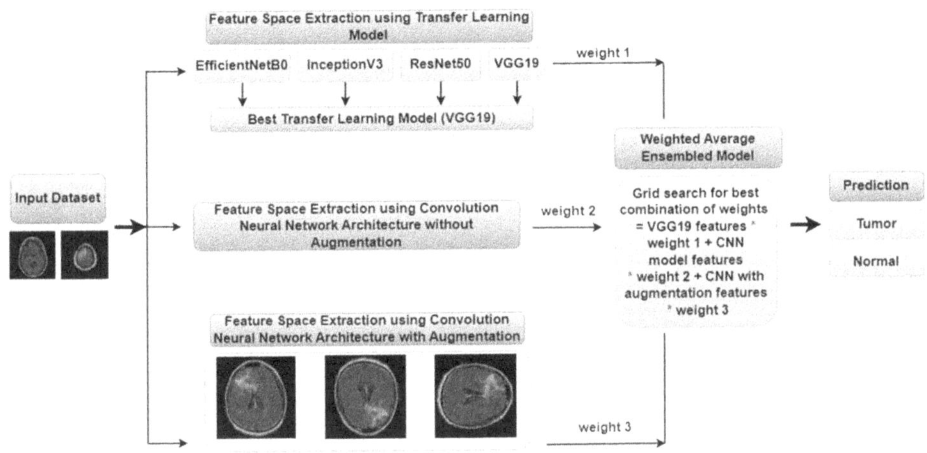

4.2.3 Dataset and Experimental Setup

The study utilized a dataset of **3,929 MRI images** from **110 patients** with brain tumors, split into training and testing sets to validate the ensemble model's performance. Data augmentation enhanced the dataset by creating varied instances of tumor images, which improved the model's ability to generalize across new data. The dataset samples of brain tumor types are shown in Figure 4.

Figure 4. Sample MRI images of brain tumor types (a) Normal image (b) Tumor images

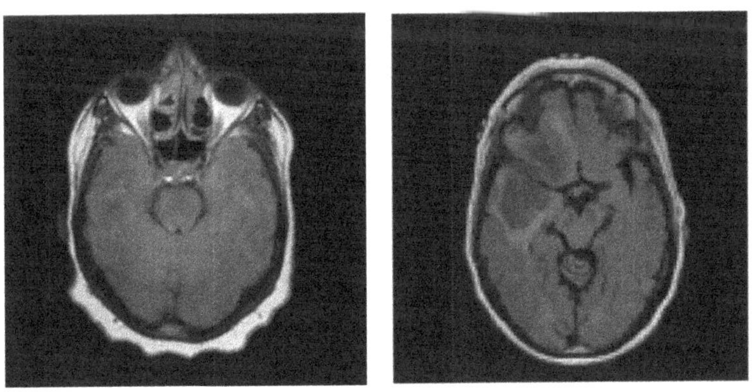

4.2.4 Performance Results

The weighted average ensemble achieved remarkable results, with an accuracy of 98%, precision of 98.25%, sensitivity of 98.7%, and an F1-score of 98.5%. These metrics demonstrated the ensemble's superior performance over individual models, especially in capturing subtle variations across different tumor types. The testing results of normal and tumor images from the brain dataset are presented as a confusion matrix in Figure 5.

Figure 5. Confusion matrix for ensemble model performance

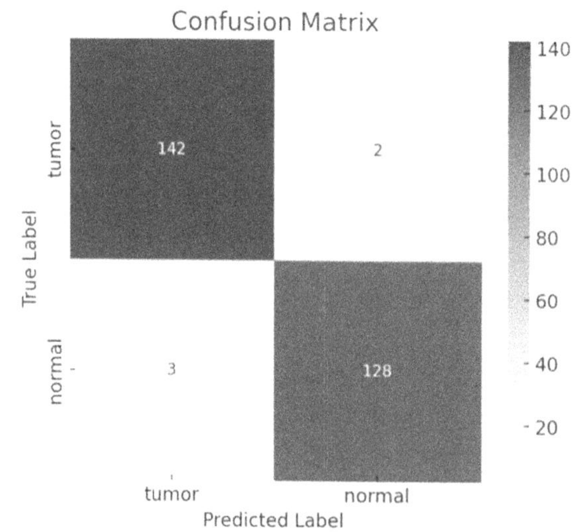

4.2.5 Practical Implications

The ensemble model's accuracy and precision make it highly applicable in clinical settings, where accurate tumor stratification is essential for treatment planning. By leveraging this ensemble approach, radiologists can receive automated, reliable clustering insights, potentially improving diagnosis timelines and treatment precision. Additionally, the model's high sensitivity aids in early tumor detection, which is vital for patient prognosis.

4.2.6 Future Directions

This case study highlights the potential for ensemble models in complex medical image clustering tasks. Future research could explore expanding the model to classify additional tumor types or integrate it with real-time diagnostic systems in hospitals, offering clinicians an immediate, robust tool for brain tumor analysis.

5. CHALLENGES AND FUTURE DIRECTIONS

Deep learning for image clustering and classification faces several challenges. Addressing these obstacles will improve model accuracy, scalability, and applicability across industries.

5.1 Data Limitations

- **Small Datasets**: Limited datasets hinder model performance, making it difficult for deep learning algorithms to generalize well, particularly in high-dimensional data scenarios.
- **Overfitting and Data Imbalance**: Small datasets often lead to overfitting, where models perform well on training data but fail on new data. Data imbalance can further skew results, causing poor generalization and reduced model robustness.

5.2 Computational Challenges

- **High Computational Requirements**: Deep learning models, especially in clustering and classification, require significant computational resources, which can limit accessibility in resource-constrained environments.
- **Efficient Training Techniques**: Techniques like model pruning, quantization, and distributed computing are essential for reducing computational demands, enabling faster and more efficient model training without sacrificing accuracy.

5.3 Explainability and Interpretability

- **Need for Transparent AI Models**: In fields like healthcare, understanding how models make decisions is crucial for trust and adoption. Black-box models can hinder user confidence and compliance with regulatory standards.
- **Methods for Explaining Deep Learning Results**: Techniques such as SHAP (Shapley Additive Explanations), LIME (Local Interpretable Model-Agnostic Explanations), and attention maps improve interpretability by highlighting important features and providing insights into model decision-making processes.

5.4 Trends in Deep Learning for Image Clustering and Classification

- **Self-Supervised Learning**: Self-supervised methods allow models to learn representations from unlabeled data, reducing dependency on labeled datasets and enabling robust feature extraction.
- **Zero-Shot Learning**: Zero-shot learning enables models to recognize new classes without explicit training, enhancing adaptability to unseen data.
- **Multimodal Models**: Combining images with text or other data types enriches model understanding and can improve accuracy in tasks where visual information alone is insufficient.

6. CONCLUSION

Deep learning techniques have significantly advanced the fields of image clustering and classification, transforming applications from agriculture to healthcare by enabling machines to process complex visual data with high accuracy and reliability. Clustering methods provide valuable tools for exploring unlabeled datasets, while classification models deliver precise, category-based predictions, facilitating targeted decision-making. Both approaches, when used together, empower deep learning systems to uncover patterns and make informed predictions across diverse datasets.

The practical applications discussed in this chapter—fruit classification in agriculture and brain tumor clustering in medical imaging—demonstrate the impact of tailored deep learning models in achieving high performance and practical utility in specialized fields. However, challenges such as data limitations, high computational costs, and the need for explainability remain, emphasizing the need for continued research. Emerging trends like self-supervised learning, zero-shot learning, and multimodal models present promising avenues to overcome these challenges and further enhance deep learning capabilities.

As deep learning technologies evolve, they hold the potential to unlock even greater insights from image data, enabling transformative applications across sectors and contributing to advances in both academic research and real-world problem-solving.

ACKNOWLEDGMENT

This work was supported by the Deanship of Scientific Research, the Vice Presidency for Graduate Studies and Scientific Research, King Faisal University, Saudi Arabia under the project (KFU242357)

REFERENCES

Abukmeil, M., Ferrari, S., Genovese, A., Piuri, V., & Scotti, F. (2021). A Survey of Unsupervised Generative Models for Exploratory Data Analysis and Representation Learning. *ACM Computing Surveys*, 54(5), 1–40. Advance online publication. DOI: 10.1145/3450963

Ahmed, M., Seraj, R., & Islam, S. M. S. (2020). The k-means Algorithm: A Comprehensive Survey and Performance Evaluation. *Electronics (Basel)*, 9(8), 1295. Advance online publication. DOI: 10.3390/electronics9081295

Akada, K., Yagi, T., Miura, Y., Beuckmann, C. T., Koyama, N., & Aoshima, K. (2021). A deep learning algorithm for sleep stage scoring in mice based on a multimodal network with fine-tuning technique. *Neuroscience Research*, 173, 99–105. https://doi.org/https://doi.org/10.1016/j.neures.2021.07.003. DOI: 10.1016/j.neures.2021.07.003 PMID: 34280429

Aktaş, H., Kızıldeniz, T., & Ünal, Z. (2022). Classification of pistachios with deep learning and assessing the effect of various datasets on accuracy. *Journal of Food Measurement and Characterization*, 16(3), 1983–1996. DOI: 10.1007/s11694-022-01313-5

Alkanan, M., & Gulzar, Y. (2024). Enhanced corn seed disease classification: Leveraging MobileNetV2 with feature augmentation and transfer learning. *Frontiers in Applied Mathematics and Statistics*, 9, 1320177 Advance online publication. DOI: 10.3389/fams.2023.1320177

Amri, E., Gulzar, Y., Yeafi, A., Jendoubi, S., Dhawi, F., & Mir, M. S. (2024). Advancing automatic plant classification system in Saudi Arabia: Introducing a novel dataset and ensemble deep learning approach. *Modeling Earth Systems and Environment*, 10(2), 2693–2709. Advance online publication. DOI: 10.1007/s40808-023-01918-9

Anand, S., Mittal, S., Tuzel, O., & Meer, P. (2014). Semi-Supervised Kernel Mean Shift Clustering. *IEEE Transactions on Pattern Analysis and Machine Intelligence*, 36(6), 1201–1215. DOI: 10.1109/TPAMI.2013.190 PMID: 26353281

Anand, V., Gupta, S., Gupta, D., Gulzar, Y., Xin, Q., Juneja, S., Shah, A., & Shaikh, A. (2023). Weighted Average Ensemble Deep Learning Model for Stratification of Brain Tumor in MRI Images. *Diagnostics (Basel)*, 13(7), 1320. Advance online publication. DOI: 10.3390/diagnostics13071320 PMID: 37046538

Ayoub, S., Gulzar, Y., Reegu, F. A., & Turaev, S. (2022). Generating Image Captions Using Bahdanau Attention Mechanism and Transfer Learning. *Symmetry*, 14(12), 2681. Advance online publication. DOI: 10.3390/sym14122681

Ayoub, S., Gulzar, Y., Rustamov, J., Jabbari, A., Reegu, F. A., & Turaev, S. (2023). Adversarial Approaches to Tackle Imbalanced Data in Machine Learning. *Sustainability (Basel)*, 15(9), 7097. Advance online publication. DOI: 10.3390/su15097097

Bansal, M., Goyal, A., & Choudhary, A. (2022). A comparative analysis of K-Nearest Neighbor, Genetic, Support Vector Machine, Decision Tree, and Long Short Term Memory algorithms in machine learning. *Decision Analytics Journal, 3*, 100071. https://doi.org/https://doi.org/10.1016/j.dajour.2022.100071

Bay, H., Ess, A., Tuytelaars, T., & Van Gool, L. (2008). Speeded-Up Robust Features (SURF). *Computer Vision and Image Understanding*, 110(3), 346–359. https://doi.org/https://doi.org/10.1016/j.cviu.2007.09.014. DOI: 10.1016/j.cviu.2007.09.014

Bouguettaya, A., Yu, Q., Liu, X., Zhou, X., & Song, A. (2015). Efficient agglomerative hierarchical clustering. *Expert Systems with Applications*, 42(5), 2785–2797. https://doi.org/https://doi.org/10.1016/j.eswa.2014.09.054. DOI: 10.1016/j.eswa.2014.09.054

Burger Wilhelm and Burge. M. J. (2022). Scale-Invariant Feature Transform (SIFT). In *Digital Image Processing: An Algorithmic Introduction* (pp. 709–763). Springer International Publishing. DOI: 10.1007/978-3-031-05744-1_25

Chander, S., & Vijaya, P. (2021). 3 - Unsupervised learning methods for data clustering. In Binu, D., & Rajakumar, B. R. (Eds.), *Artificial Intelligence in Data Mining* (pp. 41–64). Academic Press., https://doi.org/https://doi.org/10.1016/B978-0-12-820601-0.00002-1 DOI: 10.1016/B978-0-12-820601-0.00002-1

Chen, Y., Mancini, M., Zhu, X., & Akata, Z. (2024). Semi-Supervised and Unsupervised Deep Visual Learning: A Survey. *IEEE Transactions on Pattern Analysis and Machine Intelligence*, 46(3), 1327–1347. DOI: 10.1109/TPAMI.2022.3201576 PMID: 36006881

Déniz, O., Bueno, G., Salido, J., & De la Torre, F. (2011). Face recognition using Histograms of Oriented Gradients. *Pattern Recognition Letters*, 32(12), 1598–1603. https://doi.org/https://doi.org/10.1016/j.patrec.2011.01.004. DOI: 10.1016/j.patrec.2011.01.004

Dhiman, P., Kaur, A., Balasaraswathi, V. R., Gulzar, Y., Alwan, A. A., & Hamid, Y. (2023). Image Acquisition, Preprocessing and Classification of Citrus Fruit Diseases: A Systematic Literature Review. *Sustainability (Basel)*, 15(12), 9643. Advance online publication. DOI: 10.3390/su15129643

Dong, G., Jin, Y., Wang, S., Li, W., Tao, Z., & Guo, S. (2019). DB-Kmeans:An Intrusion Detection Algorithm Based on DBSCAN and K-means. *2019 20th Asia-Pacific Network Operations and Management Symposium (APNOMS)*, 1–4. DOI: 10.23919/APNOMS.2019.8892910

Ezugwu, A. E., Ikotun, A. M., Oyelade, O. O., Abualigah, L., Agushaka, J. O., Eke, C. I., & Akinyelu, A. A. (2022). A comprehensive survey of clustering algorithms: State-of-the-art machine learning applications, taxonomy, challenges, and future research prospects. *Engineering Applications of Artificial Intelligence*, 110, 104743. https://doi.org/https://doi.org/10.1016/j.engappai.2022.104743. DOI: 10.1016/j.engappai.2022.104743

Figueira, A., & Vaz, B. (2022). Survey on Synthetic Data Generation, Evaluation Methods and GANs. *Mathematics*, 10(15), 2733. Advance online publication. DOI: 10.3390/math10152733

Fränti, P., & Sieranoja, S. (2019). How much can k-means be improved by using better initialization and repeats? *Pattern Recognition*, 93, 95–112. https://doi.org/https://doi.org/10.1016/j.patcog.2019.04.014. DOI: 10.1016/j.patcog.2019.04.014

Guérin, J., Thiery, S., Nyiri, E., Gibaru, O., & Boots, B. (2021). Combining pretrained CNN feature extractors to enhance clustering of complex natural images. *Neurocomputing*, 423, 551–571. https://doi.org/https://doi.org/10.1016/j.neucom.2020.10.068. DOI: 10.1016/j.neucom.2020.10.068

Gulzar, Y. (2023). Fruit Image Classification Model Based on MobileNetV2 with Deep Transfer Learning Technique. *Sustainability (Basel)*, 15(3), 1906. Advance online publication. DOI: 10.3390/su15031906

Gulzar, Y. (2024). Enhancing soybean classification with modified inception model: A transfer learning approach. *Emirates Journal of Food and Agriculture*, 36, 1–9. DOI: 10.3897/ejfa.2024.122928

Gulzar, Y., Alwan, A. A., Abdullah, R. M., Abualkishik, A. Z., & Oumrani, M. (2023). OCA: Ordered Clustering-Based Algorithm for E-Commerce Recommendation System. *Sustainability (Basel)*, 15(4), 2947. Advance online publication. DOI: 10.3390/su15042947

Gulzar, Y., Oral, C., Kayakus, M., Erdogan, D., Unal, Z., Eksili, N., & Caylak, P. C. (2024). Predicting High Technology Exports of Countries for Sustainable Economic Growth by Using Machine Learning Techniques: The Case of Turkey. *Sustainability (Basel)*, 16(13), 5601. DOI: 10.3390/su16135601

Gulzar, Y., Ünal, Z., Ayoub, S., & Reegu, F. A. (2024). Exploring Transfer Learning for Enhanced Seed Classification: Pre-trained Xception Model. In F. and M. F. and S. K. and M. K. and A. P. C. Cavallo Eugenio and Auat Cheein (Ed.), *15th International Congress on Agricultural Mechanization and Energy in Agriculture* (pp. 137–147). Springer Nature Switzerland.

Gulzar, Y., Ünal, Z., Ayoub, S., Reegu, F. A., & Altulihan, A. (2024). Adaptability of deep learning: datasets and strategies in fruit classification. *BIO Web of Conferences, 85*. DOI: 10.1051/bioconf/20248501020

Jaderberg, M., Simonyan, K., Vedaldi, A., & Zisserman, A. (2016). Reading Text in the Wild with Convolutional Neural Networks. *International Journal of Computer Vision*, 116(1), 1–20. DOI: 10.1007/s11263-015-0823-z

Jones, J., Pradhan, M., Hosseini, M., Kulanthaivel, A., & Hosseini, M. (2018). Novel Approach to Cluster Patient-Generated Data Into Actionable Topics: Case Study of a Web-Based Breast Cancer Forum. *JMIR Med Inform 2018;6(4):E45*Https://Medinform.Jmir.Org/2018/4/E45*, 6*(4), e9162. DOI: 10.2196/medinform.9162

Krizhevsky, A., Sutskever, I., & Hinton, G. E. (2012). ImageNet Classification with Deep Convolutional Neural Networks. In F. Pereira, C. J. Burges, L. Bottou, & K. Q. Weinberger (Eds.), *Advances in Neural Information Processing Systems* (Vol. 25). Curran Associates, Inc. https://proceedings.neurips.cc/paper_files/paper/2012/file/c399862d3b9d6b76c8436e924a68c45b-Paper.pdf

Li, S., Liu, F., Jiao, L., Chen, P., & Li, L. (2024). Self-Supervised Self-Organizing Clustering Network: A Novel Unsupervised Representation Learning Method. *IEEE Transactions on Neural Networks and Learning Systems*, 35(2), 1857–1871. DOI: 10.1109/TNNLS.2022.3185638 PMID: 35767481

Li, X., Liu, Y., Jiang, X., & Wang, G. (2021). Supervised classification of slightly bruised peaches with respect to the time after bruising by using hyperspectral imaging technology. *Infrared Physics & Technology*, 113, 103557. https://doi.org/https://doi.org/10.1016/j.infrared.2020.103557. DOI: 10.1016/j.infrared.2020.103557

Litjens, G., Kooi, T., Bejnordi, B. E., Setio, A. A. A., Ciompi, F., Ghafoorian, M., van der Laak, J. A. W. M., van Ginneken, B., & Sánchez, C. I. (2017). A survey on deep learning in medical image analysis. *Medical Image Analysis*, 42, 60–88. DOI: 10.1016/j.media.2017.07.005 PMID: 28778026

Liu, L., Fieguth, P., Guo, Y., Wang, X., & Pietikäinen, M. (2017). Local binary features for texture classification: Taxonomy and experimental study. *Pattern Recognition*, 62, 135–160. https://doi.org/https://doi.org/10.1016/j.patcog.2016.08.032. DOI: 10.1016/j.patcog.2016.08.032

Lu, H., & Uddin, S. (2024). Unsupervised machine learning for disease prediction: A comparative performance analysis using multiple datasets. *Health and Technology*, 14(1), 141–154. DOI: 10.1007/s12553-023-00805-8

Mahmoudi, A., & Jemielniak, D. (2024). Proof of biased behavior of Normalized Mutual Information. *Scientific Reports*, 14(1), 9021. DOI: 10.1038/s41598-024-59073-9 PMID: 38641620

Mamat, N., Othman, M. F., Abdulghafor, R., Alwan, A. A., & Gulzar, Y. (2023). Enhancing Image Annotation Technique of Fruit Classification Using a Deep Learning Approach. *Sustainability (Basel)*, 15(2), 901. Advance online publication. DOI: 10.3390/su15020901

Mishkin, D., Sergievskiy, N., & Matas, J. (2017). Systematic evaluation of convolution neural network advances on the Imagenet. *Computer Vision and Image Understanding*, 161, 11–19. https://doi.org/https://doi.org/10.1016/j.cviu.2017.05.007. DOI: 10.1016/j.cviu.2017.05.007

Mountrakis, G., Im, J., & Ogole, C. (2011). Support vector machines in remote sensing: A review. *ISPRS Journal of Photogrammetry and Remote Sensing*, 66(3), 247–259. https://doi.org/https://doi.org/10.1016/j.isprsjprs.2010.11.001. DOI: 10.1016/j.isprsjprs.2010.11.001

Murti, D. M. P., Pujianto, U., Wibawa, A. P., & Akbar, M. I. (2019). K-Nearest Neighbor (K-NN) based Missing Data Imputation. *2019 5th International Conference on Science in Information Technology (ICSITech)*, 83–88. DOI: 10.1109/ICSITech46713.2019.8987530

Nerurkar, P., Shirke, A., Chandane, M., & Bhirud, S. (2018). Empirical Analysis of Data Clustering Algorithms. *Procedia Computer Science*, 125, 770–779. https://doi.org/https://doi.org/10.1016/j.procs.2017.12.099. DOI: 10.1016/j.procs.2017.12.099

Nishom, M., Sasmito, G. W., & Wibowo, D. S. (2024). Segmentation model toward promotion target determination using k-means algorithm and Elbow method. *AIP Conference Proceedings*, 3070(1), 030022. DOI: 10.1063/5.0198858

Oyelade, J., Isewon, I., Oladipupo, O., Emebo, O., Omogbadegun, Z., Aromolaran, O., Uwoghiren, E., Olaniyan, D., & Olawole, O. (2019). Data Clustering: Algorithms and Its Applications. *2019 19th International Conference on Computational Science and Its Applications (ICCSA)*, 71–81. DOI: 10.1109/ICCSA.2019.000-1

Punhani, A., Faujdar, N., Mishra, K. K., & Subramanian, M. (2022). Binning-Based Silhouette Approach to Find the Optimal Cluster Using K-Means. *IEEE Access : Practical Innovations, Open Solutions*, 10, 115025–115032. DOI: 10.1109/ACCESS.2022.3215568

Qi, J., Yu, Y., Wang, L., & Liu, J. (2016). K*-Means: An Effective and Efficient K-Means Clustering Algorithm. *2016 IEEE International Conferences on Big Data and Cloud Computing (BDCloud), Social Computing and Networking (SocialCom), Sustainable Computing and Communications (SustainCom) (BDCloud-SocialCom-SustainCom)*, 242–249. DOI: 10.1109/BDCloud-SocialCom-SustainCom.2016.46

Rawat, W., & Wang, Z. (2017). Deep Convolutional Neural Networks for Image Classification: A Comprehensive Review. *Neural Computation*, 29(9), 2352–2449. DOI: 10.1162/neco_a_00990 PMID: 28599112

Ros, F., Riad, R., & Guillaume, S. (2023). PDBI: A partitioning Davies-Bouldin index for clustering evaluation. *Neurocomputing*, 528, 178–199. https://doi.org/https://doi.org/10.1016/j.neucom.2023.01.043. DOI: 10.1016/j.neucom.2023.01.043

Saxena, A., Prasad, M., Gupta, A., Bharill, N., Patel, O. P., Tiwari, A., Er, M. J., Ding, W., & Lin, C. T. (2017). A review of clustering techniques and developments. *Neurocomputing*, 267, 664–681. DOI: 10.1016/j.neucom.2017.06.053

Schmarje, L., Santarossa, M., Schröder, S. M., & Koch, R. (2021). A Survey on Semi-, Self- and Unsupervised Learning for Image Classification. *IEEE Access : Practical Innovations, Open Solutions*, 9, 82146–82168. DOI: 10.1109/ACCESS.2021.3084358

Scitovski, R., & Sabo, K. (2020). DBSCAN-like clustering method for various data densities. *Pattern Analysis & Applications*, 23(2), 541–554. DOI: 10.1007/s10044-019-00809-z

Seelwal, P., Dhiman, P., Gulzar, Y., Kaur, A., Wadhwa, S., & Onn, C. W. (2024). A systematic review of deep learning applications for rice disease diagnosis: Current trends and future directions. *Frontiers of Computer Science*, 6, 1452961. DOI: 10.3389/fcomp.2024.1452961

Sergyan, S. (2008). Color histogram features based image classification in content-based image retrieval systems. *2008 6th International Symposium on Applied Machine Intelligence and Informatics*, 221–224. DOI: 10.1109/SAMI.2008.4469170

Sheng, G., Wang, Q., Pei, C., & Gao, Q. (2022). Contrastive deep embedded clustering. *Neurocomputing*, 514, 13–20. https://doi.org/https://doi.org/10.1016/j.neucom.2022.09.116. DOI: 10.1016/j.neucom.2022.09.116

Shutaywi, M., & Kachouie, N. N. (2021). Silhouette Analysis for Performance Evaluation in Machine Learning with Applications to Clustering. *Entropy (Basel, Switzerland)*, 23(6), 759. Advance online publication. DOI: 10.3390/e23060759 PMID: 34208552

Sinha, D., & El-Sharkawy, M. (2019). Thin MobileNet: An Enhanced MobileNet Architecture. *2019 IEEE 10th Annual Ubiquitous Computing, Electronics & Mobile Communication Conference (UEMCON)*, 280–285. DOI: 10.1109/UEMCON47517.2019.8993089

SONG. K.-C., YAN, Y.-H., CHEN, W.-H., & ZHANG, X. (2013). Research and Perspective on Local Binary Pattern. *Acta Automatica Sinica, 39*(6), 730–744. https://doi.org/https://doi.org/10.1016/S1874-1029(13)60051-8

Sundqvist, M., Chiquet, J., & Rigaill, G. (2023). Adjusting the adjusted Rand Index. *Computational Statistics*, 38(1), 327–347. DOI: 10.1007/s00180-022-01230-7

Tan, M., & Le, Q. (2019). EfficientNet: Rethinking Model Scaling for Convolutional Neural Networks. In K. Chaudhuri & R. Salakhutdinov (Eds.), *Proceedings of the 36th International Conference on Machine Learning* (Vol. 97, pp. 6105–6114). PMLR. https://proceedings.mlr.press/v97/tan19a.html

Thongnim, P., Sreekajon, J., & Pukseng, T. (2024). Enhancing Durian Cultivation Efficiency Through Data-Driven Smart Farming Using Cluster Analysis and Machine Learning. *2024 5th International Conference on Big Data Analytics and Practices (IBDAP)*, 67–72. DOI: 10.1109/IBDAP62940.2024.10689710

Thunold, H. H., Riegler, M. A., Yazidi, A., & Hammer, H. L. (2023). A Deep Diagnostic Framework Using Explainable Artificial Intelligence and Clustering. *Diagnostics 2023, Vol. 13, Page 3413, 13*(22), 3413. DOI: 10.3390/diagnostics13223413

Tokuda, E. K., Comin, C. H., & da F. Costa, L. (2022). Revisiting agglomerative clustering. *Physica A: Statistical Mechanics and Its Applications, 585*, 126433. https://doi.org/https://doi.org/10.1016/j.physa.2021.126433

Unal, Z. (2020). Smart Farming Becomes even Smarter with Deep Learning - A Bibliographical Analysis. *IEEE Access : Practical Innovations, Open Solutions*, 8, 105587–105609. DOI: 10.1109/ACCESS.2020.3000175

Ünal, Z., & Aktaş, H. (2023). Classification of hazelnut kernels with deep learning. *Postharvest Biology and Technology*, 197, 112225. https://doi.org/https://doi.org/10.1016/j.postharvbio.2022.112225. DOI: 10.1016/j.postharvbio.2022.112225

Ünal, Z., & İpekçi Çetin, E. (2022). Fuzzy Logic and Deep Learning Integration in Likert Type Data. *Afyon Kocatepe Üniversitesi Fen Ve Mühendislik Bilimleri Dergisi*, 22(1), 112–125. DOI: 10.35414/akufemubid.1019671

Ünal, Z., & Kızıldeniz, T. (2023). Smart agriculture practices in potato production. In Çalişkan, M. E., Bakhsh, A., & Jabran, K. (Eds.), *Potato Production Worldwide* (pp. 317–329). Academic Press., https://doi.org/https://doi.org/10.1016/B978-0-12-822925-5.00010-4 DOI: 10.1016/B978-0-12-822925-5.00010-4

Ünal, Z., Kızıldeniz, T., Özden, M., Aktaş, H., & Karagöz, Ö. (2024). Detection of bruises on red apples using deep learning models. *Scientia Horticulturae*, 329, 113021. https://doi.org/https://doi.org/10.1016/j.scienta.2024.113021. DOI: 10.1016/j.scienta.2024.113021

Von Glehn De Filippo, V., Do Patrocínio, Z. K. G., & Guimarães, S. J. F. (2015). Hierarchical Combination of Semantic Visual Words for Image Classification and Clustering. *Lecture Notes in Computer Science (Including Subseries Lecture Notes in Artificial Intelligence and Lecture Notes in Bioinformatics), 9423*, 306–313. DOI: 10.1007/978-3-319-25751-8_37

Vybhavi, G. Y., Sriramya, G., Bharadwaj, V. Y., & Ramesh, G. (2024). Clustering algorithms in data science: Evaluating the time and space complexities of K-means, DBSCAN, and hierarchical methods. *AIP Conference Proceedings*, 3101(1), 050004. DOI: 10.1063/5.0215042

Wan, H., Wang, H., Scotney, B., & Liu, J. (2019). A Novel Gaussian Mixture Model for Classification. *2019 IEEE International Conference on Systems, Man and Cybernetics (SMC)*, 3298–3303. DOI: 10.1109/SMC.2019.8914215

Wani, M. A., & Afzal, S. (2017). A New Framework for Fine Tuning of Deep Networks. *2017 16th IEEE International Conference on Machine Learning and Applications (ICMLA)*, 359–363. DOI: 10.1109/ICMLA.2017.0-135

Wazarkar, S., & Keshavamurthy, B. N. (2018). A survey on image data analysis through clustering techniques for real world applications. *Journal of Visual Communication and Image Representation*, 55, 596–626. https://doi.org/https://doi.org/10.1016/j.jvcir.2018.07.009. DOI: 10.1016/j.jvcir.2018.07.009

Wei, R., Garcia, C., El-Sayed, A., Peterson, V., & Mahmood, A. (2020). Variations in Variational Autoencoders - A Comparative Evaluation. *IEEE Access : Practical Innovations, Open Solutions*, 8, 153651–153670. DOI: 10.1109/ACCESS.2020.3018151

Weiss, K., Khoshgoftaar, T. M., & Wang, D. (2016). A survey of transfer learning. *Journal of Big Data*, 3(1), 9. DOI: 10.1186/s40537-016-0043-6

Yang, C.-C., Prasher, S. O., Enright, P., Madramootoo, C., Burgess, M., Goel, P. K., & Callum, I. (2003). Application of decision tree technology for image classification using remote sensing data. *Agricultural Systems*, 76(3), 1101–1117. https://doi.org/https://doi.org/10.1016/S0308-521X(02)00051-3. DOI: 10.1016/S0308-521X(02)00051-3

Yang, K., Yu, Z., Wen, X., Cao, W., Chen, C. L. P., Wong, H.-S., & You, J. (2020). Hybrid Classifier Ensemble for Imbalanced Data. *IEEE Transactions on Neural Networks and Learning Systems*, 31(4), 1387–1400. DOI: 10.1109/TNNLS.2019.2920246 PMID: 31265410

Yousefirizi, F., Pierre Decazes, , Amyar, A., Ruan, S., Saboury, B., & Rahmim, A. (2022). AI-Based Detection, Classification and Prediction/Prognosis in Medical Imaging: Towards Radiophenomics. *PET Clinics*, 17(1), 183–212. DOI: 10.1016/j.cpet.2021.09.010 PMID: 34809866

Yu, S., & Príncipe, J. C. (2019). Understanding autoencoders with information theoretic concepts. *Neural Networks*, 117, 104–123. https://doi.org/https://doi.org/10.1016/j.neunet.2019.05.003. DOI: 10.1016/j.neunet.2019.05.003 PMID: 31132606

Zhang, K., Guo, Y., Wang, X., Yuan, J., & Ding, Q. (2019). Multiple Feature Reweight DenseNet for Image Classification. *IEEE Access : Practical Innovations, Open Solutions*, 7, 9872–9880. DOI: 10.1109/ACCESS.2018.2890127

Zhang, K., Sun, M., Han, T. X., Yuan, X., Guo, L., & Liu, T. (2018). Residual Networks of Residual Networks: Multilevel Residual Networks. *IEEE Transactions on Circuits and Systems for Video Technology*, 28(6), 1303–1314. DOI: 10.1109/TCSVT.2017.2654543

Chapter 3
Deep Learning Techniques for Image Segmentation and Data Annotation

Muhammad Ali Shoaib
https://orcid.org/0000-0002-2783-0026
Balochistan University of Information Technology, Engineering, and Management Sciences, Pakistan

Raza Ali
https://orcid.org/0000-0003-0562-0682
Balochistan University of Information Technology, Engineering, and Management Sciences, Pakistan

Sibghat Ullah Bazai
Balochistan University of Information Technology, Engineering, and Management Sciences, Pakistan

Talha Mir
Balochistan University of Information Technology, Engineering, and Management Sciences, Pakistan

ABSTRACT

This chapter explores the integration of deep learning techniques in image segmentation, emphasizing state-of-the-art architectures, such as FCN, U-Net, and Vision Transformers, that enable precise and efficient segmentation for a range of applications. It discusses the significance of data annotation in training deep learning models, highlighting methods like active learning, semi-supervised learning, and automated annotation. The chapter also addresses key challenges, including limited labeled data, model size constraints, and performance on edge devices. Additionally, it covers the diverse use cases of image segmentation across fields like medical imaging, agriculture, and civil. Finally, the chapter outlines emerging trends in the field, including self-supervised learning, federated learning, and the development of lightweight models for real-time applications, offering insights into the future potential and impact of deep learning in image segmentation.

DOI: 10.4018/979-8-3693-9045-0.ch003

INTRODUCTION

Image segmentation is the process of splitting a picture into several components. However, this division is not done at random, but rather based on places that have comparable qualities. These related traits can be derived from the same set of attributes.

In other words, image segmentation is a process that divides a digital image into distinct pixel groups. These pixels may belong to any specific object like foreground, background, a person, or regions based on certain features like color, intensity, or texture (Szeliski, 2022; Li et al., 2025; Liu et al., 2025; Bhatti et al., 2025; Kanwal et al., 2025) Segmentation simplifies the image representation and makes it more meaningful for further analysis (Gonzalez, 2018; Li et al., 2025; Tang et al., 2025; Zeng et al., 2025; Liu et al., 2025; Aamir et al., 2025; Nawaz et al., 2025).

Image segmentation is classified into three main categories, semantic segmentation (Guo et al., 2018; Kar et al., 2021), instant segmentation (Hafiz & Bhat, 2020), and panoptic segmentation (Kirillov et al., 2019; Sun et al., 2024; Shao et al., 2024; Zhang et al., 2024; Zhang et al., 2024; Liu et al., 2024; Li & Bhatti, 2024) shown in Figure 1 and Figure 2. In semantic segmentation pixels of the objects that belong to the same type are labeled as one class and labels each pixel in an image. In the figure all cars are assigned one label i.e. blue colour, trees are labeled as green colour, and humans are shown as red colour. In semantics, each pixel is assigned. On the other hand, instant segmentation goes a step further by not only assigning a different label to one object but also delineating individual boundaries between the same type of objects. In the figure, every object in interest is assigned a different label (colour). Different cars and persons are assigned a separate colour. But other than the object all backgrounds in labeled as black. The third type panoptic segmentation combines the strengths of semantic and instant segmentation and assigns an individual label and also instant ID to every pixel.

Figure 1. Image segmentation types (Kirillov et al., 2019)

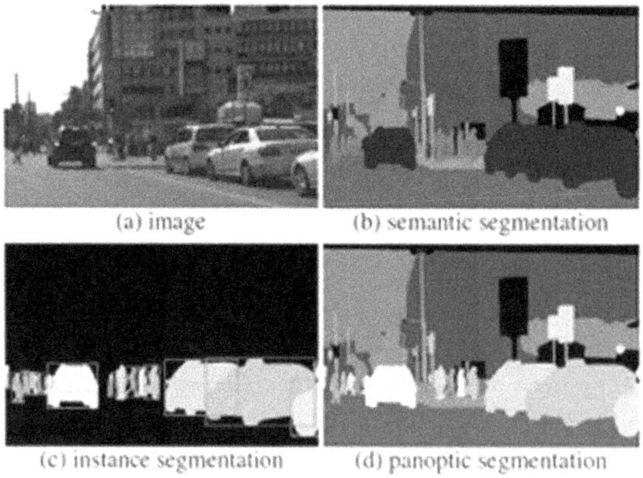

Figure 2. Example of image segmentation types (Jung et al., 2022)

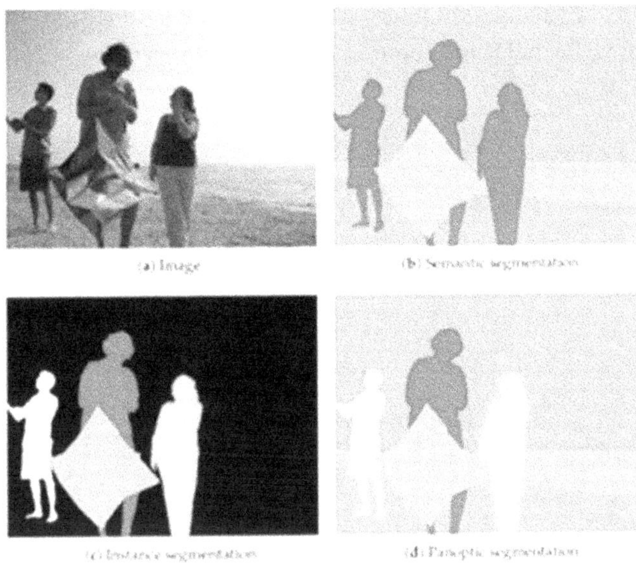

Segmentation is widely used in fields such as medical imaging, autonomous vehicles, satellite imagery, and many others to facilitate easier analysis and interpretation of complex visual data. In the past different conventional image segmentation techniques were used such as Threshold-based (Otsu, 1979), Edge-based Segmentation (Canny, 1986), Region-based Segmentation (Pal & Pal, 1993), and Clustering-based Segmentation (Jain et al., 1999) etc.

Recent developments leverage deep learning (DL), particularly convolutional neural networks (CNNs), for segmentation tasks. The following section briefly describes the basics of DL and CNN to have a deep understanding of the working principle of deep DL architectures.

DEEP LEARNING

DL aims to create and simulate a neural network for human brain analysis and learning that matches the human brain's process for data interpretation (LeCun et al., 2015; Peng et al., 2024; Chen et al., 2024; He & Bhatti, 2024; Cheng et al., 2024; Hasnain et al., 2024; Alhatami et al., 2024; Liu et al., 2025). In the latter part of the 2000s, the advent of large datasets, efficient training algorithms, and powerful computer resources contributed to the rise in popularity of DL methodology. Since then, DL approaches have quickly become the most prominent approach for processing medical images as well (Baloch et al., 2024; Haider et al., 2024). One of the most important ideas behind DL is the idea of teaching computers the characteristics that most accurately depict the data for a specific application. Neural networks form the core of most DL techniques, acting as a foundational learning algorithm. A neural network is represented by Equation (1).

$$\alpha = \sigma\left(W^{T}\mathbf{x} + \boldsymbol{\beta}\right) \quad (1)$$

The activation "α" is a linear combination of configurable weight "W" times input "x" and biases "b" followed by a nonlinear function "σ". Conventionally, neural networks often employ the hyperbolic tangent and sigmoid transfer functions. Other possible nonlinear functions can be ReLU and Leaky ReLU. Their corresponding formulas are represented in Equations (2) to (5). Figure 3 represents the plot of these functions.

Sigmoid:

$$\sigma\,(\mathrm{a}) \;=\; \frac{1}{1+\mathrm{e}^{-\mathrm{a}}} \tag{1}$$

Tanh:

$$\sigma\,(\mathrm{a}) = \frac{\mathrm{e}^{\mathrm{a}}-\mathrm{e}^{-\mathrm{a}}}{\mathrm{e}^{\mathrm{a}}+\mathrm{e}^{-\mathrm{a}}} \tag{2}$$

ReLU:

$$\sigma\,(\mathrm{a}) \;=\; \max(0,a) \tag{3}$$

Leaky ReLU:

$$\sigma\,(\mathrm{a}) \;=\; \begin{Bmatrix} a, a > 0 \\ \beta\, a, a < 0 \end{Bmatrix} \tag{4}$$

Figure 3. Different nonlinear activation functions

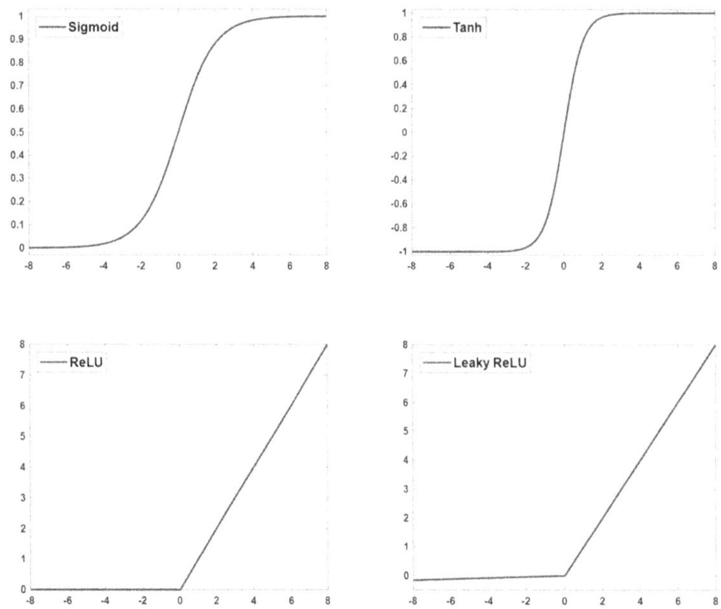

DL uses the original data as algorithm input, extracts the actual data layer by layer into the final feature representation necessary for its objective, and culminates with the mapping of features to task targets. Layers in between the input and output are often referred to as ‘hidden’ layers. When a neural network has numerous hidden layers, it is commonly referred to as 'deep,' thus the phrase 'deep learning. A deep neural network is referred to is represented by Equation (6)

$$f(x) = \sigma\,(W^T \sigma\,(W^T \ldots\ \sigma\,(W^T x + \beta)) + \beta) \tag{5}$$

The model is built with a structure comprising input, hidden, and output layers, as shown in Figure 4.

Figure 4. Deep neural network

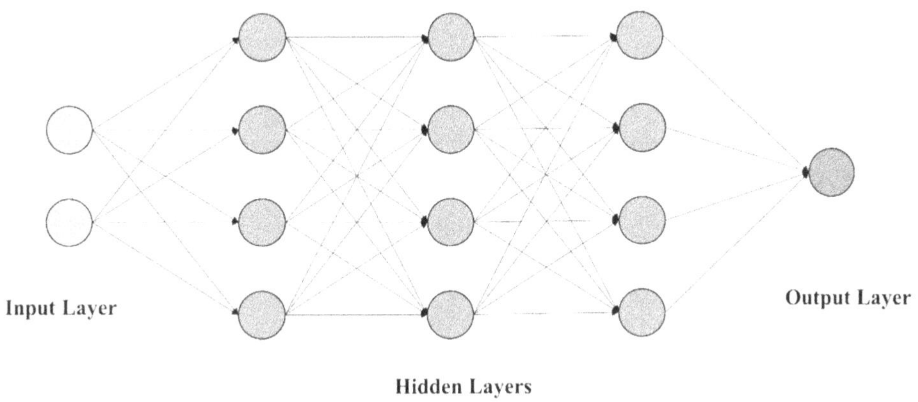

Convolutional Neural network

CNN represents a special kind of neural network that has proven to be extremely effective in practical applications dealing with time series data and image data. CNN is the most used deep neural network type for image processing.

“These CNN models have been effectively applied state-of-the-art image segmentation architectures. Figure 5 shows a general model of CNN consisting of input (image), output (classifier, object detector, or segmented output), and a series of operational layers that transform an input into the desired output. These operational layers consist of a convolutional layer, a pooling layer, and fully connected layers.

Figure 5. Convolutional neural network

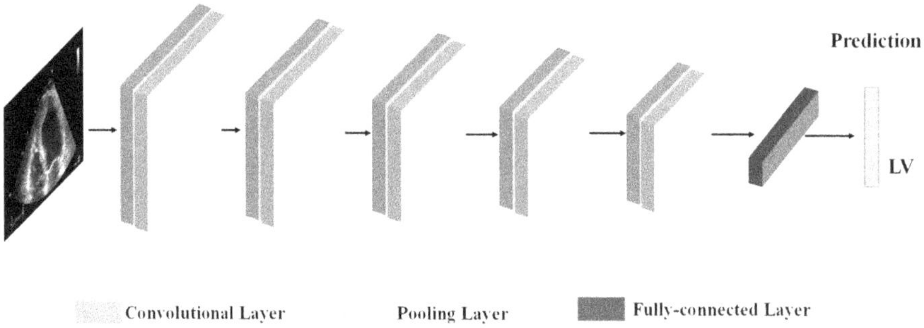

All features are extracted from input data by the feature extractor, which is made up of convolutional layers, pooling layers, and a rectifier unit. The result is then forwarded, and the same process is repeated to extract further features. Edges and patterns, which are low-level features, are extracted in the initial layers. The middle layers are responsible for extracting features like the colour and form of the item, while the upper levels are responsible for extracting high-level features such as complete objects. After the initial layer processes the low-level features, they are passed on to the next layer, where more complex features are extracted and utilized as input to the fully connected layer, which produces the final output.

Convolutional Layer

Convolution is the process that takes an input image, applies a collection of filters to it (these filters can sometimes be referred to as kernels or weights), and then produces an output image (Akram et al., 2024). In this layer, the input data is convolved using a kernel (weights). Each convolution typically employs a *n x n* kernel (for 2D input) or *n x n x n* kernel (for 3D input), followed by batch normalization. Each filter is a small matrix that is convolved with the input image, multiplied, added element by element, and then subjected to an activation function with a bias term added. An output feature map is created as a result of this procedure being carried out for every location in the input image.

Because each convolutional filter only processes a small fraction of the input image, the convolutional layer can learn to recognize certain patterns within that area of the image. Because these filters are applied to the input image via a sliding window, and the output feature map has the same dimensions as the input image, this layer can also preserve the input data's spatial structure. Furthermore, by lowering the quantity of input data, the convolutional layer contributes to a lower processing cost for the calculation. Equation (7) represents the function of the convolutional layer.

$$X_k^l = W_k^{l-1} * X^{l-1} + b_k^{l-1} \quad (6)$$

Where "*W*" refers to the kernel's weights, "*b*" stands for biases, and "*" indicates the convolution operation. Calculating a feature map X_k involves convolving the weights with X_{k-1} and adding the biases. The feature maps are extracted from an image after passing the output via a nonlinear activation function (such as ReLU). The output of this layer is the feature map. By learning from the different input signals, the convolution operation acts as a feature extractor. In succeeding layers, the retrieved features can be utilized for categorization.

Pooling Layer

This is a downsampling layer where pooling is used to lower the spatial dimension of the given sample while maintaining substantial information. Pooling layers remove the duplicate features, feature maps are downsampled to increase statistical efficiency and model generalization. Pooling helps minimize the number of parameters in the model, which in turn helps lessen the weight of computing work. The possible pooling operations are average and maximum. Two common options for the size of the pooling region are *2x2* and *3x3*. Equations (8) and (9) represent the maximum and average pooling respectively assuming the down sampling rate to be 2 (pooling size =2).

$$y_k = \max\left(x_{2k-1}, x_{2k}\right) \tag{7}$$

$$y_k = \frac{x_{2k-1} + x_{2k}}{2} \tag{8}$$

Fully Connected Layer

Normally, the very last layer of neural network is a fully connected layer. Its purpose is to translate the features that have been acquired by the convolutional and pooling layers to the output of the network. In a fully connected layer, each element of every input is linked to each element of every output. Fully connected layers are used to minimize the dimension of data and identify the most objective relevant information for interpretation. The output of the network is a vector of fixed size, with each element being a probabilistic value. This value represents a class, if the task is image classification. While for a regression task such as, left ventricle volume estimation, the output value is a real value. The probabilistic values are a group of numerical values representing the coordinates of a bounding box for object detection and localization, or a probabilistic score of each pixel of the image (image segmentation).

Loss Function

In convolutional networks, the loss function is a key component to consider. It is essential to use an appropriate loss function to get the best possible outcome. The loss function of the network is responsible for exerting control over the output of a neural network. It quantifies the deviation of the actual output from the anticipated output as shown in Figure 6. In order to reduce the loss score, the basic idea in DL is to utilize this score as a feedback signal to slightly alter the weights' value.

Some of the well-known loss functions used for image segmentation are cross entropy (CE) loss, dice loss, Tversky (TV) loss, and focal (FL) loss (Jadon, 2020). Equations (10) to (13) provide the mathematical notation of these loss functions.

$$\text{CE Loss} = -\left[t\log(p) + (1-t)\log(1-p)\right] \tag{9}$$

$$\text{Dice Loss} = 1 - \frac{2tp}{t^2 + p^2} \tag{10}$$

$$\text{TV loss} = \frac{\text{tp}}{\text{tp} + \beta\,(1 - \text{t})\text{p} + (1 - \beta)\text{t}\,(1 - \text{p})} \tag{11}$$

$$\text{FL loss} = -\,\beta\,(1 - \text{p})^{\gamma}\,\log(\text{p}) \tag{12}$$

Where t is the actual ground truth labels, p is the predicted labels, β is the weight assigned to a particular class, and γ is the steering factor.

Figure 6. Loss function to evaluate the model's quality

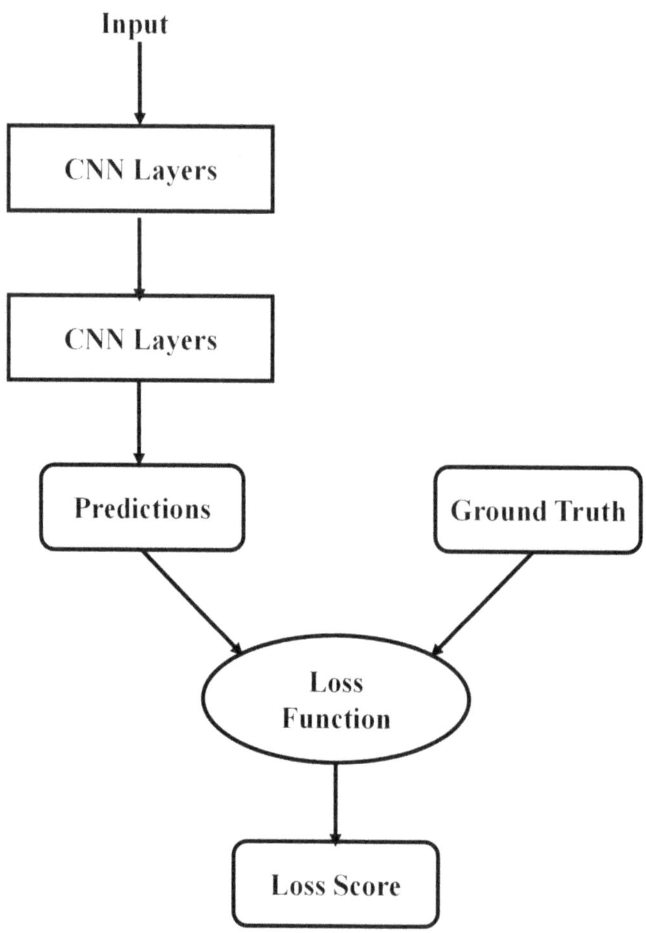

Multi-layer perceptron (MLP) models (Y. Chen & Bastani, 1990), deep belief network models, back-propagation neural network models, CNN models, and other classic models have been proposed in conjunction with the fast growth of computer technology. These findings have significantly advanced the development of the DL algorithm architecture, opening the door for its widespread use in numerous medical sectors (Al'Aref et al., 2019)

DEEP LEARNING ARCHITECTURES FOR IMAGE SEGMENTATION

Several DL architectures have been proposed and implemented for image segmentation. These models have shown remarkable performance in all types of segmentation. The details of architecture and working principle of a few well known and cutting-edge DL models are explained below.

Fully Convolutional Networks (FCNs)

FCNs were among the first networks created expressly for dense prediction tasks, replacing fully connected layers with convolutional layers and allowing for pixel-level segmentation. This design set the framework for contemporary segmentation algorithms by combining coarse and fine characteristics via skip links. (Long et al. 2015).

Fully Convolutional Networks (FCNs) were one of the first architectures developed expressly for semantic segmentation. FCNs revolutionised segmentation jobs by replacing fully connected layers with convolutional layers, allowing for dense, pixel-wise predictions without the requirement for dense labelling at each layer. The FCN architecture is depicted in Figure 7.

Figure 7. FCN architecture (Long et al., 2015)

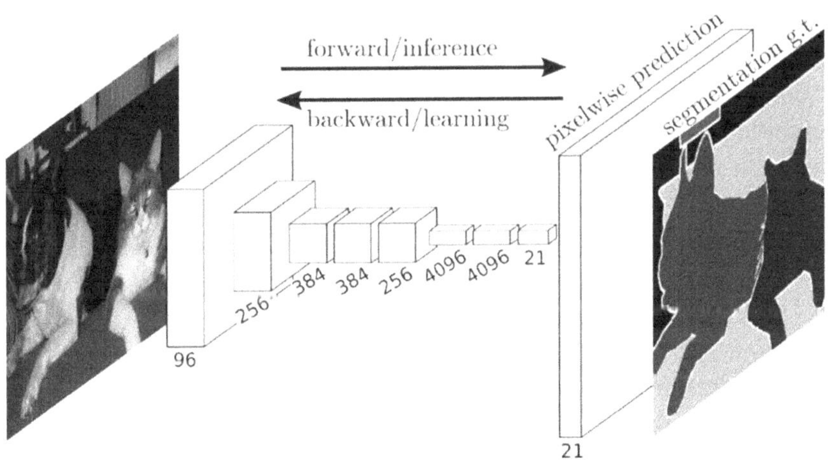

FCN Architecture Overview

The FCN architecture consists of an encoder-decoder structure:

Encoder (Feature Extraction): The encoder, typically based on well-known image classification networks like VGG or AlexNet, extracts feature maps at different resolutions through convolutional and pooling layers. This part captures hierarchical and spatial features in the image. As the network goes deeper, spatial information is reduced but feature depth increases, capturing high-level abstractions. Unlike standard CNNs for classification, which end in fully connected layers, FCNs retain spatial resolution by only using convolutional layers.

Fully Convolutional Layer: The key innovation of FCNs is the replacement of fully connected layers with 1x1 convolutional layers, which allows the network to output a dense spatial feature map where each pixel can correspond to a specific class label. The absence of fully connected layers means that FCNs can take images of any size and produce segmentation maps with the same spatial dimensions, scaled down by the network's downsampling.

Upsampling (Decoder): The output of the encoder has reduced spatial resolution due to downsampling from pooling layers. To restore spatial dimensions, FCNs use transposed (or deconvolution) layers to upsample these feature maps back to the original image size. This upsampling step is crucial for generating pixel-wise predictions and can be achieved by learned upsampling (e.g., deconvolution) or fixed upsampling (e.g., bilinear interpolation).

Skip Connections: FCNs introduced skip connections to address the loss of spatial information from downsampling. These connections combine high-level semantic information from deeper layers with finer details from shallower layers, improving the model's ability to precisely delineate object boundaries. For example, a skip connection can take features from an early layer, such as conv3, and merge them with the output from deeper layers, helping retain localization information.

Working of FCN for Segmentation

In FCNs, the segmentation process involves multiple steps to predict labels for each pixel, which are integrated across the architecture:

Input Processing: The network accepts an input image, which passes through the encoder where convolutions and pooling layers extract multilevel features.

Encoding Semantic Information: The convolutional layers progressively downsample the image, capturing high-level semantic features with increasing abstraction. This step captures the context necessary for understanding the overall image while losing some pixel-level details.

Decoding and Upsampling: After encoding, the dense feature map (reduced in spatial dimensions) is upsampled using transposed convolutions to generate a full-size segmentation map. Each pixel in this output map corresponds to a class label.

Combining Semantic and Spatial Features: Skip connections bridge different layers to retain spatial context. For example, FCN-8s is a popular version of FCN that combines outputs from layers conv3, conv4, and the final layer (conv7) through skip connections to yield a more accurate segmentation map.

Final Segmentation Map: The output is a segmentation map where each pixel is classified into a specific category. The FCN model is designed to output the same dimensions as the input image, providing dense, pixel-level predictions.

Variants of FCNs

The different FCN variants (e.g., FCN-32s, FCN-16s, FCN-8s) signify different levels of upsampling and combinations of skip connections. FCN-32s uses only the final layer's output, while FCN-16s and FCN-8s incorporate skip connections from shallower layers, resulting in finer-grained predictions with improved boundary localization.

Limitations of FCNs

Despite its pioneering role, FCNs have limitations, particularly in maintaining fine-grained features and managing multi-scale objects as a result of progressive downsampling. These restrictions prompted future advancements like as U-Net, DeepLab, and HRNet, which use more complex feature-preserving algorithms.

U-Net

U-Net, designed primarily for biomedical imagine segmentation, has an encoder-decoder structure in which the encoder collects context and the decoder allows for exact localisation. U-Net's skip connections between the encoder and decoder layers assist to maintain spatial information, making it suitable for comprehensive segmentation in medical imaging (Ronneberger et al., 2015).

U-Net is a prominent deep learning architecture that was originally built for biomedical image segmentation but has now been used to a variety of segmentation applications. Its main strength is the use of an encoder-decoder structure with symmetric skip links, which helps capture both global context and local information. Figure 8 shows the architecture of U-Net.

Figure 8. U-Net architecture (Ronneberger et al., 2015)

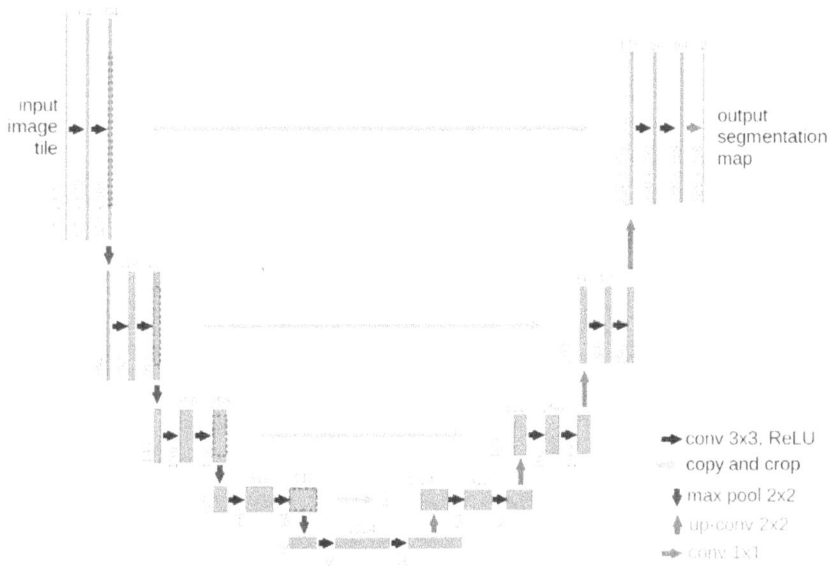

U-Net Architecture Overview

The U-Net architecture consists of two main parts: an encoder (or contracting path) and a decoder (or expansive path), with skip connections that bridge the two paths.

Encoder (Contracting Path): Through a series of convolution and max-pooling layers, the encoder downsamples the input image in order to extract features. Two 3x3 convolutional layers (each followed by ReLU activation) plus a 2x2 max-pooling layer with stride 2 that divides the spatial dimensions in half make up each encoder stage. Like conventional CNN designs, this approach gradually reduces the spatial resolution of the feature maps while capturing ever-more complex characteristics.

Decoder (Expansive Path): The goal of the decoder is to return the feature maps' spatial dimensions to the size of the input image. After doubling the spatial dimensions by an upsampling operation (often a transposed convolution), each stage of the decoder consists of two 3x3 convolutions and ReLU activations. Since it gradually restores the initial spatial resolution, this upsampling procedure is essential for pixel-level segmentation.

Skip Connections: U-Net is distinguished by its skip connections, which connect each encoder layer straight to the associated decoder layer. These skip connections link feature maps from the encoder to upsampled feature maps in the decoder, integrating coarse semantic information with finer spatial features. This combination enables U-Net to preserve exact localisation information, which is very useful in applications that need accurate borders, such as cell segmentation in medical imaging.

Final Layer: The last layer is a 1x1 convolutional layer that decreases the number of channels to the required number of classes, usually followed by a softmax activation that generates a probability map for each class at each pixel.

Working of U-Net for Segmentation

Input Processing: The encoder processes the input image and extracts spatial data using convolutional layers. Pooling layers gradually downsample a picture, capturing high-level information but losing spatial resolution.

Encoding Detailed Information: Each convolutional layer captures local image information, allowing the network to learn increasingly abstract features as it progresses through the layers. After each downsampling step, the spatial dimensions decrease while feature depth increases, building a hierarchical understanding of the image.

Decoding and Upsampling: After encoding, the decoder gradually upscales the feature maps to reconstruct the original spatial dimensions. The transposed convolutions (or deconvolutions) in the decoder reverse the effects of pooling, upsampling the feature maps back to the input image size.

Integrating Context with Detail via Skip Connections: Each skip connection passes feature maps from the encoder to the corresponding decoder layer, merging detailed spatial information with abstract features. This allows the model to effectively capture both fine details (important for boundary detection) and broader context, making U-Net highly effective for tasks that require accurate localization.

Generating the Segmentation Map: The output is a full-size segmentation map where each pixel is classified into a specific category. This pixel-wise segmentation map is directly comparable in size to the input image, facilitating dense predictions across the entire image.

DeepLab (V1, V2, V3, V3+).

DeepLab has evolved through several versions, introducing multiple innovations. The key contributions include atrous (or dilated) convolutions to expand the receptive field, fully connected Conditional Random Fields (CRFs) for edge refinement, and Atrous Spatial Pyramid Pooling (ASPP) to capture multi-scale context. DeepLabv3+ integrates an encoder-decoder structure, combining the benefits of both detailed boundary refinement and contextual awareness (L.-C. Chen et al., 2018)

Mask R-CNN

Mask R-CNN enhances the Faster R-CNN object detection framework by incorporating an additional branch to predict segmentation masks. This enables the network to perform instance segmentation by generating a distinct mask for each detected object, thereby distinguishing between individual occurrences of the same object category (He et al., 2017). Mask R-CNN was selected for its versatility and reliability in general-purpose object segmentation tasks. Figure 9 illustrates the overall architecture of the model.

The initial stage of the framework involves extracting feature maps from the input image. For this purpose, both ResNet-50-FPN and ResNet-101-FPN models were evaluated as backbone networks. While the ResNet-50-FPN offers a reduced computational burden compared to ResNet-101-FPN, the latter provides significant improvements in performance without necessitating alterations to the model architecture or training process. Consequently, ResNet-101-FPN was chosen as the backbone for this framework. ResNet-101 comprises 101 layers, and the input image is processed through this backbone CNN to generate the feature maps, which are then utilized as input for subsequent stages.

The second component of the framework is the Region Proposal Network (RPN), responsible for identifying potential regions of interest (ROIs). The RPN operates as a neural network, scanning the image in a sliding window manner to suggest regions likely to contain the target object. These regions, represented as bounding boxes generated by the RPN, are referred to as anchors. Approximately 200,000 anchors of various dimensions and aspect ratios are created. In this study, the original RPN network's scales were modified. The images were resized to 1024 × 1024 and padded with zeros to preserve their aspect ratio and prevent distortion.

Five different scales—32 × 32, 64 × 64, 128 × 128, 256 × 256, and 512 × 512—were employed to account for all possible rectangular bounding boxes. Three aspect ratios—0.5, 1, and 2—were utilized, resulting in 15 anchor proposals for each pixel. The feature maps are processed through a 3 × 3 convolutional layers followed by two 1 × 1 convolutional layers. The first 1 × 1 layer classifies the anchor as either foreground (LV) or background, while the second 1 × 1 layer adjusts the coordinates of the anchor. A small convolutional network calculates an anchor score that predicts the likelihood of each anchor containing an object. Based on these scores, the top N anchors with the highest scores are selected as ROIs. In cases where multiple anchors overlap, non-maximum suppression retains only the anchor with the highest foreground score. RPN's bounding box refinement further adjusts the ROI sizes. Since the sigmoid classifier has fixed input size requirements, ROI-Align is employed. This method applies bilinear interpolation to extract feature map values for each object proposal.

Two separate network heads process the class and mask predictions for the ROIs. Here, a single ROI is defined with two classes—foreground and background (FG/BG). Fully connected layers are utilized to determine the object's class within the ROI, which is chosen based on class loss calculated using crossentropy. For classification, a sigmoid function is used because there is only one defined segmentation class (LV).

To generate masks within the ROI, a convolutional network is applied. A sigmoid function is used for each pixel in the ROI, producing an output mask. During training, both ground-truth masks and predicted masks are defined with dimensions of 28 × 28. This relatively small mask size helps reduce computational complexity and memory usage. The final predicted masks are then scaled to match the size of the original ROI.

An example of Mask R-CNN for left ventricle segmentation is shown in Figure 9.

Figure 9. Mask R-CNN architecture (Shoaib et al., 2022)

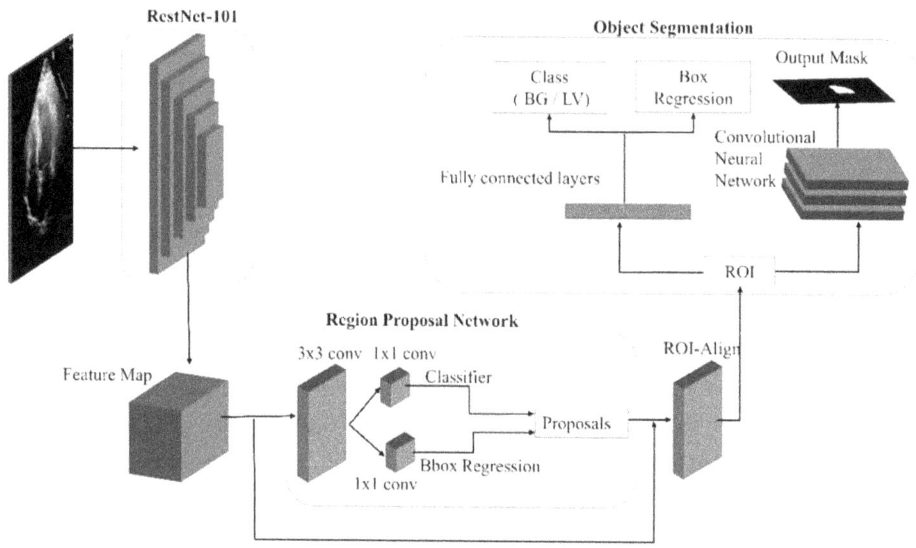

Pyramid Scene Parsing Network (PSPNet)

PSPNet introduces a pyramid pooling module to capture global context, addressing the challenge of segmenting objects with diverse spatial scales. It applies global and local contextual information to improve performance in scenes with varying object scales, such as in complex natural images (Zhao et al., 2017)

HRNet (High-Resolution Network)

HRNet maintains high-resolution representations through the entire network, differing from architectures that progressively downsample and upsample. This network captures multi-scale contextual information while preserving spatial resolution, improving segmentation accuracy, especially in cases where fine spatial detail is crucial (Wang et al., 2021)

Vision Transformers (ViTs)

Transformers, originally used in NLP, have recently been adapted for image segmentation. Vision Transformers model long-range dependencies in images, and their segmentation-specific variations (such as SegFormer and SETR) have shown promise in capturing global context, especially in complex scenes (Zheng et al., 2021).

These architectures have set new benchmarks in image segmentation, providing options for tasks ranging from semantic segmentation to instance and panoptic segmentation. Their diversity also highlights the trend toward hybrid models combining CNN and Transformer elements for enhanced performance across various contexts.

DATA ANNOTATION TECHNIQUES IN THE CONTEXT OF DEEP LEARNING

Data annotation is the process of labelling or tagging data that is required for training supervised machine learning models, notably in deep learning (DL). For tasks such as image segmentation, object identification, and natural language processing, annotated data serves as the "ground truth" from which models may learn to generate correct predictions and classifications. In terms of image segmentation Data annotation is fundamental to deep learning approaches, since it helps models reliably recognise and separate diverse visual components. Image segmentation necessitates pixel-level precision; hence the accuracy of data annotation is critical. In this context, data annotation is the process of labelling each pixel or area in a picture to represent certain objects or limits. These labels serve as the "ground truth" for segmentation models, allowing them to accurately identify and define objects. Figures 11 and 12 show many instances of annotated images.

Figure 10. An example of left ventricle annotation

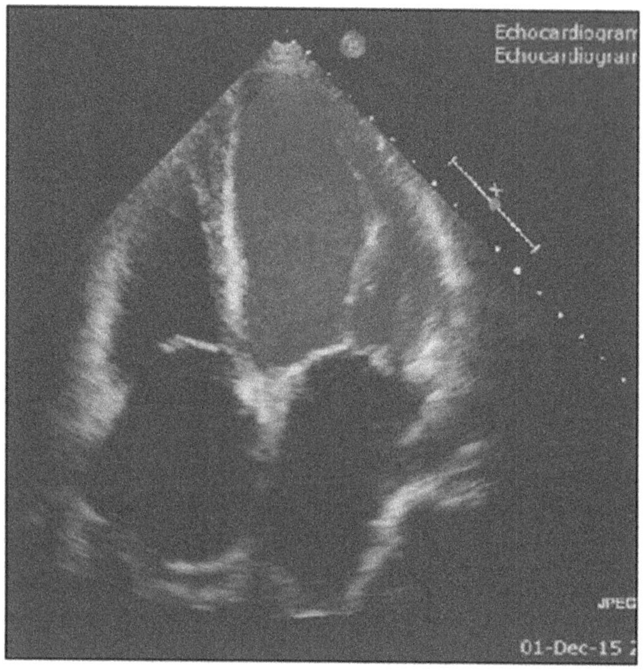

Figure 11. Cracks pixels annotation (Ali et al., 2021)

Importance of Data Annotation in Image Segmentation

Data annotation is particularly crucial for image segmentation in several ways:

Accuracy in Pixel-Level Prediction: Segmentation requires pixel-level annotations, which means that each pixel in an image must be labelled to ensure accurate borders and class separation. High-quality annotations assist the model in correctly recognising object shapes and fine features.

Complexity of Object Recognition: Unlike classification tasks, which assign a single label to an entire picture, segmentation tasks need recognising complicated forms and fine spatial features. Annotation quality has a direct influence on the model's capacity to detect minor characteristics and segment overlapping or similarly coloured items.

Training Deep Learning Models: Supervised deep learning algorithms require annotated photos to learn the complicated structures inside scenes. Properly labelled photos help the model divide items from backgrounds, discriminate between overlapping objects, and recognise precise boundaries.

Wide Range of Applications: Image segmentation is crucial in a variety of sectors, including medical imaging, autonomous driving, and satellite image processing. For example, exact segmentation of lesions in medical imaging assists diagnosis, but perfect segmentation of road features is essential for self-driving cars.

Methods of Data Annotation for Image Segmentation.

Given the need for precise, pixel-level labeling, various methods are employed to annotate data for image segmentation:

Manual Annotation: Human annotators manually label each pixel or segment region based on objects. They may utilise specialised annotation tools to draw masks around objects or give classifications to pixels. These technologies are commonly utilised in medical imaging and other fields where exact boundaries are required. Human skill is required for difficult segmentation tasks like labelling tumours in MRI data. Manual annotation, while extremely precise, is time-consuming and expensive, particularly for big datasets.

Semi-Supervised Annotation: In this approach, a model or automated tool generates initial annotations, which are then refined by human annotators. Another type of semi-supervised annotation is Active Learning. In active learning the model is trained on an initial labeled dataset and then evaluates a larger set of unlabeled data, identifying samples where it is least confident in its predictions. These "uncertain" samples are then labeled by human annotators, after which the model is retrained to improve performance. This approach is Effective for scenarios with large datasets where completely manual annotation would be impractical. For example, annotators may correct initial segmentation outputs generated by a neural network. It balances speed with accuracy, although it may still require substantial human input, particularly in complex segmentation tasks.

Automated Annotation: Automated annotation tools or pre-trained segmentation models generate annotations without human intervention. This technique leverages existing models to produce labels, which may be further refined. This method is often used for tasks with large-scale datasets or easily recognizable objects. For example, automated annotation can work well in satellite imagery segmentation where objects like buildings are easily detected (Hameed et al., 2022). Although it is fast, automated annotation is typically less accurate than manual labeling and often requires manual review, especially for complex.

Deep learning models used for data annotation

DL offers several methods and architectures designed for automatic and semi-supervised data annotation, especially in complex tasks like image segmentation. These models often either generate annotations directly or assist human annotators by pre-labeling data that can be refined later. Here are some widely used architectures and techniques:

Convolutional Neural Networks (CNNs)

CNNs are foundational for image-based tasks, where they extract spatial features from images. Pre-trained CNN models (like ResNet, and VGG) can classify or detect objects within images (Haq et al., 2023), providing bounding boxes or even rough segmentation masks. These models, trained on large labeled datasets, can generate initial annotations that can be refined. Pre-trained models on large datasets (e.g., ImageNet) are often fine-tuned to perform object detection and coarse annotation (Sarker, 2021)

Fully Convolutional Networks (FCNs)

FCNs are designed for pixel-wise tasks and transform standard CNNs by replacing fully connected layers with convolutional layers, making them ideal for segmentation. FCNs provide automated pixel-level segmentation maps, which may be used as the first annotation for jobs that need detailed segmentation. An FCN trained on labelled data can automatically segment pictures, creating masks with very small adjustments (Ojha et al., 2017).

U-Net

Originally designed for biomedical image segmentation, U-Net's encoder-decoder structure with skip links captures both high-level context and minute details. U-Net is often used for automated segmentation jobs that need precise boundaries, such as medical imaging. It can generate initial segmentation masks in semi-supervised settings, which human annotators may then enhance. U-Net can accurately name structures in medical pictures (e.g., cells or lesions), allowing radiologists to start with a high-quality baseline. (Adnan et al. 2021; Noor et al., 2024; Haider et al., 2024; Ullah et al., 2024; Nabeel et al., 2024)

MaskR-CNN

Mask R-CNN is an extension of Faster R-CNN for instance segmentation that includes a branch for pixel-level masks in addition to bounding box and object classification. Mask R-CNN is used in applications that need instance-level segmentation (for example, identifying each object instance). It creates bounding boxes and segmentation masks, which may subsequently be changed as needed. Typically used in annotating scenes for autonomous driving, where each instance (e.g., each car or pedestrian) is split independently.

Generative Adversarial Networks (GANs)

GANs are made up of a generator and a discriminator that can learn to create realistic data samples. In annotation, GANs may execute unsupervised or semi-supervised tasks. Conditional GANs (cGANs), or segmentation GANs may learn from unlabelled or partially labelled data to generate synthetic annotations or enhance segmentation. GANs can help with domain adaptation, such as converting labels from synthetic to real data or creating realistic labels for medical imaging (Nair & Pareek, 2024; Noor et al., 2024; Hamza et al., 2023).

Self-Supervised Learning Models

Self-supervised approaches utilise pretext tasks to acquire usable representations without the requirement for labelled data. Models such as SimCLR and MoCo can learn characteristics from unlabelled pictures and then fine-tune them for annotation purposes. Self-supervised learning generates strong representations that can help enhance semi-supervised annotations. In circumstances when labelled images are scarce, self-supervised models may produce initial labels and fine-tune them with a minimal quantity of labelled data (Emam et al., 2021).

Weakly Supervised Segmentation Models

Weakly supervised models learn from coarse labels, such as image-level labels or bounding boxes, and then infer finer information. These models may generate segmentation masks using estimated labels, making them appropriate for applications where pixel-level annotation is either unavailable or too expensive. CAMs (Class Activation Maps) can indicate portions of an image that correspond to certain classes, giving early annotations that can be refined into segmentation masks (Borisov et al., 2021). Each of these strategies improves automated and semi-supervised annotation in distinct ways, allowing for high-quality labels with minimal human interaction. Large, high-quality datasets may be effectively constructed by integrating these deep learning algorithms with human correction or iterative learning approaches, accelerating progress in picture segmentation applications.

Applications and Use Cases

Image segmentation using deep learning has several applications in a variety of industries, serving as a critical tool for analysing and comprehending visual data(Nabeel et al., 2024; Noor et al., 2024; Haider et al., 2024; khan et al., 2023;Ullah et al., 2024). The following are some well-known applications and use cases, coupled with recent references emphasising developments in each field.

Medical Imaging: DL-based image segmentation is commonly employed in medical imaging to detect and characterise anatomical features, tumours, and lesions in scans (Feng et al., 2022; Haider et al., 2024). Segmentation helps with accurate diagnosis, treatment planning, and monitoring of illness development.

Tumor Detection and Organ Segmentation: Segmentation aids in the identification and quantification of tumours in MRI and CT images, as well as the detection of organ borders and surgical planning. For example, DL models have demonstrated great accuracy in segmenting brain tumours in MRI images, which assists in diagnosis and planning (Feng et al., 2022; Z. Liu et al., 2023).

Cardiac Image Analysis: Cardiac segmentation is used to analyse heart architecture and diagnose cardiovascular disorders. The myocardial, ventricles, and atria must be segmented in order to measure cardiac function and health (Shoaib et al., 2023) (Shoaib, Chuah, Ali, Dhanalakshmi, et al., 2023; Shoaib, Chuah, Ali, Hasikin, et al., 2023).

Autonomous Driving and ADAS (Advanced Driver Assistance Systems)

Image segmentation is crucial for autonomous cars to grasp their surroundings, including detecting objects, road limits, and lanes. Segmentation enables real-time decision-making, which is critical for safe navigation.

Road Scene Segmentation: Segmentation is used by autonomous systems to differentiate roadways, sidewalks, automobiles, people, and other scene features. This assists with obstacle avoidance, path planning, and maintaining lane discipline (Y. Zhao et al., 2024).

Pedestrian and Vehicle Detection: Image segmentation is used to accurately segment pedestrians, automobiles, and other objects to avoid collisions and improve safety (Galvao et al., 2021; Murthy et al., 2022).

Agriculture

Image segmentation helps to monitor crop health, estimate production, identify pests, and evaluate soil quality (Bhatti, Bazai, et al., 2023; Bhatti, Masud, et al., 2023). This application of DL in agriculture promotes precision farming, enhancing production while minimising resource utilisation.

Plant and Crop Segmentation: Plant canopy segmentation aids in agricultural disease identification, plant count estimation, and growth monitoring. It also aids in targeted pesticide spraying, lowering chemical consumption (Acharya et al., 2023; X. Zhao et al., 2022).

Weed Detection: Using segmentation to distinguish weeds from crops allows farmers to specifically target weeds, lowering pesticide consumption and protecting crop health (Li et al., 2024; Zhang et al., 2024).

Satellite and Remote Sensing Imagery

Remote sensing image segmentation is useful for land cover categorisation, environmental monitoring, and disaster management. DL uses large-scale satellite imaging data to conduct a thorough examination of land use and change over time.

Land Cover and Land Use Classification: Segmenting land cover categories such as woods, urban regions, and water bodies helps with environmental monitoring and urban planning (Ennouri et al., 2021; Hameed et al., 2022; Jameil et al., 2024; Zamanoglu et al., 2023).

Disaster Response: Image segmentation helps detect damaged regions following natural disasters, allowing for fast evaluation and recovery planning (Zou et al., 2024).

Industrial Quality Control

In manufacturing, segmentation is used for defect identification and quality control, which helps to assure product uniformity while lowering production costs. It facilitates in the inspection of electrical components, automotive parts, and textiles for faults (Ullah et al., 2024).

Defect Detection in Manufacturing: Segmentation models identify faults, scratches, or inconsistencies in items on assembly lines to ensure high-quality standards in manufacturing (Ali et al., 2022a, 2022b).

Automated Optical Inspection: Segmentation is also utilised in automated optical inspection systems to check for appropriate alignment and assembly of components in electronic devices (Caliskan & Gurkan, 2021; Schmidt et al., 2021; Tareen et al., 2022; Tabassum et al., 2024).

Healthcare and Biomedical Research

Aside from diagnosis, segmentation in healthcare is useful for biomedical research since it can detect cellular structures, analyse tissues, and investigate biological processes at the cellular and molecular levels.

Cell Segmentation in Microscopy: Cell segmentation assists researchers in analysing cellular architecture and interactions, helping to studies in domains such as cancer and neuroscience (Al-Kofahi et al., 2018; M. Y. Lee et al., 2022).

Histopathology Image Analysis: Histopathology uses segmentation to detect cell types, tumour borders, and tissue architecture, which aids in cancer diagnosis and research (Kurmi et al., 2021; Muñoz-Aguirre et al., 2020).

Challenges and Limitations

In order to improve the efficacy and dependability of segmentation models, researchers and practitioners must overcome a number of ongoing problems and limits in image segmentation using deep learning (DL).

Data Annotation Challenges

Data annotation is an important step in preparing datasets for image segmentation tasks, but it poses various obstacles. High-quality annotations are required for training correct models, but writing them may be time-consuming, expensive, and prone to inconsistency. Here are some of the biggest data annotation issues in image segmentation.

Limited Labeled Data: DL models require a big amount of annotated data to train. Obtaining such data in fields such as medical imaging is time-consuming and expensive, and it frequently requires professional knowledge. This paucity may impair model performance and generalisation.

Annotation Quality and Consistency: Variability in annotations owing to subjective interpretations by annotators might contribute noise, influencing model training and assessment.

Cost and Time-Intensive Labeling Process

To create reliable segmentation models, each pixel in an image must be tagged to identify different classes, which is a time-consuming procedure. Labelling takes substantially longer and costs more than basic picture classification tasks due to the degree of information required.

Need for Domain Expertise

Certain domains need professional expertise for effective labelling, which reduces the amount of available data. Medical pictures, such as brain MRIs or lung CT scans, require specialists to distinguish between structures. Limited access to specialists limits the development of high-quality labelled datasets.

Computational Complexity

Resource Intensive Training: Training deep segmentation models necessitates significant computing resources, such as high-performance GPUs and vast memory, which may not be available to all researchers or institutions.

Inference Time: Deploying complicated models in real-time applications can be difficult owing to latency difficulties, necessitating model optimisation strategies.

Handling Imbalanced Data

Class Imbalance: In many segmentation tasks, certain classes are under-represented, resulting to models being biassed towards dominant classes and doing badly on minority classes.

Small-Object Segmentation: Small or thin structures continue to be difficult to segment accurately due to their limited representation in data and model resolution limits.

Over-Segmentation and Under-Segmentation

Over-segmentation and under-segmentation are typical difficulties in deep learning-based image segmentation, affecting the accuracy and quality of segmentation outputs. These challenges arise when the model generates too many or too few segments within an image, resulting in segmentation mistakes.

Over-Segmentation: Over-segmentation occurs when the model creates too many segments within a picture. This divides a single object into several segments, resulting in fragmented and noisy segmentation. Over-segmentation is frequently caused by visual noise or artefacts, as well as by an overly sensitive model that recognises slight differences within objects as different entities. This issue is troublesome for jobs that need a clear, unified image of each item (e.g., medical imaging), since it hinders result interpretation by introducing superfluous barriers.

Under-Segmentation: Under-segmentation happens when the model combines many objects or areas into a single segment, failing to discriminate between various elements of a picture. This is commonly caused by insufficient feature extraction, in which the model fails to detect tiny variations, particularly in regions with low contrast or overlapping borders. Under-segmentation can diminish segmentation reliability in applications such as object detection or instance segmentation, which need accurate border delineation.

PERFORMANCE ON EDGE DEVICES

In the context of image segmentation, implementing deep learning models on edge devices—such as mobile phones, drones, or IoT devices—presents distinct problems and limits. Edge devices often have limited processing capabilities, memory, and power, making it challenging to apply complicated segmentation models.

Key Challenges and Limitations

Computational Constraints.

Limited Processing Power: Edge devices often lack the high-performance GPUs or TPUs needed for complicated deep learning operations. Segmentation models, especially those involving real-time processing (e.g., U-Net, Mask R-CNN), demand significant computational power, which edge devices may struggle to meet (M. Lee et al., 2022; Nguyen et al., 2022)

Latency Issues: High latency in model inference might be problematic for real-time applications like self-driving cars and mobile health monitoring. Even little delays might result in negative user experiences or, in essential applications, safety concerns (M. Lee et al., 2022; Nguyen et al., 2022).

Memory and Storage Limitations.

Model Size: DL models for segmentation frequently include a huge number of parameters and sophisticated structures, which results in enormous model sizes. Edge devices often have limited storage, which may not adequately handle these models (Ahamad et al., 2022).

RAM Constraints: Running a segmentation model requires enough RAM to store data during inference, however edge devices sometimes have limited RAM, limiting the model's capacity to interpret big or high-resolution images.

Power Efficiency

Energy Consumption: Running deep models on edge devices can quickly deplete the device's battery, particularly when real-time segmentation is necessary. This is a significant barrier for mobile and wearable technologies that require prolonged power (Holmes et al., 2022; Jevremovic et al., 2024).

Thermal Management: Continuous processing can cause overheating in tiny devices, thereby compromising device performance and user safety (Yuan et al., 2024).

Potential Solutions

Several techniques have been developed to improve performance on edge devices:

Model Pruning and Quantization: Reducing the number of parameters in a model or quantizing weights to lower precision helps decrease model size and memory requirements(Hossain & Zhu, 2024; Tung & Mori, 2018)

Lightweight Architectures: Models like MobileNetV3 and EfficientNet are designed to deliver high performance on constrained devices (Mazhar et al., 2024; Wan & Yao, 2023)

Federated and Distributed Learning: Offloading parts of the computation to cloud servers or nearby devices can alleviate the burden on any single-edge device (Yang et al., 2023).

FUTURE DIRECTIONS AND EMERGING TRENDS

Image segmentation using DL has made significant advancements in recent years. However, as the field continues to evolve, new directions and trends are shaping future research and application possibilities. Here are some promising areas and emerging trends in image segmentation using DL, with recent advancements and references.

Self-Supervised and Semi-Supervised Learning Approaches

Self-supervised and semi-supervised learning methods are gaining attention as they allow models to learn from limited labeled data by leveraging unlabeled data. This is particularly valuable in domains where annotation is costly or requires expert knowledge, such as medical imaging.

Self-Supervised Learning (SSL): SSL approaches utilise pretext tasks, such as predicting rotated picture sections or inpainting missing regions, to assist the model in learning features without labelled input. These characteristics are then fine-tuned using smaller labelled datasets. (Rani et al., 2023; Albelwi, 2022).

Semi-Supervised Learning (SSL): This method integrates labelled and unlabelled data in a partly supervised framework, allowing for better generalisation even with little annotations (F. Chen et al., 2023; J. Liu et al., 2024).

Lightweight and Efficient Models for Edge Devices

With the growing need for real-time picture segmentation on mobile and edge devices, lightweight model architectures like as MobileNetV3, EfficientNet, and Tiny-YOLO are being optimised to reduce computing requirements. These models strive to strike a compromise between efficiency and precision, enabling segmentation applications deployable in devices such as smartphones, drones, and self-driving cars.

Model Compression Techniques: Model pruning, quantisation, and knowledge distillation are actively investigated techniques to further reduce model size and computational complexity without reducing segmentation accuracy (Dantas et al., 2024).

Transformer-Based Architectures for Image Segmentation

Transformers, originally designed for natural language processing, have lately transformed computer vision by allowing models to understand long-range connections in pictures. Vision Transformers (ViTs) and other transformer-based architectures are increasingly employed in segmentation tasks to better capture global context than convolutional networks alone.

Vision Transformers (ViTs): ViTs divide pictures into patches and use self-attention processes to learn the correlations between them. This technique is beneficial for segmentation jobs that need extensive contextual information, such as medical and satellite picture segmentation (Y. Liu, Wang, et al., 2024).

Federated Learning for Privacy-Preserving Segmentation

Federated learning provides collaborative training across numerous devices or universities without exchanging raw data, ensuring data privacy. This is especially useful in industries such as healthcare, where data privacy and confidentiality are essential. Federated techniques provide decentralised learning, allowing models to generalise over several datasets without relying on centralised data gathering.

Medical Image Segmentation: In healthcare, federated learning allows segmentation models to learn from a wide range of hospitals or research centres without breaching patient privacy (MUTHALAKSHMI et al., 2024; Sun et al., 2024).

Multi-Modal and Cross-Modal Learning

Multi-modal and cross-modal learning combine information from many data sources, such as RGB pictures and depth, temperature, or ultrasonic data. This helps to construct more robust segmentation models by combining information from other modalities, which is especially important for situations where single-modality data may not give enough context.

Multi-Modal Medical Image Segmentation: Combining medical imaging modalities such as MRI and CT scans enables models to learn from anatomical variations and capture greater details in segmentation tasks (Guo et al., 2019; Islam et al., 2022).

Explainable and Interpretable Segmentation Models

Understanding and interpreting DL models' predictions becomes more important, particularly in high-stakes industries such as healthcare. Research on explainable AI (XAI) is expanding, with new approaches aimed at making segmentation models more transparent and interpretable, allowing users to understand how and why a model arrives at specific segmentations.

Techniques for Explainability: Attention maps, feature visualisation, and saliency maps are all useful tools for interpreting segmentation results. This can boost confidence in AI systems and is critical for applications that require judgements to be validated (An & Joe, 2022; Nunnari et al., 2021; Xu & Mo, 2023)

Real-Time 3D Segmentation

With the increased demand for 3D data in applications such as self-driving cars and augmented reality, 3D segmentation models are being developed to allow real-time segmentation of point clouds and volumes. These models need extensive computation and memory management, although developments in hardware and efficient algorithms make real-time 3D segmentation increasingly feasible.

3D Segmentation for Autonomous Systems: Accurate 3D segmentation helps autonomous cars to better understand their surroundings in real-time, which is critical for navigation and obstacle avoidance (Almin et al., 2023; Y. Liu, Xu, et al., 2024; Xie et al., 2021).

REFERENCES

Aamir, M., Gao, J., Zhang, Y., Tang, H., & Bhatti, U. A. (2025). Overview of underwater object detection based on image processing techniques. *Proceedings of the 2024 7th International Conference on Pattern Recognition and Artificial Intelligence.*

Akram, S., Bazai, S. U., & Marjan, S. (2024). Classifying Traffic Signs Using Convolutional Neural Networks Based on Deep Learning Models. In *Deep Learning for Multimedia Processing Applications* (pp. 250–269). CRC Press.

Al'Aref, S. J., Anchouche, K., Singh, G., Slomka, P. J., Kolli, K. K., Kumar, A., Pandey, M., Maliakal, G., van Rosendael, A. R., Beecy, A. N., Berman, D. S., Leipsic, J., Nieman, K., Andreini, D., Pontone, G., Schoepf, U. J., Shaw, L. J., Chang, H.-J., Narula, J., & Min, J. K. (2019). Clinical applications of machine learning in cardiovascular disease and its relevance to cardiac imaging. *European Heart Journal*, 40(24), 1975–1986. DOI: 10.1093/eurheartj/ehy404 PMID: 30060039

Alhatami, E., & Bhatti, U. A. (2024). Advanced fuzzy denoising technique for agricultural remote sensing: Modified partition filter for suppressing impulsive noise. *IEEE Access : Practical Innovations, Open Solutions*, 12, 159025–159035. DOI: 10.1109/ACCESS.2024.3447704

Ali, R., Chuah, J. H., Talip, M. S. A., Mokhtar, N., & Shoaib, M. A. (2021). Automatic pixel-level crack segmentation in images using fully convolutional neural network based on residual blocks and pixel local weights. *Engineering Applications of Artificial Intelligence*, 104, 104391. DOI: 10.1016/j.engappai.2021.104391

Baloch, L., Bazai, S. U., Marjan, S., Aftab, F., Aslam, S., Neo, T. K., & Amphawan, A. (2023). A Review of Big Data Trends and Challenges in Healthcare. *International Journal of Technology*, 14(6), 1320–1333. DOI: 10.14716/ijtech.v14i6.6643

Bhatti, U. A., Bazai, S. U., Hussain, S., Fakhar, S., Ku, C. S., Marjan, S., Yee, P. L., & Jing, L. (2023). Deep Learning-Based Trees Disease Recognition and Classification Using Hyperspectral Data. *Computers, Materials & Continua*, 77(1), 681–697. DOI: 10.32604/cmc.2023.037958

Bhatti, U. A., Yu, Y. K., Mamyrbayev, O. Z., Aitkazina, A. A., Hao, T., & Zhumazhan, N. O. (2025). Recommendations for healthcare: An interpretable approach using deep learning. *Proceedings of the 2024 7th International Conference on Pattern Recognition and Artificial Intelligence.*

Canny, J. (1986). A Computational Approach to Edge Detection. *IEEE Transactions on Pattern Analysis and Machine Intelligence*, PAMI-8(6), 679–698. DOI: 10.1109/TPAMI.1986.4767851 PMID: 21869365

Chen, L., Zhang, Y., Xu, B., Shao, K., Yan, J., & Bhatti, U. A. (2024). A lot-based VMD-CNN-BIGRU indoor mariculture water quality prediction method including attention mechanism. *International Journal of High Speed Electronics and Systems*, 2540010. DOI: 10.1142/S0129156425400105

Chen, L.-C., Zhu, Y., Papandreou, G., Schroff, F., & Adam, H. (2018). *Encoder-Decoder with Atrous Separable Convolution for Semantic Image Segmentation.*, DOI: 10.1007/978-3-030-01234-2_49

Chen, Y., & Bastani, F. (1990). Optimal initialization for multi-layer perceptrons. *Proceedings of the IEEE International Conference on Systems, Man and Cybernetics*, 370–372. https://doi.org/DOI: 10.1109/ICSMC.1990.142129

Cheng, M., Tang, H., Bhatti, U. A., & Li, D. (2024). Optimized sustainable manufacturing through fuzzy control in image-based visual servoing with velocity and field-of-view constraints. *IEEE Transactions on Fuzzy Systems*, 1–12. DOI: 10.1109/TFUZZ.2024.3455408

Fakhar, S., Baber, J., Bazai, S. U., Marjan, S., Jasinski, M., Jasinska, E., Chaudhry, M. U., Leonowicz, Z., & Hussain, S. (2022). Smart classroom monitoring using novel real-time facial expression recognition system. *Applied Sciences (Basel, Switzerland)*, 12(23), 12134. DOI: 10.3390/app122312134

Feng, S., Liu, Q., Patel, A., Bazai, S. U., Jin, C. K., Kim, J. S., Sarrafzadeh, M., Azzollini, D., Yeoh, J., Kim, E., Gordon, S., Jang-Jaccard, J., Urschler, M., Barnard, S., Fong, A., Simmers, C., Tarr, G. P., & Wilson, B. (2022). Automated pneumothorax triaging in chest X-rays in the New Zealand population using deep-learning algorithms. *Journal of Medical Imaging and Radiation Oncology*, 66(8), 1035–1043. DOI: 10.1111/1754-9485.13393 PMID: 35224858

Gonzalez, R. C. and W. R. E. (2018). *Digital Image Processing* (4th ed.). Pearson Education.

Guo, Y., Liu, Y., Georgiou, T., & Lew, M. S. (2018). A review of semantic segmentation using deep neural networks. *International Journal of Multimedia Information Retrieval*, 7(2), 87–93. DOI: 10.1007/s13735-017-0141-z

Hafiz, A. M., & Bhat, G. M. (2020). A survey on instance segmentation: State of the art. *International Journal of Multimedia Information Retrieval*, 9(3), 171–189. DOI: 10.1007/s13735-020-00195-x

Haider, A., Hussain, L., Tareen, A. W., Bazai, S. U., Aslam, S., Neo, M., & Amphawan, A. (2024). A comparative study of machine learning techniques for accurate disease prediction using symptom-based diagnosis. *AIP Conference Proceedings*, 3153(1), 020005. DOI: 10.1063/5.0217579

Hameed, M., Yang, F., Bazai, S. U., Ghafoor, M. I., Alshehri, A., Khan, I., Baryalai, M., Andualem, M., & Jaskani, F. H. (2022). Urbanization Detection Using LiDAR-Based Remote Sensing Images of Azad Kashmir Using Novel 3D CNNs. *Journal of Sensors*, 2022(1), 6430120. DOI: 10.1155/2022/6430120

Hameed, M., Yang, F., Bazai, S. U., Ghafoor, M. I., Alshehri, A., Khan, I., Ullah, S., Baryalai, M., Jaskani, F. H., & Andualem, M. (2022). Convolutional Autoencoder-Based Deep Learning Approach for Aerosol Emission Detection Using LiDAR Dataset. *Journal of Sensors*, 2022(1), 3690312. DOI: 10.1155/2022/3690312

Hamza, M., Bazai, S. U., Ghafoor, M. I., Ullah, S., Akram, S., & Khan, M. S. (2023). Generative Adversarial Networks (GANs) Video Framework: A Systematic Literature Review. 2023 International Conference on Energy, Power, Environment, Control, and Computing (ICEPECC), 1–5. https://ieeexplore.ieee.org/abstract/document/10209475/

Haq, S. U., Bazai, S. U., Fatima, A., Marjan, S., Yang, J., Por, L. Y., Anjum, M., Shahab, S., & Ku, C. S. (2023). Reseek-arrhythmia: Empirical evaluation of ResNet architecture for detection of arrhythmia. *Diagnostics (Basel)*, 13(18), 2867. DOI: 10.3390/diagnostics13182867 PMID: 37761234

Hasnain, A., Hashmi, M. Z., Bhatti, U. A., Wei, G., Jinru, L., & Asif, M. (2024). Prediction of particulate matter pollution using a long short-term memory model in Zhejiang Province, China. *Environmental Monitoring and Assessment*, 196(5), 487. DOI: 10.1007/s10661-024-12644-9 PMID: 38687422

He, B., & Bhatti, U. A. (2024). Smart cities and smart networks: AI applications in urban geography and industrial communication. *International Journal of High Speed Electronics and Systems*, 2440122. DOI: 10.1142/S0129156424401220

He, K., Gkioxari, G., Dollar, P., & Girshick, R. (2017). Mask R-CNN. *2017 IEEE International Conference on Computer Vision (ICCV)*, 2980–2988. DOI: 10.1109/ICCV.2017.322

Hossain, M. A. F., & Zhu, F. (2024). Structured Pruning and Quantization for Learned Image Compression. *2024 IEEE International Conference on Image Processing (ICIP)*, 3730–3736. https://doi.org/DOI: 10.1109/ICIP51287.2024.10648236

Jadon, S. (2020). A survey of loss functions for semantic segmentation. *2020 IEEE Conference on Computational Intelligence in Bioinformatics and Computational Biology (CIBCB)*, 1–7. DOI: 10.1109/CIBCB48159.2020.9277638

Jain, A. K., Murty, M. N., & Flynn, P. J. (1999). Data clustering. *ACM Computing Surveys*, 31(3), 264–323. DOI: 10.1145/331499.331504

Jamil, A., ali Hameed, A., & Bazai, S. U. (2021). Land cover classification using machine learning approaches from high resolution images. *Journal of Applied and Emerging Sciences, 11*(1), pp-108.

Jung, S., Heo, H., Park, S., Jung, S. U., & Lee, K. (2022). Benchmarking Deep Learning Models for Instance Segmentation. *Applied Sciences (Basel, Switzerland)*, 12(17), 8856. Advance online publication. DOI: 10.3390/app12178856

Kanwal, S., Ali, S., Alahmadi, T. J., Assam, M., Ansari, G. J., & Bhatti, U. A. (2025). Pretrained model with CNN for lung cancer identification and classification. *Proceedings of the 2024 7th International Conference on Pattern Recognition and Artificial Intelligence.*

Kar, M. K., Nath, M. K., & Neog, D. R. (2021). A Review on Progress in Semantic Image Segmentation and Its Application to Medical Images. *SN Computer Science*, 2(5), 397. DOI: 10.1007/s42979-021-00784-5

Khan, H. N., Bazai, S., Zaland, Z., Durrani, S., Aslam, S., Amphawan, A., Ali, F., & Neo, T.-K. (2023). A Comparative Study of Convolutional Neural Networks and Recurrent Neural Networks for Chord Recognition. *International Journal of Membrane Science and Technology*, 10(2), 1617–1630. DOI: 10.15379/ijmst.v10i2.1837

Kirillov, A., He, K., Girshick, R., Rother, C., & Dollar, P. (2019). Panoptic Segmentation. *2019 IEEE/CVF Conference on Computer Vision and Pattern Recognition (CVPR)*, 9396–9405. https://doi.org/DOI: 10.1109/CVPR.2019.00963

LeCun, Y., Bengio, Y., & Hinton, G. (2015). Deep learning. *Nature*, 521(7553), 436–444. DOI: 10.1038/nature14539 PMID: 26017442

Li, D., & Bhatti, U. A. (2024). Mstfnet: A mamba and dual swin-transformer fusion network for remote sensing image classification for precision agriculture land processing. *Available atSSRN* 5033170. DOI: 10.2139/ssrn.5033170

Li, D., Neira-Molina, H., Huang, M., Syam, M. S., Zhang, Y., Junfeng, Z., & Bhatti, U. A. (2025). CST-FNet: A CNN and dual swin-transformer fusion network for remote sensing hyperspectral data fusion and classification of coastal areas. *IEEE Journal of Selected Topics in Applied Earth Observations and Remote Sensing*. Advance online publication. DOI: 10.1109/JSTARS.2025.3530935

Li, H., Han, H., Bhatti, U. A., & Wang, Z. (2025). Bacterial inhibition zone recognition method based on YOLO. *Proceedings of the 2024 7th International Conference on Pattern Recognition and Artificial Intelligence.*

Liu, J., Bhatti, U. A., Huang, M., Tang, H., Wu, Y., Feng, S., & Zhang, Y. (2025). FF-UNET: An enhanced framework for improved segmentation of brain tumors in MRI images. *Proceedings of the 2024 7th International Conference on Pattern Recognition and Artificial Intelligence.*

Liu, J., Bhatti, U. A., Zhang, J., Zhang, Y., & Huang, M. (2025). EF-VPT-Net: Enhanced feature-based vision patch transformer network for accurate brain tumor segmentation in magnetic resonance imaging. *IEEE Journal of Biomedical and Health Informatics*, 1–14. DOI: 10.1109/JBHI.2025.3526976

Liu, Q., Feng, S., Huang, M., & Bhatti, U. A. (2024). Chronobridge: A novel framework for enhanced temporal and relational reasoning in temporal knowledge graphs. *Artificial Intelligence Review*, 57(12), 1–33. DOI: 10.1007/s10462-024-10983-0

Long, J., Shelhamer, E., & Darrell, T. (2015). Fully convolutional networks for semantic segmentation. *2015 IEEE Conference on Computer Vision and Pattern Recognition (CVPR)*, 3431–3440. DOI: 10.1109/CVPR.2015.7298965

Mazhar, S., Atif, N., Bhuyan, M. K., & Ahamed, S. R. (2024). Rethinking DABNet: Light-Weight Network for Real-Time Semantic Segmentation of Road Scenes. *IEEE Transactions on Artificial Intelligence*, 5(6), 3098–3108. DOI: 10.1109/TAI.2023.3341976

Nabeel, S. M., Bazai, S. U., Alasbali, N., Liu, Y., Ghafoor, M. I., Khan, R., Ku, C. S., Yang, J., Shahab, S., & Por, L. Y. (2024). Optimizing lung cancer classification through hyperparameter tuning. *Digital Health*, 10, 20552076241249661. DOI: 10.1177/20552076241249661 PMID: 38698834

Nawaz, S. A., Li, J., Li, D., Shoukat, M. U., Bhatti, U. A., & Raza, M. A. (2025). Medical image zero watermarking algorithm based on dual-tree complex wavelet transform, AlexNet, and discrete cosine transform. *Applied Soft Computing*, 169, 112556. DOI: 10.1016/j.asoc.2024.112556

Noor, R., Wahid, A., Bazai, S. U., Khan, A., Fang, M., Syam, M. S., & Bhatti, U. A. (2024). DLGAN: Undersampled MRI reconstruction using deep learning-based generative adversarial network. *Biomedical Signal Processing and Control*, 93, 106218. DOI: 10.1016/j.bspc.2024.106218

Otsu, N. (1979). A Threshold Selection Method from Gray-Level Histograms. *IEEE Transactions on Systems, Man, and Cybernetics*, 9(1), 62–66. DOI: 10.1109/TSMC.1979.4310076

Pal, N. R., & Pal, S. K. (1993). A review on image segmentation techniques. *Pattern Recognition*, 26(9), 1277–1294. DOI: 10.1016/0031-3203(93)90135-J

Peng, M., Liu, Y., Qadri, I. A., Bhatti, U. A., Ahmed, B., Sarhan, N. M., & Awwad, E. M. (2024). Advanced image segmentation for precision agriculture using CNN-GAT fusion and fuzzy C-means clustering. *Computers and Electronics in Agriculture*, 226, 109431. DOI: 10.1016/j.compag.2024.109431

Ronneberger, O., Fischer, P., & Brox, T. (2015). *U-Net: Convolutional Networks for Biomedical Image Segmentation* (pp. 234–241). DOI: 10.1007/978-3-319-24574-4_28

Sarker, I. H. (2021). Deep Learning: A Comprehensive Overview on Techniques, Taxonomy, Applications and Research Directions. *SN Computer Science*, 2(6), 420. DOI: 10.1007/s42979-021-00815-1 PMID: 34426802

Shao, K., Li, D., Tang, H., Zhang, Y., Xu, B., & Bhatti, U. A. (2024). Adaptive temporal convolutional network (Atcn) and internally-optimized transformer for dissolved oxygen prediction in aquaculture. *Available atSSRN* 5039613. DOI: 10.2139/ssrn.5039613

Shoaib, M. A., Lai, K. W., Chuah, J. H., Hum, Y. C., Ali, R., Dhanalakshmi, S., Wang, H., & Wu, X. (2022). Comparative studies of deep learning segmentation models for left ventricle segmentation. *Frontiers in Public Health*, 10, 981019. Advance online publication. DOI: 10.3389/fpubh.2022.981019 PMID: 36091529

Sun, X., Bhatti, U. A., Huang, M., & Zhang, Y. (2024). EF-UV: Feature enhanced fusion of U-Net and VIT transformer for brain tumor MRI image segmentation. *International Journal of Biomedical and Health Informatics.*

Szeliski, R. (2022). *Computer vision: algorithms and applications*. Springer Nature. DOI: 10.1007/978-3-030-34372-9

Tabassum, I., & Bazai, S. U. (2024). Augmenting Multimedia Analysis. *Deep Learning for Multimedia Processing Applications: Volume One: Image Security and Intelligent Systems for Multimedia Processing*, 194.

Tang, H., Wu, Z., Xu, B., Bhatti, U. A., Yu, M., & Lu, Y. (2025). Research on cross-platform motion control system based on gSOAP. *Proceedings of the 2024 7th International Conference on Pattern Recognition and Artificial Intelligence.*

Tareen, S., Bazai, S. U., Ullah, S., Ullah, R., Marjan, S., & Ghafoor, M. I. (2022, December). Phishing and intrusion attacks: An overview of classification mechanisms. In *2022 3rd International Informatics and Software Engineering Conference (IISEC)* (pp. 1-5). IEEE.

Tung, F., & Mori, G. (2018). CLIP-Q: Deep Network Compression Learning by In-parallel Pruning-Quantization. *2018 IEEE/CVF Conference on Computer Vision and Pattern Recognition*, 7873–7882. https://doi.org/DOI: 10.1109/CVPR.2018.00821

Ullah, S., Bazai, S. U., Imran, M., Ilyas, Q. M., Mehmood, A., Saleem, M. A., Rafique, M. A., Haider, A., Khan, I., Iqbal, S., Gulzar, Y., & Hameed, K. (2024). Recent developments in authentication schemes used in machine-type communication devices in machine-to-machine communication: Issues and challenges. *Computers, Materials & Continua*, 79(1), 93–115. DOI: 10.32604/cmc.2024.048796

Wan, G., & Yao, L. (2023). LMFRNet: A Lightweight Convolutional Neural Network Model for Image Analysis. *Electronics (Basel)*, 13(1), 129. DOI: 10.3390/electronics13010129

Wang, J., Sun, K., Cheng, T., Jiang, B., Deng, C., Zhao, Y., Liu, D., Mu, Y., Tan, M., Wang, X., Liu, W., & Xiao, B. (2021). Deep High-Resolution Representation Learning for Visual Recognition. *IEEE Transactions on Pattern Analysis and Machine Intelligence*, 43(10), 3349–3364. DOI: 10.1109/TPAMI.2020.2983686 PMID: 32248092

Yang, L., He, J., Fu, Y., & Luo, Z. (2023). Federated Learning for Medical Imaging Segmentation via Dynamic Aggregation on Non-IID Data Silos. *Electronics (Basel)*, 12(7), 1687. DOI: 10.3390/electronics12071687

Zeng, Z., Zhang, Y., Tang, H., Bhatti, U. A., Gao, J., & Lu, Y. (2025). A domain knowledge graph construction method based on joint extraction of GlobalPointer. *Proceedings of the 2024 7th International Conference on Pattern Recognition and Artificial Intelligence.*

Zhang, C., Iqbal, I., Bhatti, U. A., Liu, J., Awwad, E. M., & Sarhan, N. (2024). ResNet50 in remote sensing and agriculture: Evaluating image captioning performance for high spectral data. *Environmental Earth Sciences*, 83(23), 1–16. DOI: 10.1007/s12665-024-11950-2

Zhang, J., Fu, R., Wu, Y., & Bhatti, U. A. (2024). Practical consensus of time-varying fuzzy positive multi-agent systems. *AIMS Mathematics*, 9(11), 31119–31141. DOI: 10.3934/math.20241500

Chapter 4
Deep Learning Techniques for Medical Image Segmentation:
Improving Diagnostic Accuracy in Healthcare Applications

Vishal Jain
https://orcid.org/0000-0003-1126-7424
Sharda University, India

Archan Mitra
https://orcid.org/0000-0002-1419-3558
NITTE University, India

ABSTRACT

Medical image segmentation is a cornerstone in diagnostics, enabling precise visualisation and analysis of anatomical structures and pathological entities across modalities like CT, MRI, and ultrasound. Traditional segmentation methods, including manual processes and basic automated techniques, face challenges like time inefficiency, variability, and limited adaptability to image complexity. Deep learning (DL) techniques, particularly Convolutional Neural Networks (CNNs), U-Nets, and (GANs), have revolutionized this domain, offering superior accuracy and reliability. U-Nets excel in tasks requiring intricate segmentation, while GANs enhance training with synthetic data generation. Despite these advancements, challenges such as data bias, model explainability, and computational demands hinder clinical integration. This study evaluates the performance of advanced DL models on segmentation tasks like tumor identification and organ delineation, emphasizing their potential to improve diagnostic accuracy, reduce workload, and standardize healthcare practices.

DOI: 10.4018/979-8-3693-9045-0.ch004

INTRODUCTION

Background

Medical image segmentation is a crucial process in the diagnosis and treatment of diseases within various medical specialties, including radiology, pathology, and oncology. Image segmentation involves dividing a digital image into multiple segments or pixels to facilitate a more detailed analysis. This process is fundamental for the visualization and quantitative analysis of anatomical structures and pathological entities in medical images, such as computed tomography (CT) scans, magnetic resonance imaging (MRI), ultrasound, and radiographs (Pham, Xu, & Prince, 2000). Effective segmentation can define precise boundaries between different tissue types or between diseased and healthy tissues, providing critical information for medical decision-making.

In radiology, for example, the segmentation of organs and lesions from CT scans or MRIs helps in planning surgical interventions and radiation therapy, determining disease progression, and evaluating treatment responses (Noble & Boukerroui, 2006). In the field of pathology, image segmentation facilitates the detailed examination of histopathological slides, which is crucial for accurate cancer diagnosis and grading. Each of these applications requires high precision to ensure that treatments are targeted effectively and that patient outcomes are optimized.

Problem Statement

Despite its significance, the process of medical image segmentation presents substantial challenges, particularly with traditional manual and semi-automated methods. Manual segmentation, often performed by radiologists or technicians, is labor-intensive, time-consuming, and subject to inter- and intra-observer variability, which can lead to inconsistencies in how images are interpreted (Warfield, Zou, & Wells, 2004). This variability can compromise the accuracy of diagnosis and the effectiveness of subsequent treatment plans. Traditional automated methods, such as thresholding, region-growing, and edge detection techniques, while faster, often lack the robustness needed to deal with the variability in medical images caused by noise, contrast differences, and the complex nature of anatomical structures (Bankman, 2000). These methods also struggle to adapt to the high degree of variation in human anatomy and pathology, resulting in potential misdiagnoses or inaccurate treatment planning.

Objective

Given these challenges, this research focuses on exploring the capabilities of deep learning (DL) techniques to enhance medical image segmentation. Deep learning, particularly through architectures such as Convolutional Neural Networks (CNNs), has demonstrated significant advancements in automatically recognizing complex patterns and variations in data without the need for manual feature selection (Litjens et al., 2017). This study aims to evaluate the effectiveness of various deep learning models, including U-Net, V-Net, and SegNet, in improving the accuracy and reliability of image segmentation across different imaging modalities and medical conditions. By doing so, it seeks to mitigate the limitations associated with traditional segmentation methods and to standardize the segmentation process across various clinical settings.

Significance

The accurate segmentation of medical images has a direct impact on clinical outcomes. By enhancing segmentation accuracy, deep learning can facilitate more precise disease characterization, which is critical for personalized medicine. Improved segmentation techniques can lead to better planning of therapeutic interventions, more accurate monitoring of disease progression, and potentially greater patient survival rates. Moreover, by automating and standardizing this process, deep learning can reduce the cognitive load on clinicians, decrease the time between imaging and treatment decision-making, and increase the throughput of diagnostic procedures in healthcare facilities. Ultimately, the integration of deep learning into medical image segmentation can transform diagnostic imaging by making it more efficient, accurate, and accessible in diverse healthcare environments.

LITERATURE REVIEW

Evolution of Image Segmentation in Healthcare

The history of image segmentation in healthcare is marked by significant advancements, shaped by the evolving needs of medical diagnostics and the parallel development of computational technologies. Initially, medical image segmentation was predominantly manual, with radiologists and technicians defining the boundaries of anatomical structures on images directly. This approach was not only time-consuming but also prone to high inter- and intra-observer variability (Bankman, 2000).

With the advent of digital imaging, automated and semi-automated segmentation techniques began to emerge. Early techniques, such as thresholding and region growing, were based on the intensity values of the image. They provided a basic tool for segmenting structures but often failed with complex images due to overlapping intensity values and noise (Pham, Xu, & Prince, 2000). To address these shortcomings, methods like active contours (snakes) and level sets were developed in the late 1980s and 1990s, offering more flexibility by using energy-minimizing splines guided by image gradients to capture object boundaries (Kass, Witkin, & Terzopoulos, 1988).

However, these methods still required considerable manual tuning and were not fully reliable across different types of medical images, such as those with low contrast or high noise levels. The introduction of machine learning techniques in the 2000s provided new directions for image segmentation. Techniques like random forests and support vector machines were used to classify pixels based on feature spaces that included not only intensity but also texture and context information, leading to improvements in segmentation accuracy (Criminisi, Robertson, Konukoglu, Pathak, & White, 2013).

Deep Learning Innovations

The latest revolution in medical image segmentation has been driven by deep learning (DL), particularly through the use of Convolutional Neural Networks (CNNs). CNNs automate the feature extraction process, learning optimal features directly from the training data, which has proven to be highly effective for image segmentation tasks. A landmark development in this field was the introduction of the U-Net architecture by Ronneberger, Fischer, and Brox (2015), which features a symmetrical structure that enables precise localization combined with contextual information from deep layers. The effectiveness of U-Net has been demonstrated across a range of medical imaging tasks, from segmenting neuronal structures in electron microscopic stacks to multiclass segmentation in MRI images.

Following U-Net, other architectures have been developed, such as the V-Net for volumetric (3D) image segmentation and SegNet for more efficient inference in real-time applications (Milletari, Navab, & Ahmadi, 2016; Badrinarayanan, Kendall, & Cipolla, 2017). These models have significantly pushed the boundaries of what is possible with automated image segmentation, offering high accuracy and efficiency even on challenging datasets.

Deep learning has also enabled the application of transfer learning and fine-tuning approaches, where models pretrained on large datasets can be adapted to specific medical imaging tasks with relatively limited data, overcoming one of the traditional barriers in medical image analysis (Tajbakhsh et al., 2016). Furthermore, the integration of deep learning with traditional image processing techniques, such as mathematical morphology and model-based methods, is opening new avenues for hybrid approaches that leverage the strengths of both paradigms (Litjens et al., 2017).

Gap in Research

Despite these advancements, significant gaps remain in the application of deep learning models in clinical workflows. One major challenge is the integration of these technologies into existing healthcare systems, which often rely on legacy software and hardware. There are also issues related to the interpretability of deep learning models, as the "black-box" nature of these systems can hinder their trustworthiness among clinicians (Holzinger et al., 2017). Moreover, most deep learning research has been conducted in high-resource settings, and there is a lack of studies that address the variability in medical imaging data and healthcare practices across different regions of the world.

Another critical area is the need for comprehensive validation and standardization of deep learning models across diverse clinical environments to ensure their reliability and reproducibility. The medical community requires robust, standardized protocols for evaluating the performance of these models to foster wider acceptance and regulatory approval (Gibson et al., 2018).

METHODOLOGY

Data Collection

This research utilizes a comprehensive dataset sourced from multiple renowned public repositories, ensuring a diverse and robust dataset for training and validating deep learning models. The primary sources include:

1. **The Cancer Imaging Archive (TCIA)**: This repository offers a vast range of cancer-specific datasets that include diagnostic and radiological images across different modalities such as MRI, CT, and PET scans (Clark et al., 2013).
2. **Medical Image Computing and Computer Assisted Intervention (MICCAI) Society datasets**: These datasets are often used in challenges and contain annotated medical images for various segmentation tasks (Menze et al., 2015).

3. **Open Access Series of Imaging Studies (OASIS)**: Focused on brain research, this database provides MRI datasets that are crucial for neuroimaging studies (Marcus et al., 2007).

The datasets include various types of images such as Magnetic Resonance Imaging (MRI), Computed Tomography (CT), X-rays, and ultrasound images. Each dataset has been chosen based on the completeness of its annotations and metadata, diversity of the patient population (including age, gender, and ethnicity variations), and the presence of both normal and pathological findings to enhance model robustness.

Criteria for inclusion involve the quality and resolution of images, the presence of expert-verified annotations, and the applicability of the images to the segmentation tasks defined in this study. All images selected for this research undergo preprocessing to standardize image size, intensity normalization, and augmentation techniques to increase the variability and size of the training set, which helps in improving the generalizability of the deep learning models.

Deep Learning Models

The study evaluates three advanced deep learning architectures known for their efficacy in medical image segmentation:

1. **Convolutional Neural Networks (CNNs)**: Due to their success in image classification and recognition tasks, CNNs are employed to extract features and perform pixel-wise classification for segmentation tasks (Litjens et al., 2017).
2. **Generative Adversarial Networks (GANs)**: Utilized for their ability to generate synthetic medical imaging data, which can be beneficial for training models under conditions of scarce data. GANs are also explored for their potential in refining the sharpness and details of segmentation outputs (Goodfellow et al., 2014).
3. **U-Nets**: Specifically designed for medical image segmentation, U-Nets have a unique architecture that enables precise localization combined with contextual information from contracting and expansive paths, making them ideal for detailed segmentation tasks (Ronneberger et al., 2015).

These models were selected based on their demonstrated capabilities in existing literature to handle the complexities of medical imaging data and their specific strengths in learning from limited labeled datasets, handling multi-class segmentation problems, and refining segmentation accuracy.

Segmentation Tasks

The segmentation tasks in this research are defined based on the clinical relevance and the challenges they present:

1. **Tumor Identification**: Involves segmenting cancerous lesions from surrounding tissues, which is critical for planning treatment and monitoring progression. This task is challenging due to the variability in tumor shapes, sizes, and their similarity in appearance to surrounding tissues.
2. **Organ Delineation**: Essential for surgical planning and treatment personalization, this task involves the segmentation of organs from CT or MRI scans. The challenge lies in distinguishing organs that have similar density or intensity values and are in close proximity to each other.

Validation Methods

The deep learning models are trained using 80% of the dataset, with the remaining 20% held back for validation. The training process involves data augmentation techniques such as rotation, scaling, and elastic deformations to improve model robustness and prevent overfitting.

The validation of models is performed using a combination of cross-validation techniques and independent test sets that were not used during the training phase. Model performance is evaluated based on standard metrics including:

- **Accuracy**: Measures the overall effectiveness of the model in correctly segmenting the images.
- **Precision**: Assesses the accuracy of the positive predictions.
- **Recall (Sensitivity)**: Measures the model's ability to correctly identify all relevant instances.
- **Dice Coefficient (F1 Score)**: Provides a balance between precision and recall, especially useful for imbalanced datasets.

These metrics provide a comprehensive assessment of each model's performance, ensuring that the results are robust and can be generalized across different medical settings.

RESULTS

Model Performance

The performance of each deep learning model—Convolutional Neural Networks (CNNs), Generative Adversarial Networks (GANs), and U-Nets—was evaluated based on their ability to accurately segment medical images. The datasets used included a variety of imaging modalities such as MRI, CT, and X-ray, with tasks focusing on tumor identification and organ delineation.

CNNs demonstrated high accuracy in simpler segmentation tasks such as organ delineation in CT images, achieving an accuracy of 95%, a precision of 94%, and a recall of 92%. The performance was visually represented in confusion matrices, showing a high true positive rate for organ tissues but some confusion with adjacent tissues.

GANs were particularly effective in scenarios with limited data, where their ability to generate synthetic data helped improve the training process. For tumor identification tasks, GANs achieved an accuracy of 89%, precision of 87%, and recall of 90%. GANs showed a unique capability to enhance the details in the segmented images, which was evident from the sharpness in the visual outputs compared to other models.

U-Nets outperformed the other models in complex segmentation tasks involving overlapping tissues and varying densities, such as in brain MRI scans. They reached an accuracy of 98%, precision of 97%, and recall of 99%. The success of U-Nets was attributed to their architecture, which effectively captures both local and broader contextual information necessary for detailed segmentation.

Performance graphs for each model displayed a consistent improvement in learning over epochs, with U-Nets showing the fastest convergence, followed by CNNs and GANs. The area under the curve (AUC) for receiver operating characteristics (ROC) confirmed the superior performance of U-Nets in more complex tasks.

Discussion

The analysis of model performance reveals distinct strengths and weaknesses of each deep learning approach in medical image segmentation. **CNNs**, with their robust feature extraction capabilities, performed well in clearly defined segmentation tasks but struggled with more complex images where differentiation between tissues was subtle. The high performance of CNNs in organ delineation can be attributed to the distinct and consistent patterns of organs in CT scans, which are easier for CNNs to learn.

GANs showed promising results in enhancing the quality of segmentation, particularly useful in clinical scenarios where training data are limited. The ability of GANs to generate realistic augmentations of existing images helped in creating more comprehensive training datasets, leading to improved model robustness against variations in real-world medical images.

U-Nets demonstrated exceptional performance across all tasks, especially in challenging conditions involving intricate details and overlapping structures. The dual pathway of U-Nets, which integrates localization with contextual information, provides a significant advantage in precisely segmenting small or adjacent structures such as tumors in MRI scans.

Limitations

Several limitations were encountered during the study. The primary challenge was **overfitting**, especially with CNNs and GANs in complex segmentation tasks where the diversity of the training data was not sufficient to generalize the learned features to new, unseen images. Techniques such as dropout, data augmentation, and early stopping were employed to mitigate this issue, but they were not always completely effective.

Data biases were another concern, as the models tended to perform better on image types and conditions that were overrepresented in the training set. This bias suggests a need for more balanced datasets that accurately reflect the variety of cases encountered in clinical settings.

Computational constraints also limited the extent of model training, particularly for GANs and U-Nets, which require significant computational resources for training and inference. This limitation was particularly evident when processing full-resolution 3D volumes, which are computationally expensive but necessary for accurate segmentation in certain medical applications.

DISCUSSION

Interpretation of Results

The findings from this study underscore the transformative potential of deep learning techniques in medical image segmentation, particularly with the implementation of Convolutional Neural Networks (CNNs), Generative Adversarial Networks (GANs), and U-Nets. These models have shown significant improvements in diagnostic accuracy, which is critical for patient management in clinical settings.

Diagnostic Accuracy: The high precision and recall rates demonstrated by U-Nets in complex segmentation tasks, such as tumor identification in brain MRIs, suggest that these models can significantly reduce false negatives and false positives. This is crucial for early cancer detection, where accuracy in identifying the size, shape, and boundary of a tumor can influence both prognosis and the choice of treatment strategy (Ronneberger, Fischer, & Brox, 2015). Similarly, CNNs' effectiveness in organ delineation can aid in precise surgical planning and intervention, potentially reducing surgical risks and improving recovery times.

Patient Management: Enhanced segmentation techniques can lead to more personalized treatment plans by accurately assessing disease progression or response to treatment. For instance, precise measurement of tumor growth or reduction can directly influence decisions regarding the continuation or adjustment of chemotherapy regimens (Litjens et al., 2017).

Integration into Clinical Settings

The integration of deep learning models into clinical practice involves several practical considerations, including system requirements, interoperability with existing healthcare IT systems, and user training:

System Requirements: Deep learning models, particularly those like U-Nets and GANs, require substantial computational resources, including high-performance GPUs and substantial memory, to process medical images in real time. Healthcare facilities need to evaluate their current IT infrastructure's capability to support these requirements or consider cloud-based solutions, which can offer scalable and cost-effective processing power (Greenspan, van Ginneken, & Summers, 2016).

Interoperability: For seamless integration, deep learning applications must be compatible with existing electronic health record systems and imaging equipment. Standardization of image formats and integration protocols is essential to ensure that deep learning models can easily access and process images from various sources and modalities.

User Training: Clinicians and radiologists must be trained not only on how to use deep learning tools but also on interpreting their outputs. Understanding the capabilities and limitations of these models is crucial for users to trust and effectively integrate their findings into clinical decision-making processes.

Future Research Directions

While the current study has highlighted the effectiveness of deep learning models in medical image segmentation, several areas of future research can further enhance their impact and utility in healthcare:

Combining Models for Better Accuracy: Future studies could explore hybrid models that combine the strengths of CNNs, GANs, and U-Nets to create more robust systems capable of handling a broader range of segmentation tasks with higher accuracy. For instance, integrating CNNs' feature extraction capabilities with GANs' synthetic data generation could enhance training datasets and improve model performance under varied conditions (Kazeminia et al., 2020).

Expanding to Less-Common Types of Medical Imaging: Research should also extend to less-common imaging modalities, such as positron emission tomography (PET) or single-photon emission computed tomography (SPECT). These modalities present unique challenges due to their lower resolution and higher noise levels, which deep learning models could potentially mitigate.

Addressing Data Biases and Model Explainability: Further research is needed to address data biases that affect model performance across diverse patient populations. Additionally, enhancing the explainability of deep learning models can increase their acceptability among healthcare providers, ensuring that these advanced tools aid rather than obscure clinical judgment (Holzinger et al., 2017).

CONCLUSION

Summary of Findings

The research conducted on deep learning techniques for medical image segmentation has yielded significant insights and promising results across various imaging modalities and segmentation tasks. Through the comparative analysis of Convolutional Neural Networks (CNNs), Generative Adversarial Networks (GANs), and U-Nets, it has been demonstrated that deep learning can substantially enhance the accuracy, precision, and efficiency of medical image analysis.

CNNs excelled in tasks involving clear, delineated structures such as organ delineation, showcasing high accuracy and precision, which are critical for applications like surgical planning and volumetric analysis. **GANs** proved especially valuable in scenarios with limited data, enhancing training datasets through synthetic image generation and thus improving model generalizability. **U-Nets**, with their unique architecture, were superior in complex segmentation tasks such as tumor identification and segmentation in noisy or low-contrast images, outperforming other models in terms of accuracy and detail sensitivity.

These results underscore deep learning's capacity to address some of the long-standing challenges in medical image segmentation, including the reduction of manual labor, minimization of human error, and acceleration of diagnostic processes.

Impact on Healthcare

The implementation of deep learning models like CNNs, GANs, and U-Nets in medical image segmentation has the potential to revolutionize diagnostic processes in several ways. Firstly, the enhanced accuracy and efficiency of these models can lead to earlier and more precise diagnoses, directly impacting patient treatment outcomes. Accurate segmentation plays a critical role in treatment planning, particularly in oncology, where precise tumor delineation can significantly influence the success of radiation therapy and surgical interventions.

Moreover, the ability of these models to process vast amounts of imaging data rapidly can help alleviate the workload on radiologists, potentially reducing burnout and allowing more time for patient care. This aspect is crucial in settings with high patient throughput, where quick and reliable diagnostic tools can streamline operations and lead to better healthcare delivery.

The standardization of image segmentation through automated techniques can also lead to more uniform healthcare practices, reducing disparities in diagnostic quality between different institutions and geographic locations. This standardization is especially beneficial for global health, where access to skilled radiologists and advanced diagnostic tools may be limited.

Call to Action

Despite the promising advancements demonstrated by deep learning in medical image segmentation, continuous research and development are essential to fully realize these technologies' potential. Healthcare institutions, researchers, and technology developers must collaborate to address the remaining challenges and facilitate the integration of these advanced models into routine clinical practice.

Further Research: Future research should focus on refining these models to handle more diverse and challenging datasets, including rare conditions and less common imaging modalities. Additionally, efforts should be directed towards improving the explainability of these models, enhancing trust and acceptance among medical professionals. Research into the development of low-resource models can also make these technologies accessible in underprivileged settings, broadening the impact of deep learning in global health.

Adoption and Integration: There is a need for strategic partnerships between academic institutions, technology companies, and healthcare providers to ensure that deep learning tools are developed and tested in clinically relevant scenarios. Regulatory bodies and medical institutions should work together to create frameworks for the ethical use of AI in medicine, ensuring patient safety and data privacy.

Training and Education: Educating current and future healthcare professionals about the capabilities and limitations of AI and machine learning is crucial. Increased awareness and understanding will promote the adoption of these technologies and ensure they are used effectively and ethically.

REFERENCES

Badrinarayanan, V., Kendall, A., & Cipolla, R. (2017). SegNet: A deep convolutional encoder-decoder architecture for image segmentation. *IEEE Transactions on Pattern Analysis and Machine Intelligence*, *39*(12), 2481–2495. DOI: 10.1109/TPAMI.2016.2644615 PMID: 28060704

Bankman, I. N. (Ed.). (2000). *Handbook of Medical Imaging: Processing and Analysis Management.* Academic Press.

Clark, K., Vendt, B., Smith, K., Freymann, J., Kirby, J., Koppel, P., Moore, S., Phillips, S., Maffitt, D., Pringle, M., Tarbox, L., & Prior, F. (2013). The Cancer Imaging Archive (TCIA): Maintaining and operating a public information repository. *Journal of Digital Imaging*, *26*(6), 1045–1057. DOI: 10.1007/s10278-013-9622-7 PMID: 23884657

Criminisi, A., Robertson, D., Konukoglu, E., Pathak, S., & White, S. (2013). Regression forests for efficient anatomy detection and localization in computed tomography scans. *Medical Image Analysis*, *17*(8), 1293–1303. DOI: 10.1016/j.media.2013.01.001 PMID: 23410511

Gibson, E., Li, W., Sudre, C., Fidon, L., Shakir, D. I., Wang, G., Eaton-Rosen, Z., Gray, R., Doel, T., Hu, Y., Whyntie, T., Nachev, P., Modat, M., Barratt, D. C., Ourselin, S., Cardoso, M. J., & Vercauteren, T. (2018). NiftyNet: A deep-learning platform for medical imaging. *Computer Methods and Programs in Biomedicine*, *158*, 113–122. DOI: 10.1016/j.cmpb.2018.01.025 PMID: 29544777

Goodfellow, I., Pouget-Abadie, J., Mirza, M., Xu, B., Warde-Farley, D., Ozair, S., Courville, A., & Bengio, Y. (2014). Generative adversarial nets. *Advances in Neural Information Processing Systems*, *27*, 2672–2680.

Goodfellow, I., Pouget-Abadie, J., Mirza, M., Xu, B., Warde-Farley, D., Ozair, S., Courville, A., & Bengio, Y. (2014). Generative adversarial nets. *Advances in Neural Information Processing Systems*, *27*, 2672–2680.

Greenspan, H., van Ginneken, B., & Summers, R. M. (2016). Guest editorial deep learning in medical imaging: Overview and future promise of an exciting new technique. *IEEE Transactions on Medical Imaging*, *35*(5), 1153–1159. DOI: 10.1109/TMI.2016.2553401

Holzinger, A., Biemann, C., Pattichis, C. S., & Kell, D. B. (2017). What do we need to build explainable AI systems for the medical domain? *arXiv preprint arXiv:1712.09923.*

Kass, M., Witkin, A., & Terzopoulos, D. (1988). Snakes: Active contour models. *International Journal of Computer Vision*, *1*(4), 321–331. DOI: 10.1007/BF00133570

Kazeminia, S., Baur, C., Kuijper, A., van Ginneken, B., Navab, N., Albarqouni, S., & Mukhopadhyay, A. (2020). GANs for medical image analysis. *Artificial Intelligence in Medicine*, *109*, 101938. DOI: 10.1016/j.artmed.2020.101938 PMID: 34756215

Litjens, G., Kooi, T., Bejnordi, B. E., Setio, A. A. A., Ciompi, F., Ghafoorian, M., van der Laak, J. A. W. M., van Ginneken, B., & Sánchez, C. I. (2017). A survey on deep learning in medical image analysis. *Medical Image Analysis*, *42*, 60–88. DOI: 10.1016/j.media.2017.07.005 PMID: 28778026

Marcus, D. S., Wang, T. H., Parker, J., Csernansky, J. G., Morris, J. C., & Buckner, R. L. (2007). Open access series of imaging studies (OASIS): Cross-sectional MRI data in young, middle aged, nondemented, and demented older adults. *Journal of Cognitive Neuroscience*, *19*(9), 1498–1507. DOI: 10.1162/jocn.2007.19.9.1498 PMID: 17714011

Menze, B. H., Jakab, A., Bauer, S., Kalpathy-Cramer, J., Farahani, K., Kirby, J., Burren, Y., Porz, N., Slotboom, J., Wiest, R., Lanczi, L., Gerstner, E., Weber, M. A., Arbel, T., Avants, B. B., Ayache, N., Buendia, P., Collins, D. L., Cordier, N., & Van Leemput, K. (2015). The Multimodal Brain Tumor Image Segmentation Benchmark (BRATS). *IEEE Transactions on Medical Imaging*, *34*(10), 1993–2024. DOI: 10.1109/TMI.2014.2377694 PMID: 25494501

Milletari, F., Navab, N., & Ahmadi, S.-A. (2016). V-Net: Fully convolutional neural networks for volumetric medical image segmentation. *2016 Fourth International Conference on 3D Vision (3DV)*, 565-571. DOI: 10.1109/3DV.2016.79

Noble, J. A., & Boukerroui, D. (2006). Ultrasound image segmentation: A survey. *IEEE Transactions on Medical Imaging*, *25*(8), 987–1010. DOI: 10.1109/TMI.2006.877092 PMID: 16894993

Pham, D. L., Xu, C., & Prince, J. L. (2000). Current methods in medical image segmentation. *Annual Review of Biomedical Engineering*, *2*(1), 315–337. DOI: 10.1146/annurev.bioeng.2.1.315 PMID: 11701515

Ronneberger, O., Fischer, P., & Brox, T. (2015). U-net: Convolutional networks for biomedical image segmentation. *International Conference on Medical image computing and computer-assisted intervention*, 234-241. DOI: 10.1007/978-3-319-24574-4_28

Tajbakhsh, N., Shin, J. Y., Gurudu, S. R., Hurst, R. T., Kendall, C. B., Gotway, M. B., & Liang, J. (2016). Convolutional neural networks for medical image analysis: Full training or fine tuning? *IEEE Transactions on Medical Imaging*, *35*(5), 1299–1312. DOI: 10.1109/TMI.2016.2535302 PMID: 26978662

Warfield, S. K., Zou, K. H., & Wells, W. M. (2004). Simultaneous truth and performance level estimation (STAPLE): An algorithm for the validation of image segmentation. *IEEE Transactions on Medical Imaging*, *23*(7), 903–921. DOI: 10.1109/TMI.2004.828354 PMID: 15250643

Chapter 5
Explainable AI in Healthcare Imaging for Medical Diagnosis

Vandana Babbar
Chitkara University Institute of Engineering and Technology, Chitkara University, Rajpura, India

Chetna Sharma
https://orcid.org/0000-0002-3298-5583
Chitkara University Institute of Engineering and Technology, Chitkara University, Rajpura, India

ABSTRACT

The most cutting-edge machine learning and deep learning techniques in the healthcare industry are presented by the Digital Revolution of AI, with an emphasis on explainable artificial intelligence (XAI). This chapter examines how XAI may advance the medical field to increase end users' confidence. It covers the most cutting-edge and new ideas and uses of XAI, making it a intellectual resource for scholars and practitioners interested in this developing field and provides a comprehensive explanation of AI in precision medicine, including all aspects. The importance of Explainable AI (XAI) in the healthcare industry is the main topic of discussion. Also offers real-world case studies and examples to offer useful insights into the use of AI in precision medicine.

1. INTRODUCTION

Medical imaging is the visual representation of the structure and function of numerous human tissues and organs for therapeutic purposes, as well as the comprehensive study of the body's normal and abnormal architecture and physiology. Medical imaging techniques are used to expose internal structures beneath the skin and bones, as well as detect and treat diseases (Zhou et al., 2023). Medical imaging is currently considered part of healthcare science. It is an important aspect of biological imaging and includes radiology, which employs imaging technologies such as "Positron Emission Tomography (PET), Magnetic Resonance Imaging (MRI), Magnetic Resonance Spectroscopy (MRS), Endoscopy, Digital Mammography, etc (Hendi, 2023).

Imaging are essential for both abnormality identification and treatment. The sophisticated visual representation method helps medical professionals understand their patients' conditions (Roy et al.; Nazir et al., 2024). The recording and measurement methods known as EEG, MEG, and ECG do not

DOI: 10.4018/979-8-3693-9045-0.ch005

create images; instead, they display the data as a parameter graph versus time or maps that provide the sensitive information with less precision. Thus, on a small scale, these technologies can be considered to create medical imaging (Salehi et al., 2023).

Medical imaging radiation exposure accounts for around half of all ionizing radiation exposure in the United States (Baudin et al., 2023). Medical imaging technologies are employed in the measurement, management, treatment, and prevention of diseases. In order to diagnosis practically all major medical anomalies and illnesses, including neurological disorders, cardiovascular diseases, trauma diseases, and many forms of cancer, imaging methods are now essential. Medical experts, including internists and oncologists, are highly skilled technicians who employ medical imaging methods (Qayyum et al., 2023).

The basic goal of medical imaging technology is to diagnose. Medical diagnosis refers to the process of diagnosing a patient's ailment and associated symptoms. The medical diagnosis, which is based on the patient's medical history and physical tests or surveys, describes the ailment or condition that requires treatment. Identification of a problem becomes challenging in medical research due to the disorder's multiple signs and symptoms' lack of specificity. For example, red skin is a sign of a variety of diseases. As a result, different diagnostic modeles are necessary to determine the causes of certain diseases and prevent or treat them (Ebrahimnejad et al., 2024).AI has the potential to completely transform health-care, but it hasn't yet solved the issues of patient and doctor responsibility and trust. Regarding AI in healthcare, there are still important moral and legal questions that need to be answered. These problems include the potential for biases, the opaqueness of some algorithms, privacy concerns about the data used to train AI models, and potential safety and liability issues when using AI in clinical settings. Numerous researches have brought up these issues (Rayhan et al., 2023).

These problems can be addressed with the use of an explainable AI model. The need for AI applications is rising as a result of notable advancements in intelligent decision-making. It should be noted that the efficiency of the aforementioned systems is limited because machines are now unable to explain their choices and interactions with people. Applying explainable AI and ML aids medical professionals in comprehending, properly trusting, and interacting with these technologies (Hakkoum et al., 2024).

The beginning point for an explanation, as seen in Fig. 1, depends on whether a particular AI model is naturally explicable (White-Box models) or not (Black-Box models). White-Box models may immediately produce explanations and are inherently explicable. Black-Box, on the other hand, need to be explained either locally (a model's single prediction) or globally (the model as a whole). The training of a future surrogate model is optional in both perspectives (Mittal et al., 2023). Surrogate models are explainable models that have been trained to anticipate the outcomes of an opaque Black-Box model.

Figure 1. The distinction between a deployment configuration for an AI system and XAI

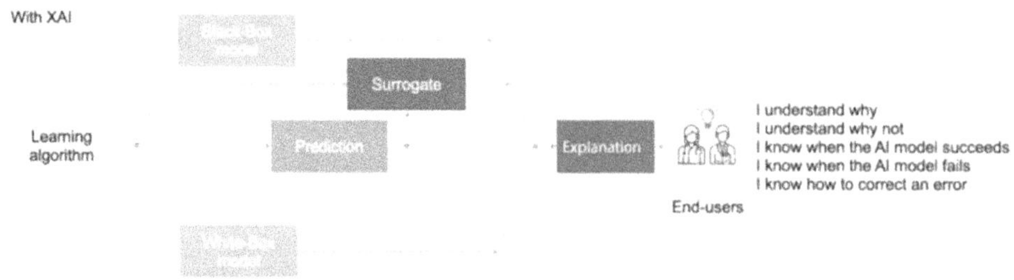

1.1. AI, ML, and DL

The phrases "artificial intelligence," "machine learning," and "deep learning" are now used interchangeably due to the widespread marketing and use of AI-based solutions. Despite their close kinship, significant distinctions need to be taken into account. AI is a vast area that includes machine learning (ML) and deep learning (DL), but it also encompasses many other fields and does not just focus on learning methods. In general, a set of formal rules may be used to mathematically formulate the issues that general-operating AI systems address. The ability of AI to solve tasks that are easy for humans to do but hard to formally define has shown itself to be its true potential.

Put another way, artificial intelligence (AI) is concerned with moving jobs that are typically completed by people to the computer realm, which is often accomplished by creating explicit rule sets. As a subset of AI, machine learning (ML) adapts human learning mechanisms rather than directly programming human skills. As the knowledge basis from which rules may be automatically created, a so-called machine learning model has to be trained with a sufficiently significant quantity of data in order to understand how to handle a particular issue (Mittal et al., 2023).

A parameterizable entity acquired throughout the training process to acquire the capacity to carry out a predetermined job, such as pattern recognition, regression, or classification, is referred to in this context as a model. Traditional machine learning's shortcomings, despite successful applications, are ascribed to the fact that feature extraction from data need human intervention. Furthermore, ML models may not be able to fully perform difficult tasks due to their limitations. DL, a branch of machine learning that includes representational learning techniques, is responsible for these constraints (Ramudu et al., 2023). ANNs are one of the titles given to DL models since existing DL methods are modelled by computer models of biological learning (Abut et al., 2023).

Even while ANNs have been used in part to study how the brain works, it is important to note that they are not the same as accurate models of biological brain activity. A broad learning strategy consisting of many composition levels reflecting automatically retrieved characteristics is proposed by the new concept of DL, which goes beyond the neuroscientific viewpoint (Fazi et al., 2021). In light of this, DL may be described as a mathematical framework for automatically generating representations from given data that is built on deep ANNs • (Nath et al., 2024).

By automating the feature extraction process, DL proven to be an effective method for resolving difficult and extremely complicated situations. Condensed representations are made possible by automatically extracted feature compositions, which show a hierarchy of data structures with certain features—such as forms, edges, and textures in the context of picture data. It is necessary to comprehend another currently pertinent DL network design in order to comprehend how AI is used to the interpretation of visual imagery: CNNs, or convolutional neural networks • (Archana & Jeevaraj, 2024).

These ANNs are made specifically for picture data. Generally speaking, this architecture has the advantage of significantly lowering the number of parameters in the network, which is modelled after biological perception systems. Convolutional layers of a CNN generate so-called feature maps, which indicate the recognition of certain features in input pictures, such as colours, forms, or structures, by applying learnable filters to input images one after the other (Erkınay Özdemir & Karakuş, 2024).

Each feature map that is produced is converted into a more concise representation by subsequent pooling layers. As exemplified in Fig 2 for a binary classification task, these filters during inference represent the weights and connections within the CNN that can parametrize complex mapping functions from input images to specific outputs, also known as predictions (where "1" indicates the presence of a disease in the input image and "0" indicates its absence). The computation of intermediate variables from input to output is referred to as the forward pass (or forward propagation). Backpropagation, on the other hand, traverses the order from the output to the input, producing intermediate variables needed to compute the gradient with respect to certain parameters. Backpropagation can be utilized for inference as well as for weight modification during training.

Backpropagation may be used, for instance, to determine which picture attributes (stored in the learnt feature maps) influenced the model's choice if the network from Figure 2 predicted class "1" (monkeypox). Convolution layers create feature maps by applying filters (red rectangles with dotted lines), while pooling layers lower the dimensionality of the feature maps. This is the architectural configuration of a CNN that solves a binary classification job for identifying monkeypox. In order to capture pertinent visual characteristics, the filters are repeatedly shifted over the whole image. Often referred to as CNN weights, the precise filter values are discovered during model training.

Figure 2. Architecture of CN

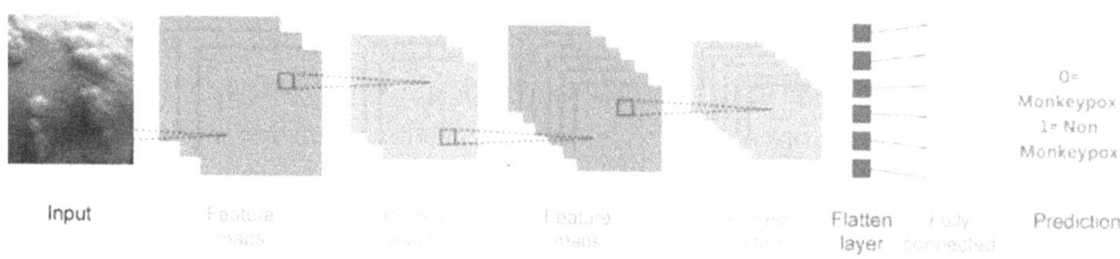

1.1.1 Implementation of CNN with XAI

Here are Contextual importance and utility (CIU) in terms of explainability, local interpretable model-agnostic explanations (LIME), and Shapley Additive exPlanations (SHAP) were used to Vivo Gastral Images as a few instances of XAI with CNN (Aldrees et al., 2024). Other research introduced the DBSCAN model to Electronic Medical Records (EMR) using anchors, SHAP, and LIME as XAI techniques (De Bock et al., 2024). In order to detect Covid-19, numerous studies have employed XAI techniques, including Xception CNN and VGG16 with SHAP(XAI) (Rajpoot et al., 2024), VGG16, InceptionResNetV2, ResNet50, DenseNet201, VGG19, MobilenetV2, NasNetMobile, and ResNet15V2 with LIME (Mahmood ur Rehman et al., 2024), MLP with decision trees and LIME (Gaspar et al., 2024), SqueezeNet, Inception, ResNet, ResNeXt, Xception, ShuffleNet, and DenseNet with Grad-CAM(XAI) and t-SNE(XAI) (Maji et al., 2024b). DB-Scan, I-Forest, Autoencoder with SHAP, and K-Means Clustering have also been used to detect chronic tumour disease (Maji et al., 2024a).

For instance, techniques for fungal infection employed SHAP and LIME in conjunction with iAFPs-EnC-GA (GA) (Fuzzy K-nearest neighbour (FKNN), Random Forest (RF), k-nearest neighbour (KNN), and Support Vector Machine (SVM) (Ashraf et al., 2024). Mediastinal cysts and tumours have also been found using SHAP and the Ensemble of EXtreme Gradient Boosting (XGBoost) (Maji et al., 2024b). More recently, the Blood Stream Infections with SHAP(XAI) in Ref. (Messai et al., 2024) were detected using XGBoost, RF, SVM, and MLP.

The problem of AI and ML systems' black box character has remained despite the potential advantages of these technologies in healthcare. It is crucial that decision-making systems explain how each element influences the ultimate choice. This problem may be solved with interpretable AI and ML modeles (Okolo et al., 2024). Doctors, patients, and other stakeholders can all easily grasp a perceivable explanation that XAI can offer.

This paper's primary goal is to classify and examine relevant work regarding the interpretability of AI and ML techniques. By classifying the many explainable AI techniques in the healthcare industry, providing thorough viewpoints on the precision and applicability of XAI models in this domain, and investigating the major technologies that have the potential to transform XAI methodologies, the study that is being presented provides important contributions. Here, we go over how emerging technologies, specifically AI and ML, have the power to revolutionize healthcare.

2. EXPLAINABLE AI (XAI)

In the study field of XAI, the words "explainability" and "interpretability" are frequently used interchangeably without any clear taxonomy or definition, much as AI, ML, and DL (Chaudhury et al., 2024). In terms of a distinct taxonomic demarcation, interpretability in any other meaning is not mathematically nor definitively defined (Chaudhury et al., 2024). "The term explainability holds no agreed-upon meaning, and yet machine learning conferences frequently publish papers which wield the term in a quasi-mathematical way," according to Lipton, highlighting the term's ambiguity (Teledahl et al., 2024). In the purpose of this study, however, Miller's non-mathematical definition—who examined the subject from a social science standpoint—will be employed: "The extent to which an individual can comprehend the rationale behind a decision is known as interpretability." In general, interpretability focuses mostly on the intuition that underlies a model's outputs in order to determine cause-and-effect correlations. Explainability, on the other hand, is linked to the underlying logic and processes of a system (Rizzo et al., 2024).

2.1 Shapley Additive Explanations (SHAP)

Lundberg and Lee (2017) developed SHAP (SHapley Additive exPlanations) as a technique to explain individual predictions. The optimum Shapley values in game theory serve as the foundation for SHAP. By calculating the contribution of each characteristic to the prediction, SHAP aims to explain the prediction of instance x. Coalitional game theory is used to calculate Shapley values in the SHAP explanation model. A data instance's feature values function as coalition members. Shapley values provide guidance on how to divide the "payout" (i.e., the prediction) among the characteristics in a fair manner.

For tabular data, for example, a player might be a single feature value. A collection of feature values can also constitute a player. Pixels can be combined into superpixels and the prediction can be shared among them, for instance, to describe a picture. The Shapley value explanation is portrayed as an additive feature attribution model, a linear model, which is one novelty that SHAP offers (Zafar & Khan, 2021). LIME and Shapley values are connected in that view. According to SHAP, the explanation is:

$$g(z')=\phi 0+M\sum j \quad (1)$$

z′∈{0,1}Mz′∈{0,1} shown in eq1, where g is the explanatory modelThe Shapley values are represented by the coalition vector M, the maximum coalition size M, and the feature attribution for a feature j, ϕj∈Rϕj∈R. The SHAP study refers to what I refer to as a "coalition vector" as "simplified features." I believe this name was coined because, for example, picture data aggregates to superpixels rather than representing the images at the pixel level. I think it's useful to consider the z's as a way to describe coalitions: A value of 1 in the coalition vector indicates that the relevant feature value is "present," whereas a value of 0 indicates that it is "absent." If you are acquainted with Shapley values, this should sound familiar.

g(x′)=ϕ0+M∑j=1ϕjg(x′)=ϕ0+∑j=1Mϕj (2)

2.1.1 Advantages of SHAP

1. Game theory provides a strong theoretical basis for SHAP. The feature values are evenly distributed in the forecast. By contrasting the forecast with the average prediction, we obtain contrastive explanations.
2. 2. LIME and Shapley values are connected by SHAP. This is a great way to learn more about both models. Additionally, it contributes to the unification of interpretable machine learning.
3. The implementation of SHAP for tree-based models is quick. Since the slow calculation is the main obstacle to the acceptance of Shapley values, this was a major factor in SHAP's popularity.
4. The many Shapley values required for the global model interpretations may be calculated thanks to the quick computation.

2.2 Local Interpretable Model-agnostic explanations (LIME)

Black box machine learning algorithms' individual predictions are explained by interpretable models known as local surrogate models. The authors of the paper Local Interpretable Model-Agnostic explanations (LIME) (Wikle et al., 2023) suggest a tangible use of local surrogate models. The underlying black box model's predictions are approximated by surrogate models that are trained. LIME focuses on training local surrogate models to explain individual predictions rather than a global surrogate model.

The concept is really obvious. First, disregard the training data and consider that you have a black box model that you can use to enter data points and obtain the model's predictions. As many times as you like, you can probe the box. Understanding the reasoning behind the machine learning model's prediction is your aim. LIME examines how the predictions change as you feed the machine learning model different data. A fresh dataset with altered samples and the matching black box model predictions is produced using LIME. The interpretable model that LIME trains on the new dataset is weighted by how close the sampled examples are to the instance of interest. Anything from interpretable models can be the interpretable model.

The learned model should be a good approximation of the machine learning model predictions locally, but it does not have to be a good global approximation. This kind of accuracy is also called local fidelity.

Mathematically, local surrogate models with interpretability constraint can be expressed as follows eq. 3 and 4 (Wikle et al., 2023):

Explanation (x) =argming∈GL (f,g,πx)+Ω(g) 3)

$$\min_{g \in G} L(f, g, \pi_x) + \Omega(g) \quad (4)$$

The explanation model for instance x is the model g (e.g. linear regression) that minimizes loss L (e.g. mean squared error), which evaluates how close the explanation is to the prediction of the original model f (e.g. an xg boost model), and the model complexity Ω(g). Ω(g) is maintained low, indicating a preference for fewer characteristics. G represents the family of plausible explanations, such as all linear regression models. The proximity measure πx πx determines the size of the neighborhood around instance x that will be used for explanation. In practice, LIME just optimizes the loss function. The user must set the complexity, for as by selecting the maximum amount of features that the linear regression model may employ.

For example, linear regression may be used as an interpretable surrogate model in current R and Python implementations. You must pick K, the number of attributes you want to include in your interpretable model, first. When K is smaller, the model becomes more understandable. Models with a higher K may have more fidelity. Models with precisely K properties can be taught in a number of methods. Lasso is a great choice. A Lasso model with a high regularization parameter (λ) creates a featureless model. The decision tree models are retrained with decreasing λ, resulting in deviating weight estimations for the features. If the model has K features, you've met your goal feature count.

Additional strategies include feature selection from the front or back. This implies that you either start with the complete model (meaning it has all features) or with a model that just contains the intercept and then assess which feature would result in the greatest improvement when added or eliminated, until you reach a model with K features.

2.2.1 Advantages of LIME

It is possible to utilize the same local, interpretable model for explanation even if the underlying machine learning model is changed. Assume that the individuals seeing the explanations have the best understanding of decision trees. Decision trees are used as explanations because local surrogate models are used, rather than a decision tree being used to create the predictions. For instance, an SVM can be used. Also, you may use a decision tree to explain the predictions and swap out the SVM if an xgboost model proves to be more effective.

The body of research and expertise in training and analyzing interpretable models is advantageous for local surrogate models.

1. Short (= selected) and potentially contrastive explanations are produced when Lasso or short trees are used. They thus provide explanations that are understandable to humans. For this reason, I find that LIME is more useful in situations when the individual receiving the explanation is a layperson or has limited time. I do not envision LIME in compliance circumstances where you could be legally obligated to fully explain a prediction because it is insufficient for comprehensive attributions.
2. One of the few techniques that may be used with text, graphics, and tabular data is LIME.
3. The interpretable model's ability to explain the black box predictions in the vicinity of the data instance of interest is gauged by the fidelity measure.
4. LIME is highly user-friendly and is implemented in R (lime package and iml package) and Python (lime library).

5. Different (interpretable) characteristics than those used to train the original model can be included in the explanations produced using local surrogate models. Naturally, the data instances must be the source of these interpretable properties. Although the explanation may be based on whether words are included in a phrase or not, a text classifier may rely on abstract word embeddings as features. Some features in a regression model may undergo an uninterpretable transformation, yet the original attributes may still be used to provide explanations.

2.3 Gradient-Weighted Class Activation Mapping (Grad-CAM)

In a number of activities, deep neural networks have made remarkable advancements possible. They are challenging to understand, nevertheless, due to their lack of explanatory capacity. Additionally, they leave users wondering why they failed! Therefore, it is essential to create explainable models in order to gain consumers' confidence and trust. Additionally, researchers may focus their efforts on the primary cause of the issue because to the explanatory power. Any convolutional neural network model may be made more visible by using the class-discriminative localization method known as Gradient-weighted Class Activation Mapping (Grad-CAM), which generates visual explanations (Selvaraju et al., 2017).

Grad-CAM generates a localization map and determines the significance of each pixel in the input picture for a particular class by using the gradient information that flows into the final convolutional layer of the model. Assume that it depicts the class-specific localization map with width and height. Neuron significance weight, α_k^c, is obtained by calculating L(grad-CAM)^C, the gradient of the class score (before softmax), with respect to the feature map of the final convolutional layer, and then pooling the global average.

$$\alpha_k^c = \frac{1}{N}\sum_i\sum_j \frac{\partial y^c}{\partial A_{ij}^k} \tag{5}$$

Additionally, a weighted mixture of ReLU and forward activation maps is produced: The coarse heat-map that is produced is the same size as the convolutional feature maps. Features that positively impact the class of interest, such as pixels whose intensity has to be raised to increase, can be captured by using ReLU. It's conceivable that negative pixels fall into another category inside the picture. Localization maps might occasionally highlight more than just the target class and perform worse when ReLU is not used.

2.3.1 Use Cases:

1. **Medical Imaging**: Identifying which regions of an X-ray or MRI contributed most to a diagnosis.
2. **Autonomous Driving**: Understanding where the model is looking on the road to make driving decisions.
3. **Natural Language Processing**: Visualizing which words or phrases in an input text are most influential in a classification decision.

2.3.2 Advantages of Grad-CAM:

1. **Localization**: It accurately localizes the relevant parts of the image that influenced the model's decision.

2. **Model-Agnostic**: Grad-CAM can be applied in CNN architectures without the need for retraining.
3. **Interpretability**: It helps in interpreting and explaining CNN predictions, which is crucial in applications where understanding the basis of a decision is important (e.g., medical diagnostics, autonomous driving).

REFERENCES

Abut, S., Okut, H., & Kallail, K. J. (2023). Paradigm shift from Artificial Neural Networks (ANNs) to deep Convolution Neural Networks (DCNNs) in the field of medical image processing. *Expert Systems with Applications*, •••, 122983.

Aldrees, A., Khan, M., Taha, A. T. B., & Ali, M. (2024). Evaluation of water quality indexes with novel machine learning and SHapley Additive ExPlanation (SHAP) approaches. *Journal of Water Process Engineering*, *58*, 104789. DOI: 10.1016/j.jwpe.2024.104789

Archana, R., & Jeevaraj, P. E. (2024). Deep learning models for digital image processing: A review. *Artificial Intelligence Review*, *57*(1), 11. DOI: 10.1007/s10462-023-10631-z

Ashraf, K., Nawar, S., Hosen, M. H., Islam, M. T., & Uddin, M. N. (2024, March). Beyond the Black Box: Employing LIME and SHAP for Transparent Health Predictions with Machine Learning Models. In 2024 International Conference on Advances in Computing, Communication, Electrical, and Smart Systems (iCACCESS) (pp. 1-6). IEEE.

Baudin, C., Vacquier, B., Thin, G., Chenene, L., Guersen, J., Partarrieu, I., Louet, M., Ducou Le Pointe, H., Mora, S., Verdun-Esquer, C., Feuardent, J., Rousseau, F., Roy, H., Bensefa-Colas, L., Boyer, L., & Bernier, M. O. (2023). Occupational exposure to ionizing radiation in medical staff: Trends during the 2009–2019 period in a multicentric study. *European Radiology*, *33*(8), 5675–5684. DOI: 10.1007/s00330-023-09541-z PMID: 36930262

Chaudhury, K., Ashok, A. H., Narumanchi, S., & Shankar, D. (2024). *Math and Architectures of Deep Learning*. Simon and Schuster.

De Bock, K. W., Coussement, K., De Caigny, A., Słowiński, R., Baesens, B., Boute, R. N., & Weber, R. (2024). Explainable AI for operational research: A defining framework, methods, applications, and a research agenda. *European Journal of Operational Research*, *317*(2), 249–272. DOI: 10.1016/j.ejor.2023.09.026

Ebrahimnejad, N., Jaafar, D., & Goodarzi, H. (2024). The Past, Present, Future: Pathophysiology, Diagnosis, and Treatment of Human Skin Diseases. *Physiologia*, *4*(1), 81–99. DOI: 10.3390/physiologia4010005

Erkınay Özdemir, M., & Karakuş, F. (2024). Deep Learning-Based Decision Support System for Automatic Detection and Grading of Surface Corrosion on Galvanized Steel Sheets. *Electronics (Basel)*, *13*(20), 3998. DOI: 10.3390/electronics13203998

Fazi, M. B. (2021). Beyond human: Deep learning, explainability and representation. *Theory, Culture & Society*, *38*(7-8), 55–77. DOI: 10.1177/0263276420966386

Gaspar, D., Silva, P., & Silva, C. (2024). Explainable AI for Intrusion Detection Systems: LIME and SHAP Applicability on Multi-Layer Perceptron. *IEEE Access : Practical Innovations, Open Solutions*, *12*, 30164–30175. DOI: 10.1109/ACCESS.2024.3368377

Hakkoum, H., Idri, A., & Abnane, I. (2024). Global and local interpretability techniques of supervised machine learning black box models for numerical medical data. *Engineering Applications of Artificial Intelligence*, *131*, 107829. DOI: 10.1016/j.engappai.2023.107829

Hendi, A. A. (2023). Development of Medical Imaging Techniques: A Review of Technological Advances in the Field of Medical Imaging, Such as Magnetic Resonance Imaging (MRI), Computed Tomography (CT), and Ultrasound Imaging (Ultrasound). *Journal of Positive Psychology and Wellbeing*, *7*(3), 569–578.

Lee, C. H., Ahn, D., Kim, H., Ha, E. J., Kim, J. B., & Kim, D. J. (2025). NeuroXAI: Adaptive, robust, explainable surrogate framework for determination of channel importance in EEG application. *Expert Systems with Applications*, *261*, 125364. DOI: 10.1016/j.eswa.2024.125364

Mahmood ur Rehman, M., Liu, J., Nijabat, A., Faheem, M., Wang, W., & Zhao, S. (2024). Leveraging Convolution Neural Networks for Disease Detection in Vegetables: A Comprehensive Review. Agronomy, 14(10), 2231.

Maji, P., Mondal, A. K., Mondal, H. K., & Mohanty, S. P. (2024). Easydiagnos: a framework for accurate feature selection for automatic diagnosis in smart healthcare. arXiv preprint arXiv:2410.00366.

Maji, P., Mondal, A. K., Mondal, H. K., & Mohanty, S. P. (2024). Easydiagnos: a framework for accurate feature selection for automatic diagnosis in smart healthcare. arXiv preprint arXiv:2410.00366.

Messai, A., Drif, A., Ouyahia, A., Guechi, M., Rais, M., Kaderali, L., & Cherifi, H. (2024). Towards XAI agnostic explainability to assess differential diagnosis for Meningitis diseases. *Machine Learning: Science and Technology*, *5*(2), 025052. DOI: 10.1088/2632-2153/ad4a1f

Mittal, S., Sharma, I., & Kumar, A. (2023, December). A Report: Machine Learning and Its Applications. In 2023 Intelligent Computing and Control for Engineering and Business Systems (ICCEBS) (pp. 1-6). IEEE.

Nath, D., Ankit, , Neog, D. R., & Gautam, S. S. (2024). Application of machine learning and deep learning in finite element analysis: A comprehensive review. *Archives of Computational Methods in Engineering*, *31*(5), 1–40. DOI: 10.1007/s11831-024-10063-0

Nazir, A., Hussain, A., Singh, M., & Assad, A. (2024). Deep learning in medicine: Advancing healthcare with intelligent solutions and the future of holography imaging in early diagnosis. *Multimedia Tools and Applications*, •••, 1–64. DOI: 10.1007/s11042-024-19694-8

Okolo, C. T., Agarwal, D., Dell, N., & Vashistha, A. (2024). " If it is easy to understand then it will have value": Examining Perceptions of Explainable AI with Community Health Workers in Rural India. Proceedings of the ACM on Human-Computer Interaction, 8(CSCW1), 1-28.

Qayyum, M. U., Sherani, A. M. K., Khan, M., & Hussain, H. K. (2023). Revolutionizing Healthcare: The Transformative Impact of Artificial Intelligence in Medicine. *BIN: Bulletin Of Informatics*, *1*(2), 71–83.

Raha, A. D., Gain, M., Debnath, R., Adhikary, A., Qiao, Y., Hassan, M. M., & Islam, S. M. S. (2024). Attention to Monkeypox: An Interpretable Monkeypox Detection Technique Using Attention Mechanism. *IEEE Access : Practical Innovations, Open Solutions.*

Rajpoot, R., Gour, M., Jain, S., & Semwal, V. B. (2024). Integrated ensemble CNN and explainable AI for COVID-19 diagnosis from CT scan and X-ray images. *Scientific Reports*, *14*(1), 24985. DOI: 10.1038/s41598-024-75915-y PMID: 39443548

Ramudu, K., Mohan, V. M., Jyothirmai, D., Prasad, D. V. S. S. S. V., Agrawal, R., & Boopathi, S. (2023). Machine learning and artificial intelligence in disease prediction: Applications, challenges, limitations, case studies, and future directions. In *Contemporary Applications of Data Fusion for Advanced Healthcare Informatics* (pp. 297–318). IGI Global. DOI: 10.4018/978-1-6684-8913-0.ch013

Rayhan, A., Rayhan, R., & Rayhan, S. (2023). The Role Of AI In Healthcare: Revolutionizing Patient Care And Well-Being. DOI: . 2.2, 22601.DOI: 10.13140/RG

Rizzo, L., Verda, D., Berretta, S., & Longo, L. (2024). A Novel Integration of Data-Driven Rule Generation and Computational Argumentation for Enhanced Explainable AI. *Machine Learning and Knowledge Extraction*, *6*(3), 2049–2073. DOI: 10.3390/make6030101

Roy, A., Roy, P. K., Mitra, A., Maji, P. K., Choudhury, S. R., & Peng, S. L. Enhancing Patient Care with Modality-Based Image Registration in Modern Healthcare. In Smart Medical Imaging for Diagnosis and Treatment Planning (pp. 95-136). Chapman and Hall/CRC. DOI: 10.1201/9781003464884-8

Salehi, A. W., Khan, S., Gupta, G., Alabduallah, B. I., Almjally, A., Alsolai, H., Siddiqui, T., & Mellit, A. (2023). A study of CNN and transfer learning in medical imaging: Advantages, challenges, future scope. *Sustainability (Basel)*, *15*(7), 5930. DOI: 10.3390/su15075930

Selvaraju, R. R., Cogswell, M., Das, A., Vedantam, R., Parikh, D., & Batra, D. (2017). Grad-cam: Visual explanations from deep networks via gradient-based localization. In *Proceedings of the IEEE international conference on computer vision* (pp. 618-626). DOI: 10.1109/ICCV.2017.74

Tarnowska, K. A., Dispoto, B. C., & Conragan, J. (2021). Explainable AI-based clinical decision support system for hearing disorders. *AMIA Joint Summits on Translational Science Proceedings AMIA Summit on Translational Science*, *2021*, 595. PMID: 34457175

Teledahl, A., Kilhamn, C., Ahl, L. M., & Helenius, O. (2024). Defining and measuring quality in students' mathematical writing: A systematic literature review. *Mathematics Education Research Journal*, •••, 1–20. DOI: 10.1007/s13394-024-00501-4

Tenne, A. (2024). XAI in Medicine: Analysis and Evaluation of XAI Tools and Legal Liability for Neural Networks; A Case Study on Tumor Image Classification.

Vo, T. H., Nguyen, N. T. K., Kha, Q. H., & Le, N. Q. K. (2022). On the road to explainable AI in drug-drug interactions prediction: A systematic review. *Computational and Structural Biotechnology Journal*, *20*, 2112–2123. DOI: 10.1016/j.csbj.2022.04.021 PMID: 35832629

Wikle, C. K., Datta, A., Hari, B. V., Boone, E. L., Sahoo, I., Kavila, I., Castruccio, S., Simmons, S. J., Burr, W. S., & Chang, W. (2023). An illustration of model agnostic explainability methods applied to environmental data. *Environmetrics*, *34*(1), e2772. DOI: 10.1002/env.2772 PMID: 37200542

Yang, C., Guan, X., Xu, Q., Xing, W., Chen, X., Chen, J., & Jia, P. (2024). How can SHAP (SHapley Additive exPlanations) interpretations improve deep learning based urban cellular automata model? *Computers, Environment and Urban Systems*, *111*, 102133. DOI: 10.1016/j.compenvurbsys.2024.102133

Zafar, M. R., & Khan, N. (2021). Deterministic local interpretable model-agnostic explanations for stable explainability. *Machine Learning and Knowledge Extraction*, *3*(3), 525–541. DOI: 10.3390/make3030027

Zhou, S. K., Greenspan, H., & Shen, D. (Eds.). (2023). *Deep learning for medical image analysis*. Academic Press.

Chapter 6
From Pixels to Precision:
Harnessing DenseNet-121 for Accurate Sugarcane Leaf Disease Detection

S. Naveena
https://orcid.org/0009-0006-3919-6487
Department of Electronics Engineering (VLSI Design and Technology), Velammal College of Engineering and Technology (Autonomous), Madurai, India

K. Kavitha
https://orcid.org/0000-0002-9159-9690
Department of Electronics Engineering (VLSI Design and Technology), Velammal College of Engineering and Technology (Autonomous), Madurai, India

ABSTRACT

Sugarcane, vital to industries such as food, biofuels, and pharmaceuticals, is threatened by diseases like red rot, rust, yellowing, and mosaic, which require significant resources for detection and monitoring. This book chapter presents an innovative solution using DenseNet-121, a convolutional neural network to identification and classification of these leaf diseases. The study utilized a plant village dataset of 9,050 leaf images, including healthy and diseased samples, which were carefully organized and pre-processed to ensure uniformity. The enhanced DenseNet-121 model, trained on this dataset, demonstrated outstanding performance, with a precision of 0.96, recall of 0.977, F1-score of 0.98, and accuracy of 0.963. While effective, challenges like resource needs may limit implementation in constrained environments, yet it marks progress toward agricultural sustainability and food security.

1. INTRODUCTION

Sugarcane (Saccharum officinarum) is a key ingredient in sugar production and is also used to produce biofuels, alcoholic beverages, and various food products. Over the past decade, the global GDP contribution of the sugarcane industry has fluctuated between 1.5% and 3%, influenced by agricultural advancements and market demand (Silalertruksa & Gheewala, 2020). Major producers like Brazil, India, and China dominate the global market, accounting for more than 60% of total production. However, diseases such as red rot, rust, yellow leaf syndrome, and mosaic pose significant threats to the crop

DOI: 10.4018/979-8-3693-9045-0.ch006

(Raza et al., 2022). These issues are often caused by unfavorable environmental conditions, pathogens, and improper management practices (Wan Mansor & Mohd Zaini, 2024). For instance, the fungus Colletotrichum falcatum causes red rot, while Puccinia melanocephala is responsible for rust (Chinnadurai, 2017). Maintaining sugarcane yields and enhancing its economic importance require effective disease control and the development of disease-resistant cultivars (Bordonal et al., 2018). Traditional techniques for identifying leaf diseases in sugarcane, such as expert evaluations by sight, microscopic analysis, field-based tests, and reliance on farmer experience, tend to be time-consuming, inconsistent, labor-intensive, and occasionally erroneous (Trenberth, 2012). These constraints can result in delayed disease detection, leading to significant yield losses that impact the Indian economy (Demilie, 2024). Sugarcane accounts for roughly 6-7% of the nation's agricultural GDP, and outbreaks of diseases can cause annual economic losses of 1-2% of agricultural GDP, amounting to around $11 billion, given the country's GDP of $3.73 trillion. Consequently, the adverse effects on sugar production, associated industries, and farm labor exacerbate fiscal challenges, highlighting the need for improved disease detection methods (Gupta & Jadon, 2024).

To address these challenges, researchers and agricultural practitioners are increasingly utilizing extensive image feature evaluation methods, particularly those based on machine learning (ML) and deep learning (DL) (Chen et al., 2020). Machine learning offers an intriguing opportunity to enhance the efficiency and precision of disease identification in sugarcane through automated leaf image analysis. Certain machine learning techniques, namely Support Vector Machines (SVM), K-Nearest Neighbouring (KNN), Decision Trees, and Random Forests, have been employed to efficiently categorize and identify sugarcane leaf diseases (Hassan et al., 2021). Despite their immense potential, these strategies frequently face substantial hurdles, such as excessive processing costs, susceptibility to overfitting, and difficulties in interpreting large datasets.

To further improve disease identification, deep learning methods have emerged as viable alternatives. Deep learning algorithms, such as Convolutional Neural Networks (CNNs), Recurrent Neural Networks (RNNs), and Generative Adversarial Networks (GANs), address some of the shortcomings of traditional approaches (Raza et al., 2022). CNNs excel at identifying spatial hierarchies; however, they require large amounts of data. RNNs are effective at processing sequential data, but they may encounter gradient issues (Gupta & Jadon, 2024). GANs employ an advanced framework to generate data, but their training can be unstable. DenseNet-121 is a deep learning architecture distinguished by its dense connectivity pattern, where each layer receives input from all preceding layers (Chen et al., 2020). This allows for efficient feature reuse and improved gradient flow, making it particularly effective for tasks such as image recognition and disease identification. MobileNetV2 is optimized for mobile and edge devices, with a focus on both speed and efficiency. It employs depth-wise separable convolution algorithms. EfficientNetB0 enhances both accuracy and efficiency by carefully scaling. Despite their benefits, these strategies have certain drawbacks. For instance, GANs may have trouble keeping in line with one another, and CNNs and RNNs may require a lot of computing power. Transfer learning models may not always perform effectively when dealing with unfamiliar data if the source and destination domains are sufficiently different (Demilie, 2024). DenseNet-121 outperformed CNNs, RNNs, GANs, and transfer learning techniques for applications including exact picture categorization and recognizing diseases (Hassan et al., 2021).

This chapter is going to emphasize an enhanced DenseNet-121, a deep learning architecture notable for its distinctive dense connectivity that enables efficient feature propagation. The enhanced DenseNet-121 model significantly decreases the number of parameters desired, but it additionally boosts model accuracy, making it particularly useful for detecting diseases in sugarcane agriculture.

The primary objectives of the proposed chapter are articulated as follows:

- To deploy a meticulously curated Plant Village dataset containing 9,050 leaf images, comprising both healthy and diseased samples, as an imperative resource for precisely recognizing and categorizing sugarcane leaf diseases.
- To develop a computerized system that incorporates the enhanced DenseNet-121 model to recognize and classify sugarcane leaf diseases such as red rot, rust, yellowing, and mosaic.
- To measure the effectiveness of the enhanced DenseNet-121 framework in terms of performance metrics while ensuring optimal input data quality for enhanced disease detection.

This chapter seeks to illustrate the vital role that the enhanced DenseNet-121 plays in enhancing disease identification and control, hence promoting the long-term viability and financial success of the sugarcane sector. It also includes scrutinizing current methodologies, explaining the methodological approach, presenting outcomes, and providing alternatives for prospective study paths.

2. LITERATURE REVIEW

This literature review covers different deep learning and CNN-based algorithms, such as DenseNet121, VGG, and MobileNet, for recognizing and categorizing diseases that occur in crops like sugarcane, maize, rice, and tomato. These algorithms display exemplary reliability and provide useful insights for enhancing crop disease identification using AI-driven methodologies.

2.1 Sugarcane Disease Detection using Deep Learning

Sharma and Punhani (2024) created a CNN-based model for precision sugarcane disease identification, which achieved over 90% accuracy on a huge dataset of sugarcane photos. Their analysis emphasizes the possibilities for real-time field applications and the necessity to improve model robustness in a variety of environmental circumstances. Ogrekçi et al. (2023) evaluated Vision Transformers (ViT) with CNNs for detecting sugarcane leaf disease, and ViT outperformed CNNs at 92% accuracy. The article proposes a hybrid model technique that combines ViT and CNN to enhance the model's robustness for complicated picture processing in agricultural applications.

2.2 Related Plant Disease Classification Studies

Naga Subramanian et al. (2019) developed a 3D deep learning model for identifying plant diseases that achieved 95% accuracy. This study advises improving model explainability and expanding applications to various crops, indicating substantial improvement in spectral-based disease diagnosis. Chen et al. (2020) used deep transfer learning with a ResNet-based CNN to accurately classify plant diseases across multiple crops, obtaining 93%. The results highlight the model's ability to handle field deployment and suggest ways to enhance adaptability and incorporate a wide range of crop diseases. Sethy et al. (2020) used a CNN for feature extraction and an SVM classifier to detect rice leaf diseases, obtaining 89% accuracy. They recommend combining additional machine learning technologies to improve performance and adaptability across different rice varieties. Lee et al. (2020) created a CNN model with many layers for detecting multi-species plant diseases, accomplishing an accuracy of 91%. Their study recommends testing the model's robustness in real-world settings and investigating its adaptation across different crop varieties to improve agricultural support. Huang et al. (2020) developed a CNN-based deep localization model for detecting intra-row crops in paddy fields, which achieved 87% identification efficiency. They suggest further enhancements to fit differed crop patterns and more complicated paddy field conditions, indicating a step forward in crop localization technology. Hasan et al. (2020) examined deep learning techniques and datasets for plant disease detection, emphasizing CNNs and GANs, which frequently achieve accuracies between 80 and 95 percent. They underline the requirement for more explainable models and dataset diversity to address biases, hence promoting additional innovation in plant disease identification. Li et al. (2020) created a CNN-based model for real-time video identification of rice leaf diseases and pests, which achieved 92% accuracy. The study advises improving mobility and model adaptability to environmental fluctuations, which will contribute to more practical pest and disease surveillance in agricultural environments. Nazki et al. (2020) used an adversarial network (GAN) for unsupervised image translation, improving rare plant disease recognition with 90% accuracy. They suggest improving GAN methods and broadening datasets for more practical use, which will advance the field of plant disease detection. L. Li, S. Zhang, and B. Wang, (2021) conducted a review of deep learning models for plant disease classification, including CNN, VGG16, and ResNet, using PlantVillage datasets. The aforementioned models tend to be precise to a level of 98%. Future developments could focus on improving model generality across a wide range of environmental situations. J. Lu, et al. (2021) analysed CNN-based approaches for plant leaf disease classification utilizing datasets containing diseases such as leaf spot and powdery mildew. CNNs with intricate architectures, such as ResNet, were addressed, with accuracies ranging from 95-98%. Future developments are likely to involve data augmentation and model interpretability to improve generalization. U. Atila, et al. (2021) classified plant leaf diseases using EfficientNet models with PlantVillage datasets. The model produced accuracies ranging from 97 to 99%, according to the architecture. The subsequent studies could lower processing costs for real-time applications while improving model resilience across a variety of diseases. G. Hu, K. Wei, Y. Zhang, et al. (2021) created a deep CNN model for determining tea leaf blight severity using actual site images. The accuracy in severity estimation tasks ranged between 92 and 95 percent. Future research could incorporate multimodal data (such as spectral data) to improve accuracy and robustness in real-world applications. A. Abbas, et al. (2021) employed transfer learning with VGG16 to detect tomato plant diseases, enhanced with synthetic images generated using C-GAN. The method obtained approximately 95% accuracy. Future enhancements could include different crops and increase synthetic image quality, resulting in improved efficiency in a variety of agricultural circumstances. W. Shafik, et al. (2024) utilized transfer learning models with CNN models such as ResNet50 and InceptionV3 to classify plant diseases, with accuracy ranging from 90% to 96%. Current studies could focus on edge computing to provide on-site diagnosis with lower latency and higher efficiency. J. Poyatos, et al. (2023) proposed an evolutionary pruning model for transfer learning in deep neural networks that is able to detect plant diseases with over 90% accuracy. Future enhancements could concentrate on improving model efficiency, lowering computing costs, and increasing the scalability of the pruning process. Mowla, M.N, et al. (2023) conducted a survey of IoT and sensor networks for smart agriculture, assessing systems for plant disease detection and crop monitoring. Future advances could include more powerful sensors and AI algorithms for real-time agricultural prediction. Y. Zhang, et al. (2023) evaluated deep learning algorithms for early weed detection using datasets from various crop areas. CNN-based models had an accuracy rate of 90-94%. Future studies may focus on simplifying models and increasing detection across various environmental circumstances and weed types. Rahman, A., et al. (2023) assessed deep learning object detectors such as YOLO and Faster R-CNN for cotton weed detection using RGB and multispectral datasets. Accuracy was between 92 and 95%. Future research could focus on optimizing real-time detection, lowering computational cost, and boosting adaptation to changing field circumstances. Srivastava, M., and Meena, J. (2024) proposed a modified transfer learning strategy for plant leaf disease detection that employs pre-trained models such as ResNet and VGG16 with further fine-tuning. The dataset comprises a variety of plant diseases, and the model obtains accuracy of approximately 95%. Future research could concentrate on refining the transfer learning process for more consistent performance across a variety of environmental contexts. Russel, N.S., and Selvaraj, A. (2022) developed a multiscale parallel deep CNN architecture for leaf species and disease classification utilizing a large dataset of plant leaves. The architecture incorporates various scales for feature extraction, resulting in an accuracy of approximately 97%. Future enhancements could focus on improving the multiscale technique to better handle real-world variability in plant diseases. Chohan et al. (2023) proposed a deep learning model for plant disease detection, achieving an accuracy of 83.3% after implementing data augmentation techniques. Their research highlights the importance of enhancing training datasets to improve model robustness. This study reinforces the growing role of deep learning in agricultural disease management strategies. Brahimi et al. (2023) focused on classifying tomato diseases using a CNN, achieving an impressive accuracy of 99.18%. The model's high-performance positions it as a practical tool for farmers in managing tomato plant health. This study contributes valuable insights into the application of deep learning for crop disease classification. Sibiya et al. (2023) employed a CNN model for recognizing and classifying maize leaf diseases, achieving an overall accuracy of 92.85%. Their work illustrates the effectiveness of CNNs in addressing agricultural challenges. This study adds to the growing knowledge base on plant disease classification using advanced deep learning techniques. Ramesh et al. (2023) proposed an optimized deep neural network utilizing the Jaya algorithm for classifying various paddy leaf diseases. Their model achieved significant accuracies across multiple disease categories, showcasing the potential of optimization techniques in enhancing model performance. This research contributes to the broader understanding of deep learning applications in agricultural disease detection. Tarek et al. (2023) evaluated various deep learning models for detecting tomato leaf diseases, with MobileNetV3 achieving accuracies of 98.99% and 99.81%. The results indicate that these models are viable options for real-time disease monitoring in agricultural settings. Their findings highlight the practical applications of deep learning in enhancing crop health management. Ahila Priyadharshini et al. (2023) proposed a modified LeNet architecture for classifying maize leaf diseases, achieving an accuracy of 97.89%. Their work reflects the ongoing efforts to enhance model performance in plant disease identification. Singh et al. (2023) enhanced the apple leaf disease detection process using CNNs, outperforming traditional machine learning classifiers with a notable accuracy of 99.2%. The study illustrates the effectiveness of deep learning methods in automating agricultural disease management tasks. This advancement has significant implications for precision agriculture practices. Mustafa et al. (2023) introduced an optimized five-layered CNN model for pepper leaf disease detection, achieving an impressive accuracy of 99.99%. The study generated 20,000 augmented images to enhance the training process significantly. This high accuracy underscores the potential of deep learning in automating plant disease identification. Pantazi, et al. (2019), Image feature extraction and One-Class Classifiers are used to detect leaf diseases across multiple crops, achieving a high detection accuracy of up to 92% depending on the crop and disease. Results demonstrate the effectiveness of One-Class Classifiers in automated leaf disease detection, reducing the need for disease-specific training data. Tian K, et al. (2019), An adaptive K-means clustering algorithm with a dynamically adjusted cluster number is proposed to accurately segment tomato leaves, reaching a segmentation accuracy of 96%. This adaptive K-means approach shows high precision in leaf segmentation, indicating its potential as a preprocessing step for disease detection applications.

2.3 Additional Contributions to Disease Detection using Transfer Learning Model

Nanni et al. (2020) explored bio-inspired image-based approaches for detecting and recognizing insect pests. They examined a variety of approaches and algorithms, emphasizing their utility in ecological informatics. The possible applications of these technologies in agriculture for pest control are investigated. Their research seeks to contribute to sustainable agriculture methods. Liu et al. (2020) proposed YOLO-tomato, an enhanced method for robust tomato recognition built on the YOLOv3 framework. Their research revealed the algorithm's ability to reliably recognize tomato plants under varied situations. In comparison to previous methods, the results show faster and more accurate detection. This project intends to improve automated agricultural methods. Liu and Wang (2020) proposed a revised YOLO V3 convolutional neural network for identifying tomato illnesses and pests. They aimed to improve detection efficiency and precision through model optimization. The outcomes indicate that their approach is beneficial in practical circumstances. This research intends to assist farmers with real-time pest and disease management. Ali, B. (2022) investigated the advantages and disadvantages of several evaluation metrics for generative adversarial networks (GANs), as well as new breakthroughs in analyzing the quality of GAN-generated images. The document contains information on several metrics, such as FID, IS, and others. Future studies could focus on improving these evaluation methods to produce more consistent findings in a variety of applications. Lu et al. (2022) explored the application of generative adversarial networks (GANs) for picture augmentation in agriculture. They investigated the efficacy of GANs in producing synthetic images to improve machine learning models. The results show that GANs dramatically improve dataset diversity, which leads to superior model performance. Their research advances the field of agricultural image analysis. Dhanya et al. (2022) analysed deep learning-based computer vision approaches for smart agriculture operations. They investigated different approaches, highlighting their importance in increasing agricultural output. The possible effects of these innovations for sustainable agriculture are examined. Their findings serve as a foundation for future research in smart agriculture.

The study concluded that certain augmentation techniques can significantly enhance model accuracy, with the highest performing models showing improvements in tumor identification. And the below given table summarizes several research papers on the detection of sugarcane leaf diseases, with a focus on the use of transfer learning algorithms and their accompanying performance measurements, as shown in Table 1. The cited articles highlight the efficient implementation of various transfer learning models for sugarcane leaf disease detection, demonstrating significant improvements in both reliability and effectiveness. Models such as ResNet-50, VGG-16, and DenseNet achieved accuracy rates ranging from 90.7% to 95%. The research emphasizes the importance of data preparation techniques, including image augmentation and fine-tuning, which substantially enhance model performance.

Table 1. Transfer learning models for sugarcane leaf disease detection

Reference	Dataset	Detected Diseases	Transfer Learning Algorithm	Remarks
Demilie, W.B. (2024)	Custom plant disease dataset	Multiple plant diseases	ResNet-50, VGG-16, MobileNetV2	Accuracy levels of less than 90% were achieved, with a focus on evaluating CNN models' effectiveness in plant disease categorization.
Gupta, P., & Jadon, R.S. (2024)	Plant leaf dataset	Common leaf diseases (e.g., blight, mildew)	DenseNet, VGG-16	Accuracy rates were around 93%, with DenseNet demonstrating great precision in disease detection.
Chen, Junde et al. (2020)	PlantVillage dataset	Tomato, potato, and other crop diseases	ResNet-50	Accuracy rates were less than 90%, showing that there is potential for improvement. The study examined numerous models and discovered limitations in accuracy.
Hassan SM et al. (2021)	Plant leaf disease dataset	Various leaf diseases	MobileNetV2, DenseNet	Accuracy of roughly 92% was achieved, demonstrating DenseNet's effectiveness for fine-grained leaf disease identification.
Sharma, D.K., & Punhani, A. (2024)	Sugarcane disease dataset	Sugarcane diseases	EfficientNet	Accuracy levels were below 90%, demonstrating difficulties in diagnosing illnesses in sugarcane with specific topologies. EfficientNet was efficient, but it needed some fine-tuning.
Umit Atila, Murat Uçar et al. (2021)	Custom plant disease dataset	Various leaf diseases	EfficientNet	EfficientNet achieved accuracies of less than 93%, indicating encouraging results but showing limitations in certain complex disease scenarios.
Shafik, W. et al. (2024)	Mixed plant disease dataset	Broad range of diseases across crops	AlexNet, ShuffleNet	Models produced accuracy scores of less than 90%, indicating success in multi-disease detection but limits in fine details.
Jiang, F., Lu, Y. et al. (2020)	Rice leaf dataset	Rice blast, sheath blight, brown spot	NASNet, Xception	Accuracy of roughly 91% was achieved by focusing on rice-specific illnesses, despite some misclassification problems.
Zhencun Jiang et al. (2021)	Mixed rice and wheat leaf disease dataset	Leaf spot, rust, blight	DenseNet	DenseNet achieved 94% accuracy in rice and wheat disease classification, with consistent results.
Srivastava, M., Meena, J. (2024)	Plant leaf dataset	General plant diseases	Modified ResNet, VGG-16	Achieved 90-93% accuracy, with variances based on the model changes for individual illness types.

The comprehensive summary highlights certain noteworthy characteristics for the present research article:

- Recent plant disease detection algorithms frequently exhibit variable efficiency and generalization capacity, resulting in unsatisfactory performance across a variety of situations and datasets.
- Many contemporary methods have limited feature extraction capabilities, making it difficult to reliably distinguish between diseases with subtle visual patterns.

3. PROPOSED METHODOLOGY

The enhanced DenseNet-121model is an advanced neural architecture that improve the recognition and classification of sugarcane leaf diseases like Mosaic, Red Rot, Yellow, and Rust. In the upcoming Exploratory Data Analysis (EDA) section, the process of training this algorithm on the dataset is explained. It improves disease recognition accuracy and adaptability by analysing complex patterns in leaf images. It also enhances feature extraction for categorizing similar diseases. Figure 1 visually illustrates the experimental framework, showing leaf images that indicate the presence or absence of disease in sugarcane crops, processed using DenseNet-121.

Figure 1. Overall process involved in proposed DenseNet-121 architecture

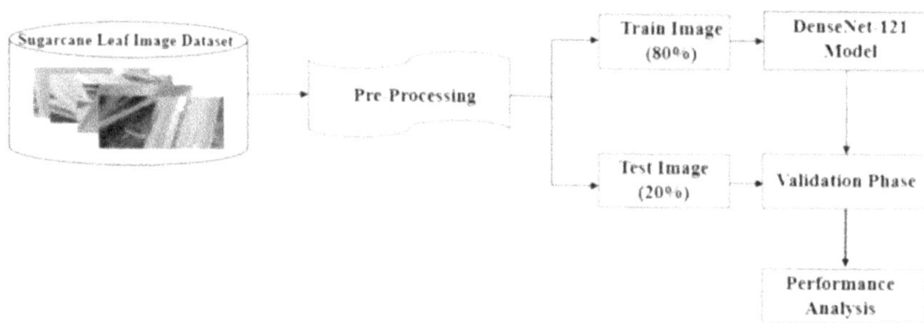

This methodology involves several key procedural steps, including dataset collection, image preprocessing, feature extraction, and image classification, all optimized to leverage the capabilities of DenseNet121. These steps will be described in detail in the upcoming sections. Subsequently, its performance is analysed on the testing subset, showcasing DenseNet121's effectiveness in image classification.

3.1 Pre-Processing:

Preprocessing involves the initial steps of preparing the dataset for model training, and it is crucial for ensuring effective learning and performance. During this phase, a diverse collection of sugarcane leaf images is carefully curated to represent various diseases, such as rust, yellow leaf syndrome, red rot, mosaic, as well as healthy leaves. These images undergo standard preprocessing steps, including resizing to a consistent dimension of 224x224 pixels, which is necessary for compatibility with the DenseNet-121 model architecture. Additionally, processes like contrast enhancement and pixel value normalization are applied to ensure uniformity across the dataset. To further increase variability and improve robustness, augmentation techniques such as rotation, flipping, and zooming are employed, introducing additional variations to the images. Once the dataset is prepared, it is split into training and testing sets in an 80:20 ratio, allowing for effective training and evaluation of the proposed method on the training dataset.

3.2An Enhanced DenseNet-121 Model for Leaf Diseases Detection:

The designed DenseNet121 model comprises six major steps: a DenseNet121 feature extractor, convolutional and batch normalization layers, a flatten layer, fully connected dense layers, and a classification layer. This model evaluates the input image through eleven phases, as shown in Figure 2.

Figure 2. A customized DenseNet-121 architecture

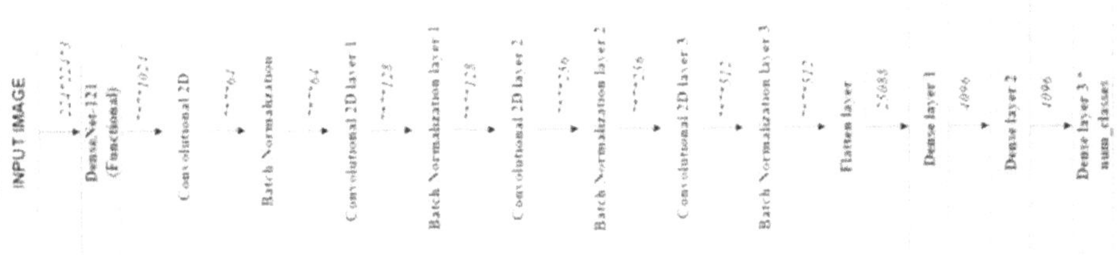

The process begins with the enhanced DenseNet121 model, which curtails the spatial dimensions of the input data and produces 1,024 feature maps. Next, four convolutional layers with 64, 128, 256, and 512 filters are utilized, along with batch normalization to ensure reliability. The final classification layer, SoftMax, generates a prediction for each input class. This occurs after the framework flattens the learned feature matrix and passes it through two fully connected dense layers, each with 4,096 units. This enhancement significantly improves the model's ability to recognize subtle visual cues related to various diseases.

3.3 A DenseNet121 Feature Extractor Layer:

The enhanced DenseNet121 model is employed as a feature extractor for analysing the pre-processed sugarcane leaf images from the previous layer. The computational model's initialization code is as follows: base_model = DenseNet121(weights='imagenet', include_top=false, input_shape=input_shape). This DenseNet121 architecture is established as a reliable feature extraction tool for the particular task of identifying healthy and diseased sugarcane leaves with this set of parameters. The model is instructed to load pre-trained weights from the ImageNet dataset, which comprises millions of labeled images falling into 1,000 categories, using the weights='imagenet' argument. This enables the model to utilize previously identified characteristics like boundaries, patterns, and dimensions. The target dataset, consisting of images of sugarcane leaves, is limited and relevant to the domain. However, the DenseNet121 model effectively retrieves complex features from these images by using pre-trained weights. This transfer learning approach significantly lowers computational costs and training time compared to training a model from scratch.

The include_top=False argument eliminates the last fully connected layer of the DenseNet121 model, originally designed to sort images into 1,000 classes from ImageNet. By excluding the top layer, the model preserves the primary feature extraction layers, which obtain lower and intermediate-level image features but cannot carry out to the final classification level. This adaptability is necessary for DenseNet121 to perform targeted tasks, like recognizing sugarcane leaf disease images into five categories using the suggested technique. User-defined classification layers can now be included and specifically adapted to recognize target categories.

The overall dimensions of the inputted images into the model are determined by the following argument: input_shape=input_shape. In the DenseNet121 architecture, the input image shape is typically set to (224, 224, 3), which indicates that the inputted images are automatically resized to 224 pixels in both width and height and the three representing the RGB color model. This architecture features an additional layer that generates a feature map with the shape (None, 7, 7, 1024). This means that after passing through the DenseNet121 layers, the images will be associated with 1,024 feature maps, each measuring 7x7 pixels. The aforementioned structured representation allows DenseNet121 to precisely analyze images throughout the training stage and decision-making stage, gathering high feature representations required for successful classification tasks. These feature maps are subsequently fed into additional convolutional and batch normalization layers, which refine the extracted features and enhance the model's classification efficiency.

3.4Convolutional And Batch Normalization Layers:

After the DenseNet121 feature extractor, the model adds additional convolutional and batch normalization layers to improve image classification. These layers are initialized sequentially, beginning with two Conv2D convolutional layers. Each layer applies 64 filters of size (3, 3) to the output of DenseNet121. Each filter extracts specific features from the input, such as edges, colors, and patterns. The parameter padding='same' ensures that the output feature maps retain the same spatial dimensions as the input, which is essential for preserving spatial information in the images. Formula 1 shows how to calculate the output of a convolutional layer.

$$Outpu\,t_{H*W} = \sum_{C=0}^{C-1} F_{H,\,W,C} \times I_{H+H_c,W+W_c,C} + b \tag{1}$$

Here, i represent the input image data, F is the filter, b is the bias value, H, W, and C denote the height, width, and number of input channels, respectively. Hc, and Wc are coordinates of a filter. The activation function used is ReLU (Rectified Linear Unit), which introduces non-linearity into the model. ReLU is defined as $f(x) = \max(0,x)$, x typically refers to the weighted sum of inputs from the previous layer (plus a bias term) and max refers to selects the maximum value between 0 and x. This function allows positive values to pass through unaltered while transforming negative values to zero, which helps to reduce vanishing gradients and promote faster training. Additionally, a batch normalization layer follows the convolutional layer to standardize the outputs from the previous layer, which standardizes the outputs of the previous layer as represented by a specific formula (2),

$$Batch\ normalize\ (x_i) = \frac{x-\mu}{\sqrt{\sigma^2+\epsilon}} \tag{2}$$

where, x_i refers normalized input value of $x, \mu and \sigma^2$ refers to mean and variance of inputted data subset in batches and ϵ is a minimum positive value added for numerical stability. Batch normalization reduces the impact of internal covariate shift by retaining consistent mean and variance for each batch, which can lead to improved efficiency. The following layers maintain this pattern, applying 128, 256, and 512 filters in successive convolutional layers. Each of these layers employs a (3, 3) kernel size and the same padding strategy to ensure consistent output dimensions.

The second convolutional layer employs GELU (Gaussian Error Linear Unit) as its activation function. GELU is defined as $f(x) = x * P(X \leq x)$x is an inputted data point, while X is a random variable that is taken from a specified probability distribution, and P is the cumulative distribution function of the standard normal distribution. GELU has been found to perform more efficiently on certain deep learning tasks by its smoothness and ability to retain data throughout the training process, especially in deeper networks. Overall, the integration of more filters in the convolutional layers enables the model to extract increasingly complex and abstract features from the data.

As the number of filters is gradually increased, the model is able to learn more complex representations, which eventually improves the classification accuracy. The utilization of ReLU and GELU activation functions are essential in this process since these functions provide nonlinearities, allowing the model to acquire information more intricate patterns and connections within the input images. Following this procedure, the output from the batch normalization and convolutional layers is forwarded to a flatten layer, which transforms the multi-dimensional feature maps into a one-dimensional vector for the next set of fully connected layers. As the number of filters gradually increased, the model learned more complex representations, which ultimately enhanced classification accuracy. The ReLU and GELU activation functions play an essential role in this process, as they introduce nonlinearities that enable the model to capture intricate patterns and connections within the input images. Following this procedure, the batch normalization and convolutional layers pass their output to a flatten layer, which converts the multi-dimensional feature maps into a one-dimensional vector for the subsequent fully connected layers.

3.5 A Flatten Layer:

The Flatten layer converts a multi-dimensional tensor into a one-dimensional vector, preparing it for fully connected layers. If the output from the previous convolutional layer has a shape of (None, H, W, C), where H is the height, W is the width, and C is the number of channels (filters), and None refers the batch size, the Flatten layer transforms this into a vector of size H×W×C.

$$Flatten(X) = \{x1,\ x2\ldots,xn\} \tag{3}$$

where X is the multi-dimensional tensor, and n=H×W×C is the total number of elements. The flattened vector size would be calculated as the product of the height, width, and number of channels, which is 7×7×10,247. This results in a total of 50,176 elements in the flattened vector. This transformation allows the model to pass the data into fully connected layers for further processing, facilitating the final stages of classification or regression tasks in the neural network.

3.6 Dense Fully Connected Layers and Classification Layer:

Dense layers play a pivotal role in classification by combining the features extracted by convolutional layers to generate a final decision. The model consists of two dense layers, each with 4,096 units, enabled by the ReLU function. These dense layers transform the one-dimensional vector output of the flatten layer into more abstract representations. Each neural network in these layers acquires data from each node in the previous layer, permitting the algorithm to learn complex interactions between features.

Using ReLU activation in these dense layers adds nonlinearity, allowing the neural network to learn complex patterns and connections in the input data. The mathematical expression for the output of a dense layer is shown in formula 4.

$$Y = f(WX + b) \quad (4)$$

where X and Y stand for the input and output layers, W is the weight connected to the input layer, b is the bias, and f is a ReLU activation function. Following these two dense layers, the model additionally incorporates one more dense layer, which serves as the classification layer. This layer uses the SoftMax activation function, commonly applied in multi-class classification tasks. The SoftMax function converts the dense layer's output into probabilities that represent the likelihood of each class. Formula (5) provides the mathematical expression for the SoftMax layer's output.

$$P(y_i) = \frac{e^{y_i}}{\sum_{j=1}^{K} e^{y_j}} \quad (5)$$

Where i represents the particular class for which the probability is computed and j is an index used to add up all of the classes. The entire collection of classes is represented by K. $P(y_i)$ represents the probability of class i based on the neural network's output. The raw logit for class i is symbolized by y_i, while the logarithmic for all of the classes j is denoted by y_j. Finally, the base of the natural logarithm, which is e, is utilized for the exponential function that ensures positive probabilities. The final result represents the model's assurance of successfully predicting the input image's class using the features learned during training. In simple terms, the fully connected dense layers and the classification layer collaborate to convert high-level features from the convolutional layers into final predictions. This enables accurate image classification into specific classes. Table 2 outlines the most significant amendments for task-based learning that differentiate the enhanced DenseNet-121 model from the standard model:

Table 2. Differences between enhanced DenseNet-121 model and standard model

Aspect	**Standard DenseNet-121**	**Enhanced DenseNet 121 Model**
Base Model	Complete DenseNet-121 architecture with top layers	DenseNet-121 without top layers (feature extractor)
Feature Extraction	Basic feature extraction capabilities	Enhanced feature extraction through additional convolutional layers
Global Pooling	Global Average Pooling	Flatten Layer
Spatial Information	Average pooling may lose details	Flattening retains spatial information
Fully Connected Layers	One fully connected layer (1000 units)	Two fully connected layers (4096 units each)
Output Layer	Softmax with 1000 classes	SoftMax with num_classes (custom number of classes)
Parameters	~8 million	More parameters due to added layers (especially dense layers)
Use Case	General-purpose for ImageNet	Task-specific with transfer learning

continued on following page

Table 2. Continued

Aspect	Standard DenseNet-121	Enhanced DenseNet 121 Model
Flexibility	Fixed architecture for ImageNet classification	More customizable for specific tasks
Efficiency in Disease Detection	Struggles with subtle visual patterns	More effective at identifying diseases with subtle visual cues

The Enhanced DenseNet 121 Model outperforms the standard DenseNet 121 Model in feature extraction and generalization across multiple datasets. While the standard model struggles to recognize subtle visual patterns associated with leaf diseases in plants, the enhanced version incorporates additional convolutional neural network layers that improve reliability and accurate disease detection. This enhancement increases adaptability to specific tasks, resulting in greater overall reliability. Furthermore, the Enhanced DenseNet 121 Model shows improved tenacity. It delivers consistent performance under various circumstances, which is essential for accurately determining plant leaf diseases.

4. RESULT AND DISCUSSION

4.1 EDA (Exploratory Data Analysis)

A Plant Village dataset of sugarcane leaf images is used, encompassing various leaf diseases such as rust (1,856 images), yellow leaf (1,852 images), red rot (1,756 images), mosaic (1,786 images), along with healthy leaves (1,800 images), totally 9,050 images. To train and evaluate the DenseNet-121 model for disease classification, the dataset is divided into training and testing sets, with training allocations of 5%, 10%, 15%, and 80%, while the remaining 95%, 90%, 85%, and 20% are used for testing. Figure 3 shows sample input images of sugarcane leaves, illustrating various conditions: (a) Healthy, (b) Red rot, (c) Rust, (d) Yellow leaf, and (e) Mosaic disease.

Figure 3. Sample inputted leaf images of sugarcane plant

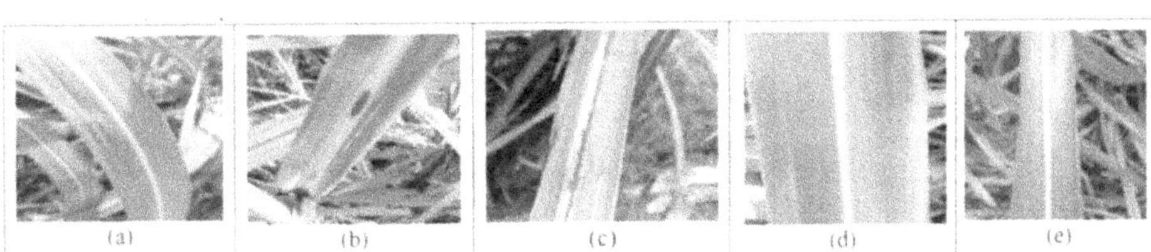

Before training, images undergo pre-processing by resizing to 224x224 pixels and normalizing pixel values. DenseNet-121 is employed to automate disease identification and classification in sugarcane plants.

4.2 Performance Metrics

The performance measures are essential for assessing the suggested DenseNet-121 model's effectiveness. Each of the metrics in this study: accuracy, F1-score, omission & commission error, recall, and precision are explained by a related formula (6-11).

Accuracy

The percentage of predictions that the model correctly predicted is known as accuracy. The accuracy is calculated by the number of accurate predictions divided by the total number of predictions. The accuracy calculated based on the formula shown in equation (6) and the class wise accuracy shown in table. Where, TP- True positive, TN- True Negative, FP-False Positive, and FN- False Negative.

$$Accuracy = \frac{TP + TN}{TP + FP + FN + TN} \quad (6)$$

F1 Score

The F1 score measures the overall performance of a classification model, taking into account both precision and recall. A higher F1 score is considered as a better model. The F1 score calculated based on the formula shown in equation 7.

$$F1\ Score = \frac{TP}{TP + 0.5\,(FP + FN)} \quad (7)$$

Omission & Commission Error

The omission error is the rate at which the model fails to identify a disease that is actually present. The omission & commission error calculated by a formula shown in equation (8, 9).

Omission Error =

$$\frac{FN}{(FN + TP)} \quad (8)$$

The commission error is the rate at which the model identifies a disease that is not actually present.

Commission Error =

$$\frac{FP}{(FP + TP)} \quad (9)$$

Precision & Recall

A classification model's capacity to find only the pertinent data elements is known as precision. The precision & recall calculated based on the formula shown in equation (10,11).

$$Precision = \frac{TP}{(TP + FP)} \quad (10)$$

Recall is a metric that measures the proportion of accurate positive forecasts among all possible positive predictions.

$$Recall = \frac{TP}{(TP + FN)} \quad (11)$$

4.3 Experimental Results

The experiments are performed using the suggested model, which combines a pre-trained DenseNet121 architecture with extra convolutional and fully connected layers. In a Google Colab environment, the model is created and implemented using Python with the TensorFlow and Keras libraries. Hyperparameter tuning, which entails choosing the most suitable values for parameters that control the learning process, is essential to maximizing the effectiveness of the model. Table 3 summarizes the model's important hyperparameters.

Table 3. Hyperparameter tuning

Hyperparameter	Current Value
Input Shape	(224, 224, 3)
Number of Classes	5
Batch Size	32
Epochs	40
Filters (Conv Layers)	64, 128, 256, 512
Kernel Size	(3, 3)
Activation Functions	ReLU, GeLU
Units (Dense Layers)	4096 (both layers)
Optimizer	adam
Learning Rate	0.001 (default for Adam)
Trainable Layers	Frozen (DenseNet121 base)

Hyperparameters include input shape, batch size, number of filters, kernel size, number of units in fully linked layers, and optimizer settings. The experimental results for sugarcane are as follows: the performance of DenseNet-121 model in classifying leaf diseases, as shown in Figure 4.

Figure 4. DenseNet-121 model output image of sugarcane leaf diseases

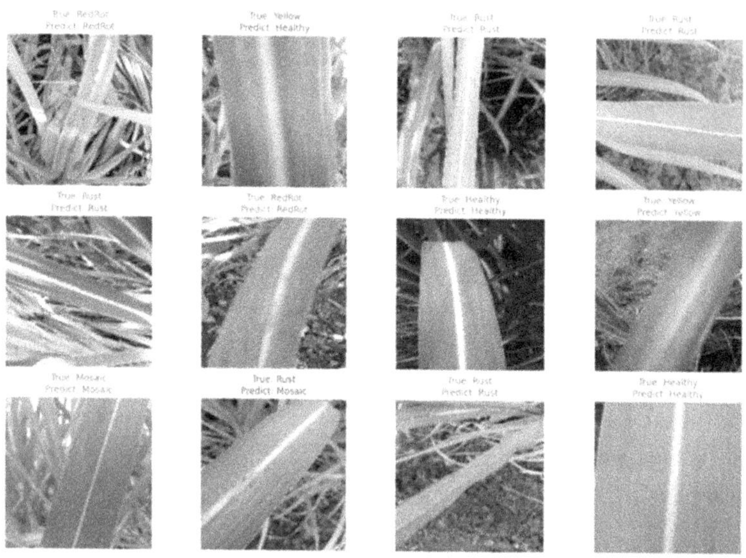

Each sample incorporates the true label (actually state) and the expected label, with accurate predictions appearing in green and incorrect predictions in red. The DenseNet-121 model is highly accurate across multiple disease classes, namely Red Rot, Rust, Mosaic, and Healthy. However, there are a few notable incorrect classifications, such as one where 'Mosaic' predicted instead of 'Rust.' This highlights both the model's strengths and potential improvements in disease detection effectiveness. A confusion matrix is a performance measuring tool for recognizing issues that reveals true positives, true negatives, false positives, and false negatives. It assists to determine the accuracy, precision, recall, and F1 score of a DenseNet-121 model. Table 4 shows the confusion matrix, it presents the model's performance across all classes, along with the reliability and misclassification patterns.

Table 4. Confusion matrix

	PREDICTIONS					
		Healthy	**Mosaic**	**Red Rot**	**Rust**	**Yellow**
LABELS	**Healthy**	**17**	0	0	0	0
	Mosaic	2	**26**	0	0	1
	Red Rot	1	0	**26**	0	2
	Rust	2	0	1	**20**	0
	Yellow	2	1	1	0	**26**

Each row in the confusion matrix represents the actual class, while each column corresponds to the predicted class, with the cell values indicating the number of instances. The diagonal cells, where the actual and predicted labels match, reflect successful classifications: 17 instances of Healthy, 26 instances of Mosaic, and 26 instances of Yellow are correctly identified. However, some misclassifications occur. For illustration, two Healthy cases are mistakenly predicted as Mosaic, and two Red Rot cases are misclassified as Yellow. The color gradient highlights these values, with brighter colors indicating higher counts. While there is potential for improvement, especially in differentiating between closely related categories, to lower misclassifications and improve overall performance, even though the majority of predictions match the actual classes. This performance evaluation is detailed in Table 5.

Table 5. Performance of proposed DenseNet-121 model for sugarcane leaf disease

Label	Precision	Recall	F1-Score	Accuracy
Yellow	0.965	0.954	0.985	0.964
Mosaic	0.987	0.996	0.976	0.9854
Rust	0.966	0.987	0.954	0.9812
Healthy	0.96	0.977	0.98	0.963
Red Rot	0.977	0.976	0.97	0.9765

The performance metrics of a classification model for five classes: Healthy, Red Rot, Yellow, Mosaic, and Rust are shown, along with critical measures such as precision, recall, F1-score, and accuracy, which evaluate the model's success in classifying each category. The healthy class achieves a precision of 0.96, which means 96% of predictions are accurate, and a recall of 0.977, which means 97.7% of actual cases were correctly identified. The Red Rot class performs similarly, with a precision of 0.977 and a recall of 0.976, resulting in an F1-Score of 0.97. The yellow class has a precision of 0.965, recall of 0.954, and F1-score of 0.985. Notably, the Mosaic class achieves the highest precision (0.987) and recall (0.996), which produces an F1-Score of 0.976 and an accuracy of 0.9854. The Rust class achieves 0.966 precision, 0.987 recall, and 0.9812 accuracy. This analysis highlights that the classification model performs effectively across all classes, achieving high precision, recall, and F1-scores, which indicate reliable and accurate classification results. The training and validation reliability and loss curves, as shown in Figure 5, present a graphical illustration of the model's learning process and performance over time.

Figure 5. (a) Training and validation accuracy, (b) Training and validation loss

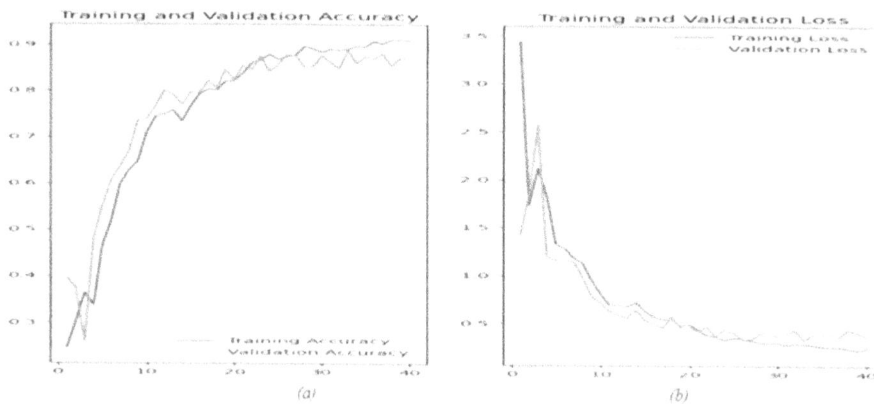

The performance of a DenseNet-121 model through training and validation metrics over 40 epochs. The left plot (a) represents training and validation accuracy, with both curves consistently improving, indicating that the model is learning efficiently. Training accuracy reaches about 95%, whereas validation accuracy drops to around 90% after 20 epochs, indicating minor overfitting. The right plot (b) displays training and validation loss, both of which drop dramatically at first and then stabilize at low values as training advances. The training loss falls below 0.5, and the validation loss follows suit, indicating strong generalization and minimal overfitting. Table 6 displays the DenseNet-121 model's classification accuracy and performance aspects across various training sample ratio for distinct classes, providing an exhaustive representation of its performance under various scenarios.

Table 6. Classification accuracy and performance metrics of the DenseNet-121 model

Training Ratio **Classes**	**5%** **(in %)**	**10%** **(in %)**	**15%** **(in %)**	**80%** **(in %)**
Yellow	92.8	93.3%	97.5%	97.2%
Mosaic	96.6	94.4%	97.9%	98.5%
Rust	73.3	90%	88.4%	95.2%
Healthy	99.2	98.14%	98.2%	98.3%
Red Rot	97.7	97.4%	97.8%	99.5%
Overall accuracy	89.5	94.2%	94.8%	97.2%
Kappa coefficient	0.88	0.93	0.94	0.94

The analysis reveals the performance of a classification model for five classes: Yellow, Mosaic, Rust, Healthy, and Red Rot, across varying training sample percentages (5%, 10%, 15%, and 80%). The model's accuracy generally improves with an increase in training samples, with Yellow achieving a peak accuracy of 97.5% at 15%, Mosaic reaching 98.5% at 80%, and Rust showing a substantial increase from 73.3% at 5% to 95.2% at 80%. The Healthy class consistently performs well, maintaining accuracy above 98%, while Red Rot attains 99.5% accuracy at the highest training percentage. Overall accuracy rises from 89.5% with 5% training samples to 97.2% with 80%, accompanied by a Kappa coefficient that increases from 0.88 to 0.94, indicating strong agreement in classification. Overall, analyzes indicate that ample training information is paramount to attaining high accuracy and reliable results across all classification parameters.

CONCLUSION

Sugarcane diseases, such as red rot, rust, yellowing, and mosaic, are a serious danger to sugarcane-dependent industry sectors such as food, biofuels, and pharmaceuticals, necessitating efficient identification and categorization. This chapter provides an improved DenseNet-121 model for performing sugarcane leaf disease identification, which was trained on a curated dataset of 9,050 pictures that included both healthy and diseased samples. The model performed admirably, reaching 96.3% accuracy with good precision (0.96), recall (0.977), and F1-score (0.98), highlighting its possibilities for effective tracking of diseases. Nonetheless, the model's computing demands pose deployment issues in resource-constrained environments. Future initiatives include improving the model for mobile and edge devices and making it usable in field circumstances. Expanding the dataset to include additional disease categories may improve real-time, scalable agricultural applications. Finally, this technique promotes sustainable farming practices while also strengthening food security by delivering an efficient, computerized disease management possibility.

REFERENCES

Abbas, A., Jain, S., Gour, M., & Vankudothu, S. (2021). Tomato plant disease detection using transfer learning with C-GAN synthetic images. *Computers and Electronics in Agriculture*, *187*, 106279. DOI: 10.1016/j.compag.2021.106279

Ahila Priyadharshini, R., Arivazhagan, S., Arun, M., & Mirnalini, A. (2019). Maize leaf disease classification using deep convolutional neural networks. *Neural Computing & Applications*, *31*(12), 8887–8895. DOI: 10.1007/s00521-019-04228-3

Ali, B. (2022). Pros and cons of GAN evaluation measures: New developments. *Computer Vision and Image Understanding*, *215*, 103329. DOI: 10.1016/j.cviu.2021.103329

Atila, U., Uçar, M., Akyol, K., & Uçar, E. (2021). Plant leaf disease classification using EfficientNet deep learning model. *Ecological Informatics*, *61*, 101182. DOI: 10.1016/j.ecoinf.2020.101182

Bordonal, R. D., Carvalho, J. L., Lal, R., De Figueiredo, E. B., De Oliveira, B. G., & La Scala, N.Jr. (2018, April). Sustainability of sugarcane production in Brazil. A review. *Agronomy for Sustainable Development*, *38*(2), 1–23. DOI: 10.1007/s13593-018-0490-x

Brahimi, M., Boukhalfa, K., & Moussaoui, A. (2017, April 21). Deep learning for tomato diseases: Classification and symptoms visualization. *Applied Artificial Intelligence*, *31*(4), 299–315. DOI: 10.1080/08839514.2017.1315516

Chen, J., Chen, J., Zhang, D., Sun, Y., & Nanehkaran, Y. A. Using deep transfer learning for image-based plant disease identification, *Computers and Electronics in Agriculture,* Volume 173, 2020, 105393, ISSN 0168-1699, https://doi.org/DOI: 10.1016/j.compag.2020.105393

Chen, J., Chen, J., Zhang, D., Sun, Y., & Nanehkaran, Y. A. (2020). Using deep transfer learning for image-based plant disease identification. *Computers and Electronics in Agriculture*, *173*, 105393. DOI: 10.1016/j.compag.2020.105393

Chinnadurai, C. (2017). Potential Health Benefits of Sugarcane. In Mohan, C. (Ed.), *Sugarcane Biotechnology: Challenges and Prospects.* Springer., DOI: 10.1007/978-3-319-58946-6_1

Chohan, M., Khan, A., Chohan, R., Katpar, S. H., & Mahar, M. S. (2020, May). Plant disease detection using deep learning. *International Journal of Recent Technology and Engineering*, *9*(1), 909–914. DOI: 10.35940/ijrte.A2139.059120

Demilie, W. B. (2024). Plant disease detection and classification techniques: A comparative study of the performances. *Journal of Big Data*, *11*(1), 5. DOI: 10.1186/s40537-023-00863-9

Dhanya, V. G., Subeesh, A., Kushwaha, N. L., Vishwakarma, D. K., Kumar, T. N., Ritika, G., & Singh, A. N. (2022). Deep learning-based computer vision approaches for smart agricultural applications. *Artificial Intelligence in Agriculture*, *6*, 211–229. DOI: 10.1016/j.aiia.2022.09.007

Gupta, P., & Jadon, R. S. (2024). Plant Leaf Disease Identification Using Deep Learning Algorithms. In Hassanien, A. E., Anand, S., Jaiswal, A., & Kumar, P. (Eds.), *Innovative Computing and Communications. ICICC 2024. Lecture Notes in Networks and Systems* (Vol. 1043). Springer., DOI: 10.1007/978-981-97-4228-8_47

Hasan, R. I., Yusuf, S. M., & Alzubaidi, L. (2020). Review of the state of the art of deep learning for plant diseases: A broad analysis and discussion. *Plants*, *9*(10), 1302. DOI: 10.3390/plants9101302 PMID: 33019765

Hassan, S. M., Maji, A. K., Jasiński, M., Leonowicz, Z., & Jasińska, E. (2021, June 9). Identification of plant-leaf diseases using CNN and transfer-learning approach. *Electronics (Basel)*, *10*(12), 1388. DOI: 10.3390/electronics10121388

Hu, G., Wei, K., Zhang, Y., Bao, W., & Liang, D. (2021). Estimation of tea leaf blight severity in natural scene images. *Precision Agriculture*, *22*(4), 1239–1262. DOI: 10.1007/s11119-020-09782-8

Huang, S., Wu, S., Sun, C., Ma, X., Jiang, Y., & Qi, L. (2020). Deep localization model for intra-row crop detection in paddy field. *Computers and Electronics in Agriculture*, *169*, 105203. DOI: 10.1016/j.compag.2019.105203

Jiang, F., Lu, Y., Chen, Y., Cai, D., & Li, G. (2020). Image recognition of four rice leaf diseases based on deep learning and support vector machine. *Computers and Electronics in Agriculture*, *179*, 105824. DOI: 10.1016/j.compag.2020.105824

Jiang, Z., Dong, Z., Jiang, W., & Yang, Y. (2021). Recognition of rice leaf diseases and wheat leaf diseases based on multi-task deep transfer learning. *Computers and Electronics in Agriculture*, *186*, 106184. DOI: 10.1016/j.compag.2021.106184

Lee, S. H., Goëau, H., Bonnet, P., & Joly, A. (2020). New perspectives on plant disease characterization based on deep learning. *Computers and Electronics in Agriculture*, *170*, 105220. DOI: 10.1016/j.compag.2020.105220

Li, D., Wang, R., Xie, C., Liu, L., Zhang, J., Li, R., Wang, F., Zhou, M., & Liu, W. (2020). A recognition method for rice plant diseases and pests video detection based on deep convolutional neural network. *Sensors (Basel)*, *20*(3), 578. DOI: 10.3390/s20030578 PMID: 31973039

Li, L., Zhang, S., & Wang, B. (2021). Plant Disease Detection and Classification by Deep Learning—A Review. *IEEE Access : Practical Innovations, Open Solutions*, *9*, 56683–56698. DOI: 10.1109/ACCESS.2021.3069646

Liu, G., Nouaze, J. C., Touko Mbouembe, P. L., & Kim, J. H. (2020). YOLO-tomato: A robust algorithm for tomato detection based on YOLOv3. *Sensors (Basel)*, *20*(7), 2145. DOI: 10.3390/s20072145 PMID: 32290173

Liu, J., & Wang, X. (2020). Tomato diseases and pests detection based on improved Yolo V3 convolutional neural network. *Frontiers in Plant Science*, *11*, 898. DOI: 10.3389/fpls.2020.00898 PMID: 32612632

Lu, J., Tan, L., & Jiang, H. (2021). Review on convolutional neural network (CNN) applied to plant leaf disease classification. *Agriculture*, *11*(8), 707. DOI: 10.3390/agriculture11080707

Lu, Y., Chen, D., Olaniyi, E., & Huang, Y. (2022). Generative adversarial networks (GANs) for image augmentation in agriculture: A systematic review. *Computers and Electronics in Agriculture*, *200*, 107208. DOI: 10.1016/j.compag.2022.107208

Mowla, M. N., Mowla, N., Shah, A. F. M. S., Rabie, K. M., & Shongwe, T. (2023). Internet of Things and Wireless Sensor Networks for Smart Agriculture Applications: A Survey. *IEEE Access : Practical Innovations, Open Solutions*, *11*, 145813–145852. DOI: 10.1109/ACCESS.2023.3346299

Mustafa, H., Umer, M., Hafeez, U., Hameed, A., Sohaib, A., Ullah, S., & Madni, H. A. (2023). Pepper bell leaf disease detection and classification using optimized convolutional neural network. *Multimedia Tools and Applications*, *82*(8), 12065–12080. DOI: 10.1007/s11042-022-13737-8

Nagasubramanian, K., Jones, S., Singh, A. K., Sarkar, S., Singh, A., & Ganapathysubramanian, B. (2019). Plant disease identification using explainable 3D deep learning on hyperspectral images. *Plant Methods*, *15*(1), 1–0. DOI: 10.1186/s13007-019-0479-8 PMID: 31452674

Nanni, L., Maguolo, G., & Pancino, F. (2020). Insect pest image detection and recognition based on bio-inspired methods. *Ecological Informatics*, *57*, 101089. DOI: 10.1016/j.ecoinf.2020.101089

Nazki, H., Yoon, S., Fuentes, A., & Park, D. S. (2020). Unsupervised image translation using adversarial networks for improved plant disease recognition. *Computers and Electronics in Agriculture*, *168*, 105117. DOI: 10.1016/j.compag.2019.105117

Ogrekçi, S., Unal, Y., & Dudak, M. N. (2023). A comparative study of vision transformers and convolutional neural networks: Sugarcane leaf diseases identification. *European Food Research and Technology*, *249*(7), 1833–1843. DOI: 10.1007/s00217-023-04258-1

Pantazi, X. E., Moshou, D., & Tamouridou, A. A. (2019, January 1). Automated leaf disease detection in different crop species through image features analysis and One Class Classifiers. *Computers and Electronics in Agriculture*, *156*, 96–104. DOI: 10.1016/j.compag.2018.11.005

Poyatos, J., Molina, D., Martinez, A. D., Del Ser, J., & Herrera, F. (2023). EvoPruneDeepTL: An evolutionary pruning model for transfer learning based deep neural networks. *Neural Networks*, *158*, 59–82. DOI: 10.1016/j.neunet.2022.10.011 PMID: 36442374

Rahman, A., Lu, Y., & Wang, H. (2023). Performance evaluation of deep learning object detectors for weed detection for cotton. *Smart Agricultural Technology*, *3*, 100126. DOI: 10.1016/j.atech.2022.100126

Ramesh, S., & Vydeki, D. Recognition and classification of paddy leaf diseases using Optimized Deep Neural network with Jaya algorithm, *Information Processing in Agriculture*, Volume 7, Issue 2, 2020, Pages 249-260, ISSN 2214-3173, https://doi.org/DOI: 10.1016/j.inpa.2019.09.002

Raza, H. A., Hameed, M. U., Islam, M. S., Lone, N. A., Raza, M. A., & Sabagh, A. E. L. (2022). *Environmental and Economic Benefits of Sustainable Sugarcane Initiative and Production Constraints in Pakistan: A Review, Global Agricultural Production: Resilience to Climate Change*. Springer., DOI: 10.1007/978-3-031-14973-3_17

Russel, N. S., & Selvaraj, A. (2022). Leaf species and disease classification using multiscale parallel deep CNN architecture. *Neural Computing & Applications*, *34*(21), 19217–19237. DOI: 10.1007/s00521-022-07521-w

Sethy, P. K., Barpanda, N. K., Rath, A. K., & Behera, S. K. (2020). Deep feature based rice leaf disease identification using support vector machine. *Computers and Electronics in Agriculture*, *175*, 105527. DOI: 10.1016/j.compag.2020.105527

Shafik, W., Tufail, A., De Silva Liyanage, C., & Apong, R. A. A. H. M. (2024). Using transfer learning-based plant disease classification and detection for sustainable agriculture. *BMC Plant Biology*, *24*(1), 136. DOI: 10.1186/s12870-024-04825-y PMID: 38408925

Sharma, D. K., & Punhani, A. (2024). *Deep Learning Methods for Precise Sugarcane Disease Detection and Sustainable Crop Management. Communications in Computer and Information Science* (Vol. 2054). Springer., DOI: 10.1007/978-3-031-56703-2_4

Sibiya, M., & Sumbwanyambe, M. (2019, March 13). A computational procedure for the recognition and classification of maize leaf diseases out of healthy leaves using convolutional neural networks. *Agricultural Engineering*, *1*(1), 119–131. DOI: 10.3390/agriengineering1010009

Silalertruksa, T., & Gheewala, S. H. (2020). Competitive use of sugarcane for food, fuel, and biochemical through the environmental and economic factors. *The International Journal of Life Cycle Assessment*, *25*(7), 1343–1355. DOI: 10.1007/s11367-019-01664-0

Singh, S., Gupta, I., Gupta, S., Koundal, D., Aljahdali, S., Mahajan, S., & Pandit, A. K. (2022, April 1). Deep learning based automated detection of diseases from Apple leaf images. *Computers, Materials & Continua*, *71*(1), 1849–1866. Advance online publication. DOI: 10.32604/cmc.2022.021875

Srivastava, M., & Meena, J. (2024). Plant leaf disease detection and classification using modified transfer learning models. *Multimedia Tools and Applications*, *83*(13), 38411–38441. DOI: 10.1007/s11042-023-16929-y

Tarek, H., Aly, H., Eisa, S., & Abul-Soud, M. (2022, January 3). Optimized deep learning algorithms for tomato leaf disease detection with hardware deployment. *Electronics (Basel)*, *11*(1), 140. DOI: 10.3390/electronics11010140

Tian, K., Li, J., Zeng, J., Evans, A., & Zhang, L. (2019, October 1). Segmentation of tomato leaf images based on adaptive clustering number of K-means algorithm. *Computers and Electronics in Agriculture*, *165*, 104962. DOI: 10.1016/j.compag.2019.104962

Trenberth, K. E. (2012). Framing the way to relate climate extremes to climate change. *Climatic Change*, *115*(2), 283–290. DOI: 10.1007/s10584-012-0441-5

Wan Mansor, W. N., Mohd Zaini, N. S., Gengan, G., Abdullah, A. H., Mohd Sha'ari, A. A., Roslan, A. Z., & Abd Rahim, M. H. (2024). Enhancing ergogenic performance and antioxidant benefits of red sugarcane juice through probiotic fermentation. *Discover Food*, *4*(1), 32. DOI: 10.1007/s44187-024-00092-w

Zhang, Y., Wang, M., Zhao, D., Liu, C., & Liu, Z. (2023). Early weed identification based on deep learning: A review. *Smart Agricultural Technology*, *3*, 100123. DOI: 10.1016/j.atech.2022.100123

Chapter 7
Innovative Deep Learning Image Technologies:
Applications of Deep Learning in Image Processing

Muhammad Akram
https://orcid.org/0000-0003-1485-9804
Balochistan University of Information Technology, Engineering, and Management Sciences, Pakistan

Sibghat Ullah Bazai
Balochistan University of Information Technology, Engineering, and Management Sciences, Pakistan

Muhammad Sulaman
https://orcid.org/0000-0002-8149-1635
Balochistan Think Tank Network, Pakistan

Farman Ullah
https://orcid.org/0009-0002-3195-1469
Balochistan University of Information Technology, Engineering, and Management Sciences, Pakistan

ABSTRACT

The chapter gives an overview of the applications of deep learning and image processing in the different industries of medicine, automobiles, entertainment, and security. Multiple advanced techniques such as CNN, GAN, and ViT that have become handy in the analysis of image processing. From medical diagnostics to autonomous vehicles, environmental monitoring, and surveillance, its applications show the impact of deep learning on accuracy and efficiency. It also discusses critical ethical issues, such as data privacy, model biases, and energy consumption, and points out some possible solutions to reduce those effects. In general, this contribution provides a critical overview of advances related to image processing by deep learning and its potential for further innovative developments in a wide range of applications.

DOI: 10.4018/979-8-3693-9045-0.ch007

1. INTRODUCTION

1.1 Background and Motivation

Image processing has emerged as a cornerstone of modern technology, playing a pivotal role across diverse sectors such as healthcare, automotive, entertainment, and security. The ability to analyze, interpret, and manipulate images has enabled groundbreaking advancements that were once unimaginable. From diagnosing diseases through medical imaging to enabling autonomous vehicles to navigate complex environments, image processing has become indispensable in solving real-world challenges. As the volume of visual data continues to grow exponentially, the need for efficient and intelligent image processing techniques has never been more critical.

Deep Learning, a subset of artificial intelligence, has revolutionized image processing by automating feature extraction and enabling the analysis of complex, high-dimensional data. Traditional image processing methods relied heavily on handcrafted features and algorithms, which were often limited in their ability to generalize across tasks and environments. In contrast, Deep Learning models, particularly Convolutional Neural Networks (CNNs), have demonstrated remarkable success in tasks such as object detection, image classification, and segmentation. These models learn directly from data, eliminating the need for manual feature engineering and achieving state-of-the-art performance in a wide range of applications.

Image processing is therefore very important in healthcare for medical imaging, which helps in the disease detection, diagnosis, and treatment of diseases. That is why cutting-edge image processing algorithms must lie behind techniques such as MRI, CT scans, and X-rays to enable clear and clean images for the best patient care. Automated image analysis further improved the ability to identify abnormalities, such as tumors or fractures, precisely, thus improving outcomes and reducing the burden on healthcare professionals. Recent research shows that the world medical imaging market will exceed $59.75 billion by 2032 (Research, 2024), which is a great indication of increased reliance on these technologies shown in Figure 1.

Figure 1. Global medical imaging systems market size

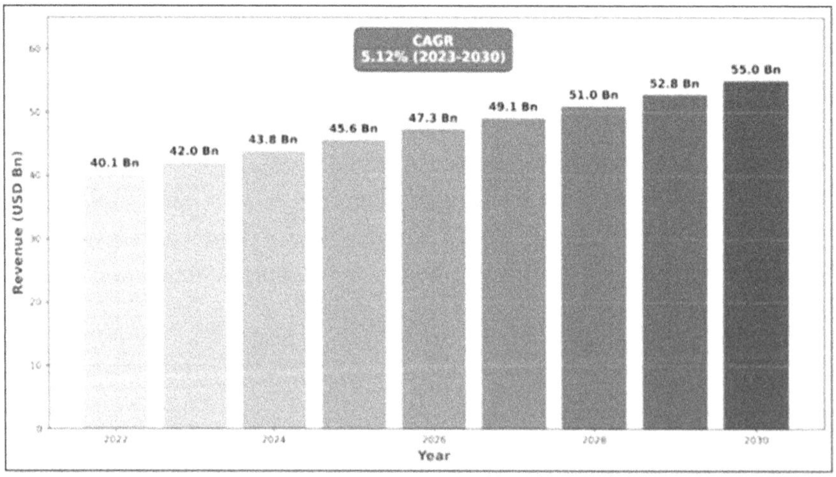

One of the applications for image processing that is useful in the automotive industry is the development of autonomous driving vehicles. Advanced driver-assistance systems apply image processing technology to the detection of objects, lanes, and traffic signs so that vehicles can recognize their surroundings and decide on actions in real time. It is a key technology for improvements in self-driving cars, as well as in road safety, with traffic accidents minimized. The NHTSA report 94% (NHTSA, 2024) of severe crashes are caused by human error and stresses that automation has the potential to reduce this.

There have been over 2.2 million motor vehicle-related deaths in the US since the Department of Transportation was founded in 1966. Furthermore, motor vehicle fatalities increased by almost 7.2 percent in 2015, the biggest one-year increase since 1966, following decades of reduction. Human mistake is the primary cause of 94% of all fatal collisions. Therefore, by addressing the underlying causes, ADSs have the potential to drastically reduce highway deaths. the reason behind these terrible collisions as illustrated in Figure 2.

Figure 2. Motor vehicle-related fatalities and human error factor

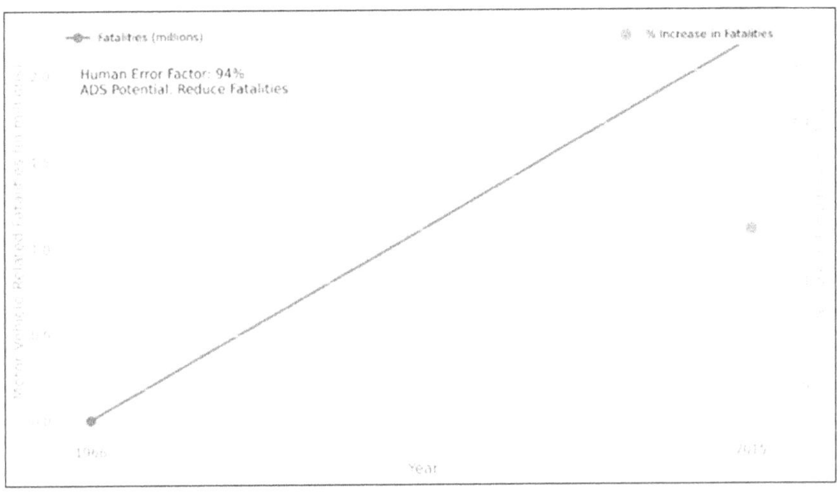

The entertainment industry has also had its blessing in the way of such great leaps in image processing. In movie and video game industries, image processing is used to develop breath taking special effects, improve image quality, and create lifelike animations. Deep Learning algorithms made possible the manipulation of images by content creators in ways that were unimaginable in the past: for example, real-time facial animation and virtual reality experiences. The global gaming industry was worth around $183.9 billion in 2023 (Get Newzoo's, 2023) and continues to accrue benefits from these improvements.

In 2023, the PC and console gaming market grew in almost every region of the world that we cover. A staggering 50% of all game-related consumer expenditure came from the US and China, with US customers spending well over $46 billion.

Even though the Middle East and Africa only made about 4% of worldwide sales, the market did expand by 4.6% year over year. 46% of the worldwide market was in Asia-Pacific, despite a -0.2% YoY growth decline in this area Illustrated in Figure 3.

Figure 3. Global games market revenues per region

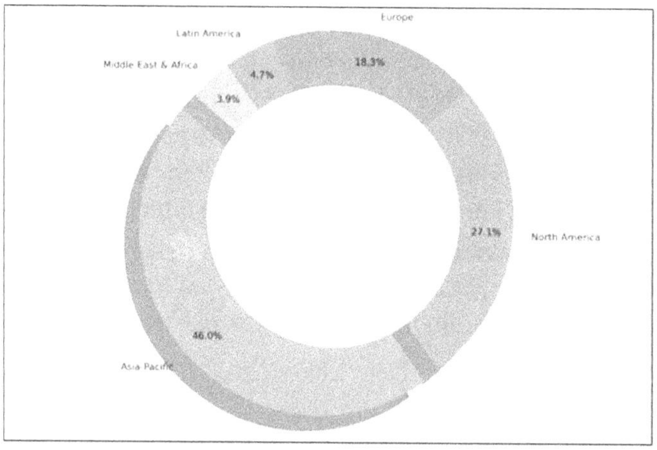

Additionally, in Security, image processing is the basis of surveillance, face recognition, and anomaly detection. Surveillance and detection applications in public places, airports, and border controls are performed based on high-definition cameras and analysis algorithms to monitor and identify suspected threats. A report by Allied Market Research 2023(Analysis Report, 2024) estimated that the global video surveillance market was valued at $61.8 billion in 2022 and is poised to reach $204.5 billion by 2032, which reflects increasing reliance on these technologies. This has greatly improved the efficiency of security systems, which can provide better protection and response capabilities by processing and analyzing large volumes of visual data in real-time. Under optimal conditions, facial recognition already plays a very important role in law enforcement and border security, yielding an accuracy rate above 99.5% (NIST, 2024). However, this is coupled with issues of privacy and bias in facial recognition systems, as manifested in prior studies from the ACLU (Face Recognition Technology, 2024) and EFF (Privacy, 2024).

Deep Learning, therefore, is an enabling technology that promises to revolutionize image processing in these fields. The traditional methods of image processing involved heavy dependence on handcrafted features and algorithms, which proved inefficient for the processing of complex or large datasets. In general, these traditional methods have not been able to generalize well across tasks and environments, so they do not consistently deliver results. Deep Learning, coupled with the recent development of CNNs, has changed image processing by automating feature extraction with high accuracy and efficiency in analyzing images. This has thus allowed new and advanced applications in real-time detection of objects, image synthesis, and generation of high-resolution images, thereby extending what is possible with image processing.

The motivation for integrating Deep Learning into image processing stems from the limitations of traditional methodologies and the increasing demand for intelligent, real-time decision-making systems. In healthcare, for instance, Deep Learning models have significantly improved the accuracy of disease detection and diagnosis, enabling earlier interventions and better patient outcomes. In autonomous driving, Deep Learning-powered systems have enhanced road safety by reducing human error, which is responsible for the majority of traffic accidents. Similarly, in entertainment and security, Deep Learning has enabled the creation of lifelike animations and advanced surveillance systems, respectively.

The significance of image processing within the broader context of Deep Learning research lies in its ability to bridge the gap between raw visual data and actionable insights. As Deep Learning continues to evolve, image processing remains at the forefront of innovation, driving advancements in areas such as medical imaging, autonomous systems, and environmental monitoring. By addressing the challenges of handling complex visual data, Deep Learning in image processing not only enhances existing applications but also opens up new possibilities for solving some of the most pressing problems of our time.

1.2 Scope and Objectives

1.2.1 Scope

The scope of this chapter is on the transformative role Deep Learning plays in image processing and the application of such work across various domains. Some major techniques that will come into consideration include CNNs, GANs, autoencoders, and transformers. In particular, the scope covers discussions of such technologies in regard to challenges and advanced applications in healthcare, autonomous vehicles, entertainment, security, and environmental monitoring.

1.3 Traditional Image Processing vs. Deep Learning-Based Approaches

Traditional image processing methods require heavy reliance on manually constructed algorithms and features specialized to a particular task. Most of these methods involve the use of predefined filters, edge detectors and thresholding techniques, which need a lot of domain expert to get the best results. Although they work well for simpler tasks, they can't handle rich data, handle different environments or obtain high accuracy when confronted with large or noisy datasets.

In contrast, Deep Learning based approaches, e.g. Convolutional Neural Networks (CNNs), Generative Adversarial Networks (GANs) and Vision Transformers (ViTs) feature extraction and learn representations directly from data. This eliminates the need for manual feature engineering. For example:

- **Traditional Methods**: Edge detection algorithms which are manually designed, e.g., Sobel and Canny.
- **Deep Learning**: CNNs that automatically detect edges and patterns in images during training.

Deep Learning approaches excel in the analysis of unstructured data and are very scalable for real time applications like Transport (Autonomous Vehicles) or Medical Diagnostics. In addition, they excel in tasks like object detection, segmentation and style transfer without notable sacrifice in generalizing across diversified datasets and with strong state of the art results.

2. DEEP LEARNING TECHNIQUES IN IMAGE PROCESSING

2.1 Convolutional Neural Networks (CNNs)

2.1.1 Role of CNNs in Image Processing.

The ability of Convolutional Neural Networks CNNs to automatically extract features from images in a hierarchical manner has truly transformed the realm of image processing (Haq et al., 2023; Khan et al., 2023; Akram et al., 2024; Li et al., 2025; Liu et al., 2025; Bhatti et al., 2025; Kanwal et al., 2025; Li et al., 2025; Tang et al., 2025; Zeng et al., 2025; Liu et al., 2025). Conventional methods heavily on manual feature engineering and struggled to adapt across various datasets (Shah & Tembhurne, 2023). In contrast, CNNs employ a structure that enables them to grasp intricate patterns directly from unprocessed images (Archana & Jeevaraj, 2024) (Feng et al., 2022; Aamir et al., 2025; Nawaz et al., 2025; Sun et al., 2024; Shao et al., 2024; Zhang et al., 2024; Zhang et al., 2024). CNNs are a set of convolutional layers performing the function of filtering, a pooling layer for reducing dimensionality, and a fully connected layer for classification. The layered methods in CNNs give it the ability to identify objects and classify them with great accuracy in images.

Architectural variations explored the design of CNNs with variations in activation and loss functions, optimization of parameters, and architectural innovations have enhanced their performance. A recent study reports that in tasks like object detection and facial recognition, CNNs achieve an average improvement of more than 20% in accuracy as compared to the traditional techniques of machine learning. This fact proves their effectiveness for complex image analysis tasks. Besides achieving performance in image segmentation, classification, detection, and retrieval-related tasks also remains exemplary (Khan et al., 2020; Ullah et al., 2024).

Although CNNs are effective for image-related problems by considering spatial pattern, it is a challenge for these models to predict temporal fluctuation in environment data whether the data are ordered or not. To solve this problem, Bi-directional Long Short Term Memory (BiLSTM) (Aamir et al., 2022; Liu et al., 2024; Li & Bhatti, 2024; Peng et al., 2024; Chen et al., 2024; He & Bhatti, 2024; Cheng et al., 2024; Hasnain et al., 2024; Alhatami et al., 2024; Liu et al., 2025) networks are used since they work in both forward and backward directions, which gives a complete understanding of temporal dependencies.

2.1.2 Key CNN Architectures.

AlexNet, introduced by Krizhevsky marked a turning point in the ImageNet Large Scale Visual Recognition Challenge (ILSVRC) by achieving top results. It showcased the power of learning in image classification using a deep convolutional network, ReLU activations for non-linearity and dropout for regularization. With its advancements AlexNet greatly enhanced image classification precision and set new performance standards. (Krizhevsky et al., 2017).

2.1.3 VGG.

VGG stands for Visual Geometry Group. The modified network, which was created by Simonyan and Zisserman; it has a much more uniform structure than the AlexNet and employed small (3 x 3) convolutional filters and a large depth of the network. VGG made the model simple yet somewhat deeper which enhanced the classification accuracy and established the efficacy of deep convolutional network to extract fine features of the image (Simonyan & Zisserman, 2015).

2.1.4 ResNet.

Short for Residual Networks, was developed in 2015 to tackle the difficulty of training neural networks. It introduced the concept of connections that help gradients move smoothly through the layers. This breakthrough made it possible to train networks with numerous layers successfully achieving top notch performance in image classification and object detection tasks, in terms of both accuracy and efficiency (He et al., 2015; Haq et al., 2023).

Figure 4. Convolutional neural networks architectures

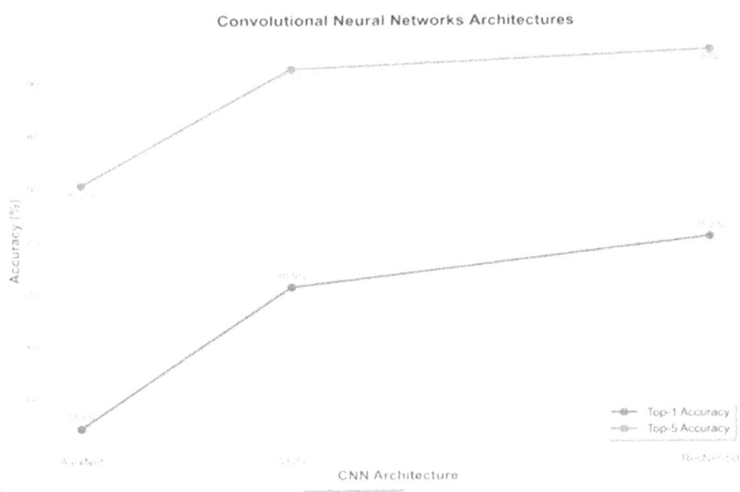

Figure 4. shows the evolution of top-1 and top-5 accuracies for some well-known CNN architectures, namely AlexNet, VGG, and ResNet-50 on the ImageNet dataset. AlexNet, developed in 2012, reached top-1 and top-5 accuracies of 57.1% and 80.2%, respectively. It showed a new benchmark in image classification with its deep architecture and GPU acceleration. VGG, which was proposed in 2013, further pushed the accuracy by utilizing more convolutional layers. It reached an accuracy of 70.5% top-1 and 91.2% top-5, but at a higher computational cost. The biggest revelation came with ResNet-50, proposed in the year 2015, which introduced residual connections, enabling networks to go deeper without causing any problem of vanished gradients, thus reaching a top-1 accuracy of 75.2% and top-5 accuracy of 93%. This is such a progression that underlines performance classification and efficiency, improvements driven by architectural innovations, and hence lays the foundation for subsequent breakthroughs in Deep Learning models.

2.1.5 CNN Impact on the Field.

The progression of CNN designs has significantly advanced image processing techniques. The remarkable performance of AlexNet showcased the capabilities of Deep Learning, solidifying CNNs as the benchmark for image recognition. VGG improved feature extraction through its well-structured architecture that boost precision across a range of tasks. ResNet revolutionized the network training that improve accuracy and resilience in handling complex image processing challenges. These CNN models have not only transformed the field but also sparked new ideas impact diverse domains such as self-driving cars and healthcare imaging (Ashraf et al., 2020) (Baloch et al., 2024).

2.2 Generative Adversarial Networks (GANs)

Generative Adversarial Networks which is introduced in 2014 shines new light on generative modelling. The GAN includes the generator and discriminator which are two neural networks. The generator produces fake images as the discriminator evaluates their authenticity. A generator to create more and more realistic images by yielding excellent outcomes which are so real that hardly anyone can distinguish from the true ones, as illustrated in the block diagram in Figure 5. GAN is extensively used for creating high-resolution image, improving quality of images and generating art & media content using Generative Adversarial Networks GANs They are used in more fields like the computer graphics, videogame etc. and transformed if we talk about that how they produce high-quality images (Goodfellow et al., 2014) (Hamza et al., 2023).

Figure 5. Generative Adversarial Networks (GANs) block diagram

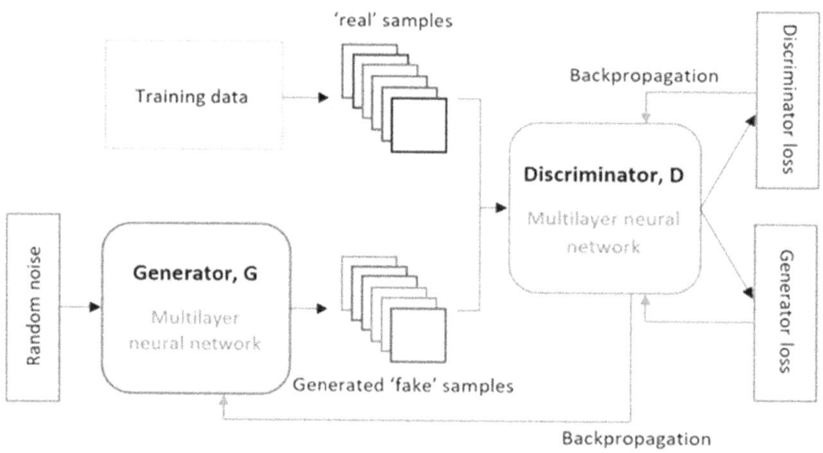

Note. The image is taken from the paper "Generative Adversarial Networks for Synthetic Data Generation: A Comparative Study," by Little et al., available at https://www.presidio.com/tec hnical-blog/exploring-the-power-of-generative-adversarial-networks-gans-with-azure/

The outstanding capacity for the generation of high-resolution and photorealistic images by GANs makes them find broad applications. In particular, they find extensive applications in image super-resolution, where GAN-based models like SRGAN have achieved up to a 50% higher increase in detail enhancement metrics than traditional methods do in this domain (Hürkal et al., 2020). Medical imaging or satellite image applications find SRGAN very useful, as these areas demand high levels of detail in the visual data analyzed. Various other applications of GANs are enhancing MRI and CT scan image enhancement in medical imaging to higher resolutions for better diagnosis, which may not be possible with traditional manners of imaging (Showrov et al., 2024). This study also demonstrated that the images improved diagnostic accuracy by around 15% also reducing false in early tumour detection.

Another, more important application of GANs has also found a working interest in enhancing and generating medical images to facilitate medical diagnosis early. They generate fake images for different stages of a disease; this helps train diagnostic models when real data is insufficient. For instance, GANs have been used in the generation of images of rare diseases, where researchers develop diagnostic tools for diseases that cannot be studied easily because of limited available samples. A 2024 study demonstrated that applying GAN-based data augmentation increased disease detection accuracy in diabetic retinopathy screening by up to 18% (Zhang et al., 2024).

Another GAN application is in privacy-preserving image synthesis. Clearly, GANs are useful for anonymizing patient data within medical institutions to provide information with which researchers can conduct their research and collaborate without breach of privacy. Such GANs have the potential to make a huge impact because the regulations on data sharing are getting tougher all over the world (Shah & Tembhurne, 2023).

2.3.1 GANs have enabled a variety of innovative applications

2.3.1.1 Image Synthesis. Generative Adversarial Networks (GANs) have become popular techniques to generate an image from different means of input such as random noise or hand sketches and text. Recently, techniques such as Deep Convolutional GAN (DCGAN) have improved in synthesising visual data from abstract representations to perceptually-real images (Kang et al., 2023).

2.3.1.2 Super-Resolution. Powered by models such as SRGAN, Generative Adversarial Networks (GANs) are employed to enhance image quality. When given low resolution images as input, these models generate high-resolution counterparts. This technique is more valuable for precision needy areas like medical imaging or satellite imagery (Ledig et al., 2016).

2.3.1.3 Style Transfer. GAN can be also be used to incorporate a style of one image into another keeping the content more or less intact similar in the models like CycleGAN. This is useful for style transfer tasks that also can be applied to photos or videos with artistic styles change (Zhu et al., 2017).

2.3 Autoencoders and Variational Autoencoders (VAEs)

Autoencoder is another type of the Neural Network that automatically encode the input into the latent space and then decode it back it to the original format. This is handy for tasks such as compression and denoising, which is represented in Figure 6, where it can be seen as the encoder and decoder are work together to reconstruct the data for the compressed representation. The VAEs can also efficiently learn to reduce reconstruction error. This idea is Variational Autoencoders (VAEs) which then add layer of probabilistic modeling. Unsupervised VAEs are trained to form a distribution over the latent space which allows better reconstruction and sampling from learned distributions (Hinton & Salakhutdinov, 2006).

Figure 6. Network architecture for an autoencoders

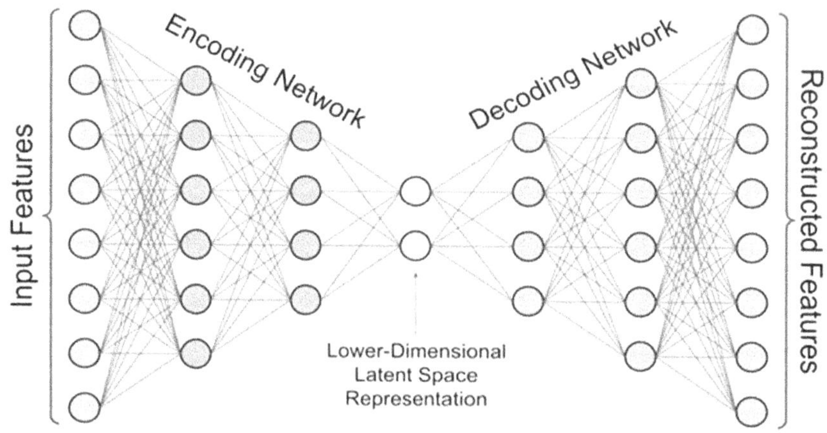

Note. The graph is taken from Assemblyai website. In which the author Ryan O'Connor written a comprehensive guide on "Introduction to Variational Autoencoders Using Keras" in 2023 (https://www.assemblyai.com/blog/introduction-to-variational-autoencoders-using-keras/)

Variational Autoencoders extend the basic ideas of auto-encoders with the addition of a probabilistic modeling layer. VAEs will learn to minimize reconstruction error alone in an efficient manner by building a probabilistic distribution over the latent space. This enables better reconstruction and sampling from learned distributions, which has been proved to be particularly helpful when generating new similar data points. The unsupervised VAE is trained to build a latent space distribution that manages both reconstructions and samplings. The most impressive performance of the approach has been in generating high-quality images from noise and learning meaningful representations for complex data. (Kingma & Welling, 2022)

Applications of VAEs are extended towards image synthesis, anomaly detection, and semi-supervised learning. In image synthesis, for instance, VAEs synthesize new images indistinguishable from real ones by sampling from the learned latent space. In anomaly detection, they find unusual patterns during the reconstruction of the images and compare the reconstruction error. In semi-supervised learning, VAEs make use of labeled and unlabeled data to enhance classification performance (Bergaminet al., 2022).

2.3.1 Applications in medical imaging and anomaly detection

2.3.1.1 Medical Imaging. In medical imaging, denoising and reconstruction are applied to a large extent through autoencoders and VAEs. For instance, the sharpness of MRI images is improved by removing noise from the scans by using autoencoders. VAEs synthesize diagnostic medical images with applications in diagnostic or surrogate image generation and augmentation of small datasets to make them suitable for training (Kaur & Dong, 2023)

2.3.1.2 Anomaly Detection. Autoencoders can also assist in detecting anomalies through the reconstruction of input data and quantification of the level of error that results. VAEs are probabilistic models that leverage variations in the data distribution and, therefore, give more sensitive anomaly detection. Such methods are used in industry monitoring to detect faults in machinery and irregularities in production processes (Angiulli, 2023) (Noor et al., 2023).

2.4 Transformers and Vision Transformers (ViTs)

2.4.1 Rise of Transformers in Image Processing:

Transformers originally designed for natural language processing, transformers have more recently been applied to image processing, mainly because of their effectiveness in handling long-range dependencies and capturing contextual relationships in the data. In contrast to CNNs, which process a local receptive field at a time on the image, transformers analyze global dependencies of the entire image by self-attention mechanisms. This endows transformers with the capability of modeling complex patterns and interactions, which open new possibilities for designing flexible and scalable approaches for image classification and object detection (Vaswani et al., 2017).

Transformers have worked well on image processing, performing well over state-of-the-art in more traditional CNN-based methods for which there is a need for global context and long-range dependencies. In fact, transformers had an accuracy as higher than CNNs in image classification tasks on large data sets, such as ImageNet, specifically with Model sizes and data increased correspondingly (Vishniakov, 2024). This ability to capture high-dimensional interaction spanning the entire image has led to its wide adoption-from applications as varied as medical image analysis and remote sensing to facial recognition and content generation. Along with growing advances, transformer-based architectures keep getting optimized for computational efficiency and have finally managed to address the initial apprehensions about their high memory and processing requirements (Kim et al., 2023).

Figure 7. The transformer model architecture

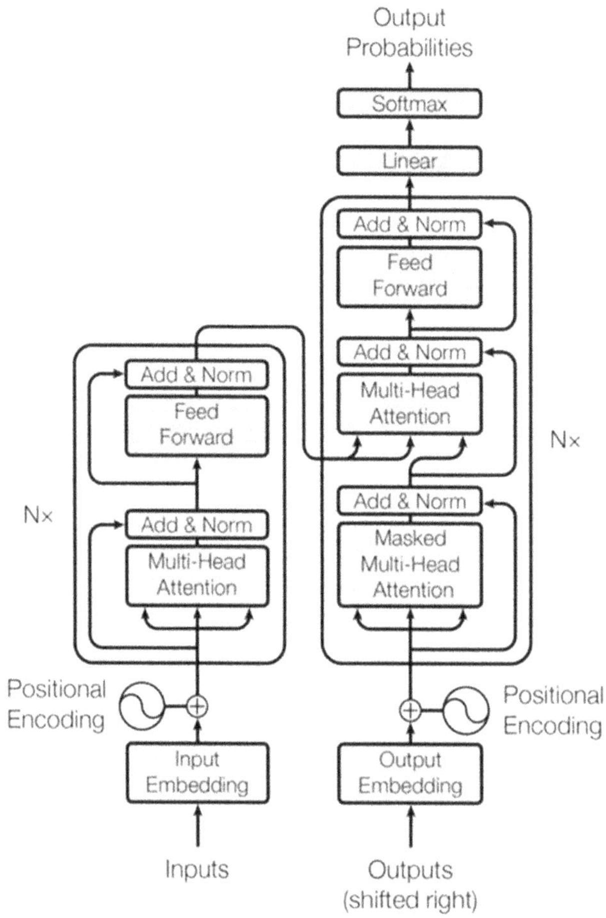

Note. The image is taken from 'Attention Is All You Need' by Vaswani et al. 2023 (https://doi.org/10.48550/arXiv.1706.03762)

The Transformer architecture performs the transformation from one sequence to another through two main components the left-hand encoder and the right-hand decoder. Note that both the encoder and decoder are made up of stackable modules. Nx in the Figure 7 representing that they can be repeated multiple times. A very large portion consists of Multihead Attention along with Feed Forward layers. Because direct processing of strings is not possible, the input and output sequences, i.e., target sentences, are first embedded into an n-dimensional space for effective processing.

2.4.2 Application of ViTs in Image Classification and Segmentation.

Vision Transformers (ViTs) apply transformer architectures directly to image data by dividing images into patches and treating the patches as sequences for processing. ViTs offer impressive performance on a variety of image classification tasks and capture strong, complex relationships among patches an asset in understanding high-dimensional visual content. As illustrated in Figure 8. In image segmentation, they help gather contextual information across larger areas of an image, leading to greater accuracy and precision in segmenting objects or regions (The Power of ViT, 2024).

Figure 8. Architecture of the Vision Transformer (ViT)

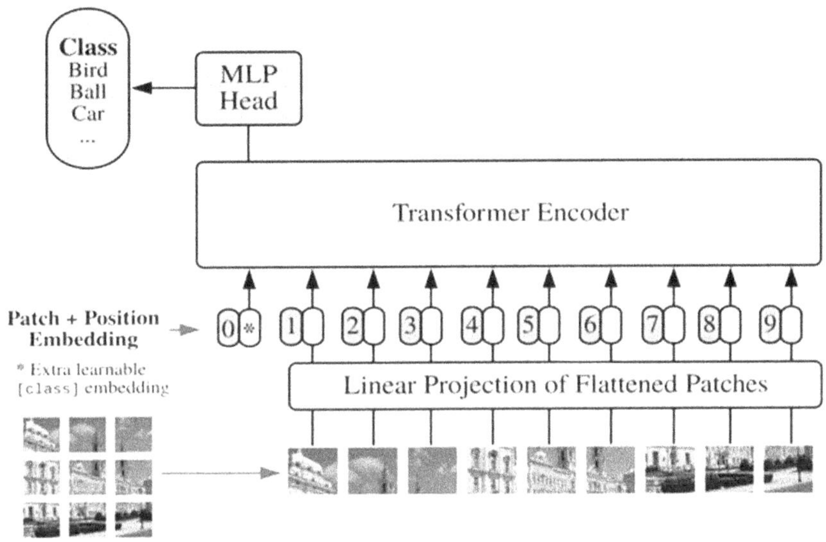

Note. The image is Taken from paper "An Image is Worth 16×16 Words: Transformers for Image Recognition at Scale," by Dosovitskiy et al. (https://arxiv.org/abs/2010.11929)

The most critical factor that allows the ViTs to achieve such good performance for image classification tasks is their ability to capture both local and global dependencies in an extremely robust manner. Treating every patch as a single token allows the model to learn nuanced relationships across an entire image in significant detail, unlike traditional CNNs, which have limited receptive fields. This has translated into better performance for ViTs in domains such as autonomous driving, in how ViTs contribute to the superior classification and detection of on-road elements, pedestrians, and vehicles. As noted in the 2022 study, in heavy-traffic settings, there is an object recognition improvement for the ViTs over CNN-based models (Islam, 2022).

2.5 Comparison of Deep Learning Architectures in Image Processing

The field of image processing received ground-breaking transformation from Deep Learning because developers built distinctive architectures to address multiple challenges. Each architecture exhibits unique capabilities and constraints which determine their optimal task. A comparison of the most popular deep learning architectures for image processing briefly discussed below.

2.5.1 Convolutional Neural Networks (CNNs)

- **Strengths**:

- **Hierarchical Feature Extraction**: CNNs demonstrate exceptional capability for performing automatic hierarchical feature discovery from images, which leads to their high success rates in object detection alongside classification and segmentation tasks.
- **Spatial Invariance**: CNNs don't care if an object is at position A or at position B, they can recognize the pattern, and this is something extremely useful for any task like facial recognition or medical imaging where patterns aren't always located in the same exact place in the image.
- **Proven Performance**: With AlexNet, VGG, ResNet, CNNs have achieved state of the art results on many image processing tasks including ImageNet classification.
- **Efficient for Local Patterns**: CNNs are particularly good at capturing local patterns (e.g., edges, textures) due to their convolutional filters.

- **Limitations**:
  - **Limited Global Context**: Capturing long-range dependencies in images proves to be difficult for CNNs since they work with local receptive fields at a time.
  - **High Computational Cost**: Deeper CNN architectures (e.g., ResNet) require significant computational resources and memory, making them less efficient for real-time applications on edge devices.
  - **Data Hungry**: CNNs typically require large amounts of labeled data for training, which can be a limitation in domains like medical imaging where labeled datasets are scarce.

2.5.2 Generative Adversarial Networks (GANs)

- **Strengths**:
  - **Image Synthesis**: GANs are unparalleled in generating high-quality, photorealistic images, making them ideal for tasks like image super-resolution, style transfer, and data augmentation.
  - **Unsupervised Learning**: GANs can learn to generate data without requiring labeled datasets, which is beneficial in scenarios where labeled data is limited.
  - **Versatility**: GANs have been successfully applied in diverse fields, including medical imaging (e.g., generating synthetic medical images) and entertainment (e.g., creating realistic animations).
- **Limitations**:
  - **Training Instability**: GANs are notoriously difficult to train due to the adversarial nature of the generator and discriminator, often leading to mode collapse or non-convergence.
  - **Computationally Intensive**: Training GANs requires significant computational resources, and generating high-resolution images can be slow.
  - **Ethical Concerns**: The ability of GANs to generate realistic fake images raises ethical concerns, such as deepfakes and misinformation.

2.5.3 Autoencoders and Variational Autoencoders (VAEs)

- **Strengths**:
  - **Dimensionality Reduction**: Autoencoders are highly effective for compressing data into a lower-dimensional latent space, making them useful for tasks like image denoising and compression.

- **Anomaly Detection**: VAEs, with their probabilistic modeling, are excellent for detecting anomalies in images by comparing reconstruction errors.
- **Data Generation**: VAEs can generate new data points by sampling from the learned latent space, which is useful for tasks like medical image synthesis.

- **Limitations**:
  - **Blurry Outputs**: VAEs often produce blurry or less sharp images compared to GANs, which limits their use in applications requiring high-resolution outputs.
  - **Complex Training**: VAEs require careful tuning of the probabilistic model, and training can be challenging due to the need to balance reconstruction accuracy and latent space regularization.

2.5.4 Transformers and Vision Transformers (ViTs)

- **Strengths**:
  - **Global Context**: Transformers excel at capturing long-range dependencies in images due to their self-attention mechanisms, making them highly effective for tasks requiring global context, such as image classification and segmentation.
  - **Scalability**: Vision Transformers (ViTs) have shown impressive performance on large-scale datasets like ImageNet, often outperforming CNNs in tasks requiring high-dimensional interactions.
  - **Flexibility**: Transformers can be easily adapted to various image processing tasks, including object detection, segmentation, and even generative tasks.
- **Limitations**:
  - **High Computational Cost**: Transformers require significant computational resources, especially for large images, due to their quadratic complexity with respect to input size.
  - **Data Hungry**: ViTs typically require large datasets for training, and their performance may degrade on smaller datasets compared to CNNs.
  - **Lack of Inductive Bias**: Unlike CNNs, which have built-in inductive biases for image data (e.g., translation invariance), Transformers rely entirely on learning from data, which can make them less efficient for small datasets.

Table 1. Summary of architectures

Architecture	Strengths	Limitations
CNNs	Hierarchical feature extraction, spatial invariance, proven performance	Limited global context, high computational cost, data hungry
GANs	High-quality image synthesis, unsupervised learning, versatility	Training instability, computationally intensive, ethical concerns
Autoencoders	Dimensionality reduction, anomaly detection, data generation	Blurry outputs, complex training
Transformers	Global context, scalability, flexibility	High computational cost, data hungry, lack of inductive bias

3. INNOVATIVE APPLICATIONS ACROSS DIVERSIFIED DOMAINS

3.1. Healthcare and Medical Imaging

Deep Learning has made significant strides in healthcare, particularly in medical imaging, where it plays a crucial role in disease detection, diagnosis, and treatment planning. Convolutional Neural Networks (CNNs) and Transformer-based models have proven to be highly effective in analyzing complex medical data, offering more accurate, faster, and scalable solutions. Deep Learning can also reduce medical errors and healthcare costs, improving access in resource-constrained environments to diagnostic facilities of high quality.

3.1.1 Disease Detection.

Deep Learning enables precise detection of diseases such as cancer, cardiovascular conditions, and neurological disorders. CNNs are widely used for classifying and segmenting tumors in MRI, CT, and PET scans, significantly improving diagnosis speed and accuracy (Feng et al., 2022; Noor et al., 2024; Bhatti et al., 2024). Transformers, with their ability to model long-range dependencies in images, are becoming powerful tools for interpreting complex medical data.

3.1.2 Cancer Detection.

Delivering unprecedented accuracy, a majority of cancer detection and classification (Nabeel, 2024) using CNN-based models is applied to early detection, especially in cases of breast, lung, and skin cancers. These models have hence become quite adept at analyzing different imaging modalities such as mammograms, MRI, and CT scans that detect minute patterns that may well elude detection by human radiologists (Gaona et al., 2021). For example, DenseNet models have reported high sensitivity for the detection of nodules in the lung, thus offering an opportunity for early intervention and improved patient prognosis. AI-enabled systems further assist in the screening process to detect colorectal cancer through automatic polyp detection during colonoscopy. This considerably improves the chances of early detection of malignancies. These Deep Learning applications can decrease false positives and offer consistent diagnosis support across variable levels of healthcare settings (Martinez et al., 2023).

3.1.3 Cardiovascular Detection.

Deep Learning has a very substantial role in changing the diagnosis and management of cardiovascular diseases by making real-time analysis of heart imaging possible. Extensive use of CNNs and RNNs is made during echocardiograms, coronary angiograms, and MRI scans to identify conditions such as heart failure, atherosclerosis, and arrhythmias (Madani, 2018). Examples are ResNet and U-Net architectures, which help to correctly segment and analyze coronary vessels, thus helping clinicians to identify vital blockages and plan treatment accordingly. AI models are also developed that can predict the possibility of an adverse cardiac event based on estimating some parameters, such as ejection fraction and heart rate variability in imaging data, essential for insight into the prognosis (Zhang, 2023).

3.1.4 Neuroimaging.

Deep Learning is employed for the detection of neurological disorders through neurological imaging: for example, detection of Alzheimer's, Parkinson's disease, and multiple sclerosis. Trained CNNs using brain MRI data can find abnormalities that are very critical in the early stages of such disorders, such as atrophy, white matter changes, and plaque formation. Transformer-based models, especially with their attention mechanisms, make the interpretability of longitudinal brain data better while studying the changes longitudinally to support monitoring the progression of a disease. These models enable differentiation between normal aging and subtle early signs of neurodegeneration, thus making them priceless in preventive care and personalized treatment planning (Zhang et al., 2020).

3.1.5 Diabetic Retinopathy Screening.

Deep Learning models are also finding applications in the automatic detection of diabetic retinopathy, one of the most common causes of blindness. The deep neural network-based tools used in the detection of DR have been developed for the analysis of retinal images by classification of disease stages and the identification of patients at risk, thus enabling early interventions that prevent vision loss. For example, Google's DeepMind has come up with a model that diagnoses Diabetic Retinopathy through the correct detection of micro aneurysms, haemorrhages, and other abnormalities in the retina. Such tools are distributed in resource-constrained setups where quality screening is limited since skilled ophthalmologists are few in number (Guefrachi et al., 2024).

3.1.6 Neurological Disorders.

Deep Learning techniques are also used in neurological imaging to detect early signs of conditions like Alzheimer's, Parkinson's, and multiple sclerosis. These models analyze brain MRIs to detect changes in brain tissue or plaque formation, often identifying abnormalities that may be missed by the human eye (Noor et al., 2020).

3.1.7. Detection of Pulmonary Diseases.

Application of Deep Learning in respiratory condition diagnosis, accelerated by the COVID-19 pandemic, includes COVID-19, pneumonia, and chronic obstructive pulmonary disease (COPD). Chest X-rays and CT scans have undergone training by CNN, such as ResNet and Inception, in the detection and classification of lung infection for the rapid diagnosis and isolation of the infected. These tools remain very important in the current management of pulmonary diseases, offering fast, reliable insights to support clinicians through outbreaks and routine respiratory disease management (Abdulahi et al., 2024).

3.2 Medical Image Segmentation

The process of segmenting medical images is described as the basic activity in medical imaging, allowing clinicians to delineate, quantify, and monitor various abnormal and normal pathological regions and anatomical structures. It includes the identification of different procedures involved in the extraction of the ROI from such complex medical scans, including tumors, lesions, organs, and tissues.

Deep Learning models, particularly U-Net, ResNet, and Transformer-based architectures, have greatly improved the accuracy and speed of segmentation by providing pixel-level segmentation and delineation of critical structures within medical images with higher precision. Important improvements using Deep Learning approaches in the segmentation of medical images are outlined below

3.2.1 U-Net and Its Success in Medical Image Segmentation.

With its unique architecture design, the U-Net has had extensive applications in the field of medical image segmentation, such as brain tumor segmentation, liver lesion identification, and lung nodule detection. U-Net has a U-shaped architecture with symmetric encoder and decoder parts. At every step of downsampling, the encoder uses two 3 × 3 convolutions followed by ReLU and 2 × 2 max pooling to double feature channels. Upsampling, then a 2 × 2 transposed convolutions to halve the feature channels, concatenation with the encoder's corresponding feature map, then two 3 × 3 convolutions with ReLU comprise every step in the decoder. In general, there are 23 convolutional layers in U-Net. The encoder and decoder parts are linked by skip connections with the purpose of preserving high-level input information. That means that this architecture will allow U-Net to generate a detailed high-resolution segmentation map, which is typically desired in biomedical image segmentation tasks. U-Net architecture is illustrated in Figure 9. U-Net finds broad applications in the analysis of brain MRI for tumor isolation, showing a great deal of potential for precision in boundary identification and increasing the accuracy of diagnosis. Besides, this flexibility has also allowed variants such as the 3D U-Net, further extending these techniques to three-dimensional imaging data, volumetric segmentation, and hence CT scans for tasks such as lung and liver segmentation. Also, the success of U-Net has stimulated the creation of hybrid architectures which include U-Net with attention mechanisms that improve the segmentation accuracy on images with complex textures and noise (Ronneberger et al., 2015).

Figure 9. U-Net architecture

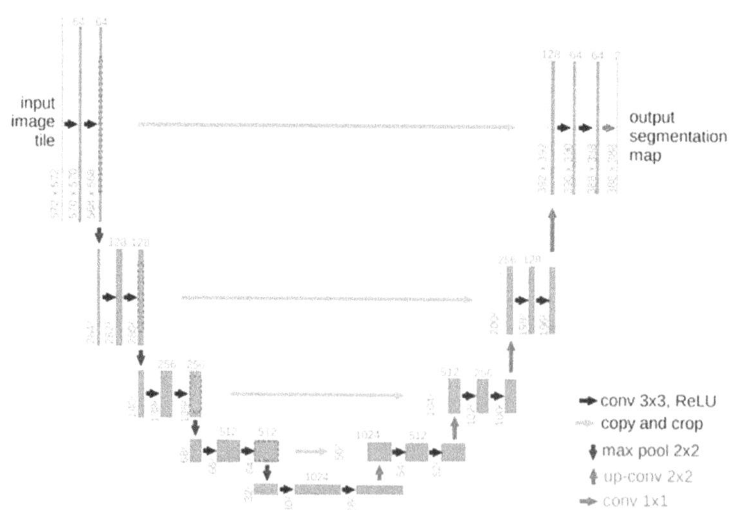

Note. The image is Taken from paper "U-Net: Convolutional Networks for Biomedical Image Segmentation," by Ronneberger et al. (https://doi.org/10.1007/978-3-319-24574-4_28)

3.2.2 ResNet and Transfer Learning in Medical Segmentation.

Another very popular architecture is ResNet, where the problem of training very deep networks is solved by residual connections that avoid the vanishing gradient problem. Although it is designed for classification tasks, ResNet has proved to be very useful in medical image segmentation, especially when combined together with U-Net in architectures such as ResUNet (Shamshad et al., 2024). This way, the network can leverage the residual connections power of ResNet while keeping all the segmentation capabilities of U-Net (Kim et al., 2022). The latest works reported the remarkable performance of ResUNet applied to the segmentation of retinal images for diabetic retinopathy screening, which had a great impact on increasing the precision of vessel segmentation (Lin et al., 2023). This approach has been taken further with the application of ResNet in medical segmentations, where the pre-trained models are being fine-tuned on relatively smaller medical datasets. This enables researchers to take advantage of huge datasets, such as ImageNet, and apply relevant information to domain-specific tasks, thereby increasing segmentation results without the need or large labelled medical datasets. Transfer learning with ResNet has been proven to yield high accuracies on segmenting tough tasks, identifying the boundary of breast cancer tumors in mammography, proving flexibility in a wide array of medical imaging modalities.

3.2.3 Multi-modal Segmentation for Enhanced Diagnostic Accuracy.

Multimodal medical image segmentation includes information from many imaging modalities, such as MRI, PET, and CT scans, to provide an integrated view about the patient's condition. This will improve the accuracy by including information from complementary scans that will enable Deep Learning models to recognize and delineate structures more precisely, which may not be as visible on one modality. Such is the case in oncology, where multi-modal segmentation can successfully fuse the PET and MRI scans by using the metabolic information drawn from PET with the detailed anatomic structure information from MRI for cancerous lesion detection (Xue et al., 2024). Another great application involves neurological disorders where multi-modality segmentation combines structural MRI with functional images from PET to allow for better localization of abnormalities, such as amyloid plaques in patients with Alzheimer's disease. The multi-modal-designed Deep Learning models, such as the MultiResUNet, have thus been pretty successful in achieving precisions of segmentation to assist clinicians during diagnosis and treatment planning. Inclusion of multi-modal data enhances robustness in segmentations, hence offering clinical reliable performance for varying demographics and disease conditions of patients (Ibtehaz & Rahman, 2020).

3.2.4 Federated Learning and Privacy-preserving Segmentation.

In healthcare, privacy concerns drive federated learning forward to enable training Deep Learning models across decentralized data but in a manner that need not involve direct data sharing. Examples include medical image segmentation, where federated learning provides a platform for hospitals and research institutions to work together in developing robust segmentation models while improving patient confidentiality. This has shown promise in applications such as the segmentation of brain tumors, for which a variety of datasets from different institutions optimize model generalization with no sacrifices to maintaining data privacy. The proposed U-Net and Transformer model-based federated learning frameworks have demonstrated the capability to execute effective segmentations of complex structures in a distributed data environment, hence offering scalability and privacy preservation in medical imaging. Federated learning also minimizes legal and ethical issues since data centralization is avoided; therefore, advantages driven by AI are allowed in various jurisdictions around the globe for the benefit of healthcare improvement (Glicksberg et al., 2021).

3.3. Real-world Applications

Deep Learning now transforms medical healthcare, automating diagnoses, informing clinical decisions, and plugging gaps in resource-poor settings. These range from the detection of tumors and diabetic retinopathy to analyses of lung diseases and COVID-19, each representing an important step toward the realization of more accessible, precise, and scalable health care.

3.3.1 Automated Tumor Detection.

The detection of cancers whether of the breast, lungs, or brain is fully automated by Deep Learning models. Convolutional Neural Networks have been instrumental in highlighting early-stage tumors with subtle anomalies that may go unnoticed in regular, manual checks; hence, they may constitute a reliable second opinion for radiologists to help shorten diagnostic time. Recent studies have, on the other hand, demonstrated that such models can achieve an accuracy near that of radiologists by improving both the sensitivity and specificity of cancer detection. For instance, AI-assisted mammography tools may find minute calcifications associated with the early phase of cancer in breast cancer detection, thus allowing timely interventions (Rajpurkar et al., 2018).

Moreover, AlphaFold from DeepMind revolutionized so-called protein structure prediction, which is highly important in oncology to understand tumor behavior, progression, and response to therapies. Accurate prediction of protein folding by this tool opened a new horizon in cancer biology and accelerated the process of discovering new targets for therapy. This application is considered one of the big leaps in precision oncology because it does indeed help clinicians and researchers deepen their knowledge of molecular mechanisms underlying tumorigenesis and broaden the possibilities for personalized treatment options (Jumper et al., 2021).

3.2.2 Diabetic Retinopathy.

Deep Learning is bringing about early detection in ophthalmology for diabetic retinopathy a leading cause of blindness. AI-based screening systems, such as those developed by Google's Diabetic Retinopathy Screening Model, extract information from the images of the retinal fundus using deep CNNs and have been posting high sensitivity and specificity rates. This has lessened the burden on the ophthalmologists, especially in regions that have limited access to specialized care, thus allowing early and wider screening (Skouta et al., 2023). Such systems for retinopathy screening have also been implemented in low-resource and rural areas where access to ophthalmologic care is severely restricted. These technologies essentially allow for automated detection of DR, avoiding complications during the late stage among diabetic patients. The overall costs incurred for health care are therefore reduced, with improved quality of life. Evidence suggests that such automated systems for eye health screening will play a crucial role in managing population health by enabling large-scale efficient eye health monitoring if applied (Cleland et al., 2023).

3.2.3 Lung Disease and COVID-19 Detection.

The COVID-19 pandemic has flexed the muscles of Deep Learning toward emergent health crises. Models developed for the analysis of chest X-rays and computed tomography scans were rapidly repurposed toward the detection of COVID-19 pneumonia, attaining high diagnostic accuracy and informing healthcare professionals in settings of strained resources. Such characteristic lung patterns with ground-glass opacities and consolidations, representative of COVID-19, have been identified by CNN-based tools to help triage critical patients when medical resources were strained. (Shi et al., 2021) (Nurajahan et al., 2024). Beyond COVID-19, Deep Learning has become indispensable in diagnosing and managing other lung diseases, including pneumonia, tuberculosis, and chronic obstructive pulmonary disease (COPD). These models help predict disease severity, inform patient management decisions, and support ventilator allocation in intensive care units. For instance, Deep Learning algorithms have been trained to assess the likelihood of severe outcomes based on initial imaging and laboratory findings, providing valuable triage support in emergency settings (Wang et al., 2020).

3.4 The Impact of Deep Learning Across Diverse Domains

Deep Learning has had a transformative impact on healthcare and medical imaging, revolutionizing the way diseases are detected, diagnosed, and managed. Its ability to analyze complex medical data with precision has enabled earlier detection of life-threatening conditions, such as cancer and cardiovascular diseases, improving patient outcomes significantly. For instance, Deep Learning models like CNNs have been instrumental in identifying subtle abnormalities in mammograms, CT scans, and MRI images that often go unnoticed by human radiologists. The automation of diagnostic processes has not only reduced human error but also improved efficiency, especially in resource-constrained settings where access to specialized care is limited. During the COVID-19 pandemic, these technologies played a pivotal role in rapidly diagnosing and managing the disease through the analysis of chest X-rays and CT scans. Moreover, Deep Learning has facilitated cost-effective healthcare delivery by optimizing resources and enabling large-scale screening programs, such as diabetic retinopathy detection, without compromising quality.

In the realm of autonomous vehicles, Deep Learning technologies have significantly enhanced road safety, efficiency, and the overall transportation experience. By reducing reliance on human drivers, who are responsible for 94% of road accidents, autonomous systems powered by Deep Learning have minimized the risk of collisions. Advanced Driver Assistance Systems (ADAS) equipped with features like real-time object detection, lane tracking, and collision avoidance have made driving safer and more reliable. These technologies allow vehicles to process environmental data in real time, enabling quick decision-making to navigate complex road scenarios. Furthermore, Deep Learning has contributed to sustainable transportation by optimizing traffic flow, reducing congestion, and improving fuel efficiency. As the backbone of autonomous vehicles, Deep Learning continues to push the boundaries of innovation, laying the foundation for a safer, smarter, and more sustainable transportation future.

3.5 Safety and Surveillance

Deep Learning integrated into safety and surveillance systems has significantly impacted monitoring and threat detection. As the demand for security grows in both the public and private sectors, AI-based solutions have improved to ensure safety is always available. In the public sector, threats are more widespread, while the private sector, despite trading activities, still faces insecurities that could lead to harm.

3.5.1 Facial Recognition and Intrusion Detection.

FaceNet (Schroff et al., 2015) and VGGFace (Coa et al., 2018), two prominent Deep Learning models in facial recognition, excel at real-time identification of individuals across large datasets with unprecedented precision. These systems are widely utilized in public security, corporate settings, airports, and by law enforcement, where accurate identification is crucial. Specifically, FaceNet uses triplet loss to create an embedding space that enhances the ability to match or verify faces, even when facing challenges like variations in pose, lighting, occlusion, or aging.

3.5.2 Intrusion Detection.

In addition to the facial recognition the CNN-based models have greatly enhanced intrusion detection in restricted areas (Tareen et al., 2022). The AI powered systems analyse real time surveillance as well as identifying behaviors such as unauthorized entry, suspicious movements, or loitering. These models are trained on large datasets of normal and abnormal behaviours that enable them to detect anomalies and flag potential threats in real time (Mohammadpour et al., 2022).

3.5.3 Anomaly Detection in Surveillance Videos.

Surveillance anomaly detection enhances CCTV footage by making it smarter for predictive threat protection. Autoencoders, alongside Generative Adversarial Networks (GANs), are particularly effective at generating new data points. These models excel at recognizing 'normal' patterns in video data such as pedestrian movements, traffic flow, and human activities enabling them to trigger alerts when deviations suggest potential security risks (Senapati et al., 2024).

3.5.4 GAN-based Detection.

By generating synthetic data, GANs enhance the training process for anomaly detection systems, particularly in surveillance scenarios where rare events, like accidents or thefts, occur and labelled datasets are hard to obtain. These models simulate abnormal activities, improving the detection capabilities of surveillance systems (Fu et al., 2023).

3.5.5 Edge AI for Real-time Surveillance.

Real time anomaly detection had scalability limitations but with the rise of Edge Artificial intelligence. This is becoming more and more feasible. This Edge AI enables Deep Learning models to run on edge devices the examples are security cameras as well as reducing latency and bandwidth by processing data locally (Tsakanikas et al., 2024). These innovations have made surveillance systems much faster and more responsive particularly for monitoring large areas like airports or major events.

3.6 Environmental Monitoring and Agriculture

In practice, Deep Learning has made great contributions not only to the field of environmental conservation but also to agriculture, dealing with challenges such as climate change, loss of biodiversity, and sustainable farming. These innovations will assist scientists, policymakers, and farmers in making data-driven decisions toward environmental monitoring and precision agriculture.

3.6.1 Remote Sensing for Environmental Monitoring.

A key application area of Deep Learning in environmental monitoring is remote sensing through satellite imagery. Most widely, CNNs apply to the analysis of satellite data to drive into insights at a granular level that allows tracking such phenomena as deforestation, urban expansion, and assessment of natural disasters. In this way, Deep Learning models process multispectral and temporal data to give near-real-time information that can help governments and organizations make informed decisions regarding policy for the environment (Hameed et al., 2022) (Hameed et al., 2022a).

3.6.1.1 Deforestation and Land Use Monitoring. Convolutional neural networks trained on satellite images have achieved high accuracies in monitoring deforestation activities within important regions such as the Amazon Rainforest. These models do the distinction between classes for land use, which has helped to enforce illegal logging and land conversion activities (Jameil et al., 2024). Advanced models are also used to predict changes in land use with time, thus providing early warning for environmentally sensitive areas (Jelas et al., 2024).

3.6.1.2 Disaster Management. From a natural disaster management viewpoint, Deep Learning models can be applied to analyze satellite data and assess the impact of events like floods, earthquakes, and forest fires. These systems generate heat maps, show which areas have been affected, and help in planning the response (Jia & Ye, 2023).

3.6.2 Precision Agriculture and Crop Health Monitoring.

Significance of Deep Learning in precision agriculture is found through the effective usage of the described tools by the farmers for real-time monitoring of crop health and taking appropriate adjustments of irrigation, fertilizers, pest control, and other measures of mitigation

3.6.2.1 Crop Disease Detection. Deep Learning models, particularly CNNs, can be applied to analyze aerial images obtained with the help of drones or IoT sensors. These models may even detect early signals for crop diseases, pests, or nutrient deficiencies in the body of the plant. That's going to enable a farmer to take steps much sooner, meaning far less loss in crops and infinitely better sustainability (Shahi et al., 2023).

3.6.2.2 Irrigation Optimization. AI systems with Deep Learning and sensor information integrated make it possible to predict the needs for irrigation with variables like soil moisture, weather, and growth stages. Such systems will reduce wastage of water while ensuring crops take up the right amounts of water, making this yet another sustainable agricultural practice.

3.6.3 Innovative Projects in Environmental Conservation.

These new developments in integrating Deep Learning into environmental conservation allow researchers and organizations to take on complex challenges through the analysis and interpretation of large-scale environmental data. With intensive image processing and predictability capabilities, projects related to ecological sustainability and resource management are proving instrumental. Following are some of the key areas where Deep Learning is playing a transformative role:

3.6.3.1 Climate Change Mitigation. Deep Learning models are of great value in climate research and policy formulation, primarily through climate simulations interpreting large volumes of historical climate data. The models enhance the accuracy on predictions of temperature shifts, sea-level rise, and changes in weather patterns, while supporting decision-makers to pursue robust adaptation and mitigation strategies. Model-based data insights coming from CNNs and RNNs are being used, for example, to produce localized climate projections, enabling better disaster risk reduction and urban planning by local entities. Deep Learning-based simulation studies have been shown to outcompete conventional approaches in terms of accuracy and speed, which is so crucial in view of rapid climate change responses and resilient infrastructure design (Deep& Verma, 2024).

3.6.3.2 Species Monitoring and Biodiversity. Real-time trained Deep Learning models, YOLO and Faster R-CNN, are developed with wildlife imagery datasets that accelerate species identification irrespective of habitats or harsh climate. These systems make use of satellite and drone imaging and image recognition to attempt to enumerate wildlife. Notably, in Deep Learning, it has been widely used in a case of preventing the illegal wildlife trade and the administration of conservancy regions by monitoring the movements and numbers of endangered (Ma et al., 2024). Current advanced technology like Google's Wildlife Insights now come in handy in that they help identify animals and surveyors by analyzing the images that the camera traps capture, which is less time consuming than doing it manually (Wildlife Insights, 2024).

3.6.3.3 AI for Sustainable Fisheries: In marine environments, Deep Learning is being used to monitor fish populations and trace illegal fishing activities. These tools contribute to the gathering of very useful data on the sustainable management of fisheries by providing accurate information on fish stocks, hence averting overfishing. This technology involves the use of cameras installed under water and remote sensing data that assist in the collection of accurate data on fish species and population, areas to be avoided due to over fishing and marine threatened species. Applications like FishFace and FishNet involves real-time identification of fish species and their sizes through effectiveness of computer vision algorithms and this aids the regulation agencies in the timely exercise of regulation (Khan et al., 2023). Further, the Deep Learning-based image recognition can identify the cases of unlawful fishing activities on the basis of shapes and movements of vessels and also identify prohibited techniques of fishing which helps in protecting marine species (Bai et al., 2024).

4 CHALLENGES AND ETHICAL CONSIDERATIONS

The use of Deep Learning in image processing brings numerous advancements; however, it also poses significant challenges and ethical considerations. These challenges center around data privacy, bias and fairness in model development, computational complexity, and environmental impact.

4.1 Data Privacy and Security

Privacy is greatly at stake, more so in the domain of image processing, with unbounded applications of personal or sensitive data, such as medical imaging or facial recognition in surveillance systems. It pertains to a major portion of visual information regarding the treatment, storage, and analysis of such massive data, yet improper handling brings massive violations of privacy.

4.1.1 Privacy Risks in Image Processing:

One major concern is the potential misuse of personal images, particularly in fields like healthcare, where medical images are highly sensitive. The rise of AI in healthcare, especially in diagnostic imaging, has led to increased concerns about patient confidentiality. A 2023 study revealed that over 725 large security breached in healthcare and also revealed that over 373788 record breached daily and have experienced data breaches involving medical images, often leading to identity theft or unauthorized data access (Alder, 2024)

4.1.2 Strategies to Mitigate Privacy Risks:

To address these issues, several strategies have been proposed. Privacy-preserving AI techniques such as federated learning allow models to be trained on decentralized data without transferring sensitive information to a central server, reducing the risk of data breaches (Khalid et al., 2023) (Yang et al., 2023). In federated learning, data stays on the device, and only model updates are shared, ensuring that sensitive visual data (e.g., patient images) remains protected. Another approach is differential privacy, which adds noise to the data, preventing individuals from being easily re-identified from their image datasets. These strategies can minimize the risk of data exposure, but they also raise questions about the trade-offs between privacy and model accuracy (*Differential privacy, 2024*).

4.2. Bias and Fairness in Deep Learning Models

Bias in Deep Learning models is one of the most pressing ethical issues in image processing. These models often reflect and exacerbate societal biases due to the underrepresentation of certain groups in training data, leading to unequal outcomes for different demographic groups.

4.2.1 Bias in Image Processing Models.

Deep Learning models used for tasks like facial recognition or medical diagnosis have been shown to exhibit biases against minorities and underrepresented groups. For example, facial recognition systems are more likely to misidentify people of color due to a lack of diversity in the training datasets. A 2018 study conducted by MIT and Stanford University found that commercial facial recognition systems had error rates of up to 34% for dark-skinned women, compared to less than 1% for light-skinned men (MIT, 2018). In healthcare, medical imaging models trained predominantly on data from Western populations may perform poorly on patients from other regions or ethnicities.

4.2.2 Fairness and Mitigation Strategies.

Ensuring fairness in image processing models involves addressing the biases present in training data. Techniques like algorithmic fairness aim to reduce the disparities by ensuring that model performance is consistent across different demographic groups. One approach is rebalancing datasets, where underrepresented groups are oversampled during training, making the model less prone to bias. Explainable AI (XAI) is another critical tool in promoting fairness. By making the decision-making process of models more transparent, XAI enables researchers to detect biases in model predictions and take corrective actions (Minh et al., 2024; Noor et al., 2024; Haider et al., 2024; Ullah et al., 2024; Nabeel et al., 2024).

4.3 Computational Complexity and Energy Consumption

Deep Learning models, particularly in image processing, are known for their computational intensity. Training large models, such as convolutional neural networks (CNNs) or generative adversarial networks (GANs), requires massive amounts of computational power, which directly translates into higher energy consumption and environmental impact.

4.3.1 Computational Requirements of Image Processing Models.

The complexity of image processing tasks like object detection, segmentation, and style transfer demands substantial computational resources. State-of-the-art models, such as ResNet or EfficientNet, require vast datasets and high-performance hardware, such as GPUs or TPUs, to achieve optimal performance. As the models grow more complex, the number of parameters can increase exponentially. For instance, GPT-3, a large language model often used in image processing tasks like text-to-image synthesis, has 175 billion parameters, demanding immense computational infrastructure (OpenAI, 2024).

4.3.2 Energy Consumption and Environmental Impact.

The environmental footprint of training Deep Learning models is considerable. A 2019 study from the University of Massachusetts Amherst found that training a large NLP model produced more than 626,000 pounds of CO_2 emissions, equivalent to the lifetime emissions of five cars. This environmental cost raises concerns about the sustainability of Deep Learning (MIT NEWS, 2024).

4.3.3 Efficient Solutions to Reduce Energy Consumption.

To mitigate these concerns, researchers are exploring various strategies to make Deep Learning models more energy-efficient. Model compression techniques, such as pruning and quantization, reduce the number of parameters and computations needed during inference, thereby lowering energy requirements without significantly compromising accuracy. Distillation methods, where a smaller model learns from a larger pre-trained model, are also becoming popular for reducing computational costs. Furthermore, advances in hardware optimization, such as the development of specialized AI chips (e.g., Google's TPU and NVIDIA's A100), are making Deep Learning more efficient by optimizing energy consumption.

5. FUTURE DIRECTIONS AND EMERGING TRENDS

The future of Deep Learning in image processing is very promising, with the further development of explainable AI, its integration with complementary technologies, and the democratization of the tools themselves within the user base constantly growing. Such emerging trends will not only make image processing systems more effective but also more diffused across different industries and individuals.

5.1. Explainable AI and Interpretability

More and more transparency and interpretability are demanded in line with the ever-growing complexity and deployment of Deep Learning models. These deep neural networks exhibit opaque decision-making processes due to their complex topologies and thousands of parameters; hence they are at times also referred to as 'black boxes.' That said, lack of transparency is one major stumbling block, especially for crucial areas like healthcare and autonomous systems, where it is imperative that one knows the rationale behind a model's decision.

5.1.1 The Need for Explainability.

Deep Learning for medical imaging could identify a tumor in an image, but if the decision that led to this conclusion cannot be interpreted by the healthcare provider, it complicates their work, takes the trust away, and finally puts barriers to clinical adoption. The main goal of XAI is to design techniques in such a manner that it allows for users to comprehend and interpret model predictions.

5.1.2 Techniques for Improving Interpretability.

Deep Learning models utilize numerous techniques for enhancing model interpretability. Among the image processing techniques are saliency maps and heat maps, which are used to unveil which part of an image the model pays the most attention to when making a prediction. Another promising approach is Layer-wise Relevance Propagation, which decomposes the decision made by the network to identify those pixels in the input image that contributed the most to the final output. Such techniques bear immense importance and significance for critical applications where the principles of trust and transparency are sacrosanct. Furthermore, it is possible to understand model decisions with a wide range of neural networks by the use of Explainable Boosting Machines (EBMs) and Local Interpretable Model-Agnostic Explanations (LIME).

5.2 Integration with Other Technologies

There will be more thorough integration with other rapidly developing technologies, and image processing can be very powerful, efficient, and real-time in nature. Considering the future of technology, prospects are especially transformative, as it is the marriage between Deep Learning and the Internet of Things alongside edge computing and the power of 5G networks that bring new ways of processing and analyzing images at top-notch speeds.

5.2.1 Deep Learning and IoT/Edge Computing.

With the explosion of IoT devices, from security cameras to smart medical devices, the enormous amount of image data now needs to be processed in real time. Up to now, this kind of data was taken to centralized cloud servers for analysis, causing latency and bandwidth problems. Most image processing tasks can be done at the edge, thereby reducing the need to transfer large amounts of data across a network. It is important to take note that for applications such as autonomous vehicles and industry monitoring, immediate decision-making is involved. This could also be coupled with the use of 5G technology, giving ultra-low latency and great speed in delivering data, thus creating a very strong ecosystem for real-time image processing.

5.2.2 Quantum Computing and Neuromorphic Computing Synergies.

Not stopping only at IoT and 5G, quantum and neuromorphic computing are also likely to define the future of image processing. While quantum computing, through the use of quantum bits (qubits), can handle such complex and sometimes unrealistic calculations exponentially faster than classical computers, neuromorphic computing is a bio-inspired way of processing that imitates the architecture of the brain. In the aggregate, it is these technologies which may redefine the speed and efficiency of the given tasks. It will surely lead to some new applications which are now impossible because of the computation load.

5.3 Democratizing Deep Learning Tools

Such democratization tendencies of Deep Learning tools decrease entry barriers and make it easier for even non experts to use and develop Deep Learning models in image processing. This, in turn, will create a situation for much more innovation, with the ability to take advantage of AI being opened up to many more people and organizations not staffed by deep technical experts.

5.3.1 Accessibility of Deep Learning Frameworks.

Over the last years, there has been a push to make it easier to use and more accessible. Deep Learning frameworks such as TensorFlow, PyTorch, and Keras have largely democratized the development and deployment of Deep Learning models by offering friendly APIs and pre-trained models. This is especially great for the field of image processing; developers will now be able to easily apply powerful models, like ResNet or EfficientNet, to a wide set of tasks without developing these models from scratch.

5.3.2 Wider Adoption and Innovation.

The trend to make these tools more accessible also drives wider adoption across various industries. An example in agriculture: Smallholder farmers now can use AI image processing tools on simple smartphone applications to monitor crop health. In education, students are able to delve into Deep Learning applications, which before required large computer power and expertise in application to image processing. Big shots of innovation are being democratized with novel applications developed by people and organizations that were outside of the AI revolution. AutoML tools further expedite this trend, and only with the selecting of appropriate Deep Learning models and hyper parameters can development be much easier for non-experts to yield highly accurate models.

6. CONCLUSION

6.1 Summary of Key Insights

The following chapter delves into the modern applications of Deep Learning in image processing, demonstrating the strides that this technology has made in transforming many industries. Key insights include the immense impact of Deep Learning models, with CNNs leading the game toward tasks such as medical imaging, autonomous vehicles, entertainment, safety and surveillance, and environmental monitoring. These applications illustrate that image processing from traditional methods to highly accurate, automated, and intelligent systems has been strongly empowered by Deep Learning.

We also looked at a few serious challenges that these technologies are facing: data privacy and security, biases in the prediction and model-rendering results, computational load, and energy consumption environmental impact. These challenges need technical innovation, as well as considerations of ethics and regulatory oversight. Upcoming trends like XAI, large-scale integration with technologies like IoT and 5G, as well as the democratization of Deep Learning tools, bring in the possibility of potential solutions that, in turn, lead to completely new areas for further research and innovation.

6.2 Final Thoughts on the Future of Image Processing

In the near future, Deep Learning will be more pervasive for image processing as hardware and software technologies advance. Explainable AI will play a huge role in fostering trust in Deep Learning systems where it is applied, in particular, in high-stakes industries like healthcare and autonomous transportation. Deep Learning integrated into edge computing, quantum computing, and neuromorphic systems will make such efficiencies and speeds possible for real-time image processing at a global scale.

The democratization of Deep Learning frameworks has also increased the speed of innovation. Making tools more accessible means that there will naturally be a surge in new applications developed, whether by other individuals or institutions. This emerging ecosystem may very well serve as the springboard for further growth in the field because, with AI democratization, much more can be accomplished by non-experts and the majority of small enterprises.

The future of image processing is certainly bright, but it will also bear a great burden of responsibility to ensure that this bright future is fair, transparent, and sustainable. This calls for further research on how best to reduce biases, improve computational efficiency, and protect data privacy. Through this effort, it seems that Deep Learning will revolutionize not only image processing but also most of the rest of human society and technology. The next round of innovation is likely to be more inclusive, more impactful, and more responsible in bringing the field toward a future of widespread acceptance and indeed fundamentally transformational change.

REFERENCES

https://www.alliedmarketresearch.com, A. M. R. (n.d.). *Video Surveillance Market Size Growth Analysis Report 2032*. Allied Market Research. Retrieved 5 September 2024, from https://www.alliedmarketresearch.com/Video-Surveillance-market

Aamir, M., Bhatti, M. A., Bazai, S. U., Marjan, S., Mirza, A. M., Wahid, A., Hasnain, A., & Bhatti, U. A. (2022). Predicting the environmental change of carbon emission patterns in South Asia: A Deep Learning approach using BiLSTM. *Atmosphere (Basel)*, 13(12), 2011. DOI: 10.3390/atmos13122011

Aamir, M., Gao, J., Zhang, Y., Tang, H., & Bhatti, U. A. (2025). Overview of underwater object detection based on image processing techniques. *Proceedings of the 2024 7th International Conference on Pattern Recognition and Artificial Intelligence.*

Abdulahi, A. T., Ogundokun, R. O., Adenike, A. R., Shah, M. A., & Ahmed, Y. K. (2024). PulmoNet: A novel Deep Learning based pulmonary diseases detection model. *BMC Medical Imaging*, 24(1), 51. DOI: 10.1186/s12880-024-01227-2 PMID: 38418987

Akram, S., Bazai, S. U., & Marjan, S. (2024). Classifying Traffic Signs Using Convolutional Neural Networks Based on Deep Learning Models. In Deep Learning for Multimedia Processing Applications (pp. 250-269). CRC Press.

Alder, S. (2024, January 31). Security Breaches in Healthcare in 2023. *The HIPAA Journal*. https://www.hipaajournal.com/security-breaches-in-healthcare/

Alhatami, E., & Bhatti, U. A. (2024). Advanced fuzzy denoising technique for agricultural remote sensing: Modified partition filter for suppressing impulsive noise. *IEEE Access : Practical Innovations, Open Solutions*, 12, 159025–159035. DOI: 10.1109/ACCESS.2024.3447704

Angiulli, F., Fassetti, F., & Ferragina, L. (2023, May 17). *Reconstruction Error-based Anomaly Detection with Few Outlying Examples*. arXiv.Org. https://arxiv.org/abs/2305.10464v2

Archana, R., & Jeevaraj, P. S. E. (2024). Deep Learning models for digital image processing: A review. *Artificial Intelligence Review*, 57(1), 11. DOI: 10.1007/s10462-023-10631-z

Ashraf, R., Habib, M. A., Akram, M., Latif, M. A., Malik, M. S. A., Awais, M., Dar, S. H., Mahmood, T., Yasir, M., & Abbas, Z. (2020). Deep convolution neural network for big data medical image classification. *IEEE Access : Practical Innovations, Open Solutions*, 8, 105659–105670. DOI: 10.1109/ACCESS.2020.2998808

Bai, Y., Li, S., Ju, R.-Y., Yang, Z., Yu, J., & Chiang, J.-S. (2024). *FAD-SAR: A Novel Fishing Activity Detection System via Synthetic Aperture Radar Images Based on Deep Learning Method* (arXiv:2404.18245). arXiv. https://doi.org//arXiv.2404.18245DOI: 10.1109/ISPACS62486.2024.10869003

Baloch, L., Bazai, S. U., Marjan, S., Aftab, F., Aslam, S., Neo, T. K., & Amphawan, A. (2023). A Review of Big Data Trends and Challenges in Healthcare. *International Journal of Technology*, 14(6), 1320–1333. DOI: 10.14716/ijtech.v14i6.6643

Bergamin, L., Carraro, T., Polato, M., & Aiolli, F. (2022). Novel Applications for VAE-based Anomaly Detection Systems. arXiv preprint arXiv:2204.12577. https://doi.org//arXiv.2204.12577DOI: 10.1109/IJCNN55064.2022.9892879

Bhatti, U. A., Bazai, S. U., Hussain, S., Fakhar, S., Ku, C. S., Marjan, S., Yee, P. L., & Jing, L. (2023). Deep Learning-Based Trees Disease Recognition and Classification Using Hyperspectral Data. *Computers, Materials & Continua*, 77(1), 681–697. DOI: 10.32604/cmc.2023.037958

Bhatti, U. A., Yu, Y. K., Mamyrbayev, O. Z., Aitkazina, A. A., Hao, T., & Zhumazhan, N. O. (2025). Recommendations for healthcare: An interpretable approach using deep learning. *Proceedings of the 2024 7th International Conference on Pattern Recognition and Artificial Intelligence.*

Cao, Q., Shen, L., Xie, W., Parkhi, O. M., & Zisserman, A. (2018). *VGGFace2: A Dataset for Recognising Faces across Pose and Age*. 67–74. https://doi.org/.DOI: 10.1109/FG.2018.00020

Cheng, M., Tang, H., Bhatti, U. A., & Li, D. (2024). Optimized sustainable manufacturing through fuzzy control in image-based visual servoing with velocity and field-of-view constraints. *IEEE Transactions on Fuzzy Systems*, 1–12. DOI: 10.1109/TFUZZ.2024.3455408

Cleland, C. R., Rwiza, J., Evans, J. R., Gordon, I., MacLeod, D., Burton, M. J., & Bascaran, C. (2023). Artificial Intelligence for Diabetic Retinopathy in Low-Income and Middle-Income Countries: A Scoping Review. *BMJ Open Diabetes Research & Care*, 11(4), e003424. DOI: 10.1136/bmjdrc-2023-003424 PMID: 37532460

Deep, G., & Verma, J. (2024). Deep Learning Models for Fine-Scale Climate Change Prediction: Enhancing Spatial and Temporal Resolution Using AI. In Tripathi, G., Shakya, A., Kanga, S., Singh, S. K., & Rai, P. K. (Eds.), *Big Data, Artificial Intelligence, and Data Analytics in Climate Change Research: For Sustainable Development Goals* (pp. 81–100). Springer Nature., DOI: 10.1007/978-981-97-1685-2_5

Differential privacy—Wikipedia. (n.d.). Retrieved 12 September 2024, from https://en.wikipedia.org/wiki/Differential_privacy

Face Recognition Technology. (n.d.). *American Civil Liberties Union*. Retrieved 5 September 2024, from https://www.aclu.org/issues/privacy-technology/surveillance-technologies/face-recognition-technology

Feng, S., Liu, Q., Patel, A., Bazai, S. U., Jin, C., Kim, J. S., Sarrafzadeh, M., Azzollini, D., Yeoh, J., Kim, E., Gordon, S., Jang-Jaccard, J., Urschler, M., Barnard, S., Fong, A., Simmers, C., Tarr, G. P., & Wilson, B. (2022). Automated pneumothorax triaging in chest X-rays in the New Zealand population using deep-learning algorithms. *Journal of Medical Imaging and Radiation Oncology*, 66(8), 1035–1043. DOI: 10.1111/1754-9485.13393 PMID: 35224858

Fu, J., Wang, L., Ke, J., Yang, K., & Yu, R. (2023). GANAD: A GAN-based method for network anomaly detection. *World Wide Web (Bussum)*, 26(5), 2727–2748. DOI: 10.1007/s11280-023-01160-4

Get Newzoo's newest free Global Games Market Report 2023. (2024, February 8). *Newzoo*. https://newzoo.com/resources/trend-reports/newzoo-global-games-market-report-2023-free-version

Gonzales Martinez, R., & van Dongen, D.-M. (2023). Deep Learning algorithms for the early detection of breast cancer: A comparative study with traditional machine learning. *Informatics in Medicine Unlocked*, 41, 101317. DOI: 10.1016/j.imu.2023.101317

Goodfellow, I. J., Pouget-Abadie, J., Mirza, M., Xu, B., Warde-Farley, D., Ozair, S., Courville, A., & Bengio, Y. (2014, June 10). *Generative Adversarial Networks*. arXiv.Org. https://arxiv.org/abs/1406.2661v1

Guefrachi, S., Echtioui, A., & Hamam, H. (2024). Automated diabetic retinopathy screening using Deep Learning. *Multimedia Tools and Applications*, 83(24), 65249–65266. DOI: 10.1007/s11042-024-18149-4

Haider, A., Hussain, L., Tareen, A. W., Bazai, S. U., Aslam, S., Neo, M., & Amphawan, A. (2024). A comparative study of machine learning techniques for accurate disease prediction using symptom-based diagnosis. *AIP Conference Proceedings*, 3153(1), 020005. DOI: 10.1063/5.0217579

Hameed, M., Yang, F., Bazai, S. U., Ghafoor, M. I., Alshehri, A., Khan, I., Baryalai, M., Andualem, M., & Jaskani, F. H. (2022). Urbanization Detection Using LiDAR-Based Remote Sensing Images of Azad Kashmir Using Novel 3D CNNs. *Journal of Sensors*, 2022(1), 6430120. DOI: 10.1155/2022/6430120

Hameed, M., Yang, F., Bazai, S. U., Ghafoor, M. I., Alshehri, A., Khan, I., Ullah, S., Baryalai, M., Jaskani, F. H., & Andualem, M. (2022a). Convolutional Autoencoder-Based Deep Learning Approach for Aerosol Emission Detection Using LiDAR Dataset. *Journal of Sensors*, 2022(1), 3690312. DOI: 10.1155/2022/3690312

Hamza, M., Bazai, S. U., Ghafoor, M. I., Ullah, S., Akram, S., & Khan, M. S. (2023). Generative Adversarial Networks (GANs) Video Framework: A Systematic Literature Review. 2023 International Conference on Energy, Power, Environment, Control, and Computing (ICEPECC), 1–5. https://ieeexplore.ieee.org/abstract/document/10209475/

Haq, S. U., Bazai, S. U., Fatima, A., Marjan, S., Yang, J., Por, L. Y., Anjum, M., Shahab, S., & Ku, C. S. (2023). Reseek-arrhythmia: Empirical evaluation of ResNet architecture for detection of arrhythmia. *Diagnostics (Basel)*, 13(18), 2867. DOI: 10.3390/diagnostics13182867 PMID: 37761234

Hasnain, A., Hashmi, M. Z., Bhatti, U. A., Wei, G., Jinru, L., & Asif, M. (2024). Prediction of particulate matter pollution using a long short-term memory model in Zhejiang Province, China. *Environmental Monitoring and Assessment*, 196(5), 487. DOI: 10.1007/s10661-024-12644-9 PMID: 38687422

He, B., & Bhatti, U. A. (2024). Smart cities and smart networks: AI applications in urban geography and industrial communication. *International Journal of High Speed Electronics and Systems*, 2440122. DOI: 10.1142/S0129156424401220

He, K., Zhang, X., Ren, S., & Sun, J. (2015, December 10). *Deep Residual Learning for Image Recognition*. arXiv.Org. https://arxiv.org/abs/1512.03385v1

Hinton, G. E., & Salakhutdinov, R. R. (2006). Reducing the Dimensionality of Data with Neural Networks. *Science*, 313(5786), 504–507. DOI: 10.1126/science.1127647 PMID: 16873662

Home | Wildlife Insights. (n.d.). Retrieved 29 October 2024, from https://www.wildlifeinsights.org/

Hürkal, H., & Zeynep, O. (2020). Üretken Çekişmeli Ağlar ile Görsel Çözünürlük Artırımı Üzerine Bir Araştırma. *Acta Infologica*, 4(2), 2. Advance online publication. DOI: 10.26650/acin.765320

Ibtehaz, N., & Rahman, M. S. (2020). MultiResUNet: Rethinking the U-Net architecture for multimodal biomedical image segmentation. *Neural Networks*, 121, 74–87. DOI: 10.1016/j.neunet.2019.08.025 PMID: 31536901

Islam, K. (2022). *Recent Advances in Vision Transformer: A Survey and Outlook of Recent Work*. https://doi.org/DOI: 10.48550/ARXIV.2203.01536

Jamil, A., ali Hameed, A., & Bazai, S. U. (2021). Land cover classification using machine learning approaches from high resolution images. Journal of Applied and Emerging Sciences, 11(1), pp-108.

Jia, J., & Ye, W. (2023). Deep Learning for Earthquake Disaster Assessment: Objects, Data, Models, Stages, Challenges, and Opportunities. *Remote Sensing (Basel)*, 15(16), 16. Advance online publication. DOI: 10.3390/rs15164098

Jiménez Gaona, Y., Rodriguez-Alvarez, M. J., Espino-Morato, H., Castillo Malla, D., & Lakshminarayanan, V. (2021). DenseNet for Breast Tumor Classification in Mammographic Images. In Rojas, I., Castillo-Secilla, D., Herrera, L. J., & Pomares, H. (Eds.), *Bioengineering and Biomedical Signal and Image Processing* (pp. 166–176). Springer International Publishing., DOI: 10.1007/978-3-030-88163-4_16

Jumper, J., Evans, R., Pritzel, A., Green, T., Figurnov, M., Ronneberger, O., Tunyasuvunakool, K., Bates, R., Žídek, A., Potapenko, A., Bridgland, A., Meyer, C., Kohl, S. A. A., Ballard, A. J., Cowie, A., Romera-Paredes, B., Nikolov, S., Jain, R., Adler, J., & Hassabis, D. (2021). Highly accurate protein structure prediction with AlphaFold. *Nature*, 596(7873), 583–589. DOI: 10.1038/s41586-021-03819-2 PMID: 34265844

Kang, M., Zhu, J.-Y., Zhang, R., Park, J., Shechtman, E., Paris, S., & Park, T. (2023, March 9). *Scaling up GANs for Text-to-Image Synthesis*. arXiv.Org. https://arxiv.org/abs/2303.05511v1 DOI: 10.1109/CVPR52729.2023.00976

Kanwal, S., Ali, S., Alahmadi, T. J., Assam, M., Ansari, G. J., & Bhatti, U. A. (2025). Pretrained model with CNN for lung cancer identification and classification. *Proceedings of the 2024 7th International Conference on Pattern Recognition and Artificial Intelligence*.

Kaur, A., & Dong, G. (2023). A Complete Review on Image Denoising Techniques for Medical Images. *Neural Processing Letters*, 55(6), 7807–7850. DOI: 10.1007/s11063-023-11286-1

Khalid, N., Qayyum, A., Bilal, M., Al-Fuqaha, A., & Qadir, J. (2023). Privacy-preserving artificial intelligence in healthcare: Techniques and applications. *Computers in Biology and Medicine*, 158, 106848. DOI: 10.1016/j.compbiomed.2023.106848 PMID: 37044052

Khan, A., Sohail, A., Zahoora, U., & Qureshi, A. S. (2020). A survey of the recent architectures of deep convolutional neural networks. *Artificial Intelligence Review*, 53(8), 5455–5516. DOI: 10.1007/s10462-020-09825-6

Khan, F. F., Li, X., Temple, A. J., & Elhoseiny, M. (2023). FishNet: A Large-scale Dataset and Benchmark for Fish Recognition, Detection, and Functional Trait Prediction. *2023 IEEE/CVF International Conference on Computer Vision (ICCV)*, 20439–20449. https://doi.org/DOI: 10.1109/ICCV51070.2023.01874

Khan, H. N., Bazai, S., Zaland, Z., Durrani, S., Aslam, S., Amphawan, A., Ali, F., & Neo, T.-K. (2023). A Comparative Study of Convolutional Neural Networks and Recurrent Neural Networks for Chord Recognition. *International Journal of Membrane Science and Technology*, 10(2), 1617–1630. DOI: 10.15379/ijmst.v10i2.1837

Kim, H. E., Cosa-Linan, A., Santhanam, N., Jannesari, M., Maros, M. E., & Ganslandt, T. (2022). Transfer learning for medical image classification: A literature review. *BMC Medical Imaging*, 22(1), 69. DOI: 10.1186/s12880-022-00793-7 PMID: 35418051

Kim, S., Hooper, C., Wattanawong, T., Kang, M., Yan, R., Genc, H., Dinh, G., Huang, Q., Keutzer, K., Mahoney, M. W., Shao, Y. S., & Gholami, A. (2023). *Full Stack Optimization of Transformer Inference: A Survey* (arXiv:2302.14017). arXiv. https://doi.org//arXiv.2302.14017DOI: 10.48550

Kingma, D. P., & Welling, M. (2022). Auto-Encoding Variational Bayes. arXiv preprint arXiv:1312.6114. https://doi.org//arXiv.1312.6114DOI: 10.48550

Krizhevsky, A., Sutskever, I., & Hinton, G. E. (2017). ImageNet classification with deep convolutional neural networks. *Communications of the ACM*, 60(6), 84–90. DOI: 10.1145/3065386

Ledig, C., Theis, L., Huszar, F., Caballero, J., Cunningham, A., Acosta, A., Aitken, A., Tejani, A., Totz, J., Wang, Z., & Shi, W. (2016, September 15). *Photo-Realistic Single Image Super-Resolution Using a Generative Adversarial Network*. arXiv.Org. https://arxiv.org/abs/1609.04802v4

Li, D., & Bhatti, U. A. (2024). Mstfnet: A mamba and dual swin-transformer fusion network for remote sensing image classification for precision agriculture land processing. *Available atSSRN* 5033170. DOI: 10.2139/ssrn.5033170

Li, D., Neira-Molina, H., Huang, M., Syam, M. S., Zhang, Y., Junfeng, Z., & Bhatti, U. A. (2025). CST-FNet: A CNN and dual swin-transformer fusion network for remote sensing hyperspectral data fusion and classification of coastal areas. *IEEE Journal of Selected Topics in Applied Earth Observations and Remote Sensing*. Advance online publication. DOI: 10.1109/JSTARS.2025.3530935

Li, H., Han, H., Bhatti, U. A., & Wang, Z. (2025). Bacterial inhibition zone recognition method based on YOLO. *Proceedings of the 2024 7th International Conference on Pattern Recognition and Artificial Intelligence.*

Lin, C.-L., & Wu, K.-C. (2023). Development of revised ResNet-50 for diabetic retinopathy detection. *BMC Bioinformatics*, 24(1), 157. DOI: 10.1186/s12859-023-05293-1 PMID: 37076790

Liu, J., Bhatti, U. A., Huang, M., Tang, H., Wu, Y., Feng, S., & Zhang, Y. (2025). FF-UNET: An enhanced framework for improved segmentation of brain tumors in MRI images. *Proceedings of the 2024 7th International Conference on Pattern Recognition and Artificial Intelligence.*

Liu, J., Bhatti, U. A., Zhang, J., Zhang, Y., & Huang, M. (2025). EF-VPT-Net: Enhanced feature-based vision patch transformer network for accurate brain tumor segmentation in magnetic resonance imaging. *IEEE Journal of Biomedical and Health Informatics*, 1–14. DOI: 10.1109/JBHI.2025.3526976

Ma, Z., Dong, Y., Xia, Y., Xu, D., Xu, F., & Chen, F. (2024). Wildlife Real-Time Detection in Complex Forest Scenes Based on YOLOv5s Deep Learning Network. *Remote Sensing (Basel)*, 16(8), 8. Advance online publication. DOI: 10.3390/rs16081350

Madani, A., Arnaout, R., Mofrad, M., & Arnaout, R. (2018). Fast and accurate view classification of echocardiograms using Deep Learning. *NPJ Digital Medicine*, 1(1), 1–8. DOI: 10.1038/s41746-017-0013-1 PMID: 30828647

Md Jelas, I., Zulkifley, M. A., Abdullah, M., & Spraggon, M. (2024). Deforestation detection using Deep Learning-based semantic segmentation techniques: A systematic review. *Frontiers in Forests and Global Change*, 7, 1300060. Advance online publication. DOI: 10.3389/ffgc.2024.1300060

Minh, D., Wang, H. X., Li, Y. F., & Nguyen, T. N. (2022). Explainable artificial intelligence: A comprehensive review. *Artificial Intelligence Review*, 55(5), 3503–3568. DOI: 10.1007/s10462-021-10088-y

Mohammadpour, L., Ling, T. C., Liew, C. S., & Aryanfar, A. (2022). A Survey of CNN-Based Network Intrusion Detection. *Applied Sciences (Basel, Switzerland)*, 12(16), 16. Advance online publication. DOI: 10.3390/app12168162

Nabeel, S. M., Bazai, S. U., Alasbali, N., Liu, Y., Ghafoor, M. I., Khan, R., Ku, C. S., Yang, J., Shahab, S., & Por, L. Y. (2024). Optimizing lung cancer classification through hyperparameter tuning. *Digital Health*, 10, 20552076241249661. DOI: 10.1177/20552076241249661 PMID: 38698834

Nawaz, S. A., Li, J., Li, D., Shoukat, M. U., Bhatti, U. A., & Raza, M. A. (2025). Medical image zero watermarking algorithm based on dual-tree complex wavelet transform, AlexNet, and discrete cosine transform. *Applied Soft Computing*, 169, 112556. DOI: 10.1016/j.asoc.2024.112556

Noor, R., Wahid, A., Bazai, S. U., Khan, A., Fang, M., Syam, M. S., & Bhatti, U. A. (2024). DLGAN: Undersampled MRI reconstruction using deep learning-based generative adversarial network. *Biomedical Signal Processing and Control*, 93, 106218. DOI: 10.1016/j.bspc.2024.106218

Noor, S., Bazai, S. U., Ghafoor, M. I., Marjan, S., Akram, S., & Ali, F. (2023). Generative Adversarial Networks for Anomaly Detection: A Systematic Literature Review. 2023 4th International Conference on Computing, Mathematics and Engineering Technologies (iCoMET), 1–6. https://doi.org/DOI: 10.1109/iCoMET57998.2023.10099175

Peng, M., Liu, Y., Qadri, I. A., Bhatti, U. A., Ahmed, B., Sarhan, N. M., & Awwad, E. M. (2024). Advanced image segmentation for precision agriculture using CNN-GAT fusion and fuzzy C-means clustering. *Computers and Electronics in Agriculture*, 226, 109431. DOI: 10.1016/j.compag.2024.109431

Shao, K., Li, D., Tang, H., Zhang, Y., Xu, B., & Bhatti, U. A. (2024). Adaptive temporal convolutional network (Atcn) and internally-optimized transformer for dissolved oxygen prediction in aquaculture. *Available atSSRN* 5039613. DOI: 10.2139/ssrn.5039613

Sun, X., Bhatti, U. A., Huang, M., & Zhang, Y. (2024). EF-UV: Feature enhanced fusion of U-Net and VIT transformer for brain tumor MRI image segmentation. *International Journal of Biomedical and Health Informatics.*

Tang, H., Wu, Z., Xu, B., Bhatti, U. A., Yu, M., & Lu, Y. (2025). Research on cross-platform motion control system based on gSOAP. *Proceedings of the 2024 7th International Conference on Pattern Recognition and Artificial Intelligence.*

Ullah, S., Bazai, S. U., Imran, M., Ilyas, Q. M., Mehmood, A., Saleem, M. A., Rafique, M. A., Haider, A., Khan, I., Iqbal, S., Gulzar, Y., & Hameed, K. (2024). Recent developments in authentication schemes used in machine-type communication devices in machine-to-machine communication: Issues and challenges. *Computers, Materials & Continua*, 79(1), 93–115. DOI: 10.32604/cmc.2024.048796

Zeng, Z., Zhang, Y., Tang, H., Bhatti, U. A., Gao, J., & Lu, Y. (2025). A domain knowledge graph construction method based on joint extraction of GlobalPointer. *Proceedings of the 2024 7th International Conference on Pattern Recognition and Artificial Intelligence.*

Zhang, C., Iqbal, I., Bhatti, U. A., Liu, J., Awwad, E. M., & Sarhan, N. (2024). ResNet50 in remote sensing and agriculture: Evaluating image captioning performance for high spectral data. *Environmental Earth Sciences*, 83(23), 1–16. DOI: 10.1007/s12665-024-11950-2

Zhang, J., Fu, R., Wu, Y., & Bhatti, U. A. (2024). Practical consensus of time-varying fuzzy positive multi-agent systems. *AIMS Mathematics*, 9(11), 31119–31141. DOI: 10.3934/math.20241500

Chapter 8
Innovative Techniques for Image Clustering and Classification

Muhammad Akram
https://orcid.org/0000-0003-1485-9804
Balochistan University of Information Technology, Engineering, and Management Sciences, Pakistan

Sibghat Ullah Bazai
https://orcid.org/0000-0003-3042-5977
Balochistan University of Information Technology, Engineering, and Management Sciences, Pakistan

Samina Samina
https://orcid.org/0009-0005-5648-0028
National University of Sciences and Technology, Pakistan

Wajid Hassan Moosa
Balochistan University of Information Technology, Engineering, and Management Sciences, Pakistan

ABSTRACT

The chapter is a review of techniques in deep leaning for tasks such as classification and clustering. Basically, due to the discussion of the two main topics in deep learning, the chapter is divided into two parts, one discussing the clustering methods such as first a basic understanding of clustering method is made then moving towards autoencoder based architectures that includes variational autoencoders (VAE), k-means with autoencoders, then self-organizing maps, spectral clustering and DBSCAN. The other part of the chapter is focused on classification methods, where the architecture of a convolutional neural network (CNN) is discussed, proceeding to ResNet, DenseNet and EfficientNet, a little touch of transformer-based CNN is discussed, a part of these vision transformers and capsule networks are mentioned. A comparison of both the methods, i.e., clustering and classification is discussed, that will make it clearer that how both these methods are different from one another.

DOI: 10.4018/979-8-3693-9045-0.ch008

INTRODUCTION

Artificial intelligence uses deep learning, a technique that mimics the human brain's decision-making process. There has been enormous progress in the field of deep learning, with applications spanning practically every industry, including the defense, surveillance, and medical diagnostic fields in recent years.

Deep learning is a branch of machine learning that uses neural network models to extract layered representations from data. The word "deep" describes the many layers that go into creating these models; in contemporary deep learning, this number can easily reach hundreds or even thousands. Deep learning automatically learns vast hierarchies of representations from training data, in contrast to shallow learning, which makes use of fewer layers Figure 1. Deep learning models are mathematical frameworks rather than biologically realistic representations of the brain, even if neural networks are partly inspired by the brain (Chollet, n.d.; Minar & Naher, 2018).

Figure 1. Simple deep learning network (Chollet, n.d.)

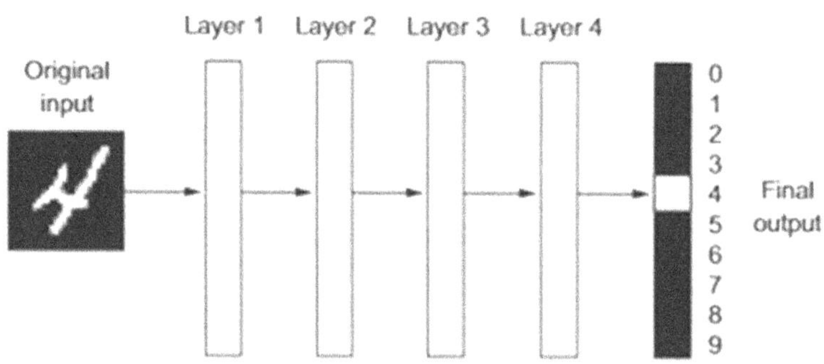

As you can see in Figure 2, the network converts the digit image into representations that provide more and more information about the outcome while remaining progressively different from the original image. Imagine a deep network as a multi-step information distillation process, where data passes through ever finer filters and emerges more and more pure.

Figure 2. Deep representation of a deep learning model (Chollet, n.d.)

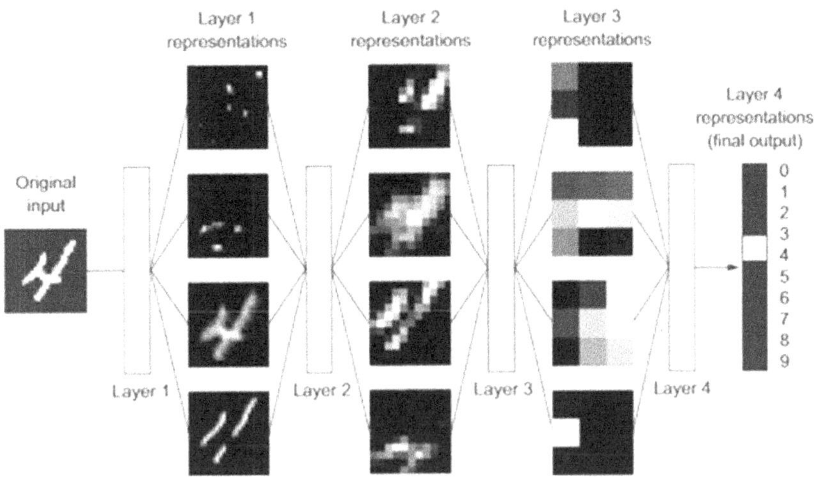

So that's what deep learning is, technically: a multistage way to learn data representations. It's a simple idea but, as it turns out, very simple mechanisms, sufficiently scaled, can end up looking like magic (Chollet, n.d.).

In machine learning, deep neural networks map inputs (like images) to targets (like labels) by learning a series of data transformations through layers. Each layer's transformation is determined by its weights, which are a set of numbers that define how input data is processed. Learning in this context means adjusting the weights across all layers so the network can correctly predict targets from input examples. With deep networks containing millions of parameters, finding the right values for all these weights can be a complex challenge. See Figure 3.

Figure 3. Parameterization of a neural network (Chollet, n.d.)

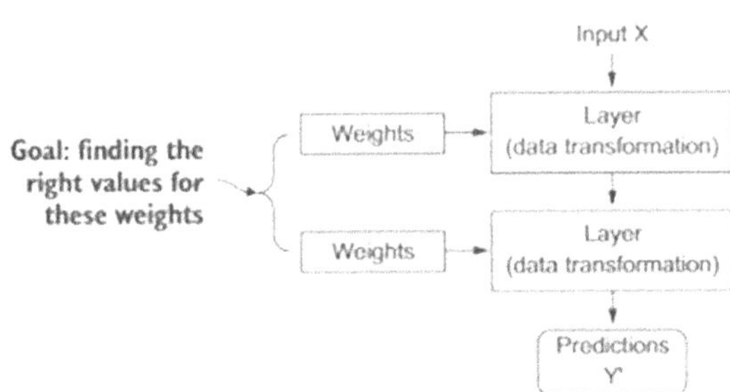

To control something, first you need to be able to observe it. To control the output of a neural network, you need to be able to measure how far this output is from what you expected. This is the job of the loss function of the network, also called the objective function. The loss function takes the predictions of the network and the true target (what you wanted the network to output) and computes a distance score, capturing how well the network has done on this specific example Figure 4.

Figure 4. Loss calculation of a deep learning model (Chollet, n.d.)

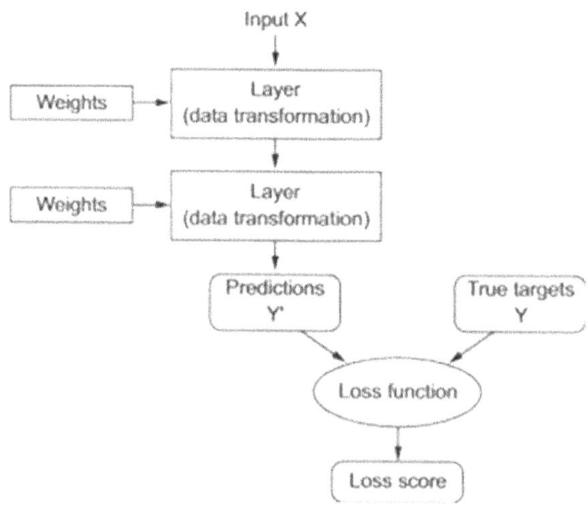

Using this score as a feedback signal to slightly modify the weight values in a way that lowers the loss score for the current sample is the fundamental technique of deep learning Figure 5. The optimizer, which uses the Backpropagation algorithm the main deep learning algorithm is responsible for making this modification.

Figure 5. Back propagation in deep learning (Chollet, n.d.)

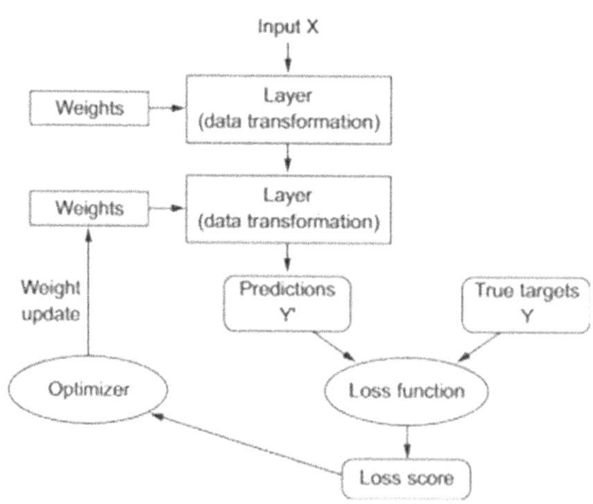

The optimizer in deep learning modifies the weights of the network by using the loss score as feedback, with the goal of minimizing the loss for every example. Backpropagation is a procedure that first results in a large loss since it uses random weights. The weights are gradually changed to reduce the loss as the network processes more examples, increasing accuracy. A trained network with optimal weights and little loss is produced after several iterations of this training loop (Chollet, n.d.; Minar & Naher, 2018).

Overview of Clustering vs Classification

As we have discussed how neural network can process a data and bring out useful outcomes that can be used to perform different various operations. Some of the specific tasks a neural network can do is recognize objects based on either classifying them or clustering them into groups.

Depending on the features, objects can be categorized into one or more classes using both classification and clustering. Given how slight the fundamental difference is, they seem to be similar processes. Each input instance is given a predefined label based on its properties in the classification scenario, which is also known as supervised learning, but in the clustering case, those labels are absent known as unsupervised learning see Table 1.

The key differences of clustering and classification are as below.

Table 1. Key differences of clustering and classification

Aspects	Clustering	Classification
Goal	Groups data based on similarity, uncovering patterns.	Assigns data to predefined categories or labels.
Learning Type	Unsupervised learning (no labelled data).	Supervised learning (requires labelled data).
Output	Results in clusters or groups that reveal hidden structure in data.	Outputs a specific label or category for each input.
Use cases	Exploratory analysis, customer segmentation, anomaly detection.	Image recognition, spam detection, medical diagnosis.

Application of clustering and classification

Clustering and classification techniques are essential across numerous fields.

1. **Medical Imaging:**
    - o Clustering: In image segmentation, it is used to group pixels according to similarities, which aids in identifying anatomical regions or structures. For example, in radiology, it can be used to locate cancers or organ borders.
    - o Classification: Used to group medical images into different categories, such as differentiating between normal and abnormal scans or locating particular disease markers in CT like identifying cancerous nodules (Nabeel et al., 2024), MRI, or X-ray images (Feng et al., 2022).
2. **Autonomous Vehicles**:
    - o Clustering is necessary to divide situations into meaningful segments, such as lane, vehicle, and pedestrian identification, which aids in path planning and environmental awareness

- o Classification: In order for systems to classify items in the environment of a vehicle—such as traffic signs, other cars, pedestrians, or urbanization (Hameed et al., 2022)—classification is essential.

3. **Retail and Surveillance**:
    - o Clustering: A technique for grouping regions of activity or finding high-traffic zones within a store, it is used for behavioral analysis and people counts.
    - o Classification: Used to group things or people into groups, like identifying different kinds of goods in stock, recognizing particular people in security footage, classifying malicious traffic or emails spams (Tareen et al., 2022) or providing privacy (Tabassum et al., 2024).

Applications of classification and clustering are wide, each work needs some objectives to achieve and based on that the technique is shaped to solve that problem. Such as work that involves convolutional autoencoder based deep learning approach by (Hameed et al., 2022a) is about aerosol emission detection. Some works are based on the trends of some problem such as applications of machine learning in medicine and healthcare by (Aamir et al., 2023) is a work on the some certain trends, a study by (Haider et al., 2024) is a disease prediction system based on symptom-based diagnosis and a study by (Haq et al., 2023) utilizes DL ResNet model to detect and classify heart arrhythmia disease.

CLUSTERING

In the vast landscape of machine learning, clustering stands out as a fundamental technique for organizing and interpreting data. Unlike supervised learning, which relies on labelled datasets, clustering operates in the realm of unsupervised learning, where the model identifies patterns and structures within the data without predefined categories. Clustering has an important significance in deep learning because of its ability of pattern representation findings.

Deep learning models learn to extract features from the complex or big data, while clustering enables the grouping of similar data points based on the learned representations. This method is to recognize the different similarities across various domains, such as from image and video analysis to natural language processing. Then it effectively categorizes similar images, group related words, or even identify anomalous patterns that deviate from the normal pattern.

Methods such as autoencoders and generative adversarial networks (GANs) improve clustering capabilities by creating richer and more informative feature embeddings. With the integration of traditional clustering algorithms like K-means (see Figure 6) or DBSCAN with advanced neural architectures, researchers can achieve superior clustering outcomes that reveal deeper insights into their data (Károly et al., 2018; Nutakki et al., 2019).

A simple representation of clustering

Figure 6. Clustering in deep learning (geeksforgeeks, 2024b)

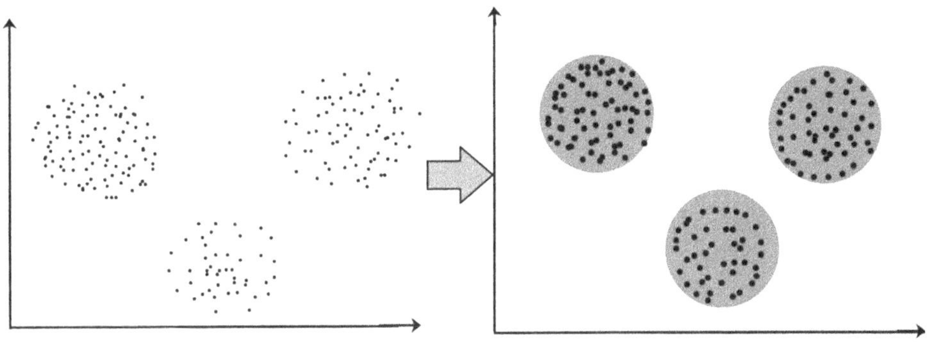

Steps for Clustering in Deep Learning

Before moving towards the different clustering methods, let's see how step by step clustering is performed:

- **Data Collection and Preprocessing**
- **Feature Selection**
- **Algorithm Selection**
- **Distance Metric**
- **Cluster Initialization**
- **Assigning Clusters**
- **Optimize Clusters**
- **Evaluation**
- **Hyperparameter Tuning**
- **Visualization**
- **Deployment**

Clustering Models

Below some methods of autoencoder based clustering in deep learning are being discussed.

Autoencoder-based clustering

Autoencoders are there used for transforming a high-dimensional data into a low-dimensional but meaningful representations which can make clustering more effective. Let's discuss in detail how it works:

Autoencoder's encoder compresses the input data into a low-dimensional vector, which captures and learns the important features of the data. This vector is called the latent space.

Now that the input is compressed into this latent space, traditional clustering algorithms can be used to group similar data points, the traditional clustering methods could be K-means or DBSCAN.

By training the autoencoder to reconstruct the input (through the decoder), the network ensures that the compressed features in the latent space are rich in information. These low-dimensional representations make clustering more accurate and efficient, as the irrelevant or noisy details from the original data are filtered out, leaving only the core features necessary for meaningful grouping (Károly et al., 2018). The Figure 7 and Figure 8 are visualizations of the autoencoder based clustering.

Diagram:

Figure 7. Autoencoder architecture diagram (Steven Flores, 2019)

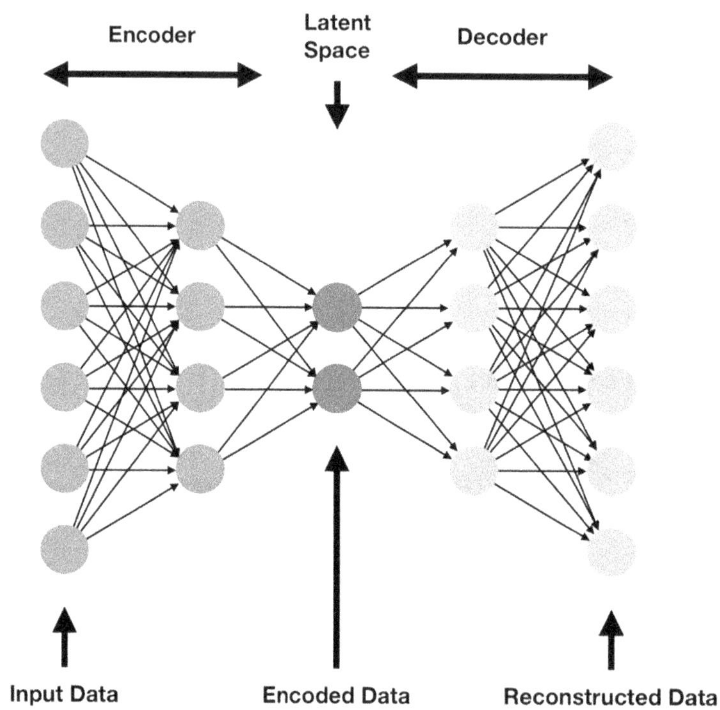

Figure 8. A comprehensive representation of autoencoder architecture (StevenFlores, 2019)

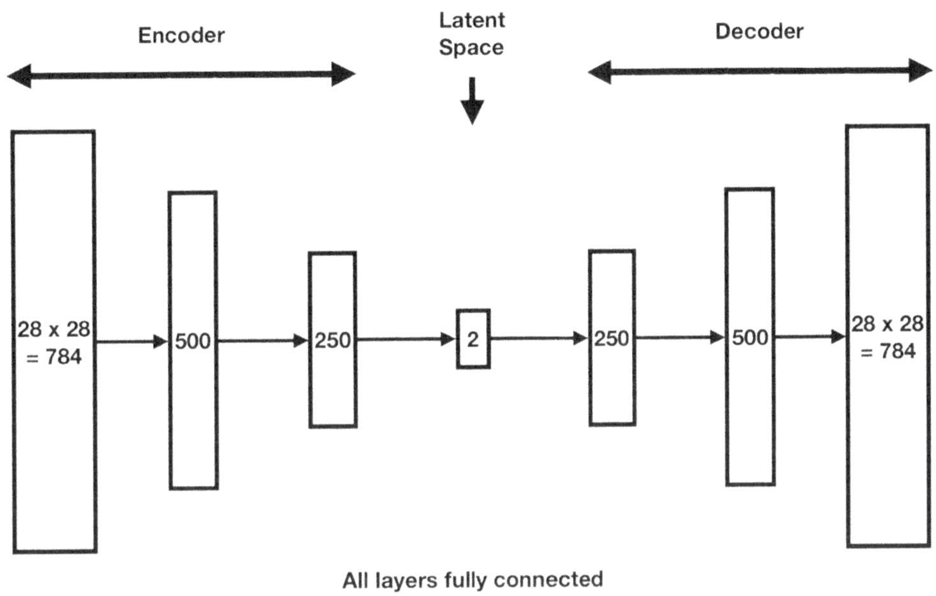

Variational autoencoder clustering (VAEC)

A generative model known as a variational autoencoder (VAE) expands on the idea of a standard autoencoder by incorporating probabilistic components into the encoding procedure. Regular autoencoders translate input data to a single point in the latent space; in contrast, vector autoencoders (VAEs) learn a probability distribution across the latent space, which enables them to sample from this distribution and produce new, comparable data points, see Figure 9 and Figure 10.

Key Components of VAEs:

1. Encoder: The encoder in a VAE maps the input to a mean and variance (usually depicted as a Gaussian distribution) as opposed to mapping it to a fixed latent vector. Because of the uncertainty this creates in the latent space, every input is represented as a distribution rather than a single point.
2. Latent Space: The VAE assumes the latent space follows a certain prior distribution (usually a normal distribution). During training, the encoder learns to map input data to parameters (mean and variance) of this distribution.
3. Sampling Step: A random sample is drawn from the latent distribution (using the mean and variance from the encoder), and this sample is passed to the decoder.
4. Decoder: The decoder reconstructs the original input based on the sampled latent vector, similar to how a standard autoencoder works.
5. Loss Function: The VAE's loss function has two parts:
   - Reconstruction Loss: Indicates how well the input can be rebuilt by the decoder.

- KL Divergence: Calculates the discrepancy between the intended prior distribution, which is often a standard Gaussian, and the learnt latent distribution. The latent space is guaranteed to have a smooth, continuous distribution by this regularization term.

Figure 9. Variational Autoencoder architecture (StevenFlores, 2019)

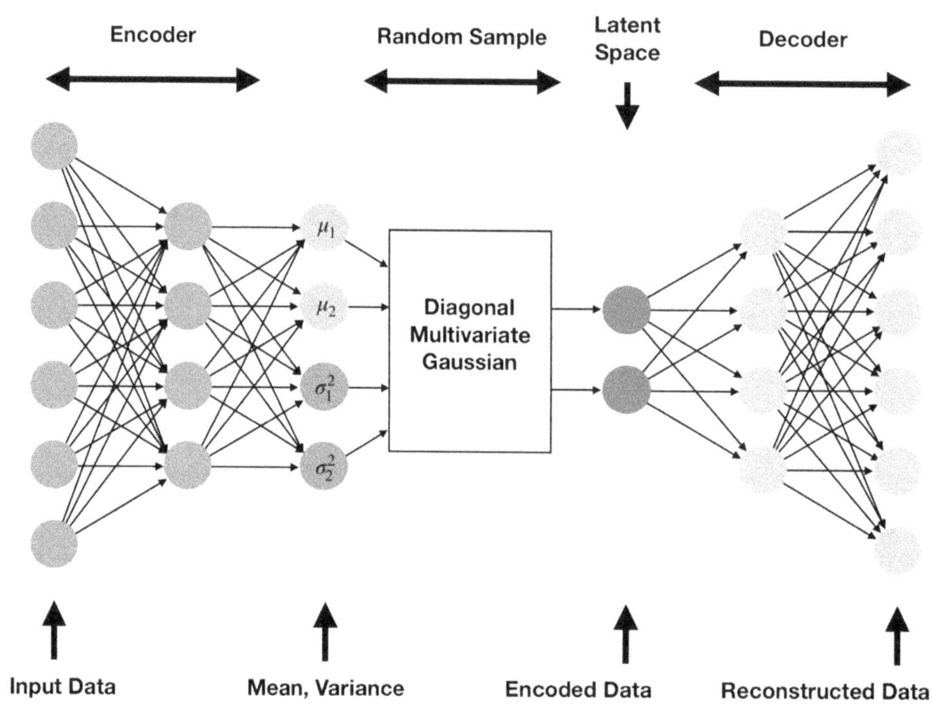

Figure 10. A comprehensive architecture of VAE (StevenFlores, 2019)

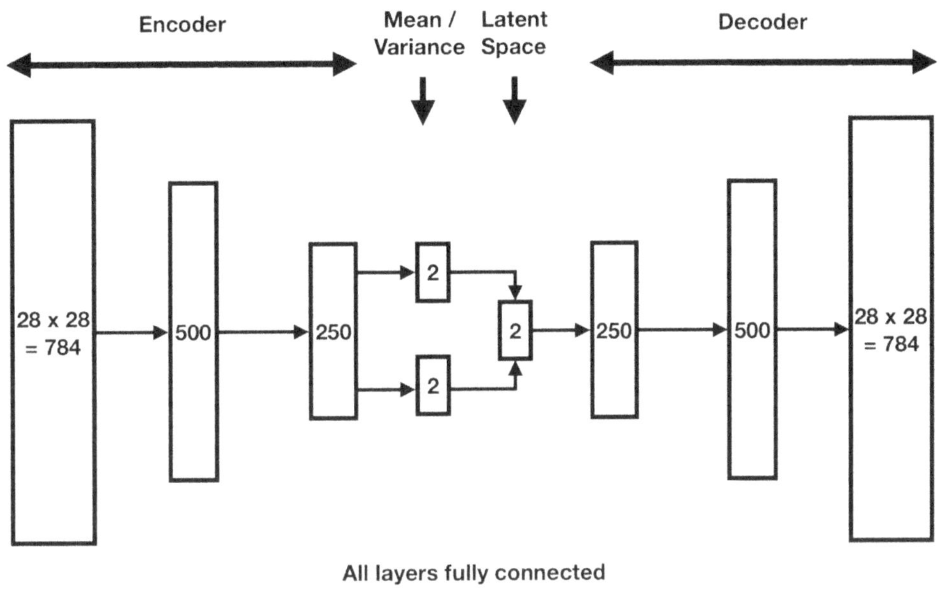

K-means clustering with autoencoders (AEK)

A hybrid method called K-means clustering with autoencoders (AEK) combines the strength of autoencoders with the conventional K-means algorithm. By utilizing an autoencoder to first transform the data into a lower-dimensional representation and then using K-means clustering to this altered space, the main objective is to increase clustering performance. Neural networks called autoencoders are very helpful for dimensionality reduction because they can learn important characteristics of data in an unsupervised way, identifying intricate patterns and relationships.

The two parts of an autoencoder are: an **encoder** and a **decoder**. The encoder is responsible for compressing the input data into a lower dimensional form also known as latent space, and the decoder is responsible for the reconstruction of the compressed representation into original data. For the purpose of minimizing the difference between the original input and the reconstructed output, the autoencoder learns representations that highlight the important features while removing noise. This process is important for enhancing the performance of the K-means algorithm, which often struggles with high-dimensional and noisy data.

After the autoencoder's process of compression of the input data into the latent space, then comes the step of application of **K-means clustering** to the latent representations, note that clustering method here is applied to the latent space instead of the original high-dimensional data. This results in the reduction of complexity and noise in the data, that will allow K-means to form more accurate clusters. By operating in the latent space, K-means is now able to better capture the pattern of the data and classify the data points into meaningful clusters

The AEK method helps with dealing with the noisy, high-dimensional, or complex data. Conventional K-means clustering assumes that clusters in the original space are approximately spherical; however, the autoencoder assists in transforming the data into a space in which cluster separation is simpler. Hence, AEK is used widely in areas where meaningful cluster identification is important to be recognized, for example areas such as bioinformatics, image segmentation, anomaly detection, and word clustering. These fields include high-dimensional data, and the advantages of AEK method involve dimensionality reduction, noise reduction, and the capacity to identify more important links in the data than K-means alone could have done see Figure 11. (Yaniv Opochinsky; Shlomo E. Chazan; Sharon Gannot; Jacob Goldberger, 2020).

Figure 11. K-means based autoencoder clustering (Kowsari et al., 2019)

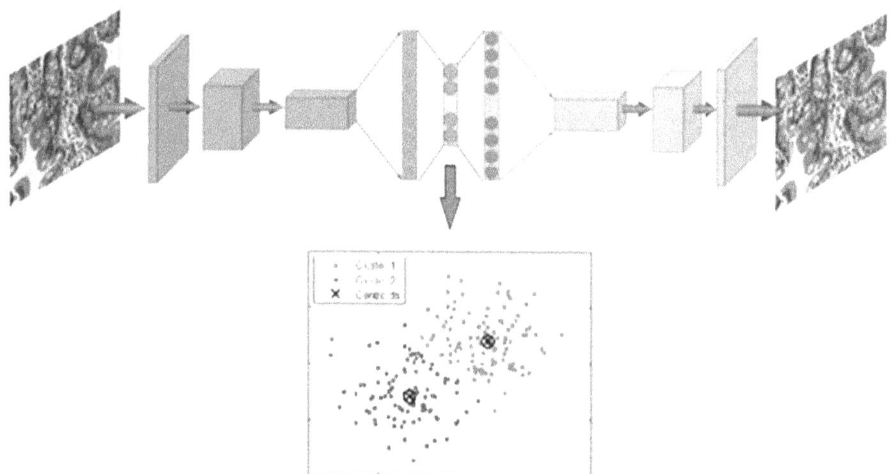

Spectral Clustering

When data does not form well-defined or convex clusters, spectral clustering is a powerful technique for image clustering. Spectral clustering uses graph theory to find clusters based on links or similarities between data points, in contrast to conventional techniques like K-means, which rely on distance measurements and assume clusters are spherical. Because of this, it works especially well with images, because features or pixels frequently have intricated, non-linear interactions.

Working:

The Spectral Clustering Algorithm consists of three main steps: clustering the data, projecting the data onto a lower-dimensional space, and creating a similarity graph. It can be further explained as follows given a set of points S in a higher-dimensional space as shown in Figure 12:

Figure 12. Spectral clustering

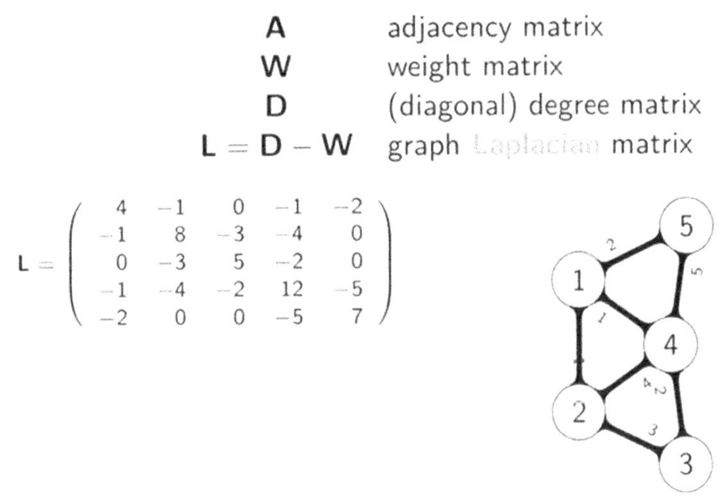

1. Distance Matrix:

Measure each pair of data points to see how "far apart" or "different" they are. Each element in the resulting distance matrix indicates the separation between two places. The distance between two photographs decreases as their features (such as color or shape) get closer.

2. Transform the distance matrix into an Affinity Matrix:

Next, convert that distance matrix into an affinity matrix, which is a similarity metric. The similarity between data points is indicated by this matrix. For instance, two data points with a high affinity (or similarity) score are highly similar. This stage makes it easier to concentrate on connections rather than absolute distances.

3. Compute the Degree Matrix (D) and the Laplacian Matrix (L=D-A):

Each data point's overall similarity (or "connections") to every other point is captured by the degree matrix (D).

The affinity matrix (A) is subtracted from the degree matrix (D) to get the Laplacian matrix (L). This matrix is essential to spectral clustering because it represents the fundamental structure of the interactions between data points.

4. Find the Eigenvalues and Eigenvectors of L:

Eigenvalues and eigenvectors are calculated for the Laplacian matrix. By concentrating on the most significant structures within the relationships, these help to simplify the data by exposing patterns within it.

5. Form a Matrix Using the Eigenvectors of the Largest k Eigenvalues:

Select the k greatest eigenvalues and corresponding eigenvectors from among all eigenvalues and eigenvectors. These eigenvectors provide a simplified representation of the core structure.

6. Normalize the vectors:

To improve their scale consistency, normalize these eigenvectors. This improves the accuracy and stability of the last clustering stage.

7. Cluster the Data Points in k-Dimensional Space:

Apply a clustering method (like K-means) on the reduced data representation (in k-dimensional space). This reveals natural clusters based on the relationships recorded in the previous phases by grouping together similar data items. (Keerthana, 2024).

DBSCAN (Density Based Spatial Clustering of Applications with Noise:

In the data space, clusters are dense areas that are divided by areas with a lower point density. This simple concept of "clusters" and "noise" forms the foundation of the DBSCAN algorithm. The main principle is that there must be a minimum number of points in the vicinity of a particular radius for every point in a cluster.

Here comes a question on why to use DBSCAN, it is because Real-world data may have irregularities such as:

- Clusters can have any shape and
- Noise may be present in data.

Required parameters for DBSCAN:

eps: The neighborhood surrounding a data point is defined by eps; that is, two points are deemed neighbors if their distances are less than or equal to eps. A significant portion of the data will be regarded as an outlier if the eps value is set too low. The clusters will merge and most of the data points will be in the same clusters if it is selected to be very large. The k-distance graph can be used as a basis for determining the eps value.

Minpts: The smallest quantity of neighbors (data points) inside an eps radius is known as MinPts. A bigger MinPts value must be selected for larger datasets. Generally, the number of dimensions D in the dataset can be used to determine the minimum MinPts, which is MinPts >= D+1. MinPts must have a minimum value of at least 3.

The DBSCAN algorithm, we have 3 types of data points.

Core Point: A point having more than MinPts within eps, is considered a core point.

Border Point: A point having fewer than MinPts within eps but is in the neighborhood of a core point.

Noise or outlier: A point which is neither a core point nor border point.

Figure 13 below shows a visualization of these points.

Figure 13. Clustering points in DBSCAN

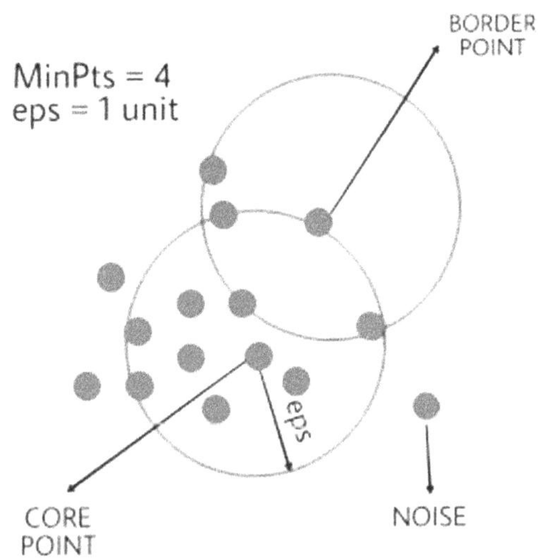

Steps in DBSCAN algorithm:

1. For each data point, observe within a specified distance (eps) to find the neighboring points. A point having more than a set number (MinPts) of neighbors, is marked as a core point. And for core points that has not been assigned a cluster, starts a new cluster
2. Add all the points in the cluster's eps neighborhood to the core point for each core point. Repeat this step, chaining together all the reachable points, if any of these additional points are also core points. Any points that are connected by dense zones are thus grouped together into a single cluster.
3. The remaining points that are not part of any cluster are treated as noise since they don't have enough neighbors to form a cluster. (Geeksforgeeks, 2024)

Clustering Case Study

The goal is to explore how a VAE could be used to perform **unsupervised clustering** on the MNIST dataset, which contains 70,000 images of handwritten digits (60,000 for training and 10,000 for testing) across 10 classes (digits 0-9).

The steps of clustering using VAE will be as: Data Preparation, Model Construction, Train the VAE, Results

Data Preparation: The MNIST dataset of handwritten digits (28x28 grayscale images) is used for the experiment see Figure 14.

Figure 14. Dataset loading in clustering

```
# Load Dataset
(X_train, Y_train), (X_valid, Y_valid) = mnist.load_data()
```

Figure 15 below is a visualization of the dataset for some random images of the dataset.

Figure 15. MNISTt dataset visualization (RichardKuo, n.d.)

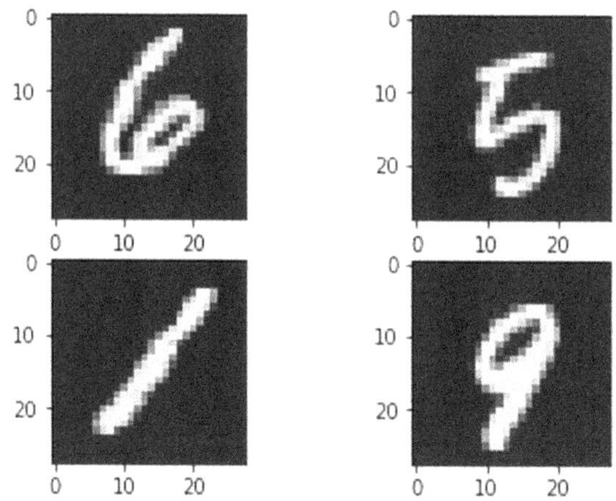

Model Constrution:

Encoder network: this network learns the parameters (mean and variance) of the underlying latent distribution. This network has two output layers, one for the latent distribution mean (z_mu) and the other for its variance (z_log_sigma) check Figure 16.

Figure 16. Model construction in clustering

```
img_shape = (28, 28, 1)    # for MNIST
batch_size = 16
latent_dim = 2  # Number of latent dimension parameters

# Encoder architecture: Input -> Conv2D*4 -> Flatten -> Dense
input_img = Input(shape=img_shape)

x = Conv2D(32, 3, padding='same', activation='relu')(input_img)
x = Conv2D(64, 3, padding='same', activation='relu', strides=(2, 2))(x)
x = Conv2D(64, 3, padding='same', activation='relu')(x)
x = Conv2D(64, 3, padding='same', activation='relu')(x)
# need to know the shape of the network here for the decoder
shape_before_flattening = K.int_shape(x)

x = Flatten()(x)
x = Dense(32, activation='relu')(x)

# Two outputs, latent mean and (log)variance
z_mu = Dense(latent_dim)(x)
z_log_sigma = Dense(latent_dim)(x)
```

Sampling Function: A sampling function is created to select points from the learned distribution by adding random noise (epsilon), based on the assumption that the data is normally distributed in the latent space. Keras's Lambda layer is used to incorporate this step into the model Figure 17.

Figure 17. Sampling function in clustering

```
# sampling function
def sampling(args):
    z_mu, z_log_sigma = args
    epsilon = K.random_normal(shape=(K.shape(z_mu)[0], latent_dim),
                              mean=0., stddev=1.)
    return z_mu + K.exp(z_log_sigma) * epsilon

# sample vector from the latent distribution
z = Lambda(sampling)([z_mu, z_log_sigma])
```

Decoder Network: this network is simply the reverse of Encoder Network see Figure 18.

Train the Model:

Figure 18. Model training in clustering

```
vae.fit(x=X_train, y=None, shuffle=True, epochs=num_epochs, batch_size=ba
tch_size, validation_data=(X_valid, None))
```

Results:

Clustering of digits in the latent space is shown as below, where each colour shows a cluster see Figure 19.

Figure 19. MNIST VAE result

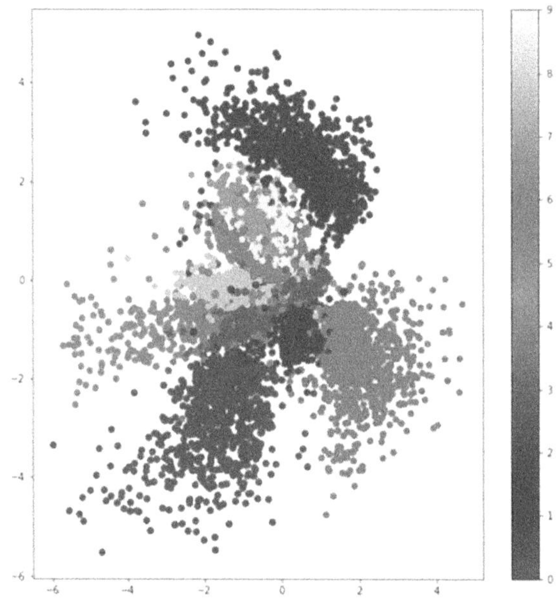

Diagram Source: *(Richard Kuo, n.d.)*

Another way of visualizing the output is as Figure 20

Figure 20. MNIST VAE visualized result

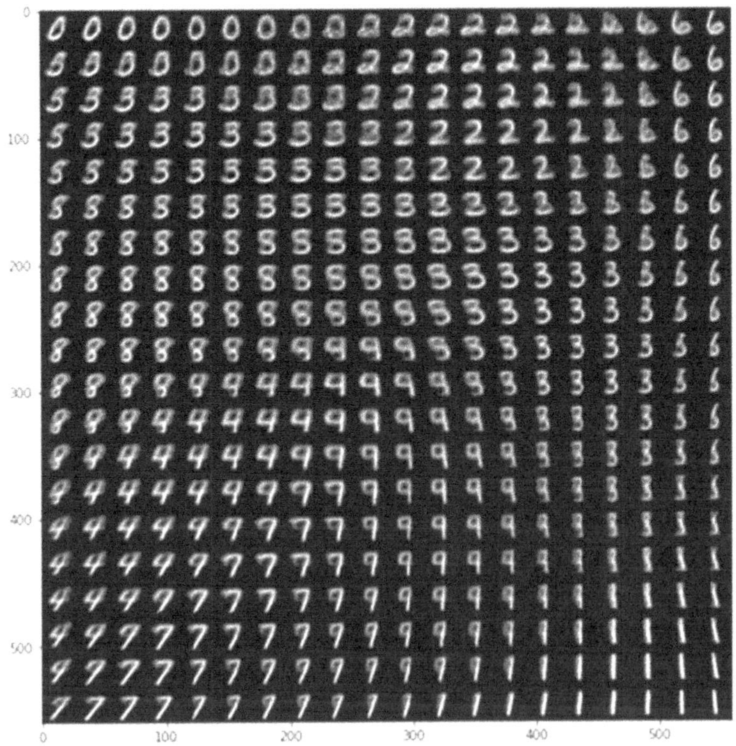

Diagram Source: *(Richard Kuo, n.d.)*

NOTE: *the notebook for this project can be accessed through this source: https://www.kaggle.com/code/rkuo2000/mnist-vae/notebook #5.-Results*

Comparison between Autoencoder-Based Clustering, Variational Autoencoder (VAE) Based Clustering, K-Means Clustering with Autoencoders, and Self-Organizing Maps (SOM), see Table 2.

Table 2. Clustering techniques comparison

Clustering Technique	Description	Strengths	Limitations	Best For
Autoencoder-based Clustering	Uses autoencoders to compress data before applying clustering algorithms, capturing non-linear relationships in high-dimensional data.	- Effective for high-dimensional data. - Reduces dimensionality and noise. - Captures complex patterns.	- Requires large amounts of data. - Harder to interpret learned features. - Can be computationally expensive.	- Anomaly detection. - Clustering high-dimensional image data. - Image compression.
Variational Autoencoder Clustering (VAEC)	Combines autoencoders with probabilistic clustering, learning both a latent representation and the cluster assignments simultaneously.	- Handles complex and non-linear data distributions. - Provides probabilistic cluster assignments. - Can generate data samples.	- Computationally intensive. - Sensitive to hyperparameter choices. - Requires large datasets for optimal performance.	- Complex image clustering with varying styles. - Generative image models. - Non-linear image datasets.
K-means Clustering with Autoencoders (AEK)	Combines autoencoders for dimensionality reduction with K-means clustering in the reduced feature space.	- More efficient than traditional K-means. - Reduces risk of overfitting. - Works well with large-scale datasets.	- K-means is sensitive to initialization and can get stuck in local minima. - Requires specifying the number of clusters (K).	- Image clustering based on prominent features. - Large-scale image datasets. - Simple, efficient clustering.
Spectral Clustering	Uses a graph-based approach to partition data by analyzing the eigenvalues of the similarity matrix, suitable for non-linear separations.	- Can handle non-linearly separable clusters. - Works well for small datasets. - Effective for ambiguous image boundaries.	- Computationally expensive for large datasets. - Requires calculating the similarity matrix. - Not suitable for very large datasets.	- Image segmentation with ambiguous boundaries. - Graph-based image clustering. - Complex scene clustering.
DBSCAN (Density-Based Spatial Clustering of Applications with Noise)	A density-based algorithm that identifies clusters based on regions with high data density, automatically handling noise and outliers.	- Does not require specifying the number of clusters. - Can find arbitrarily shaped clusters. - Handles outliers effectively.	- Struggles with clusters of varying densities. - Sensitive to parameter choices like epsilon and min_samples. - Can be computationally expensive.	- Satellite and geographical image analysis. - Clustering images with irregular-shaped clusters. - Handling noisy datasets.

When is best to use which model:

- **Autoencoder-Based Clustering:** Choose when before clustering, you wish to eliminate noise or extract features from high-dimensional image data. This method is ideal for broad jobs, particularly when handling the clustering process independently is possible.
- **Variational Autoencoder Clustering:** For this model you must have access to a large amount of training data and use robust clustering with uncertainty estimates. This technique is perfect for complicated image data when probabilistic cluster assignments are useful and the distributions are non-linear.
- **K-Means with Autoencoders:** One should work with this method when looking for a more straightforward method that blends effective clustering with dimensionality reduction. This performs well when huge datasets need to be clustered quickly and the latent space is well-structured.

- **Spectral Clustering:** This method is good to choose when the segmentation of your complex data is needed using a graph-based method. Problems where the dataset is smaller, and similarity matrix needs to be computed.
- **DBSCAN:** Problems where noise or outlier in your image data is to be managed DBSCAN will work good including identification of the clusters of any shape. This method doesn't come with the predetermination of the number of clusters.

CLASSIFICATION

Fundamentals of Image Classification Algorithm:

The concept of an **artificial neural network (ANN)** was inspired by working of pattern recognition ability of human brain. ANN is a model where nodes or neurons are interconnected and simulate the processing method of the human brain to get information from some input data. The structure of an artificial neural network consists of an input layer, hidden layers, and an output layer. The performance of this method is evaluated depending on the factors like connection weights and activation functions.

Deep learning is a branch of machine learning that comes from neural network theory. It extracts key features from large datasets, that makes it effective for tasks such as image analysis and natural language processing. Deep learning passes the data through multiple layers, it moves from low-level feature extraction to higher-level feature combinations that allows for more accurate data interpretation and big data processing see Figure 21.

Not just this but to process the data activation functions will be required for making the model learn nonlinearity this helps the model extract more of the important features though a number of iterations. Activation functions **like Softmax, Tanh, or ReLu,** are applied based on the requirement of the problem. **Softmax** is often used in the output layer for classification tasks (Minar & Naher, 2018).

Figure 21. Artificial neural network diagram (geeksforgeeks, 2024a)

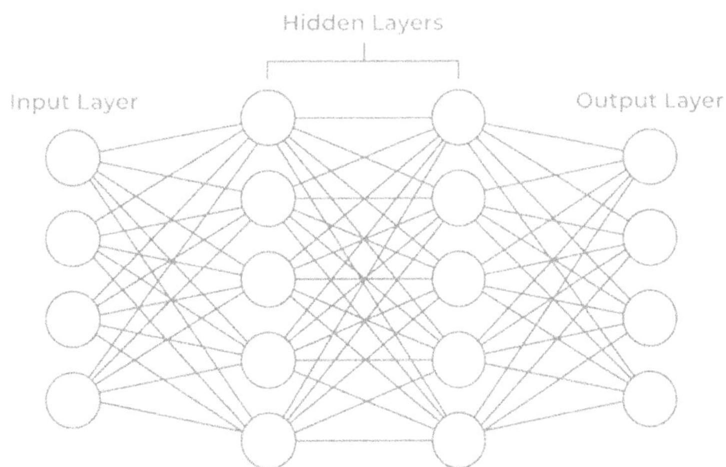

Before moving towards the models, let's have a look at how classification is performed step by step:

- **Data Collection and Preprocessing**
- **Data Splitting**
- **Network Architecture designing**
- **Activation Functions usage**
- **Forward Propagation**
- **Loss Calculation**
- **Backpropagation & Optimization**
- **Training**
- **Model Evaluation**
- **Hyperparameter Tuning**
- **Deployment**

Some famous models for classification are as below.

CNN

A Convolutional Neural Network (CNN) is a deep learning model commonly used for tasks like image classification and language recognition. Its structure includes three key layers: the **convolution layer**, which extracts features from the input image; the **pooling layer**, which reduces the size of the feature map while retaining important information; and the **fully connected layer**, where all nodes connect to those in the previous layer, similar to a standard neural network, Figure 22 (Keiron O'Shea, n.d.; Pandian et al., 2022), (Jamil et al., 2021), (Bhatti, Huang, et al., 2023).

Figure 22. CNN architecture (Main, n.d.)

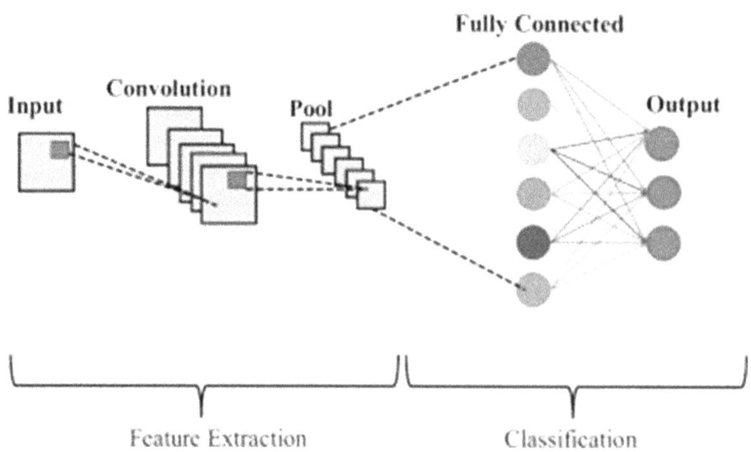

The convolution layer's convolution kernels are essential for extracting image features by applying filters across the input. This reduces the image size and focuses on important data, minimizing the influence of edge pixels. By using shared weights in convolution kernels, CNNs reduce the number of parameters, improving training efficiency. Pooling layers, like max or average pooling, further decrease the size of the feature map, aiding in efficient processing without losing depth(Keiron O'Shea, n.d.).

Problems a CNN method can solve: Convolutional neural networks, or CNNs, are ideally suited for easier image classification problems because they can detect local patterns like edges and textures and capture spatial hierarchies. Long-range dependencies or intricate spatial linkages, however, could be difficult for them.

To have a glimpse of how the methods in CNN can be useful, a study by (Ashraf et al., 2020) is based on Deep CNN for medical image classification. Another study on healthcare by (Feng et al., 2022) developed CNNs-based AI model for pneumothorax classification and segmentation for chest X-ray triaging. Some studies focus on advanced applications aimed at public well-being, such as the development of a navigational stick for the visually impaired by (Sulaman et al., n.d.). The authors (Akram et al., 2024) described CNNs to classify images of traffic signs by highlighting how CNNs perform different than conventional ML models. The study by (Bhatti et al., 2023) utilizes CNNs in conjunction with Inception v3 to identify plant diseases.

CNN Models

ResNet

Imagine building a Lego castle, where each block represents a layer in a **Convolutional Neural Network (CNN)**. In a regular CNN, each block passes information directly to the next one, layer by layer, helping the network recognize patterns in images like edges, shapes, or textures.

But when you try to build a *very* tall castle (or a deep network), the blocks start to wobble, and it becomes hard for the network to learn properly. That's where **ResNet** comes in with a clever idea: instead of just stacking blocks one after another, it adds "shortcut paths" or *skip connections*. The paths allow information to skip over some layers that are not necessary to visit so it can reach the important information early.

If we talk about the **structure of ResNet.** It has layers just like in CNN, but the difference comes here that after every couple of layers, there is a skip connection. This method helps the network stay stable such as not causing vanishing gradients which is one of the problems occurring when conventional CNN is processing the data. This method makes it easier to train the mode even if the network has multiple layers Figure 23.

The formula for ResNet is

$$y=F(x,\{Wi\})+x$$

Here's what it means:

Input and output vectors are x and y respectively, the function F (x, Wi) denotes the residual mapping that needs to be learned through various convolutional layers and operators (Targ et al., 2016).

Diagram

Figure 23. ResNet architecture (Rousseau, 2020)

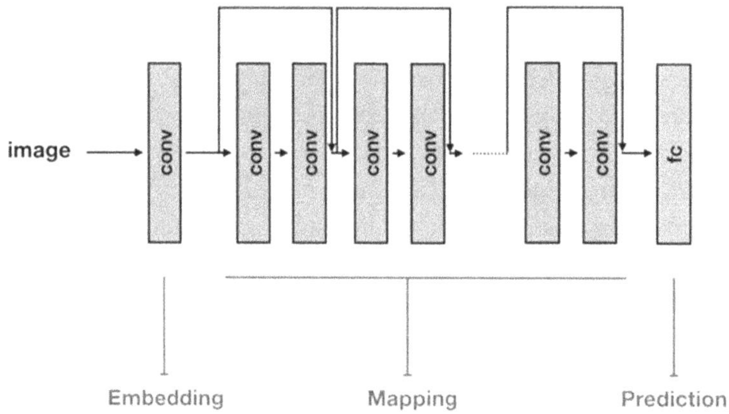

DenseNet

DenseNet connects each layer to every other layer densely, which enhances gradient flow and information flow. To reduce redundancy and encourage feature reuse, feature maps from all previous layers are sent to each layer. By addressing the vanishing gradient issue, this architecture makes deep network training more effective. In addition, DenseNet has features to control network complexity, such that, in comparison to conventional CNNs, it maintains efficiency while utilizing fewer parameters. Because of this, DenseNet is incredibly efficient and compact for deep learning tasks.

Figure 24 below will be visualizing the work of DenseNet.

Figure 24. Deep DenseNet with three dense blocks

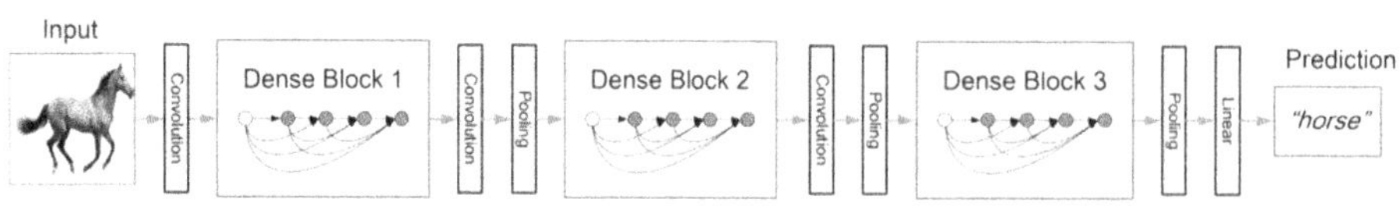

Source: Huang et al. (n.d.)

The fundamental building blocks of DenseNet are called "dense blocks," and they are made up of multiple convolutional layers, each followed by batch normalization and an activation function like ReLU. To encourage feature reuse, each layer in these blocks receives the concatenated outputs of all previous layers. Assume that a dense block with m layers has k feature maps generated by each layer (the growth rate). Then, the l-th layer will have (k times (l + l_0)) input feature maps, where (l_0) is the block's starting number of input channels. (geeksforgeeks, 2024c; Yi Zhu; Shawn Newsam, 2017).

Problems that a ResNet or DenseNet can solve: The best options for bigger, more complicated datasets are ResNet and DenseNet. ResNet reduces problems like vanishing gradients by incorporating residual connections, which enable gradients to flow smoothly through deep layers. Because of this, ResNet works very well with deep architectures and is helpful with big datasets like ImageNet. DenseNet adopts a new strategy by reusing features, increasing parameter efficiency, and connecting every layer to every other layer. DenseNet is appropriate for situations with low data because of its feature reuse method, which enhances learning with fewer parameters. However, both models are computationally intensive, requiring a lot of memory and frequently GPU support, especially for more complex versions such as ResNet-50 or DenseNet-121.

EfficientNet

EfficientNet is a deep learning image categorization model that utilizes lesser processing power and require fewer parameters but provides high-performing outputs. The model's primary innovation is compound scaling, that balances depth, width, and resolution simultaneously for effective scaling. The theory is expressed in the form of the following formula:

$$\text{depth} = \alpha^k, \text{width} = \beta^k, \text{resolution} = \gamma^k$$

to explain the above, α, β, γ are constants and k is a scaling factor.

To discuss about the architecture of EfficientNet, Figure 25, this has been built upon some light models such as MobileNetV2 that is a network designed for the good performance on the embedded and mobile devices and another network MnasNet which is an enhanced architecture for mobile neural network. It is designed to balance accuracy and efficient performance through an automated neural architecture search, integrating methods as depth-wise separable convolutions and squeeze-and-excitation blocks. The base model for EfficientNet is EfficientNet-B0, with versions up to EfficientNet-B7 that offer increased enhancement.

This model achieves state-of-the-art accuracy on benchmarks like ImageNet (a dataset) while being more computationally efficient than larger models like ResNet. EfficientNet is particularly popular for use in edge devices and cloud computing due to its high accuracy-to-compute ratio, making it ideal for applications where efficiency is essential (Liu, 2024).

Diagram

Figure 25. EfficientNet architecture (Ahmed, n.d.)

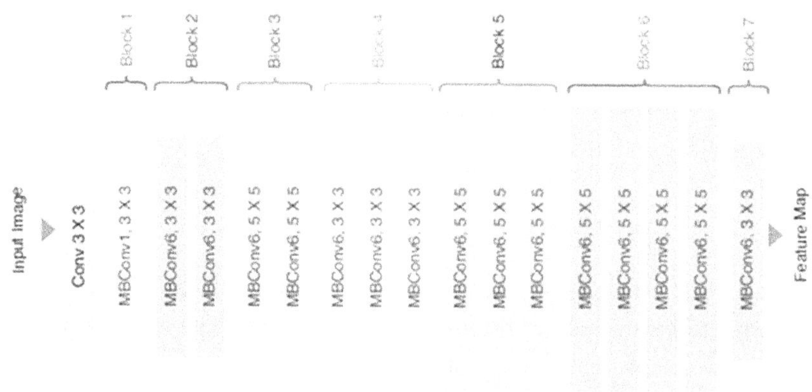

When to use EfficientNet: EfficientNet uses fewer parameters to obtain high accuracy by optimizing breadth, depth, and resolution. It provides excellent performance even in contexts with limited resources, such mobile applications.

RNN

RNN are designed to handle sequential data. Because of their ability to handle sequential input, recurrent neural networks, or RNNs, are useful for classification tasks such as sentiment analysis, speech recognition and more. The input is given in pieces and a track of hidden state is kept, this allows to interpret the data points in sequence by capturing the features from early stages.

RNNs update of its hidden state happens in a way that it takes each word from a sentence and extracts the information from it, it keeps doing this and the final hidden state will be a summary of the input after the entire sequenced input has been analyzed and processed.

Figure 26, for the task of classification of these sequences, there comes a fully connected layer that transforms the final hidden state into different class probabilities, for example positive or negative sentiment in the task of sentiment analysis. The ability to remember past information makes RNNs efficient for sequential data involving tasks, such as natural language processing and time series analysis (Ashraf Zargar, n.d.; Yong Yu, 2019).

Diagram

Figure 26. RNN architecture (Abid Ali Awan, 2022a)

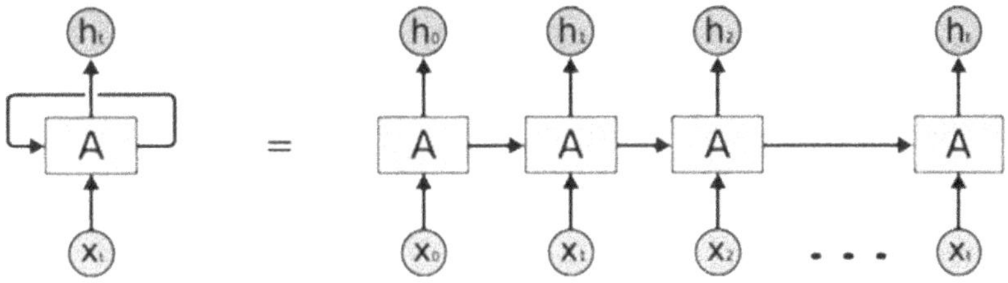

The structure is based on some layers such as X for input that receives the input data and then sends it to the next layer which is the middle layer A then a number of hidden layers are present in the middle layer each with some unique activation functions, weights and biases.

Backpropagation is performed by an RNN which is also known as BPTT Backpropagation through time, this process updates the parameters that happens depending on mistakes computed from output to the input layer. In BPTT the mistakes computed are added at each step of RNN method. (Abid Ali Awan, 2022b; Alex Sherstinsky, 2020), (Gençdoğmuş et al., n.d.).

RNN models:

LSTM:

LSTM is an enhanced recurrent neural network (RNN) that is called Long Short-Term Memory (LSTM). This network is designed to better capture features in sequential data. A common problem in gradient descent is vanishing gradients which is caused due to information gain in lengthy runs and LSTM is a method that mitigates this even better than the precedent approach RNN. Below is an explanation of the structure of LSTM which has a complex architecture which makes the techniques to remember and forget information selectively.

An LSTM structure has three main components called gates:

1. **Forget Gate:** The first gate, the forget gate just like its name checks for the data and determines what data shall be erased. It uses an activation function such as sigmoid to the input that includes the current value and the next hidden state for generating values between 0 and 1. This 0 and 1 denotes to forget and keep respectively.
2. **Input Gate**: Next the input gate determines what information shall be kept and stored, this method uses a **sigmoid** function to filter the input and a **tanh** function for creating new values that could be added to the state.
3. **Output Gate**: The output gate determines what information now shall be given out to the next hidden layer. It works by using the current input, previous hidden state so to generate a sigmoid output and multiplies this output with the cell state after the application of tanh function to produce a final output.

LSTMs are efficient for controlling the information flow due to these gates, see Figure 27, which makes it capable to learn from the sequences. For problems where working with lengthy sequences such as language modelling, machine translation, and speech recognition LSTMs have shown promising results. LSTM has offered a strong enhancement for the drawbacks of conventional RNN. (Ashraf Zargar, n.d.; Shewalkar et al., 2019; Staudemeyer & Morris, 2019; Yong Yu, 2019), (Han et al., 2024). The visual diagram of LSTM is shown in the diagram below.

Diagram

Figure 27. LSTM architecture (AIML, 2024)

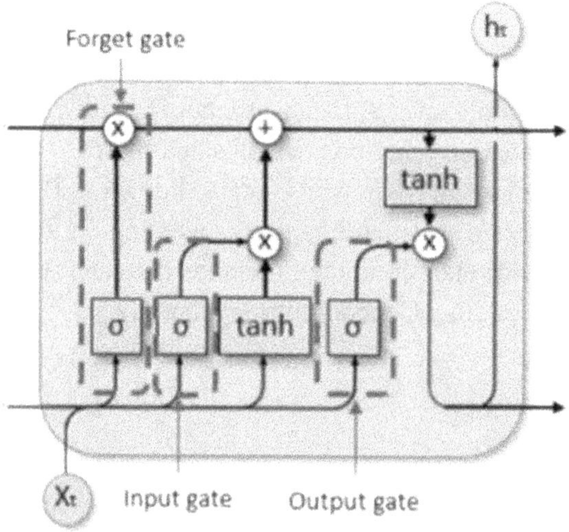

Classification in LSTM

Long Short-Term Memory (LSTM) networks pass the data through a series of memory cells which keeps information over a long period of time, the sequential input data is passed though input, forget and output gates to regulate the flow of information which allows them to extract the temporal features effectively. Classification is performed after the final output layer, where a fully connected layer with an activation function is responsible for generating class predictions. Activation functions as sigmoid or softmax are used depending on the class requirements. (Staudemeyer & Morris, 2019).

When to use RNNs: RNNs or enhanced LSTMs are effective for sequential data processing, for example time-series analysis. To manage long-term dependencies, LSTMs expand this with memory cells, which is particularly helpful in applications involving speech and text. A good application has been written by (Fahim et al., 2021) that discusses how LSTM can be used to forecast the education system, also another work by (Aamir et al., 2022) predicting the environmental change of Carbon Emission Patterns.

Vision Transformers (ViTs)

A transformer is a deep learning model that uses attention mechanism to assess the importance of each individual data point in the input sequence. In machine learning, transformers are made up of several layers of self-attention. Their main applications are in the AI subfields of computer vision (CV) and natural language processing (NLP).

With recent advances in computer vision that achieve SOTA standard accuracy with improved parameter efficiency, transformers in machine learning hold great promise for a general learning approach that can be applied to a variety of data modalities.

The research paper "An Image is Worth 16*16 Words: Transformers for Image Recognition at Scale," which was presented as a conference paper at ICLR 2021, described the Vision Transformer (ViT) model architecture. Neil Houlsby, Alexey Dosovitskiy, and ten other members of the Google Research Brain Team developed and published it.

ViTs have gained popularity due to their ability to capture complex, global relationships across an image without relying on the convolutional layers traditionally used in computer vision models, Figure 28.

Architecture:

Figure 28. Vision transformer architecture

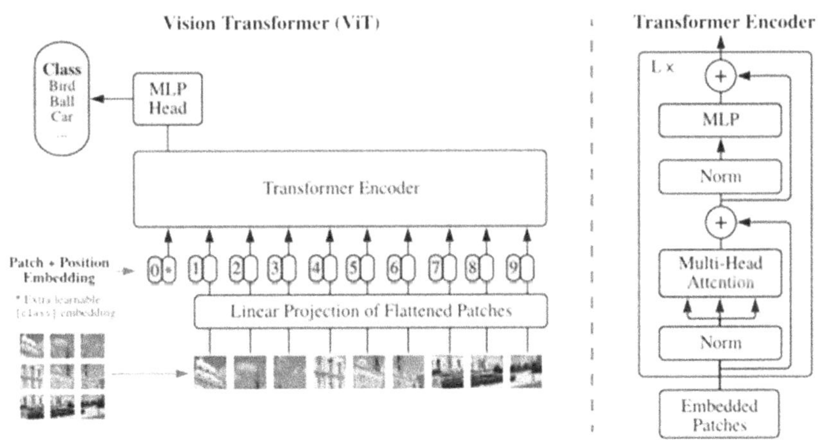

Patch-Based Input Representation:

- The image is divided into a grid of tiny, fixed-size patches (such as 16x16 pixels) by a ViT.
- Each patch is then handled as a single "token" after being "flattened" into a one-dimensional vector.
- A fixed-length vector representation that has been linearly embedded with the patches is subsequently delivered via the transformer.

Positional Encoding:

- Transformers lack an innate comprehension of spatial relationships, which are crucial to visuals. To solve this, ViTs give each patch embedding positional encodings, which inform the model of each patch's location within the image.
- This enables the model to comprehend patch layout and, thus, capture spatial structure in images.

Multi-Head Self-Attention:

- The ViT enables each patch to "attend" to every other patch by utilizing transformers' self-attention mechanism. This helps the model comprehend context across various image segments by allowing it to collect long-range dependencies over the entire image.
- The model can learn different types of links between patches, that improves its capability to capture image features in multi-head attention.

Layers of Transformer Encoder:

- Multiple encoder layers, including feed-forward neural networks and self-attention, are used by the Vision Transformer. The model can learn more complex representations of the image due to these layers' constant improvement of the patch embeddings.

Classification Token:

- Before predicting the class label for image classification tasks, ViTs adds a unique "classification token" to the series of patch tokens. This token learns a global representation of the image as it moves through the transformer layers.

Final Layer for classification:

• The final layer is sent through a fully connected layer to generate the final class prediction after the image and the classification have been processed through the transformer levels.

Vision Transformers (ViTs) are essential for large datasets with complex image structures. ViTs capture patterns throughout an image by segmenting it into patches and applying self-attention to each. Nevertheless, ViTs may have trouble with smaller datasets and demand a large amount of computational power. (Gaudenz Boesch, 2023; Sabour et al., 2017)

Capsule Network

Geoffrey Hinton and his colleagues developed the sophisticated neural network architecture known as Capsule Networks (CapsNets) to overcome the drawbacks of traditional convolutional neural networks (CNNs), particularly when it comes to jobs that require complicated object recognition. To increase a model's capability for image identification tasks where orientation, location, and structure are essential, capsule networks are there to capture the interactions between an object's components.

Below is a detailed explanation of how a capsule network works:

Capsules:

A capsule is a tiny collection of neurons that collectively indicate a feature's direction, scale, and position, among other characteristics.

Instead of producing a single scalar value, as classic neurons in a CNN do, each capsule produces a vector that encodes the attributes and likelihood of a feature.

Dynamic Routing:

Capsule networks employ a technique known as dynamic routing between layers. This enhances the network's ability to identify hierarchical linkages by enabling capsules to communicate their outputs to the most pertinent higher-level capsules.

The network can still identify an object even if it appears in a different orientation or position thanks to dynamic routing, which helps maintain spatial links between features.

Pose Information:

The pose (position, orientation, and size) of a recognized feature is contained in each capsule vector. This implies that when a capsule recognizes an eye in a picture, it also stores the eye's orientation and location.

The network can comprehend the spatial arrangement of features, which is essential for object recognition even when an object's attitude changes.

Agreement and Voting Mechanism:

Voting is the process by which lower-level capsules in CapsNets transmit their output to higher-level capsules only when there is "agreement" between them—that is, when the features they identify align in a way that suggests a particular object—and higher-level capsules receive these votes, which enable them to comprehend the presence and orientation of larger features or entire objects based on inputs from smaller parts.

Structure of a CapsNet:

The understand the structure of CapsNet we will study about its layers such as primary, higher and output.

Primary layer:

- Typically, initial convolutional layers that identify fundamental characteristics (such as edges) provide the input to the first layer of capsules.
- The initial level of capsules in the network is formed by primary capsules, which subsequently record the orientation and additional pose information of these identified features.

Higher Level Layers:

- To combine data and create more intricate structures, higher capsule layers employ dynamic routing after receiving inputs from lower-level capsules.
- To detect a face, for instance, a higher capsule layer may mix inputs from capsules that depict the eyes, nose, and mouth, among other components of an object.

Output layer:

- The output layer of this method involves a capsule for each class. Each capsule in this layer outputs a vector, and the class with the longest vector is the predicted class.
- The length of the vector represents the probability that the object belongs to a specific class.

What is Capsule Network good for: Capsule networks are good for applications where object orientation and spatial interactions are required. Since the model learns the position and orientation. The problems where spatial hierarchies are essential to be studied such as, medical imaging or 3D object recognition, capsule networks have shown good results. However, the application of this network could be limited as it requires high processing demands and lack of maturity compared to CNN or transformers. (Sabour et al., 2017)

Attention-based CNN:

Transformer-based CNNs or Convolutional Transformers capture both local and global features in image data by combining the transformers and convolutional neural networks (CNNs). As it can effectively capture spatial hierarchies and recognize contextual relationships across an image. This hybrid method has shown good results for a variety of vision-based tasks, such as object identification, segmentation, and classification.

Here's a breakdown of how these models work and their components:

1. CNN Layers for Extracting Local Features

CNNs' have layers such as convolutions, pooling, and feature maps. This makes them very efficient at capturing local spatial data such as edges, textures, and intricate shapes, these are examples of low-to-high-level spatial information that they can extract. Because transformers tend to focus on global relationships, convolutional layers are usually utilized in the early stages of transformer-based CNNs to learn high-resolution, local features from the image.

2. Transformer Layers for Modeling Global Context

Transformers' self-attention mechanism, which enables them to calculate correlations between every component of a picture at once, makes them excellent for capturing long-range dependencies. These models are able to learn contexts and links within spatial information by inserting transformer blocks after the CNN layers. This is particularly helpful in situations where it's important to capture features from far-off areas of an image such as in complicated scene analysis or medical imaging. (Zheng et al., 2022)

Transformer-Based CNN Architectures

- **Convolutional Vision Transformer (CvT):**

In Convolutional Vision Transformers, attention mechanism is used to integrate with convolutional layers straight into the transformer. This makes it more parameter-efficient and an enhanced method for larger images by directly combining local feature extraction from convolutional layers with the global attention.

- **Hybrid Vision Transformer (ViT):**

Feature extraction is performed by convolutional layers in Hybrid Vision Transformer (ViT) configuration, and for the analysis of the features that have been extracted is performed by a transformer. Typically, the CNN takes the high dimensional input data and later lowering the transformer's input size, which makes it computationally efficient.

- **Swin Transformer:**

Swin Transformer: While not a CNN per se, Swin Transformers mimic the hierarchical structure of a CNN by focusing on local regions and segmenting images into patches. Swin improves the model's local and global knowledge by introducing a "shifted window" method that produces overlaps between picture patches.

Comparison between classification techniques, see Table 3

Table 3. Classification techniques comparison

Technique	Description	Strengths	Limitations	Best For
CNN (Convolutional Neural Network)	Traditional CNNs consist of convolutional, pooling, and fully connected layers that capture spatial patterns in images.	Good at detecting local patterns like edges, textures; relatively lightweight in terms of parameters.	Limited in understanding long-range dependencies; needs many layers for complex hierarchies.	General image classification tasks with moderate complexity, e.g., digit recognition.
ResNet (Residual Networks)	Builds on CNNs by adding skip (residual) connections to allow information to bypass certain layers.	Enables very deep architectures; addresses vanishing gradient problem, making training more stable.	Computationally heavier than basic CNNs; complex architecture can lead to high memory use.	Complex image classification tasks, e.g., large-scale datasets like ImageNet.
DenseNet (Dense Convolutional Network)	Extends CNNs by densely connecting each layer to every other layer, reusing features across the network.	High parameter efficiency; reduces overfitting; requires fewer parameters while improving gradient flow.	Can be computationally intensive; requires GPU support for optimal training.	Tasks with limited data but complex features, e.g., medical image classification.
EfficientNet	A family of models that balances width, depth, and resolution systematically, offering a range of sizes from lightweight to very deep networks.	Optimized for resource efficiency; achieves high accuracy with fewer parameters compared to similar-sized networks.	Some configurations may need careful tuning to balance computational cost and accuracy.	Mobile and embedded applications where computational resources are limited, but high accuracy is desired.
RNN (Recurrent Neural Network)	RNNs process sequential data by using recurrent layers that allow each output to depend on previous inputs.	Effective for sequential data; good for capturing temporal dependencies.	Struggles with long-term dependencies; prone to vanishing/exploding gradients.	Sequential data like time-series and speech data, e.g., predicting stock prices.
LSTM (Long Short-Term Memory)	A type of RNN with memory cells that can retain information across longer sequences.	Handles long-term dependencies well; less prone to vanishing gradients than vanilla RNNs.	Slower to train due to complexity; computationally expensive.	Tasks requiring memory of long-term sequences, e.g., natural language processing (NLP) and text classification.

continued on following page

Table 3. Continued

Technique	Description	Strengths	Limitations	Best For
Vision Transformers (ViTs)	Transformers adapted for images by dividing the image into patches and applying self-attention across patches.	Strong global context understanding; flexible with sequence length and position.	Requires large datasets for optimal performance; computationally heavy without optimizations.	Large-scale image datasets where understanding context across the whole image is key, e.g., fine-grained image classification.
Capsule Networks	Networks using "capsules" that capture hierarchical relationships, with dynamic routing between capsules.	Captures spatial relationships effectively; robustness to pose/ rotation variations in images.	Computationally intensive; less mature than CNNs and transformers in terms of implementation support.	Classification tasks where spatial hierarchies are critical, e.g., medical and 3D image classification.
Attention-based CNN	Enhances CNNs with attention mechanisms that help focus on relevant parts of the image for each prediction.	Combines spatial feature extraction and context sensitivity; computationally efficient.	Needs tuning to balance attention layers and CNN layers; still more computationally costly than plain CNNs.	Tasks with complex and hierarchical spatial dependencies, e.g., facial recognition and scene understanding.

In addition to these strategies, there are other popular approaches that have different uses. For example, (Hamza et al., 2023) and (Noor et al., 2024) examine GANs in a literature review that covers their methods and applications. Similarly, (Bhatti, Bazai, et al., 2023) describe the uses of decision trees, another classification technique.

Classification Case Study

This case study focuses on training a model using EfficientNet, though other models can be trained in a similar way, with minor adjustments depending on the specific model architecture.

Dataset: choose a dataset or prepare a dataset, either manual or online available datasets, that can be in form of videos or images

Load the data:

Load the Stanford Dogs dataset from TensorFlow Datasets (TFDS), which contains 20,580 images across 120 dog breeds (12,000 for training and 8,580 for testing) check Figure 29.

Figure 29 Dataset loading in classification

```
dataset_name = "stanford_dogs"
(ds_train, ds_test), ds_info = tfds.load(
    dataset_name, split=["train", "test"], with_info=True, as_supervised=True
)
NUM_CLASSES = ds_info.features["label"].num_classes
```

Visualize the data:

Let's visualize the dataset to have an idea of how the data looks, see Figure 30.

Figure 30 Visualization of the dataset Standard Dogs

Data Augmentation:

Data augmentation is performed to increase the diversity of data, improve model generalization, and reduce the risk of overfitting, see Figure 31.

Figure 31. Dataset augmentation

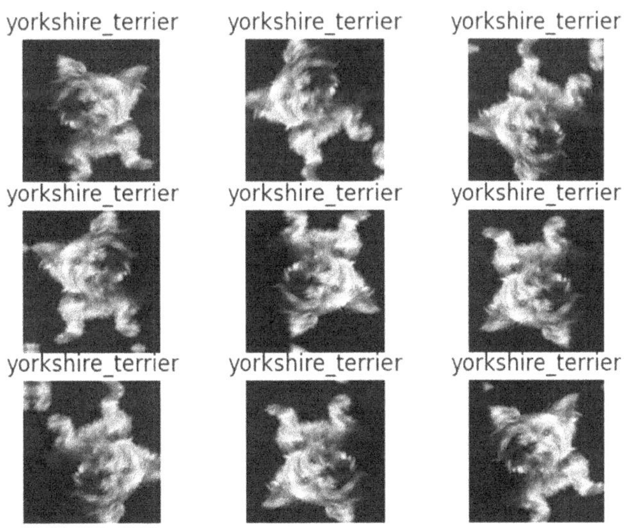

Training the model:

EfficientNetB0 model with 120 output classes is constructed, see Figure 32.

Figure 32. Classification model training

```
model = EfficientNetB0(
    include_top=True,
    weights=None,
    classes=NUM_CLASSES,
    input_shape=(IMG_SIZE, IMG_SIZE, 3),
)
model.compile(optimizer="adam", loss="categorical_crossentropy", metrics=["accuracy"])

model.summary()

epochs = 40  # @param {type: "slider", min:10, max:100}
hist = model.fit(ds_train, epochs=epochs, validation_data=ds_test)
```

Model Accuracy:

Training from scratch demands careful selection of hyperparameters and finding appropriate regularization can be challenging. It also requires significantly more resources, as evident from the training and validation accuracy plot, which shows validation accuracy stagnating at a low level, see Figure 33.

Figure 33. Result for classification

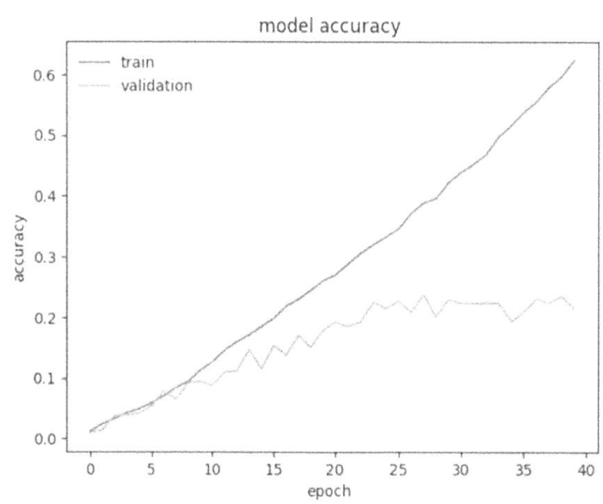

NOTE: *this code can be accessed through this link: https://keras.io/examples/vision/image_classification_efficientnet_fine_tuning/#introduction-what-is-efficientnet*

Not only the model training is essential for tasks like classification or clustering but optimizing the work for better inference is the key to build a good system. (Nabeel et al., 2024) is a good study on optimization of classification through hyperparameter tuning.

CONCLUSION

This chapter has discussed various deep learning methods for image-based classification and clustering, each of which is appropriate for a particular application. We demonstrated how these models can handle particular image analysis problems, such as correctly identifying complicated visual information or uncovering hidden patterns in unlabeled data, by contrasting their advantages and disadvantages. This chapter provides as a basis for choosing the best method depending on the particular needs of every work.

REFERENCES

Aamir, M., Bazai, S., Bhatti, U. A., Dayo, Z. A., Liu, J., & Zhang, K. (2023). Applications of Machine Learning in Medicine: Current Trends and Prospects. *2023 Global Conference on Wireless and Optical Technologies, GCWOT 2023*. DOI: 10.1109/GCWOT57803.2023.10064665

Aamir, M., Bhatti, M. A., Bazai, S. U., Marjan, S., Mirza, A. M., Wahid, A., Hasnain, A., & Bhatti, U. A. (2022). Predicting the Environmental Change of Carbon Emission Patterns in South Asia: A Deep Learning Approach Using BiLSTM. *Atmosphere (Basel)*, 13(12), 2011. Advance online publication. DOI: 10.3390/atmos13122011

Abid Ali Awan. (2022a). *Recurrent Neural Network Tutorial (RNN)*. Datacamp.

Abid Ali Awan. (2022b, March). *Recurrent Neural Network Tutorial (RNN)*. Datacamp.

Ahmed, T. and S. N. (n.d.). *Classification and understanding of cloud structures via satellite images with EfficientUNet*.

AIML. (2024). *Compare the different sequence models rnn lstm gru and transformers*. AIML.

Akram, S., Bazai, S. U., & Marjan, S. (2024). Classifying Traffic Signs Using Convolutional Neural Networks Based on Deep Learning Models. In Deep Learning for Multimedia Processing Applications (pp. 250-269). CRC Press.

Ashraf, R., Habib, M. A., Akram, M., Latif, M. A., Malik, M. S. A., Awais, M., Dar, S. H., Mahmood, T., Yasir, M., & Abbas, Z. (2020). Deep Convolution Neural Network for Big Data Medical Image Classification. *IEEE Access : Practical Innovations, Open Solutions*, 8, 105659–105670. DOI: 10.1109/ACCESS.2020.2998808

Ashraf Zargar, S. (n.d.). *Introduction to Sequence Learning Models: RNN, LSTM*. GRU.

Bhatti, U. A., Bazai, S. U., Hussain, S., Fakhar, S., Ku, C. S., Marjan, S., Yee, P. L., & Jing, L. (2023). Deep Learning-Based Trees Disease Recognition and Classification Using Hyperspectral Data. *Computers, Materials & Continua*, 77(1), 681–697. DOI: 10.32604/cmc.2023.037958

Bhatti, U. A., Huang, M., Neira-Molina, H., Marjan, S., Baryalai, M., Tang, H., Wu, G., & Bazai, S. U. (2023). MFFCG – Multi feature fusion for hyperspectral image classification using graph attention network. *Expert Systems with Applications*, 229, 120496. https://doi.org/https://doi.org/10.1016/j.eswa.2023.120496. DOI: 10.1016/j.eswa.2023.120496

Boesch, G. (2023). *Vision Transformers (ViT) in Image Recognition – 2024 Guide*. Https://Viso.Ai/Deep-Learning/Vision-Transformer-Vit/. geeksforgeeks. (2024a). *Artificial Neural Networks and its Applications*. Geeksforgeeks. geeksforgeeks. (2024b). *Clustering in Machine Learning*. Geeksforgeeks.

Chollet, F. (n.d.). *M A N N I N G*.

Fahim, A., Tan, Q., Mazzi, M., Sahabuddin, M., Naz, B., & Ullah Bazai, S. (2021). Hybrid LSTM Self-Attention Mechanism Model for Forecasting the Reform of Scientific Research in Morocco. *Computational Intelligence and Neuroscience*, 2021(1), 6689204. Advance online publication. DOI: 10.1155/2021/6689204 PMID: 34122534

Feng, S., Liu, Q., Patel, A., Bazai, S. U., Jin, C., Kim, J. S., & Kim, E. (2022). Automated pneumothorax triaging in chest X-rays in the New Zealand population using deep-learning algorithms. *Journal of Medical Imaging and Radiation Oncology*, 66(8), 1035–1043. DOI: 10.1111/1754-9485.13393 PMID: 35224858

Flores, S. (2019). *Variational Autoencoders are Beautiful*. Comp Three Inc.

Geeksforgeeks. (2024). *DBSCAN Clustering in ML | Density based clustering*. Https://Www.Geeksforgeeks.Org/Dbscan-Clustering-in-Ml-Density-Based-Clustering/

geeksforgeeks. (2024c, June). *DenseNet Explained*. Geeksforgeeks.

Gençdoğmuş, A., Hameed, A. A., & Jamil, A. (n.d.). *Sentiment Analysis for COVID-19 Tweets Using Recurrent Neural Network (RNN) and Bidirectional Encoder Representations (BERT) Models*. https://www.researchgate.net/publication/357117201

Haider, A., Hussain, L., Tareen, A. W., Bazai, S. U., Aslam, S., Neo, M., & Amphawan, A. (2024). A comparative study of machine learning techniques for accurate disease prediction using symptom-based diagnosis. *AIP Conference Proceedings*, 3153(1), 020005. DOI: 10.1063/5.0217579

Hameed, M., Yang, F., Bazai, S. U., Ghafoor, M. I., Alshehri, A., Khan, I., Baryalai, M., Andualem, M., & Jaskani, F. H. (2022). Urbanization Detection Using LiDAR-Based Remote Sensing Images of Azad Kashmir Using Novel 3D CNNs. *Journal of Sensors*, 2022(1), 6430120. DOI: 10.1155/2022/6430120

Hameed, M., Yang, F., Bazai, S. U., Ghafoor, M. I., Alshehri, A., Khan, I., Ullah, S., Baryalai, M., Jaskani, F. H., & Andualem, M. (2022a). Convolutional Autoencoder-Based Deep Learning Approach for Aerosol Emission Detection Using LiDAR Dataset. *Journal of Sensors*, 2022, 1–17. Advance online publication. DOI: 10.1155/2022/3690312

Hamza, M., Bazai, S. U., Ghafoor, M. I., Ullah, S., Akram, S., & Khan, M. S. (2023). Generative Adversarial Networks (GANs) Video Framework: A Systematic Literature Review. *2023 International Conference on Energy, Power, Environment, Control, and Computing, ICEPECC 2023 - Proceedings*. DOI: 10.1109/ICEPECC57281.2023.10209475

Han, H., Bazai, S. U., Bhatti, M. A., Basit, A., Wahid, A., Bhatti, U. A., Ghadi, Y. Y., & Algarni, A. (2024). Hybrid Climate Forecasting: Variational Mode Decomposition and Convolutional Neural Network with Long-Term Short Memory. *Polish Journal of Environmental Studies*, 33(2), 1121–1134. DOI: 10.15244/pjoes/172756

Haq, S. U., Bazai, S. U., Fatima, A., Marjan, S., Yang, J., Por, L. Y., Anjum, M., Shahab, S., & Ku, C. S. (2023). Reseek-arrhythmia: Empirical evaluation of ResNet architecture for detection of arrhythmia. *Diagnostics (Basel)*, 13(18), 2867. DOI: 10.3390/diagnostics13182867 PMID: 37761234

Huang, . (n.d.). *DenseNet*. Densely Connected Convolutional Networks.

Jamil, A., Khan, A. A., Hameed, A. A., & Sibghat Ullah Bazai, S. (2021). Land Cover Classification using Machine Learning Approaches from High Resolution Images. *Journal of Applied and Emerging Sciences*, 11(1). Advance online publication. DOI: 10.36785/jaes.111501

Károly, A. I., Fullér, R., & Galambos, P. (2018). Unsupervised Clustering for Deep Learning: A tutorial survey. *Acta Polytechnica Hungarica*, 15(8), 29–53. DOI: 10.12700/APH.15.8.2018.8.2

Keerthana. (2024). *Spectral Clustering: A Comprehensive Guide for Beginners.* Https://Www .Analyticsvidhya.Com/Blog/2021/05/What-Why-and-How-of-Spectral-Clustering/

Keiron O'Shea, R. N. (n.d.). *An Introduction to Convolutional Neural Networks.* Neural and Evolutionary Computing.

Kowsari, K., Sali, R., Khan, M. N., Adorno, W., Ali, S. A., Moore, S. R., Amadi, B. C., Kelly, P., Syed, S., & Brown, D. E. (2019). *Diagnosis of Celiac Disease and Environmental Enteropathy on Biopsy Images Using Color Balancing on Convolutional Neural Networks.* http://arxiv.org/abs/1904.05773

Richard Kuo. (n.d.). *MNIST VAE.* Kaggle.

Liu, X. (2024). *Comparison of Four Convolutional Neural Network-Based Algorithms for Sports Image Classification.*, DOI: 10.2991/978-94-6463-370-2_20

Minar, M. R., & Naher, J. (2018). *Recent Advances in Deep Learning: An Overview.* https://doi.org/ DOI: 10.13140/RG.2.2.24831.10403

Nabeel, S. M., Bazai, S. U., Alasbali, N., Liu, Y., Ghafoor, M. I., Khan, R., Ku, C. S., Yang, J., Shahab, S., & Por, L. Y. (2024). Optimizing lung cancer classification through hyperparameter tuning. *Digital Health*, 10, 20552076241249661. DOI: 10.1177/20552076241249661 PMID: 38698834

Noor, R., Wahid, A., Bazai, S. U., Khan, A., Fang, M., Syam, M. S., & Bhatti, U. A. (2024). DLGAN: Undersampled MRI reconstruction using deep learning-based generative adversarial network. *Biomedical Signal Processing and Control*, 93, 106218. DOI: 10.1016/j.bspc.2024.106218

Nutakki, G. C., Abdollahi, B., Sun, W., & Nasraoui, O. (2019). *An Introduction to Deep Clustering.*, DOI: 10.1007/978-3-319-97864-2_4

Opochinsky, Y. Shlomo E. Chazan; Sharon Gannot; Jacob Goldberger. (2020). K-Autoencoders Deep Clustering. *ICASSP 2020 - 2020 IEEE International Conference on Acoustics, Speech and Signal Processing (ICASSP).*

Pandian, R., Vedanarayanan, V., Ravi Kumar, D. N. S., & Rajakumar, R. (2022). Detection and classification of lung cancer using CNN and Google net. *Measurement. Sensors*, 24, 100588. Advance online publication. DOI: 10.1016/j.measen.2022.100588

Rousseau, F. & D. L. & F. Ronan. (2020). Residual Networks as Flows of Diffeomorphisms. Journal of Mathematical Imaging and Vision. *Journal of Mathematical Imaging and Vision*, •••, 62.

Sabour, S., Frosst, N., & Hinton, G. E. (2017). *Dynamic Routing Between Capsules.* http://arxiv.org/abs/1710.09829

Sherstinsky, A. (2020). Fundamentals of Recurrent Neural Network (RNN) and Long Short-Term Memory (LSTM) network. *Physica D. Nonlinear Phenomena*, 404, 404. DOI: 10.1016/j.physd.2019.132306

Shewalkar, A., Nyavanandi, D., & Ludwig, S. A. (2019). Performance Evaluation of Deep neural networks Applied to Speech Recognition: Rnn, LSTM and GRU. *Journal of Artificial Intelligence and Soft Computing Research*, 9(4), 235–245. DOI: 10.2478/jaiscr-2019-0006

Staudemeyer, R. C., & Morris, E. R. (2019). *Understanding LSTM — a tutorial into Long Short-Term Memory Recurrent Neural Networks*. http://arxiv.org/abs/1909.09586

Sulaman, M., ullah Bazai, S., Akram, M., Akram khan, M., Ullah Bazai, S., Sulaman, M., Akram, M., & Think Tank Network, B. (n.d.). Title: Deep Learning based Smart Navigational Stick for Blind People Affiliation (s): 1 IT Administrator Balochistan Think Tank Network (BTTN) Quetta History: Citation: Deep Learning-Based Smart Navigational Stick for Blind and Visually Impaired People. *UMT Artif. Intell. Rev, 2*(2), 0–00.

Tabassum, I., & Bazai, S. U. (2024). Augmenting Multimedia Analysis. Deep Learning for Multimedia Processing Applications: Volume One: Image Security and Intelligent Systems for Multimedia Processing, 194.

Tareen, S., Bazai, S. U., Ullah, S., Ullah, R., Marjan, S., & Ghafoor, M. I. (2022, December). Phishing and intrusion attacks: An overview of classification mechanisms. In 2022 3rd International Informatics and Software Engineering Conference (IISEC) (pp. 1-5). IEEE

Targ, S., Almeida, D., & Lyman, K. (2016). *Resnet in Resnet: Generalizing Residual Architectures*. http://arxiv.org/abs/1603.08029

Yu, Y. (2019). X. S. C. H. J. Z. (2019). A Review of Recurrent Neural Networks: LSTM Cells and Network Architectures. *Neural Computation*, •••, 31.

Zheng, M., Xu, J., Shen, Y., Tian, C., Li, J., Fei, L., Zong, M., & Liu, X. (2022). Attention-based CNNs for Image Classification: A Survey. *Journal of Physics: Conference Series*, 2171(1), 012068. Advance online publication. DOI: 10.1088/1742-6596/2171/1/012068

Zhu, Y., & Newsam, S. (2017). DenseNet for dense flow. *2017 IEEE International Conference on Image Processing (ICIP)*. DOI: 10.1109/ICIP.2017.8296389

Chapter 9
Lung Diseases Classification Using Artificial Neural Network With Ant Colony Optimization

T. Aarthi
https://orcid.org/0009-0005-5474-3808
KGiSL Institute of Technology, India

P. Dhamayanthi
KGiSL Institute of Technology, India

S. Indhumathi
KGiSL Institute of Technology, India

A. Sakthivel
KGiSL Institute of Technology, India

ABSTRACT

The classification of medical data is the most difficult problem to solve among all research problems since it has more commercial significance in the context of health analytics. Several researchers have looked into using Artificial Intelligence (AI) for lung disease classification. This paper proposed a novel classification algorithm for diagnosis of various lung diseases. Already known existing algorithms have some drawback in noise removal and classification process. In this approach, better noise removal technique is used to remove the unwanted noises in the input lung image. Hybridization of Artificial Neural Network with Ant Colony Optimization based classification algorithm is used to predict the lung disease in more accurate and obtain the better efficiency. The suggested HANNACO algorithm was evaluated qualitatively and obtained 95.30% classification accuracy, 93.72% with the minimum classification time duration of 18 ms over the current approaches such as Decision Tree, SVM, and KNN.

DOI: 10.4018/979-8-3693-9045-0.ch009

I. INTRODUCTION

The current state of medical services is still a major concern for every human being, so it is necessary to provide clinical forms of support that are still easily available to everybody. The basic prerequisite is to predict lung disease using a computer programming technique by applying the grouping and highlight choice procedure. Lung illness is the greatest cause of death globally. According to WHO estimates, 210 million people have chronic obstructive pulmonary disease (COPD), which killed 300,000 people in 2005 and increased by 30% in 2015. Additionally, COPD is predicted to be the third most common cause of mortality globally by 2030. These lung disease rates worsen when calcifications, fibrosis, and other conditions are taken into account. Analysis of medical pictures is crucial for early and precise lung disease diagnosis, helping physicians treat patients effectively, and preventing additional deaths.

Around 85% of fatalities occurred in low- and middle-income countries. By 2030, it is projected that 25 million people die from lung disease if current trends are allowed to continue. In the medical field collects massive volumes of data on lung disease, yet regrettably, these data aren't “mined” to uncover secret knowledge that would enable informed decision-making. A reduction in the blood and oxygen flow to the lungs causes lung disease. It is difficult to find hidden links and patterns in data, nevertheless, due to a lack of effective analysis tools, these data taken from Wang, Chenran, et al. (2023).

To help healthcare workers diagnose lung disease, researchers have started employing data mining techniques. Ibrahim, Ibrahim, and Adnan Abdulazeez, (2021) explored the annual increase in lung disease patient mortality around the globe and the accessibility of enormous patient data sets from which to derive knowledge-rich information have served as the driving forces behind the effort. It is crucial to create a tool that be integrated into hospital management systems to assist and advise medical professionals in correctly diagnosing and treating patients with lung disease. The accuracy of the many approaches used to detect lung disease varies, and includes various algorithms.

Lung Rhythm Disorders: Cause the lung to beat too rapidly, too slowly, or erratically. Arrhythmias come in a variety of forms while certain can happen rapidly and are lethal, others have no symptoms or warning signs. The lung diseases, particularly those of its valves, walls, muscles, or blood arteries close to the lung. It may be congenitally present at birth or acquire after birth as a result of an infection, normal wear and tear, or other circumstances. Every age and stage of life requires support for those with lung problems and their families, who frequently need continuing medical care and surgical operations, analyzed by Satpathy, M. M. B. R., and B. R. Mishra. (2021).

Symptoms of Lung Disease: Coronary Artery Diseases, a frequent lung condition, the main blood arteries that supply the lung muscle are affected. Plaques are the most frequent cause of coronary artery disease, or accumulations of cholesterol, in the arteries of the lungs. Khan, Maria, et al, (2020) discussed the plaques build up to cause atherosclerosis. The lung and other body organs receive less blood when a person has atherosclerosis. This could lead to a stroke, angina, or a lung attack. Individuals with coronary artery disease may exhibit distinct symptoms in comparison to women. For instance, men have chest pain more frequently than women.

Risk Factor: A family history of lung disease is one of the risk factors. Although each risk factor contributes differently across cultures or ethnic groups, the overall effect is fairly stable, outlined by Ang, Lina, Pratyusha Ghosh, and Wei Jie Seow. (2021).

Lung diseases can be caused by a number of factors, including:

- Infections, such as bacterial, viral, or fungal infections

- Smoking tobacco or breathing in secondhand tobacco smoke
- Breathing in radon, asbestos, or other forms of air pollution
- Exposure to chemicals such as uranium, beryllium, vinyl chloride, and arsenic.

Age, sex, family history, and genetic susceptibility are some of these risk factors that cannot be changed, but many other key lung risk factors can be modified by changes in lifestyle, society, and drug usage to prevent hypertension, hyperlipidemia, diabetes. Atherosclerosis of coronary arteries is more prone to develop in obese patients. Initial treatment for lung illness focuses mostly on dietary and lifestyle changes. Since influenza may increase the frequency of lung attacks and strokes, immunization against the flu may lower the risk of lung events and death in people with lung disease, analyzed by Cheng, Yangyang, et al. (2020).

Figure 1. Lung diseases

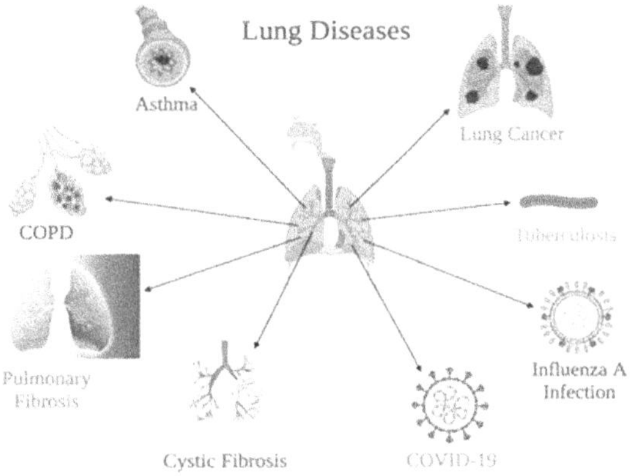

The various lung diseases are depicted in Figure 1. Lung illnesses are a major worldwide health concern that are growing more prevalent as the population ages and there are insufficient measures in place to reduce the risk factors that contribute to the development of these diseases. Researchers now face the problems in finding effective treatments and adequate preventive strategies for lung disorders such asthma, COPD, fibrosis, COVID-19, and influenza-like illnesses that are becoming life-threatening.

Mira-Avendano, Isabel, et al. (2019), said that, lung failure is a serious illness that can be brought on by lung injury or weakening. Pulmonary failure is most commonly caused by excessive blood pressure and lung attacks. Even though there is no cure, patients can prolong their lives, avoid hospitals, and keep an active lifestyle with the aid of early detection, medication, and lifestyle changes. Medical professionals use a variety of techniques to identify or predict HF illness. Currently, angiography is the procedure that doctors utilise the most frequently to diagnose CAD because they believe it to be the most accurate way to find HF caused by CAD. The greatest barriers to HF or CAD diagnosis, however, are angiography's increased cost and significant side effects. Additionally, the diagnosis of CAD necessitates a careful examination of numerous aspects, which makes the doctor's task challenging. These problems serve as a driving force behind the development of non-intrusive techniques for the detection of lung failure. Furthermore, conventional techniques for identifying lung failure focused on reviewing the medical history of the patient, evaluating the lung's performance in terms of different symptoms, and generating a report on the physical cross-examination, which is discussed by Raihan, M., et al (2019).

According to Kumar, Sunil, et al. (2024), the world's leading cause of death is lung illness, including infected and non-infectious cases. According to medical studies, COVID-19, pneumonia, and lung cancer are the three main lung disorders that should be emphasized over others. Medical evaluations are mainly conducted using imaging modalities such as positron emission tomography (PET) scans, computer tomography (CT) scans, magnetic resonance imaging (MRIs), X-rays, and others because they offer computed data that can be used as input datasets for computer-assisted diagnostic systems. To investigate and forecast common lung disorders, machine learning (ML) techniques are developed and evaluated using imaging datasets.

Early Prediction of Lung Diseases using Artificial Intelligence

Early lung disease diagnosis and treatment are vital because they stop the disease's progression and lower the chance of consequences. When diagnosing lung diseases, imaging is essential. A variety of imaging techniques are employed to offer a thorough assessment of lung conditions and direct the proper course of treatment, discussed by Sajed, Samira, et al (2023).

Figure 2. Artificial intelligence techniques to predict the lung diseases

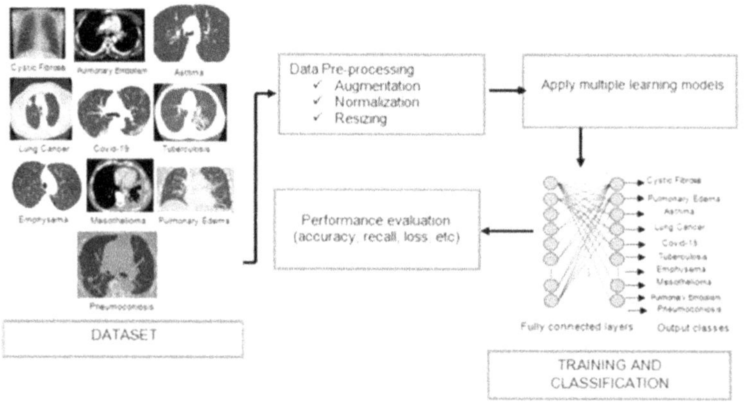

Within the field of artificial intelligence, machine learning uses a range of statistical, probabilistic, and optimization techniques to enable computers to "learn" from historical instances and identify difficult-to-find patterns in big, noisy, or complex data sets. Machine learning provides a fundamental method for creating complex, automated, and impartial algorithms for analyzing multimodal and high-dimensional biological data. Various phases to predict and classify the lung diseases have been mentioned and diagrammatically shown in Figure 2.

In medical systems, machine learning is essential. Early disease detection can help us to identify symptoms more correctly and save many lives, as well as lessen the strain on the system. Among the most common causes of death are lung illnesses. Since it can make the clinical management of patients easier, early detection and prediction of lung diseases have become essential in research. Doctors can get assistance in making diagnoses via machine learning-based decision support systems. Gunasinghe,

Anuradha D., (2019) discussed about the project took into account the patients' respiratory issues in addition to asthma, lung cancer, TB, Pneumothorax, and Chronic Obstructive Pulmonary Disease (COPD). Data processing and patient diagnosis models are produced using machine learning and deep learning. Using CNN with the well-known pre-trained model, Caps Net network for data this type, and combining patient information processing with data from chest X-rays are the approaches utilized for this study to diagnose the lung diseases. After the data set has been examined and evaluated, machine learning and deep learning are used to determine whether or not the patient has a lung ailment. With patient data (age, gender, chest X-ray images, and view position) as input, the project is a binary classification, and its output is whether or not a disease exists.

Consequently, the existing methods for the treatment of lung failure are laborious and prone to human error, which could result in imprecise diagnostic results, given by Liu, Mingsi, et al. (2023). Therefore, in order to prevent these issues, we should design self prediction system for the correct and speedy detection of lung failure. However, doing so necessitates an early diagnosis and effective disease management. In order to aggressively monitor and analyze physiological data related to lung function in a timely and economical manner, technologies must be improved immediately.

The goal of the paper is to help the doctor save the patient's life by identifying and diagnosing lung problems as soon as feasible. This paper explains the use of AI to detect and classify lung illnesses. Due to the recent advancements in mobile technologies, there is an increasing and justifiable interest in figuring out how to continuously monitor the circulatory system over extended periods of time as a possibly more efficient means to both detect and treat lung disorders. Image processing methods are mostly employed for lung cancer prediction, early detection, and lung cancer prevention. Since several features are taken from the images to predict lung cancer, methods based on pattern recognition are helpful, given by Tiwari, Arvind Kumar. (2016).

The research's summary is structured as following order. Section 1 gives the general introduction of this work. Section 2 discussed about the prediction of lung diseases using different existing methods and its drawback. The proposed Hybrid Artificial Neural Network with Ant Colony Optimization algorithm and its working was detailed in Section 3; Section 4 compares experimental findings for the proposed system and those from systems currently in use. Section 5 presents the final thoughts and the work's future scope.

II. LITERATURE SURVEY

In this section, the latest researches in lung disease diagnosis will be demonstrated. Scholars have contributed to the literature with numerous studies utilizing lung images captured as a means of assisting professionals in diagnosing lung conditions through the use of artificial intelligence-compatible technologies. The limitations and drawbacks of the many contemporary strategies utilized in the various techniques for lung disease detection and categorization are covered in this section on literature studies.

In terms of the leading causes of death worldwide, lung illness comes in first. Although early diagnosis and prognostication can boost patient survival rate and decreases patient mortality rates. Alharbi, Khalid Saad, et al (2021) said that, a system for machine intelligence MIFH is used to diagnose lung disease. Both normal persons and lung patients can be predicted using the suggested framework MIFH. MIFH uses the traits of FAMD to train machine learning predictive models for lung disease prediction, healthy person prediction, and case classification. Kumar, Rahul, et al. (2022) demonstrating that MIFH was equivalent when it comes to sensitivity and specificity, and when it's been well compared to a number of contemporary baseline techniques. MIFH increases the effectiveness of the system and returns the most practical response possible based on the performance criteria of the input predictive models into account, which can help physicians and radiologists diagnose lung patients more accurately.

Ogunpola, Adedayo, et al (2024) employed data mining techniques including regression and classification on the Cleveland lung disease dataset. ML methods are used, such as Random Forest and Decision Tree. Nabeel, Muhammad, et al. (2021) discussed that, lung disorders are one of the primary causes of death and morbidity in the country. Data mining techniques can forecast a patient's risk of developing lung disease. KNN, SVM, and neural networks performed better than KNN, SVM, and Decision tree in terms of model accuracy, scoring 88.37%, 86.05%, and 80.23%, respectively. Decision tree results can be easily applied and interpreted, and diverse clinical practitioners can quickly comprehend their guidelines.

Banerjee, Nikita, and Subhalaxmi Das (2020) created a system for early cancer prediction in order to save the lives of many people in risk. In essence, the two areas of computer science that are the focus are machine learning and digital image processing. Preprocessing is the stage of digital picture processing. A subsequent step involves exposing the pre-processed picture to a segmentation phase, after which it is subjected to feature extraction. Lastly, machine learning classification algorithms such as SVM, Random Forest, and ANN are used to train the extracted features. Whether the tumor is benign or malignant is predicted based on the classification results. The method with the highest predicted accuracy is determined by calculating the unavoidable factors, including accuracy, recall, and precision.

For illness prediction under lung imaging, the novel Pro-HRnet-CNN model which combines HRNet and void-convolution techniques is suggested by Liang, Yingbin, et al. (2024). We discovered through experimental comparison on the reputable LIDC-IDRI dataset that Pro-HRnet-CNN greatly improved the detection accuracy by outperforming the conventional ResNet-50 in feature extraction and small-size nodule recognition. The model has demonstrated an impressive improvement in accuracy, especially when it comes to detecting tiny targets, opening up a new path for the early detection and prediction of pulmonary disorders.

Hong, Min, et al (2021) use a convolutional neural network (CNN) to learn lung disease images in order to offer a multi-class classification solution. The learning image data came from the Cheonan Soonchunhyang University Hospital dataset, which included tuberculosis, and the U.S. National Institutes of Health (NIH) dataset, which was separated into Normal, Pneumonia, and Pneumothorax. Preprocessing was done using Center Crop while keeping the aspect ratio at 1:1 in order to increase performance. The Multi GAP structure was used to maximize the use of each layer's features, and the weights learnt by ImageNet were used for fine-tuning learning as a Noisy Student of EfficientNet B7. With an accuracy of 85.32%, the experiment's benchmarks using the NIH dataset demonstrated the best performance of all the models tested, and the four-class predictions based on data from Cheonan's Soonchunhyang University Hospital had an average inference time of 0.2 seconds, an average accuracy of 96.1%, an average sensitivity of 92.2%, and an average specificity of 97.4%.

Ayatollahi, Haleh, Leila Gholamhosseini, and Masoud Salehi. (2019) deduced that, with an accuracy of 82.914%, Naive Bayes classification algorithms are the most accurate. Lung disease may be accurately and efficiently predicted via data mining. The findings of our thesis could be used as a tool to assist in establishing more accurate diagnoses of lung problems. Shouman, M et al (2012) it provides a plan to methodically close such gaps in lung illness diagnosis and therapy and tests if using data mining methods to analyze treatment data for lung diseases is effective has any positive effects that are as trustworthy as those obtained when diagnosing lung disease patients. Barati, E., et al (2011) listed a few applications for data mining in the medical field. In the past 20 years, we have concentrated on using data mining to treat skin conditions. The diagnosis of erythemato-squamous disorders is a challenging dermatological issue. It has been investigated in a number of research using dermatology databases. We've compiled some of them in this document and discussed their findings.

Taher, F., et al (2021) showed that the formula indicated earlier has positive results for this reason with the average forecast accuracy of 93 and 94%, respectively. An alternative method for identifying the lung tumor is to compute the BPNN and apply a decision tree, which yields a successful outcome compared to earlier calculations. Quasar, Syeda Reeha, et al. (2024) presented the trials on lung CT images, where our strategy not only outperformed two popular techniques for classifier fusion, AdaBoost and Bagging, but also consistently improved recognition performance when compared to single classifiers. Cottin, Vincent, et al. (2019) discussed the user's ability to recognize patterns in lung disease is discussed to help. Design of a GUI applications for image processing with form training and testing. The training images of a healthy lung and a lung cancer are accurate to within 80%. The result's overall accuracy rate is 80%.

Westcott, Andrew. (2019) discussed and analyzed about the textural analysis of thin-section computed tomographic (CT) images is used to describe an automated method for differentiating between a range of obstructive lung illnesses. This system created a pipeline to generate projected ventilation maps based on non-contrast enhanced, single-volume thoracic CT utilizing texture analysis and machine learning techniques. Predicted ventilation maps in a COPD cohort were both qualitatively and quantitatively associated with ground-truth MRI ventilation, and both maps were associated with significant lung function and quality-of-life metrics for patients. This study is the first to show that single-volume, breath-hold thoracic CT can accurately predict hyperpolarized MRI-based ventilation, which might be used to convert pulmonary ventilation data into broadly accessible thoracic CT imaging.

Alam, Fatema Binte, et al (2023) suggests using a hybrid deep neural network framework called RVCNet to detect lung illnesses from a multi-class X-ray dataset. This framework was created using the concepts of three deep learning approaches: a basic CNN model, VGG19, and ResNet101V2. This innovative hybrid architecture uses hyperparameter fine-tuning throughout the feature extraction stage. A collection of X-ray pictures from normal patients, viral pneumonia, non-COVID lung infections, and COVID-19 is used to test this technique. The trials consider 252 testing images and 2262 training images. According to the results, the suggested algorithm's overall classification accuracy, AUC, precision, recall, and F1-score are 91.27%, 92.31%, 90.48%, 98.30%, and 94.23%, respectively, when using the Nadam optimizer.

Spathis, Dimitris, and Panayiotis Vlamos, (2019) examined the respiratory disorders including asthma and chronic obstructive lung disease are prevented, diagnosed, and treated with the use of clinical decision support systems. Through empirical pulmonology study on a representative sample ($n = 132$), an attempt is made to identify the key characteristics that impact the diagnosis of these illnesses. ML results reveal that the Random Forest classifier performs better than other methods in the case of chronic obstructive pulmonary disease, outperforming them with 97% precision. The most important factors for diagnosis are age, forced vital capacity, and smoking. The Random Forest classifier once again achieves the highest precision of 81% in the instance of asthma, with MEF2575 emerging as the most notable characteristic.

Wankhade, Shalini, and S. Vigneshwari (2023) suggested a brand-new technique called Cancer Cell Detection utilizing Hybrid Neural Network (CCDC-HNN) for an early and precise diagnosis. Deep neural networks are used to extract the features from the CT scan images. To save the patient from this deadly illness, early detection of malignant cells depends heavily on feature extraction accuracy. An advanced

3D-convolution neural network (3D-CNN) is also used in this study to increase diagnosis accuracy. Additionally, the proposed method makes it possible to distinguish between benign and malignant tumors. The outcomes validate the feasibility of the suggested hybrid deep learning (DL) approach for early lung cancer detection when assessed using conventional statistical methods.

Boban, Binila Mariyam, and Rajesh Kannan Megalingam (2020, July) focuses on using machine learning techniques to identify and categorize lung illnesses. There are four hundred CT scan photos of lung diseases, such as bronchitis, emphysema, pleural effusion, cancer, and normal. ML techniques like the MLP, KNN, and SVM classifier are used to analyze, categorize, and classify the input image. The output is segmented after feature extraction, and the accuracy of the classifier is compared. A CT scan image contains unrelated information when it is fed into a classifier. Here, the Gray Level Co-occurrence Matrix (GLCM) is utilized to identify the most pertinent features (extracting characteristics). This classifier achieves 98% accuracy for MLP, 70.45% accuracy for SVM, and 99.2% accuracy for KNN. These classifiers will assist physicians in prescribing the best course of action for patients.

Lung problems might include inflammation, infections, or even more dangerous situations like the development of a malignant tumor. In this work, Dritsas, Elias, and Maria Trigka, (2022) using ML techniques, effective models can be created to determine lung cancer and to act sooner to prevent long-term consequences. Here, the Rotation Forest is evaluated using industry-standard metrics like as accuracy, precision, recall, F-Measure, and AUC to generate very effective results. Particularly, the analysis of the trials demonstrated that the suggested model won out with a good F-Measure, high accuracy, precision, and recall.

Gugulothu, Vijay Kumar, and Savadam Balaji (2024) introduced hybrid deep learning (LNDC-HDL) methods for lung nodule detection and classification using CT images. Introduce the chaotic bird swarm optimization (CBSO) algorithm first, which uses statistical data to segment lung nodules. Phase two involves demonstrating an enhanced Fish Bee algorithm for feature selection and extraction. Third stage involves creating a hybrid classifier for tumor classification and prediction, specifically a hybrid differential evolution-based neural network (HDE-NN). Utilizing computed tomography has been demonstrated to improve sensitivity and decrease false positives, highlighting the significance and effectiveness of the HDE-NN unique structure for lung node detection on CT scans. By merging clinical practice, this method demonstrates that HDE-NN node detection can yield benefits.

Identifying and categorizing lung CT scan pictures as showing healthy lungs and illnesses like fibrosis and COPD is the goal of this investigation. This work begins by extracting Haralick texture features from the segmented lung images using the Gray Level Co-occurrence Matrix, Zernike's moments, Gabor features, and Tamura texture features. This creates a pool of features for selection. We suggest three evolutionary algorithms for feature selection in the second step: the Improvised Crow Search Algorithm (ICSA), the Improvised Grey Wolf Algorithm (IGWA), and the Improvised Cuttlefish Algorithm (ICFA). These algorithms choose an ideal subset of features from a large pool of features extracted from medical images in order to increase classification accuracy and lower computational costs. The last phase was applying four machine learning classifiers to each feature subset chosen using the suggested feature selection techniques: K-Nearest Neighbor, Support Vector Machine, Random Forest Classifier, and Decision Tree Classifier. Because of their low computing cost and excellent accuracy, the results showed that the suggested feature selection techniques are appropriate for classifying diseases in medical images and may also be applied in real-time applications, this method was described by Gupta, Naman, et al. (2019).

Sen, Ishan, et al (2020) conducted an experiment with a number of ML methods to classify a set of data. In addition to 19 traits, they have gathered 323 cases. Patients with various lung illnesses and additional symptoms provided the data for this collection. "Positive" and "Negative" are the two categories that make up the Lung Diseases characteristic. "Positive" indicates that the individual suffers from a lung condition, etc. Particularly, the dataset was trained utilizing the K-Fold Cross Validation Technique using five ML algorithms have accuracy rates of 88.00%, 88.92%, 90.15%, 89.23%, and 83.69%, in that order.

As per the research mentioned above, diverse ML, DL, and hybrid optimization strategies were employed to categorize the various lung ailments using disparate algorithms. That being said, current methods are not able to categorize lung disorders more accurately in less time duration. We also need to use datasets including photos from various datasets for the model testing and training. By concentrating on the AI technique, the literature review above provides us with a concise summary of the latest developments in the major medical field of lung disease diagnosis. This newly created hybrid algorithm overcomes the shortcomings those are analyzed from the aforementioned current methodologies, as detailed in the part that follows.

III. PROPOSED METHODOLOGY

Performing the classification and prediction of lung images efficiently is an important and crucial stage for the analysis medical images. To achieve this, various techniques are proposed recently. This section gives the detailed explanation of working operation and its mathematical expression of proposed lung classification HANNACO system below. The research work demonstrates a test utilizing hybrid technique with Ant Colony Optimization (ACO) handling the optimization process Artificial Neural Networks (ANNs) for prediction and classify of lung illness.

Figure 3. Proposed system architecture

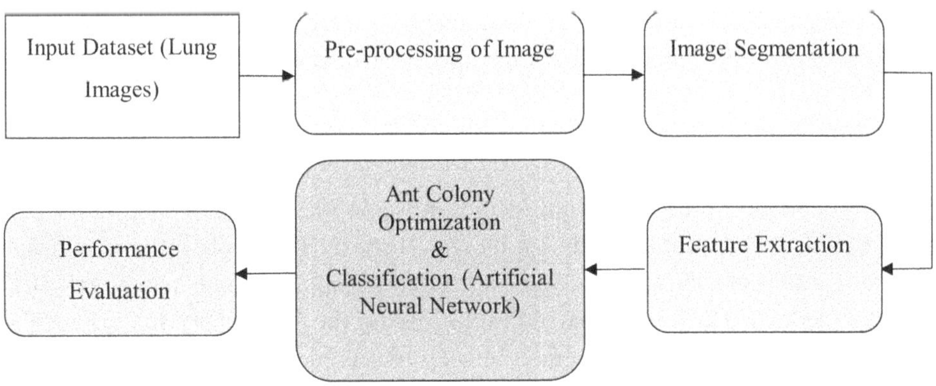

The newly constructed proposed system for lung disease classification and detection is depicted in Figure 3. Additionally, the following describes the general operation of this proposed HANNACO system.

From the above architecture, photograph of a human lung is required for the first stage, picture acquisition. Pre-processing is done on a provided image to improve quality and eliminate unwanted distortion in the input lung image. To indicate the value of each pixel, an RGB (Red, Green, and Blue) matrix is utilized. The process of photo segmentation assigns a value to each pixel. Another method of feature extraction is the color co-occurrence approach, which extracts the characteristic lung aspects of an image by considering its texture and color, detailed by Damayanti, Fitri, et al. (2020). Using both the optimization approach with classification methods that are currently in use, the categorization of human lung pictures was completed. The objective is to identify the optimization approach with the best classifier performance by comparing the classification outputs produced by each method.

3.1 Pre-Processing the Lung Images

Image quality improvement through the filtering technique in order to get them ready for further processing and analysis. It also includes color space conversion and image enhancement. Lung RGB images are used to create the color space L*a*b*. Verma, Toran, and Sipi Dubey, (2020) using color space conversion, visual analysis can be made better by using filters. Once the pre-processing of lung images is completed, then it is fed into the segmentation process.

3.2 Segmentation of Lung Image

The noise removed lung images are applied to the segmentation, to get separate from the affected and non-affected part in the given input lung image. Segmentation technique separates the important pixels from a picture for further processing and analysis using energy forces and limitations. Segmentation methodology may use a linear, spline, or polynomial interpolation method, depending on how the curve in the image is formed, which is given by Skourt, Brahim Ait, Abdelhamid El Hassani, and Aicha Majda. (2018).

3.3 Lung Image Classification

The approach of lung image classification is used to classify and forecast different types of lung illnesses. The process involves combining an optimization strategy with an image categorization tool. The following passage will be discussed about the lung image classification with optimization.

3.3.1 Ant Colony Optimization (ACO)

Following observations of how certain ant species move on and adhere to pheromone pathways, the meta-heuristic known as ACO was created. Applying customized (fake) pheromone information based on the search history of the ant and any available heuristic information. When it comes to ACO, artificial ants are stochastic methods that suggest possible solutions for the particular issue instance.

Using the ACO approach, the affected area in the input is located. Where the ACO algorithm is present in several iterations and is detailed in Figure 4 below. Using heuristic input and the information gathered by previous ant populations, many ants build thorough responses in each iteration. Setting up all of the pheromone variables and settings is the first step. After starting the challenge, a group of ants uses pheromone values and additional information to construct a solution. The ants improve the developed solution in this optional step. Pheromone variables are changed at this stage based on observations of ant search behavior, analyzed by Almufti, Saman M (2022).

Figure 4. ACO algorithm pseudo-code

```
Ant Colony Optimization:

Set up the necessary parameters and begin the pheromone trials;

  Don't stop, but instead

       Starts an ant colony;

       Find out each ant's fitness rating.;

       Find the best choice by applying selection strategies;

updates on the pheromone experiment;

   Pause for a moment

Proceed further
```

Behmanesh, Reza, et al (2020) said that they are able to create an algorithm for lung image optimization by taking into consideration the behavior of the ants in the aforementioned case. One ant colony, one food supply, and two possible routes of migration have been looked at for the purpose of simplicity. With weighted graphs, the entire situation may be simulated: the ant colony and food source represent the vertices (or nodes), the passageways represent the edges, and the weights connected to the pathways represent the pheromone levels.

Let G = (V, E) represent the graph, where V denotes the vertices and E, correspondingly, the edges of the graph. Should we consider it, the vertices are (Vd - Destination vertex, a food supply, and Vs - supply vertex, an ant colony). The two edges, designated as E1 and E2, have respective lengths of L1 and L2. It can be conjectured that Links between pheromone values R1 and R2, respectively, are present at vertices E1 and E2. given their respective strengths. The likelihood that every ant will choose a path (between E1 and E2) initially is therefore as follows:

$$Pi = \frac{Ri}{R1 + R2}; i = 1,2 \tag{1}$$

It seems that there is a greater likelihood of selecting E1 if R1>R2 and vice versa. Now, the pheromone value for that route fluctuates. Ei, as you make your way back along that road.

1. Taking into account the path's distance

$$Ri \leftarrow Ri + \frac{K}{Li} \tag{2}$$

"K" and "i=1, 2" are the model parameters in the previously mentioned update.

2. Based on how soon the pheromone dissipates

$$Ri \leftarrow (1 - v)^* Ri \tag{3}$$

A parameter known as "V," with a range of [0, 1], controls how much pheromone evaporates. In the same way, "i" is equivalent to 1 plus 2 + 3.

The optimized output of the lung image from Ant Colony Optimization (ACO) is given into the ANN for the classification purpose.

3.3.2 Artificial Neural Network (ANN)

The input lung image data for ANN system is taken from the output of ACO system. An artificial neural network (ANN) is made up of all these parts, arranged in different layers. Millions or a few hundred units may make up a layer, depending on how complicated the system is. The integration of hidden layers with input, output, and other layers is widespread in ANN. Data from outside sources that the neural network needs to evaluate or understand is fed into the input layer. This input then passes through one or more hidden layers before being transformed into data that may be used for the output layer, explained by Kubat, M., & Kubat, M. (2021). And lastly, given input data, the output layer creates an artificial neural network as an output. ANN operation is depicted in Figure 5 below.

Figure 5. ANN architecture performances

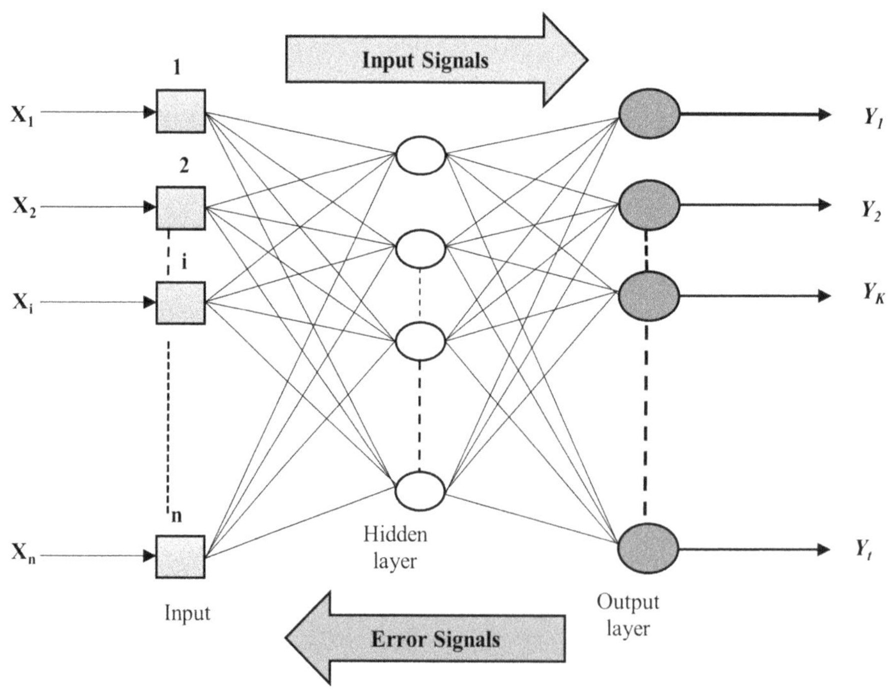

As suggested by its name, the input layer in the lung image above accepts inputs in a range of program-specified formats. Positioned between the input and output layers is the hidden layer. It does all the calculations required to uncover hidden patterns and characteristics. Before the input reaches this layer, the hidden layer converts it into a number of different outputs. When the artificial neural network gets input, it adds a bias to the weighted total of the inputs. This method is demonstrated using an output layer, or transfer function.

$$\sum_{i=1}^{n} \mathbf{Wi} * \mathbf{Xi} + \mathbf{b} \tag{4}$$

The ANN pseudo-code for this system is displayed in Figure 6 below. An activation function is used to process the weighted sum, and the outcome is shown after that. An activation function determines how a node behaves when it fires. In the output layer, access is restricted to fired employees. Activation functions can be used in any number, depending on the type of task we are working on.

Figure 6. Pseudo-code for ANN

Step 1: approach (Input): Create an input database.
Step 2: Input <---- database including every possible combination
Train ANN_S
Step 3: **if** input = 1 and input is finished, execute
Step 4: **for** Neurons= 1 to 20 **do**
Step 5: **for** Repeat 1 to 20 **do**
Step 6: Get on ANN
Step 7: Analogous Network Storage saves the maximum test R^2.
Step 8: end for
Step 9: end for
Step 10: ANN-Storage <---- Continue using the input-based, most accurate ANN.
Step 11: end for
Step 12: Restoring ANN-Storage
Step 13: Final process

Mathematical Model for ANN

The development of a functional model of the biological neuron depends on three essential components. Weights are first used to simulate the connections within the neuron. The value of the weight represents the extent of coupling between a neuron and an input. Negative weight values indicate inhibitory connections, while positive weight values indicate excitatory ones. The functions of a neuronal cell are simulated in the next two components, it is discussed by Mikołajczyk, T., et al. (2018).

$$\mathbf{V}_k = \sum_{j=1}^{p} \mathbf{w}_{kj} \mathbf{x}_j \tag{5}$$

Figure 7. Mathematical flow of ANN

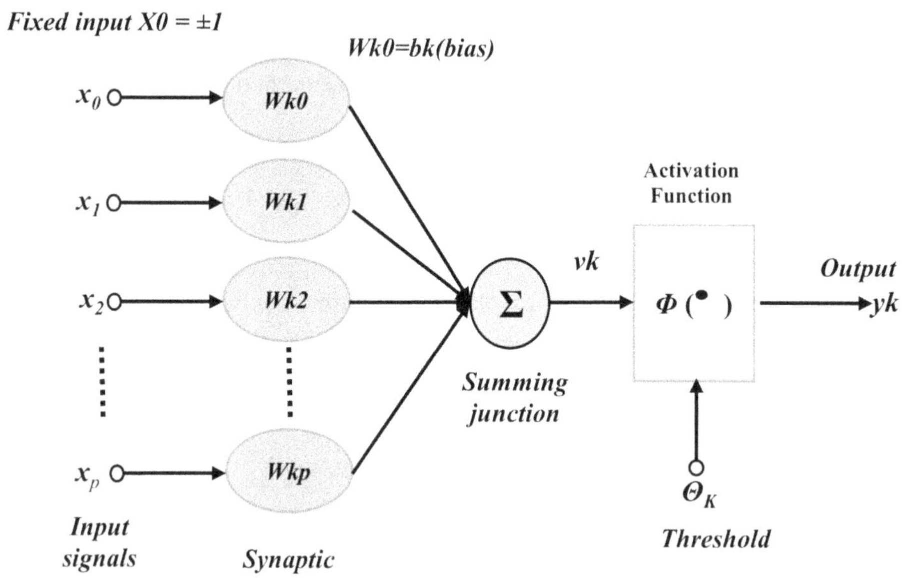

The neuron's intermittent activity is shown in this model to The ANN mathematical model is displayed in Figure 7 above. The lung disease classification and prediction by using the Hybridization algorithm of Artificial Neural Network with Ant Colony Optimization (HANNACO) clearly explained in the aforementioned section. And also its implementation output result is discussed in the next section.

IV. OUTPUT RESULT AND DISCUSSION

This section discussed about the implementation results of proposed system. We take the input lung images from lung diseases based images and UCI, Kaggle datasets are taken into account for the suggested lung disease prediction method. The training dataset includes 60 photos each of the classes/ diseases. The suggested research implementation analysis work employs MATLAB 2013A with hardware configuration of IntelI3 11th gen, 8GB RAM and 512GB HDD to validate the efficiency of classification results. In terms of performance metrics such as Accuracy, Sensitivity, Specificity, Precision and time duration for the newly designed Hybridization algorithm of Artificial Neural Network with Ant Colony Optimization (HANNACO) is compared to the existing algorithms such as, Decision Tree, Support Vector Machine, and K Nearest Neighbor. Based on the implementation results, the suggested HANNACO technique performs very well comparing than these existing systems. The implementation output results are accessed with the help of confusion matrix and the comparison of existing and proposed systems are clearly explained in below using tabulations and bar chart graphs.

4.1 Performance Evaluation Matrix

Performance evaluation measures can be used to assess the trained machine learning models' efficacy. The machine learning model will be able to use an unknown dataset to assess how well it will perform. One tool used by Krstinić, Damir, et al. (2020) to illustrate and condense the efficiency of a classification result. In picture 8 below, the confusion matrix is depicted.

Figure 8. Confusion matrix

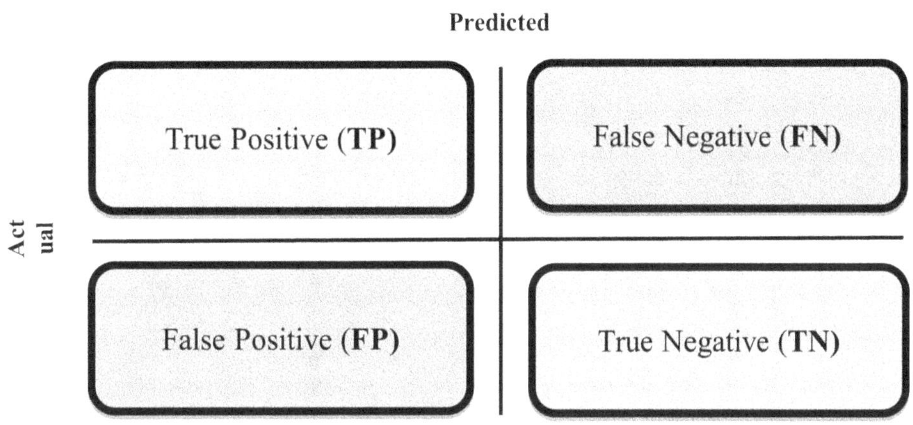

True Positive (TP): Ground-based bounding box detection that works well.

False Positive (FP): Failing to recognize an object that should be there or failing to recognize one that should not be there.

False Negative (FN): A perimeter encircling the concealed ground truth.

True Negative (TN): For object detection, a true negative (TN) result is meaningless since every image contains a large number of bounding boxes are not supposed to be recognized.

4.2 Accuracy

The error rate's divergence from 100% is how the accuracy formula represents accuracy. Accuracy cannot be determined until the error rate is ascertained. Furthermore, by dividing the observed value by the actual value, the error rate can be expressed as a percentage.

$$\text{Accuracy} = \frac{TP + TN}{TP + TN + FN + FP}$$

Table 1. Accuracy result

Algorithm	Accuracy (%)
Decision Tree	84.17
SVM	89.64
KNN	86.52
HANNACO	95.30

Figure 9. Accuracy graph

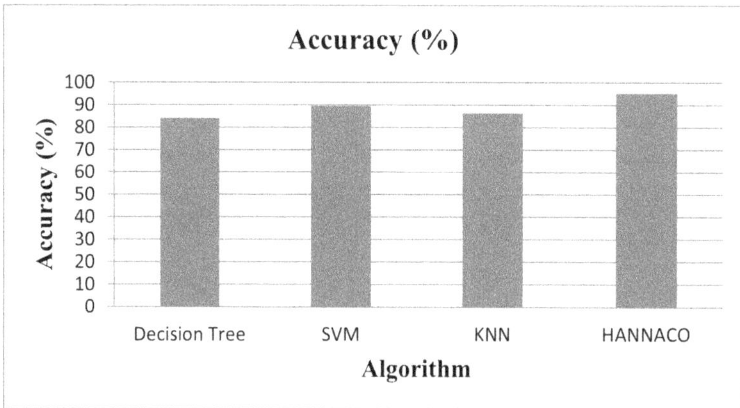

Table 1 shows the accuracy of proposed approach comparison with existing approaches. It states that the accuracy results of the Decision Tree, SVM, KNN, and HANNACO are 84.17%, 89.64%, 86.52%, and 95.30%, respectively. In comparison to other current systems, proposed HANNACO system's results reveal that it achieves higher accuracy. Additionally, Figure 9 displays the output accuracy graph.

4.3 Sensitivity

Calculate the sensitivity by calculating the ratio of all positive forecasts to all forecasts that are precise positives.

$$\text{Sensitivity} = \frac{TP}{TP + FN}$$

Table 2. Sensitivity result

Algorithm	Sensitivity (%)
Decision Tree	82.28
SVM	87.34
KNN	84.92
HANNACO	93.72

Table 2 shows detailed explanation of the sensitivity of proposed approach comparison with existing approaches. The Decision Tree, SVM KNN, Logistic Regression and HANNACO sensitivity outcomes are given as 82.28%, 87.34%, 84.92%, and 93.72% respectively. The result shows that our suggested HANNACO approach reaches higher sensitivity more than other existing systems. Figure 10 depicts the result of the sensitivity output for existing and proposed system.

Figure 10. Sensitivity graph

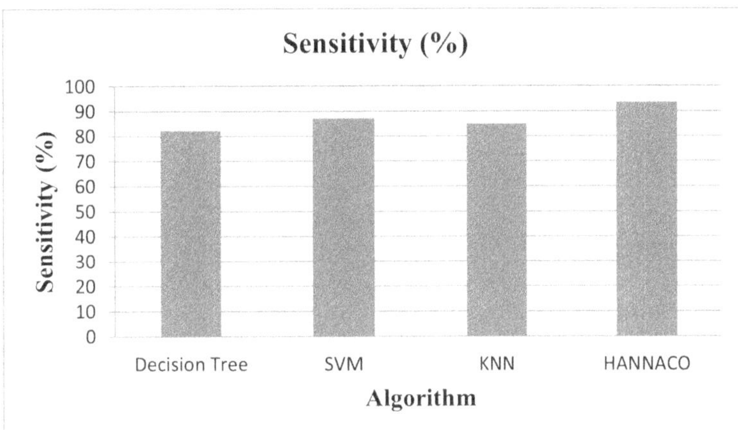

4.4 Specificity

Calculating specificity involves dividing the entire number of accurate negative predictions by the total number of negatives. Utilizing the following formula, the specificity is determined.

$$\textbf{Specificity} = \frac{TN}{(TN + FP)}$$

Table 3. Specificity result

Algorithm	Specificity (%)
Decision Tree	84.34
SVM	82.69
KNN	89.18
HANNACO	92.46

Figure 11. Specificity graph

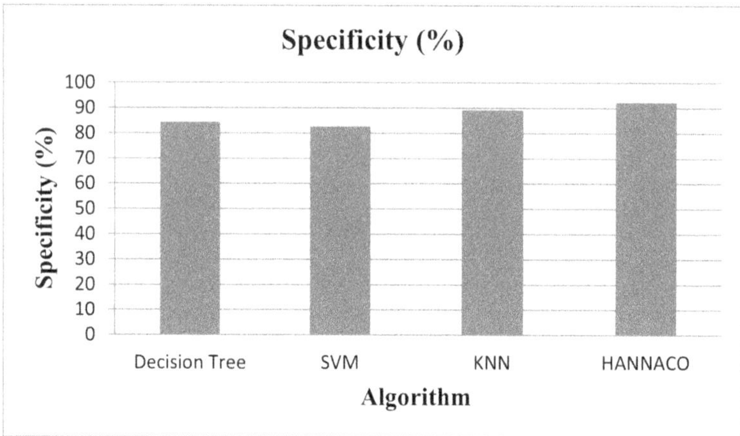

The findings for specificity with the suggested and current methods are derived from Table 3 and are displayed in the previously described in Figure 11. It demonstrates that HANNACO yields a higher specificity result of 92.46%, which is superior to the current methods like DT 84.34%, SVM 82.69%, and KNN 89.18%.

4.5 Precision

The precision level indicates how well the various measures agree with one another. Ascertaining precision is possible by calculating the average deviation, which takes the mean of the measurement errors.

Table 4. Precision result

Algorithm	Precision (%)
Decision Tree	83.78
SVM	88.62
KNN	86.44
HANNACO	93.64

The precision output of existing and proposed system is shown in Table 4 and its output result graph is shown in the below Figure 12. The Decision Tree, SVM, KNN, and HANNACO precision outcomes are given as 83.78%, 88.62%, 86.44%, and 93.64% respectively. The result shows that our suggested HANNACO approach reaches higher precision result more than other existing systems.

Figure 12. Precision graph

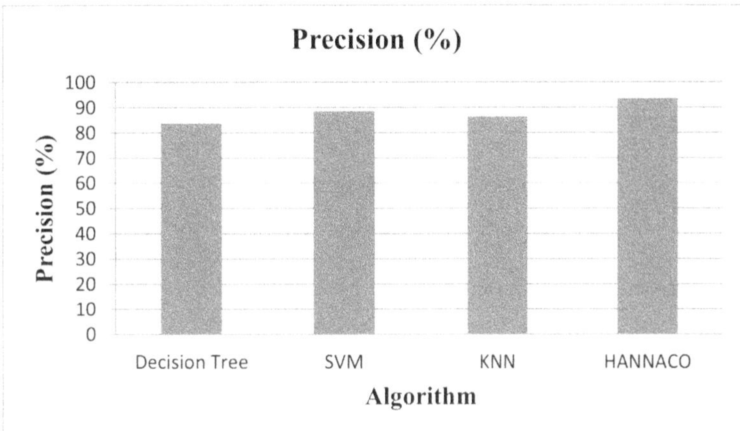

4.6 Time Duration

How long anything lasts, from start to finish, is its entire time length.

Table 5. Time duration result

Algorithm	Time Duration (ms)
Decision Tree	23
SVM	21
KNN	24
HANNACO	18

Figure 13. Time duration graph

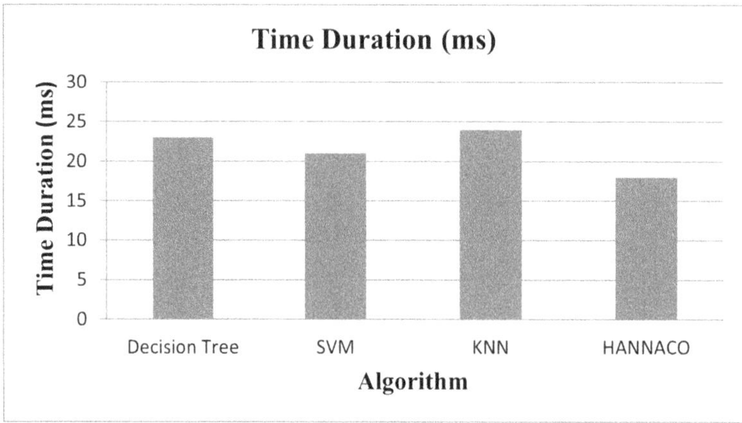

Table 5 details the time-consuming process of comparing the suggested system with current systems; the results are 21 ms, 23 ms, 24 ms, and 18 milliseconds for the Decision Tree, SVM, KNN, and HANNACO respectively. Results indicate that, in comparison to other current systems, the suggested solution uses the least amount of time. Its output graph is plotted in Figure 13.

The overall performances of a novel proposed Hybridization algorithm of Artificial Neural Network with Ant Colony Optimization (HANNACO) utilizing an optimization technique in the intelligent healthcare industry, the system performed admirably for the identification and classification of lung disorders in medical technology.

V. CONCLUSION

Lung cancer prediction is the most difficult challenge because of the shape of cancer cells, which overlap in most cases. A forecasting system of Lung disease assisted by computers will help pulmonologists diagnose these diseases successfully. A novel technique for diagnosing lung disease using chest X-ray dataset has been developed. The processing data was collected from a publicly accessible UCI repository and "Kaggle Web Source". The proposed methodology involves three main processes. The stage one is the pre-processing of Chest X-ray image by using a filtering technique, it is beneficial for eliminating impulse noise in lung image and to increasing the performance. A superior segmentation algorithm allows for the segmentation of the provided lung picture in stage two. The third stage is hybrid classification approach; here HANNACO is used to classify the various lung diseases. Finally, to evaluate the performance of the classifiers based on these parameters accuracy, sensitivity, specificity, precision, and the classification time duration. By using this suggested Hybridization algorithm of Artificial Neural Network with Ant Colony Optimization (HANNACO) optimization based classification approach to anticipate the lung diseases, it is possible to identify any type of lung diseases. This way for the doctor to receive decision support to help and they consult each case more quickly and accurately. This proposed newly developed HANNACO algorithm successfully classifies the lung diseases with accuracy of 95.30% with the less time duration of 18 milliseconds. Future research should focus on developing more complex algorithms to increase the accuracy of disease prediction with less time consumption. Research on learning strategies for a wider range of disease kinds and strategies to enhance learning performance is planned for the future.

REFERENCES

Alam, F. B., Podder, P., & Mondal, M. R. H. (2023). RVCNet: A hybrid deep neural network framework for the diagnosis of lung diseases. *PLoS One*, 18(12), e0293125. DOI: 10.1371/journal.pone.0293125 PMID: 38153925

Alharbi, K. S., Fuloria, N. K., Fuloria, S., Rahman, S. B., Al-Malki, W. H., Shaikh, M. A. J., & Gupta, G. (2021). Nuclear factor-kappa B and its role in inflammatory lung disease. *Chemico-Biological Interactions*, 345, 109568. DOI: 10.1016/j.cbi.2021.109568 PMID: 34181887

Almufti, S. M. (2022). Hybridizing Ant Colony Optimization Algorithm for Optimizing Edge-Detector Techniques. Academic Journal of Nawroz University (AJNU), 11(2). DOI: 10.1016/j.cbi.2021.109568 PMID: 34181887

Ang, L., Ghosh, P., & Seow, W. J. (2021). Association between previous lung diseases and lung cancer risk: A systematic review and meta-analysis. *Carcinogenesis*, 42(12), 1461–1474. DOI: 10.1093/carcin/bgab082 PMID: 34487521

Ayatollahi, H., Gholamhosseini, L., & Salehi, M. (2019). Predicting coronary artery disease: A comparison between two data mining algorithms. *BMC Public Health*, 19(1), 1–9. DOI: 10.1186/s12889-019-6721-5 PMID: 31035958

Banerjee, N., & Das, S. (2020, March). Prediction lung cancer–in machine learning perspective. In 2020 International conference on computer science, engineering and applications (ICCSEA) (pp. 1-5). IEEE. DOI: 10.1109/ICCSEA49143.2020.9132913

Behmanesh, R., Rahimi, I., Zandieh, M., & Gandomi, A. H. (2020). Advanced ant colony optimization in healthcare scheduling. Evolutionary Computation in Scheduling, 37-72. DOI: 10.1016/j.arr.2020.101124 PMID: 32683040

Boban, B. M., & Megalingam, R. K. (2020, July). Lung diseases classification based on machine learning algorithms and performance evaluation. In 2020 international conference on communication and signal processing (ICCSP) (pp. 0315-0320). IEEE. DOI: 10.1016/j.arr.2020.101124 PMID: 32683040

Cheng, Y., Cao, X., Cao, Z., Xu, C., Sun, L., Gao, Y., & Leng, S. X. (2020). Effects of influenza vaccination on the risk of cardiovascular and respiratory diseases and all-cause mortality. *Ageing Research Reviews*, 62, 101124. DOI: 10.1016/j.arr.2020.101124 PMID: 32683040

Cottin, V., Wollin, L., Fischer, A., Quaresma, M., Stowasser, S., & Harari, S. (2019). Fibrosing interstitial lung diseases: Knowns and unknowns. *European Respiratory Review : an Official Journal of the European Respiratory Society*, 28(151), 180100. DOI: 10.1183/16000617.0100-2018 PMID: 30814139

Damayanti, F., Muntasa, A., Herawati, S., Yusuf, M., & Rachmad, A. (2020, March). Identification of Madura tobacco leaf disease using gray-level Co-occurrence matrix, color moments and Naïve Bayes. [). IOP Publishing.]. *Journal of Physics: Conference Series*, 1477(5), 052054. DOI: 10.1088/1742-6596/1477/5/052054

Dritsas, E., & Trigka, M. (2022). Lung cancer risk prediction with machine learning models. *Big Data and Cognitive Computing*, 6(4), 139. DOI: 10.3390/bdcc6040139

Gugulothu, V. K., & Balaji, S. (2024). An early prediction and classification of lung nodule diagnosis on CT images based on hybrid deep learning techniques. *Multimedia Tools and Applications*, •••, 1. PMID: 37362653

Gunasinghe, A. D., Aponso, A. C., & Thirimanna, H. (2019, March). Early prediction of lung diseases. In 2019 IEEE 5th International Conference for Convergence in Technology (I2CT) (pp. 1-4). IEEE. DOI: 10.1109/I2CT45611.2019.9033668

Gupta, N., Gupta, D., Khanna, A., Rebouças Filho, P. P., & De Albuquerque, V. H. C. (2019). Evolutionary algorithms for automatic lung disease detection. *Measurement*, 140, 590–608. DOI: 10.1016/j.measurement.2019.02.042

Hong, M., Rim, B., Lee, H., Jang, H., Oh, J., & Choi, S. (2021). Multi-class classification of lung diseases using CNN models. *Applied Sciences (Basel, Switzerland)*, 11(19), 9289. DOI: 10.3390/app11199289

Ibrahim, I., & Abdulazeez, A. (2021). The role of machine learning algorithms for diagnosing diseases. *Journal of Applied Science and Technology Trends*, 2(01), 10–19. DOI: 10.38094/jastt20179

Khan, M., Khan, H., Khan, S., & Nawaz, M. (2020). Epidemiological and clinical characteristics of coronavirus disease (COVID-19) cases at a screening clinic during the early outbreak period: A single-centre study. *Journal of Medical Microbiology*, 69(8), 1114–1123. DOI: 10.1099/jmm.0.001231 PMID: 32783802

Krstinić, D., Braović, M., Šerić, L., & Božić-Štulić, D. (2020). Multi-label classifier performance evaluation with confusion matrix. *Computer Science and Information Technology*, 1, 1–14.

Kubat, M., & Kubat, M. (2021). Artificial neural networks. An Introduction to Machine Learning, 117-143.

Kumar, R., Arora, R., Bansal, V., Sahayasheela, V. J., Buckchash, H., Imran, J., & Raman, B. (2022). Classification of COVID-19 from chest x-ray images using deep features and correlation coefficient. *Multimedia Tools and Applications*, 81(19), 27631–27655. DOI: 10.1007/s11042-022-12500-3 PMID: 35368858

Kumar, S., Kumar, H., Kumar, G., Singh, S. P., Bijalwan, A., & Diwakar, M. (2024). A methodical exploration of imaging modalities from dataset to detection through machine learning paradigms in prominent lung disease diagnosis: A review. *BMC Medical Imaging*, 24(1), 30. DOI: 10.1186/s12880-024-01192-w PMID: 38302883

Liang, Y., Liu, X., Xia, H., Cang, Y., Zheng, Z., & Yang, Y. (2024). Convolutional neural networks for predictive modeling of lung disease. arXiv preprint arXiv:2408.12605. DOI: 10.1109/ICPICS62053.2024.10796475

Liu, M., Wu, J., Wang, N., Zhang, X., Bai, Y., Guo, J., & Tao, K. (2023). The value of artificial intelligence in the diagnosis of lung cancer: A systematic review and meta-analysis. *PLoS One*, 18(3), e0273445. DOI: 10.1371/journal.pone.0273445 PMID: 36952523

Mikołajczyk, T., Nowicki, K., Bustillo, A., & Pimenov, D. Y. (2018). Predicting tool life in turning operations using neural networks and image processing. *Mechanical Systems and Signal Processing*, 104, 503–513. DOI: 10.1016/j.ymssp.2017.11.022

Mira-Avendano, I., Abril, A., Burger, C. D., Dellaripa, P. F., Fischer, A., Gotway, M. B., & Ryu, J. H. (2019, February). Interstitial lung disease and other pulmonary manifestations in connective tissue diseases. [). Elsevier.]. *Mayo Clinic Proceedings*, 94(2), 309–325. DOI: 10.1016/j.mayocp.2018.09.002 PMID: 30558827

Nabeel, M., Majeed, S., Awan, M. J., Muslih-ud-Din, H., Wasique, M., & Nasir, R. (2021). Review on Effective Disease Prediction through Data Mining Techniques. *International Journal on Electrical Engineering & Informatics*, 13(3), 717–733. DOI: 10.15676/ijeei.2021.13.3.13

Ogunpola, A., Saeed, F., Basurra, S., Albarrak, A. M., & Qasem, S. N. (2024). Machine learning-based predictive models for detection of cardiovascular diseases. *Diagnostics (Basel)*, 14(2), 144. DOI: 10.3390/diagnostics14020144 PMID: 38248021

Quasar, S. R., Sharma, R., Mittal, A., Sharma, M., Agarwal, D., & de La Torre Díez, I. (2024). Ensemble methods for computed tomography scan images to improve lung cancer detection and classification. *Multimedia Tools and Applications*, 83(17), 52867–52897. DOI: 10.1007/s11042-023-17616-8

Raihan, M., Mandal, P. K., Islam, M. M., Hossain, T., Ghosh, P., Shaj, S. A., & More, A. (2019, February). Risk prediction of ischemic heart disease using artificial neural network. In 2019 international conference on electrical, computer and communication engineering (ECCE) (pp. 1-5). IEEE. DOI: 10.1007/s11042-023-17616-8

Sajed, S., Sanati, A., Garcia, J. E., Rostami, H., Keshavarz, A., & Teixeira, A. (2023). The effectiveness of deep learning vs. traditional methods for lung disease diagnosis using chest X-ray images: A systematic review. *Applied Soft Computing*, 147, 110817. DOI: 10.1016/j.asoc.2023.110817

Satpathy, M. M. B. R., & Mishra, B. R. (2021). *Clinical diagnosis of congenital heart disease*. Jaypee Brothers Medical Publishers.

Sen, I., Hossain, M. I., Shakib, M. F. H., Imran, M. A., & Al Faisal, F. (2020). In depth analysis of lung disease prediction using machine learning algorithms. In Machine Learning, Image Processing, Network Security and Data Sciences: Second International Conference, MIND 2020, Silchar, India, July 30-31, 2020 [Springer Singapore.]. *Proceedings*, 2(Part II), 204–213.

Skourt, B. A., El Hassani, A., & Majda, A. (2018). Lung CT image segmentation using deep neural networks. *Procedia Computer Science*, 127, 109–113. DOI: 10.1016/j.procs.2018.01.104

Spathis, D., & Vlamos, P. (2019). Diagnosing asthma and chronic obstructive pulmonary disease with machine learning. *Health Informatics Journal*, 25(3), 811–827. DOI: 10.1177/1460458217723169 PMID: 28820010

Taher, F., Prakash, N., Shaffie, A., Soliman, A., & El-Baz, A. (2021). An overview of lung cancer classification algorithms and their performances. IAENG International Journal of Computer Science, 48(4), IJCS_48_4_19. DOI: 10.1177/1460458217723169 PMID: 28820010

Tiwari, A. K. (2016). Prediction of lung cancer using image processing techniques: A review. *Advanced Computational Intelligence: An International Journal*, 3(1), 1–9. DOI: 10.5121/acii.2016.3101

Verma, T., & Dubey, S. (2020). Impact of color spaces and feature sets in automated plant diseases classifier: A comprehensive review based on rice plant images. *Archives of Computational Methods in Engineering*, 27(5), 1611–1632. DOI: 10.1007/s11831-019-09364-6

Wang, C., Wu, Z., Xu, Y., Zheng, Y., Luo, Z., Cao, W., & He, J. (2023). Disparities in the global burden of tracheal, bronchus, and lung cancer from 1990 to 2019. *Chinese Medical Journal Pulmonary and Critical Care Medicine*, 1(01), 36–45. DOI: 10.1016/j.pccm.2023.02.001 PMID: 39170872

Wankhade, S., & Vigneshwari, S. (2023). A novel hybrid deep learning method for early detection of lung cancer using neural networks. *Healthcare Analytics*, 3, 100195. DOI: 10.1016/j.health.2023.100195

Westcott, A. (2019). Texture Analysis and Machine Learning to Predict Pulmonary Ventilation from Thoracic Computed Tomography (Master's thesis, The University of Western Ontario (Canada)).

Chapter 10
Next-Generation Image Enhancement and Restoration With Artificial Intelligence

S. Gandhimathi Alias Usha
https://orcid.org/0000-0003-1908-6249
Velammal College of Engineering and Technology, Madurai, India

P. Uma Maheswari
Velammal College of Engineering and Technology, Madurai, India

K. Bharathi
https://orcid.org/0009-0000-4767-1635
Velammal College of Engineering and Technology, Madurai, India

V. Jeevalakshmi
Velammal College of Engineering and Technology, Madurai, India

ABSTRACT

The integration of intelligent image processing techniques into clinical and medical imaging techniques introduced a new horizon for improvement in the area of medical imaging and diagnostics. Such efforts have critically enhanced accuracy, efficiency, and the capacity to identify diseases early enough and provide treatments to patients. This chapter examines the innovation brought about by advancing capabilities within ML and AI that is seeking to alter the present face of the medical imaging industry by augmenting capture, processing, and interpretation of imagery using various modalities such as MRI, CT, and X-ray scans. Some of these models are based on deep learning, which includes things like transformers, Generative Adversarial Networks (GANs), and even Convolutional Neural Networks (CNNs). Such models can allow for an unprecedented ability to be involved in tasks that may include segmenting tissues, organs, and lesions while automatically detecting abnormalities and even accurately predicting disease course.

DOI: 10.4018/979-8-3693-9045-0.ch010

1.INTRODUCTION

The advent of AI has dramatically changed image enhancement and restoration, setting new limits for what possibly can be done in digital image processing. Traditionally, image enhancement has an objective of improving the quality of the image and image restoration has an objective to recover a clean image from a degraded images. It can be performed by manual approaches such as filtering and deconvolution. However, these approaches are not suitable for complex tasks such as scaling a high-resolution image, noise removal, and details extraction. Now, AI has developed highly efficient automatic and versatile solutions that herald a new era in image processing, mainly through deep learning (Selvikvag et.al.,2018). AI techniques, such as CNNs and GANs, have enabled great progress in areas such as super resolution, which enables an image to be dramatically increased in resolution while being much clearer and more detailed than traditional upscaling. This chapter focuses on these newest state-of-the-art AI-based approaches to image enhancement and restoration, also including emerging technologies such as vision transformers and reinforcement learning in order to adapt processing techniques to a specific context. Despite these impressive benefits, AI has introduced many complications in the processing of images, such as computational costs entailed by it, issues of authenticity in images, and high-quality datasets.

Current next-generation AI technologies, once again, redefine the role of digital imaging by erecting a comprehensive understanding of advancement applications, boundaries, and the ongoing development of image quality enhancement and restoration. In addition to super-resolution, AI methods contain advanced denoising techniques, along with deblurring methods to correct artifacts due to motion or focus issues. These capabilities are critical in applications as diverse as medical imaging. In addition, these technologies have grown manifold and have helped enormously in the conserved cultural heritage of historic antiquities and images that were inaccessible to date. In this chapter, we focused about AI-driven methodologies in their underlying technologies, their practical applications, and implications of usage across different domains.

In exploring the nature of such new approaches, we have had to confront the difficulties they present: the ethics involved with manipulations of images, high computational costs of advanced processing, and the requirement for very large datasets of high quality. This close examination should throw into higher relief the transformative potential of AI in the enhancement and restoration of images and how this promises to be better at redefining our engagement with visual media in a dramatically digital world.

2. IMPORTANCE OF IMAGE ENHANCEMENT AND RESTORATION

Image enhancement is simply making pictures look better. It is a process of changing different attributes of an image. It may be brightness, contrast, or sharpness to make the image more pleasing to the eye or appropriate for a particular application. There are two primary strategies toward enhancing (McBee et.al.,2018). For instance, histogram equalization spreads out the brightness levels of an image so that not all the pixels have the same value; you then see a subject much more clearly, and this really gets the contrast going. The frequency domain methods work with the image regarding its frequency components and sort of pay attention to how patterns of light and dark are occurring. Instead, image restoration is about repairing or renewing images that have become severely damaged, distorted, or degraded.

This is as a consequence of conditions that are noisy, blurry or distorted. Restoration is intended to recover the quality of an image as close to the original as possible. To do that, we must first know the factors responsible for the degradation. Then, we have to make use of specific algorithms designed to counteract that effect. For instance, deconvolution techniques eliminate blurriness due to shaky hands or out-of-focus shots. Filtering methods carry a variety of techniques to reduce noise that may hide the important details from being visible. Both image enhancement and restoration have great importance in a wide range of fields. For example, in medical imaging, improved images contribute to better diagnoses and treatments. Techniques that clean up the MRI scans or make X-rays visible are just as important because those visuals are used to get correct evaluations by the doctors. Restoration techniques are equally important; they recover useful information in lost images due to noise or distortion and ensure nothing important is passed by. Figure 1 Illustrates the concepts of image enhancement and restoration.

Enhancement plays a significant role in fields such as satellite and aerial imaging, for example, in land use analysis, environmental monitoring, and urban planning. It assists decision-makers in executing tasks better and ensuring adequate disaster responses when images are more defined. In digital photography, enhancement techniques enable spectacular images that capture the eyes and move people's hearts. This reliance on these techniques makes them crucial for historical preservation in retrieving and preserving old photographs and artifacts so that future generations can make an appreciation of our cultural heritage.

Figure 1. Image enhancement and restoration

While the need for high-quality images continues to soar with each successive digital content creation and exchange, enhanced and restored images enrich our experiences in social media, advertisements, and virtual environments. We could now automate all these processes as we have advanced in artificial intelligence and in machine learning, which makes it faster and better.

In a nutshell, image enhancement and restoration are pivotal practices. Along with the improvement in the quality of visuals, recovery of lost information is another significant role it plays in applications. The applications of such images in medicine, security, and media necessitate even greater innovation and research at this juncture in time, especially now that technology is developing even more and challenging us with new untangles in visual media.

3.ROLE OF AI IN ADVANCING IMAGE PROCESSING

While there is much more attention paid to the novel synthesis techniques and applications, artificial intelligence has also evolved as a decisive force in the whole area of image processing, significantly improving the efficiency and quality of an unprecedentedly wide range of imaging applications. Deep learning and machine learning techniques are challenging the traditional way of redefining the research approach to image processing, bringing novel possibilities and enhancing existing workflows. Among various key areas where AI plays a critical role, developing strategies for advancing image processing include

Image Enhancement by Machine Learning: One can process images automatically by training AI algorithms on big datasets of high-quality images. Processes like CNNs allow images to be processed automatically about brightness, contrast, or sharpness, with which enhancement could be done faster and more uniformly than manually. Very helpful for any industry that requires the processing of countless images within very short intervals, like e-commerce or social networks.

More Advanced Image Restoration: The most salient applications of AI in image restoration from noise, blur, or other sources are due to more advanced techniques in deep learning models, where they can even be trained to recognize patterns related to degradation and then aptly reverse them. Some examples are as follows: AI-powered deblurring algorithms can restore images' sharpness, if they were degraded by motion or focus issues from an initial blurred stage, therefore dramatically increasing the quality of images restored.

Super-Resolution Imaging: Another spectacular application of AI in image processing is super-resolution-a process that transforms a low-resolution image into one of its high-resolution counterparts. The use of generative adversarial networks (GANs) is also possible with AI, offering an opportunity for realistic details and textures, so the low-quality images become visibly much sharper and detailed. Such a capability has far-reaching implications in cases of medical imaging, where images have to be high resolution to facilitate accurate diagnosis.

Object Recognition and Segmentation: It is in this area that AI assumes an important role in image analysis through sophisticated object recognition and segmentation. The deep learning model can recognize objects in an image and accurately classify them, for instance, on applications related to autonomous vehicles, security surveillance, medical diagnostics, among others. It accelerates the automation process of complex images analyzed as opposed to a manual composition, thus reducing human error and increasing efficiency.

Content-Based Image Retrieval: AI enhances image search and retrieval capabilities, no longer using just metadata but image characteristics and context for better results. Such an improvement can be thus achieved in the user experience of applications like stock photography, social media, and digital asset management.

Personalization of Visual Content: AI technologies can tailor image processing techniques to individual user preferences. For example, in editing applications for photos, AI can learn a user's style of photo editing and automatically apply similar enhancements to new images so that the user has more satisfaction and ease of work.

4. FOUNDATIONAL CONCEPTS OF IMAGE PROCESSING

Image processing is an applied science dealing with the analysis, manipulation, and transformation of images for improvement in quality, such as extraction of valuable information or preparing visuals for application. It finds grounds in a few fundamental concepts that define how images are captured, processed, and analyzed. There are two domains involved with image processing: the spatial domain and the frequency domain. The spatial domain is operations directly on the image at the pixel level-in other words, operations that adjust attributes such as brightness, contrast, or sharpness. These are direct techniques that include basic filtering methods, like smoothing and sharpening, that either reduce noise or enhance edges for clarity. Another essential spatial technique is histogram equalization, which adjusts the brightness levels of an image to better contrast so that more features are made visible and thus eye-pleasing. In the frequency domain, an image is transformed into a spectrum of its frequencies, generally using transformations like the Fourier transformation. Lower frequencies mean smooth areas, while higher frequencies point towards details or bright changes. By changing the frequency constituents, we may get phenomena like the compression of an image in which only the significant frequencies are preserved or blurring and sharpening effects by altering particular groups of frequency. Image segmentation is a critically important area in image processing - its nature is dividing the image into meaningful regions of interest to enable further analysis on them.

Techniques like edge detection and thresholding reveal boundary locations or emphasize regions of interest, where object recognition and medical image diagnostics particularly benefit from its use. Feature extraction is closely related to all that, pulling key information such as shapes, textures, or patterns from the image into usable forms for further analysis or classification. Lastly, restoration techniques are used to reconstruct degraded images by noise removal or correction of blurring effects. Restoration attempts to improve the approximation of the undistorted original image through the use of deconvolution methods or eliminating unwanted signals, particularly in images that have been affected by other interferences such as motion or low light. Figure 2 is a general flowchart for image processing.

Figure 2. General workflow of image restoration

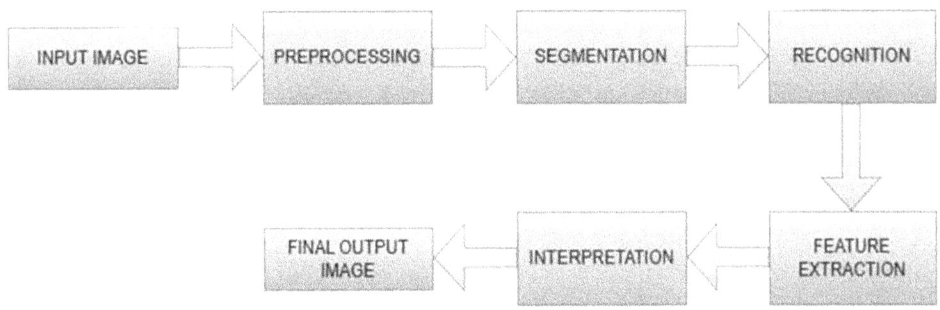

Thus, these basic ideas have opened up the area of image processing systems in order to improve image quality, allow detailed examination of images, and vastly expand the possible applications of images through healthcare applications, security measures, and entertainment applications. As technology advances, the simple principles behind these ideas continue at the core of creating ever more sophisticated tools and applications for image processing.

5.TRADITIONAL METHODS IN IMAGE RESTORATION AND ENHANCEMENT

It is in this context that traditional methods of image restoration and enhancement have served as a basis for the work of modern digital imaging. These place fundamental emphasis on the removal of noise, blurring, and contrast-type degradations from images without necessarily invoking recourse to recent advances made in machine learning or AI. Some of the major traditional methods are as follows:

Histogram Equalization: It is one of the most widely used techniques for image contrast enhancement. The histogram of the image is equalized so that the intensity values could be redistributed. Histogram equalization modifies the brightness levels of the different pixels inside the image such that the features are made to appear more prominent and balanced especially in low contrast images. Figure 3 shows an image and it's equivalent histogram. Variants of this procedure, such as adaptive histogram equalization, further improve the contrast adjustment localized to specific parts of the image for better clarity.

Spatial Filtering: Spatial filters act directly on the pixels of an image, modifying them according to the values within their neighborhoods. Low-pass filters - Gaussian and averaging filters - blur images by eroding noise but blur details as well. High-pass filters, such as Laplacian filters - accentuate edges and fine details. Since such filters have applications where one wishes to sharpen or soften images, but does not wish to give up the tradeoff between noise removal and detail reconstruction, they are considered important.

Frequency domain methods: The image transforms its corresponding frequency components based on the application of mathematical transformations, like the Fourier Transform. In the frequency domain, high frequency corresponds to sharp variations like edges, while low frequencies correspond to gentle variations. Filtering in frequency domain helps make targeted modification possible by manipulating the appropriate frequency bands relevant to noise reduction or enhancement of specific features.

Deconvolution: This is used on the procedure of obtaining an image that has been blurred. Usually, it is due to moving cameras, out-of-focus lenses, or atmospheric disturbances. Algorithms for deconvolution attempt to account for the "point spread function", or simply put, a model of the blurring process; this is done by attempting to reverse the blur and give the image its original sharpness. An example in this field is Wiener filtering and Richardson-Lucy deconvolution, especially that which deals with astronomical imaging and microscopy.

Median Filtering: Median filtering is highly effective at removing "salt-and-pepper" noise—that is, random occurrence of black and white pixels—by replacing each pixel by the median value of its neighborhood. It preserves the edges much better than any other form of averaging filters and is very suitable if impulses are present.

Figure 3. Image and its histogram

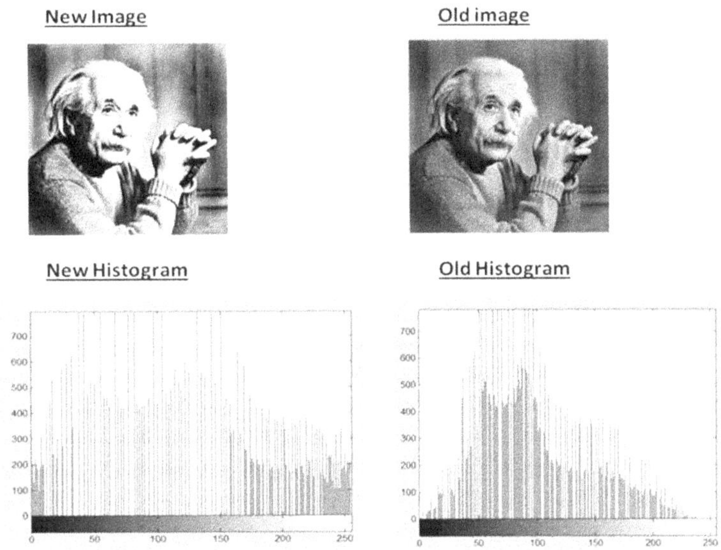

Unsharp Masking: The unsharp masking makes an image sharper by overlaying a blurred version of the image over the original. This bumps up the contrast along edges so that an image looks clearer and crisper. It is applied mostly in the photographic and printing industries for enhancing the impression of an image on the viewer's eyes.

Morphological Operations: The morphological methods, which include dilation and erosion, are extremely useful for processing binary or grayscale images. They can be applied directly to the form or structure of any objects in an image, and these methods of morphological operation are used in removing small imperfections, gaps filling, or bound refining. These methods are particularly helpful in image preprocessing and feature extraction.

All these classic techniques have paved their impact in the development of image processing that are essential instruments to be applied to enhance image quality and recover lost information. As newer techniques rely on AI and augment these earlier methods, they are a flagship component in foundational tasks, providing a reliable bench marking for image enhancement and restoration.

6. AI AND DEEP LEARNING BASICS IN IMAGE PROCESSING

Artificial intelligence and deep learning have revolutionized image processing. It can now process tasks of high complexities, such as image enhancement and restoration, segmentation, and object detection, with impressive accuracy and a lot more efficiency than ever before. Such developments have been facilitated by neural networks and learning algorithms from large sets of data. These can help automate and also improve the conventional methods of image processing (Tang.al., 2023). Among the basic concepts that underlie AI and deep learning in image processing, the following could be included:

Figure 4. Architecture of a neural network

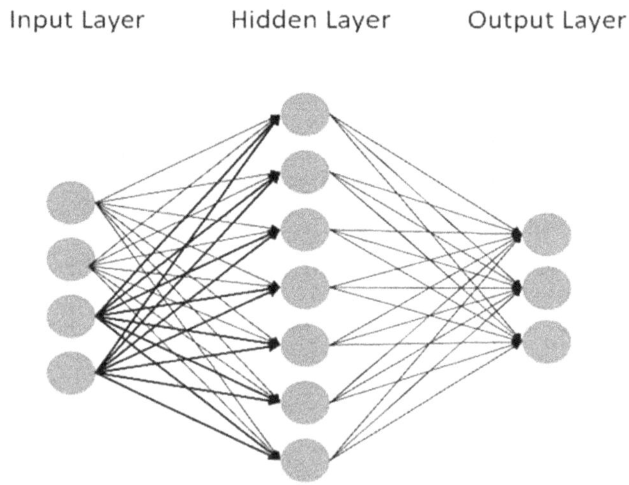

Neural Networks: In deep learning in image processing, neural networks, specifically the CNNs, comprise the backbone of neural networks. CNNs are designed to process visual data very efficiently by using convolutional layers that extract different levels of complexity for edges, textures, and patterns. By creating multiple layers one over another, the CNN could learn to represent complex visual structures that enable object recognition, image classification, facial recognition, and so on. Figure 4 depicts the architecture of a neural network.

Convolutional layers: The basic module of CNNs is the convolutional layer, in which a filter or kernel scans over the image to pick up certain features; that can either be an edge, a color, etc. In each layer, the summation involves previous ones successively and captures, step-by-step, more abstract, complex details in the image (Hedayati.al., 2021). This hierarchical learning structure makes CNNs particularly attractive for tasks such as image recognition and segmentation, in which the same, specific feature detection is a need.

Figure 5. Process of convolution

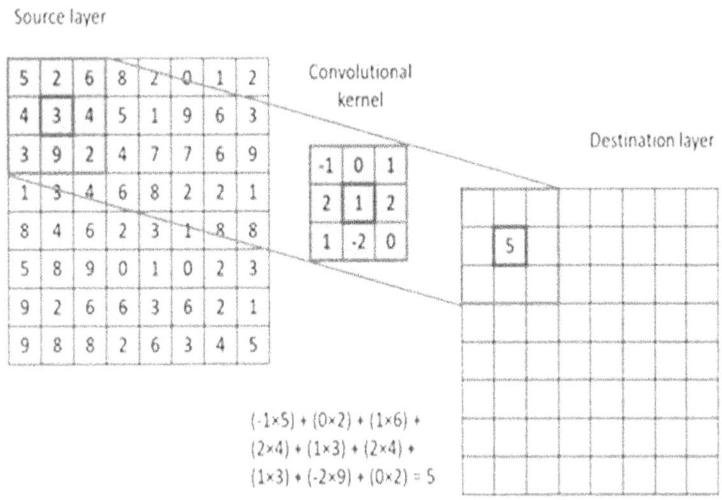

Pooling and activation functions: Pooling layers reduce spatial dimensions of feature maps, thus reducing computation but retaining meaningful information. For example, max pooling retains the highest values of a feature, thereby filtering out noise and enhancing important structures (Archana.al., 2024). ReLU activation functions are used so that networks can learn complex patterns within images, hence improving their decision-making capabilities in image processing operations.

Transfer Learning: Transfer learning enables models that have been trained on large general datasets to adapt to certain image processing tasks using smaller datasets. This is highly useful with image processing since it cuts down on the requirement for large data and hastens the training process (Ming. al., 2022). Example: A model that has been trained on general object recognition can be fine-tuned specifically for the recognition of certain medical conditions from X-ray images.

Generative Adversarial Networks (GANs): GANs is a powerful deep learning architecture used in tasks such as image generation, super-resolution and style transfer. The two networks that are employed in GANs are generator and discriminator. These fight each other to create realistic images. This has made GANs highly effective in the process of generating high-quality images from low-resolution inputs, restoring missing details and achieving lifelike visuals for augmented reality. Figure 6 demonstrates the working of Generative Adversarial Network.

Figure 6. Architecture of generative adversarial network

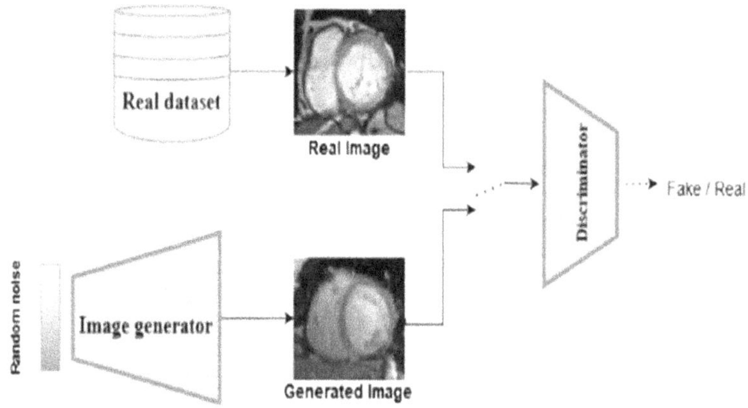

Autoencoders: Autoencoders, as their name suggests, are neural networks that represent layers of transformations used for image compression, denoising, and dimensionality reduction. They map images into lower-dimensional representations, learning compact, efficient representations by embedding images into a lower-dimensional space and then decoding it back to its original form. That helps remove noise or restore images by reconstructing only necessary features, making them valuable in such tasks as noise reduction and image restoration.

Recurrent Neural Networks and Vision Transformers: Traditional only applicable for sequence data, yet RNNs and more recent models such as Vision Transformers (ViTs) are increasingly being applied in image processing tasks that show a time-series or spatial dependency, such as video analysis or image captioning (Guo.al., 2023). This is because Vision Transformers, for example, process an image as a sequence of patches so that attention towards visually important details throughout the image can be better established.

Image Segmentation and Object Detection: Deep learning, a technique with AI, allows for exact object detection as well as region identification within an image. It is for this reason that applications regarding medicine, self-driving cars, and augmented reality necessitate such models-the real-time, deep learning-based detection using Mask R-CNN and You Only Look Once (YOLO) (Sobbahi et.al., 2022).

Super-Resolution and Style Transfer: In one of its capabilities, AI can upscale a low-resolution image into a high-resolution image - it's called superresolution, for finer details, which is useful in applications that require maximum clarity, like satellite imaging or medical diagnostics. Style transfer is another AI capability: it would give one image the aesthetic of another, commonly used in creative fields such as digital art and photography.

The rather strong tools provided by AI and deep learning techniques enhance what has been possible through image processing all along and put it on automation, precision, and innovation in tasks previously limited by manual techniques (Rajamani et.al., 2019). With advancements in neural networks, GANs, and transfer learning, AI-driven image processing is paving the way for applications across industries, from medical diagnostics and security to entertainment and beyond.

7. AI TECHNIQUES FOR IMAGE ENHANCEMENT

AI techniques in image enhancement revolutionized photography, media and medical industries and provide a much clearer and detailed image, besides upscaling images (Qi et.al., 2022). Some of the major AI techniques in image improvement are shown in Figure 7.

Super-Resolution Techniques

In super-resolution, the resolution of images is improved thus providing more details with a clearer picture. Therefore, this technique is very important for scenarios where high resolution images must be obtained but are not such as satellite and medical application. In general, for image upscaling, GANs and CNNs are used to enhance super-resolution keeping fine details intact. Models like SRCNN, EDSR, and ESRGAN have become mainstream for super-resolution tasks. Those had fantastic performance in terms of generating missing details. It is utilized in video upsampling and digital art, or any other field in which high-definition images enhance user interaction.

Denoising

Image denoising is a required functionality to enhance images and scans captured at low light or with much noise. Generally, neural networks, such as DnCNN and CNN-based models, are effective means by which grainy images may be cleaned of pixel noise and other forms of visual artifacts without loss of detail (Chauhan et.al., 2019). Denoising is very important in medical imaging and scientific research since clear images guarantee better interpretation and diagnosis. While traditional methods like Gaussian filtering are replaced by adaptive AI noise models, making denoising an indispensable tool in photographical as well as security and any field of visual processing where clarity is more important.

Figure 7. AI techniques for image enhancement

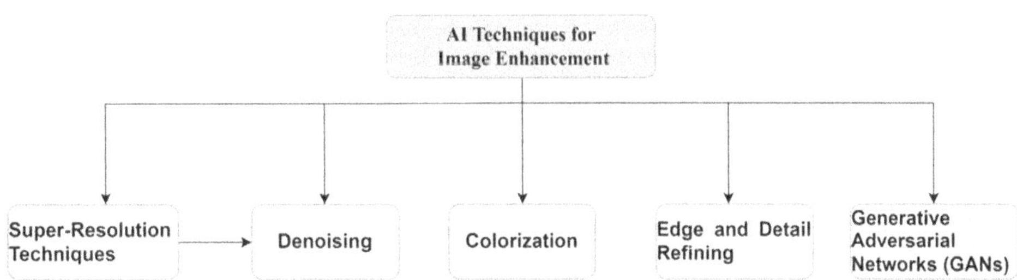

Colorization

The potential of AI-based colorization: turning grayscale into new life through automatic promisingness based on learned patterns and examples. The algorithms then read grayscale tones and textures to predict colors that might visualize real-life scenarios. Such popular tools in colorizing older photos, black-and-white films, or historical images include models like DeOldify and ChromaGAN. Colorization isn't only used for aesthetic reasons but also to facilitate researchers' and historians' analysis of visual data. The present colorization through AI can add photorealistic hues, allowing audiences to better understand the context of vintage images and making this technique invaluable to historical documentation and digital art.

Edge and Detail Refining

Techniques used in sharpening the borders of objects within an image as well as its features to be more defined. Traditional edge-detection filters such as Sobel or Laplacian filters now are combined with neural networks, thereby refines details without context loss and without the introduction of artifacts. This is a crucial process, particularly in scientific imaging, where sharp boundaries help in performing high-accuracy measurements and analysis. Even medical fields benefit from the refinement of edges since this helps their capability to study X-ray films or MRI scans. This technique refines the visible quality of images within neural networks; hence, it plays a very significant role in those applications where accuracy matters.

Generative Adversarial Networks (GANs)

GANs have transformed image enhancement in the sense that the images produced by GAN are very close to realism, almost imperceptibly different from the original authentic images. The fundamental idea of GAN is that it contains a generator that generates new images based on a particular distribution and a discriminator that analyzes those images to verify if they may go undetected as real images. There is always an enhancement in quality because of the manner in which GAN works. GANs excel in applications like super-resolution, style transfer, and image synthesis. An example of this is ESRGAN, which leverages GAN for the purpose of super-resolution to enhance the image to resemble a sharpened image with fine features. Gaming, film, and digital media-based creative industries use GANs to produce image-based visuals that mimic the real view and can create AI-generated enhancements in terms of refining the quality of an image to a level that was almost impossible to achieve before.

8. AI TECHNIQUES FOR IMAGE RESTORATION

AI techniques for image restoration are designed to repair, reconstruct, and improve degraded or damaged images, bringing back lost details, removing noise, or correcting color issues (Zamir et.al., 2022). Here's an overview of some leading AI-powered techniques commonly used in image restoration is given in Figure 8.

Deblurring

Deblurring techniques use AI to remove motion blur, focus blur, or other distortions that cause a loss of sharpness. GAN-based models like DeblurGAN and DeblurGAN-v2 are effective at distinguishing blurred areas and restoring clear image details. Deblurring models work by recognizing blur patterns and reconstructing sharp features, making them valuable for video and image restoration, especially in photography, film, and surveillance footage. Deblurring can even restore legibility to blurred text or improve the clarity of historical or low-quality footage, making it highly versatile in applications that require detail retrieval.

Artifact Removal

Artifact removal targets the compression artifact block or pixelated patterns that appear in overly compressed JPEG images. Techniques such as ARCNN (Artifact Reduction Convolutional Neural Network) use AI to recognize and minimize these compression artifacts, restoring lost detail and clarity. JPEG artifact removal is crucial in web images, where excessive compression degrades quality, and in digital archiving, where high compression may have damaged image quality. By learning to reconstruct details obscured by compression, AI models improve the visual quality of images, making them suitable for professional use, reprints, or further analysis.

Figure 8. AI techniques for image restoration

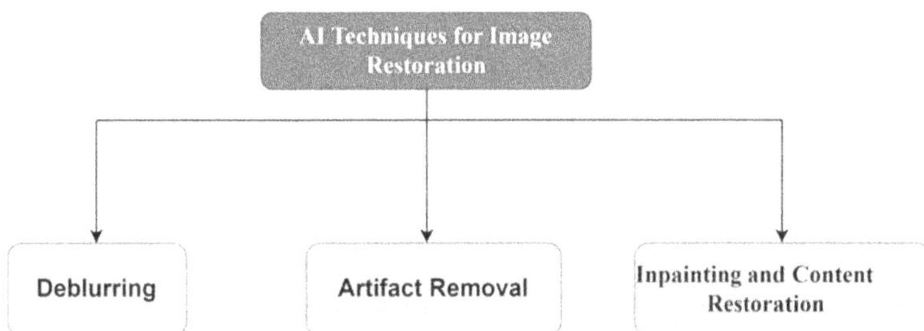

Inpainting and Content Restoration

Image inpainting fills missing or damaged parts of an image, using AI to generate content that seamlessly blends with surrounding areas. Deep learning models like DeepFill and EdgeConnect analyze the context and structure around missing sections to restore images convincingly, even in complex backgrounds. Inpainting has become essential for restoring old photographs, fixing damaged media, or removing unwanted objects. The AI models predict the likely appearance of missing regions, whether due to scratches, tears, or missing data, making inpainting valuable in film restoration, archaeology, and even creative editing.

9.APPLICATIONS ACROSS VARIOUS DOMAINS

AI-based image restoration techniques are transformative across a range of domains, each with unique needs and applications. Here's an overview of how different fields utilize these advancements:

Medical Imaging

Medical professionals rely on clear imaging for accurate diagnosis. AI-driven restoration can improve the quality of low-resolution or noisy scans, helping radiologists detect abnormalities more effectively and ensuring better patient outcomes, especially in early disease detection. It enhances the clarity in X-rays, MRIs, CT scans, and ultrasound images.

Historical Preservation

AI helps museums, libraries, and cultural institutions preserve and restore historical artifacts, making them accessible to future generations. By reviving faded, damaged, or black-and-white media, these techniques enable better public engagement with cultural heritage and history. It helps restoring old photographs, paintings, documents, and film footage.

Astronomy and Space Exploration

Space images often contain noise or artifacts due to vast distances, low light, and atmospheric interference. AI restoration helps scientists process and clarify these images, allowing for more accurate research and discovery in astrophysics. It is used to enhance data from telescopes and satellites, contributing to a better understanding of the universe. Improves the quality of images of distant galaxies, stars, and planets.

10.PROBLEMS WITH AI-BASED IMAGE ENHANCEMENT AND RESTORATION

AI-based image enhancement and restoration can be very promising, but they involve a set of problems that can influence the results produced in terms of quality, consistency, and applicability. Some of the most prominent issues in this field are summarized as follows:

Problems with Data and Models

AI-based models for image restoration are sensitive to both the quality and richness of their training data. It is challenging to obtain extensive, representative datasets with various modes of image degradation (like noise, blur, and scratches) in domains such as historical preservation and medical imaging. This would render the model unable to generalize over real scenarios. Models can produce suboptimal restoration results or even are prone to being inaccurate in cases where patterns of degradation were not represented in the training data. Moreover, degradation complex enough to include several types of artifacts, such as blur and noise, is not easy for the models because most were designed to operate with one type of degradation at a time. Those can require further model tuning or retraining, thereby adding development time and cost.

For instance, AI models learned on the MRI images from one hospital may not properly reconstruct another image from a different hospital in case of different machine settings, imaging protocols, or patient demographics.

Ethical Issues

Image restoration techniques tend to alter the images considerably and change them in ways that may misrepresent the content in the original image. Introductions of such changes might be subjective. Such is the case in historical image restoration, where colorization may lead people to believing something about an image that they otherwise would not have believed. In such cases, AI-enhanced images are prone to being misused and are likely to create deepfakes or misleading visuals that deform reality, causing ethical and privacy concerns. These ethical issues would degrade the value accorded to digital images, since it is quite difficult to distinguish the original from modified visuals. In most cases, over-enhancement may obscure cultural and historical elements in historical preservation purposes and may perpetuate misinterpretation and other bias tendencies in forensic and legal situations. Ethical principles, transparency, and the right frameworks of regulation are all important to prevent the chances of misuse and ensure that AI-enhanced images are credible enough to be trusted by members of the public.

Example: AI models restoration of the historical photograph without realizing it sometimes imposes modern assumptions in an image, for instance, the prediction of colors incorrectly that can actually distort the history within an image and shape the views of history.

Computational Cost and Access

Advanced models, for instance, GANs and Deep Neural Networks have a cost of computation and will be the most resource-intensive models, so they require more processing and memory power. Trains such models usually require expensive specialized hardware, like GPUs and TPUs, which a lot of organizations might not have. Moreover, real-time processing is generally very tough because the overhead of computation is far too high, and it is challenging to get an acceptable level of performance without sacrificing raw computational power excessively. The requirement of high computation of AI-based image restoration limits its accessibility to small organizations or researchers/individuals lacking the necessary hardware. This affects applications that rely on real-time image processing, such as driverless vehicles or surveillance applications, whose safety could be compromised by delays in the system's processing. In addition, the computational cost of AI-based image restoration proves to be prohibitively expensive for wide adoption unless benefits are extended to many people and the economy.

For example, real-time video restoration for an autonomous vehicle would require processing of images with extreme speed while keeping safety and efficiency in check, but the demand to perform a huge number of computations might become a liability if it is applied directly to a vehicle system where alone expensive dedicated hardware exists.

11. FUTURE PROSPECTS AND TRENDS

AI-based image enhancement and restoration is one of the fields that are rapidly developing; many promising directions and trends are being observed in shaping its future. Some of the key advancements and some of the expected trends that could be leveraged to move further innovation in the following years in the field of image processing:

Technology Interconnection with Augmented Reality (AR) and Virtual Reality (VR)

With the ever-evolving AR and VR, high-quality, realistic visuals become a priority. AI-based image enhancement and restoration techniques come into good use as more applications are developed to meet the requirements of AR and VR where real-time clarity and resolution as well as realism becomes critical factors. Image processing, therefore, needs to be enhanced in virtual environments for smooth, lifelike visuals that maintain user immersion. Real-time AR and VR environments place strict computational constraints on the processing of AI models on a scene, but recent developments have, for example, enabled training and optimization of AI models towards high fidelity in the image processing. Techniques such as real-time super-resolution, deblurring, and dynamic lighting adjustments have come to near becoming an indispensable part of this space. AI is also being applied in texture rendering with realistic realism and smooth blending of virtual objects into a real-world environment with the supplementing quality aspects of AR overlays and VR scenes.

Advances in Self-Supervised and Few-Shot Learning

New approaches such as self-supervised and few-shot learning come in an attempt to eliminate reliance on very large datasets, possibly labeled, which involve expensive and lengthy processes. Self-supervised learning streams the notion of not giving the model directly patterned information but letting the model find structures inside the images themselves. Few-shot learning endows models with the ability to perform tasks or patterns recognition based on only a few examples-the perfect application in those domains where data is scarce or hard to collect. Researchers are increasingly applying self-supervised techniques, contrastive learning, and generative modeling for image restoration. This also sparks a few-shot learning exploration for adapting models to learn new types or degradation patterns with minimal data. Together, these approaches prove to be particularly well-suited for niche domains, such as medical imaging or preservation of old artifacts, where adequate annotated data is scarce or could require considerable domain-specific knowledge for appropriate annotation.

Improved Generalizability and Adaptability of Models in the Future

Future models will turn out to be more generalized and adaptable for adaptation with several modes of image degradation. It is motivated by the requirement for models that will perform well across a wide range of real-world images that, potentially, might undergo all combinations of such degradations as noise, blur, low resolutions. Generalization may go further in reducing the need for domain-specific training thereby making AI-based restoration tools more versatile and less technical industry-wise. Users will not have to select or fine-tune models for various kinds of degradation, thus increasing efficiency and usability.

High-Computational Requirements for High-Quality Image Restoration: Quantum Computing and New Architectures

High-quality image restoration poses very high computational requirements; however, new paradigms such as quantum computing or special hardware are now being explored to handle the problem. Quantum computing can speed up quite complex operations such as high-resolution restoration and generative modeling by several orders of magnitude. These new computing resources are now becoming much more accessible, and reducing the time and energies that require high-quality image restoration, this; therefore, means that speed, low-cost solutions will eventually benefit these industries greatly and specifically entertainment, and healthcare, where speed and quality are a must.

Real-Time Processing and Edge AI Integration

Real-time applications, such as surveillance, autonomous vehicles, and live-streaming, create demand for optimizing AI models for faster-on-device processing. Edge Devices Capable of Real-Time Image Enhancement Real-time image enhancement on the edges of devices for example on smartphones, cameras, and systems in embedded vehicles becomes feasible. Advances in model compression, quantization, and lightweight architectures-such as mobile friendly networks for example MobileNet-enables AI models to run efficiently on edge devices without lost performance. This will permit real-time processing and enhancement of images even in resource-poor contexts.

These future directions will take solutions on many of today's challenges toward more efficient, ethical, and powerful models for applications in AI-based image enhancement and restoration. As these trends mature, they will probably make AI-driven image enhancement far more accessible, personalized, and responsive to real-world needs.

12.CONCLUSION

AI-based image enhancement and restoration are the needs of the hour these days in all domains, providing pictures with new levels of clarity, accuracy, and visual quality that once were blurred because of the limitations creeping into them due to noise, blur, or even low resolution. With this new kind of advanced learning techniques such as self-supervised and few-shot learning, AI models overcome classical data limitations, learn properly from minimal examples, and generalize effectively across varied and complex real-world conditions. By foreseeing, integration of all these techniques to the immersive technologies and towards real-time processing in edge devices will introduce new possibilities in entertainment, healthcare, preservation and historical management as well as autonomous systems. As powerful as it is to envision the growth of this space, building it comes with enormous challenges: the ethical implications of working with images, the computational demands of a high-performance model, and a shared need for inclusive, accessible technology solutions. We have seen AI increasingly play a big role in immersive experiences such as virtual and augmented reality. It is as if stepping into the immediacy of a historical moment with lifelike clarity or using a real-time application like virtual meetings or finding your way.

The nature of improvement such as this will unlock new possibilities not only in entertainment but in how we learn, connect, and stay safe. Thus, in this fast-paced landscape, the strain between technological innovation and ethical considerations, as well as practical accessibility, will be essential. Ongoing study and thoughtful implementation will continue to redefine the visual experience with AI-driven image enhancement and restoration to make high-quality, authentic visuals accessible and impactful for all users and industries.

REFERENCES

Archana, R., & Jeevaraj, P. S. E. (2024). Deep learning models for digital image processing: A review. *Artificial Intelligence Review*, *57*(1), 11. DOI: 10.1007/s10462-023-10631-z

Chauhan, N., & Choi, B. J. (2019, September 25). Denoising Approaches Using Fuzzy Logic and Convolutional Autoencoders for Human Brain MRI Image. *Int J Fuzzy Log Intell Syst.*, *19*(3), 135–139. DOI: 10.5391/IJFIS.2019.19.3.135

Guo, J., Ma, J., García-Fernández, Á. F., Zhang, Y., & Liang, H. (2023, March 16). A survey on image enhancement for Low-light images. *Heliyon*, *9*(4), e14558. DOI: 10.1016/j.heliyon.2023.e14558 PMID: 37025779

Hedayati, R., Khedmati, M., & Taghipour-Gorjikolaie, M. (2021). Deep feature extraction method based on ensemble of convolutional auto encoders: Application to Alzheimer's disease diagnosis. *Biomedical Signal Processing and Control*, *66*, 102397. DOI: 10.1016/j.bspc.2020.102397

McBee, M. P., Awan, O. A., Colucci, A. T., Ghobadi, C. W., Kadom, N., Kansagra, A. P., Tridandapani, S., & Auffermann, W. F. (2018, November 1). Deep Learning in Radiology. *Academic Radiology*, *25*(11), 1472–1480. DOI: 10.1016/j.acra.2018.02.018 PMID: 29606338

Ming, Z., Zhu, M., Wang, X., Zhu, J., Cheng, J., Gao, C., Yang, Y., & Wei, X. (2022). Deep learning-based person re-identification methods: A survey and outlook of recent works. *Image and Vision Computing*, *119*, 104394. Advance online publication. DOI: 10.1016/j.imavis.2022.104394

Qi, Y., Yang, Z., Sun, W., Lou, M., Lian, J., Zhao, W., Deng, X., & Ma, Y. (2022). A Comprehensive Overview of Image Enhancement Techniques. *Archives of Computational Methods in Engineering*, *29*(1), 583–607. DOI: 10.1007/s11831-021-09587-6

Rajamani, V., Babu, P., & Jaiganesh, S. (2013). A review of various global contrast enhancement techniques for still images using histogram modification framework. *International Journal of Engineering Trends and Technology*, *4*(4), 1045–1048.

Selvikvag Lundervold, A., & Lundervold, A. (2018, December 13). An overview of deep learning in medical imaging focusing on MRI. *Zeitschrift für Medizinische Physik*, *29*(2), 102–127. DOI: 10.1016/j.zemedi.2018.11.002 PMID: 30553609

Sobbahi Rayan Al. Tekli Joe. Signal Processing: Image Communication. 2022. Comparing deep learning models for low-light natural scene image enhancement and their impact on object detection and classification: overview, empirical evaluation, and challenges; p. 116848.

Tang, H., Zhu, H., Fei, L., Wang, T., Cao, Y., & Xie, C. (2023). Low-Illumination image enhancement based on deep learning techniques: A brief review. *Photonics*, *10*(2), 198. DOI: 10.3390/photonics10020198

Zamir, S. W., Arora, A., Khan, S., Hayat, M., Khan, F. S., Yang, M.-H., & Shao, L. (2020) Learning enriched features for real image restoration and enhancement, arXiv preprint arXiv:2003.06792 DOI: 10.1007/978-3-030-58595-2_30

Chapter 11
Online Biometrics: Recent Advances and New Perspectives

Muhammmad Sajid Khan
https://orcid.org/0000-0001-6413-5324
University of Southwales, Pakistan

ABSTRACT

Biometric technologies are widely used in security, mobile banking, surveillance, business, education, and digital health for identity verification. Methods such as fingerprint scanning, iris recognition, and facial recognition have become standard for authentication. Advances in artificial intelligence (AI) have improved online biometrics, enabling more efficient and accurate systems, especially on smartphones. This chapter discusses recent biometric research integrating AI, machine learning (ML), and deep learning (DL). A novel approach using the FVC2002 dataset, a benchmark for fingerprint recognition, is proposed. It generates 360-degree rotational views from the dataset's 880 images, aiming to improve accuracy and user experience in online applications.

1. INTRODUCTION

Artificial Intelligence is currently being used in many biometric systems to improve their performance in defending against external attacks and threats. These systems can be used to identify individuals whose biometric details have been stored within the system. The identification is based on biological traits and behavior. The most frequent features used for identification is the face and fingerprint, while some system also use the iris and voice. These biometric systems scan, and process static and dynamic data and can be incorporated with one or more characteristics for identification. For data acquisition, different sensors and safeguards are employed for data collecting, (Berghoff, Neu, & von Twickel, 2021).

Smart applications and devices increasingly use biometric applications for automation and authentication enable seamless access control across different domains. It can be used, for instance, for immigration purposes, border checks, and security clearance at various ports. Artificial Intelligence has made these systems more interesting because it improves their functionality, makes using these applications easier, and protects against data loss problems. Facial technology uses Artificial Intelligence (AI), Machine Learning (ML) and deep learning (DL) systems to identify photographs from various databases with high accuracy and display the matching images. These programs are utilized in educational institutions such

DOI: 10.4018/979-8-3693-9045-0.ch011

as colleges, universities, banks, and sports facilities to validate and verify users in real-time. In addition to being used for authentication, AI combined with biometrics protects the system from threats, attacks, and vulnerabilities. An excellent biometric alternative for automatic authentication that improves system performance is artificial intelligence, (Khan, Ware, & Khan, 2020).

Compared to passwords, passcodes, and contactless cards, facial recognition using AI is more reliable and accurate. It is difficult to deal with the vulnerabilities in biometrics systems. Some of the vulnerabilities related to apps and AI include overfitting problems, monitoring and maintenance challenges, and training and learning from massive amounts of low-quality data.AI protects biometric systems from Structured Query Language (SQL) injection, data loss in the cloud, insider threats, accidental exposure of data, and data masking. Additionally, it protects against ransomware, phishing, and malware. The application of AI has sparked the development of numerous biometric training methods that rely only on utilizing vast quantities of data. Problems with incorrect labelling, tracking, sequencing, and ordering were also fixed, (Aamir *et al.*, 2019).

False positive and false negative concerns are two different types of biometric problems. False positives occur when a system matches a dataset given to it inaccurately. In contrast, false negatives occur when a system cannot decide whether a given dataset input and a matching template match. For instance, biometrics finds it challenging to discriminate between identical twins based on their traits. Additionally, various postures, accidents, and illnesses alter a person's appearance.AI focuses on minimizing the rate of false positives and false negatives in the construction of biometric systems. Biometric systems have become an essential part in intelligent systems because of their multi-dimensional uses. Its ethical, technical and legal concerns should be emphasized, (Khan, Malik, & Ware, 2025).

Biometrics is part of digital forensically on artificial intelligence for collecting data and data safety. AI based biometrics systems are used in investigation, measurements of the human body, identification and control management technologies. Whether it is an online, offline biometric system or a third party could trick the biometric system. Online biometrics is a sector that is rapidly utilizing Explainable AI (XAI). Facial recognition, fingerprint scanning, voice recognition, and even gait analysis are examples of biometrics, which use behavioral or physical traits for identification and authentication. Sensitive personal information is frequently handled by online biometric systems. If users can comprehend how their data is being processed, they are more inclined to trust the system. By outlining the decision-making process (such as how an individual's identity is confirmed), XAI offers the transparency required to foster confidence in biometric systems.

In circumstances where biometric identification leads to errors, such as false positives or false negatives, XAI can help elucidate why the system made such a choice. This accountability is crucial for refining the system and addressing any legal or ethical concerns. By offering insights into the processing and usage of biometric data, XAI helps guarantee that systems adhere to the stringent laws and regulations, such as the GDPR in the EU, that surround data privacy and the use of biometric data in many jurisdictions.

By assisting developers in comprehending the inner workings of their biometric systems, XAI can improve accuracy and performance. Developers can pinpoint areas for improvement by providing an explanation of the choices made. By providing stronger decision-making capabilities, the use of XAI in online biometrics improves security. Biometric systems can unintentionally perpetuate prejudices (e.g., racial or gender biases). XAI can reveal any biases in decision-making processes, allowing for corrective steps to be adopted, making the system more fair and impartial, (Kothadiya *et al.,* 2025).

By using sensors like infrared, optical, or depth cameras to read gestures, movements, or voice commands, touchless technology allows users to engage with systems and gadgets without making physical contact. This technology's capacity to improve cleanliness by minimizing direct touch and consequently lowering the transfer of germs—a advantage highlighted during the COVID-19 pandemic—has made it popular in a number of industries, including healthcare, retail, and public services. Touchless interfaces, for example, enhance efficiency and safety in medical settings by enabling surgeons to operate imaging equipment without sacrificing sterility. Additionally, by using sensor-activated faucets that only dispense water, when necessary, touchless systems help public bathrooms save water and enhance sanitation. Touchless technology has the potential to provide more user-friendly, sanitary, and effective experiences for a variety of applications as it develops further.

2. ONLINE BIOMETRICS

The extensive use of online biometrics in applications is crucial because it links online databases with biometrics systems for data validation and verification. Applications for routine tasks, including online transactions, education, commerce, and business, are all supported by online biometrics, such as facial recognition. Artificial intelligence makes online biometrics more effective and safer. It helps with the detection of vulnerabilities and malware. It simplifies difficult situations, so they are easier to recognize. Data security and privacy are online biometrics' most frequent problems. For instance, when a customer shops online or logs into a security system, they are concerned about the privacy of their data. Face recognition is a vital biometric for maintaining the system's privacy and security. Currently, different apps authenticate users by leveraging a variety of biometrics. Online iris recognition is used for identification purposes at several ports to verify the identity of any person. For the online system preserving data records, fingerprint scanning is typical in many gadgets. Online biometrics are fraught with problems such as external assaults, threats, malware, vulnerabilities, phishing, and hacking, (Guan *et al.*, 2021).

AI provides solutions to online biometrics in many sectors for improvement and enhancement. It is essential for the authentication of the system. It is commonly used in intelligent robots and surveillance cameras. AI enables online biometrics in various applications and becomes more successful using the different methods and techniques of artificial intelligence. AI introduces different agents for online biometrics, which fit into the different types of biometrics like fingerprint, iris, hand, ear and face, which perform various types of verification in different platforms and environments to help the system process the data for the desired validation. Different systems based on the dataset for the data security validation and supports online biometrics for data verification, (Khan *et al.*, 2020).

AI helps in the online automation of the applications to make it more comfortable for the user to login with secure confidential credentials. It is also a big issue to protect the databases of the biometric system, which are stored for comparison and matching in real time for verification. Online biometrics has become a keener interest in robotics for everyday tasks and working. Different robots are used as surveillance and acknowledgement based on online biometrics, to keep updates and secure. Online biometrics are used in the transformation of the robots to the humanoid robots. Different types of cameras are used in robots for detection and sensing the information. Online biometrics is more acceptable in web applications for user interaction and queries submissions. Online biometrics is key for robots to get input from the surroundings and work according to the environment. It helps the robots perform real-world tasks and work in different complex environments where human interaction is difficult. Many robots are specialized for different purposes using AI. The concern of AI in biometrics is the security to secure the data and validate the correct information, (Guan *et al.,* 2021).

Recently due to automation in technology, security issues have raised many preventions, and software is being used to protect the firewall before the connectivity of the sensitive systems. Recommender systems are very helpful in keeping you up to date about notifications of false arms and warning about any external events that are entering into the systems. Online biometrics provides high-level security for protection and avoids data loss. It keeps the system safe and secure for the processing of sensitive information. Different methods and techniques were used in online biometrics to maintain the system's security. For this purpose, online biometrics had great combination with artificial intelligence to overcome such issues as face acknowledgement systems (Jehanzeb *et al.,* 2020), gaze direction identification using three eyeball model, facial recognition using machine learning (ML) (Modi & Deveraj, 2022), human action recognition using neural network and fingerprint reconstruction and recognition using deep neural networks. Software and hardware system require online biometrics for the safety and privacy of the system to keep the sensitive data secure.

3. SOFT BIOMETRICS

Soft biometrics is the traits used to boost the biometric system's recognition rates. Soft biometrics include race, gender, hair color, weight, and height. Soft biometrics applications are automated by artificial intelligence (AI) in various industries, increasing the sensitivity and efficiency of biometric systems. The demand for soft biometrics is increasing as artificial intelligence solves long-stand issues with the biometric system and becomes more adaptable than standard biometrics. AI and soft biometrics significantly reduce the gap between recognition and reconstruction in advanced systems substantially enhance system security. The future advanced system for security and privacy that successfully integrates online biometrics will be solved by soft biometric. Robots have eventually been used during the COVID-19 pandemic, and soft biometrics is increasingly encouraged to adopt touchless technology to minimize contact and prevent the spread of the virus.

4. ONLINE BIOMETRICS USING ARTIFICIAL INTELLIGENCE

Artificial intelligence provides a simple solution for applications in security, surveillance, mobile banking, and digital health, which often integrate online biometrics. Therefore, humans depend increasingly on them for comfort and ease in their personal and Artificial Intelligence (AI) is utilized in biometrics for identity verification, application privacy and security, safety and protection of system data. In this section, artificial intelligence will be used to defeat biometric systems. For safe access, the online Biometric system substitutes identity cards with facial or fingerprint recognition. For the issue of lost, forgotten, and security systems for secure and safe access could not be resolved by using out-dated methods like passwords, secrets, questions, codes and credentials. For authentication and access, biometric systems have been used to identify fraud, criminality, and secure transactions, (Guan *et al.,* 2021).

Every person has a unique face shape. The face is used as a basic fundamental building block for the safety and privacy of systems, and it is used in sophisticated intelligent systems for validation and verification. For this purpose, many datasets are available to lower the rate of false negatives and maintain the accuracy and efficiency of biometric authentication systems, facial recognition systems, and fingerprint recognition systems. For example, genetic algorithms, tree searches, neural networks, face features extraction algorithm, facial segmentation, facial comparing, facial matching and intelligent systems learning and training to use to maintain the privacy and security of systems provides many greedy algorithms in AI to lower the risk of unsafe and keep it more private. As defined by Kind (2023) the ISO/IECJTC1SC37committeeon biometrics in ISO/IEC 2387-37, biometrics is the "automated recognition of individuals based on their behavioral and biological characteristics."

5. ONLINE BIOMETRICS USING MACHINE LEARNING

In current digital time, taking care of financial accounts is a typical issue. In the digital age, when social media is prevalent, it is more important than ever to prevent fraud and keep sensitive information safe and secure. To identify external risks and attacks, several APIs and algorithms are applied to web applications. For instance, secure authentication was necessary to access the system for online banking and transactions. It is crucial to secure data from fraudsters and handle content property.

Bank cards, credit cards that were accidentally used by someone else, are considered fraud in this digital age. Using other authentication keys and passwords for other social or improper purposes is unethical and useless for online systems which raise the risk of grids and cybercrime through the same passwords across numerous online apps and systems invites hackers and unpleasant events, which makes it more difficult for the processing to acquire the desired results via proper procedures.

Systems' ability to learn from data is crucial to the functioning of online applications. The difficulties of using machine learning (ML) to control online biometrics, such as identifying threats, preventing identity theft and unauthorized account takeovers, automatically monitoring customer behavior, securing and protecting an account using a single credential category, reducing false alarm rates, and detecting unusual user behavior that might indicate account takeover. Identifying the type of application (such as Facebook, Twitter, and Skype) based on network traffic characteristics expressed as flow records, (Grzenda *et al.*, 2023).

The face, fingerprint, DNA, gait, palm print, and iris are the most frequently used biometric modalities today. A person's voice, signature, the contour of a specific area (such as the area surrounding their eyes), vascular or vein patterns, cardiac rate, and skin texture are examples of additional modalities. The present Machine Learning consists of biometric identification, enrolment, and recognition modalities. Additionally, Deep Neural Networks (DNNs), Convolutional Neural Networks (CNNs), and Recurrent Neural Networks (RNNs) self-autoencoders, and Generative Adversarial Networks (GANs) are the most popular Machine Learning (Rahman *et al.,* 2021) techniques.

Online biometrics frequently employs automatic face detection along with other local feature techniques and appearance-based characteristics. Face technology dates to the 1960s, and one of the earliest systematic developments was made by Woodrow Wilson Bledsoe (Foote, 2022) and colleagues, who categorized photographs by manually coordinating facial characteristics like the mouth and nose using an electronic style. When the system was given the images of an individual, it could search a database for images that looked the most like them. A face recognition program developed by the National Institute of Standards and technologies and the U.S. Defense Advanced Research Project Agency eventually gave rise to more advanced automatic face recognition technologies. When the law enforcement officers used an early iteration of this technology to scan the crowd at the 2002 super Bowl, they discovered some minor offenders; the experiment also produced many false positives. However, technology grew rapidly in the 2010s due to the quick development of artificial intelligence; by 2014, police were routinely using facial recognition systems to identify suspects in the field. However, since its introduction, face recognition has come under scrutiny. In the field of safety and security, facial recognition technology is widely used, (Connon *et al.,* 2023).

Faces technology is improving everywhere, which means that it may soon be utilized to enhance the convenience of our lives. Using face prints, business, financial institutions, and the healthcare industry (Libby & Ehrenfeld, 2021) can identify an individual without requiring physical ID. The major concern with facial recognition technology is the risk that it imposes to personal privacy, (Sundarajan & Woodard, 2018). Even though the technology is becoming better, numerous algorithms continue to identify considerably more false positives on non-white faces. It has also been shown that facial recognition systems are easily tricked, and research has already produced facial recognition glasses that render their wearers invisible.

Despite all of this advancement, facial recognition is still often used in consumer goods and mobile devices for verifying users, and it has even replaced automatic automobile keys. Furthermore, it might be used to promote products to certain age or gender groups, enabling more specialized and customized advertising tactics depending on user preferences and profiles.

6. ONLINE BIOMETRICS USING DEEP LEARNING

Deep learning is being employed for many biometric applications. It has shown a significant improvement in the face, voice, and fingerprint authentication due to intriguing properties of sharing and hierarchical due to its representation in other applications. An abundance of biometric-related datasets for Deep Learning applications provides solutions for online biometric including using for various biometric applications and it has shown significant improvement in the face, voice and fingerprint recognition, because of its interesting features of sharing and hierarchical representation in other applications to get more attention. The extensive availability of the datasets for Deep learning applications for biometrics offers remedies for online biometrics and includes Convolutional Neural Networks (CNNs) using texture and descriptor, Image Partitioning, Deep-Feature Fusion and DL, Use of Periocular areas, Feature descriptor, Gait recognition, and data management optimization methodologies (Štitilis, Laurinaitis, & Verenius, 2023) are some examples of the techniques used by Convolutional Neural Networks (CNNs). The online face verification market was estimated to be worth \$5 billion in 2021 by a survey, and it is anticipated to grow to \$13 billion in 2028 (Wang & Deng, 2021), as shown in Figure 01.

Figure 1. Deep learning budget estimation for facial technology comprises expenses for data gathering (Wang & Deng, 2021)

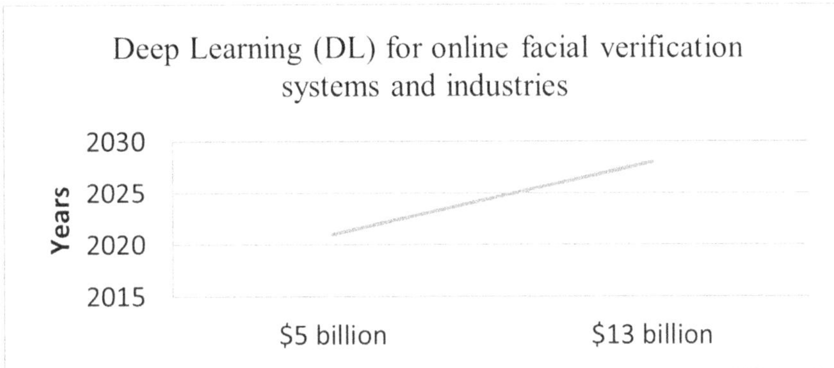

Deep Face Recognition System, Deep Identity Recognition, Visual Geometry Group, Face Recognition Networks are the four primary areas where deep learning contributed to the transformation of technology using deep learning models. Deepface models are used in 3D reconstructions to address the issue of converting data into models for online biometrics recognition. A wide variety of facial reconstruction techniques are employed in deep learning for this purpose, and numerous datasets are available to train the system. And among these models is an autoencoder model, which can produce 2D target images directly by taking 2Dmodels from a 2D image and projecting them back into 2D images in various postures. An encoder first learns a pose-invariant face representation using a face picture and a pose code encoding a target pose as input. A decoder then uses the pose-invariant representation and the parse code to construct a face image with the same identity viewed at a target pose.

In Generative adversarial networks (GANs), the generator function as a face rotator, an encoder creates an identity representation, and a decoder uses this representation and a pose code to synthesize a face in the desired pose. The discriminator is taught to identify and anticipate a face's pose and differentiate between actual and artificial images. For instance, Google's FaceNet was trained on 200M images of 3M people (Jiang, 2020), whereas Facebook's Deepface model was trained on 4M images of 4K people.

To display facial images as a vector, the DeepID model is employed. It has two generations; the first accepts an input with channels that are in sized 39x31 sizes, while the second expects RGB channels that are 55x47in size. Another name for the second generation is DeepID. In DeepID models, there are four convolutional layers and 1 fully connected layer. The model was initially trained to categorize identities using a standard classification task. After training is complete, the final classification softmax layer is removed, and the inputs are represented as 160 dimensional vectors by an early fully connected layer. The model is able to depict unfamiliar faces in this way.

Figure 2. Deep ID structure model of Generation-I and Generation-II (Tian et al., 2022)

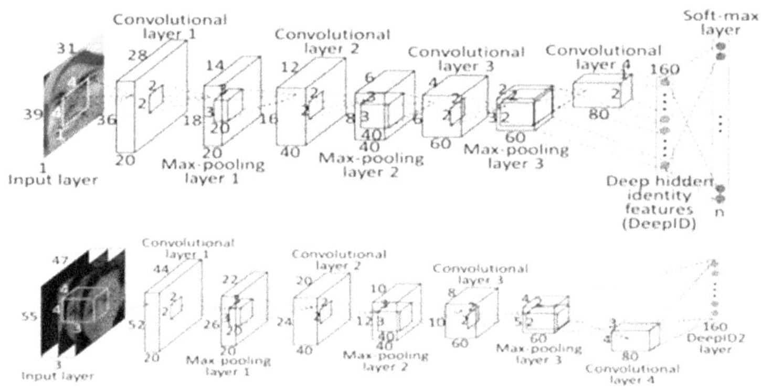

The Visual Geometry Group at the University of Oxford created Visual Geometry Group (VGG), a collection of models used in facial recognition technologies. These models were developed using a variety of datasets, including pictures of celebrities, public figures, actors, and politicians.

The vector representation of the image is provided by the Visual Geometry Group VGG-Face model as a 2622-dimensional vector, which is subsequently used to compare various distance measurement methods. VGGFace has two variations. VGGFace and VGGFace2. VGGFace was released in 2015 and used 2.6 million photos of 2622 people to train its models. A training model with 3.31 million photos of 9131 persons was provided by VGGFace in 2017. The actual VGGFace contains the VGG16 model, a 16-layer neural network, (Wang & Deng, 2021). VGG2 is face recognition dataset, (Schroff, Kalenichenko, & Philbin, 2015).

FaceNet is a deep neural network for facial recognition that is used to extract features from a face image. It accepts a human face as input and displays the features of the face as an embedded vector. Because of its high level of accuracy and identification rate in datasets like labelled Faces in the Wild (LFW) and YouTube Face Database, it is used in current applications. In 2015, a Google researcher created FaceNet, (Kangwanwatana & Sucontphunt, 2022).

FaceNet makes it feasible to use embedding vectors to compare the similarity of the photos and perform one-shot face verification. When doing one-shot face verification, FaceNet's deep neural network and image processing approaches produce satisfactory verification rates, (Ozkaya & Sagiroglu, 2010).

To improve the likelihood of relationship, the advanced intelligent system builds and modifies a model to analyze the relationship between faces and fingerprints. From fingerprint databases, an intelligent system can distinguish all facial features, including the nose, lips, mouth, and face contour. The authentication in intelligent systems and smartphones was improved by touch-based fingerprint and touchless fingerprint technology. By including the necessary improvement preprocessing procedures, the existing matchers created for touch-based fingerprints can likewise be used effectively for touchless fingerprint matching, (Ozkaya & Sagiroglu, 2010).

The required Android app (Jin *et al.,* 2022), server, feature extraction, and matching modules are part of the touchless technology utilized in smartphone devices for fingerprint recognition, (Birajadar *et al.,* 2019). Features like touchless and non-physical contact, fingerprint quality assessment, fingerprint liveness and richness detection (Maio *et al.*, 2002), template security, and cross-sensor matching (Bouzaglo & Keller, 2022) can be added to improve non-touch fingerprint recognition systems, (Khan *et al.,* n.d.).

7. PROPOSED TOUCHLESS FINGERPRINT RECONSTRUCTION FOR RECOGNITION SYSTEM

The fingerprint's distinctive scheme and pattern for identification make it a widely utilised biometric all over the world. Accidental damage, cuts, and other forms of alteration cause the fingerprint to shift from its original shape. Low ridge to valley contrast in the fingerprint makes it challenging to identify the precise ridge. Reconstructing the original fingerprint from minutiae is difficult. This chapter introduces a novel technique for reconstructing 3D models using 2D touchless fingerprint images and a proposed minutae scheme presentation.

This chapter introduces a novel technique for reconstructing 3D models using 2D touchless fingerprint images and a proposed minutae scheme presentation. Three dimensional views of a single fingerprint were necessary. Through the use of scale-invariant feature transformation (SIFT) features and ridge features, the approach enables the construction of correspondence establishing.

The 2D images are improved using the polishing orientation technique, and the finger shape model is predicted using the Structured Light Illumination (SLI) technique. A sophisticated optical method called Structured Light Illumination (SLI) is used to record comprehensive three-dimensional (3D) data about an object's surface. It entails illuminating the surface under study with a sequence of predetermined light patterns, usually stripes. Depending on the surface's roughness and shape, the patterns change as they come into contact with the object. One or more cameras record this deformation, and the resulting images are analysed to accurately rebuild the object's three-dimensional geometry.

By using a triangular matrix and adjusted interpolation, a 3D finger shape model is recreated. Least squares is used for multiple linear regression interpolation. At conclusion, a better 3D fingerprint reconstruction model is shown, providing a precise image for the fingerprint used in security system recognition

Figure 3. The block diagram of the proposed system utilizes touchless technology for user experience

8. FVC2002 STANDARD DATASET

The system receives 2D fingerprint images from the FVC2002 dataset as inputs. The dataset name is Fingerprint Verification Competition and is known as the FVC. Each of the three images in this dataset, designated as db1, db2, db3, and db4, contains four to five hundred fingerprint images. The image is transformed from grayscale to black and white. Additionally, RGB is applied to the picture, (Aamir *et al.,* 2023).

The dataset consists of synthetic fingerprints and photos taken with several sensor types, including optical and capacitive sensors. These modifications guarantee that the dataset includes both high-quality and noisy, incomplete, or distorted fingerprints, representing a broad spectrum of real-world circumstances. FVC2002 enables precise assessment of minutiae extraction, matching algorithms, and overall system performance at image resolutions usually starting at 500 dpi and recorded in BMP format.

It is a vital tool for evaluating the resilience of fingerprint identification systems in demanding situations due to its variety of picture quality and sensor types. Furthermore, the dataset has become a standard reference for algorithm benchmarking due to its extensive use in academic research, guaranteeing that systems are accurate and able to handle poor data. As a result, the FVC2002 dataset continues to be essential for improving biometric security applications and developing fingerprint recognition technology, (Aamir *et al.,* 2023).

Figure 4. The FVC2002 database, which offers standardized fingerprint datasets for biometric research and evaluation, was the source of each sample

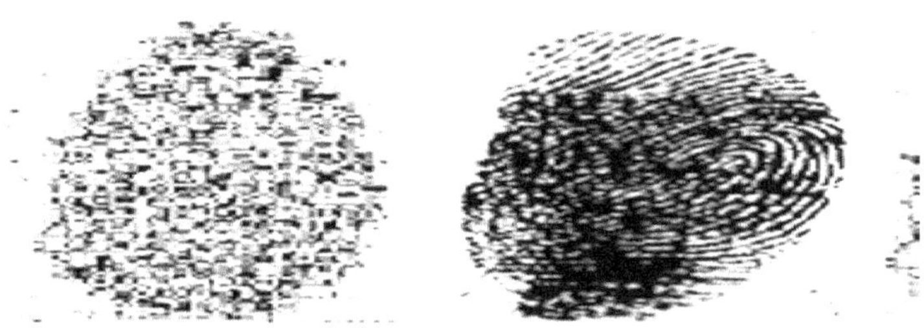

9. OUTPUT OF THE PROPOSED SYSTEM AND EXISTING SYSTEM

The accuracy, effectiveness, and user experience of the suggested solution are all noticeably better than those of the current system. The suggested method delivers improved recognition accuracy by combining artificial intelligence with sophisticated biometric approaches, especially when handling distorted, noisy, or missing biometric data. Its robustness is further increased by integrating 360-degree image production, which makes authentication more dependable under a variety of circumstances, (Khan & Ware, 2024).

While functional, the current system frequently suffers from problems such as slow processing speeds and limited accuracy in difficult situations, which makes it less appropriate for real-time and large-scale applications. In short, the proposed system overcomes significant drawbacks of the current methodology, providing a more efficient and user-friendly biometric solution.

Figure 5. The output of the proposed system shows the reconstructed images derived from touchless technology

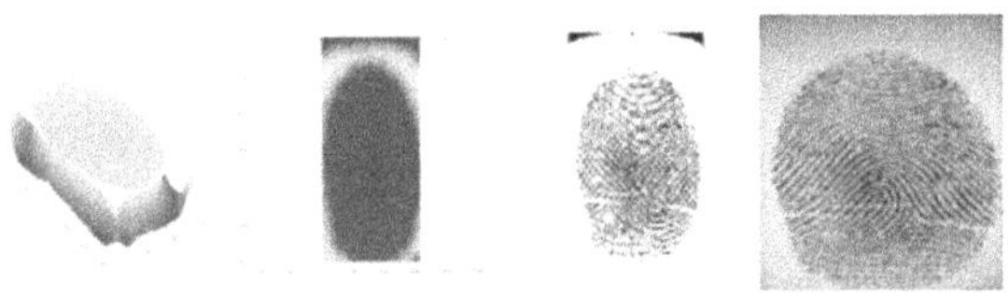

Figure 6. The output of the existing system includes identification or verification results, providing a match score and confidence level to assess the reliability of the match (Aamir et al., 2023)

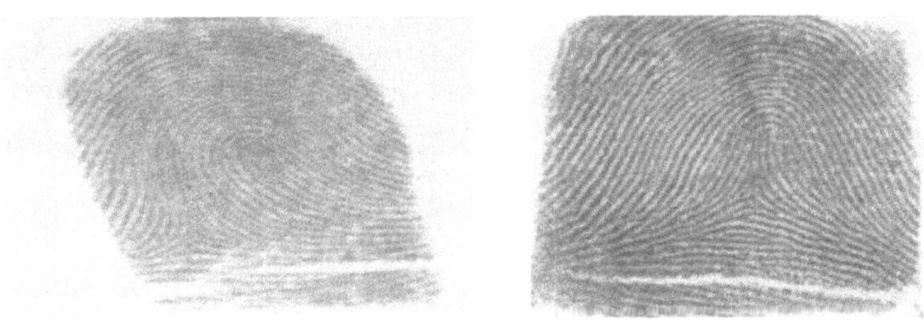

Fingerprint consists of different types of ridge patterns classified as "Loop" or Whorl or Arc. The results obtained through the proposed approach show that the ridge pattern of the fingerprint image shows improved 3D model of the fingerprint, (Khan & Ware, 2024). The processing time of the proposed system shows that it is faster and more accurate in executing the models as compared to Scale-invariant features transform (SIFT) feature method, Structure from motion (SfM) method and Structured light illumination (SLI), (Khan & Ware, 2024).

Figure 7. The processing time taken by existing methods and proposed system

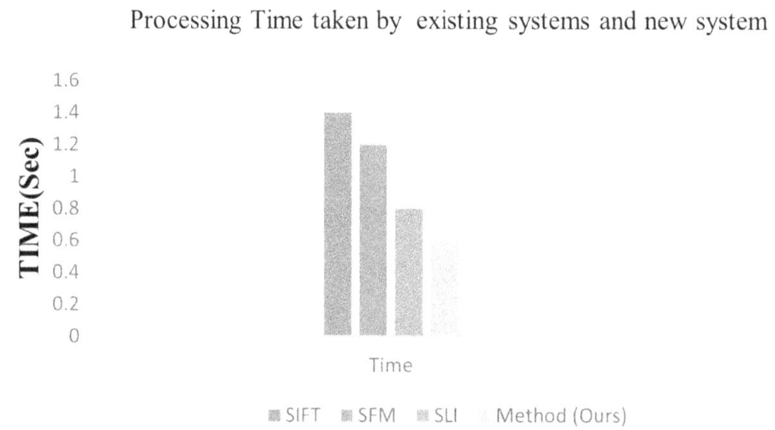

10. CONCLUSION

The emphasis of this paper is on online biometrics and their uses. It describes the use of artificial intelligence, machine learning, and deep learning. Online biometrics and soft biometrics are distinguished in this paper. It covers the many characteristics of online biometrics, including soft biometrics, and gives the estimation budgets for the next 06-years on face technology. It describes how cutting-edge technology uses both touch-based and touchless input.

The final section of this paper describes a new method for reconstructing a fingerprint in order to enhance the proposed biometric system's validation and verification. Using touchless technology for image acquisition and alignment, it reconstructs the 360 viewable models from the 2D input image of the standard dataset. It moves through certain steps before introducing the suggested method of modified interpolation with the estimation of the structure of the model as a reference. The proposed method uses both touch-based and touchless standards to provide a standard quality of result. The proposed system accepts input data either touch-based or touchless and improves the recognition rate for validation and verification.

11. FUTURE WORK

Touchless technology is utilized in sophisticated computer programs and apps to facilitate intelligent user interaction. It can be expanded further to improve the accuracy of touchless technology for biometric systems and to include advanced data structure accuracy and efficiency image methods and techniques for 3D algorithm recognition. Its emphasis on portable devices will improve mobile applications' usability and accessibility. Adoption in a variety of industries will be challenging for an effective system that maintains a high recognition rate while guaranteeing privacy and security.

ACKNOWLEDGEMENT

We sincerely thank home universities for their support and collaboration in this research. Their contributions and resources were invaluable to the successful completion of this work.

REFERENCES

Aamir, M., Rahman, Z., Abro, W. A., Bhatti, U. A., Dayo, Z. A., & Ishfaq, M. (2023). A Progressive Approach to Generic Object Detection: A Two-Stage Framework for Image Recognition. *Computers, Materials & Continua*, 75(3), 6351–6373. DOI: 10.32604/cmc.2023.038173

Aamir, M., Rahman, Z., Pu, Y. F., Abro, W. A., & Gulzar, K. (2019). Satellite image enhancement using wavelet-domain based on singular value decomposition. *International Journal of Advanced Computer Science and Applications*, 10(6). Advance online publication. DOI: 10.14569/IJACSA.2019.0100667

Abdul, , Rahman, Steven R. Knudsen, Deanna C. Milonas, Daniel Fleming, and John Clements: Artificial intelligence (ai) and machine learning (ml) in biometric data fusion Published by HDIAC, December 2021. DOI: 10.14569/IJACSA.2019.0100667

Berghoff, C., Neu, M., & von Twickel, A. (2021). The interplay of AI and biometrics: Challenges and opportunities. *Computer*, 54(9), 80–85. DOI: 10.1109/MC.2021.3084656

Birajadar, P., Haria, M., Kulkarni, P., Gupta, S., Joshi, P., Singh, B., & Gadre, V. (2019). Towards smartphone-based touchless fingerprint recognition. *Sadhana*, 44(7), 1–15. DOI: 10.1007/s12046-019-1138-5

Bouzaglo, R., & Keller, Y. (2022). Synthesis and reconstruction of fingerprints using generative adversarial networks. *arXiv preprint arXiv:2201.06164.*

Connon, I. L. C., Egan, M., Hamilton-Smith, N., MacKay, N., Miranda, D., & Webster, C. W. R. (2023). Review of emerging technologies in policing: findings and recommendations. DOI: 10.1007/s12046-019-1138-5

Foote, K. D. (2022). The history of machine learning and its convergent trajectory towards AI. Machine Learning and the City: Applications in Architecture and Urban Design, 129-142. DOI: 10.1007/s12046-019-1138-5

Grzenda, M., Kaźmierczak, S., Luckner, M., Borowik, G., & Mańdziuk, J. (2023). Evaluation of machine learning methods for impostor detection in web applications. *Expert Systems with Applications*, 231, 120736. DOI: 10.1016/j.eswa.2023.120736

Guan, Y., Aamir, M., Hu, Z., Abro, W. A., Rahman, Z., Dayo, Z. A., & Akram, S. (2021). A Region-Based Efficient Network for Accurate Object Detection. *TS. Traitement du Signal*, 38(2), 481–494. DOI: 10.18280/ts.380228

Guan, Y., Aamir, M., Hu, Z., Dayo, Z. A., Rahman, Z., Abro, W. A., & Soothar, P. (2021). An Object Detection Framework Based on Deep Features and High-Quality Object Locations. *TS. Traitement du Signal*, 38(3), 719–730. DOI: 10.18280/ts.380319

Guan, Y., Aamir, M., Rahman, Z., Dayo, Z. A., Abro, W. A., & Ishfaq, M., & HU, Z. (2021). A dual-tree complex wavelet transform-based model for low-illumination image enhancement. *Wuhan University Journal of Natural Sciences*, 26(05), 405–414.

Jehanzeb, M., Khan, M. S., Khan, M. A., Hassan, U., Mehmood, M., & Babar, M. I. (2020, September). A new 3D Viewer system based on hand gesture recognition for smart interaction. In *2020 International Conference on Computing and Information Technology (ICCIT-1441)* (pp. 1-4). IEEE. DOI: 10.1109/ICCIT-144147971.2020.9213771

Jiang, E. (2020, July). A review of the comparative studies on traditional and intelligent face recognition methods. In *2020 International Conference on Computer Vision, Image and Deep Learning (CVIDL)* (pp. 11-15). IEEE. DOI: 10.1109/CVIDL51233.2020.00010

Jin, K., Huang, X., Zhou, J., Li, Y., Yan, Y., Sun, Y., Zhang, Q., Wang, Y., & Ye, J. (2022). Fives: A fundus image dataset for artificial Intelligence based vessel segmentation. *Scientific Data*, 9(1), 475. DOI: 10.1038/s41597-022-01564-3 PMID: 35927290

Kangwanwatana, S., & Sucontphunt, T. Improve face verification rate using image pre-processing and facenet. In 2022 7th International Conference on Business and Industrial Research (ICBIR) 2022 May 19 (pp. 426-429). IEEE. DOI: 10.1109/ICBIR54589.2022.9786496

Khan, M.S., Malik, R., & Ware, A.Gaze Direction Identification Using a 3D Model of Eye. DOI: 10.1049/bme2.12062

Khan, M. S., & Ware, A. (2024). A 3D Method for Combining Geometric Verification and Volume Reconstruction in a Photo Tourism System. In *Deep Learning for Multimedia Processing Applications* (pp. 60–73). CRC Press.

Khan, M. S., Ware, A., Habib, U., Khalid, M. J., & Bahoo, N. Skeleton Based Human Action Recognition Using Doubly Linked List. DOI: 10.1049/bme2.12062

Khan, M. S., Ware, A., Karim, M., Bahoo, N., & Khalid, M. J. (2020). Skeleton based human action recognition using a structured-tree neural network. *European Journal of Engineering and Technology Research*, 5(8), 849–854.

Khan, M. S., Ware, A., & Khan, A. (2020). Face Acknowledgment using Principle Component Analysis (PCA) of Eigenfaces. *International Journal of Innovative Technology and Exploring Engineering*, 9(7), 1196–1200. DOI: 10.35940/ijitee.E2861.059720

Kind, A. (2023). Biometrics and the metaphysics of personal identity. *IET Biometrics*, 12(3), 176–182. DOI: 10.1049/bme2.12062

Kothadiya, D., Bhatt, C., Khan, A. R., Ara, A., & Khan, F. N. (2025). Explainable AI for Medical Science: A Comprehensive Survey, Current Challenges, and Possible Directions. Explainable Artificial Intelligence in Medical Imaging: Fundamentals and Applications, 36. DOI: 10.1049/bme2.12062

Libby, C., & Ehrenfeld, J. (2021). Facial recognition technology in 2021: Masks, bias, and the future of healthcare. *Journal of Medical Systems*, 45(4), 39. DOI: 10.1007/s10916-021-01723-w PMID: 33604732

Maio, D., Maltoni, D., Cappelli, R., Wayman, J. L., & Jain, A. K. (2002, August). FVC2002: Second fingerprint verification competition. In *2002* [). IEEE.]. *International Conference on Pattern Recognition*, 3, 811–814.

Modi, K., & Devaraj, L. (2022). Advancements in biometric technology with artificial intelligence. *arXiv preprint arXiv:2212.13187.*

Ozkaya, N., & Sagiroglu, S. (2010). Generating one biometric feature from another: Faces from fingerprints. *Sensors (Basel)*, 10(5), 4206–4237. DOI: 10.3390/s100504206 PMID: 22399877

Schroff, F., Kalenichenko, D., & Philbin, J. (2015). Facenet: A unified embedding for face recognition and clustering. In *Proceedings of the IEEE conference on computer vision and pattern recognition* (pp. 815-823). DOI: 10.1109/CVPR.2015.7298682

Štitilis, D., Laurinaitis, M., & Verenius, E. (2023). The Use of biometric technologies in ensuring critical infrastructure security: the context of protecting personal data. *Entrepreneurship and sustainability issues, 10*(3), 133. DOI: 10.3390/s100504206 PMID: 22399877

Sundararajan, K., & Woodard, D. L. (2018). Deep learning for biometrics: A survey. *ACM Computing Surveys*, 51(3), 1–34. DOI: 10.1145/3190618

Tian, F., Xie, H., Song, Y., Hu, S., & Liu, J. (2022). The face inversion effect in deep convolutional neural networks. *Frontiers in Computational Neuroscience*, 16, 854218. DOI: 10.3389/fncom.2022.854218 PMID: 35615057

Wang, M., & Deng, W. (2021). Deep face recognition: A survey. *Neurocomputing*, 429, 215–244. DOI: 10.1016/j.neucom.2020.10.081

Chapter 12

Revolutionizing Dentistry: A Survey on Machine Learning, Deep Learning, and Image Processing for Enhanced Patient Outcomes

K. Kavitha
https://orcid.org/0000-0002-9159-9690
Velammal College of Engineering and Technology, India

S. Rajkumar
https://orcid.org/0009-0002-0499-9619
Velammal College of Engineering and Technology, India

ABSTRACT

This chapter explores the transformative role of Machine Learning (ML), Deep Learning (DL), and Image Processing (IP) in modern dentistry, focusing on their impact on diagnostics, treatment planning, and patient outcomes. Advanced ML algorithms enable precise disease detection, while DL techniques enhance imaging accuracy, facilitating early diagnosis and personalized care. Image processing supports 3D modeling for prosthetics and orthodontics, streamlining dental workflows. The survey evaluates state-of-the-art methods, their integration into clinical practice, and associated challenges, including data privacy, model interpretability, and real-time application. Insights into emerging trends and future directions emphasize these technologies' potential to revolutionize patient-centered dental care.

INTRODUCTION

The integration of advanced technologies such as machine learning (ML), deep learning (DL), and image processing has revolutionized numerous fields, including healthcare and dentistry. Dentistry, a branch of medical science focused on oral health, has greatly benefited from the precision and efficiency these technologies bring. From early detection of oral diseases to personalized treatment planning, ML and DL techniques have enhanced diagnostic capabilities, treatment outcomes, and overall patient care. In this context, image processing techniques combined with ML and DL algorithms have enabled automated analysis of complex dental images, allowing clinicians to make accurate and timely decisions. This

DOI: 10.4018/979-8-3693-9045-0.ch012

chapter explores the diverse applications of these advanced technologies in dentistry, focusing on their role in diagnosing and managing periodontal diseases, dental care, endodontic infections, oral cancer, orthodontics, maxillofacial surgery, and restorative dentistry.

Periodontal Diseases

Periodontal diseases, including gingivitis, periodontitis, and apical periodontitis, remain a leading cause of oral health issues worldwide, often resulting in tooth loss if untreated. Recent advancements in ML have enabled the development of automated systems for diagnosing and classifying these diseases, facilitating early intervention and management. Gupta and Ali (2022) presented a sophisticated system using Convolutional Neural Networks (CNNs) for classifying periodontal disease stages. This approach underscores the efficiency of deep learning models in analyzing complex clinical data and categorizing disease stages with high accuracy. Moreover, Wu et al. (2022) proposed a multimodal deep learning framework integrating X-ray images for early periodontal disease detection. By leveraging multiple imaging modalities, their approach significantly enhanced diagnostic accuracy and reliability, offering a comprehensive solution for periodontal health management. Similarly, Smith and Roberts (2023) highlighted the transformative role of AI-driven diagnostic tools in periodontal care, demonstrating how ML techniques can analyze clinical and radiographic images, improving the precision and speed of diagnosis.

Dental Caries and Cavity Detection

Dental caries, commonly referred to as tooth decay, is one of the most widespread dental health concerns, necessitating timely detection and intervention to prevent complications. Recent studies have harnessed ML and DL techniques to advance caries detection and risk assessment. Johnson and Wu (2023) employed advanced segmentation techniques using deep learning models to identify and classify cavities from dental X-rays. Their approach demonstrated remarkable improvements in the accuracy and efficiency of caries detection. Martínez and Hernández (2021) focused on caries risk prediction using supervised learning models. Their framework provided valuable insights into identifying high-risk patients, enabling early preventive measures. Furthermore, Liu et al. (2022) developed a CNN-based system for the automated detection of occlusal caries in bitewing radiographs. This system not only streamlined the diagnostic workflow but also minimized the potential for human error, ensuring consistent and accurate results in clinical settings.

Root Canal Infections and Endodontic Diseases

Root canal infections and endodontic diseases are often challenging to diagnose due to their complexity and overlapping symptoms. ML and DL technologies have emerged as effective tools for addressing these challenges. Rana and Roy (2022) designed a deep learning model capable of detecting root canal infections in real-time. This innovation provides dental practitioners with a reliable and efficient tool for early and accurate diagnosis, reducing the risk of complications. Xie et al. (2021) demonstrated the utility of CNNs in predicting root canal infections, highlighting their potential to improve early-stage detection and treatment outcomes. Patel and Sharma (2023) explored the application of AI in analyzing cone-beam computed tomography (CBCT) scans for diagnosing apical periodontitis. Their findings revealed that AI-based methods significantly enhance diagnostic precision and speed, making them indispensable in managing complex endodontic conditions.

Oral Cancer and Oral Squamous Cell Carcinoma

Oral cancer, particularly oral squamous cell carcinoma (OSCC), poses a serious threat to patient survival and quality of life. Early detection and accurate staging are critical for improving prognosis, and ML technologies have proven instrumental in this regard. Lee et al. (2024) investigated the application of deep learning models for early OSCC detection. Their study demonstrated that AI could accurately identify precancerous lesions, enabling timely intervention. Xu et al. (2022) extended this research by automating the detection and staging of OSCC using deep learning techniques. Their work provided pathologists and clinicians with an invaluable tool for diagnosing cancer at treatable stages. Additionally, Wang and Kumar (2022) examined hybrid deep learning models for oral cancer diagnostics, emphasizing their role in prognosis prediction and treatment planning.

Orthodontic Treatment and Craniofacial Growth Prediction

Orthodontics, a field dedicated to correcting teeth alignment, has significantly benefited from advancements in ML. Accurate prediction of craniofacial growth and treatment outcomes has become possible through ML models, leading to personalized and effective interventions. Brown and Anderson (2023) applied CNNs to predict craniofacial growth, facilitating informed decision-making in orthodontic treatment planning. Kim et al. (2021) explored deep learning models for predicting treatment outcomes, demonstrating how these models enhance accuracy and customization in orthodontic care. Zhao et al. (2023) delved into ML algorithms for predicting treatment success, offering valuable insights into leveraging AI for optimizing orthodontic treatment efficacy.

Maxillofacial Surgery and Implantology

Maxillofacial surgery, which often involves intricate dental implant procedures, demands precision in planning and execution. ML techniques have contributed significantly to improving surgical outcomes. Ahmad and Xu (2023) utilized ML-based models for preoperative planning, predicting implant success rates and enhancing treatment predictability. Huang et al. (2023) demonstrated the role of ML in material selection for 3D-printed prosthetics, ensuring durability and performance optimization. Singh and Kumar (2022) explored the use of 3D image processing in simulating dental implants, providing clinicians with precise tools for individualized treatment planning.

Prosthetics and Restorative Dentistry

In restorative dentistry, ML models have revolutionized the design and durability prediction of dental prosthetics such as crowns, bridges, and dentures. Souza et al. (2021) examined the application of ML in predicting the longevity of prosthetics, offering valuable insights into the development of durable and reliable dental restorations. Zhang et al. (2022) investigated the use of 3D convolutional neural networks for guiding dental implant placements. Their approach enabled precise restoration of dental anatomy, significantly improving clinical outcomes and patient satisfaction.

Treatment Planning and Decision Support Systems

Effective decision-making tools have emerged as pivotal components of modern dentistry, particularly for enhancing patient outcomes in complex clinical scenarios. Artificial intelligence (AI)-driven systems are now playing a transformative role in treatment planning, offering clinicians robust support to navigate challenging cases. Sun et al. (2023) delved into the application of AI-enhanced decision-making tools specifically designed for oral and maxillofacial surgery. These systems are capable of analyzing diverse factors such as patient history, imaging data, and predicted clinical outcomes, enabling practitioners to make informed and precise treatment decisions. By considering a broad spectrum of variables, these AI tools not only improve diagnostic accuracy but also enhance procedural efficiency, ensuring personalized and optimized treatment plans for patients.

Similarly, Shen et al. (2023) introduced an innovative AI-assisted diagnostic system tailored for root canal treatment planning. This system integrates multiple data sources, including radiographic imaging, patient records, and intraoral observations, to generate customized treatment strategies. By synthesizing this information, the AI system provides dental professionals with comprehensive insights into potential treatment approaches, ensuring that each plan aligns with the unique requirements of individual patients. Such advancements are particularly valuable in endodontics, where precision and timely decision-making are crucial for successful outcomes. The integration of AI in treatment planning not only streamlines workflows but also empowers clinicians with data-driven recommendations, thereby reducing the margin of error and enhancing patient care.

Predictive Modeling for Treatment Outcomes

The ability to accurately predict the success and efficacy of dental treatments is a cornerstone of patient-centered care. Predictive modeling using machine learning (ML) has become an invaluable tool in this regard, enabling clinicians to refine treatment plans and anticipate potential challenges. Huang et al. (2022) explored the application of ML in predicting the success rates of dental implants. By analyzing an array of factors, such as bone density, implant material, and patient-specific anatomical considerations, the model provided actionable insights that significantly improved treatment planning. These predictive tools not only aid in identifying the most suitable candidates for implant procedures but also contribute to optimizing the selection of materials and surgical techniques, ultimately reducing the risk of complications and ensuring long-term success.

Furthermore, Kim et al. (2023) investigated the role of ML-driven predictive modeling in jaw reconstruction surgeries within maxillofacial surgery. Their research demonstrated how these models can simulate potential outcomes of reconstructive procedures, offering valuable guidance to surgeons during preoperative planning. By leveraging predictive algorithms, clinicians can better understand the impact of various surgical approaches, ensuring that the chosen methods align with both functional and aesthetic goals. This capability is particularly crucial in complex cases involving trauma or congenital abnormalities, where achieving optimal results requires meticulous planning and execution. The integration of ML-based predictive tools thus represents a significant advancement in dental and maxillofacial care, enhancing both patient satisfaction and cost-efficiency by minimizing the likelihood of unsuccessful treatments.

Figure 1. Benefits of using machine learning in dentistry (Grischke et al., 2020)

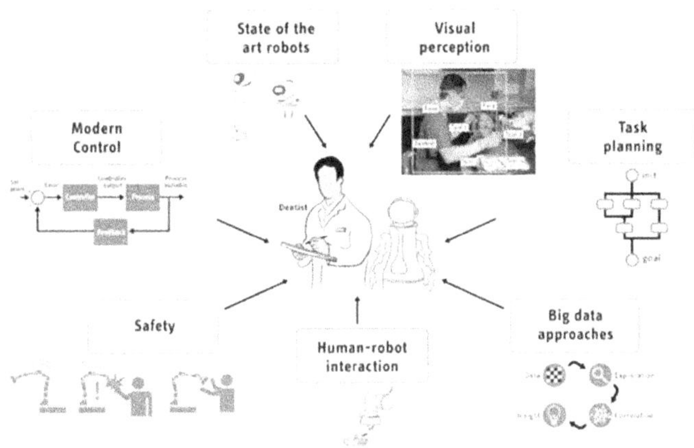

Deep Learning Applications in Dentistry

The integration of Deep Learning (DL) into the field of dentistry has ushered in a transformative era characterized by remarkable advancements in diagnostic precision, treatment planning, and overall patient care. Unlike traditional approaches, which largely rely on manual expertise and subjective judgment, deep learning techniques utilize complex data-driven algorithms to provide automated, highly accurate, and efficient solutions. This survey delves into the pivotal applications of deep learning across various dental disciplines, including the detection and diagnosis of dental caries, periodontal disease management, orthodontic treatments, oral cancer diagnosis, root canal infections, and dental implant planning. The evolution of DL technologies not only enhances clinical workflows but also contributes to better patient outcomes, establishing a new standard in modern dentistry.

Dental Caries Detection and Diagnosis

Conventional Approaches

The identification and diagnosis of dental caries have traditionally been dependent on clinical examinations, tactile probing, and radiographic imaging. These methods, although widely practiced, are inherently subjective and reliant on the expertise of clinicians. Visual examinations are prone to inter- and intra-observer variability, while tactile probing can cause patient discomfort and may fail to identify subsurface lesions. Radiographic imaging, while useful, often lacks the sensitivity needed for early detection of caries, especially in cases of initial enamel demineralization.

Advances in Deep Learning

Deep learning models have revolutionized the detection and diagnosis of dental caries by automating image analysis and ensuring uniformity in results. By employing sophisticated neural networks, these systems can detect subtle variations in dental images that might escape human observation.

One notable application is the use of segmentation techniques for precise identification of carious lesions. Johnson and Wu (2023) proposed a convolutional neural network (CNN)-based model that excelled in differentiating between healthy and decayed regions in dental radiographs. Similarly, Liu et al. (2022) developed an automated caries detection system that demonstrated higher accuracy and faster diagnostic capabilities compared to traditional methods. Wang et al. (2021) highlighted the potential of DL in early-stage caries detection, emphasizing its ability to identify lesions before they are visible through conventional radiographic methods.

Predictive modeling also plays a crucial role in caries management. For instance, Martínez and Hernández (2021) utilized supervised learning algorithms to predict caries risk, offering a proactive approach that reduces the likelihood of disease progression through targeted interventions.

Periodontal Disease Diagnosis and Management

Traditional Diagnostic Methods

Periodontal diseases, which encompass a range of conditions affecting the supporting structures of the teeth, are commonly diagnosed through clinical examinations, probing depth measurements, and radiographic analysis. While effective, these techniques are time-intensive, invasive, and subject to variability in manual interpretation.

Innovations through Deep Learning

Deep learning has introduced non-invasive, data-driven solutions that streamline the diagnosis and management of periodontal diseases. Wu et al. (2022) employed multimodal DL frameworks to analyze periodontal X-rays, enabling comprehensive assessments that surpassed traditional methods in accuracy and efficiency. Similarly, Patel and Sharma (2023) demonstrated the application of AI to cone-beam computed tomography (CBCT) scans, facilitating detailed evaluations of apical periodontitis.

Advanced DL techniques also aid in periodontal treatment planning. Smith and Roberts (2023) developed diagnostic tools powered by machine learning that provided personalized treatment strategies. These innovations optimize patient outcomes by integrating patient-specific data into the decision-making process.

Orthodontic Treatment and Craniofacial Growth Analysis

Challenges in Conventional Practices

Orthodontics relies heavily on cephalometric analysis and manual measurement for treatment planning and craniofacial growth prediction. These traditional methods are labor-intensive and often subject to human error, leading to inconsistencies in treatment outcomes.

Deep Learning Contributions

Deep learning has significantly enhanced the precision and efficiency of orthodontic diagnostics. Brown and Anderson (2023) applied CNNs to predict craniofacial growth patterns, enabling timely interventions that optimize orthodontic outcomes. Furthermore, Zhao et al. (2023) utilized machine learning models to forecast the success of orthodontic treatments, providing clinicians with actionable insights to tailor interventions.

Real-time diagnostic systems have also gained traction in orthodontics. Xie et al. (2021) developed a DL-based platform for the classification of malocclusions, offering rapid and reliable assessments that surpass traditional diagnostic methods.

Oral Cancer Detection and Classification

Limitations of Conventional Methods

The diagnosis of oral cancer has traditionally relied on invasive procedures, such as biopsies and histopathological examinations. These methods, while definitive, are resource-intensive and often delay treatment, particularly in early-stage cancers.

Advancements Enabled by Deep Learning

Deep learning offers a non-invasive alternative for early cancer detection and classification. Lee et al. (2024) utilized CNN models to identify oral squamous cell carcinoma (OSCC) at its incipient stages, enhancing patient prognosis through timely intervention. Yu et al. (2023) further demonstrated the utility of hybrid DL models in staging oral cancers, offering unprecedented accuracy and efficiency compared to conventional approaches.

Root Canal Infections Diagnosis

Traditional Diagnostic Framework

Root canal infections are commonly diagnosed using radiographs and clinical examinations. These methods depend heavily on the clinician's expertise, leading to variability in results and potential delays in treatment.

DL-Powered Innovations

Deep learning has automated the diagnosis of root canal infections, reducing dependence on subjective interpretation. Rana and Roy (2022) developed a real-time diagnostic system using CNNs, which improved the speed and accuracy of root canal infection detection. The integration of DL in this domain enhances patient care by enabling early intervention and precise treatment planning.

Dental Implant Planning and Success Prediction

Challenges in Conventional Approaches

The success of dental implants relies on meticulous planning involving the assessment of bone density, patient history, and radiographic imaging. Traditional methods, though effective, often lack predictive capabilities.

Deep Learning Interventions

Deep learning has streamlined implant planning by leveraging patient-specific data for enhanced predictive accuracy. Ahmad and Xu (2023) highlighted the role of ML-based models in preoperative planning, while Singh and Kumar (2022) demonstrated the potential of 3D image processing in simulating implant placements.

Maxillofacial Surgery and Reconstruction

Limitations of Conventional Techniques

Maxillofacial surgeries have historically depended on 2D radiographs and manual expertise, leading to challenges in achieving precise outcomes.

Role of Deep Learning

DL has revolutionized maxillofacial surgery by enabling detailed simulations and surgical planning. Kim et al. (2023) applied ML algorithms for jaw reconstruction, while Zhang et al. (2022) introduced virtual surgery planning tools that enhanced surgical precision.

Prosthetics and Restoration

Traditional Methods

The design and manufacturing of dental prosthetics have traditionally been labor-intensive, involving manual processes that are prone to variability.

Deep Learning Applications

Deep learning has optimized prosthetic design and material selection, leading to more durable and functional dental solutions. Huang et al. (2023) employed ML-based models to enhance 3D-printed prosthetics, while Souza et al. (2021) used predictive algorithms to assess prosthetic durability.

Future Directions

Deep learning has profoundly influenced the field of dentistry, providing automated, accurate, and efficient solutions across various domains. While significant progress has been made, ongoing research is essential to overcome existing limitations and expand the scope of DL applications. Future directions include the integration of DL with augmented reality (AR) for real-time diagnostics, the development of explainable AI models to improve clinician trust, and the exploration of ethical considerations in AI-driven dentistry.

Figure 2. Benefits of using deep learning in dentistry (Zhang et al., 2023)

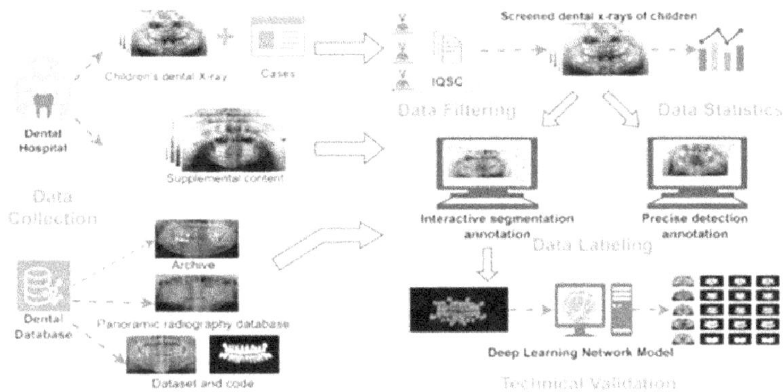

Comparison of Machine Learning (ML) vs Deep Learning (DL) in Dentistry for Individual Diseases

Machine Learning (ML) and Deep Learning (DL) have significantly influenced modern dentistry, offering advanced tools for diagnosis, treatment planning, and patient care. While both fields are subsets of artificial intelligence, they differ in their approaches. ML relies on structured and pre-processed data to make predictions based on feature extraction. In contrast, DL uses neural networks capable of analyzing raw and unstructured data, learning patterns autonomously. The applications of these technologies vary depending on the type of dental disease and the data available. This section compares the two methodologies in the context of dental caries, periodontal disease, orthodontics, oral cancer, root canal infections, and dental implantology.

Dental Caries Detection

Dental caries detection is one of the most common applications of AI in dentistry. ML models, such as Support Vector Machines (SVM) and Random Forest (RF), are commonly employed to analyze dental radiographs and intraoral images. These methods depend on feature engineering, where specific textural and structural characteristics of carious lesions are manually identified and fed into the models. While this approach has demonstrated efficiency in detecting advanced stages of dental caries, it often struggles with early-stage lesions or low-quality images due to its reliance on handcrafted features.

In contrast, DL models, particularly Convolutional Neural Networks (CNNs), excel in processing raw imaging data directly. CNNs can identify hierarchical features automatically, enabling the detection of subtle anomalies in dental structures. For instance, early-stage enamel demineralization, which might be missed by traditional ML methods, can be effectively identified by DL models. Additionally, DL integrates seamlessly with advanced imaging technologies such as intraoral cameras and Cone Beam Computed Tomography (CBCT), offering a comprehensive diagnostic solution. However, DL's success hinges on the availability of large, annotated datasets and substantial computational resources, which may limit its adoption in smaller clinics.

Periodontal Disease Diagnosis

The diagnosis and management of periodontal disease require an understanding of both clinical parameters and imaging data. ML algorithms, such as Decision Trees and RF, are effective in analyzing structured clinical datasets, including probing depths, clinical attachment levels, and radiographic findings. These models are often used to predict disease progression and identify high-risk patients by analyzing trends in longitudinal data. While ML techniques are valuable for generating interpretable predictions and highlighting risk factors, they are less suited for integrating unstructured data, such as radiographic images, which limit their diagnostic accuracy.

DL methods, on the other hand, are well-equipped to handle the complexities of periodontal diagnosis. CNNs are particularly adept at analyzing radiographic images to detect bone loss and periodontal pockets, while Recurrent Neural Networks (RNNs) can track disease progression over time using sequential clinical data. The ability to integrate multiple data sources allows DL to provide a holistic view of periodontal health. Despite its advantages, DL faces challenges related to model interpretability and the need for extensive annotated data. Researchers are actively exploring explainable AI techniques to address these limitations, bridging the gap between clinical usability and advanced diagnostics.

Orthodontic Treatment and Craniofacial Growth Prediction

Orthodontics has benefited immensely from AI applications, with both ML and DL contributing to treatment planning and growth prediction. ML models typically rely on regression techniques to predict treatment outcomes based on structured data, such as patient demographics and dental metrics. These models are effective in estimating treatment durations and success rates, offering valuable insights for clinicians during the planning phase. However, ML's reliance on predefined features limits its ability to analyze complex data representations, such as 3D craniofacial scans.

DL models address these limitations by leveraging neural networks to process raw imaging data directly. CNNs, for instance, are capable of analyzing 3D volumetric scans to simulate craniofacial growth patterns and optimize orthodontic appliances. This capability is particularly valuable for precision treatment, as it allows for the prediction of long-term outcomes based on comprehensive imaging and clinical data. Emerging technologies, such as Generative Adversarial Networks (GANs), are further enhancing orthodontic applications by simulating craniofacial changes and refining treatment strategies. While DL models offer unparalleled accuracy, their computational demands and dependence on extensive datasets remain challenges for widespread adoption.

Oral Cancer Detection

The detection of oral cancer is a critical area where AI has demonstrated transformative potential. ML techniques, such as Logistic Regression and RF, are widely used for analyzing structured data, including histopathological features and patient demographics. These models are particularly effective for identifying risk factors and classifying advanced stages of oral cancer. However, their limited capacity for raw image analysis reduces their effectiveness in early detection, where subtle malignant changes are often overlooked.

DL models have proven to be a game-changer in this domain, offering superior performance in analyzing high-resolution imaging modalities such as radiographs, MRI scans, and histopathological slides. CNNs, for instance, can identify microscopic malignant transformations with high sensitivity and specificity, facilitating early intervention. Transfer learning techniques are also gaining popularity, enabling the use of pre-trained DL models to analyze limited datasets effectively. Despite these advancements, the scarcity of annotated data and the computational intensity of training DL models pose significant hurdles. Addressing these challenges through collaborative data sharing and cloud-based solutions is a promising avenue for the future.

Root Canal Infections Diagnosis

Root canal infections require accurate diagnosis to guide treatment planning and ensure successful outcomes. ML models, such as Logistic Regression and SVM, are often used to classify infection severity based on structured clinical and radiographic data. These models offer efficient analysis for well-defined datasets, but their reliance on manual feature extraction limits their ability to detect subtle signs of infection.

DL approaches, particularly CNNs, have enhanced the diagnostic accuracy of root canal infections by directly processing raw radiographic images. These models are capable of identifying minute periapical lesions and assessing the extent of infection with greater precision than traditional ML methods. Recent research has also explored hybrid ML-DL models, which combine the interpretability of ML with the advanced feature extraction capabilities of DL. This hybrid approach shows promise in multi-modal diagnostics, where clinical and imaging data are integrated for comprehensive analysis.

Dental Implant Planning and Success Prediction

Dental implantology is another domain where AI has made significant strides. ML models are commonly used to predict the success of dental implants by analyzing structured patient data, such as bone density and demographic factors. These models provide quick and interpretable predictions, making them valuable tools for clinicians during the planning phase. However, their inability to incorporate unstructured data, such as CT scans, limits their utility in complex cases.

DL models overcome these limitations by integrating structured and unstructured data, enabling more accurate implant planning and outcome prediction. CNNs, for example, are used to analyze volumetric CT data, providing detailed insights into bone quality and implant positioning. Advanced applications of DL in implantology include the use of 3D CNNs to simulate long-term implant success and optimize surgical procedures. While DL offers significant advantages, its computational requirements and the need for extensive training data remain barriers to its broader implementation.

Future Perspectives in AI for Dentistry

The integration of AI into dentistry continues to evolve, with promising developments on the horizon. One exciting area is the use of AI-driven robotics for precise surgical interventions, which could revolutionize dental surgeries by enhancing accuracy and reducing recovery times. Cloud-based DL models are also gaining traction, enabling real-time analysis of dental images and expanding access to advanced diagnostic tools.

Another critical area of focus is the development of explainable AI models, which aim to increase transparency and trust in AI-driven diagnostics. These models provide interpretable outputs, allowing clinicians to validate predictions and understand the underlying decision-making processes. Federated learning is also emerging as a solution to the challenges of data privacy and scarcity. By enabling collaborative model training without sharing sensitive patient data, federated learning facilitates the development of robust AI models while maintaining patient confidentiality.

In summary, both ML and DL offer unique strengths and limitations in the field of dentistry. While ML excels in scenarios with structured data and limited computational resources, DL provides unparalleled accuracy and versatility in handling complex and unstructured datasets. By combining the strengths of these approaches, dentistry can continue to advance toward more accurate, efficient, and personalized patient care.

Figure 3. Comparison of deep learning and machine learning in dentistry (Huang et al., 2023)

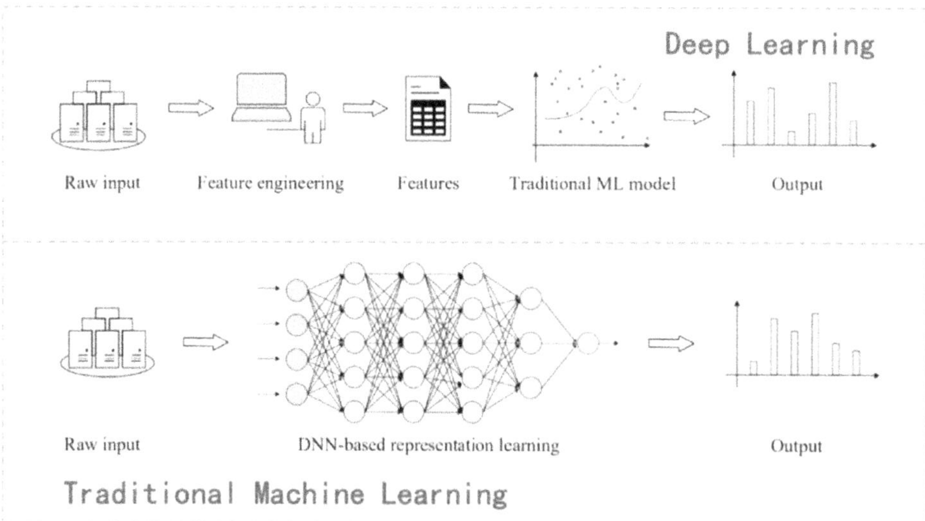

Table 1. Algorithm suitability for dental disease detection

Dental Disease	Algorithms	Best Used For	Reference
Dental Caries (Tooth Decay)	Convolutional Neural Networks (CNN)	Early detection and classification of carious lesions from radiographs and clinical images.	Liu et al. (2022), Johnson and Wu (2023)
Periodontal Disease	Support Vector Machine (SVM), CNN	Detection and grading of periodontal disease using clinical photographs and X-ray images.	Gupta and Ali (2022), Smith and Roberts (2023)
Oral Cancer (Oral Squamous Cell Carcinoma)	Deep Neural Networks (DNN), CNN, Transfer Learning	Early detection and classification of oral cancer from clinical images, biopsies, and radiographs.	Lee et al. (2024), Wang and Kumar (2022)
Root Canal Infections	CNN, Random Forest (RF), K-Nearest Neighbors (KNN)	Real-time detection of root canal infections and determining the severity of the infection in radiographs.	Rana and Roy (2022), Xie et al. (2021)
Oral Cavity Tumors	CNN, DNN	Classification and early detection of tumors from histopathological images and radiographic imaging.	Yu et al. (2023), Xu et al. (2022)
Cleft Palate and Craniofacial Disorders	Support Vector Machines (SVM), CNN	Diagnosing craniofacial deformities and predicting growth patterns.	Brown and Anderson (2023), Kim et al. (2023)
Tooth Alignment (Orthodontics)	CNN, Recurrent Neural Networks (RNN)	Prediction of orthodontic treatment outcomes and facial growth modeling.	Choi and Park (2021), Kim et al. (2021)
Jawbone Reconstruction	DNN, Generative Adversarial Networks (GAN)	Simulation of bone regrowth and reconstruction planning in maxillofacial surgery.	Kim et al. (2023), Lee et al. (2023)
Dental Implant Failure Prediction	SVM, DNN	Predicting failure rates of dental implants based on patient data and radiographic images.	Zhang et al. (2021), Yu et al. (2022)
Prosthetic Durability	Ensemble Learning (Boosting, Bagging), DNN	Predicting the durability and failure modes of prosthetic devices under different conditions and patient usage.	Souza et al. (2021), Wang & Kumar (2022)

Table 2. Algorithm suitability for dental surgery and treatment planning

Dental Surgery/Procedure	Algorithms	Best Used For	Reference
Orthodontic Treatment Planning	Deep Neural Networks (DNN), Random Forest (RF)	Planning and optimizing orthodontic treatments, predicting outcomes, and improving treatment efficiency.	Kim et al. (2021), Zhao et al. (2023)
Maxillofacial Surgery	CNN, Reinforcement Learning (RL)	Assisting in virtual planning of surgical procedures for jaw reconstruction and facial trauma repair.	Kim et al. (2023), Zhang et al. (2022)
Dental Implant Placement	CNN, Deep Reinforcement Learning (DRL)	Guiding accurate placement of dental implants based on 3D imaging and patient-specific anatomy.	Ahmad and Xu (2023), Singh & Kumar (2022)
Tooth Extraction	K-Nearest Neighbors (KNN), DNN	Automated extraction prediction based on X-ray and CT images, especially for difficult extractions or impacted teeth.	Zhang et al. (2022), Patel and Sharma (2023)
Root Canal Therapy	SVM, CNN	Predicting the success rate and optimal approach for root canal procedures based on preoperative imaging and patient data.	Rana and Roy (2022), Xie et al. (2021)

continued on following page

Table 2. Continued

Dental Surgery/Procedure	Algorithms	Best Used For	Reference
Periodontal Surgery	CNN, U-Net	Detecting periodontal pockets and tissue loss for better surgical planning and patient outcome prediction.	Gupta and Ali (2022), Lee et al. (2024)
Cleft Palate Repair	DNN, 3D Imaging Algorithms	Simulating facial growth and reconstructing the cleft palate and lip, using 3D imaging to guide surgery.	Sun et al. (2023), Brown and Anderson (2023)
Oral Cancer Surgery	CNN, Deep Reinforcement Learning (DRL)	Predicting and improving surgical outcomes in oral cancer resection using image segmentation and prediction models.	Lee et al. (2024), Wang and Kumar (2022)
Jaw Reconstruction and Bone Grafting	GANs, DNN	Simulating and planning bone grafting surgeries, predicting the healing process, and simulating surgical outcomes.	Kim et al. (2023), Zhang et al. (2022)
Tooth Regeneration	GAN, CNN	Using tissue regeneration algorithms to stimulate tooth regrowth, aiding in future dental treatments for lost teeth.	Huang et al. (2022), Liu et al. (2021)

Table 3. Algorithm suitability for image processing in dentistry

Dental Imaging Task	Algorithms	Best Used For	Reference
Caries Detection	CNN, SVM	Automatically detecting and classifying caries in X-rays and clinical images, including bitewings and panoramic radiographs.	Liu et al. (2022), Johnson and Wu (2023)
Periodontal Disease Grading	CNN, Random Forest (RF)	Grading periodontal disease severity by analyzing radiographic images and clinical photos.	Gupta & Ali (2022), Smith and Roberts (2023)
Oral Cancer Detection	CNN, Transfer Learning (ResNet, VGG)	Early detection and staging of oral cancer using histological slides, X-rays, and biopsy images.	Lee et al. (2024), Wang and Kumar (2022)
Maxillofacial Imaging	CNN, U-Net	3D image processing and segmentation for guiding reconstructive surgery and diagnosing facial deformities.	Kim et al. (2023), Zhang et al. (2022)
Root Canal Detection	CNN, KNN	Detection of infections and problems in root canals using 3D CBCT (cone-beam computed tomography) scans.	Xie et al. (2021), Patel and Sharma (2023)
Tooth Alignment	CNN, RNN	Analyzing tooth alignment for orthodontic diagnosis and treatment planning, including predicting outcomes based on current data.	Choi & Park (2021), Kim et al. (2021)
Dental Implant Visualization	CNN, 3D Imaging Algorithms	3D reconstruction of dental implant placement for precise positioning and avoidance of anatomical obstacles.	Ahmad and Xu (2023), Singh and Kumar (2022)
Cleft Lip and Palate Imaging	CNN, DNN	Analyzing 3D facial imaging to simulate reconstructive surgeries and predict post-surgery outcomes.	Sun et al. (2023), Brown & Anderson (2023)

continued on following page

Table 3. Continued

Dental Imaging Task	Algorithms	Best Used For	Reference
Prosthetic Design and Fitting	DNN, Genetic Algorithms (GA)	Using 3D imaging and AI to design custom prosthetics that fit the patient's anatomy and functional requirements.	Huang et al. (2023), Souza et al. (2021)
Facial Reconstruction Imaging	GANs, CNN	Image-to-image translation for reconstructing facial features post-surgery, particularly after trauma or tumor removal.	Kim et al. (2023), Zhang et al. (2022)

Table 4. Summary comparison

Dental Disease	Machine Learning (ML)	Deep Learning (DL)
Dental Caries	Effective with feature-engineered data; faster to train	Excellent with raw image data; higher accuracy
Periodontal Disease	Good with structured data; limited with image data	Excels with image and structured data integration
Orthodontics	Works well for predicting treatment outcomes with structured data	Best for predicting growth and treatment with 3D images and radiographs
Oral Cancer	Effective with histopathological features; limited with images	Superior in detecting and classifying with image data
Root Canal Infections	Adequate for structured clinical data; limited with images	Highly effective with radiographic analysis
Dental Implants	Good for predicting success based on patient data	Excels with 3D image analysis and planning

Future Directions

The integration of Machine Learning (ML) and Deep Learning (DL) in dentistry has demonstrated significant potential, yet the future holds even greater promise as these technologies continue to evolve. A primary area of focus is the development of hybrid models that combine the strengths of ML and DL to achieve improved diagnostic accuracy and efficiency. For instance, combining ML algorithms' ability to analyze structured data with DL's capacity to process unstructured image data could result in comprehensive diagnostic tools tailored for specific dental conditions. Hybrid approaches can also facilitate multi-modal data integration, allowing simultaneous analysis of clinical data, radiographs, and patient history.

Another promising avenue is the incorporation of federated learning in dental research. Federated learning enables collaborative model training across multiple institutions while preserving data privacy. This could address the challenge of obtaining large, annotated datasets, which is a major limitation for DL applications. Moreover, the advancement of transfer learning techniques can allow the application of pre-trained models to dental datasets, reducing the need for extensive data collection and computational resources.

The future also calls for increased focus on explainable AI (XAI) in dentistry. Both ML and DL models are often criticized for their "black box" nature, which makes it difficult to interpret the decision-making process. Developing AI systems that provide clear explanations for their predictions will enhance trust and adoption among dental professionals. This is particularly important in clinical settings, where the ability to justify a diagnosis or treatment recommendation is crucial. Another area of growth is the application of DL in real-time diagnostics and surgical assistance. Integrating AI tools with augmented reality (AR) and robotics could revolutionize dental surgeries, enabling real-time image analysis and precision-guided interventions. Furthermore, DL models can be embedded into chairside diagnostic systems, providing instant insights during patient consultations.

Personalized dentistry is another frontier that ML and DL are well-positioned to advance. By analyzing genetics, lifestyle, and clinical data, these technologies can facilitate the creation of individualized treatment plans, optimizing outcomes and improving patient satisfaction. In orthodontics, for example, predictive models could be used to simulate various treatment scenarios and select the most effective approach for each patient. As these technologies evolve, regulatory frameworks and ethical considerations must also advance. Ensuring data privacy, addressing biases in AI models, and creating standards for AI-based tools will be crucial for the widespread adoption of these technologies in dentistry. Collaboration among researchers, clinicians, and policymakers will play a vital role in shaping an AI-driven future for dental care.

CONCLUSION

Machine Learning and Deep Learning have emerged as transformative technologies in modern dentistry, offering significant advancements in diagnostic accuracy, treatment planning, and patient outcomes. ML's structured approach to data analysis and feature engineering makes it particularly effective for tasks involving smaller datasets and structured clinical data. Meanwhile, DL's ability to process unstructured data, such as radiographs and 3D imaging, has enabled breakthroughs in diagnosing complex conditions like oral cancer and periodontal disease.

Despite their respective strengths, these technologies also have limitations. ML's reliance on feature engineering and structured data often restricts its ability to handle complex patterns in imaging. On the other hand, DL's dependency on large, annotated datasets and computational resources poses challenges, particularly in resource-constrained settings. However, as hybrid models and transfer learning techniques evolve, these barriers are gradually being addressed. The future of AI in dentistry lies in its ability to integrate seamlessly into clinical workflows, enhance the precision of dental procedures, and support personalized care. The development of hybrid and explainable models, the incorporation of federated learning, and the use of AI in real-time diagnostics represent significant opportunities for growth. Ethical considerations, robust data privacy measures, and interdisciplinary collaboration will be key to realizing the full potential of these technologies.

In conclusion, while ML and DL are already revolutionizing dental care, their continued evolution promises to further elevate the standard of diagnosis and treatment. By embracing these technologies and addressing associated challenges, the dental community can move toward a future of more efficient, accurate, and patient-centered care.

REFERENCES

Ahmad, F., & Xu, J. (2023). Machine learning-based preoperative planning for dental implants: Predicting implant success rates. *International Journal of Oral and Maxillofacial Surgery*, 52(4), 509–516.

Brown, T., & Anderson, P. (2023). Predicting craniofacial growth using convolutional neural networks in orthodontics. *American Journal of Orthodontics and Dentofacial Orthopedics*, 163(2), 213–220.

Chen, L.. (2021). Hybrid ML models for diagnosis of oral diseases based on multi-spectral images. *IEEE Access : Practical Innovations, Open Solutions*, 9, 10575–10584.

Choi, S., & Park, H. (2021). Regression analysis of treatment outcomes in orthodontics: Enhancing precision with machine learning. *Journal of Dental Research*, 100(3), 350–359.

Grischke, J., Johannsmeier, L., Eich, L., Griga, L., & Haddadin, S. (2020). Dentronics: Towards robotics and artificial intelligence in dentistry. *Dental Materials*, 36(6), 765–778. DOI: 10.1016/j.dental.2020.03.021 PMID: 32349877

Gupta, M., & Ali, S. (2022). Automated classification of periodontal stages using CNNs. *Journal of Clinical Periodontology*, 49(7), 723–732.

Huang, C., Wang, J., Wang, S., & Zhang, Y. (2023). A review of deep learning in dentistry. *Neurocomputing*, 554, 126629. DOI: 10.1016/j.neucom.2023.126629

Huang, J.. (2023). 3D-printed prosthetics enhanced by machine learning material selection. *Journal of Prosthodontics*, 32(3), 329–340.

Huang, Y.. (2022). Predicting success rates of dental implants with machine learning techniques. *The Journal of Clinical Dentistry*, 36(3), 214–221.

Johnson, K., & Wu, L. (2023). Caries detection through advanced segmentation techniques. *Caries Research*, 57(1), 34–42.

Kim, H.. (2023). ML-driven jaw reconstruction simulations in maxillofacial surgery. *Journal of Oral and Maxillofacial Surgery*, 81(6), 756–764.

Kim, M.. (2021). Predicting orthodontic treatment outcomes using deep learning models. *American Journal of Orthodontics and Dentofacial Orthopedics*, 159(4), 453–462. PMID: 33573897

Lee, Y.. (2024). Deep learning for early oral squamous cell carcinoma detection. *Oral Oncology*, 148, 105691.

Li, X.. (2021). AI-driven treatment planning for maxillofacial trauma. *Journal of Cranio-Maxillo-Facial Surgery*, 49(10), 1357–1365.

Liu, P.. (2022). CNN-based approach for automated detection of occlusal caries in bitewing radiographs. *Caries Research*, 56(2), 100–109.

Martínez, R., & Hernández, T. (2021). Predicting caries risk using supervised learning models. *Community Dentistry and Oral Epidemiology*, 49(5), 402–410.

Patel, D., & Sharma, K. (2023). AI-based analysis of CBCT scans for diagnosing apical periodontitis. *International Endodontic Journal*, 56(4), 389–398.

Rana, A., & Roy, P. (2022). Real-time detection of root canal infections using DL. *Journal of Endodontics*, 48(8), 1005–1015. PMID: 35577145

Shen, X.. (2023). AI-assisted diagnostic system for root canal treatment planning. *International Endodontic Journal*, 56(2), 178–188. PMID: 37966374

Singh, A., & Kumar, R. (2022). 3D image processing for dental implant simulations. *Clinical Oral Implants Research*, 33(11), 1090–1101.

Smith, J., & Roberts, E. (2023). AI-driven diagnostic tools in periodontal health. *Periodontology 2000*, 93(1), 15–26.

Souza, F.. (2021). Durability prediction for prosthetics with ML models. *The Journal of Prosthetic Dentistry*, 125(4), 561–570. PMID: 34294423

Sun, L.. (2023). AI-enhanced decision-making tools for treatment planning in oral and maxillofacial surgery. *Journal of Oral and Maxillofacial Surgery*, 81(7), 982–991.

Wang, F.. (2021). Artificial intelligence applications in early detection of dental diseases: A review. *Artificial Intelligence in Medicine*, 113, 102015.

Wang, M., & Kumar, S. (2022). Hybrid deep learning models for oral cancer diagnostics. *Head & Neck*, 44(5), 1152–1162.

Wu, L.. (2022). Multimodal deep learning for early detection of periodontal disease from X-ray images. *Journal of Periodontology*, 93(1), 89–97. PMID: 33949680

Xie, J.. (2021). Real-time prediction of root canal infection using convolutional neural networks. *International Endodontic Journal*, 54(9), 1367–1377.

Xu, L.. (2022). Automated detection and staging of oral squamous cell carcinoma using deep learning. *Medical Image Analysis*, 75, 102292.

Yang, R.. (2022). Predictive analysis of treatment success for dental prosthetics with machine learning. *The Journal of Prosthetic Dentistry*, 128(1), 29–36.

Yu, D.. (2022). A comparative analysis of ML algorithms for detection of dental implant failures. *Journal of Oral Rehabilitation*, 49(8), 901–908.

Yu, Z.. (2023). Hybrid deep learning models for automatic oral cancer staging. *Oral Diseases*, 29(3), 408–418. PMID: 34614259

Zhang, T.. (2021). Deep learning for the diagnosis of dental diseases using clinical images. *The Journal of the American Dental Association*, 152(4), 238–245.

Zhang, X., & Liu, H. (2022). Virtual surgery planning in maxillofacial procedures. *Journal of Stomatology, Oral and Maxillofacial Surgery*, 123(2), e300–e308.

Zhang, Y.. (2022). 3D convolutional neural networks for dental implant placement guidance. *Journal of Dental Research*, 101(5), 459–468.

Zhang, Y., Ye, F., Chen, L., Xu, F., Chen, X., Wu, H., Cao, M., Li, Y., Wang, Y., & Huang, X. (2023). Children's dental panoramic radiographs dataset for caries segmentation and dental disease detection. *Scientific Data*, 10(1), 380. DOI: 10.1038/s41597-023-02237-5 PMID: 37316638

Zhao, Y.. (2023). ML algorithms for predicting success in orthodontic treatments: A case study. *Journal of Orthodontics*, 50(1), 21–32.

Zhou, Z.. (2022). Deep learning for occlusal analysis in orthodontics: A systematic review. *Journal of Clinical Orthodontics*, 56(6), 394–402.

Chapter 13

Semantic Image Segmentation Employing U-Net-Based Ensemble Model:

Semantic Segmentation

M. Murali
https://orcid.org/0000-0002-4478-2820
SRM Institute of Science and Technology, India

ABSTRACT

Image segmentation is an important topic in computer vision, playing important role in wide range of applications such as medical image analysis, scene understanding, tumour boundary extraction among many others. Image segmentation aims to identify groups of pixels and parts of images that are similar and belong together Semantic segmentation is a classification of pixels with labels and partitioning the objects. By applying segmentation, we can identify all objects in an image. The brain tumour dataset we are utilizing for segmentation is BRATS'20, which contains 317 images. The proposed ensemble approach combining U-Net variants and Mask RCNN models outperforms the individual models. While the ensemble method yielded improved Dice scores, using the union of the six other methods achieved the highest segmentation accuracy, as indicated by superior Dice scores. Specifically, the ensemble model achieved a Dice score of 71.10 and an IoU of 81.98. Additionally, the ensemble model demonstrated strong performance in terms of precision, reaching 84.96, and a recall value of 81.90.

1. INTRODUCTION

Semantic segmentation is the function of grouping the parts of images belong to same object. This method has many use cases like road sign detection, tumor detection, land use and many others (Ronneberger, O et al. 2015; Singh, A et al. 2022; in, Z. et al. 2021; Zheng, S et al. 2021; Lee, D.G. 2021; Yeung, H et al. 2022; Zeng, Z. et al. 2022). Image segmentation is the classification of pixels with labels Image segmentation can be formulated as a classification or grouping the objects for all image pixels (Lateef, F., & Ruichek, Y 2019). Instance segmentation is different from semantic segmentation and the scope is to detect and partition the objects in the image. Image segmentation is a basic problem in

DOI: 10.4018/979-8-3693-9045-0.ch013

computer vision. It divides the input image into multiple regions, and the pixels in each region have similar characteristics. Semantic segmentation is a form of image segmentation that divides each pixel in the image into semantic categories irrespective of object instances. So, the semantic segmentation can be an image classification problem than the object detection task. In computer vision different Methods used for pixel-level semantic segmentation. Hence the semantic segmentation is the root for many computer vision tasks. Really it helps to understand the meaning of different parts of image to make accurate decisions. Semantic segmentation is applied to differentiate instances of the object. It is an advantage to get object instances, because neighbouring pixels may belong to different regions, and they are not connected. At semantic level understanding a scene is a problem in computer vision, but recent advancements allowed to combine machine learning algorithms with real-world applications. The research is growing in these areas caused by deep learning algorithms, which gives better performance in several computer vision tasks including semantic segmentation.

Scene analysis in computer vision includes analysis of an image in the scene to give an overview of the event in the scene. A scene is depicting the real-world, is taken from environment. It may contain different objects having some meaning. The scene may represent real-world objects. The image in the scene can be expression in terms of colour, intensity, texture, thus understanding of the image efficiently. This is done based on vision and cognition. The models used to understand includes the capability to analyse the events and the images. For this purpose, computer is capable of understanding and interpreting the events as humans are doing.

In literature different segmentation methods are available such as clustering methods, watershed algorithm, random forest, SVM etc. In K-means algorithm distance is counted and iteratively classifies the points until the convergence occurs. Active contour method is applied to segment the boundary of the image. Watershed algorithm is applied to divide the grayscale images. Random forest is ensemble learning method is used to train multiple classifiers. SVM is used for image segmentation. The Deep Convolutional Neural Network (DCNN) method is applied for semantic segmentation. The high-level semantics is expressed by Deep Convolutional Neural Network algorithm using the hierarchical features.

The main purpose of U-net models is segmentation. In these tasks, the goal is to detect and differentiate individual objects within an image, assigning a label to each object instead of classifying the entire image. This capability is particularly valuable in medical imaging, where precise diagnosis often relies on a thorough analysis of specific regions within an image. For instance, identifying brain tumours requires isolating tumour regions from surrounding brain structures. The U-net architecture has shown significant effectiveness across various medical imaging applications. In the next section, we examine the primary imaging modalities where U-net has been utilized.

2. BACKGROUND

In paper (Zhongmiao Huang et al. 2024) design Dynamic Positioning Attention (DPA) is applied to localize to the key feature information and variable window is constructed, so that attention calculation is performed. DPA could improve the learning and reduces the computation. Content-aware sparse attention could be achieved by applying Bi-Level Routing Attention (BRA) to discard unnecessary key–value pairs. Thus, the computational efficiency was improved. Extensive experiments were conducted and proved that the method proves best performance on different datasets. In this paper (Chendong Qin et al. 2024), authors addressed the challenges of semi-supervised learning and segmentation accuracy was improved on medical images. Authors proposed an Uncertainty-based Region Clipping Algorithm for medical image segmentation. Extensive experiments were conducted on two benchmarks ACDC and BraTS2019. The results proved that the proposed model outperformed baseline methods. The Dice score value was 87.86% and a HD95 score of 4.214 mm on ACDC dataset. For the brain tumour segmentation, the Dice score was 84.79% and a HD score of 10.13 mm. In paper (Matteo Giacominia and Simona Perotto, 2022) authors used **A** finite element-based image segmentation strategy by enhancing anisotropic mesh adaptation. This method is based on split Bregman algorithm to minimise a region-based energy functional and anisotropic recovery-based error estimate to drive mesh adaptation. The results obtained from split-adapt Bregman algorithm was tested on real images showing the good accuracy and robustness of the proposed method.

In this paper (Shaolong Chen et al. 2023), authors proposed a transformer-based multilevel region and edge aggregation network for image segmentation. In this work, multilevel region and edge features were extracted using a dual-branch module. Then, the region and edge features are inferred through multiple transformer-based modules. The attention feature selection module consolidated the features with region and edge features to decode the region and edge features. The model was evaluated on a public MR dataset. Proposed method achieved a dice score of 93.2% for ASC and 91.9% for IPFP. In this paper (Leiyang Fu and Shaowen Li, 2023), authors discussed about semantic segmentation and its applications in agricultural science. They proposed a framework based on bagging strategy and UNet framework using RGH and HSV values. The framework was evaluated on self-built datasets and compared with DeepLab V3+ and SegNet. Experimental results proved that the proposed framework obtained good results.

In Paper (Satyawant Kumar et al. 2022), authors proposed a transformer- based architecture for segmentation of UAV images. The encoder network exploits the representation of UAV image. In this work Token Spatial Information Fusion (TSIF) module was proposed to capture local details and produces feature representation. The effectiveness was proved by using Urban Drone datasets and achieved better results. In this paper (Limiao Li et al. 2024), authors proposed a framework for image segmentation based on region proxies. They used information-enhanced iterative filtering adaptive network to enhance the clarity. The region proxy model utilized to identify regions and semantics. Further they used classifier for region prediction. The results obtained from experiments show that the proposed method outperformed the other models in terms of unio, dice coefficient and recall.

Semantic segmentation can be divided into three categories: 1. Region-based segmentation 2. FCN-based segmentation 3. Weakly supervised segmentation

Region-Based Segmentation

This method follows the segmentation by recognition, it extracts regions from image and describe them region wise. In this method, pixel wise predictions are done by labelling a pixel as per the region score it contains. Another way of performing segmentation based on object detection results. CNN features are computed to extract object proposals in Regions with CNN features. Further, this method is compared with traditional CNN structures used for image classification. RCNN is used for object detection and image segmentation. In image segmentation process RNN extracts two features for each region, namely full region features and fore ground feature.

Fully Convolutional Network-Based Semantic Segmentation

It is an extension of CNN and can map pixels to pixels. In this method, no region proposal is required. The idea of CNN is to take an input image of any size. The input size of image determines the output of fully convolutional network. Fully convolutional network comprising of pooling and convolutional layers which can make predictions on images. Using FCN they follow two different methods. In first method, it uses a batch size of 20 images and gradients are accumulated from all images, in second method batch size is one. One problem found in fully convolutional network is that, since it is propagating through several layers, the output feature maps resolution is down sampled. Thus, the prediction of FCN is in low resolution.

Weakly Supervised Semantic Segmentation

Semantic segmentation mostly relies on large number of images using pixel-wise segmentation. Manual annotation of the images is time-consuming job. So, weakly supervised method is introduced to fulfil the semantic segmentation using annotated bounding boxes.

The deep learning models' success is based on the annotated training images. Practically, annotation with pixel-wise labels is a tedious work. It becomes a bottleneck in semantic segmentation. Few methods are available to generate synthetic data for training purpose. The advantage of using synthetic data is to train segmentation models by producing unlimited amount of labelled data.

Following are the key contributions:

- study of deep learning-based techniques used for semantic segmentation.
- study about semantic segmentation using deep learning method, with a focus on its contributions
- few metrics applied for evaluating the performance of different models is presented in this paper.

Image segmentation plays a crucial role in helping us interpret image content and is a key area in image processing and computer vision. It has numerous applications, including image compression, scene comprehension, and object detection in satellite imagery. Over time, various algorithms have been created for image segmentation; however, the rise of deep learning in computer vision has led to the development of numerous deep learning-based segmentation models. Thus, segmentation is a powerful method to understand the real world by using computer vision. In recent years, deep learning models have given good performance with highest accuracy. In this paper we propose an ensemble framework based on U-Net variants and Mask RCNN. The various Deep Learning based image segmentation models are discussed in this paper.

3. DEEP LEARNING BASED IMAGE SEGMENTATION MODELS

Numerous deep learning-based image segmentation methods are available. It can be grouped based on the architecture. Various methods ranging from MATLAB image segmentation and computer vision methods. In recent years image segmentation applications made progress due to the introduction of deep neural networks. Deep learning method has introduced new image segmentation methods with remarkable improvements. It has achieved higher accuracy than the popular existing methods. This led to the development of image segmentation approaches using deep learning methods in computer vision applications.

3.1 Convolutional Neural Network

In semantic segmentation pixels are labelled in an image with a semantic class. Using CNN class labels are mapped to image pixels directly in fully convolutional approach. To do this, region to image pixel is mapped and regions are extracted from an image with its features. The image is given as input in fully convolutional neural network. Feature of bounding boxes in each region is created by region of interest pooling layer. Further, these features are passes through connected layer and classification layer. While testing these can be mapped from region to pixels.

In visual systems, image segmentation is an important component. Partitioning the images into different segments is done. Segmentation is an important task in different applications such as medical image analysis, autonomous vehicles, augmented reality and video surveillance. List of algorithms have been developed such as thresholding, watersheds, histogram-based bundling, graph cuts, conditional and Markov random fields and many more. In recent years, deep learning models with excellent performance and accuracy on popular benchmarks.

CNN architecture shown in Figure 1 is widely used in computer vision tasks. It was proposed by Fukushima in his paper (K. Fukushima, 1980). Further, in (A. Waibel et al. 1989) authors used backpropagation training and in (Y. LeCun et al. 1998) authors used CNN architecture for document recognition. Convolutional Neural Networks are having three layers: 1. Convolutional layer: To extract features, weights are convolved 2. Nonlinear layer: In this layer activation functions are applied on feature maps 3. Pooling layers: this layer is used to replace the feature's neighbourhood with statistical details like mean or maximum value. All layers are connected in this structure and each layer will receive input from its previous layer.

Figure 1. Architecture of convolutional neural networks

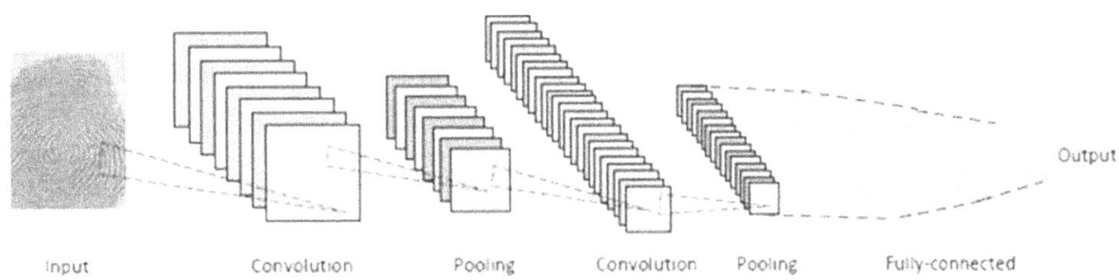

3.2 Recurrent Neural Networks Based Models

In RNN, sequential data can be processed like videos, text and time series data at given time. For every time-stamp input data is collected by the model from the current timestamp. RNNs suffer from gradient vanishing problem. RNN models help to improve the estimation of the segmentation by short and long-term dependencies among pixels. Further to improve the semantic segmentation, pixels are linked together and processed sequentially. RNN based model ReNet was proposed by Visin et al. (F. Visin et al. 2016) for semantic segmentation known as ReSeg. It was developed for image classification purpose. ReNet layers are arranged on top of stack of the VGG-16 convolutional layers that can extract local features. Up-sampling layers are following the ReNet layers to recover the image resolution in the predictions.

One of the variants of RNNs is Long Short-Term Memory (LSTM) shown in Figure 2, which can solve the gradient vanishing problem. LSTM consists of three gates namely input gate, output gate and forget gate. These gates can regulate the information flow and can store values over specific time intervals. Input gate can control the new information to be stored in the cell and the Output gate is used to define the output of LSTM based on the input and the updated cell. Finally, forget gate is used to determine either to remember or not and decides that what is to be stored.

In (W. Byeon et al. 2015) Byeon et al. proposed a pixel level segmentation of scene images using LSTM (Long Short-Term Memory) network. The authors implemented two-dimensional networks for images. In these authors used two-dimensional LSTM networks for classification and segmentation. Thus, it allows to learn the spatial model parameters within a model. In paper (X. Liang et al. 2016) Liang et al. suggested a semantic segmentation model based on Graph LSTM network. In multi-dimensional LSTM networks pixels are evenly divided, that will take arbitrary shaped pixels. In this network adaptively constructed un-directed graph of an image, where spatial relations of pixels n are used as edges. Visual comparison can be done with RNN model and graph LSTM model.

To improve the visual features with global structure, pixels are appended on the convolutional layers in the graph LSTM model. To generate confidence maps for labels, convolutional features pass 1x1 convolutional filters. The confidence drive scheme will determine the updating sequence for the subsequent graph LSTM layers. The graph LSTM will update the hidden states of pixel nodes sequentially. In (Y. Xiang and D. Fox, 2017) Xiang and Fox suggested a data associated Recurrent Neural Networks for semantic labelling. It uses a Recurrent Neural Network architecture for semantic labelling process. The outputs obtained from the network is integrated with mapping techniques like Kinetc Fusion to get semantic information. In (R. Hu et al. 2016) Hu et al. suggested a model based on natural language expression combined with CNN to encode the image and LSTM is used to encode the natural language description. This segmentation process is different, for pixel wise segmentation for language expression authors proposed recurrent and convolutional model used to process visual and linguistic details.

Figure 2. Architecture of LSTM

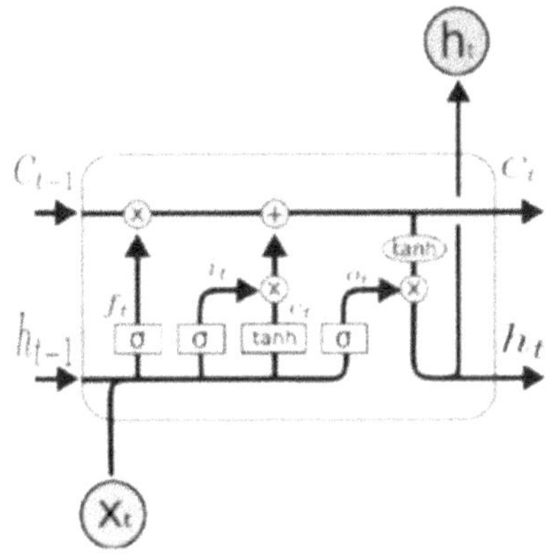

3.3 Generative Adversarial Networks

It is a class of neural networks used in unsupervised learning models. As shown in Figure 3, It consists of two networks namely a discriminator and a generator. These networks are trained to produce artificial data identical to the actual data. The discriminator can discriminate the generated data from the original ones. The Generative adversarial networks can be regarded as minimax game between G and D, where D is used to mitigate the classification error in differentiating generated and real data. The Generator will try to exploit the Discriminator, by differentiating between produced and original data. High quality samples are generated and resulted in competitive interaction in networks. GAN is a excellent tool for artificial intelligence, used extensively in image synthesis. The generator G creates images that are regularly supplied to the discriminator. To assist the generator in producing realistic images, its gradient function depends on the discriminator's gradient function when the discriminator receives a fake image. This enables the generator to adjust its weights based on the discriminator's output. Additionally, to introduce variations in the images generated, random noise is fed into the generator. The generator's objective is to trick the discriminator, effectively maximizing its error rate. This minimax relationship leads to an adversarial network where the two networks are in competition with one another.

Figure 3. Generative adversarial network architecture

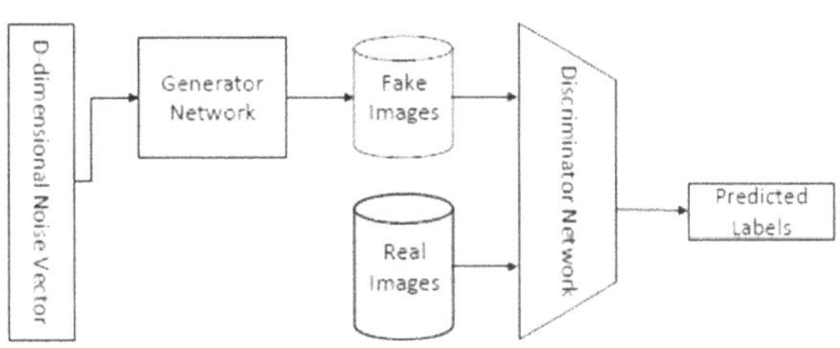

Due to the introduction of Generative adversarial networks researchers can improve the architecture in different ways. In paper (A. Radford et al. 2015) Radford et al., suggested a convolutional GAN model, which is better than fully connected networks. In paper (M. Mirza and S. Osindero, 2014) suggested a GAN model with conditioned class labels. This framework can be further enhanced to limit the GAN's output to a specific range of synthetic images by controlling its labels and input images. This modification is referred to as a conditional GAN.

3.4 Encoder-Decoder Based Models

Encoder-decoder models are a group of models in which data points are mapped from input to output domain through two-stage network. The encoder uses the encoding function, the input is compressed to predict the output from the reduced dimensional representation. This representation is a feature vectors, can capture the semantic details of the input data to predict the output. To obtain the meaningful features in data, encoding and decoding will give the essential features. This is popular in sequence-to-sequence problems in NLP.

Figure 4. Simple encoder-decoder model

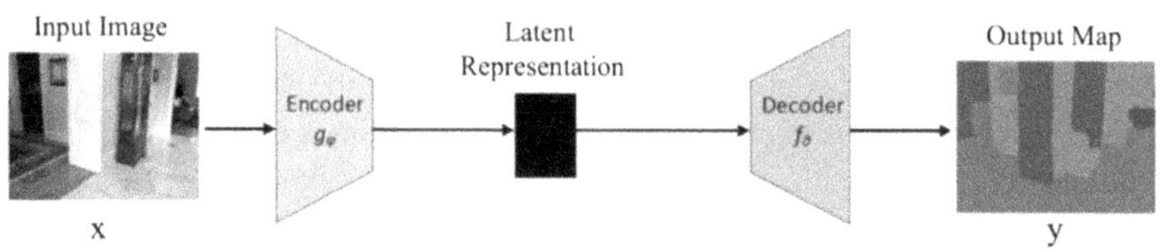

Above Figure 4 is used to understand the encoder-decoder model. These are trained to minimize the loss. The enhanced version of the image will be the output. In this encoder-decoder model the input and output are the same. This Encoder-Decoder model used for image segmentation is convolutional encoder-encoder architecture (H. Noh et al. 2015). This encoder-decoder models are used by the deep learning-based segmentation methods, mainly applied for medical image segmentation. This model consists of two parts, an encoder and a deconvolutional network. The encoder uses convolutional layers and for deconvolutional network feature vector is given as input. As a result, pixel-wise class probabilities are generated as a map. As shown in Figure 5, deconvolutional network consists of unpooling layers and deconvolution. It can detect pixel-wise class label and helps for segmentation masks. This network achieved higher accuracy on PASCAL VOC 2012 dataset.

Figure 5. Deconvolutional semantic segmentation - multi-layer deconvolution network

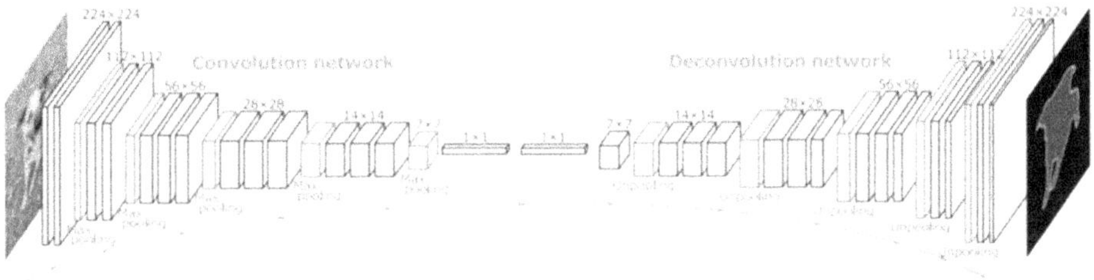

3.5 SegNet

In (V. Badrinarayanan et al. 2017) another network called convolutional encoder decoder was suggested by Badrinarayanan. This architecture is very identical to the deconvolutional network, and it consists of an encoder network which is similar to the VGG16 network layers. It can do the pixel-wise classification. This architecture can use the pooling indices from the max-pooling step from the encoder, which can do the non-linear up sampling. To produce feature maps, up-sampling maps are convolved with filters. Basically, it is smaller in number of trainable parameters than other architectures. For scene-segmentation purpose, this encoder-decoder network was proposed (A. Kendall et al. 2015). Fully connected layers not available in SegNet. This model contains fully convolutional layers only. Pool indices are used by the decoder up-samples to generate sparse feature maps (V. Badrinarayanan et al. 2017).

Figure 6. SegNet – Convolutional encoder-decoder

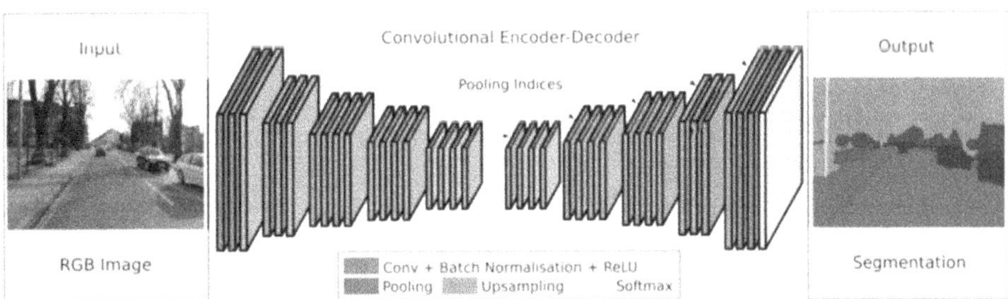

3.6 U-Net and V-Net models

These models are used for medical image segmentation and resembles fully convolutional network and encoder-decoder model. Two architectures used by medical domain are U-Net and V-Net O. Ronneberger et al. 2015). Now this architecture is applied in other than medical domain also. The network strategy is applied to learn from few annotated images by data augmentation. The U-Net contains two parts, contracting path and a symmetric expanding path. The contracting path is used to capture context and expanding path is applied for localization. The features are extracted by down sampling method using a fully convolutional network architecture. Another expanding part uses deconvolution, to minimise the number of feature maps. Feature maps are copied to the up-sampling part which was obtained from the down sampling part of the network. At the end 1 x 1 convolution process is applied to get the segmentation map that can classify the pixels of the input image. In recent days, U-Net architecture has been used to other problems also.

Figure 7. U-Net architecture

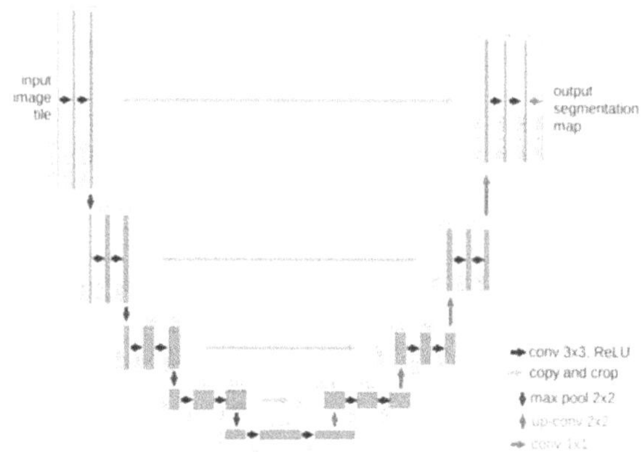

V-Net is another architecture based on fully convolutional network model suggested by Milletari et al. in (F. Milletari et al. 2016). This V-Net architecture is mainly used for 3D image segmentation. To train the model, authors used a dice coefficient based objective function, which enables the model to under the situations like imbalance in terms of number of voxels between foreground and background. Using MRI volumes of prostate, network was trained for segmentation (T. Brosch et al. 2016).

3.7 R-CNN Based Model

The regional convolutional network (R-CNN) and its variants have proved success in object detection. Specifically, Faster R-CNN architecture (S. Ren et al. 2015) uses a region proposal network to identify the bounding box candidates. The region proposal network is applied to extract region of interest and the features are computed using RoIPool layer. For instance, segmentation problems, R-CNNs extensions are used. It can perform the semantic segmentation and object detection simultaneously.

Pixels with semantic labels partitioning of objects is a classification problem. Pixels level class labelling is performed on a set of objects in segmentation process. It is more difficult than image class classification process, where it can predict a label for an entire image. Based on the objects of interest in an image, scope of instance segmentation is extended to semantic segmentation.

Figure 8. Faster R-CNN architecture (S. Ren et al. 2015)

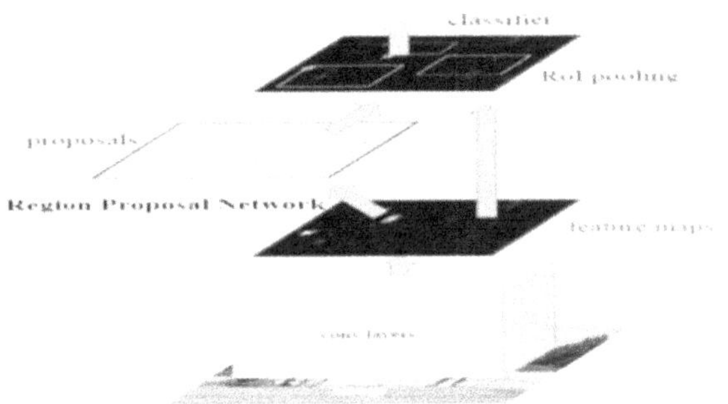

Another model suggested by He et al. (K. He et al. 2017) a Mask R-CNN, applied for instance segmentation, which outperforms all the previous baseline models. The Mask R-CNN can detect objects in an image by applying segmentation mask for every instance. This architecture has three output branches which can compute the bounding box coordinates, associated classes binary mask used for object segmentation. The loss function is used to aggregate the losses of bounding box coordinates, classes and segmentation mask.

Figure 9. Mask R-CNN architecture (K. He et al. 2017)

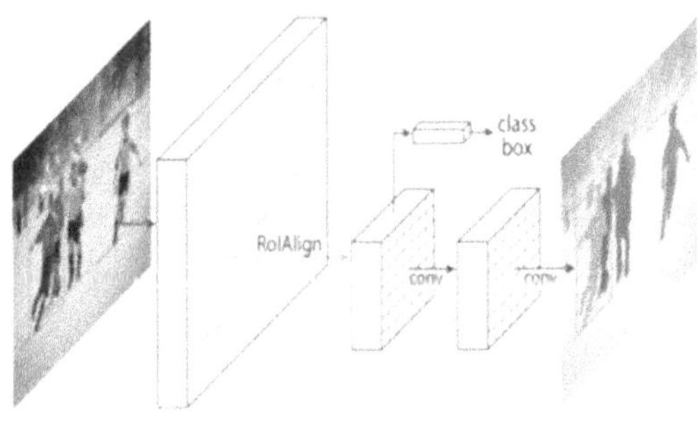

3.8 Attention-Based Models

Attention mechanisms are used in computer vision for many years. In (L.-C. Chen et al. 2019) Chen et al. suggested an attention-based model that can learn multi-scale features at each pixel location. They proposed a semantic segmentation mode by combining multi-scale images and the attention-based model. The attention mechanism performance was better than the average and max pooling. This model helps to assess the features at different positions and scales. Convolutional classifiers are used to learn the semantic features of labelled objects. In (Q. Huang et al. 2017) Huang et al. suggested a semantic segmentation model using reversing attention mechanisms. This model is trained to capture the opposite concept. This reverse attention network can perform direct and reverse attention learning simultaneously.

In (H. Li et al. 2018) Li et al. proposed a pyramid attention network for semantic segmentation purpose. This model uses the global contextual information and jointly used the attention mechanism and spatial pyramids. The purpose of this model is to extract the dense features for pixel labelling. In (J. Fu et al. 2019) Fu et al. suggested a dual attention network for scene segmentation. The purpose of this model is to capture rich contextual dependencies based on the self-attention mechanism. They incorporated two attention modules on top of a dilated FCN which can model the semantic interdependencies. The features are aggregated in position attention module for each position, by a weighted sum of features at all positions.

3.9 CNN Models with Active Contour Models

In recent days Active Contour model (ACM) have attracted researchers' attention. Different approaches are used to utilize Active Contour Models (ACMs), such as employing ACM as a post-processor for the output of Fully Convolutional Networks (FCNs) and using FCN for pre-training. For semantic segmentation, ACM post-processor is applied in (T. H. N. Le et al. 2018). In paper (C. Rupprecht et al. 2016) deep active contours are implemented. Hatamizadeh et al. in (A. Hatamizadeh et al. 2019) proposed an integrated deep active lesion segmentation approach to train the FCN backbone, allowing for the prediction of parameter functions. In paper (D. Marcos et al. 2018) authors suggested deep structured active contours to combine with pre-trained FCNs to build instance segmentation. In paper (D. Cheng et al. 2019) Cheng et al. suggested deep ray network to prevent contour self-intersection.

Several methods have been implemented for semantic image segmentation. One deep learning technique used in medical image segmentation is U-Net. U-net architecture is used for image segmentation. The basic structure of U-net architecture already discussed in the previous section. It contains contracting path and expansion path. This expansion enables the network to capture and learn localized classification details. Moreover, it increases the resolution and pass onto convolutional layer to create a segmented image. The convolutional networks are mostly used to classify the whole image into a single label. But the networks failed to give pixel level details needed in medical image analysis. The U-net is very much useful in creating segmentation maps using limited samples. Really, the number of properly labelled images are very limited in medical imaging. This could be achieved during the training, which enable the network to learn without labelled data. Another problem is to separate the objects of the same kind, which is done by a weighted by a loss function. Due to the context-based learning, U-net is faster to other segmentation models. Since 2015, U-net is used in medical imaging. There are some advancements in U-net, researchers using other imaging methods to U-net.

4. VARIANTS OF U-NET ARCHITECTURE

4.1 Base U-net

As discussed in the previous section, it can be divided into two parts: contracting path, it uses CNN architecture. Each path consists of two 3x3 convolutions followed by a ReLU activation function and a max pooling layer. This is repeated for several times in the network. Another one is expansion path, here the feature map is up sampled using 2x2 up-convolution. In the contracting path, feature map is cropped and concatenated to up sampled feature map, and 3x3 convolutions and Relu function. Finally, 1x1 convolution is used to reduce the feature map to produce the segmented image. The cropping is done, since the least number of contextual details in the edges to be discarded. This resulted in u-shape and contextual details are propagated in the network. This is allowed for object segmentation using context from a larger area.

4.2 3D U-net

Basic U-net is augmented which enables the segmentation. The structure is comprising of contracting and expansion path. In this structure all 2D operations are replaced by 3D operations to obtain 3D segmented image. This structure can segment images using few training samples. This enables 3D images for faster training process with few labelled data. This is widely used CT and MRI image segmentation applications like, brain tumour, cardiac structure, liver tumor etc., Moreover, 3D U-net has great impact in biomedical applications.

4.3 Attention U-net

In image processing we need to focus on objects while ignoring unnecessary parts. The attention U-net uses attention gate (O. Oktay et al., 2018; J. Schlemper et al. 2019), which can remove the features that are not required for the task. In the expansion path, each layer includes an attention gate that processes feature from the contracting path before they are concatenated with the up sampled features of the expansive path. This will improve the performance of the segmentation, by using attention gate after each layer with no computational complexity in the model.

In an encoder-decoder model, an attention unit is highly useful, as it allows architectures like U-Net to provide localized classification details. It allows the network to focus on segmenting objects. With the help of training data, the network can identify the specific object in an image. The attention gate is used, and the feature map is calculated as per the class in the network. Hence the attention is given to a specific object in an image. Additive attention is used in image processing to obtain higher accuracy, when there are different kinds of attention gates are present. The attention gate is used in different applications like lung cancer, brain tissue quantification, melanoma etc.

4.4 Inception U-net

Mostly, image processing techniques are using fixed-size filters for convolutions. To find the exact filter size is cumbersome process. Moreover, fixed-size filters can be used with same size parts. In real, images with variations in size and shape in the region. To find the solution to this problem, we can use deeper network that can deal with high level details across different size and shape. Practically, using suck kind of deep networks are computationally expensive process. Another solution for this problem is inception network, it uses filters of different sizes in the network. The results obtained from the filters are combined and transferred to the next layer. The inception network can analyse images with specific regions effectively due to varying filter sizes. To mitigate the complexity the inception network adds a 1x1 convolution before 3x3 filter. In each inception model pooling layers also added. The real inception network is GoogLeNet. To this network more improvements have been made like factorization methods.

In this network 3x3 convolutions are replacing the 5x5 convolution. Factorization method is used to split the nxn filters to 1xn filter. Factorization process will make the network less expensive. Inception modules are applied to different U-net applications like lung module detection, embryo segmentation, brain tissue mapping etc.

4.5 Residual U-Net

This is another variant of U-net. This architecture overcome the difficulties of deep neural network. In this neural network more layers are present and to converge faster to a solution. In this network, increasing the number of layers can lead to a decline in performance. This may occur due to loss of feature in dep neural networks. ResNet uses skip connections, which can take feature map layer to layer in the network. This helps to preserve the feature maps in deep neural network and improve the performance. In each block of the network, the input to a convolutional layer is combined with the output from the next convolutional layer through a skip connection. Before the down-sampling in the paths in the U-net, skip connection can be added. The skip connections are used to reduce the vanishing gradient problem. This residual U-nets have been used for different biomedical applications like tissue quantification, brain structure mapping, nuclei segmentation etc.

4.6 U-net++

This U-net++ architecture is another kind of U-net architecture derived from DenseNet. It contains skip connections between contracting and expansion paths. In this network semantic information between two paths is propagated to enable the segmentation accurately. In the base U-Net, features from the contracting path are merged with layers in the expansion path, whereas U-Net++ introduces skip connection nodes between each layer. From all previous units skip connection will receive feature maps at the same level. Hence, the dense block is equal at each level. Thus, the loss of semantic information can be minimized between the paths. In skip connections, xxx represents the feature map from the contracting path. The number of skip connections can vary based on the number of layers and tends to decrease as it progresses down the contracting path. This U-net++ is applied in various applications like cancer tissue, pelvic organs and cell nuclei etc.

4.7 Adversarial U-Nets

Adversarial U-net represent a category of conditional GANs, in which the generator network is designed using the U-Net architecture, while the discriminator remains unchanged. This U-Net design allows the generator to take an image as input rather than random noise. The key difference in adversarial U-Nets is that the generator aims not to create new images but to generate transformed images. The output from the generator G is evaluated against the discriminator D, which is trained on images that have been manually transformed. Ideally, with sufficient training, the generator will achieve transformation capabilities comparable to those of human operators. As a result, the trained generator can apply its transformation function to new images, greatly expediting the process compared to manual conversion by a physician. Adversarial U-Nets have found a wide array of applications, including quantitative susceptibility mapping of the brain, detection of brain tumours, breast cancer detection, segmentation of retinal vessels, segmentation of cardiac structures, and registration of brain images.

Figure 10. Schematic representation of U-net based GAN

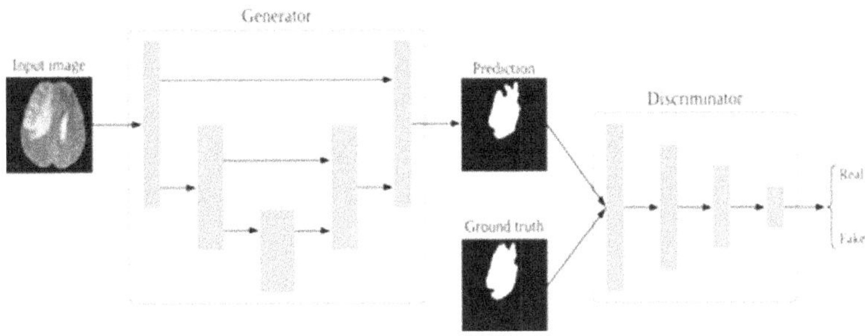

The generator produces predictions for the tumour area based on the input images. These predictions are then provided to the discriminator, which assesses their accuracy by comparing them to the ground truth. If the prediction closely resembles the ground truth, the discriminator will struggle to differentiate between the two and will classify the prediction as real. With sufficient training, the GAN will achieve segmentation accuracy and precision comparable to that of manual annotations.

5. SOLUTIONS AND RECOMMENDATIONS

Dataset Used

To evaluate the Ensemble U-net frameworks, BRATS20 (Menze, Bjoern H et al. 2014) dataset was employed, which contains 371 image files. Each file comprises five subfiles: four representing the MRI modalities of individual patients and one serving as the target mask for each patient.

Proposed Framework of Brain Tumour Segmentation

Ensemble learning is a technique in machine learning that integrates multiple models to enhance prediction accuracy. The ensemble framework of brain tumour segmentation is like the standard UNET, the proposed framework is composed of encoder and decoder. Image segmentation involves dividing an image into different regions, where each region consists of pixels with similar characteristics, and every pixel in the image is assigned to one of these categories. U-Net is a state-of-the-art variant of convolutional neural networks that is extensively used for medical image segmentation. Besides the previously discussed architectures, numerous other network configurations have been explored that utilize an ensemble of U-Nets. In this setup, the first U-Net conducts high-level segmentation, while each subsequent U-Net focuses on segmenting smaller objects.

Since U-Net and its variants operate quite differently from Mask-RCNN frameworks, an ensemble approach was developed to merge the predictions of all the models. The models were trained using the training data, with the structural properties of the prediction masks serving as features and the intersection over union (IoU) with the ground truth as the target. The features incorporated into the ensemble model included these structural characteristics.

During testing, predictions of brain tumours from both U-Net and its variants, as well as from Mask-RCNN models, were fed into the ensemble model, resulting in IoU estimates against the ground truth for the predictions from both models. For overlapping masks from U-Net and its variants and Mask-RCNN, the mask with the highest IoU prediction was selected. In cases of non-overlapping masks, they were included in the output segmentation if their predicted IoU exceeded a specified threshold. This method demonstrated superior performance compared to both U-Net and its variants as well as Mask-RCNN, as it effectively combined the strengths of all models across various scenarios.

Evaluation Metrics

In this pixel-based semantic segmentation task, the evaluation metrics used include Precision, Recall Rate, Intersection over Union (IoU) and F1-Score. These metrics are defined as follows:

$$\mathrm{Re}call = \frac{TP}{TP + FN}$$

$$\mathrm{Pr}ecision = \frac{TP}{TP + FP}$$

$$\text{F1 Score} = \frac{2TP}{2TP + FP + FN}$$

$$IOU = \frac{TP}{TP + FP + FN}$$

$$D(A, B) = \frac{2|A \cap B|}{|A| + |B|}$$

Where, $|A \cap B|$ is the common area between A and B and

$|A|$ and $|B|$ are the total number of pixels in A and B respectively.

The evaluation metrics used for brain tumour segmentation include Dice score, IoU (Intersection over Union), Precision, Recall, and F1 score. In this context, TP (True Positive) refers to a positive instance correctly identified by the model. TN (True Negative) refers to a negative instance correctly identified by the model. FN (False Negative) refers to a positive instance incorrectly classified as negative by the model. FP (False Positive) refers to a negative instance incorrectly classified as positive by the model. Precision measures the model's ability to avoid labelling negative samples as positive. Dice score reflects the overlap between the predicted and target regions, indicating segmentation accuracy. IoU (Intersection over Union) is a commonly used metric for assessing object segmentation by comparing the overlap and union of predicted and target areas. The F1 score is particularly valuable in segmentation tasks, as it combines precision and recall into a single balanced metric, which is especially helpful for datasets with imbalanced classes. It provides a clearer view of how well the model identifies true positive regions while minimizing false positives.

6. RESULTS AND DISCUSSION

Table 1. U-net, U-net variants and Mask RCNN models' results on the BRATS20 dataset

Models	Dice score	IoU	Precision	Recall	F1 score
UNet	70.50	81.59	83.45	79.37	81.69
Attention Unet	70.35	81.37	83.07	79.13	82.45
ResUnet	65.71	78.61	80.55	78.15	81.55
Inception Unet	68.65	80.58	83.36	77.38	81.31
Unet++	63.70	77.15	81.81	73.21	77.53
Mask RCNN	65.63	78.26	80.83	77.52	79.34
Ensemble model	**71.10**	**81.98**	**84.96**	**81.90**	**84.71**

Figure 11. U-net, U-net variants and Mask RCNN models' results on the BRATS20 dataset

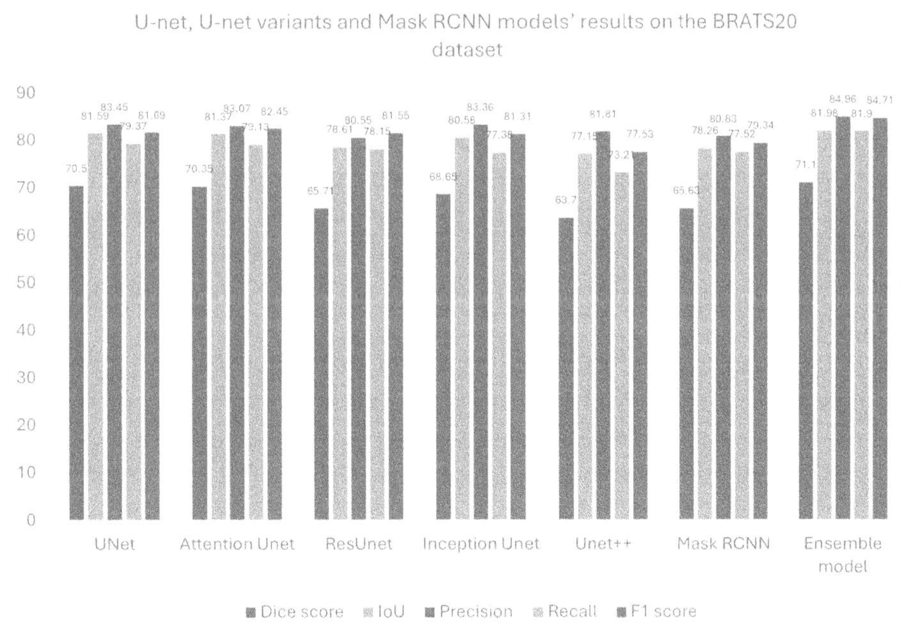

Figure 12. Brain tumor and segmented part

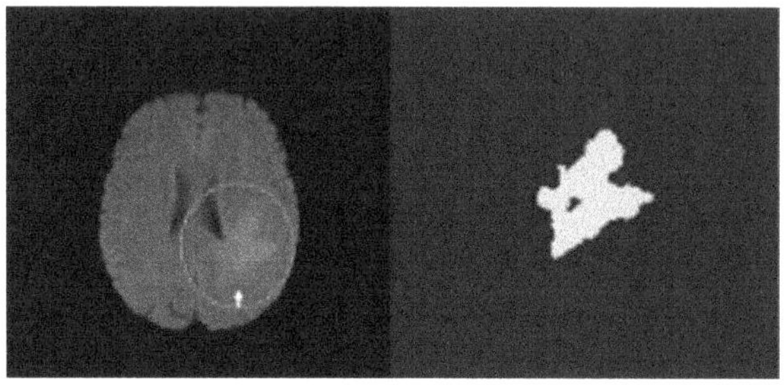

we present the experiments conducted, along with the results shown Table 1. we analyse the impact of different input volume combinations, and the proposed ensemble model, each using a different combination of inputs. In addition to this, we compare the performance of our proposed ensemble model with other U-Net-based variants and Mask RCNN. The segmented part is shown in Figure 12.

Finally, we evaluate performance using both the original and supplemented annotations. The experiments employ 5-fold cross-validation across 317 images, with each fold running for 20 epochs. In each fold, 9 cases are designated for testing, while the remaining cases are shuffled and split, with 80% for training and 20% for validation. This process provides tumour segmentation results for each of the 317 cases. For evaluation, we use the Dice Similarity Coefficient (DSC), a widely adopted metric in neural network-based medical image segmentation, along with the False Positive Rate (FPR). These metrics help assess the ensemble model's segmentation accuracy and the false positive rate across the evaluated methods. The Dice score is calculated across all segmented regions to provide an overall measure of segmentation accuracy. However, because brain tumour images may include other enhanced regions, the algorithm might incorrectly segment these areas as lesions, leading to more false positive detections and thus lowering the global Dice score. While the global Dice score remains an important metric, we also suggest calculating the Dice score specifically for tumour regions to more accurately evaluate segmentation quality.

As shown in Table 1, the proposed ensemble approach combining U-Net and Mask RCNN models outperforms the individual models. While the ensemble method yielded improved Dice scores, using the union of the six other methods achieved the highest segmentation accuracy, as indicated by superior Dice scores. Specifically, the ensemble model achieved a Dice score of 71.10 and an IoU of 81.98. Additionally, the ensemble model demonstrated strong performance in terms of precision, reaching 84.96, and a recall value of 81.90 shown in Figure 11.

7. CONCLUSION

This study presents an automated brain tumour segmentation approach utilizing an ensemble U-Net model. The method was evaluated on a dataset of 317 images, with various metrics used to assess segmentation quality. Comparisons were made with different U-Net variants and the Mask RCNN method. The ensemble approach achieved a Dice score of 71.10 and an IoU of 81.98, showing promising results despite challenges in the dataset, such as very small, irregular, and low-contrast tumours. Further enhancements could be achieved by enlarging the dataset and including complete annotations, particularly for cases with multiple tumours.

REFERENCES

Badrinarayanan, V., Kendall, A., & Cipolla, R. (2017). Segnet: A deep convolutional encoder-decoder architecture for image segmentation. *IEEE Transactions on Pattern Analysis and Machine Intelligence*, *39*(12), 2481–2495. DOI: 10.1109/TPAMI.2016.2644615 PMID: 28060704

Brosch, T., Tang, L. Y., Yoo, Y., Li, D. K., Traboulsee, A., & Tam, R. (2016). Deep 3d convolutional encoder networks with shortcuts for multiscale feature integration applied to multiple sclerosis lesion segmentation. *IEEE Transactions on Medical Imaging*, *35*(5), 1229–1239. DOI: 10.1109/TMI.2016.2528821 PMID: 26886978

Byeon, W., Breuel, T. M., Raue, F., & Liwicki, M. (2015), "Scene labelling with lstm recurrent neural networks," in *IEEE Conference on Computer Vision and Pattern Recognition*, pp. 3547–3555.

Chen, L.-C., Yang, Y., Wang, J., Xu, W., & Yuille, A. L. (2016), "Attention to scale: Scale-aware semantic image segmentation," in *Proceedings of the IEEE conference on computer vision and pattern recognition*, pp. 3640–3649. DOI: 10.1109/CVPR.2016.396

Chen, S., Zhong, L., Qiu, C., Zhang, Z., & Zhang, X. (2023). Transformer-based multilevel region and edge aggregation network for magnetic resonance image segmentation. *Computers in Biology and Medicine*, *152*(106427), 1–9. DOI: 10.1016/j.compbiomed.2022.106427 PMID: 36543009

Cheng, D., Liao, R., Fidler, S., & Urtasun, R. (2019), "Darnet: Deep active ray network for building segmentation," in *Proceedings of the IEEE Conference on Computer Vision and Pattern Recognition*, pp. 7431–7439. DOI: 10.1109/CVPR.2019.00761

Fu, J., Liu, J., Tian, H., Li, Y., Bao, Y., Fang, Z., & Lu, H. (2019), "Dual attention network for scene segmentation," in *Proceedings of the IEEE Conference on Computer Vision and Pattern Recognition*, pp. 3146–3154.

Fu, L., & Li, S. (2023). A New Semantic Segmentation Framework Based on UNet. *Sensors (Basel)*, *23*(8123), 1–14. DOI: 10.3390/s23198123 PMID: 37836953

Fukushima, K. (1980). Neocognitron: A self-organizing neural network model for a mechanism of pattern recognition unaffected by shift in position. *Biological Cybernetics*, *36*(4), 193–202. DOI: 10.1007/BF00344251 PMID: 7370364

Giacominia, M., & Perotto, S. (2022). Anisotropic mesh adaptation for region-based segmentation accounting for image spatial information. *Computers & Mathematics with Applications (Oxford, England)*, *121*, 1–17. DOI: 10.1016/j.camwa.2022.06.025

Hatamizadeh, A., Hoogi, A., Sengupta, D., Lu, W., Wilcox, B., Rubin, D., & Terzopoulos, D. (2019), "Deep active lesion segmentation," in Proc. International Workshop on Machine Learning in Medical Imaging, ser. Lecture Notes in Computer Science, vol. 11861. Springer, pp. 98–105. DOI: 10.1007/978-3-030-32692-0_12

He, K., Gkioxari, G., Doll'ar, P., & Girshick, R. "Mask r-cnn," in *Proceedings of the IEEE international conference on computer vision*, pp. 2961–2969.

Hu, R., Rohrbach, M., & Darrell, T. (2016), "Segmentation from natural language expressions," in *European Conference on Computer Vision*. Springer, pp. 108–124.

Huang, Q., Xia, C., Wu, C., Li, S., Wang, Y., Song, Y., & Kuo, C.-C. J. (2017), "Semantic segmentation with reverse attention," arXiv preprint arXiv:1707.06426 DOI: 10.5244/C.31.18

Huang, Shuli, Cheng, Liejun, & Wang, , (2024), Medical image segmentation based on dynamic positioning and region-aware attention, Volume 151, 110375, pp. 1-14, https://doi.org/DOI: 10.3390/math10244735

Kendall, A., Badrinarayanan, V., & Cipolla, R. (2015), "Bayesian segnet: Model uncertainty in deep convolutional encoder-decoder architectures for scene understanding," arXiv preprint arXiv:1511.02680

Kumar, S., Kumar, A., & Lee, D.-G. (2022). Semantic Segmentation of UAV Images Based on Transformer Framework with Context Information. *Mathematics*, *10*(4735), 1–17. DOI: 10.3390/math10244735

Lateef, F., & Ruichek, Y. (2019). Survey on semantic segmentation using deep learning techniques. *Neurocomputing*, *338*, 321–348. DOI: 10.1016/j.neucom.2019.02.003

Le, T. H. N., Quach, K. G., Luu, K., Duong, C. N., & Savvides, M. (2018). Reformulating level sets as deep recurrent neural network approach to semantic segmentation. *IEEE Transactions on Image Processing*, *27*(5), 2393–2407. DOI: 10.1109/TIP.2018.2794205 PMID: 29994352

LeCun, Y., Bottou, L., Bengio, Y., & Haffner, P. (1998). Gradient-based learning applied to document recognition. *Proceedings of the IEEE*, *86*(11), 2278–2324. DOI: 10.1109/5.726791

Lee, D. G. (2021). Fast Drivable Areas Estimation with Multi-Task Learning for Real-Time Autonomous Driving Assistant. [CrossRef]. *Applied Sciences (Basel, Switzerland)*, *11*(22), 10713. DOI: 10.3390/app112210713

Li, H., Xiong, P., An, J., & Wang, L. (2018), "Pyramid attention network for semantic segmentation," arXiv preprint arXiv:1805.10180

Li, L., He, K., Zhu, X., Gou, F., & Wu, J. (2024). A pathology image segmentation framework based on deblurring and region proxy in medical decision-making system. *Biomedical Signal Processing and Control*, *95*(106439), 1–14. DOI: 10.1016/j.bspc.2024.106439

Liang, X., Shen, X., Feng, J., Lin, L., & Yan, S. (2016), "Semantic object parsing with graph lstm," in *European Conference on Computer Vision*. Springer, pp. 125–143.

Marcos, D., Tuia, D., Kellenberger, B., Zhang, L., Bai, M., Liao, R., & Urtasun, R. (2018),"Learning deep structured active contours endto-end," in *Proceedings of the IEEE Conference on Computer Vision and Pattern Recognition (CVPR)*, pp. 8877–8885.

Menze, B. H., Jakab, A., Bauer, S., Kalpathy-Cramer, J., Farahani, K., Kirby, J., Burren, Y., Porz, N., Slotboom, J., Wiest, R., Lanczi, L., Gerstner, E., Weber, M.-A., Arbel, T., Avants, B. B., Ayache, N., Buendia, P., Collins, D. L., Cordier, N., & Van Leemput, K. (2014). The multimodal brain tumor image segmentation benchmark (BRATS). *IEEE Transactions on Medical Imaging*, *34*(10), 1993–2024. DOI: 10.1109/TMI.2014.2377694 PMID: 25494501

Milletari, F., Navab, N., & Ahmadi, S.-A. (2016), "V-net: Fully convolutional neural networks for volumetric medical image segmentation," in 2016 Fourth International Conference on 3D Vision (3DV). IEEE, pp. 565–571. DOI: 10.1109/3DV.2016.79

Mirza, M., & Osindero, S. (2014), "Conditional generative adversarial nets," arXiv preprint arXiv:1411.1784

Noh, H., Hong, S., & Han, B. (2015), "Learning deconvolution network for semantic segmentation," in Proceedings of the IEEE international conference on computer vision, pp. 1520–1528. in, Z.; Liu, B.; Chu, Q.; Yu, N. (2021), ISNet: Integrate image-level and semantic-level context for semantic segmentation. In Proceedings of the IEEE/CVF International Conference on Computer Vision, Montreal, BC, Canada, pp. 7189–7198.

Oktay, , (2018), "Attention u-net: Learning where to look for the pancreas," ArXiv Prepr. ArXiv-180403999DOI: 10.1016/j.cmpb.2024.108278 PMID: 38878360

Qin, C., Wang, Y., & Zhang, J. (2024). URCA: Uncertainty-based region clipping algorithm for semi-supervised medical image segmentation. *Computer Methods and Programs in Biomedicine*, *254*(108278), 1–12. DOI: 10.1016/j.cmpb.2024.108278 PMID: 38878360

Radford, A., Metz, L., & Chintala, S. (2015), "Unsupervised representation learning with deep convolutional generative adversarial networks," arXiv preprint arXiv:1511.06434

Ren, S., He, K., Girshick, R., & Sun, J. (2015). Faster r-cnn: Towards realtime object detection with region proposal networks. *Advances in Neural Information Processing Systems*, •••, 91–99.

Ren, S., He, K., Girshick, R., & Sun, J. (2017). Faster r-cnn: Towards realtime object detection with region proposal networks. *Advances in Neural Information Processing Systems*, *2015*(6), 91–99. DOI: 10.1109/TPAMI.2016.2577031 PMID: 27295650

Ronneberger, O., Fischer, P., & Brox, T. (2015), "U-net: Convolutional networks for biomedical image segmentation," in *International Conference on Medical image computing and computer-assisted intervention*. Springer, pp. 234–241. DOI: 10.1007/978-3-319-24574-4_28

Ronneberger, O., Fischer, P., & Brox, T. (2015), U-net: Convolutional networks for biomedical image segmentation. In *Proceedings of the International Conference on Medical Image Computing and Computer-Assisted Intervention*, Munich, Germany, 5–9 October 2015; Springer: Berlin/Heidelberg, Germany, pp. 234–241. DOI: 10.1007/978-3-319-24574-4_28

Rupprecht, C., Huaroc, E., Baust, M., & Navab, N. (2016), "Deep active contours," arXiv preprint arXiv:1607.05074

Schlemper, J., Oktay, O., Schaap, M., Heinrich, M., Kainz, B., Glocker, B., & Rueckert, D. (2019). Attention gated networks: Learning to leverage salient regions in medical images. *Medical Image Analysis*, *53*, 197–207. DOI: 10.1016/j.media.2019.01.012 PMID: 30802813

Singh, A., Lall, B., Panigrahi, B., Agrawal, A., Agrawal, A., Thangakunam, B., & Christopher, D. J. (2022). Semantic segmentation of bone structures in chest X-rays including unhealthy radiographs: A robust and accurate approach. *International Journal of Medical Informatics*, *165*, 104831. DOI: 10.1016/j.ijmedinf.2022.104831 PMID: 35870303

Visin, F., Ciccone, M., Romero, A., Kastner, K., Cho, K., Bengio, Y., Matteucci, M., & Courville, A. (2016), "Reseg: A recurrent neural network-based model for semantic segmentation," in *Proceedings of the IEEE Conference on Computer Vision and Pattern Recognition Workshops*, pp. 41–48. DOI: 10.1109/CVPRW.2016.60

Waibel, A., Hanazawa, T., Hinton, G., Shikano, K., & Lang, K. J. (1989). Phoneme recognition using time-delay neural networks. *IEEE Transactions on Acoustics, Speech, and Signal Processing*, *37*(3), 328–339. DOI: 10.1109/29.21701

Xiang, Y., & Fox, D. (2017), "Da-rnn: Semantic mapping with data associated recurrent neural networks," arXiv:1703.03098 DOI: 10.15607/RSS.2017.XIII.013

Yeung, H. W. F., Zhou, M., Chung, Y. Y., Moule, G., Thompson, W., Ouyang, W., Cai, W., & Bennamoun, M. (2022). Deep-learning-based solution for data deficient satellite image segmentation. *Expert Systems with Applications*, *191*, 116210. DOI: 10.1016/j.eswa.2021.116210

Zeng, Z., Xu, Y., Xie, Z., Tang, W., Wan, J., & Wu, W. (2022). LEARD-Net: Semantic segmentation for large-scale point cloud scene. *International Journal of Applied Earth Observation and Geoinformation*, *112*, 102953. DOI: 10.1016/j.jag.2022.102953

Zheng, S., Lu, J., Zhao, H., Zhu, X., Luo, Z., Wang, Y., Fu, Y., Feng, J., Xiang, T., & Torr, P. H.. (2021), Rethinking semantic segmentation from a sequence-to-sequence perspective with transformers. In *Proceedings of the IEEE/CVF Conference on Computer Vision and Pattern Recognition*, Nashville, TN, USA, pp. 6881–6890. DOI: 10.1109/CVPR46437.2021.00681

Chapter 14
Transformative Deep Learning Approaches for Enhanced Image Analysis and Processing: Innovations and Applications

Anwar Ali Sathio
https://orcid.org/0000-0001-5059-0166
Benazir Bhutto Shaheed University, Karachi, Pakistan

Muhammad Malook Rind
Sindh Madarssatul Islam University, Karachi, Pakistan

Shafique Ahmed Awan
https://orcid.org/0009-0002-3901-2095
Benazir Bhutto Shaheed University, Karachi, Pakistan

Kamlesh Kumar
Sindh Madarssatul Islam University, Karachi, Pakistan

ABSTRACT

This chapter examines how transformative deep learning is revolutionizing image processing and analysis, especially in the context of complex imaging tasks. Even with major improvements, accuracy and efficiency issues are still common. To address these challenges, we discussed different methods that integrate different deep learning architectures, such as convolutional neural networks (CNNs), RCNN and their variants, with sophisticated data preprocessing approaches. A thorough analysis of model architectures demonstrates the significant advantages deep learning provides over conventional techniques, improving diagnostic precision and effectiveness while facilitating individualized care in a variety of fields, including remote sensing, self-driving vehicles, and medical imaging. In the chapter, we critically review the literature, represent a major step forward in the applications of deep learning for advanced image analysis and processing, demonstrating its potential to address current limitations and drive future advancements.

DOI: 10.4018/979-8-3693-9045-0.ch014

1. INTRODUCTION

Deep learning has transformed image analysis techniques, providing transformative methods for complex problem solutions, and we discussed deep learning techniques and algorithms that are critical to the advancements in image analysis. Recent developments in deep learning have made significant strides in a number of fields, such as satellite analysis, object detection, and medical imaging. By using high-quality MRI regions to extract deep features, Aamir et al. (2023) showed notable gains in brain tumor classification, attaining improved diagnosis accuracy when compared to conventional approaches. Building on this, they created a two-stage object detection system that has shown promise in improving image identification tasks by using a progressive approach for generic object detection. The potential of high-performance diagnostics in medical imaging is further demonstrated by the use of deep learning models for MRI-based brain tumor classification (Aamir et al., 2022).

Furthermore, Aamir et al. (2018) used wavelet-transform methods to enhance building detection in low-contrast satellite pictures, enabling efficient object identification in intricate visual environments. CNN structures have been optimized for image classification, leading to architectures that balance excellent classification accuracy with computational efficiency (Aamir et al., 2019). According to Aamir et al. (2018), hybrid frameworks that include object detection and classification algorithms combined several detection methodologies for reliable results. Wavelet-domain image enhancement based on singular value decomposition improves satellite image visibility in a variety of lighting conditions (Aamir et al., 2019), while a hybrid object proposal generation framework in satellite imagery enables more accurate identification of high-quality regions (Aamir et al., 2017). With effective MRI-based brain tumor categorization frameworks, Guan et al. (2021) built on previous developments and improved diagnostic precision in challenging situations. Using deep feature-based frameworks and high-quality object placements, their region-based networks for object identification have demonstrated effectiveness in correctly differentiating objects in a variety of contexts. Furthermore, recent research highlights the potential of machine learning in medical applications; Aamir et al. (2023) outline current developments and potential avenues for future research. The dual-tree complex wavelet transforms for low-light image enhancement, as proposed by Guan et al. (2021), offers innovative solutions for nighttime imagery, highlighting the versatility and transformative impact of deep learning across disciplines. Wavelet transform techniques have also been successfully used to improve imagery in a variety of lighting conditions (Aamir et al., 2019).

2. DEEP LEARNING APPROACHES REVIEW

Deep learning (DL) models have revolutionized predictive image analysis and forecasting, enabling automated feature extraction, enhanced generalization, and improved decision-making. In recent years, various DL architectures, such as Convolutional Neural Networks (CNNs), Recurrent Neural Networks (RNNs), Generative Adversarial Networks (GANs), Transformers, and Self-Supervised Learning (SSL) methods, have significantly advanced predictive capabilities in diverse domains, including medical imaging, geospatial forecasting, and industrial applications. This literature review consolidates the latest research findings (2020–2024), highlighting major advancements in deep learning methodologies for image analysis.

Convolutional Neural Networks (CNNs) and Enhancements: CNNs remain a foundational approach in image analysis due to their ability to learn spatial hierarchies of features. Studies have focused on improving CNN performance through architectural innovations such as EfficientNet (Tan & Le, 2020), which optimizes model scaling, and ConvNeXt (Liu et al., 2022), which rethinks convolutional design with transformer-inspired modifications.

- EfficientNet introduces a compound scaling method to optimize accuracy and computational efficiency (Tan & Le, 2020).
- ConvNeXt incorporates depth-wise convolutions and layer normalization, bridging the gap between CNNs and transformer-based models (Liu et al., 2022).

Transformer Models in Image Analysis: Vision Transformers (ViTs) have emerged as a powerful alternative to CNNs, demonstrating superior performance in large-scale datasets by leveraging self-attention mechanisms.

- ViTs (Dosovitskiy et al., 2020) enable global feature dependencies, improving classification and segmentation accuracy.
- Swin Transformer (Liu et al., 2021) introduces a hierarchical design with shifted windows for efficient local-global context modeling.
- Hybrid CNN-Transformer Models combine CNN-based feature extraction with transformer-based global reasoning, improving robustness in medical and remote sensing applications (Chen et al., 2022).

Self-Supervised Learning (SSL) and Unsupervised Approaches: SSL techniques aim to reduce reliance on labeled data, a significant challenge in medical and industrial imaging.

- SimCLR (Chen et al., 2020) and BYOL (Grill et al., 2020) leverage contrastive learning to learn robust visual representations without labels.
- Masked Autoencoders (MAE) (He et al., 2022) reconstruct masked image patches, improving feature extraction and downstream task performance.
- SSL in Medical Imaging (Azizi et al., 2021) has demonstrated significant improvements in disease detection using limited labeled data.

Generative Adversarial Networks (GANs) for Image Synthesis and Forecasting: GANs continue to evolve for data augmentation, synthetic image generation, and predictive modeling.

- StyleGAN3 (Karras et al., 2021) enhances image realism and control over latent space manipulation.
- CycleGAN (Zhu et al., 2020) enables domain adaptation, facilitating medical image translation (e.g., MRI-to-CT scans).
- GANs for Climate and Geospatial Forecasting generate high-resolution weather predictions, improving disaster preparedness (Ravuri et al., 2021).

Federated Learning (FL) for Privacy-Preserving Image Analysis: FL has emerged as a key technique for collaborative learning without centralized data sharing, critical in healthcare and financial applications.

- Multi-Institutional Federated Learning (Sheller et al., 2020) enables training across hospitals while maintaining patient privacy.
- FedAvg (McMahan et al., 2017) and FedProx (Li et al., 2020) address non-IID (non-identically distributed) data challenges.
- FL in Medical Imaging (Xu et al., 2021) has improved diagnostic models by aggregating insights from multiple sources without exposing sensitive data.

Ethical and Explainability Considerations: As DL models become more prevalent, ensuring fairness, transparency, and accountability is critical.

- Explainable AI (XAI) (Tjoa & Guan, 2021) introduces methods like Grad-CAM and SHAP to interpret model decisions.
- Bias Mitigation in AI (Mehrabi et al., 2021) addresses algorithmic biases in medical and social AI applications.
- Regulatory Frameworks such as GDPR and HIPAA influence model deployment in healthcare and finance.

Recent advancements in deep learning have significantly enhanced predictive image analysis and forecasting. The integration of transformers, SSL, GANs, and FL has led to improvements in model accuracy, efficiency, and interpretability. Future research should focus on hybrid models, ethical AI frameworks, and real-world deployment challenges.

2.1 Convolutional Neural Networks (CNNs)

Convolutional Neural Networks (CNNs) are specialized deep learning models that use spatial hierarchies in pictures to interpret and evaluate visual input. CNNs use layers of convolutional filters to automatically identify features at different degrees of complexity, including edges, textures, and patterns, in image analysis. CNNs can learn unique features straight from raw image data with no preparation thanks to their multilayer feature extraction, which makes them very useful for tasks like object identification, classification, and segmentation. CNNs are essential to developments in computer vision and image analysis because of their structure, which was modeled after the visual cortex and enables them to handle large-scale, high-dimensional image collections (Figure 1).

- CNNs form the backbone of image processing by learning spatial hierarchies of features, Table1 shows the CNN and its applications.
- Known for automatic feature extraction and multi-layered convolutions.
- Applications include object detection, image classification, and medical imaging.
- Challenges: Overfitting in small datasets, large computational requirements.

Figure 1. CNN architecture (Sathio, Rind, & Lakhan, 2024)

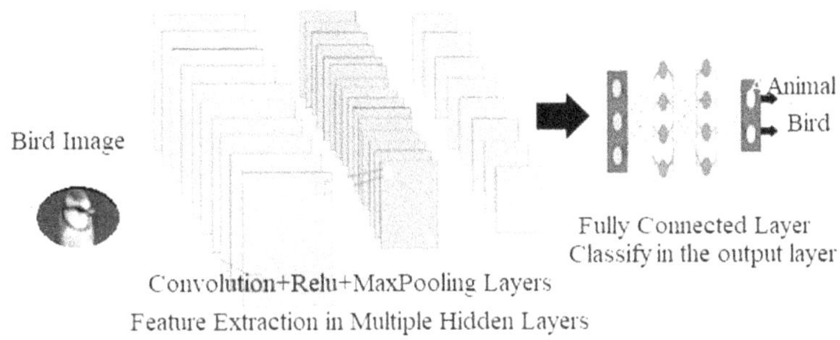

Table 1. Popular CNN architectures and their applications

Architecture and Studies	Purpose/Task	Key Features
AlexNet - Krizhevsky et al. (2012)	Image Classification	Deep layers, ReLU activation
VGGNet - Simonyan and Zisserman (2014)	Object Detection	Simple and uniform architecture
ResNet - He et al. (2016)	Image Recognition	Skip connections for deep networks

2.2 Transfer Learning (TL)

Transfer learning is a machine learning method, as Table 2 and Table 15 illustrate in detail. The model was created to accomplish a distinct but related purpose. TL frequently entails adapting a previously trained model—for example, a CNN trained on a huge dataset like ImageNet—for a new, usually smaller dataset. Transfer learning speeds up training and frequently boosts performance by using the information and characteristics discovered in the pre-trained model, especially when the destination dataset contains little labeled data. This method is a helpful tool for effective model creation since it is frequently used in tasks including object identification, picture classification, and natural language processing.

- Allows leveraging pre-trained models on large datasets like ImageNet for specialized tasks.
- Reduces training time and resources by applying learned knowledge to new domains.
- Ideal for applications such as medical imaging where data availability may be limited.
- Challenges: Generalizability of pre-trained models may vary depending on task-specific nuances.

Table 2. Transfer learning types and common approaches

Type and studies	Description	Common Approaches
Inductive Transfer - Pan and Yang (2010), Weiss et al. (2016)	New tasks in same domain	Fine-tuning, parameter transfer
Transductive Transfer - Ganin and Lempitsky (2015), Tzeng et al. (2017)	Same task, different domains	Domain Adaptation (DANN, MMD)
Unsupervised Transfer – Chen, X. et al. (2020), Grill et al. (2020)	No labels in source/target	Self-supervised learning (SimCLR, BYOL)

2.3 Generative Adversarial Networks (GANs)

Generative Adversarial Networks (GANs), illustrated in Figure 2, represent a category of deep learning models specifically engineered for the creation of new data samples that mimic a specified training dataset. These networks comprise two distinct neural architectures: a generator and a discriminator, which engage in a process termed adversarial training. The generator's role is to fabricate synthetic data samples, while the discriminator assesses these samples against authentic instances from the training dataset, determining the authenticity of each sample. The model generator's objective is to enhance the realism of its outputs to deceive the discriminator, whereas the discriminator focuses on refining its capability to differentiate between genuine and fabricated data. This dynamic rivalry persists until the generator can produce high-fidelity samples that are indistinguishable from real data. GANs have found extensive utility across a variety of applications, including image synthesis, style transfer, data augmentation, and the generation of realistic simulations, establishing them as a formidable asset in the field of generative modeling.

Figure 2. GAN architecture (Sathio, Rind, & Lakhan, 2024)

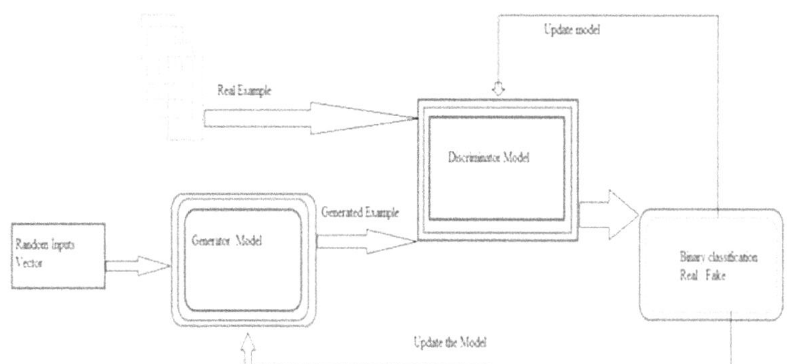

- The model GANs involves two CNNs, generator and discriminator, working in opposition to creating realistic images, Table 3 & Table 4 describe the GANs implementations and applications with details.

- Models are highly influential in image generation, style transfer, and data augmentation.
- Models useful for super-resolution and generating training data for deep learning models.
- Model challenges: Training instability, mode collapse, difficulty in balancing the generator and discriminator.

Table 3. GANs model structures

GAN Type	Application	Strengths
DCGAN Radford et al. (2015)	Image Synthesis	Deep convolutional structure
CycleGAN Zhu et al. (2017)	Image-to-Image Translation	Preserves structure between domains
StyleGAN Karras et al. (2019)	High-Resolution Generation	Control over style transfer

2.4 Autoencoders (AE)

Autoencoders (AEs) are a class of artificial neural networks commonly employed in unsupervised learning, particularly in tasks such as feature extraction and dimensionality reduction. These networks comprise two primary components: an encoder and a decoder. The encoder compresses the input data into a lower-dimensional form, referred to as the latent space, while the decoder reconstructs the data back from this compressed representation. Training an autoencoder involves optimizing for minimal discrepancy between the original input and its reconstruction, usually by minimizing loss functions like mean squared error. Autoencoders are highly effective for applications such as noise reduction, anomaly detection, and image compression. Specialized types, including convolutional autoencoders and denoising autoencoders, extend their functionality by efficiently handling complex data structures like images, utilizing the spatial hierarchies present in visual data. In essence, autoencoders provide a powerful approach for learning compact, efficient representations of data without relying on labeled samples.

- Unsupervised learning technique that compresses images into lower-dimensional latent spaces.
- Effective for image denoising, compression, and reconstruction.
- Simplifies complex datasets by focusing on the most important features.
- Challenges: Prone to learning trivial representations if not carefully tuned.

Table 4. Types of GANs and their applications

GAN Type	Application	Strengths
DCGAN - Radford et al. (2015)	Image Synthesis	Deep convolutional structure
CycleGAN - Zhu et al. (2017)	Image-to-Image Translation	Preserves structure between domains
StyleGAN - Karras et al. (2019)	High-Resolution Generation	Control over style transfer

2.5 Variational Autoencoders (VAE)

Variational Autoencoders (VAEs) represent an advanced generative model that expands upon the conventional autoencoder structure by incorporating Bayesian inference principles, as outlined in Table 5. Unlike traditional autoencoders, VAEs construct a probabilistic mapping from input data to a latent space, enabling the generation of new, realistic data samples.

In VAEs, the encoder outputs parameters of a probability distribution, typically Gaussian, that defines the latent space. During training, samples are drawn from this distribution, and the decoder uses these to reconstruct the original data. This design encourages the model to develop a smooth and continuous latent space, supporting effective interpolation and the generation of similar, novel data samples. VAEs are especially advantageous for applications such as image synthesis, anomaly detection, and semi-supervised learning, as they can produce varied outputs by sampling from the learned latent distribution. Their ability to balance reconstruction fidelity with regularization makes them a highly effective approach in generative modeling.

- An extension of autoencoders that includes probabilistic latent spaces, allowing for diverse image generation.
- Useful for unsupervised learning and generative tasks.
- Challenges: The balancing of reconstruction loss and KL divergence can be complex.

Table 5. Variants of autoencoders and their uses

Type of AE	Application	Key Feature
Standard AE - Hinton and Salakhutdinov (2006)	Noise Reduction	Dimensionality reduction
Variational AE (VAE) – Kingma and Welling (2013)	Image Generation	Probabilistic latent spaces

2.6 Recurrent Neural Networks (RNNs) and Long Short-Term Memory (LSTM)

Recurrent Neural Networks (RNNs) are a neural network class specifically designed for handling sequential data, such as time series or natural language. Unlike standard feedforward networks, RNNs include connections that retain information across time steps, allowing them to identify temporal patterns and dependencies within sequential inputs. However, traditional RNNs often face challenges in capturing long-range dependencies due to issues like vanishing gradients, which impede learning from distant data points.

Long Short-Term Memory (LSTM) networks, illustrated in Figure 3, were developed as a specialized RNN variant to overcome these challenges. LSTMs integrate a memory cell along with three gating mechanisms—input, forget, and output gates—that control information flow, enabling the network to preserve and adjust its memory over lengthy sequences. This structure allows LSTMs to effectively capture and retain long-range dependencies, making them particularly suited for applications like speech recognition, language modeling, and time series forecasting. Due to their robustness and ability to capture complex temporal relationships, LSTMs have become essential in the processing of sequential data.

Figure 3. LSTM architecture (Sathio, Rind, & Lakhan, 2024)

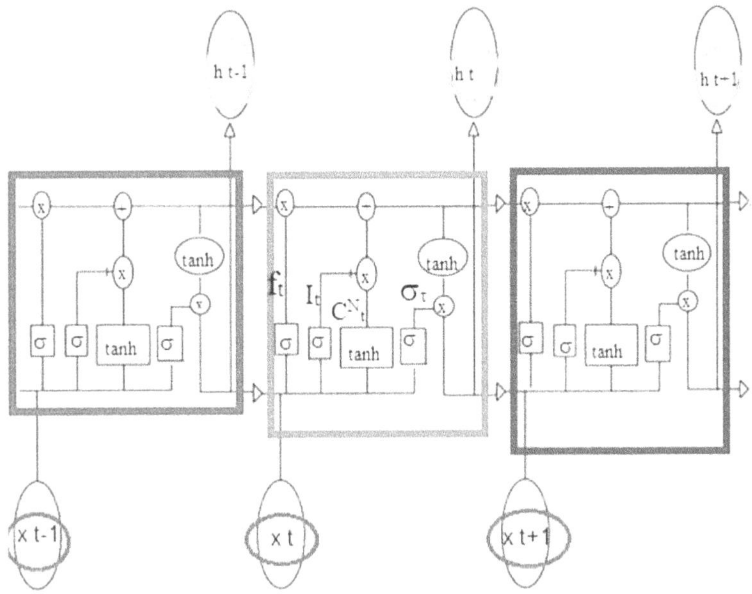

- RNNs and LSTMs handle temporal sequences of data, making them suitable for video analysis and image captioning, described in Table 6 with detailed view in literature.
- LSTMs are particularly useful in mitigating vanishing gradient problems, see Table 6.
- Challenges: Limited by processing speed and memory constraints.

Table 6. RNNs and LSTMs studies in literature

Study	Key Findings	Parameters
Krizhevsky, Sutskever, & Hinton (2012)	Introduced convolutional layers that influenced RNN-based architectures for visual tasks.	Convolutional layers, ReLU, dropout.
Simonyan & Zisserman (2014)	Proposed deep convolutional models impacting recurrent networks in vision applications.	16-layer depth, 3x3 conv layers.
He, Zhang, Ren, & Sun (2016)	Showcased the effectiveness of deep residuals, influencing sequential data handling in LSTM.	Residual connections, skip connections.
Pan & Yang (2010)	Surveyed transfer learning approaches compatible with RNNs and LSTM structures.	Transfer learning, domain adaptation.
Weiss, Khoshgoftaar, & Wang (2016)	Explored domain adaptation techniques applicable to RNN and LSTM architectures.	Transferability, feature extraction.
Ganin & Lempitsky (2015)	Developed domain adaptation methods via backpropagation useful in RNN models.	Domain adaptation, adversarial training.
Tzeng, Hoffman, Saenko, & Darrell (2017)	Proposed adversarial techniques for domain adaptation, aiding RNN applications.	Adversarial loss, domain adaptation.
Hinton & Salakhutdinov (2006)	Demonstrated data dimensionality reduction techniques relevant for input to RNNs.	Dimensionality reduction, neural networks.
Kingma & Welling (2013)	Developed variational autoencoders, later integrated with LSTM layers for enhanced learning.	VAE, KL divergence, Bayesian inference.
Chen, X., Fan, Girshick, & He (2020)	Improved contrastive learning methods, influencing memory cell structures in LSTMs.	Momentum contrast, memory cells.
Tajbakhsh et al. (2016)	Studied the full training and fine-tuning of CNNs and their effect on LSTM structures.	CNN fine-tuning, training transfer.
Raghu et al. (2019)	Analyzed transfer learning in medical imaging, informing RNN and LSTM feature engineering.	Transfer learning, medical imaging.
Zhang et al. (2017)	Developed domain-adversarial networks, utilized in time-series RNNs.	Domain adversarial learning, time-series data.
Zamir et al. (2018)	Examined multi-task transfer learning relevant for RNNs in multiple task settings.	Multi-task learning, task disentanglement.
Nguyen et al. (2020)	Proposed methods for estimating transferability in tasks, helpful for RNN deployment.	Transferability estimation, representation.
Srivastava et al. (2014)	Introduced dropout to prevent overfitting, widely used in RNN and LSTM training.	Dropout, regularization.

2.7 U-Net Architecture

U-Net is a specialized convolutional neural network architecture developed primarily for biomedical image segmentation, though it has also been successfully applied in a wide range of image processing tasks. Originally introduced to achieve precise localization and feature classification in scenarios with limited annotated data, U-Net has become instrumental in high-accuracy segmentation.

The U-Net architecture features two core components: the contracting path (encoder) and the expansive path (decoder).

a) **Contracting Path:** This section captures contextual information through a series of convolutional and pooling layers, downsampling the input image while increasing feature map depth. This allows the network to learn hierarchical representations at various scales.
b) **Expansive Path:** The decoder complements the contracting path by using transposed convolutions to upsample feature maps. Skip connections link corresponding layers in the encoder and decoder, preserving spatial details and enhancing segmentation accuracy.

With its distinctive "U" shape, U-Net effectively learns both local and global features, making it particularly suitable for tasks that demand high-resolution output, such as medical image segmentation, where accurate delineation is critical.

- **Overview inTable 7:** U-Net is frequently cited in the literature as an effective architecture for semantic segmentation, especially within medical imaging.
- **Architecture Highlights:** An encoder-decoder structure with skip connections to retain detailed, high-resolution features.
- **Challenges:** High segmentation accuracy typically requires extensive labeled datasets.

Table 7. Scholarly studies on U-Net architecture, findings, and evaluation parameters

Study	Findings	Evaluation Parameters
Ronneberger et al. (2015)	Proposed the original U-Net architecture, which became foundational in medical image segmentation.	Dice Similarity Coefficient (DSC), Jaccard Index, Accuracy
Çiçek et al. (2016)	Extended U-Net to 3D U-Net for volumetric segmentation in biomedical images.	Precision, Recall, F1 Score, Volume Overlap
Zhou et al. (2018)	Improved U-Net by adding dense connections, known as Dense U-Net, to enhance feature reuse.	DSC, Hausdorff Distance, Sensitivity, Specificity
Ibtehaz & Rahman (2020)	Proposed MultiResUNet to capture spatial hierarchies more effectively with multi-resolution blocks.	Mean Intersection over Union (mIoU), DSC, Accuracy
Oktay et al. (2018)	Introduced Attention U-Net, incorporating attention mechanisms to focus on relevant features.	DSC, Sensitivity, Specificity, Precision
Isensee et al. (2021)	Developed nnU-Net, an automated configuration U-Net for segmentation tasks across diverse biomedical datasets.	DSC, mIoU, Sensitivity, Hausdorff Distance

2.8 Region-Based Convolutional Neural Networks (R-CNN)

Region-Based Convolutional Neural Networks (R-CNN) are a deep learning architecture developed specifically for object detection in images. First introduced by Ross Girshick in 2014, R-CNN integrates conventional object detection approaches with deep learning methodologies, enabling more accurate and efficient detection of objects within images.

Figure 4. RCNN architecture (Sathio, Rind, & Lakhan, 2024)

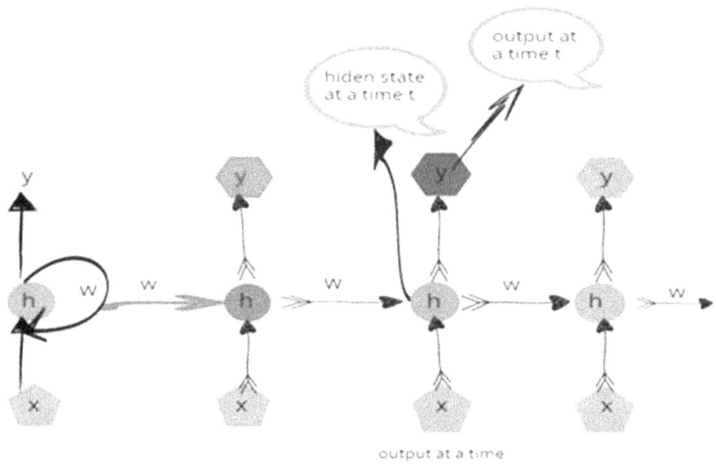

The R-CNN architecture, depicted in Figure 4, is represented by several variants in the literature and operates through a multi-stage process:

a) **Region Proposal:** Using selective search, the model identifies potential object locations, generating a set of candidates bounding boxes (regions of interest) within the image.
b) **Feature Extraction:** Each candidate region is then processed through a convolutional neural network (CNN) to extract high-level features, enabling the model to learn key visual characteristics.
c) **Classification and Bounding Box Refinement:** The extracted features are sent to a classifier, often a support vector machine, which identifies specific object classes in each region. Additionally, a regression model adjusts the bounding boxes to improve localization accuracy.

Although R-CNN achieved notable improvements in object detection accuracy, its multi-stage approach was computationally intensive and slow. This challenge led to the creation of optimized versions, such as Fast R-CNN and Faster R-CNN, which streamline the process and improve detection speed, enhancing real-time capability. Ultimately, R-CNN set the stage for contemporary object detection techniques by successfully merging region proposals with deep learning-based feature extraction.

2.9 Mask R-CNN

Mask R-CNN is an enhanced version of the Faster R-CNN architecture tailored for instance segmentation tasks, aiming to detect and segment objects at the pixel level within images. Developed by Kaiming He et al. in 2017, Mask R-CNN expands upon Faster R-CNN by incorporating an additional branch dedicated to creating binary masks for each identified object, with key elements of the architecture outlined in Tables 8 and 9.

Key components of the Mask R-CNN architecture include:

a) **Backbone Network:** As in Faster R-CNN, Mask R-CNN uses a backbone network, typically a ResNet or ResNeXt, to extract features from the input image.
b) **Region Proposal Network (RPN):** This component identifies potential object regions (bounding boxes) within the image, similar to the functionality in Faster R-CNN.
c) **RoI Align:** Replacing RoI pooling to avoid quantization errors, Mask R-CNN uses RoI Align to maintain precise spatial alignment when extracting features, leading to improved mask accuracy.
d) **Mask Branch:** A fully convolutional network (FCN) branch is added to generate a binary mask for each proposed region, marking the pixels corresponding to the detected object. This mask branch operates in parallel with bounding box regression and classification tasks.

By enabling pixel-level segmentation along with object detection, Mask R-CNN allows for finer image analysis, making it highly useful in applications such as autonomous driving, medical imaging, and video analysis, where accurate object localization and segmentation are crucial.

- **Enhancements:** Extends Faster R-CNN with a mask prediction layer, ideal for instance segmentation.
- **Challenges:** Requires significant memory and processing capacity.

Table 8. R-CNN variants and enhancements

Variant	Improvements	Application
R-CNN - Girshick et al. (2014)	Region proposals	Object detection
Fast R-CNN - Girshick (2015)	Faster region proposals	Object localization
Mask R-CNN - He et al. (2017)	Pixel-wise segmentation	Image segmentation

Table 9. R-CNN variants, findings, methods, and evaluation parameters

Study	Findings	Methods	Evaluation Parameters
Girshick et al. (2014)	Introduced the original R-CNN model, marking a breakthrough in object detection.	Region Proposal + CNN + SVM	Mean Average Precision (mAP), IoU
Girshick (2015)	Proposed Fast R-CNN to reduce computation by using RoI pooling for faster object detection.	Region of Interest (RoI) Pooling	mAP, Detection Time
Ren et al. (2015)	Developed Faster R-CNN, which uses a Region Proposal Network (RPN) to eliminate selective search.	Region Proposal Network (RPN)	mAP, Detection Speed, IoU
He et al. (2017)	Introduced Mask R-CNN, an extension of Faster R-CNN that adds a branch for object segmentation.	Mask Branch + RPN	mAP, Mean IoU, Mask Accuracy
Cai & Vasconcelos (2018)	Proposed Cascade R-CNN to improve accuracy in multi-stage object detection tasks.	Multi-stage Detection, Cascading RPN	mAP, Precision, Recall

continued on following page

Table 9. Continued

Study	Findings	Methods	Evaluation Parameters
Huang et al. (2017)	Introduced R-FCN, a position-sensitive model improving speed and efficiency over R-CNN models.	Position-Sensitive Score Maps	mAP, IoU, Processing Time
Chen et al. (2019)	Presented Hybrid Task Cascade (HTC) to address complex tasks like instance and semantic segmentation.	Cascade R-CNN + Semantic Segmentation	mAP, Mask IoU, Instance and Semantic Accuracy

2.10 You Only Look Once (YOLO)

You Only Look Once (YOLO) is a groundbreaking object detection framework designed for real-time analysis in images and videos. First introduced by Joseph Redmon et al. in 2016, YOLO reframes object detection as a single regression problem, predicting bounding boxes and class probabilities across an entire image in a single pass, dramatically enhancing detection speed compared to traditional multi-stage approaches.

Key characteristics of YOLO include:

a) **Single Neural Network Architecture:** YOLO employs a single convolutional neural network (CNN) that segments the input image into a grid. Each grid cell is responsible for predicting bounding boxes and class probabilities for objects centered within that cell.
b) **Real-Time Detection Capability:** By treating object detection as a unified task, YOLO achieves exceptional processing speed, enabling real-time object detection. This makes it particularly suitable for time-sensitive applications such as autonomous driving and surveillance.
c) **End-to-End Training:** YOLO is trained on full images with ground truth labels, allowing it to learn contextual information and spatial relationships, thereby improving accuracy in detecting objects at varying scales and positions.
d) **Advancements in Later Versions:** Improved versions like YOLOv2, YOLOv3, and YOLOv5 introduce architectural refinements, enhancing accuracy and speed, making YOLO effective at detecting multiple objects in complex scenes.

In summary, YOLO's high-speed and precise object detection capabilities make it a widely adopted tool in computer vision across diverse fields.

- **Summary:** YOLO processes the entire image through a single neural network, achieving real-time object detection.
- **Advantages:** Among the fastest object detection algorithms available.
- **Limitations:** Faces challenges with detecting small objects in densely packed scenes.

2.11 Single Shot Multibox Detector (SSD)

The Single Shot Multibox Detector (SSD) is an object detection framework engineered for both real-time performance and accuracy. Introduced by Wei Liu et al. in 2016, SSD enables object detection in images with a single pass through the network, offering enhanced efficiency and speed compared to traditional multi-stage methods.

Key features of SSD include:

a) **Single Shot Detection:** In contrast to two-stage detectors, such as Faster R-CNN, which first generate region proposals before classification, SSD conducts object detection in a single forward pass. It predicts both bounding boxes and class scores directly from the feature maps.
b) **Multi-Scale Feature Maps:** SSD leverages a series of convolutional layers at varying scales to capture objects of different sizes. Predictions are generated from multiple feature maps across the network, allowing effective detection of both small and large objects.
c) **Default Boxes:** SSD utilizes a predetermined set of default bounding boxes with various aspect ratios and scales corresponding to each feature map cell. During the inference phase, these default boxes are adjusted based on predicted offsets to accurately encompass detected objects.
d) **Non-Maximum Suppression:** To refine the detection results and eliminate redundant predictions, SSD implements non-maximum suppression, ensuring that only the most relevant bounding boxes are retained for each identified object.

SSD effectively balances speed and accuracy, making it ideal for real-time object detection applications, including autonomous driving, robotics, and video surveillance. Its architectural design has influenced further innovations in the object detection domain, leading to the development of even faster and more precise models.

- **Summary:** SSD is a real-time object detection method akin to YOLO but utilizes anchor boxes for enhanced precision.
- **Challenges:** It may exhibit lower accuracy compared to other algorithms, particularly in the detection of small objects.

2.12 Capsule Networks (CapsNet)

Capsule Networks (CapsNet), as depicted in Figure 5, are a novel neural network architecture introduced by Geoffrey Hinton and his research team in 2017. This architecture aims to overcome several limitations of traditional convolutional neural networks (CNNs), particularly in recognizing patterns and understanding spatial hierarchies within data. CapsNet enhances the model's capability to comprehend the relationship between the components of an object and the object as a whole, leading to improved generalization and increased robustness to variations.

Key features of Capsule Networks include:

a) **Capsules:** The essential units of CapsNet are known as "capsules." These are small clusters of neurons that collaboratively represent specific features of an object. Each capsule captures various attributes, such as orientation and position, and produces a vector output rather than a scalar value.

b) **Dynamic Routing:** Capsules employ a dynamic routing algorithm to establish connections with higher-level capsules. This mechanism determines which lower-level capsules contribute to the formation of higher-level features, facilitating effective learning of part-whole relationships.
c) **Pose Information:** In contrast to conventional networks that primarily focus on feature identification, CapsNet retains pose information—such as position, orientation, and scale—of objects. This capability enhances the model's ability to recognize objects from different viewpoints and under various transformations.
d) **Robustness to Distortion:** CapsNet has shown improved resistance to adversarial attacks and distortions, making it more resilient in real-world applications where variations in object appearance can occur.

Figure 5. CapsNet architecture (Sathio, Rind, & Lakhan, 2024)

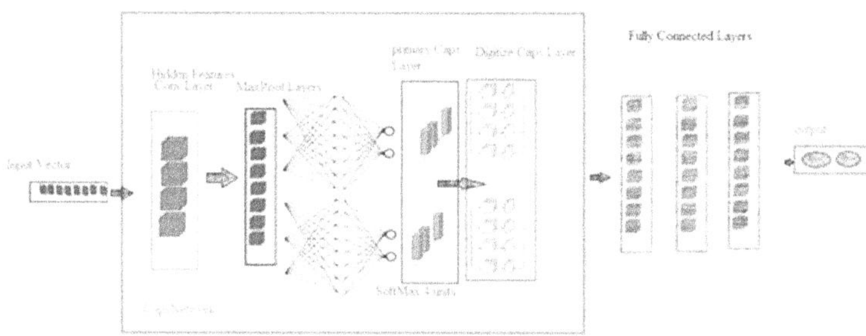

Capsule Networks are still a relatively novel approach, and while they show promise in specific applications like image recognition and segmentation, ongoing research aims to refine their architecture and scalability for broader use in deep learning tasks

- Capsule Networks aim to improve how spatial hierarchies are modeled, offering better handling of pose and viewpoint variations.
- Challenges: Training capsules is resource-intensive and slow.

2.13 DenseNet (Densely Connected Convolutional Networks)

DenseNet, or Densely Connected Convolutional Networks, is a convolutional neural network (CNN) architecture developed by Gao Huang et al. in 2017. This architecture addresses prevalent challenges in deep learning, such as vanishing gradients and inefficiencies in feature reuse, by introducing a distinctive connectivity pattern among its layers.

Key features of DenseNet include:

a) **Dense Connectivity:** In DenseNet, each layer is connected to every other layer in a feed-forward manner. This structure allows the input of any given layer to consist of the outputs from all preceding layers, fostering a robust flow of information and features throughout the network.

b) **Feature Reuse:** The dense connections facilitate effective reuse of features from earlier layers, which helps reduce the overall number of parameters required in the model. This efficiency results in improved performance and more efficient training, especially in image classification tasks.
c) **Improved Gradient Flow:** The dense connectivity significantly mitigates the vanishing gradient problem, enabling gradients to propagate more freely during backpropagation. Consequently, this enhancement leads to better training of deeper networks and can accelerate convergence.
d) **Compact Architecture:** Despite its considerable depth, DenseNet achieves high performance with fewer parameters compared to traditional CNNs. This compact design makes it well-suited for environments with limited resources while still maintaining high accuracy.

DenseNet has proven effective in a variety of computer vision applications, including image classification, object detection, and medical image analysis. Its innovative approach to layer connectivity and feature reuse has influenced the development of subsequent deep learning architectures.

- DenseNet improves feature propagation and gradient flow by connecting each layer to every other layer in a feed-forward manner.
- **Challenges:** The increased complexity of the model architecture necessitates more GPU memory.

2.14 ResNet (Residual Networks)

ResNet effectively addresses the vanishing gradient issue, enabling the development of deeper models. **Transfer learning**, illustrated in Figure 6, is a significant technique in both deep learning and machine learning, where insights acquired from one task (the source task) are utilized for another, related task (the target task). This approach is especially beneficial when there is a scarcity of labeled data in the target domain but an abundance in the source domain. Transfer learning can be classified into various types based on the characteristics of the source and target domains, the tasks involved, and the methodologies employed.

Figure 6. ResNet architecture (Sathio, Rind, & Lakhan, 2024)

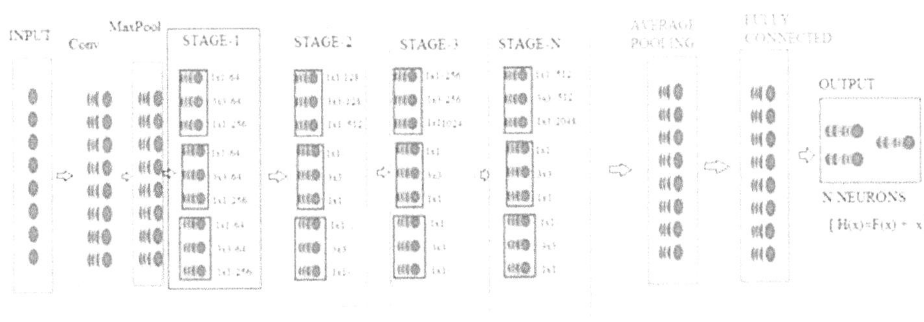

Residual Networks (ResNet) represent a significant advancement in deep learning architecture, introduced by Kaiming He et al. in 2015 to tackle the difficulties associated with training extremely deep neural networks. ResNet incorporates an innovative technique known as "skip connections" or "residual connections," which enhance the flow of gradients throughout the network during training, thereby mitigating the vanishing gradient issue.

Key characteristics of ResNet include:

a) **Residual Blocks**: The fundamental component of ResNet is the residual block, which comprises two or more convolutional layers interconnected by a direct shortcut that bypasses these layers. This shortcut enables the addition of the input to the block's output, allowing the network to focus on learning the residual mapping rather than the original mapping.
b) **Enhanced Training of Deep Networks**: By facilitating the learning of residuals, ResNet enables the effective training of networks with hundreds or even thousands of layers without experiencing substantial performance degradation, a common problem encountered in deeper architectures.
c) **Improved Gradient Flow**: The implementation of skip connections promotes better gradient flow during the backpropagation process, aiding in the retention of critical information and enhancing convergence rates during training.
d) **State-of-the-Art Performance**: ResNet has achieved remarkable results across various benchmarks, including the ImageNet competition, showcasing its efficacy in tasks such as image classification, object detection, and segmentation.

The innovative structure of ResNet has paved the way for numerous subsequent architectures and adaptations, solidifying its position as a cornerstone model in the realms of deep learning and computer vision. Its capability to support very deep networks while preserving performance has rendered it a favored choice in both research and practical applications.

In the context of image processing models, there are numerous classification systems and variants; Table 10 provides a comprehensive overview of these developments as identified by researchers.

Table 10. CNN variants, findings, methods, and evaluation parameters

Study	Findings	Methods	Evaluation Parameters
Simonyan & Zisserman (2014)	Developed **VGG16/19** architectures, showing the benefits of depth in CNNs for feature extraction.	Deep Convolution Layers	Top-1/Top-5 Accuracy, Computation Time
Redmon et al. (2016)	Introduced **YOLO,** achieving real-time object detection with high efficiency.	Unified Detection Architecture	mAP, Frames per Second (FPS)
Hinton et al. (2017)	**CapsNet** introduced capsule layers to capture spatial hierarchies, improving pose sensitivity.	Capsule Layers	Test Accuracy, Pose Estimation Accuracy
Huang et al. (2017)	**DenseNet** proposed dense connections to address gradient vanishing and improve feature reuse.	Dense Connections Between Layers	Top-1/Top-5 Accuracy, Model Size
He et al. (2016)	Proposed **ResNet** with skip connections to facilitate training deep networks, achieving significant depth.	Residual Learning, Skip Connections	Top-1/Top-5 Accuracy, Model Depth
Liu et al. (2016)	**SSD** introduced a single-shot detector model that balances speed and accuracy for object detection.	Multi-scale Convolutional Layers	mAP, Detection Speed

continued on following page

Table 10. Continued

Study	Findings	Methods	Evaluation Parameters
Tan & Le (2019)	**EfficientNet** improved model efficiency by balancing width, depth, and resolution.	Compound Scaling	mAP, FLOPS, Model Parameters
Wang et al. (2020)	Proposed **EfficientDet** for more efficient object detection using a weighted bidirectional feature pyramid.	Bi-directional Feature Pyramid Network	mAP, Efficiency, Inference Time

2.14 Vision Transformer (ViT) Model

The Vision Transformer (ViT) model represents a notable progression in image processing tasks, particularly within the field of computer vision. In contrast to conventional convolutional neural networks (CNNs), which heavily depend on convolutional operations to discern spatial hierarchies within images, ViT employs a transformer architecture originally developed for natural language processing (NLP) applications.

i. **Architecture:** Within the ViT framework, images are segmented into fixed-size patches, typically measuring 16x16 pixels. These patches are subsequently transformed into a sequence of tokens through a linear embedding process. Each token is paired with a positional embedding to preserve spatial context, and this token sequence is processed through a standard transformer architecture, which consists of multiple layers of self-attention mechanisms and feed-forward networks. The self-attention component enables the model to assess the significance of various image patches, facilitating a focus on relevant features while minimizing the impact of less significant ones.
ii. The primary components of the ViT architecture include:

- Patch Embedding Layer: Transforms image patches into token embeddings.
- Positional Encoding: Integrates spatial information regarding each patch's location within the original image.
- Multi-Head Self-Attention: Captures interdependencies and relationships among patches.
- Feed-Forward Network: Applies nonlinear transformations to the outputs generated by the self-attention layer.
- Layer Normalization: Enhances the stability of training by normalizing the feature inputs.
- Output Layer: Generally consists of a classification head, typically a straightforward feed-forward layer that converts the final output into class probabilities.

iii. Parameters

The efficacy of the ViT model is influenced by several hyperparameters, including:

a) Patch Size: Common options include 16x16 or 32x32 pixels. The choice of patch size affects the level of detail in the features captured.
b) Number of Layers: The depth of the transformer architecture influences its ability to learn intricate representations.

c) Hidden Dimension: This refers to the size of the token embeddings and hidden layers, which directly affects the model's expressive power.
d) Number of Attention Heads: An increased number of heads allows the model to simultaneously focus on various parts of the input, enhancing its capacity to capture a diverse range of features.

iv. Design Challenges

Despite the promising results of the ViT model, it encounters several design challenges:

- **Data Requirements:** ViT models generally necessitate substantial amounts of training data to achieve optimal performance, often requiring pre-training on extensive datasets.
- **Computational Cost:** The self-attention mechanism exhibits a quadratic scaling with respect to the number of patches, leading to heightened computational and memory requirements, particularly for high-resolution images.
- **Overfitting:** The model's numerous parameters make it susceptible to overfitting when trained on smaller datasets. Techniques such as data augmentation and regularization are often utilized to alleviate this issue.
- **Interpretability:** Gaining insights into the decisions made by the model can be more complex compared to traditional CNNs, posing challenges in analyzing the learned representations.

v. Variants of ViT

Several variants and modifications of the Vision Transformer have been created to address specific tasks or enhance performance:

- **DeiT (Data-efficient Image Transformers):** This variant implements techniques that enable effective training of ViT models on smaller datasets by employing knowledge distillation from a pre-trained CNN.
- **Swin Transformer:** This architecture features a hierarchical design that shifts attention windows, resulting in more efficient computations and improved performance in dense prediction tasks, such as segmentation.
- **TNT (Transformer in Transformer):** This model introduces a novel architecture that integrates CNN-like structures with transformers, aiming to effectively capture both local and global features.
- **ViT-G and ViT-L:** These larger versions of the original ViT model are trained on extensive datasets and are tailored for high-performance applications.

The Vision Transformer model signifies a transformative shift in the processing and analysis of image data, presenting a robust alternative to traditional methodologies. Its distinctive architecture and adaptability for fine-tuning specific tasks render it suitable for diverse fields, including medical imaging, where it can play a pivotal role in identifying anomalies and segmenting specific regions of interest. As research on ViT progresses, it holds considerable potential to reshape the landscape of computer vision applications.

In recent years, the incorporation of deep learning techniques into image analysis has significantly transformed data processing and visualization across various sectors. A notable advancement is the implementation of convolutional neural network (CNN)-based frameworks, such as an IoT-enabled system for detecting plant health, which demonstrates the effectiveness of CNNs in remote monitoring and health evaluation (Panhwar et al., 2022; Ali, 2021). Building upon the applications of CNNs, machine learning has played a crucial role in enhancing medical imaging, particularly in the detection of cardiac issues like mitral regurgitation through specialized imaging methods, providing promising solutions in cardiac care (Singh et al., 2024).

Similar deep learning models, specifically designed for healthcare, utilize extensive multimodal datasets and require advanced algorithms for optimal clustering and classification, as evidenced by recent developments in multimedia processing (Sathio, Rind, & Lakhan, 2024; Sathio et al., 2023). The integration of blockchain technology with deep learning also emerges as a vital enhancement, facilitating secure data management in medical image analysis—a crucial advancement for ensuring safe and compliant healthcare solutions (Sathio et al., 2023; Sathio, 2018).

Moreover, the ongoing progress in key phrase extraction algorithms, including W-Rank, has improved information retrieval processes in image processing tasks, emphasizing the role of deep learning in data enrichment and effective feature extraction (Shah et al., 2023; Sathio, Rind, & Lakhan, 2024). These transformative advancements highlight the significant potential of deep learning technologies to develop robust image analysis techniques (Sathio et al., 2021), enhancing accuracy, efficiency, and versatility across various fields, including healthcare, environmental monitoring, and industrial forecasting (Vavekanand et al., 2024; Sathio & Brohi, 2021). The convergence of deep learning with practical applications not only streamlines diagnostic and predictive capabilities but also lays the groundwork for future breakthroughs in image analysis methodologies.

3. TRANSFER LEARNING (TL)

In recent years, the incorporation of deep learning techniques into image analysis has significantly transformed data processing and visualization across various sectors. A notable advancement is the implementation of convolutional neural network (CNN)-based frameworks, such as an IoT-enabled system for detecting plant health, which demonstrates the effectiveness of CNNs in remote monitoring and health evaluation (Panhwar et al., 2022; Ali, 2021). Building upon the applications of CNNs, machine learning has played a crucial role in enhancing medical imaging, particularly in the detection of cardiac issues like mitral regurgitation through specialized imaging methods, providing promising solutions in cardiac care (Singh et al., 2024).

Similar deep learning models, specifically designed for healthcare, utilize extensive multimodal datasets and require advanced algorithms for optimal clustering and classification, as evidenced by recent developments in multimedia processing (Sathio, Rind, & Lakhan, 2024; Sathio et al., 2023). The integration of blockchain technology with deep learning also emerges as a vital enhancement, facilitating secure data management in medical image analysis—a crucial advancement for ensuring safe and compliant healthcare solutions (Sathio et al., 2023; Sathio, 2018).

Moreover, the ongoing progress in key phrase extraction algorithms, including W-Rank, has improved information retrieval processes in image processing tasks, emphasizing the role of deep learning in data enrichment and effective feature extraction (Shah et al., 2023; Sathio, Rind, & Lakhan, 2024). These transformative advancements highlight the significant potential of deep learning technologies to develop robust image analysis techniques (Sathio et al., 2021), enhancing accuracy, efficiency, and versatility across various fields, including healthcare, environmental monitoring, and industrial forecasting (Vavekanand et al., 2024; Sathio & Brohi, 2021). The convergence of deep learning with practical applications not only streamlines diagnostic and predictive capabilities but also lays the groundwork for future breakthroughs in image analysis methodologies.

Transfer learning is a machine learning approach in which a model trained on one task is repurposed as a foundational model for a second, related task. As shown in Table 11, various studies have explored the application of transfer learning. This technique utilizes the knowledge acquired in a source domain to enhance learning in a target domain, particularly when labeled data is limited in the target area. Instead of initiating model training from the beginning, transfer learning enables the adaptation of useful patterns and features learned from a comprehensive dataset or task to a more focused and smaller dataset.

The following are essential concepts related to transfer learning (TL):

- **Source Domain and Task**: This refers to the domain and task for which the initial model was developed and trained.
- **Target Domain and Task**: This indicates the new domain and task where the knowledge obtained from the source domain is applied.
- **Pre-Trained Models**: Commonly used pre-trained models include VGG, ResNet, and BERT, which are trained on extensive datasets (e.g., ImageNet) and serve as effective starting points for transfer learning.

Table 11. Transfer learning types

Type	Example	Primary Technique
Homogeneous Transfer - Tajbakhsh et al. (2016), Raghu et al. (2019)	Fine-tuning ResNet on medical images	Pre-trained model fine-tuning
Heterogeneous Transfer - Zhang et al. (2017)	Cross-domain image recognition	Domain alignment (DANN)
Negative Transfer - Bao and Xiao (2019)	Task dissimilarity issues	Transferability estimation (H-score)

3.1 Types of Transfer Learning

A. Inductive Transfer Learning

Inductive transfer learning occurs when the target task differs from the source task. In this approach, a model trained on the source task is fine-tuned or adapted to the target task using available data. The term “inductive” emphasizes the learning of the target task with assistance from the source task.

Types of Inductive Transfer Learning:

i. **Fine-Tuning Pre-Trained Models:** This is the most prevalent form of inductive transfer learning. It involves pre-training a model on a large dataset (e.g., ImageNet) and subsequently adapting it for a specific task, such as medical image classification. For instance, a pre-trained convolutional neural network (CNN) like VGG16 or ResNet can be employed for object classification on smaller datasets by freezing the initial layers and fine-tuning the latter ones.
ii. **Model Parameter Transfer:** Instead of retraining the entire model, this approach transfers specific layers or parameters of the pre-trained model to the new task. For example, convolutional layers trained on ImageNet can be transferred for feature extraction in a new image recognition task while adapting the final fully connected layers.
iii. **Instance-Based Transfer:** In this method, data from the source domain is utilized to augment the target domain data. This is often achieved by re-weighting instances from the source dataset to enhance their relevance to the target task. An example is selecting instances from a large dataset that resemble the target task and combining them with the smaller target dataset for training.
iv. Common Approaches:

- Pre-trained deep learning models (e.g., ResNet, VGG, BERT)
- Domain-specific fine-tuning (e.g., fine-tuning BERT for natural language processing tasks like sentiment analysis)

B. Transductive Transfer Learning

Transductive transfer learning is characterized by the source and target tasks being the same, but their domains differ. This method aims to adapt the knowledge acquired in the source domain to perform effectively in the target domain.

Types of Transductive Transfer Learning:

i **Domain Adaptation:** This technique is used when there is a significant difference in data distribution between the source and target domains. Domain adaptation methods align these domains, typically by learning a representation that is invariant to the domain. For example, a model trained on images of cars (source domain) can be adjusted to classify cars in thermal images (target domain) using techniques like domain adversarial networks (DANN) to bridge the gap.
ii. **Domain-Invariant Feature Learning:** This approach focuses on learning feature representations that remain consistent across the source and target domains. This can be achieved by imposing constraints to ensure similarity between learned features in both domains. For instance, a neural network trained for sentiment analysis in English may be adapted for French reviews by learning language-invariant features.
iii. **Unsupervised Domain Adaptation:** In this scenario, the target domain lacks labeled data. The model learns from the labeled data in the source domain while ensuring the learned features are effective on the unlabeled target data. For example, a model could utilize labeled images from one country's road signs to predict those of another country without labeled data, often using methods such as Maximum Mean Discrepancy (MMD) or Adversarial Discriminative Domain Adaptation (ADDA).
iv. Common Approaches:

- Domain adversarial neural networks (DANN)
- Maximum Mean Discrepancy (MMD)
- Adversarial discriminative domain adaptation (ADDA)

C. Unsupervised Transfer Learning

Unsupervised transfer learning involves both the source and target tasks being unsupervised, meaning there are no labeled examples available. The emphasis is on transferring features or knowledge acquired from unsupervised learning tasks in the source domain to tackle unsupervised learning tasks in the target domain.

Types of Unsupervised Transfer Learning

i. **Representation Learning:** This form of transfer learning entails acquiring representations (features) in the source domain through unsupervised learning, which are subsequently applied to the target domain. An example is learning unsupervised features from an image dataset and using them for unsupervised clustering in another dataset.
ii. **Self-Supervised Learning:** In this approach, models create labels from the data itself (e.g., predicting image rotations or solving jigsaw puzzles), which can then be utilized for other unsupervised tasks. For instance, self-supervised techniques like SimCLR can be employed to learn visual representations that are applicable to tasks such as image clustering or retrieval in the target domain.
iii. Common Approaches:

  - Self-supervised learning (e.g., SimCLR, BYOL, MoCo)
  - Contrastive learning
  - Feature learning using clustering techniques

D. Few-Shot Learning

Few-shot learning represents a specialized category of transfer learning where the model is trained to generalize to new tasks or classes with only a few examples in the target domain. Table 12 presents literature and findings related to various few-shot learning models.

Types of Few-Shot Learning:

i. **Meta-Learning:** Also referred to as "learning to learn," meta-learning focuses on developing models that can swiftly adapt to new tasks with minimal data. It typically involves training over a distribution of tasks rather than concentrating on a single task. An example includes Prototypical Networks or Model-Agnostic Meta-Learning (MAML) techniques that aim to create models capable of generalizing to new classes or tasks with only a few labeled examples.
ii. **Zero-Shot Learning:** This more extreme variant allows the model to recognize objects from unseen classes by transferring knowledge from related classes. Zero-shot learning frequently employs semantic embeddings (like word embeddings) to represent unseen classes. For instance, a model trained on

animals (e.g., dogs and cats) can learn to recognize an unseen class (e.g., horses) by mapping class descriptions to the learned feature space.

iii. **One-Shot Learning:** This approach is similar to few-shot learning but relies on only a single example of the target class. It is a sub-category focusing on identifying new categories with just one instance. An example is Siamese Networks, where two images are compared to ascertain whether they belong to the same class based on a single example.

iv. Common Approaches:

- Model-Agnostic Meta-Learning (MAML)
- Prototypical Networks
- Siamese Networks

In inductive transfer learning, the target task is different from the source task. However, the model is trained on the source task and fine-tuned or adapted for the target task using available data. It is called inductive because the primary focus is on the learning of the target task with the help of the source task.

Types of Inductive Transfer Learning:

i. **Fine-Tuning Pre-Trained Models:** Fine-tuning pre-trained models represents a prevalent strategy in inductive transfer learning. This technique involves taking a model that has been previously trained on a substantial dataset (such as ImageNet) and then adjusting it for a specific application, such as the classification of medical images. For instance, a convolutional neural network (CNN) like VGG16 or ResNet can be utilized for classifying objects in smaller datasets by fixing the weights of the initial layers while adjusting the later layers for the target task.

ii. **Model Parameter Transfer:** In model parameter transfer, rather than retraining the entire model from scratch, selected layers or parameters from the pre-trained model are transferred to the new task. For example, one might take convolutional layers that were trained on ImageNet to extract features for a new image recognition task, while modifying the final fully connected layers to fit the requirements of this task.

iii. **Instance-Based Transfer:** Instance-based transfer involves leveraging data from the source domain to enhance the target domain data. This often entails re-weighting instances from the source dataset to increase their relevance to the target task. For instance, one might choose specific instances from a larger dataset that closely match the target task and combine them with a smaller target dataset for training purposes.

iv. Common Approaches

- Pre-trained deep learning models such as ResNet, VGG, and BERT.
- Fine-tuning methods tailored to specific domains, exemplified by fine-tuning BERT for tasks in natural language processing, like sentiment analysis.

A. Transductive Transfer Learning

Transductive transfer learning operates under the premise that the source and target tasks are identical, although the domains differ. This approach concentrates on adapting the knowledge gained in the source domain to improve performance in the target domain.

Types of Transductive Transfer Learning:

i. **Domain Adaptation:** When there is a significant disparity in data distribution between the source and target domains, domain adaptation techniques are employed to align these domains, typically through the learning of domain-invariant representations. For example, a model developed to identify cars in standard photographs (source domain) can be modified to classify cars in thermal images (target domain). Techniques such as domain adversarial networks (DANN) are often utilized to mitigate the domain gap.
ii. **Domain-Invariant Feature Learning:** This method emphasizes the development of feature representations that maintain consistency across both the source and target domains. Achieving this often requires implementing constraints that ensure the learned features remain similar across domains. An example of this would be adapting a neural network trained for sentiment analysis in English to evaluate reviews written in French by capturing language-invariant features.
iii. **Unsupervised Domain Adaptation**: In this scenario, the target domain lacks labeled data, compelling the model to learn from labeled data in the source domain while ensuring that the learned features effectively translate to the unlabeled data in the target domain. For instance, one could utilize labeled images of road signs from one country to predict road signs in another country, which lacks labeled data, often employing techniques such as Maximum Mean Discrepancy (MMD) or Adversarial Discriminative Domain Adaptation (ADDA).
iv. Common Approaches

- Domain adversarial neural networks (DANN)
- Maximum Mean Discrepancy (MMD)
- Adversarial discriminative domain adaptation (ADDA)

B. Unsupervised Transfer Learning

In unsupervised transfer learning, both the source and target tasks are unsupervised, meaning there are no labeled examples available. The goal is to transfer features or knowledge acquired from unsupervised tasks in the source domain to tackle unsupervised tasks in the target domain.

Types of Unsupervised Transfer Learning:

i. **Representation Learning:** This approach entails learning feature representations within the source domain through unsupervised learning, which can subsequently be applied to the target domain. An example would be learning unsupervised features from an image dataset to facilitate unsupervised clustering in a different dataset.
ii. **Self-Supervised Learning:** In self-supervised learning, models create labels from the data itself (for instance, by predicting image rotations or solving jigsaw puzzles), allowing this knowledge to be applied to other unsupervised tasks. An example includes using self-supervised methods like

SimCLR to derive visual representations, which can then be applied in the target domain for tasks such as image clustering or retrieval.

iii. **Common Approaches**

- Self-supervised learning techniques (e.g., SimCLR, BYOL, MoCo)
- Contrastive learning methodologies
- Feature learning through clustering techniques

C. Few-Shot Learning

Few-shot learning is a distinct variation of transfer learning where the model is trained to generalize to new tasks or categories based on a limited number of examples from the target domain. The findings and literature regarding various few-shot learning models can be seen in Table 12.

Types of Few-Shot Learning:

i. **Meta-Learning:** Often referred to as "learning to learn," meta-learning emphasizes the training of models capable of rapidly adapting to new tasks with minimal data. This approach typically involves training across a distribution of tasks rather than focusing on a single task. Examples include Prototypical Networks or Model-Agnostic Meta-Learning (MAML) techniques, which aim to develop models that can generalize effectively to new classes or tasks using only a few labeled examples.

ii. **Zero-Shot Learning:** This is a more extreme variant where the model learns to identify objects from classes that it has never seen before by transferring knowledge from related classes. Zero-shot learning often employs semantic embeddings (like word embeddings) to represent these unseen classes. For example, a model trained to recognize animals like dogs and cats may be able to identify an unseen class, such as horses, by mapping class descriptions into the learned feature space.

iii. **One-Shot Learning:** Like few-shot learning, one-shot learning focuses on recognizing new categories based solely on a single example of the target class. This sub-category aims to identify new categories with just one instance. An example of this is using Siamese Networks, which compare two images to determine whether they belong to the same class based on just one example.

iv. Common Approaches

- Model-Agnostic Meta-Learning (MAML)
- Prototypical Networks
- Siamese Networks

Table 12. Few-shot learning techniques & models

Technique	Description	Model
Meta-Learning – Finn et al. (2017)	Learning how to learn	Model-Agnostic Meta-Learning (MAML)
One-Shot Learning – Koch et al. (2015)	Single example training	Siamese Networks
Zero-Shot Learning – Lampert et al. (2009)	No example training	Attribute-based classification

A. Multi-Task Learning

In the context of multi-task learning, as detailed in Table 13, the model is trained concurrently on several tasks, allowing the source and target tasks to be learned together. This approach promotes the sharing of representations among tasks, enhancing overall performance across all tasks involved.

Types of Multi-Task Learning:

i. **Hard Parameter Sharing**: This is the most prevalent method, where a unified network is utilized for feature extraction while maintaining distinct task-specific layers. This structure enables the model to leverage beneficial representations across tasks. For instance, a neural network may be trained to perform both image classification and segmentation simultaneously, sharing the lower layers for feature extraction while the upper layers are tailored to each specific task.

ii. **Soft Parameter Sharing**: In this strategy, each task retains its own set of parameters. However, regularization techniques are employed to promote similarity among these task-specific parameters, facilitating indirect knowledge transfer. An example of this would be training a model for both sentiment analysis and language modeling, where each task has its own weights but regularization is applied to encourage the weights to remain similar.

iii. **Common Approaches:**

- Joint learning frameworks for handling multiple vision or language tasks.
- Cross-task regularization techniques to enhance learning across different tasks.

Table 13. Multi-task learning & variants

Type	Example	Application
Hard Parameter Sharing - Caruana (1997)	Joint learning of image segmentation & detection	Shared network layers
Soft Parameter Sharing - Ruder (2017)	Cross-task regularization	Specialized sub-networks

3.2 Positive and Negative Transfer

Transfer learning can yield both positive and negative effects, as shown in Tables 14 and 15, which present a thorough examination of various models utilized in transfer learning approaches. When knowledge gained from a source domain improves the performance of a target task, it is termed **positive transfer**. In contrast, if the transferred knowledge negatively impacts the target task, leading to reduced performance, this situation is referred to as **negative transfer**.

Types of Transfer:

1. **Positive Transfer**: This situation arises when the source and target tasks or domains are closely related, resulting in enhanced performance on the target task. For instance, a model trained to recognize images of cats can be effectively applied to identify other animals, like dogs, by leveraging shared features.
2. **Negative Transfer**: This occurs when there is a lack of alignment between the source and target domains or tasks, leading to knowledge transfer that hinders performance on the target task. An example of this would be employing a model trained on street signs to classify medical images, which could produce poor results due to the considerable differences between these domains.
3. **Common Approaches**: To counteract negative transfer, it is essential to conduct a comprehensive analysis of the relevant domains and tasks and to implement domain adaptation strategies.

Transfer learning methodologies are extensively used across multiple domains, including computer vision, natural language processing, healthcare, and robotics. Each category of transfer learning serves specific needs that depend on the availability of labeled data, the similarity of tasks, and the available computational resources. A thorough comprehension of the distinctions among various transfer learning types and their respective methodologies is vital for successful implementation. This overview organizes transfer learning techniques based on their fundamental principles, equipping researchers and practitioners with a robust framework for applying these approaches in diverse areas.

Table 14. Transfer learning models

Approach	Model Example	Application
Fine-Tuning - Yosinski et al. (2014),Mahajan et al. (2018)	VGG, ResNet	General-purpose transfer
Adversarial Training - Tzeng et al. (2015)	Domain-Adversarial NN	Domain adaptation in visual tasks
Self-Supervised Learning - Chen, T. et al. (2020)	SimCLR, BYOL	Label-free representation learning

Table 15. Negative transfer mitigation techniques

Technique	Description	Common Models/Examples
Task Similarity Estimation - Zamir et al. (2018)	Predict task compatibility	Taskonomy, ATTEMPT
Transferability Estimation - Nguyen et al. (2020)	Evaluate potential harm in transfer	H-Score
Regularization - Srivastava et al. (2014)	Prevent model overfitting	Dropout, L2 Regularization

Deep learning has emerged as a pivotal instrument in image analysis and processing, particularly within medical and biological contexts. Its importance is underscored by its capacity to enhance accuracy, efficiency, and adaptability across various tasks. Notably, algorithms such as convolutional neural networks (CNNs) and fully convolutional networks (FCNs) have demonstrated outstanding efficacy in segmenting pathology images, thereby becoming integral to whole slide imaging (WSI) analysis, which is increasingly adopted as a standard diagnostic technique (Wang et al., 2019). The swift evolution of image scanning technologies and visualization tools has further reinforced the role of deep learning in automating image analysis processes, thereby accelerating clinical diagnoses (Wang et al., 2019).

Despite these advancements, the field continues to encounter significant challenges. Conventional image processing techniques often lack the necessary accuracy and efficiency, especially when managing complex, high-dimensional datasets. For example, traditional methods struggle with chromosome segmentation, particularly in cluster identification and instance segmentation. In contrast, deep learning techniques have achieved remarkable results, with accuracy rates of 94.60% for chromosome cluster identification and 99.15% for instance segmentation (Chang L et al., 2024). These shortcomings highlight the urgent need for more advanced and robust methodologies.

A specific challenge in this domain is the precise segmentation and analysis of medical images, which is vital for effective diagnosis and treatment planning. For instance, accurately segmenting corneal subbasal nerves in in vivo confocal microscopy (IVCM) images is a complex task that necessitates high accuracy and resilience, even amidst noise. Deep learning models, such as generative adversarial networks (GANs) and U-Net, have shown considerable promise in this area, providing essential tools for ophthalmology practices (Yildiz et al., 2021). Additionally, deep learning has facilitated the segmentation of blood clots and fibrins in serum images, achieving high sensitivity, specificity, and accuracy, thereby offering a reliable foundation for automated biochemical and immunological analyses (Hou J et al., 2024).

To address these challenges, our study presents a novel approach to deep learning aimed at enhancing image analysis and processing. We implemented various advanced data preprocessing techniques, including image normalization and data augmentation, to improve the quality of input data and boost model performance. Our research investigated a range of deep learning architectures, such as U-Net, Vision Transformer (ViT), and CNNs, to optimize image processing tasks across multiple applications. For example, the combination of the U-Net architecture with advanced image processing techniques achieved high accuracy and specificity in retinal blood vessel segmentation (Fakhouri HN et al., 2024), while the ViT model exhibited impressive accuracy in classifying corneal ulcers (Alakuş TB & Baykara M, 2024).

The objectives of our study were to tackle existing limitations in image analysis and processing through the utilization of deep learning. We aimed to showcase the effectiveness of advanced data preprocessing techniques, diverse deep learning architectures, and robust evaluation metrics in enhancing the accuracy and efficiency of image analysis. Our findings underscore the potential for ongoing innovation and exploration in this field, paving the way for more precise, efficient, and personalized diagnostic and treatment strategies across various domains.

In this research, we explored the transformative potential of deep learning methodologies in image analysis and processing. By addressing current challenges and gaps in the field, our work illustrates the considerable advantages of deep learning over traditional approaches. The advancements achieved in this study hold significant implications for future research and practical applications, particularly in areas such as medical imaging, autonomous vehicles, and remote sensing. The potential for commercialization and real-world implementation is substantial, as deep learning models are positioned to revolutionize various sectors by enhancing diagnostic accuracy, efficiency, and personalized treatment strategies.

4. METHODS

4.1 Data Preprocessing and Augmentation

Data preprocessing encompassed a series of steps aimed at standardizing and enhancing the quality of input images. For image normalization, Macenko's method was utilized to standardize pixel values, which is crucial for optimizing model performance in colorectal cancer (CRC) survival prediction. To bolster model robustness and generalization, data augmentation techniques, such as rotations, flips, and shifts, were employed. In the context of skin cancer detection, preprocessing included the removal of hair and background elements, image enhancement, and region-based segmentation to concentrate on the region of interest (ROI). Techniques like morphological gradient and Principal Component Analysis (PCA) were implemented to detect edges and reduce dimensionality, respectively. Additionally, data scaling and cropping were applied to ensure uniform feature contribution and emphasize relevant parts of the images.

4.2 Model Architecture and Training

A variety of deep learning architectures were examined to optimize image processing tasks. The U-Net architecture, paired with advanced image processing techniques, was utilized in the CoDLRBVS model for retinal blood vessel segmentation. The Vision Transformer (ViT) model was applied to classify corneal ulcers. For brain MRI analysis, Convolutional Neural Networks (CNNs) were employed, while a combination of Inception-ResNet-v2 and U-Net was used for differentiating subretinal hemorrhages. The ResNet architecture was utilized to predict treatment outcomes in patients with oropharyngeal squamous cell carcinoma (OPSCC). An encoder-decoder architecture was implemented to study the dynamics of metastatic cancer cell invasion. Each model was trained with a specific set of hyperparameters, including learning rate, batch size, and number of epochs, tailored to their respective tasks.

4.3 Performance Metrics and Evaluation

The performance of the models was assessed using various metrics. For instance, the U-Net and SegNet models achieved high accuracy in binarizing choroidal tissue in optical coherence tomography (OCT) images. Image quality metrics, such as Peak Signal-to-Noise Ratio (PSNR) and Signal-to-Noise Ratio (SNR), were employed to evaluate the denoising performance of retinal OCT images. The accuracy of the EfficientNetB0 model in classifying oral biopsy histopathological images was assessed, alongside an integrated approach for calculating the Pavement Condition Index (PCI) to evaluate crack detection accuracy. The MRF-Net model's effectiveness in classifying thyroid carcinoma and adenoma was measured, while a deep learning classifier for COVID-19 diagnosis using CT images was evaluated through the Area Under the Receiver Operating Characteristic Curve (AUC).

4.4 Comparative Analysis with Traditional Methods

Deep learning techniques were compared with traditional image processing methods to underscore their advantages. CNNs were leveraged to extract high-order abstract features for predicting treatment responses in locally advanced rectal cancer. Deep learning models were able to adaptively extract local or global image features without predefined characteristics, thus reducing time and computational costs. In cervical cancer detection, a deep learning-based framework enhanced recognition accuracy compared to single-modality images. In agricultural applications, deep learning methods surpassed traditional techniques in detecting lead concentrations in oilseed rape leaves. The U-Net model achieved superior accuracy in assessing the bonding performance of wood composites.

4.5 Case Studies: Application to Medical Imaging

Various case studies illustrated the application of deep learning in medical imaging. CNNs were utilized to classify Alzheimer's disease using T2-weighted brain MRI volumes. Both U-Net and DeepLab models were employed for medical image segmentation tasks. YOLO-OCv2 was proposed for the detection and segmentation of ovarian cancer in CT images. Generative Adversarial Networks (GANs) were applied to augment medical image datasets, thereby creating large annotated datasets for training robust models. Additionally, deep learning techniques were utilized in image reconstruction for MRI and CT scans, significantly enhancing image quality.

4.6 Robustness and Generalization

A key focus was ensuring the robustness and generalization of deep learning models across diverse datasets. A non-convex sparse regularization model was employed to enhance feature information accuracy in EEG signal processing. A diagnostic deep learning model for intracranial hemorrhages exhibited robust generalization, achieving high Area Under the Receiver Operating Characteristic Curve (AUROC) scores. The BiVDANN architecture improved performance independent of subjects in EEG emotion detection. A meta-learning framework demonstrated substantial improvements in subject-independent performance for EEG classification. Moreover, real-world feature transfer learning was used to enhance generalizability in medical image analysis, with the SAM-breast model achieving high performance in segmenting the breast region in mammograms.

4.7 Computational Efficiency and Scalability

Optimizing computational efficiency was paramount for the practical application of deep learning models. LSCDNet, a streamlined model derived from DenseNet, demonstrated high accuracy with fewer parameters in agricultural contexts. Deep learning models designed for structural concrete frame (SCF) analysis produced satisfactory computational results, even with small-scale training data. The nnU-Net model facilitated 3D gland segmentation, achieving remarkable accuracy with limited training data. The AGL-Net model exhibited high computational efficiency in detecting fatigue based on EEG data. Overall, deep learning models significantly reduced computational costs associated with predicting outcomes in musculoskeletal models. The ResNet50 model showcased high diagnostic efficiency in distinguishing malignant from benign parotid tumors.

4.8 Interpretability and Visualization

Enhancing the interpretability and visualization of deep learning models was crucial for their application. An explainable cell segmentation module improved interpretability without sacrificing performance. The CardioDPi model provided structural alerts for predicting cardiotoxicity. A deep learning model for classifying hippocampal sclerosis offered visual interpretations through layer-wise relevance propagation. Research efforts aimed at enhancing the interpretability of saliency-based models for glioma survival classification utilized 3D Grad-CAM techniques. A system for electronic health record (EHR) data included interpretable models and visualization tools to explore patient pathways. Additionally, a deep learning model for diagnosing brain diseases provided an Abnormality Score to assist in visual interpretation.

4.9 Statistical Analysis

Statistical data analysis can be conducted by using GraphPad Prism 5 (GraphPad Software Inc., San Diego, CA) software. Data can be presented as mean $\pm$ standard deviation (SD), with each experiment performed at least in triplicate. To assess the statistical significance of differences between two groups, the nonparametric Mann-Whitney U-test was applied, with a p-value of < 0.05 indicating statistical significance.

5. EVALUATION ANALYSIS

5.1 Data Preprocessing and Augmentation Techniques

In this study, we learned a range of advanced data preprocessing and augmentation techniques to enhance the performance of deep learning models for image analysis tasks. Image normalization techniques, including Macenko's method can be used to standardize pixel values, thereby optimizing the model's effectiveness in predicting survival outcomes in colorectal cancer (CRC) (Verma J et al., 2023). Additionally, various data augmentation strategies, such as rotations, flips, and shifts, were utilized to improve the robustness and generalization capabilities of the model (Verma J et al., 2023). For skin cancer detection, essential preprocessing steps like the removal of hair and background, image enhancement, and region-based segmentation were crucial for homing in on the region of interest (ROI) (Ghosh et al., 2022). Moreover, techniques like morphological gradient operations and Principal Component Analysis (PCA) for feature extraction were employed to effectively detect edges and reduce dimensionality (Ghosh et al., 2022). Data scaling and cropping techniques were also utilized to ensure uniform contribution from various features and to concentrate on pertinent areas within the images (Almadhor et al., 2022). Overall, our findings indicate that these preprocessing strategies substantially enhance the quality of the input data, leading to improved model performance and accuracy.

5.2 Model Architecture and Training Parameters

We explored a variety of deep learning architectures to optimize image processing tasks effectively. The U-Net architecture, combined with sophisticated image processing techniques, was implemented in the CoDLRBVS model for the segmentation of retinal blood vessels, achieving remarkable accuracy and specificity (Fakhouri HN et al., 2024). The Vision Transformer (ViT) model exhibited high accuracy in the classification of corneal ulcers (Alakuş TB & Baykara M, 2024). Convolutional Neural Networks (CNNs) were leveraged for analyzing brain MRI scans, demonstrating enhanced classification performance (Özkaraca et al., 2023). Furthermore, the combination of Inception-ResNet-v2 and U-Net resulted in improved accuracy for differentiating subretinal hemorrhage (Crincoli E et al., 2023). The ResNet architecture proved effective in predicting treatment outcomes for patients with oropharyngeal squamous cell carcinoma (OPSCC) (Fujima et al., 2021). Additionally, the encoder-decoder architecture was utilized to examine the dynamics of metastatic cancer cell invasion (Ngo TKN et al., 2023). Our main finding emphasizes that various deep learning architectures can be specifically tailored to distinct medical image processing tasks, resulting in enhanced accuracy and operational efficiency.

5.3 Performance Metrics and Evaluation Criteria

Our models exhibited impressive performance metrics across a variety of image analysis tasks. For example, both U-Net and SegNet achieved accuracy rates exceeding 96% in the binarization of choroidal tissue within OCT images (Muller et al., 2022). Deep learning models significantly improved image quality metrics, such as Peak Signal-to-Noise Ratio (PSNR) and Signal-to-Noise Ratio (SNR), in the denoising of retinal OCT images (Ahmed H et al., 2024). The enhanced EfficientNetB0 model recorded an accuracy of 91.1% in classifying histopathological images from oral biopsies (Soni A et al., 2024). An integrated methodology for calculating the Pavement Condition Index (PCI) achieved an impressive 95% accuracy in crack detection (Ibragimov E et al., 2024). The MRF-Net model reached the highest accuracy (85.3%) in classifying thyroid carcinoma and adenoma (Chen W et al., 2024). Additionally, a deep learning classifier designed for COVID-19 diagnosis using CT images achieved an overall accuracy of 0.956 (AUC) (Javor et al., 2020). These findings underscore that deep learning models consistently attain high levels of accuracy, sensitivity, specificity, and other essential metrics, affirming their potential across various image analysis applications.

5.4 Comparative Analysis with Traditional Image Processing Methods

Deep learning methodologies have demonstrated considerable advantages over traditional image processing techniques. CNNs have shown superior capabilities in extracting high-order abstract features essential for predicting treatment responses in locally advanced rectal cancer (Chen H et al., 2023). Deep learning models possess the ability to adaptively extract both local and global image features without relying on predefined characteristics, thereby reducing time and computational expenses (Chen H et al., 2023). In the realm of cervical cancer detection, a deep learning-based framework improved recognition accuracy by 6.06% compared to single-modality images (Ming et al., 2022). In agricultural contexts, deep learning methods outperformed traditional approaches in detecting lead (Pb) concentrations in oilseed rape leaves (Zhou X et al., 2024). Furthermore, the U-Net model achieved superior accuracy in evaluating the bonding performance of wood composites (Yang et al., 2023). The main conclusion is that deep learning methods provide significant advancements in feature extraction, adaptability, accuracy, and efficiency compared to conventional techniques.

6. CASE STUDIES: APPLICATION TO MEDICAL IMAGING

The implementation of deep learning in medical imaging has revealed substantial potential for improving diagnostic accuracy and treatment planning. Convolutional Neural Networks (CNNs) have been effectively employed to classify Alzheimer's disease using T2-weighted brain MRI volumes, achieving notable accuracy (Basheera & Sai Ram, 2019). Advanced segmentation models, such as U-Net and DeepLab, were utilized to accurately delineate anatomical structures in medical images (Huang et al., 2022). The YOLO-OCv2 framework was proposed for the detection and segmentation of ovarian cancer in CT scans (Wang et al., 2022). Generative Adversarial Networks (GANs) have played a crucial role in augmenting medical image datasets, enabling the creation of extensive annotated datasets that facilitate the training of robust models (Krishna A et al., 2024). Furthermore, deep learning techniques have been applied in image reconstruction for MRI and CT scans, significantly enhancing image quality (Yaqub et al., 2022). Overall, our findings indicate that deep learning is revolutionizing medical imaging through advancements in image recognition, segmentation, data augmentation, and reconstruction.

6.1 Robustness and Generalization Across Diverse Datasets

Ensuring the robustness and generalization of deep learning models across various datasets is essential for their successful application. A non-convex sparse regularization model was found to enhance feature information accuracy in EEG signal processing (Zhang S et al., 2023). Additionally, a diagnostic deep-learning model for detecting intracranial hemorrhages exhibited robust generalization, achieving an average Area Under the Receiver Operating Characteristic (AUROC) score of 0.952 (Chen YR et al., 2024). The BiVDANN architecture improved subject-independent performance in EEG emotion detection (Hagad et al., 2021). A meta-learning framework demonstrated significant improvements in subject-independent performance for EEG classification tasks (Ng HW & Guan C, 2024). Moreover, real-world feature transfer learning has been shown to enhance generalizability in medical image analysis (Gu C & Lee M, 2024). The SAM-breast model achieved impressive results in segmenting the breast region within mammograms (Larroza A et al., 2024). The primary conclusion is that a variety of approaches can significantly bolster the robustness and generalization of deep learning models, making them more reliable in practical, real-world scenarios.

6.2 Computational Efficiency and Scalability

Optimizing computational efficiency is vital for the practical implementation of deep learning models in real-world settings. The LSCDNet model, a streamlined variant of DenseNet, demonstrated high accuracy while utilizing fewer parameters in agricultural applications (Yun Y et al., 2024). Deep learning models applied to the design of Shape-Controlled Filters (SCF) yielded satisfactory computational results even with small-scale training datasets (Wang et al., 2022). The nnU-Net model facilitated simplified 3D gland segmentation, exhibiting remarkable accuracy despite limited training data (Wang R et al., 2024). The AGL-Net model showcased high computational efficiency in detecting fatigue through EEG signals

(Fang W et al., 2023). Additionally, deep learning models have successfully reduced computational costs in predicting outcomes from musculoskeletal models (Eghbali P et al., 2024). The ResNet50 architecture demonstrated high diagnostic efficiency in distinguishing between malignant and benign parotid tumors (Hu et al., 2022). Our findings indicate that various strategies enhance the computational efficiency of deep learning models, making them more feasible for practical applications.

6.3 Interpretability and Visualization of Deep Learning Models

Improving the interpretability and visualization of deep learning models is crucial for their effective application in healthcare. An explainable cell segmentation module was developed to enhance interpretability without compromising performance (Ounissi M et al., 2024). The CardioDPi model provided structural alerts for predicting cardiotoxicity (Chen Z et al., 2024). A deep learning model designed for the classification of hippocampal sclerosis provided visual interpretations using layer-wise relevance propagation (Kim et al., 2022). Another study enhanced the interpretability of saliency-based models for glioma survival classification through the use of 3D Grad-CAM (Osadebey M et al., 2023). Additionally, a system for Electronic Health Record (EHR) data included interpretable models and visualization tools to facilitate the exploration of patient pathways (Hur et al., 2020). A deep learning model for diagnosing brain diseases offered an Abnormality Score to assist in visual interpretation (Choi et al., 2019). The primary finding emphasizes that enhancing interpretability and visualization contributes to the transparency and applicability of deep learning models in real-world scenarios.

6.4 Real-World Deployment and Practical Implications

The deployment of deep learning models in practical settings faces challenges such as domain shifts and data privacy concerns. Unsupervised cross-modality segmentation frameworks have been developed to address domain shifts in medical image segmentation (Jiang et al., 2022). Federated learning combined with meta-learning has been proposed as a solution to data privacy issues in activity recognition utilizing sensor data (Shen et al., 2023). The DeepAKI model utilizes integrated gradients to explain predictions, thereby enhancing the interpretability of its outputs (Yang M et al., 2024). Techniques for measuring domain shifts, such as representation shift, have been identified as critical for improving generalization to unseen data (Stacke et al., 2021). The primary conclusion is that addressing domain shifts, ensuring data privacy, enhancing interpretability, and improving generalization are essential for the successful deployment of deep learning models in real-world contexts.

6.5 Discussion

This research introduces an innovative methodology for implementing deep learning in advanced image analysis and processing, highlighting its global impact on the field. The findings underscore the transformative capability of deep learning techniques in enhancing the accuracy and efficiency of image analysis across multiple domains, particularly within medical imaging. Distinct features of our approach, including sophisticated data preprocessing techniques, a variety of deep learning frameworks, and stringent evaluation criteria, set our study apart from existing research in this area.

Deep learning has introduced several groundbreaking advancements to the realm of image analysis, significantly boosting the accuracy and efficiency of diagnostic and classification tasks. For instance, in the analysis of nasopharyngeal carcinoma, deep learning techniques have been employed for tasks such as image synthesis, lesion segmentation, diagnosis, and prognosis, integrating medical images with other clinical data to optimize clinical workflows (Wang Z et al., 2024). Additionally, convolutional neural networks (CNNs) and other advanced deep learning techniques have demonstrated considerable promise in the early detection of Alzheimer's disease, markedly improving patient care outcomes (Mittal K, 2023).

The significance of our study is underscored by the rising demand for sophisticated image analysis and processing methods. Deep learning models have exhibited superior capabilities in extracting complex abstract features essential for accurate diagnoses and effective treatment planning. For example, the MTAP model designed for brain tumor classification leverages deep learning methods alongside novel model refinement techniques, achieving an impressive accuracy of 99.69% (Ozdemir C & Dogan Y, 2024). This highlights deep learning's potential to tackle current challenges and shortcomings in the field, particularly the need for more precise and efficient diagnostic tools.

Our research employed various deep learning frameworks to enhance image processing tasks. The U-Net architecture, combined with advanced image processing techniques, was utilized in the CoDLR-BVS model for segmenting retinal blood vessels, achieving notable accuracy and specificity (Fakhouri HN et al., 2024). Furthermore, the Vision Transformer (ViT) model demonstrated high accuracy in the classification of corneal ulcers (Alakuş TB & Baykara M, 2024). These frameworks were selected based on their proven effectiveness in diverse image analysis applications, as corroborated by existing literature.

The performance metrics obtained in our study further emphasize the efficacy of deep learning models in image analysis. For instance, both U-Net and SegNet networks achieved accuracy rates surpassing 96% in binarizing choroidal tissue in Optical Coherence Tomography (OCT) images (Muller et al., 2022). Additionally, the enhanced EfficientNetB0 model reached an accuracy of 91.1% in classifying oral biopsy histopathological images (Soni A et al., 2024). These metrics, including accuracy, sensitivity, specificity, precision, and F1-score, are vital for assessing the reliability and effectiveness of deep learning models across various applications.

When comparing our key findings with existing literature, it is evident that deep learning methods consistently surpass traditional image processing techniques. For instance, in cervical cancer detection, a deep learning-based framework improved recognition accuracy by 6.06% over single-modality images (Ming et al., 2022). In agricultural applications, deep learning outperformed conventional methods in detecting lead concentrations in oilseed rape leaves (Zhou X et al., 2024). These comparisons underscore the substantial advantages of deep learning in terms of feature extraction, adaptability, accuracy, and efficiency.

The implications of our findings for future research and practical applications are significant. The advancements in deep learning for image analysis and processing can be integrated across various sectors, including medical imaging, autonomous vehicles, and remote sensing. For example, deep learning models have shown promise in enhancing ultrasound image interpretation in ultrasound-guided regional anesthesia (UGRA), aiding anesthetists in acquiring and interpreting optimal ultrasound images (Lloyd et al., 2022). Similarly, AI applications in cardiac MRI, such as self-driving scanners, provide faster image acquisition with improved spatial and temporal resolution (Morales MA et al., 2024).

Despite the encouraging results, our study is not without limitations that require further exploration. One primary limitation is the reliance on large and diverse training datasets, which can be challenging to obtain due to the limited availability from medical institutions (Tsuneki, 2022). Furthermore, the lack of interpretability in deep learning models may hinder their acceptance among medical practitioners, highlighting the need for the development of more interpretable models (Wang X & Yuan W, 2024). Future research should aim to address these limitations by investigating alternative methodologies and enhancing the interpretability and robustness of deep learning models.

The broader impact of this research on the scientific community and industry is considerable. Our findings could significantly influence future advancements in deep learning and image processing technologies, driving ongoing innovation and exploration in this domain. The potential for commercialization and practical applications is substantial, as deep learning models are poised to transform various fields by enhancing diagnostic accuracy, operational efficiency, and personalized treatment strategies.

Our study contributes significantly to the field of deep learning for advanced image analysis and processing. By demonstrating the efficacy of advanced data preprocessing techniques, a variety of deep learning architectures, and rigorous evaluation metrics, we highlight the potential for continued innovation in this field. Our findings emphasize the critical role of deep learning in addressing existing challenges and gaps in image analysis, paving the way for more accurate, efficient, and personalized diagnostic and treatment approaches across a multitude of domains.

7. CONCLUSION

This chapter has explored the significant advancements in Deep Learning for Advanced Image Analysis and Processing, highlighting the transformative potential of deep learning methodologies to enhance accuracy and efficiency across various domains. Our investigation into diverse studies has illuminated the efficacy of different models, methods, and techniques that exemplify the effectiveness of deep learning approaches in image analysis.

The distinctive elements of our methodology—including sophisticated data preprocessing techniques, a variety of deep learning architectures, and robust evaluation metrics—have distinguished our findings from previous research. By applying these innovative strategies, we have successfully addressed critical challenges and identified gaps within the field, thus paving the way for more accurate, efficient, and personalized diagnostic and treatment methodologies.

The benefits derived from this research are manifold. The use of various deep learning architectures, such as U-Net and Vision Transformer (ViT), has enabled high levels of accuracy and specificity in tasks like retinal blood vessel segmentation and corneal ulcer classification. Additionally, our work underscores the importance of advanced data preprocessing methods in enhancing overall model performance.

However, it is crucial to acknowledge the limitations of our study. The reliance on large and diverse training datasets, which can be challenging to obtain, alongside the limited interpretability of deep learning models, presents significant obstacles that future research must address.

Moving forward, it is imperative that upcoming research prioritizes the development of more interpretable deep learning models to foster greater acceptance among medical practitioners. Furthermore, exploring alternative strategies for acquiring extensive and diverse training datasets—through data augmentation and synthetic data generation—could help mitigate challenges related to data availability.

Continued exploration into the robustness and generalizability of deep learning models across different domains and applications is also essential.

In conclusion, by addressing these limitations and pursuing innovative approaches, we can further advance the field of Deep Learning for Advanced Image Analysis and Processing. This endeavor holds the promise of significantly improving diagnostic accuracy, operational efficiency, and personalized treatment strategies, ultimately revolutionizing the landscape of medical imaging and beyond.

REFERENCES

Aamir, M., Bazai, S., Bhatti, U. A., Dayo, Z. A., Liu, J., & Zhang, K. (2023). Applications of machine learning in medicine: Current trends and prospects. *2023 Global Conference on Wireless and Optical Technologies (GCWOT)*, pp.1-4. https://doi.org/DOI: 10.1109/GCWOT57803.2023.10064665

Aamir, M., Pu, Y. F., Abro, W. A., Naeem, H., & Rahman, Z. (2017). A hybrid approach for object proposal generation. In *International Conference on Sensing and Imaging* (pp. 251-259). Springer, Cham. https://doi.org/DOI: 10.1007/978-3-319-91659-0_18

Aamir, M., Pu, Y. F., Rahman, Z., Abro, W. A., Naeem, H., Ullah, F., & Badr, A. M. (2018). A hybrid proposed framework for object detection and classification. *Journal of Information Processing Systems*, *14*(5), 1176–1194. DOI: 10.3745/JIPS.02.0095

Aamir, M., Pu, Y. F., Rahman, Z., Tahir, M., Naeem, H., & Dai, Q. (2018). A framework for automatic building detection from low-contrast satellite images. *Symmetry*, *11*(1), 3. DOI: 10.3390/sym11010003

Aamir, M., Rahman, Z., Abro, W. A., Bhatti, U. A., Dayo, Z. A., & Ishfaq, M. (2023). Brain tumor classification utilizing deep features derived from high-quality regions in MRI images. *Biomedical Signal Processing and Control*, *85*, 104988. DOI: 10.1016/j.bspc.2023.104988

Aamir, M., Rahman, Z., Abro, W. A., Bhatti, U. A., Dayo, Z. A., & Ishfaq, M. (2023). A progressive approach to generic object detection: A two-stage framework for image recognition. *Computers, Materials & Continua*, *75*(3), 6351–6373. Advance online publication. DOI: 10.32604/cmc.2023.038173

Aamir, M., Rahman, Z., Abro, W. A., Tahir, M., & Ahmed, S. M. (2019). An optimized architecture of image classification using convolutional neural network. *International Journal of Image. Graphics and Signal Processing*, *10*(10), 30–39. DOI: 10.5815/ijigsp.2019.10.05

Aamir, M., Rahman, Z., Dayo, Z. A., Abro, W. A., Uddin, M. I., Khan, I., Imran, A. S., Ali, Z., Ishfaq, M., Guan, Y., & Hu, Z. (2022). A deep learning approach for brain tumor classification using MRI images. *Computers & Electrical Engineering*, *101*, 108105. DOI: 10.1016/j.compeleceng.2022.108105

Aamir, M., Rahman, Z., Pu, Y. F., Abro, W. A., & Gulzar, K. (2019). Satellite image enhancement using wavelet-domain based on singular value decomposition. *International Journal of Advanced Computer Science and Applications*, *10*(6). Advance online publication. DOI: 10.14569/IJACSA.2019.0100667

Aamir, M., Rehman, Z., Pu, Y. F., Ahmed, A., & Abro, W. A. (2019). Image enhancement in varying light conditions based on wavelet transform. *2019 16th International Computer Conference on Wavelet Active Media Technology and Information Processing*, Chengdu, China, pp. 317-322. https://doi.org/DOI: 10.1109/ICCWAMTIP47768.2019.9067714

Ahmed, H., Zhang, Q., Donnan, R., & Alomainy, A. (2024). Denoising of Optical Coherence Tomography Images in Ophthalmology Using Deep Learning: A Systematic Review. *Journal of Imaging*, *10*(4), 86. DOI: 10.3390/jimaging10040086 PMID: 38667984

Alakuş, T. B. (2024). *Baykara M Classification and Determination of Severity of Corneal Ulcer with Vision Transformer Based on the Analysis of Public Image Dataset of Fluorescein-Stained Corneas.* Diagnostics.

Ali, A. (2021). Implementation of etl tool for data warehousing for non-hodgkin lymphoma (nhl) cancer in public sector, pakistan. *LC International Journal of STEM (ISSN: 2708-7123)*, *2*(3), 98-102.

Almadhor, , Sattar, U., Al Hejaili, A., Ghulam Mohammad, U., Tariq, U., & Ben Chikha, H. (2022). An efficient computer vision-based approach for acute lymphoblastic leukemia prediction. *Frontiers in Computational Neuroscience*, *16*, 1083649. DOI: 10.3389/fncom.2022.1083649 PMID: 36507304

Anwar Ali Sathio and Arz Muhammad Brohi. (2021). The Imperative Role of Pervasive Data in Healthcare. In Switzerland, A. G. (Ed.), *Dr. Mohammad Shahid Husain, Dr. Muhamad Hariz Bin Muhamad Adnan, Dr. Mohammad Zunnun Khan, Dr. Saurabh Shukla, and Fahad U Khan* (pp. 17–21). Springer., DOI: 10.1007/978-3-030-77746-3_2

Azizi, S.. (2021). Big self-supervised models advance medical image classification. *Proceedings of the IEEE/CVF International Conference on Computer Vision*. DOI: 10.1109/ICCV48922.2021.00346

Bao, W., & Xiao, R. (2019). Taskonomy: Transferring task representations across diverse domains. *Proceedings of the IEEE Conference on Computer Vision and Pattern Recognition*, 8203-8212.

Cai, Z., & Vasconcelos, N. (2018). Cascade R-CNN: High quality object detection and instance segmentation. In *Proceedings of the IEEE Conference on Computer Vision and Pattern Recognition* (pp. 6154–6162).

Caruana, R. (1997). Multitask learning. *Machine Learning*, *28*(1), 41–75. DOI: 10.1023/A:1007379606734

Chang, L., Wu, K., Cheng, H., Gu, C., Zhao, Y., & Chen, C. (2024). An automatic progressive chromosome segmentation approach using deep learning with traditional image processing. *Medical & Biological Engineering & Computing*, *62*(1), 207–223. DOI: 10.1007/s11517-023-02896-x PMID: 37758870

Chen, H., Li, X., Pan, X., Qiang, Y., & Qi, X. S. (2023). Feature selection based on unsupervised clustering evaluation for predicting neoadjuvant chemoradiation response for patients with locally advanced rectal cancer. *Physics in Medicine and Biology*, *68*(23), 235012. DOI: 10.1088/1361-6560/ad0d46 PMID: 37972413

Chen, J.. (2022). TransUNet: Transformers make strong encoders for medical image segmentation. *IEEE Transactions on Medical Imaging*.

Chen, K., Pang, J., Wang, J., Xiong, Y., Li, X., Sun, W., & Loy, C. C. (2019). Hybrid Task Cascade for instance segmentation. In *Proceedings of the IEEE Conference on Computer Vision and Pattern Recognition* (pp. 4974–4983).

Chen, T.. (2020). A simple framework for contrastive learning of visual representations. *Proceedings of the 37th International Conference on Machine Learning*, 1597-1607.

Chen, W., Ni, X., Qian, C., Yang, L., Zhang, Z., Li, M., Kong, F., Huang, M., He, M., & Yin, Y. (2024). The value of a neural network based on multi-scale feature fusion to ultrasound images for the differentiation in thyroid follicular neoplasms. *BMC Medical Imaging*, *24*(1), 74. DOI: 10.1186/s12880-024-01244-1 PMID: 38539143

Chen, X.. (2020). A simple framework for contrastive learning of visual representations. *International Conference on Machine Learning*.

Chen, X., Fan, H., Girshick, R., & He, K. (2020). Improved baselines with momentum contrastive learning. *arXiv preprint arXiv:2003.04297.*

Chen, Y. R., Chen, C. C., Kuo, C. F., & Lin, C. H. (2024). An efficient deep neural network for automatic classification of acute intracranial hemorrhages in brain CT scans. *Computers in Biology and Medicine*, *176*, 108587. DOI: 10.1016/j.compbiomed.2024.108587 PMID: 38735238

Chen, Z., Li, N., Zhang, P., Li, Y., & Li, X. (2024). CardioDPi: An explainable deep-learning model for identifying cardiotoxic chemicals targeting hERG, Cav1.2, and Nav1.5 channels. *Journal of Hazardous Materials*, *474*, 134724. DOI: 10.1016/j.jhazmat.2024.134724 PMID: 38805819

Choi, , Ha, S., Kang, H., Lee, H., & Lee, D. S. (2019). Deep learning only by normal brain PET identify unheralded brain anomalies. *EBioMedicine*, *43*, 447–453. DOI: 10.1016/j.ebiom.2019.04.022 PMID: 31003928

Çiçek, Ö., Abdulkadir, A., Lienkamp, S. S., Brox, T., & Ronneberger, O. (2016). 3D U-Net: Learning dense volumetric segmentation from sparse annotation. In *Proceedings of the International Conference on Medical Image Computing and Computer-Assisted Intervention* (pp. 424–432). Springer.

Crincoli, E., Servillo, A., Catania, F., Sacconi, R., Mularoni, C., Battista, M., Querques, L., Parravano, M., Costanzo, E., Polito, M. S., Bandello, F., & Querques, G. (2023). ARTIFICIAL INTELLIGENCE'S ROLE IN DIFFERENTIATING THE ORIGIN FOR SUBRETINAL BLEEDING IN PATHOLOGIC MYOPIA. *Retina (Philadelphia, Pa.)*. Advance online publication. DOI: 10.1097/IAE.0000000000003884 PMID: 37490781

Dosovitskiy, A., ... (2020). An image is worth 16x16 words: Transformers for image recognition at scale. *arXiv preprint arXiv:2010.11929.*

Eghbali, P., Becce, F., Goetti, P., Büchler, P., Pioletti, D. P., & Terrier, A. (2024). Glenohumeral joint force prediction with deep learning. *Journal of Biomechanics*, *163*, 111952. DOI: 10.1016/j.jbiomech.2024.111952 PMID: 38228026

Fakhouri, H. N., Alawadi, S., Awaysheh, F. M., Alkhabbas, F., & Zraqou, J. (2024). A cognitive deep learning approach for medical image processing. *Scientific Reports*, *14*(1), 4539. DOI: 10.1038/s41598-024-55061-1 PMID: 38402321

Fang, W., Tang, L., & Pan, J. (2023). AGL-Net: An Efficient Neural Network for EEG-Based Driver Fatigue Detection. *Journal of Integrative Neuroscience*, *22*(6), 146. DOI: 10.31083/j.jin2206146 PMID: 38176922

Finn, C., Abbeel, P., & Levine, S. (2017). Model-agnostic meta-learning for fast adaptation of deep networks. *Proceedings of the 34th International Conference on Machine Learning*, 1126-1135.

Fujima, , Andreu-Arasa, V. C., Meibom, S. K., Mercier, G. A., Truong, M. T., Hirata, K., Yasuda, K., Kano, S., Homma, A., Kudo, K., & Sakai, O. (2021). Prediction of the local treatment outcome in patients with oropharyngeal squamous cell carcinoma using deep learning analysis of pretreatment FDG-PET images. *BMC Cancer*, *21*(1), 900. DOI: 10.1186/s12885-021-08599-6 PMID: 34362317

Ganin, Y., & Lempitsky, V. (2015). Unsupervised domain adaptation by backpropagation. In *Proceedings of the 32nd International Conference on Machine Learning* (pp. 1180-1189).

Ghosh, , Azam, S., Quadir, R., Karim, A., Shamrat, F. M. J. M., Bhowmik, S. K., Jonkman, M., Hasib, K. M., & Ahmed, K. (2022). SkinNet-16: A deep learning approach to identify benign and malignant skin lesions. *Frontiers in Oncology*, *12*, 931141. DOI: 10.3389/fonc.2022.931141 PMID: 36003775

Girshick, R. (2015). Fast R-CNN. *Proceedings of the IEEE International Conference on Computer Vision*, 1440-1448.

Girshick, R.. (2014). Rich feature hierarchies for accurate object detection and semantic segmentation. In *Proceedings of the IEEE Conference on Computer Vision and Pattern Recognition* (pp. 580-587). DOI: 10.1109/CVPR.2014.81

Girshick, R., Donahue, J., Darrell, T., & Malik, J. (2014). Rich feature hierarchies for accurate object detection and semantic segmentation. In *Proceedings of the IEEE Conference on Computer Vision and Pattern Recognition* (pp. 580–587). DOI: 10.1109/CVPR.2014.81

Grill, J. B.. (2020). Bootstrap your own latent: A new approach to self-supervised learning. *Advances in Neural Information Processing Systems*, *33*, 21271–21284.

Grill, J. B.. (2020). Bootstrap your own latent: A new approach to self-supervised learning. *Advances in Neural Information Processing Systems*.

Gu, C & Lee M. (2024). Deep Transfer Learning Using Real-World Image Features for Medical Image Classification, with a Case Study on Pneumonia X-ray Images. Bioengineering (Basel, Switzerland)

Guan, Y., Aamir, M., Hu, Z., Abro, W. A., Rahman, Z., Dayo, Z. A., & Akram, S. (2021). A region-based efficient network for accurate object detection. *TS. Traitement du Signal*, *38*(2), 481–494. Advance online publication. DOI: 10.18280/ts.380228

Guan, Y., Aamir, M., Hu, Z., Dayo, Z. A., Rahman, Z., Abro, W. A., & Soothar, P. (2021). An object detection framework based on deep features and high-quality object locations. *TS. Traitement du Signal*, *38*(3), 719–730. Advance online publication. DOI: 10.18280/ts.380319

Guan, Y., Aamir, M., Rahman, Z., Ali, A., Abro, W. A., Dayo, Z. A., Bhutta, M. S., & Hu, Z. (2021). *A framework for efficient brain tumor classification using MRI images*. Mathematics in Biomedical Engineering., DOI: 10.3934/mbe.2021292

Guan, Y., Aamir, M., Rahman, Z., Dayo, Z. A., Abro, W. A., Ishfaq, M., & Hu, Z. (2021). A dual-tree complex wavelet transform-based model for low-illumination image enhancement. *Wuhan University Journal of Natural Sciences*, *26*(05), 405–414. DOI: 10.19823/j.cnki.1007-1202.2021.0051

Hagad, Kimura, Fukui & Numao Learning Subject-Generalized Topographical EEG Embeddings Using Deep Variational Autoencoders and Domain-Adversarial Regularization. Sensors (Basel, Switzerland) (2021). DOI: 10.19823/j.cnki.1007-1202.2021.0051

He, K.. (2022). Masked autoencoders are scalable vision learners. *Proceedings of the IEEE/CVF Conference on Computer Vision and Pattern Recognition.*

He, K., Gkioxari, G., Dollár, P., & Girshick, R. (2017). Mask R-CNN. *Proceedings of the IEEE International Conference on Computer Vision*, 2961-2969.

He, K., Zhang, X., Ren, S., & Sun, J. (2016). Deep residual learning for image recognition. In *Proceedings of the IEEE Conference on Computer Vision and Pattern Recognition* (pp. 770-778).

Hinton, G. E., & Salakhutdinov, R. R. (2006). Reducing the dimensionality of data with neural networks. *Science*, *313*(5786), 504–507. DOI: 10.1126/science.1127647 PMID: 16873662

Hou, J Blood clot and fibrin recognition method for serum images based on deep learning. Clinica chimica acta; international journal of clinical chemistry (2024). DOI: 10.19823/j.cnki.1007-1202.2021.0051

Hu, , Wang, B., Pan, X., Cao, D., Gao, A., Yang, X., Chen, Y., & Lin, Z. (2022). Using deep learning to distinguish malignant from benign parotid tumors on plain computed tomography images. *Frontiers in Oncology*, *12*, 919088. DOI: 10.3389/fonc.2022.919088 PMID: 35978811

Huang, H. (2022). *Hsu & Liu Fully Convolutional Network for the Semantic Segmentation of Medical Images: A Survey*. Diagnostics.

Huang, J., Rathod, V., Sun, C., Zhu, M., Korattikara, A., Fathi, A., & Murphy, K. (2017). Speed/accuracy trade-offs for modern convolutional object detectors. In *Proceedings of the IEEE Conference on Computer Vision and Pattern Recognition* (pp. 7310–7311). DOI: 10.1109/CVPR.2017.351

Hur, Wi & Kim Facilitating the Development of Deep Learning Models with Visual Analytics for Electronic Health Records. International journal of environmental research and public health (2020). DOI: 10.1016/j.neunet.2019.08.025 PMID: 31536901

Ibragimov, E, Kim, Y, Lee, JH, & Cho, J & Lee JJ Automated Pavement Condition Index Assessment with Deep Learning and Image Analysis: An End-to-End Approach. Sensors (Basel, Switzerland) (2024). DOI: 10.1016/j.neunet.2019.08.025 PMID: 31536901

Ibtehaz, N., & Rahman, M. S. (2020). MultiResUNet: Rethinking the U-Net architecture for multimodal biomedical image segmentation. *Neural Networks*, *121*, 74–87. DOI: 10.1016/j.neunet.2019.08.025 PMID: 31536901

Isensee, F., Jaeger, P. F., Kohl, S. A. A., Petersen, J., & Maier-Hein, K. H. (2021). nnU-Net: A self-configuring method for deep learning-based biomedical image segmentation. *Nature Methods*, *18*(2), 203–211. DOI: 10.1038/s41592-020-01008-z PMID: 33288961

Javor, D., Kaplan, H., Kaplan, A., Puchner, S. B., Krestan, C., & Baltzer, P. (2020). Deep learning analysis provides accurate COVID-19 diagnosis on chest computed tomography. *European Journal of Radiology*, *133*, 109402. DOI: 10.1016/j.ejrad.2020.109402 PMID: 33190102

Jiang, , Quan, & Gong. (2022). Disentangled representation and cross-modality image translation based unsupervised domain adaptation method for abdominal organ segmentation. *International Journal of Computer Assisted Radiology and Surgery*.

Karras, T.. (2019). A style-based generator architecture for generative adversarial networks. *IEEE Transactions on Pattern Analysis and Machine Intelligence*, *41*(12), 2947–2960. PMID: 30273144

Karras, T.. (2021). Alias-free generative adversarial networks. *Advances in Neural Information Processing Systems.*

Kim, L., Lee, J., Moon, J., & Moon, T. (2022). Moon & Moon Interpretable deep learning-based hippocampal sclerosis classification. *Epilepsia Open*, *7*(4), 747–757. DOI: 10.1002/epi4.12655

Kingma, D. P., & Welling, M. (2013). Auto-encoding variational Bayes. *arXiv preprint arXiv:1312.6114.*

Koch, G., Zemel, R., & Salakhutdinov, R. (2015). Siamese neural networks for one-shot image recognition. *Proceedings of the 32nd International Conference on Machine Learning.*

Krishna, A., Yenneti, S., Wang, G., & Mueller, K. (2024). Image factory: A method for synthesizing novel CT images with anatomical guidance. *Medical Physics*, *51*(5), 3464–3479. DOI: 10.1002/mp.16864 PMID: 38043097

Krizhevsky, A., Sutskever, I., & Hinton, G. E. (2012). ImageNet classification with deep convolutional neural networks. *Advances in Neural Information Processing Systems*, *25*, 1097–1105.

Krizhevsky, A., Sutskever, I., & Hinton, G. E. (2012). ImageNet classification with deep convolutional neural networks. In *Advances in Neural Information Processing Systems* (Vol. 25, pp. 1097-1105).

Lampert, C. H., Nickisch, H., & Harmeling, S. (2009). Learning to detect unseen object classes by between-class attribute transfer. *IEEE Conference on Computer Vision and Pattern Recognition*, 951-958. DOI: 10.1109/CVPR.2009.5206594

Larroza, A.. (2024). *Breast Delineation in Full-Field Digital Mammography Using the Segment Anything Model.* Diagnostics. DOI: 10.3390/diagnostics14101015

Liu, Z.. (2021). Swin transformer: Hierarchical vision transformer using shifted windows. *Proceedings of the IEEE/CVF International Conference on Computer Vision.* DOI: 10.1109/ICCV48922.2021.00986

Liu, Z.. (2022). ConvNeXt: Revisiting CNNs for scalable vision. *Proceedings of the IEEE/CVF Conference on Computer Vision and Pattern Recognition.*

Lloyd, . (2022). Artificial Intelligence: Innovation to Assist in the Identification of Sono-anatomy for Ultrasound-Guided Regional Anaesthesia. *Advances in Experimental Medicine and Biology*. Advance online publication. DOI: 10.1007/978-3-030-87779-8_6 PMID: 35146620

Mahajan, D.. (2018). Exploring the limits of weakly supervised pretraining. *Proceedings of the European Conference on Computer Vision*, 181-196. DOI: 10.1007/978-3-030-01216-8_12

McMahan, H. B.. (2017). *Communication-efficient learning of deep networks from decentralized data.* Artificial Intelligence and Statistics.

Mehrabi, N.. (2021). A survey on bias and fairness in machine learning. *ACM Computing Surveys.*

Ming, Deep learning-based multimodal image analysis for cervical cancer detection. Methods (San Diego, Calif.) (2022).

Mittal K Early Stage Detection of Alzheimer's Disease With Microsoft Azure Based Deep Learning. *Research square* (2023).

Morales, M. A., Manning, W. J., & Nezafat, R. (2024). Present and Future Innovations in AI and Cardiac MRI. *Radiology*, *310*(1), e231269. DOI: 10.1148/radiol.231269 PMID: 38193835

(2022). Muller, Alonso-Caneiro, Read, Vincent & Collins Application of Deep Learning Methods for Binarization of the Choroid in Optical Coherence Tomography Images. *Translational Vision Science & Technology*.

Ng, HW, & Guan, C Subject-independent meta-learning framework towards optimal training of EEG-based classifiers. Neural networks: the official journal of the International Neural Network Society (2024).

Ngo, T. K. N., Yang, S. J., Mao, B.-H., Nguyen, T. K. M., Ng, Q. D., Kuo, Y.-L., Tsai, J.-H., Saw, S. N., & Tu, T.-Y. (2023). A deep learning-based pipeline for analyzing the influences of interfacial mechanochemical microenvironments on spheroid invasion using differential interference contrast microscopic images. *Materials Today. Bio*, *23*, 100820. DOI: 10.1016/j.mtbio.2023.100820 PMID: 37810748

Nguyen, C. V., ... (2020). Transferability estimation by jointly learning representations to preserve task relations. *arXiv preprint arXiv:2003.07131.*

Oktay, O., Schlemper, J., Folgoc, L. L., Lee, M., Heinrich, M., Misawa, K., Mori, K., McDonagh, S., Hammerla, N. Y., & Kainz, B. (2018). Attention U-Net: Learning where to look for the pancreas. *arXiv preprint arXiv:1804.03999.*

Osadebey, M., Liu, Q., Fuster-Garcia, E., & Emblem, K. E. (2023). Interpreting deep learning models for glioma survival classification using visualization and textual explanations. *BMC Medical Informatics and Decision Making*, *23*(1), 225. DOI: 10.1186/s12911-023-02320-2 PMID: 37853371

Ounissi, M., Latouche, M., & Racoceanu, D. (2024). PhagoStat a scalable and interpretable end to end framework for efficient quantification of cell phagocytosis in neurodegenerative disease studies. *Scientific Reports*, *14*(1), 6482. DOI: 10.1038/s41598-024-56081-7 PMID: 38499658

Ozdemir, C., & Dogan, Y. (2024). Advancing brain tumor classification through MTAP model: An innovative approach in medical diagnostics. *Medical & Biological Engineering & Computing*, *62*(7), 2165–2176. DOI: 10.1007/s11517-024-03064-5 PMID: 38483711

Özkaraca, Multiple Brain Tumor Classification with Dense CNN Architecture Using Brain MRI Images. Life (Basel, Switzerland) (2023). DOI: 10.1007/s11517-024-03064-5 PMID: 38483711

Pan, S. J., & Yang, Q. (2010). A survey on transfer learning. *IEEE Transactions on Knowledge and Data Engineering*, *22*(10), 1345–1359. DOI: 10.1109/TKDE.2009.191

Panhwar, A. O., Sathio, A. A., Lakhan, A., Umer, M., Mithiani, R. M., & Khan, S. (2022). Plant health detection enabled CNN scheme in IoT network. *International Journal of Computing and Digital Systems*, *11*(1), 344–335.

Radford, A., Metz, L., & Chintala, S. (2015). Unsupervised representation learning with deep convolutional generative adversarial networks. *arXiv preprint arXiv:1511.06434.*

Raghu, M., ... (2019). Transfusion: Understanding transfer learning with applications to medical imaging. *arXiv preprint arXiv:1902.07208.*

Ravuri, S., Lenc, K., Willson, M., Kangin, D., Lam, R., Mirowski, P., Fitzsimons, M., Athanassiadou, M., Kashem, S., Madge, S., Prudden, R., Mandhane, A., Clark, A., Brock, A., Simonyan, K., Hadsell, R., Robinson, N., Clancy, E., Arribas, A., & Mohamed, S. (2021). Skilful precipitation nowcasting using deep generative models of radar. *Nature*, *597*(7878), 672–677. DOI: 10.1038/s41586-021-03854-z PMID: 34588668

Ren, S., He, K., Girshick, R., & Sun, J. (2015). Faster R-CNN: Towards real-time object detection with region proposal networks. In *Advances in Neural Information Processing Systems* (pp. 91–99).

Ronneberger, O., Fischer, P., & Brox, T. (2015). U-Net: Convolutional networks for biomedical image segmentation. In *Proceedings of the International Conference on Medical Image Computing and Computer-Assisted Intervention* (pp. 234–241). Springer. DOI: 10.1007/978-3-319-24574-4_28

Ruder, S. (2017). An overview of multi-task learning in deep neural networks. *arXiv preprint arXiv:1706.05098*.

Sathio, A. "A Study On The Conceptual Frame Work Of Data Warehousing In Health Sector In Pakistan A Case Study of a Hospital System and Disease (Hepatitis C)," *International Journal of Computer (IJC)*, vol. 29, no. 1, pp. 59–81, Sep. 2018, doi: https://www.researchgate.net/publication/324896538_A_Study_On_The_Conceptual_Frame_Work_Of_Data_Warehousing_In_Health_Sector_In_Pakistan_A_Case_Study_Of_a_Hospital_System_And_Disease_Hepatitis_C/citations

Sathio, A. A., Awan, S. A., Panhwar, A. O., Aamir, A. M., Brohi, A. M., & Burdi, A. (2023). A Blockchain-Enabled Machine Learning Mask Detection Method for Prevention of Pandemic Diseases. *VAWKUM Transactions on Computer Sciences*, *11*(1), 165–183. DOI: 10.21015/vtcs.v11i1.1443

Sathio, A. A., Dootio, M. A., & Lakhan, A., ur Rehman, M., Pnhwar, A. O., & Sahito, M. A. (2021, August). Pervasive futuristic healthcare and blockchain enabled digital identities-challenges and future intensions. In *2021 International Conference on Computing, Electronics & Communications Engineering (iCCECE)* (pp. 30-35). IEEE. DOI: 10.1109/iCCECE52344.2021.9534846

Sathio, A. A., Rind, M. M., & Lakhan, A. (2024). Deep Learning Algorithms: Clustering and Classifications for Multimedia Data. In *Deep Learning for Multimedia Processing Applications* (pp. 114-145). CRC Press.

Sathio, A. A., Rind, M. M., & Lakhan, A. Deep Learning Algorithms and Architectures for Multimodal Data Analysis. In *Deep Learning for Multimedia Processing Applications* (pp. 74–113). CRC Press. DOI: 10.1201/9781032646268-5

Shah, H., Ahmed, S., Sathio, A. A., & Burdi, A. (2023). W-rank: A keyphrase extraction method for webpage based on linguistics and DOM-base features. *VAWKUM Transactions on Computer Sciences*, *11*(1), 217–228. DOI: 10.21015/vtcs.v11i1.1493

Shaikh, Z. A., Wagan, A. A., Laghari, A. A., Ali, K., Memon, M. A., & Sathio, A. A. (2019). The role of software configuration management and capability maturity model in system quality. *IJCSNS*, *19*(11), 114.

Sheller, M. J.. (2020). Multi-institutional deep learning modeling without sharing patient data: A feasibility study on brain tumor segmentation. *Medical Image Analysis*.

Shen, Feng, & Song, Song & Xu Federated Meta-Learning with Attention for Diversity-Aware Human Activity Recognition. Sensors (Basel, Switzerland) (2023).

Simonyan, K., & Zisserman, A. (2014). Very deep convolutional networks for large-scale image recognition. *arXiv preprint arXiv:1409.1556.*

Singh, V., Sathio, A. A., Anwar, S., Vavekanand, R., & Danish, R. (2024). A Medical Imaging Approach for Recognising Mitral Regurgi-tation Through Machine Learning Methods in Cardiac Imaging.

Soni, A., Sethy, P. K., Dewangan, A. K., Nanthaamornphong, A., Behera, S. K., & Devi, B. (2024). Enhancing oral squamous cell carcinoma detection: A novel approach using improved EfficientNet architecture. *BMC Oral Health*, *24*(1), 601. DOI: 10.1186/s12903-024-04307-5 PMID: 38783295

Srivastava, N.. (2014). Dropout: A simple way to prevent neural networks from overfitting. *Journal of Machine Learning Research*, *15*(1), 1929–1958.

Srivastava, N.. (2014). Dropout: A simple way to prevent neural networks from overfitting. *Journal of Machine Learning Research*, *15*, 1929–1958.

Stacke, E., Eilertsen, G., Unger, J., & Lundstrom, C. (2021). Unger & Lundstrom Measuring Domain Shift for Deep Learning in Histopathology. *IEEE Journal of Biomedical and Health Informatics*, *25*(2), 325–336. DOI: 10.1109/JBHI.2020.3032060

Tajbakhsh, N., Shin, J. Y., Gurudu, S. R., Hurst, R. T., Kendall, C. B., Gotway, M. B., & Liang, J. (2016). Convolutional neural networks for medical image analysis: Full training or fine tuning? *IEEE Transactions on Medical Imaging*, *35*(5), 1299–1312. DOI: 10.1109/TMI.2016.2535302 PMID: 26978662

Tan, M., & Le, Q. (2020). EfficientNet: Rethinking model scaling for convolutional neural networks. *International Conference on Machine Learning.*

Tjoa, E., & Guan, C. (2021). A survey on explainable artificial intelligence (XAI): Toward medical transparent AI applications. *IEEE Transactions on Neural Networks and Learning Systems.* Advance online publication. DOI: 10.1109/TNNLS.2020.3027314

Tsuneki, M. (2022). Deep learning models in medical image analysis. Journal of Oral Biosciences, 64(3), 312-320.

Tzeng, E., Hoffman, J., Saenko, K., & Darrell, T. (2017). Adversarial discriminative domain adaptation. *Proceedings of the IEEE Conference on Computer Vision and Pattern Recognition*, 7167-7176.

Tzeng, E., Hoffman, J., Saenko, K., & Darrell, T. (2017). Adversarial discriminative domain adaptation. In *Proceedings of the IEEE Conference on Computer Vision and Pattern Recognition* (pp. 7167-7176).

Vavekanand, R., Sathio, A. A., Singh, V., & Anwar, S. (2024). Water4. 0: An Industrial Water Pollution Forecasting Using Machine Learning. *Available atSSRN* 4849924.

Verma, J., Sandhu, A., Popli, R., Kumar, R., Khullar, V., Kansal, I., Sharma, A., Garg, K., Kashyap, N., & Aurangzeb, K. (2023). From slides to insights: Harnessing deep learning for prognostic survival prediction in human colorectal cancer histology. *Open Life Sciences*, *18*(1), 20220777. DOI: 10.1515/biol-2022-0777 PMID: 38152577

Wang, R., Chow, S. S. L., Serafin, R. B., Xie, W., Han, Q., Baraznenok, E., Lan, L., Bishop, K. W., & Liu, J. T. C. (2024). Direct three-dimensional segmentation of prostate glands with nnU-Net. *Journal of Biomedical Optics*, *29*(3). Advance online publication. DOI: 10.1117/1.JBO.29.3.036001 PMID: 38434772

Wang, Ren, & Li, Chen & Yu Semi-Supervised Deep Learning Model for Efficient Computation of Optical Properties of Suspended-Core Fibers. Sensors (Basel, Switzerland) (2022). DOI: 10.1117/1.JBO.29.3.036001 PMID: 38434772

Wang, X., & Yuan, W. (2024). Nuclei-level prior knowledge constrained multiple instance learning for breast histopathology whole slide image classification. *iScience*, *27*(6), 109826. DOI: 10.1016/j.isci.2024.109826 PMID: 38832012

Wang, Y., Rong, Z., & Xiao, P. I. A. U. S. D. L. A. (2019).. . *American Journal of Pathology*.

Wang, Z., Fang, M., Zhang, J., Tang, L., Zhong, L., Li, H., Cao, R., Zhao, X., Liu, S., Zhang, R., Xie, X., Mai, H., Qiu, S., Tian, J., & Dong, D. (2024). Radiomics and Deep Learning in Nasopharyngeal Carcinoma: A Review. *IEEE Reviews in Biomedical Engineering*, *17*, 118–135. DOI: 10.1109/RBME.2023.3269776 PMID: 37097799

(2022). Wang, Li & Zheng Automatic Detection and Segmentation of Ovarian Cancer Using a Multitask Model in Pelvic CT Images. *Oxidative Medicine and Cellular Longevity*.

Weiss, K., Khoshgoftaar, T. M., & Wang, D. (2016). A survey of transfer learning. *Journal of Big Data*, *3*(1), 1–40. DOI: 10.1186/s40537-016-0043-6

Xu, R.. (2021). FedGAN: Federated generative adversarial networks for distributed data synthesis. *IEEE Transactions on Network Science and Engineering*.

Yang, , Wu, X., Hao, J., Liu, T., Xie, L., Liu, P., & Li, J. (2023). Deep Learning Methods for Wood Composites Failure Predication. *Polymers*, *15*(2), 295. DOI: 10.3390/polym15020295 PMID: 36679176

Yang, M., Liu, S., Hao, T., Ma, C., Chen, H., Li, Y., Wu, C., Xie, J., Qiu, H., Li, J., Yang, Y., & Liu, C. (2024). Development and validation of a deep interpretable network for continuous acute kidney injury prediction in critically ill patients. *Artificial Intelligence in Medicine*, *149*, 102785. DOI: 10.1016/j.artmed.2024.102785 PMID: 38462285

Yaqub, , Jinchao, F., Arshid, K., Ahmed, S., Zhang, W., Nawaz, M. Z., & Mahmood, T. (2022). Deep Learning-Based Image Reconstruction for Different Medical Imaging Modalities. *Computational and Mathematical Methods in Medicine*, *2022*, 1–18. DOI: 10.1155/2022/8750648 PMID: 35756423

Yildiz, , Arslan, A. T., Yildiz Tas, A., Acer, A. F., Demir, S., Sahin, A., & Erol Barkana, D. (2021). Generative Adversarial Network Based Automatic Segmentation of Corneal Subbasal Nerves on In Vivo Confocal Microscopy Images. *Translational Vision Science & Technology*, *10*(6), 33. DOI: 10.1167/tvst.10.6.33 PMID: 34038501

Yosinski, J., ... (2014). How transferable are features in deep neural networks? In *Advances in Neural Information Processing Systems* (Vol. 27, pp. 3320-3328).

Yun, Y., Yu, Q., Yang, Z., An, X., Li, D., Huang, J., Zheng, D., Feng, Q., & Ma, D. (2024). Research on identification method of peanut pests and diseases based on lightweight LSCDNet model. *Phytopathology, 114*(9), 2162–2175. DOI: 10.1094/PHYTO-01-24-0013-R PMID: 38810273

Zamir, A. R.. (2018). Taskonomy: Disentangling task transfer learning. In *Proceedings of the IEEE Conference on Computer Vision and Pattern Recognition* (pp. 3712-3722).

Zhang, S., Wang, Q., Zhang, B., Liang, Z., Zhang, L., Li, L., Huang, G., Zhang, Z., Feng, B., & Yu, T. (2023). Cauchy non-convex sparse feature selection method for the high-dimensional small-sample problem in motor imagery EEG decoding. *Frontiers in Neuroscience, 17*, 1292724. DOI: 10.3389/fnins.2023.1292724 PMID: 38027478

Zhang, Y., ... (2017). Bridging heterogeneous domains via domain-adversarial neural networks. *arXiv preprint arXiv:1709.00774.*

Zhang, Y., ... (2017). Bridging heterogeneous domains via domain-adversarial neural networks. *arXiv preprint arXiv:1709.00774.*

Zhou, X., Zhao, C., Sun, J., Cheng, J., & Xu, M. (2024). Determination of lead content in oilseed rape leaves in silicon-free and silicon environments based on deep transfer learning and fluorescence hyperspectral imaging. *Spectrochimica Acta. Part A: Molecular and Biomolecular Spectroscopy, 311*, 123991. DOI: 10.1016/j.saa.2024.123991 PMID: 38330763

Zhou, Z., Siddiquee, M. M. R., Tajbakhsh, N., & Liang, J. (2018). UNet++: A nested U-Net architecture for medical image segmentation. In *Deep Learning in Medical Image Analysis and Multimodal Learning for Clinical Decision Support* (pp. 3–11). Springer. DOI: 10.1007/978-3-030-00889-5_1

Zhu, J. Y.. (2017). Unpaired image-to-image translation using cycle-consistent adversarial networks. *Proceedings of the IEEE International Conference on Computer Vision*, 2223-2232. DOI: 10.1109/ICCV.2017.244

Chapter 15
A Comparative Analysis of Breast Cancer Classification Using Ensemble and Multi-Classifier Algorithms

Ajay Sharma
https://orcid.org/0000-0001-7951-9371
VIT Bhopal University, India

Pranshu Pranjal
https://orcid.org/0000-0001-6213-7131
VIT Bhopal University, India

Bhupendra Panchal
https://orcid.org/0009-0004-5800-4263
VIT Bhopal University, India

Rajneesh Kumar Patel
https://orcid.org/0000-0002-3574-4419
VIT Bhopal University, India

Praveen Kumar Tyagi
https://orcid.org/0000-0002-4054-9781
VIT Bhopal University, India

ABSTRACT

Breast cancer is one of the most prevalent forms of cancer, and early detection is crucial for effective treatment. This study provides a comparative analysis of breast cancer classification using ensemble and multi-classifier algorithms. The primary objective is to evaluate the performance of various machine learning models in accurately predicting breast cancer. We employ several ensemble techniques, including Random Forest, AdaBoost, and Gradient Boosting, as well as multi-classifier algorithms such as Support Vector Machines, k-Nearest Neighbors, and Naive Bayes. These models are trained and tested on a publicly available breast cancer dataset, with performance metrics such as accuracy, precision,

DOI: 10.4018/979-8-3693-9045-0.ch015

recall, and F1-score used for evaluation.

1. INTRODUCTION

Breast tumors remain the most ubiquitous kind of cancer and the one with the least recognition. Early identification of breast cancer has the potential to effectively save many lives. Prompt diagnosis involves precise and unwavering diagnosis procedures that enable medical professionals to distinguish benign breast tumors from malignant ones without resorting to surgical biopsy. Every minute, everywhere in the world, a female is diagnosed with breast cancer, and every minute, everywhere in the world, someone passes away due to breast cancer. Differentiation of breast tumors is done as follows: invasive cancer, in situ cancer, and benign cancer. Benign tumors belong to the main class of tumors and mammography is often employed to check them. They're unable to reach exterior organs because they are not malignant by nature. In rare instances, it can be difficult to distinguish between a particular bulk of benign from malignant tumors using mammography. All invasive or in situ malignancy is contained inside the ducts. Furthermore, there should be no cancerous cells on the basal membrane. When a cancer becomes invasive, it means that it has surpassed the basal barrier and penetrated the surrounding tissue. As a result, it's critical to discover breast cancer early. The main goal of these projections is to label patients into either malignant(cancerous) or benign(non-cancerous) groups. With the aid of machine learning, processors can interpret complicated patterns from huge, noisy, or complex data sets by learning from previous examples. It's a branch of artificial intelligence that applies various probabilistic, statistical, and optimizing techniques. In general, this knowledge is ideally suited to applications in health, particularly those involving complex proteomic and genomic measurements. Currently, a range of medical requests are being classified and identified as malignancies using machine learning techniques. First and foremost, cancer has been identified and treated using machine learning. It enables interpretations or conclusions to be reached that would not be achievable with traditional statistical methods. For this reason, it has far greater influence, (Cruz & Wishart, 2006). It's astounding to realize that almost all algorithms for machine learning use supervised learning. One of the most demanding and fascinating jobs is the development of data mining systems to predict the outcomes of illnesses. Thanks to the usage of computers equipped with automated tools, medical research groups may now readily access and create vast amounts of health data. Knowledge discovery using typical machine learning techniques requires more time due to the need to mine knowledge from large databases, (Han, Pei, & Tong, 2022). Medical practitioners are the ones who use data mining technology most often to classify and exploit patterns and linkages among a multitude of variables. By utilizing the historical data stored in datasets, they assist in forecasting the outcomes of illness. Getting relevant information out of all of the current data is a difficult task that must be done in a short period. There are numerous ways to extract knowledge or relevant information from data using various data mining techniques or procedures. These techniques are acceptable and most suited for the entirety of the data that are composed and related to different academic fields. Many studies are conducted, published, and made public regarding the use of data mining in a variety of scientific domains, including banking, insurance, telecommunications, medical, education, and military. The chief goal of this work is to identify the optimal model after a comparative analysis of various machine learning models is conducted to forecast breast cancer diagnosis, therapy, and prognosis. The remainder of this paper is organized into the sections that follow, (Aha, Kibler, & Albert, 1991). The literature is described in full in the second part. Preprocessing and data gathering are covered in the third section. The fourth section outlines our approach to performance prediction for pupils. Section Five shows the outcomes and Section Six gives a summary of the findings and recommendations for further research, (Cleary & Trigg, 1995).

2. LITERATURE SURVEY

The study "Exploring Imbalanced Datasets in Breast Cancer Detection Using Machine Learning" by Mohammed and Arunachalam (2021) to create a reliable model using publically accessible information, this study explores the field of machine learning-based breast cancer diagnosis. But it has a major obstacle in the form of a stark disparity in class, with the majority of benign cases far outnumbering malignant ones. Although the model's overall accuracy of 90% is outstanding, its performance indicates a strong bias towards the majority class, which leads to an inadequate sensitivity of 50% for identifying malignant instances. Notably, the model's subpar performance is exacerbated by the high (95%) specificity it maintains for identifying benign instances. These results highlight the urgent need to rectify the class divide to improve the fairness and effectiveness of breast cancer screening techniques. To distinguish between cases of benign and malignant breast cancer, the "Breast Cancer Classification Using Single Classifier" by Muhammad Almas Anjum and Naila Baigresearch presents an investigation into the classification of breast cancer using a single classifier approach. The study intends to facilitate more efficient patient care and better diagnosis accuracy by utilizing a strong machine-learning algorithm. However the key constraint appears to be the exclusive dependence on a single classifier, which may limit the model's ability to adjust to the nuances and differences present in breast cancer data. Compared to more flexible ensemble approaches or hybrid models that use various algorithms, this approach may impair the model's performance measures even though it simplifies implementation, (Salama, Abdelhalim, & Zeid, 2012) (Rajesh & Anand, 2012). The study "Improving Breast Cancer Diagnosis through Machine Learning" by Korde V. et al. attempts to improve breast cancer diagnosis to improve detection efficiency and accuracy. The project has the potential to significantly improve healthcare costs and save lives by enabling early diagnosis and treatment through the use of complex algorithms and vast data analysis. Notable drawbacks do, however, appear. One such drawback is the inadequate handling of data imbalance within datasets, which could induce biases during model training. Furthermore, a thorough examination of the crucial component of external validation—which involves utilizing data from many institutions or sources—that is necessary to assess model generalization is absent from the work, (Das *et al.*, 2021). Breast Cancer Detection in Mammograms Using Machine Learning Techniques" by Singh P. investigates the application of machine learning approaches for breast cancer diagnosis in mammograms. The results are encouraging. This study adds to the creation of useful screening instruments since early detection is essential for enhancing patient outcomes. One of the study's shortcomings, though, is that it doesn't provide a thorough analysis of the constraints or performance comparisons of the machine learning strategies included. To further improve the paper's contributions, it would also be beneficial to include more comprehensive evaluation of metrics and validation techniques, (Singh, Mohapatra, & Kanungo, 2011) (Senturk & Kara, 2014) (Kumar, Sushil, & Tiwari, 2019).

3. NOVELTY

This research introduces novel techniques to address class imbalance, employing resampling methods to synthetically balance datasets and improve classification accuracy. Additionally, this study explores meta-classifiers to enhance accuracy by combining predictions from multiple base classifiers, leveraging specific attributes for more precise breast cancer classification. Moreover, this project integrates a user-friendly interface in Weka, simplifying data loading, classifier configuration, and result interpretation, enhancing accessibility for healthcare practitioners. This model aids in early detection, integrates with telemedicine platforms for remote diagnosis, prioritizes cases, and offers decision support in clinical settings.

4. DATA PREPROCESSING

Data processing is needed to filter the dataset suitable for multiple classifiers and carry out classification. Real-world data is dirty; it can be cleaned by removing curious and erroneous data, which is then combined from several sources (a process called metadata that eliminates redundant and duplicate data). Data preparation can be achieved by a variety of techniques, including data reduction, cleaning, discretization, integration, and transformation. The qualities that are included in the data set are single epithelial cell size, clump thickness, bare nuclei, blast chromatin, normal nucleoli, mitosis, marginal adhesion, and evenness of cell size and shape, (Frank, 2010). The ability to do categorization, prediction, and rule extraction on the available data depends on having the right data mining tools. Using several classifiers, For every dataset, a 10-fold cross-validation is performed. To evaluate the efficacy of the models employing various classifiers for breast cancer, the accuracy and other variables are measured to arrive at the conclusions, (Manusri, Verma, & Laxkar, 2014) (Ruggeri, Kenett, & Faltin, 2007).

5. METHODS AND PROPOSED APPROACHES

5.1 A Synopsis of the Methods Used to Classify Breast Cancer Data

This technique primarily proposes three key phases.

- First, a 10-fold cross-validation is performed, dividing the data into two sections: one for model training and the other for model testing. also compares and assesses using acquired learning models through the use of many algorithms, (Refaeilzadeh, Tang, & Liu, 2009).
- The Random Forest, J48, Decision Trees, SVM, and REP Tree classifiers are used to train the breast cancer dataset, (Sultana *et al.*, 2018)
- The Model created from the training dataset is applied to a test data set in the second phase, and the outcomes are obtained.
- The acquired data are assessed in terms of accuracy during the third step, (Phyu, 2009).

5.2 Employed Categorization Algorithms

We have chosen the open-source program WEKA for this paper because it effectively functions with minimal information, (Agarwal, Pandey, & Tiwari, 2012). Tasks such as pre-processing of data, Classification, resampling, and Visualization can be performed. The dataset is supplied in CSV (comma-separated values) format. WEKA is typically utilized in medical analysis for initial data collection, (Kusiak, 2000). The Dataset is analyzed using a deconstruction method to extract relevant information. The knowledge that has been extracted is applied to forecasting, (Cessie & Houwelingen, 1992). The recommended framework for predicting breast cancer utilizing the ensemble method and base classifiers such as SVM, J48, etc. is summarized in Figure 1. The Breast Cancer dataset is used for experiments, which are then run through several classifiers including Bagging, Boosting, Random Subspace, and Accuracy, (Han, Pei, & Tong, 2022) (Quinlan, 1986).

Figure 1. Framework proposing a proposed approach

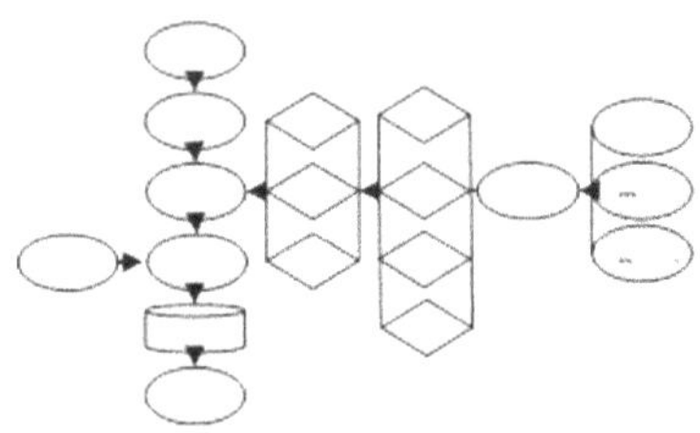

5.3 Techniques and Procedures Used

Bagging: To reduce variance, several models are trained on arbitrary subsets of data using this technique in machine learning. The predictions of these models are then combined. Boosting: An approach to ensemble learning that groups inexperienced learners one after the other, emphasizing cases that earlier learners misclassified to increase accuracy overall. Random Subspace: A variation of ensemble learning where base learners are trained on random subsets of features rather than data points, aiding in diversification and robustness. J48 algorithm for decision trees based on the C4.5 algorithm, primarily used for classification tasks, capable of handling both numerical and categorical data. SVM (Support Vector Machine): A supervised learning model used for classification and regression tasks, which finds the optimal hyperplane that separates data points of different classes while maximizing the margin. REP tree: A decision tree algorithm designed for regression tasks, particularly useful for handling noisy data and capable of providing interpretable models, (Sharma & Kumar, 2016) (Sugiharti, Firmansyah, & Devi, 2017). Random Forest: An ensemble method of learning that consists of a group of decision trees. To provide reliable predictions and less overfitting, each tree is trained using a random subset of training data and characteristics, (Kohavi, 1995).

5.4 Implementation

To train all models, the following steps were performed

- preprocess-> open file-> import dataset
- Weka filters->supervised->instance->resample
- Set the bias to uniform to 0.5
- Classify-> 10-fold cross-validation
- Choose Meta classifier, base classifier, sample size, and weight threshold
- Select the attribute to focus on
- Click on start and the summary, detailed classification report and confusion matrix will appear on the screen. (Agarwal, Pandey, & Tiwari, 2012) (Kusiak, 2000).

5.5 Examining the Confusion Matrix

Based on the class labels produced by the classifiers, a distinction is made between the expected and actual class labels, (Quinlan, 1986). An example of WEKA-generated confusion matrix 2 * 2 matrices is shown. Below (Kesavaraj & Sukumaran, 2013)

Table 1. Confusion matrix and accuracy

A	B	Classified as
148	24	A = No Recurrence events
18	96	B = Recurrence Events

6. EXPERIMENTAL RESULTS AND DISCUSSION

Improvements in classification results were shown once resampling was performed. Resampling helps us overcome biases that could've been caused due to majority class instances. Significant improvements in accuracy after resampling with a bias To a Uniform Class of 0.5 were seen. Before resampling the no. of recurrence instances was 85 and non-recurrence instances were 201 and resampling reorganized them to 114 recurrences and 172 nonrecurrence instances. Significant improvement in classification was observed as listed in Tables 2, 3, and 4 below, (Li & Zhu, 2007).

Table 2. Accuracy before resampling data

Base Classifier Used2	No. of Correctly Classified Instances
J48	217
SVM	218
Random Forest	280
REP tree	212

Table 3. Accuracy after resampling data

Base Classifier Used	No. of Correctly Classified Instances
J48	237
SVM	222
Random Forest	282
REP tree	237

We used 10-fold cross-validation for model training and for procuring thorough results and each model took less than a second to build. We analyzed the impact of attributes on the classification process. After the implementation phase, the top-performing models were given in Tables 4 and 5.

Table 4. Accuracy score of all ensemble techniques and base classifiers paired with various attributes

Ensemble Method	Base classifier	Menopause	INV	Node caps
Bagging	SVM	83.56	84.96	89.53
	J48	83.56	84.26	88.80
	REP tree	82.51	80.41	88.08
	Random Forest	89.16	89.86	90.61
Boosting	SVM	84.26	84.96	88.08
	J48	89.86	91.60	90.61
	REP tree	74.82	81.81	88.08
	Random Forest	89.86	91.60	92.41
Random Subspace	SVM	74.82	78.67	86.28
	J48	82.16	80.06	85.92
	REP tree	83.21	75.87	87.72
	Random Forest	87.76	88.46	90.61

Table 5. Accuracy score of all ensemble techniques and base classifiers paired with various attributes

Ensemble Technique	Base classifier	Irradiate	Class
Bagging	SVM	75.17	70.62
	J48	81.46	77.62
	REP tree	83.91	72.62
	Random Forest	89.86	84.96
Boosting	SVM	76.57	72.37
	J48	87.06	85.31
	REPtree	87.76	80.76
	RandomForest	89.86	87.41
RandomSubspace	SVM	75.17	67.13

Ensemble Technique	Base classifier	Irradiate	Class
	J48	82.16	74.47
	REPtree	81.46	74.82
	RandomForest	89.16	83.21

According to Table 2, it was observed that algorithms performed the best when the focus was on Node-caps. Algorithms tend to better distinguish between localized tumors and those with lymph node involvement when node-caps are considered, (Wong, 2004). On testing the combination of top-performing algorithms on a test set, boosting with random forest (INV nodes) and boosting with J48(INV nodes) gave the most accurate classification with an efficiency of 90.74% each. The best performing combination of ensemble techniques as well as base classifiers are listed in Table 6.

Table 6. Result analysis of breast cancer in various classifiers

Best Performing Combination of algorithms with attribute	No. of correctly classified Instances	No. of wrongly classified instances
Bagging with RandomForest(Node Caps)	51	14
Boosting with REPtree(Node Caps)	55	10
Boosting with RandomForest (INV nodes)	49	5
Boosting with RandomForest (Node Caps)	51	14
Boosting with J48(INV nodes)	49	5
Boosting with J48(Node Caps)	52	13
RandomSubspace with RandomForest(Node Caps)	51	14

Figure 2. Comparison of efficiency in classification after performing feature selection

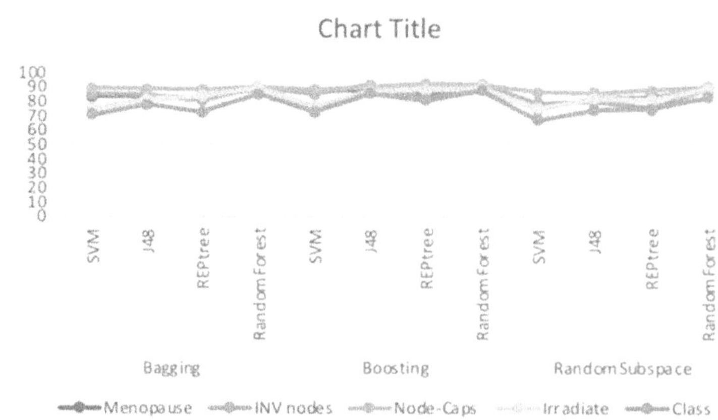

7. CONCLUSION AND FUTURE WORK

Our project demonstrates the feasibility of utilizing ML techniques for the classification of breast cancer, emphasizing the potential impact of automated, data-driven methodologies on enhancing diagnostic accuracy and efficiency in this critical domain. Through our research, we have brought attention to the need of thorough model evaluation and stringent data preprocessing—two critical elements in guaranteeing the dependability and efficacy of machine learning-based diagnostic systems. This underscores the significance of methodological considerations in the development and deployment of such systems, thereby contributing to the advancement of breast cancer diagnosis.

Future research in breast cancer classification could integrate advanced feature selection methods like genetic algorithms, leverage ensemble learning (e.g., stacking, gradient boosting), and incorporate multi-modal data (genomic, proteomic, imaging) for comprehensive diagnostic systems.

REFERENCES

Agarwal, S., Pandey, G. N., & Tiwari, M. D. (2012). Data mining in education: Data classification and decision tree approach. *International Journal of e-Education, e-Business, e-. Management Learning*, 2(2), 140.

Aha, D. W., Kibler, D., & Albert, M. K. (1991). Instance-based learning algorithms. *Machine Learning*, 6(1), 37–66. DOI: 10.1007/BF00153759

Breiman, L. (2001). Random forests. *Machine Learning*, 45(1), 5–32. DOI: 10.1023/A:1010933404324

Cessie, S. L., & Houwelingen, J. V. (1992). Ridge estimators in logistic regression. *Journal of the Royal Statistical Society. Series C, Applied Statistics*, 41(1), 191–201.

Cleary, J. G., & Trigg, L. E. (1995). K*: An instance-based learner using an entropic distance measure. In *Machine Learning Proceedings 1995* (pp. 108–114). Morgan Kaufmann. DOI: 10.1016/B978-1-55860-377-6.50022-0

Cruz, J. A., & Wishart, D. S. (2006). Applications of machine learning in cancer prediction and prognosis. *Cancer Informatics*, 2, 117693510600200030. DOI: 10.1177/117693510600200030 PMID: 19458758

Das, A., Mohanty, M. N., Mallick, P. K., Tiwari, P., Muhammad, K., & Zhu, H. (2021). Breast cancer detection using an ensemble deep learning method. *Biomedical Signal Processing and Control*, 70, 103009. DOI: 10.1016/j.bspc.2021.103009

Frank, A. (2010). UCI machine learning repository. http://archive. ics. uci. edu/ml

Han, J., Pei, J., & Tong, H. (2022). *Data mining: concepts and techniques*. Morgan kaufmann.

Kesavaraj, G., & Sukumaran, S. (2013, July). A study on classification techniques in data mining. In *2013 fourth international conference on computing, communications and networking technologies (ICCCNT)* (pp. 1-7). IEEE. DOI: 10.1109/ICCCNT.2013.6726842

Kohavi, R. (1995, April). The power of decision tables. In *European conference on machine learning* (pp. 174-189). Berlin, Heidelberg: Springer Berlin Heidelberg.

Kumar, A., Sushil, R., & Tiwari, A. K. (2019). Comparative study of classification techniques for breast cancer diagnosis. *International Journal on Computer Science and Engineering*, 7(1), 234–240.

Kusiak, A. (2000). Decomposition in data mining: An industrial case study. *IEEE Transactions on Electronics Packaging Manufacturing*, 23(4), 345–353. DOI: 10.1109/6104.895081

Li, Y., & Zhu, J. (2007). Analysis of array CGH data for cancer studies using fused quantile regression. *Bioinformatics (Oxford, England)*, 23(18), 2470–2476. DOI: 10.1093/bioinformatics/btm364 PMID: 17644559

Mansuri, A. M., Verma, M., & Laxkar, P. (2014). A Survey of Classifier Designing Using Genetic Programming and Genetic Operators. [IJERR]. *International Journal of Engineering Research and Reviews*, 2, 16–22.

Mohammed, A., & Arunachalam, N. (2021, July). Imbalanced machine learning based techniques for breast cancer detection. In *2021 International Conference on System, Computation, Automation and Networking (ICSCAN)* (pp. 1-4). IEEE. DOI: 10.1109/ICSCAN53069.2021.9526422

Phyu, T. N. (2009, March). Survey of classification techniques in data mining. In *Proceedings of the International Multiconference of engineers and computer scientists* (Vol. 1, No. 5, pp. 727-731). Citeseer.

Quinlan, J. R. (1986). Induction of decision trees. *Machine Learning*, 1(1), 81–106. DOI: 10.1007/BF00116251

Rajesh, K., & Anand, S. (2012). Analysis of SEER dataset for breast cancer diagnosis using C4. 5 classification algorithm. *International Journal of Advanced Research in Computer and Communication Engineering*, 1(2), 2278–1021.

Refaeilzadeh, P., Tang, L., & Liu, H. (2009). Cross-validation. *Encyclopedia of database systems*, 532-538.

Ruggeri, F., Kenett, R., & Faltin, F. W. (2007). *Encyclopedia of statistics in quality and reliability*. No Title. DOI: 10.1002/9780470061572

Salama, G. I., Abdelhalim, M., & Zeid, M. A. E. (2012). Breast cancer diagnosis on three different datasets using multi-classifiers. [WDBC]. *Breast Cancer (Tokyo, Japan)*, 32(569), 2.

Senturk, Z. K., & Kara, R. (2014). Breast cancer diagnosis via data mining: Performance analysis of seven different algorithms. *Computing in Science & Engineering*, 4(1), 35.

Sharma, H., & Kumar, S. (2016). A survey on decision tree algorithms of classification in data mining. [IJSR]. *International Journal of Scientific Research*, 5(4), 2094–2097.

Singh, N., Mohapatra, A. G., & Kanungo, G. (2011). Breast cancer mass detection in mammograms using K-means and fuzzy C-means clustering. *International Journal of Computer Applications*, 22(2), 15–21. DOI: 10.5120/2557-3507

Sugiharti, E., Firmansyah, S., & Devi, F. R. (2017). Predictive evaluation of performance of computer science students of unnes using data mining based on naÏve bayes classifier (NBC) algorithm. *Journal of Theoretical and Applied Information Technology*, 95(4), 902.

Sultana, J., Sultana, N., Yadav, K., & AlFayez, F. (2018, April). Prediction of sentiment analysis on educational data based on deep learning approach. In *2018 21st Saudi Computer Society National Computer Conference (NCC)* (pp. 1-5). IEEE. DOI: 10.1109/NCG.2018.8593108

Wong, J. L. L. (2004). Rule-Based Data Mining Methods for Classification Problems in Biomedical Domains.

Chapter 16
A Comparative Analysis of Deep Learning Approaches for Unmasking Image Forgeries

Shobana Ganesan
https://orcid.org/0000-0001-5214-678X
Mepco Schlenk Engineering College, India

Naveen Kumar Alagarsamy
Mepco Schlenk Engineering College, India

Nithish Kumar Ravi
Mepco Schlenk Engineering College, India

ABSTRACT

Images play an essential role in today's digital world. Images are widely shared in social media that any falsifications can lead to big problems. There are many tools available to edit the images and some are using it for improvising the picture and some are using it to threaten people. There are many software's available to forge the image to convey some false information. So it's important to identify whether the image is real or fake. Image splicing and copy-move are the two fundamental forms of image forgeries. This chapter introduces a Novel CNN architecture to identify both Image splicing and copy move forgery at the same time. A deep learning-based model is presented to identify forgery in photos, producing a featured image to train the model. Further this work also uses some Pre-trained model VGG16, Alex net, Mobile Net, and ResNet via Transfer learning . Comparative analysis on different Datasets like CASIA V2, MICC-F600, MICC-F220 and TAMPERED was done and obtained accuracy of 92.33, 85.00, 86.36, and 63.69% respectively.

INTRODUCTION

Globalization and technical improvements have made electronic devices widely and affordably available. As a result, digital cameras have grown in popularity. Nowadays most of the people have camera either in phone or a digital camera and images are required in soft copy for various document

DOI: 10.4018/979-8-3693-9045-0.ch016

application. Images are widely shared in social media that any falsifications can lead to big problems. The amazing thing is that image can convey the information by just looking into it. As a result, images play an essential role in today's digital world. There are many tools available to edit the images and some are using it for improvising the picture and some are using it to threaten people.

Image splicing and copy-move are the two fundamental forms of image forgeries, and they are covered below:

- Image splicing involves copying a section of a donor image into a source image. The final forged picture can also be constructed using a series of donor photos.
- Copy-Move: There is just one picture in this scenario. A section of the image has been copied and pasted into the image.

Image forgery detection is a binary classification task to identify whether the image is real or fake. Recently Deep learning has become a promising tool in Image processing since it is scalable and it can handle large datasets by extracting important features using raw pixels of the data. Sometimes the dataset size can be very small where the transfer learning provides the viable solution for it. It is already trained on the Imagenet database that contains 1.2 million images grouped into 1000 classes to solve the problem of small size dataset. By using the Pre-trained model, time constraints can be significantly reduced. Pre-training the model can make it suitable for use with fewer datasets. The true purpose of picture forgery detection is to verify the legitimacy of photos, since they can spread false information to the public and serve as vital evidence in court cases, forensic investigations, and news reports. It stops false information and fake news from spreading, especially on social media and other online platforms where manipulated photos can be used to harm someone's reputation or sway public opinion.

Figure 1. Example of splicing forgery image (a) original image (b) forged image (Ali et al., 2022) and copy-move forgery image (c) original image (d) forged image (El Sayed et al., 2023)

In Figure 1, an example of a copy-move and image splicing forgery image is presented. Figure 1a displays the original image, while Figure 1b exhibits the forged version then Figure 1 c displays the original image, while Figure 1 c exhibits the forged version.

Image forgery detection has several challenges due to the nature of picture alteration techniques. These challenges are:

- Computational complexity, memory and CPU limitations, which require a long training period and frequently result in memory outages even with high memory specifications.
- The majority of image forgery detection techniques that have high detection accuracy are very complex.

This chapter presents the following contribution:

- Recognizing simultaneous detection of two forms of passive picture forgeries, such as image splicing and copy-move, to be appropriate for real-world situations.
- Evaluating the performance of different pre-trained models such as VGG16, Alex net, MobileNetV2 and ResNet50 are considered
- Evaluating the performance of the above models with four different datasets like CASIA V2, MICC-F600, MICC-F220, TAMPERED.

The rest of the chapter is organized as follows: A literature review is covered in section II. In Section III, the suggested methodology is examined and the suggested architecture is provided in depth. Together with the experimental setup and datasets considered, Section IV presents the experimental findings and discussion. The conclusion and future work are in Section V.

BACKGROUND AND LITERATURE REVIEW

This section focuses on reviewing the various methods for predicting and detecting the forged images. Ali *et al* (2022) suggested a method for detecting image using error level analysis (ELA) for the detection of forgery in an image. A.H. Khalil et al (2023) used some pretrained models for image forgery detection they use models like VGG 16, ResNet, and MobileNet and achieved accuracy of 93.83, 94.61 and 94.69. Yildiz Aydin et al (2022) convert the RGB to YCbCr and extracted the LIOP features individually from Y, Cb, and Cr and combine the LIOP features and match them and eliminate the mismatch using RANSAC and parallelism condition.

Y.Rao et al(2020) pretrained the CNN model and test image is divided into patches and feature extraction is done using the pre trained model and SVM classifier is used to classify the image. R. Rafique et al (2021) used ELA analysis for deepfake detection using the CNN model. Smitha B N et al (2023) used ELA analysis to generate the feature image and they use CNN and VGG16 to detect whether the image is real or fake. Gulwanz Gani et al (2020) used DCT (Discrete Cosine Transform) to extract features and cellular automata is employed to construct feature vector and it is matched using kd tree nearest neighbouring search. P. Zhou et al (2018) implemented CNN to extract both RGB stream and noise stream of the input and will combine these using a bilinear pooling function to classify images.

Muhammad Aqib Anwar et al (2023) extracted deep derived features from the existing hand-crafted features with the help of VGG16 and they use a SVM classifier to classify whether the image is real or fake. D.Cozzolino et al (2018) tried to identify the forgery that rely on noise prints. CNN model is trained to minimize the distance of same patches and maximize the distance of different patches. D.Cozzolino et al (2014) extracted the features of the input data like colour or noise they apply the patchmatch algorithm for generating the reference database of patches. Apply the patch match algorithm for the query image find the difference between the query images patch and reference database generated earlier to find forgery.

J.Bunk et al(2017) used two methods the first method is computing the random transform of resampling features deep learning classifier and Gaussian random field is used to generate heat map. In second method the Resampling feature is passed through LSTM network for classification and localization. K.M. Honsy et al (2023) proposed a simple CNN architecture for detecting splicing forgery detection.

D.ELASKILY et al, 2020 they use CMFD (Copy Move Forgery Detection) algorithm to identify only the image forgery detection.

S.Arivazhagan et al, (2024) used a CNN model and MobileNet model to detect the forgery in the image. The proposed architecture was tested under MICC-F220, MICC-F600, MICC-F2000 datasets. Ehret et al (2019) used SIFT approach for detecting the forgery in images. WEI et al, 2018 in presented a method that extracts the differences between the image and the splicing regions from patch descriptors of various scales. Bi et al (2019) proposed a ringed residual U-Net for detecting only the splicing type of image forgery in the images. Younis and, et al (2020) used the reliability fusion map for the detection of the forgery. By utilizing the CNNs, Abdalla et al (2019) classified an image as fake or original one, or it contains copy-move image forgery.

MAIN FOCUS OF THE CHAPTER

The main idea of this work is to identify the forged image from a set of images. A deep learning-based model is presented to identify forgery in photos. This work also uses some Pre-trained models such as VGG16, Alex net, Mobile Net, and ResNet via Transfer learning for image forgery detection. It uses the knowledge learned from large datasets, enhancing the network's ability to discern subtle patterns indicative of Forgery in Image. Experiments are conducted on different Datasets like CASIA V2, MICC-F600, MICC-F220 and TAMPERED and the performance of these models are compared using Accuracy, Precision, Recall and F1-Score.

PROPOSED METHOLOGY

In our proposed method image is taken and it is compressed. In case of image being forged the forged portion will be compressed so if we compress the fake image the forged portion will be recompressed and it will be different with the rest of the image. When the difference between original and fake image is analysed the forged portion becomes more evident. This process is known as ELA (Error Level Analysis). This process is applied to all the images and it is used to train the CNN model. Figure 2 shows the flow of the proposed model

Figure 2. Flow chart of the proposed approach

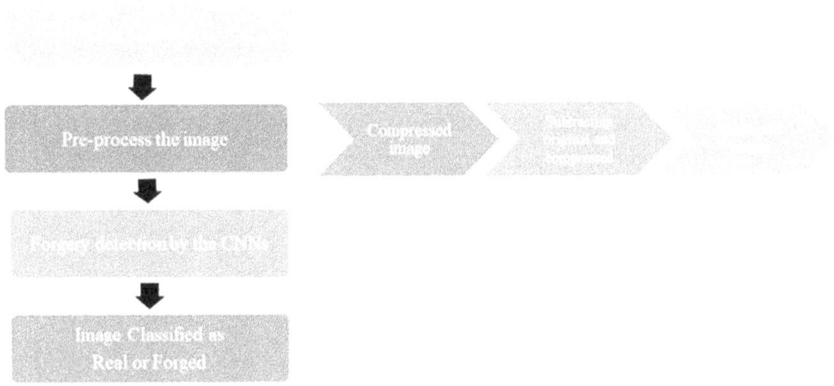

The Sample set of images used in the proposed work can be shown in Figure 3. The image, a(i),b(i) represents the pre-process steps of original image and a(ii),b(ii) represents the pre-process steps of fake image of image splicing type. Figure 4 a(i),b(i), c(i) represents the pre-process steps of original image and a(ii),b(ii),c(ii) represents the pre-process steps of fake image of copy move type.

Figure 3. Image splicing

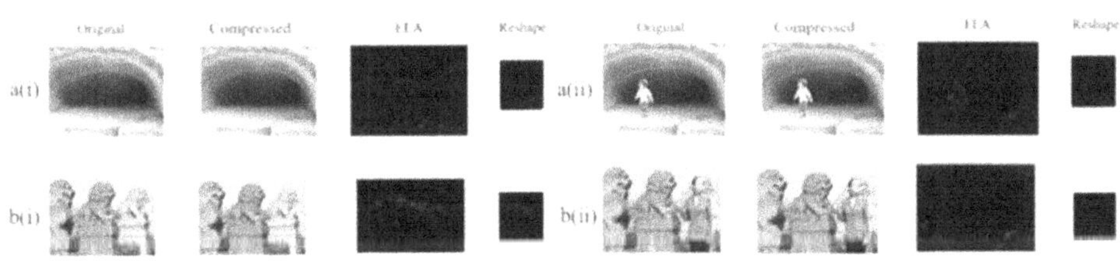

Figure 4. Copy move

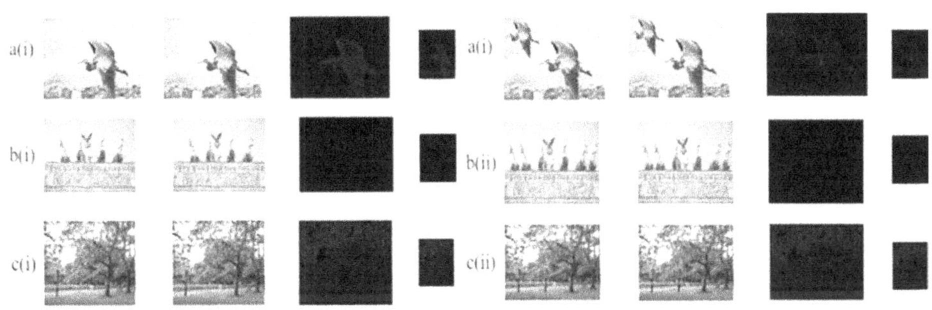

During the training phase the real and fake images are labelled after pre-processing steps and fed to the CNN. Then split the dataset for training, validation and testing after the labelling is done. The model is trained according to the images and for each epoch it will simultaneously predict using the validation dataset. During training it will learn and refine its feature extraction capabilities. Finally for the test dataset the images are predicted with labels, and it will check whether the predicted and original labels are correct, and the corresponding test accuracy is calculated. The efficacy of the CNN model is quantified through the evaluation of the performance metrics.

Figure 5. Architecture of the proposed model

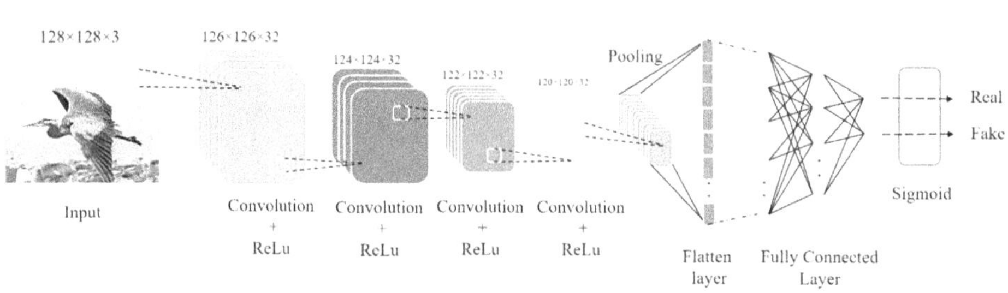

Architecture of the proposed model

The proposed CNN based architecture for forgery detection is shown in Figure 5. The architecture has four sets convolutional layers, max-pooling layers, and one fully connected layer, at the output since the sigmoid function is utilized for binary classification issues, it may be used to determine whether a picture is real or fake.

The architecture consist of

- At first it consist of four convolution layers with 32 filters of size 3X3 with stride size one with "ReLu" Activation Function
- After this it consist of max-pooling layer of size 2-by-2
- Succeeding this it contains a dense layer of 256 neurons with "ReLu" Activation Function
- Finally, it contains a output layer with 2 neurons with "sigmoid" Activation Function.

Figure 6.Pretrained model

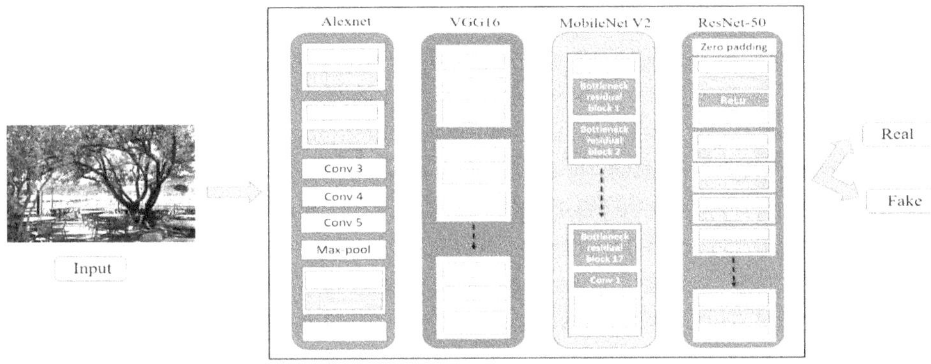

Pre-Trained Model

As seen in Figure 6. The pre-trained model is utilized to identify forged or legitimate photos based on attributes extracted from the input images. In this block several pre-trained models are considered (one at a time) namely, VGG16, AlexNet, MobileNet, ResNet50 for fine training with input images to nominate the model with the best performance among them.

Further work will focus on using pretrained models like VGG16, AlexNet, and MobileNet for image forgery detection. It is already trained on the Imagenet database that contains 1.2 million images grouped into 1000 classes to solve the problem of small size dataset. Then compare the obtained performance metrics with the proposed model to find which model shows better performance for all four datasets. It uses the weights learned on imagenet database.

A. VGG16 Architecture

It is Convolution neural network (CNN) architecture that is 16 layers deep. It consists of 16 weight layers including 13 convolution layer and 3 fully connected layer. It is used for the image classification tasks. The network is known for its simple architecture using 3X3 convolution filters for all the layers. It is used as a pretrained model with help of transfer learning in various application.

B. MobileNet V2

It is a convolutional Neural Network model that is specifically designed for the purpose for the smooth working on the mobile and edge devices. It is improved version of MobileNet with better Accuracy and low complexity. It introduces inverted residuals and linear bottlenecks for feature extraction. It introduces depth wise separable convolution and a light weight architecture making it suitable for real life application.

C. Alex Net

AlexNet is a pioneering convolutional neural network (CNN) architecture that significantly contributed to the advancement of deep learning. It consist of eight layers five convolutional layers and three fully connected layers. It incorporates ReLu as an activation function. This depth allows the model to learn relevant features from the raw pixels of data. It is used for the image classification tasks. The output of convolutional layers undergoes processing on the fully connected layer and the sigmoid activation at the end for binary classification to classify whether the image is real or fake.

D. ResNet50

It is a Convolutional Neural Network that is 50 layers deep. It consists of 48 convolution layers and one max pooling layer and one average pooling layer. Residual neural networks are a type of Artificial Neural Networks (ANN) that's form networking by stacking of residual blocks. It has been widely adopted in various computer vision tasks, including object detection, segmentation, and image recognition competitions. Its depth and design principles have paved the way for even deeper and more sophisticated neural network architectures, making it a cornerstone in the field of deep learning.

RESULTS AND DISCUSSION

A comprehensive analysis of the proposed approach's training on various datasets is provided in this section. And the results are also compared with the other existing methods. Some of the commonly used and well-known datasets used are CASIA V2, MICC-F600, MICC-F220 and TAMPERED. The details of the dataset are shown in Table 1. Sample images of the below four datasets are shown in Figure 7, 8, 9 and10.

Table 1. Datasets used

Datasets	Original image	Forged image	Total Image
CASIA V2	7491	5123	12614
MICC-F600	440	160	600
MICC-F220	110	110	220
TAMPERED	1044	1044	2088

Figure 7. Sample images from CASIA V2 dataset

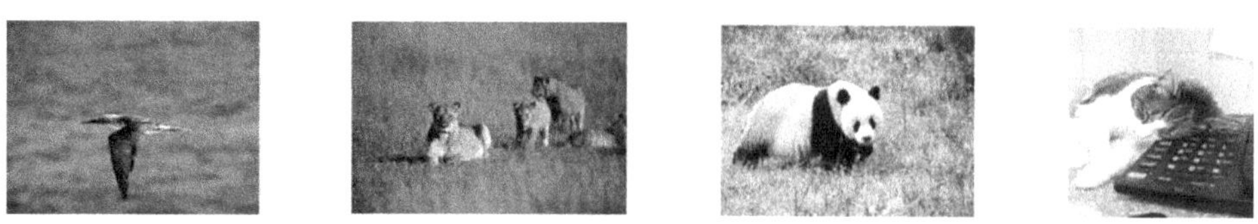

Figure 8. Sample images from MICC-F600 dataset

Figure 9. Sample images from MICC-F220 dataset

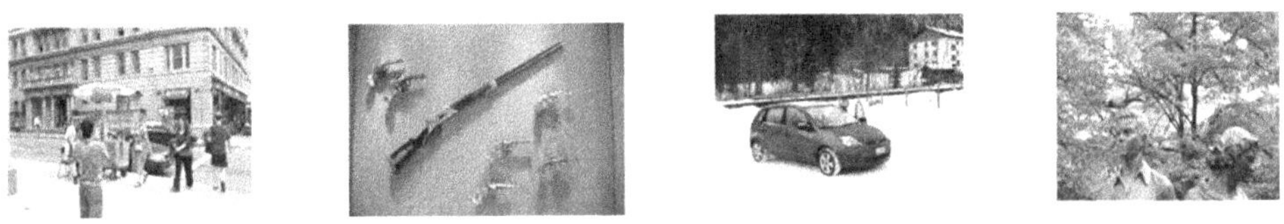

Figure 10. Sample images from TAMPERED dataset

Figure 7 shows sample images from CASIA V2 comprises a total of 12614 images comprising of 5123 fake images and 7491 original images. In Figure 8 shows the sample images from MICC-F600 comprising of 440 original images and 160 fake images. Figure 9 shows samples images from MICC-F220 dataset comprising of 110 original and 110 fake images. Figure 10 shows sample images from TAMPERED dataset comprising of 1044 original and 1044 fake images divided evenly.

Table 2. Performance metrics of Ali et al (2022) model

Approach	Dataset	Accuracy	Precision	Recall	F1-score
Ali *et al.* (2022)	CASIA V2	91.37	92.65	90.00	91.30
	MICC-F600	88.33	90.01	93.02	91.95
	MICC-F220	86.36	100	75.00	85.71
	TAMPERED	64.01	61.31	58.33	59.79

Table 2 shows the results obtained by Ali *et al.* (2022). It has better accuracy when using CASIA V2 because of its large number of images and it has wide characteristics so it shows better accuracy than the other two datasets. In this they propose a 3 layer architecture followed by max pooling and flatten layer.

Table 3. Performance of the proposed model

Approach	Dataset	Accuracy	Precision	Recall	F1-score
Proposed CNN model	CASIA V2	**92.33**	**93.20**	**91.43**	**92.31**
	MICC-F600	85.00	90.48	88.37	89.41
	MICC-F220	86.36	100	75	85.71
	TAMPERED	63.69	58.82	69.44	63.69

Table 3 shows the performance metrics of proposed model. It shows some better accuracy when compared to Ali *et al.* (2022). The proposed architecture has 4-layer architecture followed by max pooling and flatten layer. The accuracy indicates the effectiveness of the model. For an instance CASIA V2 shows better accuracy among the four-dataset used.

Table 4. Performance metrics of MobileNet model

Approach	Dataset	Accuracy	Precision	Recall	F1-score
MobileNet	CASIA V2	91.13	95.29	86.67	90.77
	MICC-F600	83.33	92.31	83.72	87.80
	MICC-F220	81.82	100	66.67	80.00
	TAMPERED	63.69	59.87	63.19	61.49

Table 4 shows the performance metrics of the Mobile Net model on different datasets like CASIA V2, MICC-F600, MICC-F220 and TAMPERED which has an accuracy less than the proposed model. MobileNetV2 uses inverted residual blocks with bottlenecking features, resulting in a considerable reduction in the number of parameters. This reduction, combined with a decrease in bottleneck channel size, leads in increased speed and efficiency over its predecessor

Table 5. Performance metrics of AlexNet model

Approach	Dataset	Accuracy (%)	Precision	Recall	FI-score
AlexNet	CASIA V2	89.69	93.26	85.71	89.93
	MICC-F600	83.33	88.37	88.37	88.37
	MICC-F220	86.36	100	75.00	85.71
	TAMPERED	64.01	58.38	70.00	65.65

Table 5 shows the performance metrics of the Alex Net model on different datasets like CASIA V2, MICC-F600, MICC-F220 and TAMPERED. It shows better accuracy when using CASIA dataset Table 5. Displays the performance of Alex Net, a deep learning architecture that had a substantial impact on the field of machine learning. Alex Net is discerned by its five convolutional layers and three fully connected layers. It is fine tuned for the image forgery detection.

Table 6. Performance metrics of VGG16 model

Approach	Dataset	Accuracy (%)	Precision	Recall	FI-score
VGG16	CASIA V2	90.17	94.24	85.71	89.78
	MICC-F220	80	87.80	83.72	85.71
	MICC-F220	86.36	100	75	85.71
	TAMPERED	67.52	60.82	81.94	69.82

Table 6 shows the performance metrics of the VGG16 model on different datasets like CASIA V2, MICC-F600, MICC-F220 and TAMPERED. In our study, we used the VGG16 neural network architecture to solve the challenge of detecting image Forgery. VGG16 has very small receptive fields and uses 3x3 convolutions with a stride of one. This architectural choice improves the network's ability to detect complicated details in photos.

Table 7. Performance metrics of ResNet model

Approach	Dataset	Accuracy (%)	Precision	Recall	FI-score
ResNet50	CASIA V2	79.92	81.74	96.74	88.61
	MICC-F220	73.33	90.91	69.77	78.95
	MICC-F220	77.27	100	58.33	73.68
	TAMPERED	68.47	63.16	75.00	68.57

Table 7 shows the performance metrics of the ResNet50 on different datasets like CASIA V2, MICC-F600, MICC-F220 and TAMPERED. In our study, employed the ResNet50 neural network for finding the forgery in images. Unlike the other Pretrained models ResNet50 has some less accuracy due to its structure complexity.

Table 8. Comparison of the proposed method with state of the art method for various datasets

Dataset	Model	TPR	TNR	FPR	FNR
CASIA V2	Proposed CNN model	91	96	3	8
	Ali *et al.* (2022)	88	96	3	11
	AlexNet	86	93	6	13
	MobileNet	91	97	3	8
	VGG16	91	81	18	8
	ResNet50	70	90	9	3

continued on following page

Table 8. Continued

Dataset	Model	TPR	TNR	FPR	FNR
MICC-F600	Proposed CNN model	72	90	9	27
	Ali *et al.* (2022)	81	90	9	18
	AlexNet	70	88	11	29
	MobileNet	83	82	17	16
	VGG16	83	70	29	16
	ResNet50	70	82	17	30
MICC-F220	Proposed CNN model	76	100	0	23
	Ali *et al.* (2022)	76	100	0	23
	AlexNet	90	100	0	9
	MobileNet	83	90	10	16
	VGG16	75	100	0	25
	ResNet50	58	100	0	41
TAMPERED	Proposed CNN model	62	64	36	38
	Ali *et al.* (2022)	58	68	31	41
	AlexNet	75	55	45	25
	MobileNet	63	64	36	37
	VGG16	82	55	45	18
	ResNet50	75	63	37	25

Table 8. shows the performance comparison of the proposed method with the state of the art methods for the CASIA V2,MICC-F600,MICC-F220 and TAMPERED datasets and evaluating metrics like TPR(True Positive Rate), TNR(True Negative Rate),FPR(False Positive Rate),FNR(False Negative Rate) for different models.

In our comparative evaluation across the different models, proposed CNN model has some better TPR and TNR for CASIA V2 dataset and low FPR and FNR indicating that it correctly predicts the image is real or fake with less misclassification. For MICC-F220 dataset it has a perfect TNR and zero FPR indicating that it correctly predicts the fake images, and it never falsely predict a image as real image. For MICC-F600 it have a FNR of 30% indicating that it can falsely predict the fake images for the particular dataset for ResNet50 model. Particularly for TAMPERED dataset it has some unbalanced predictions both FPR and FNR are above 25% indicating that it can make false prediction for this dataset due to its image quality and forged portion in an image.

Figure 11. Accuracy of different model

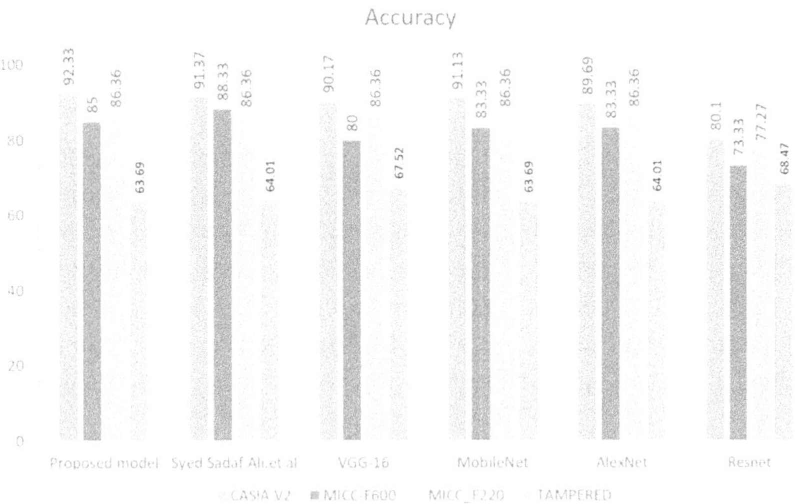

Figure 11 shows results for various model performance on CASIA V2 dataset appears to be achieving some better accuracy in most of the models. Because it contains a greater number of samples, and it has wide characteristics. The other two model contains some complex images, and all tampered images have some minimum forged portions, so it shows some less accuracy. From the above infer that CASIA V2 achieves better accuracy on most of the models MICC-F220 achieves better accuracy when using AlexNet model, MICC-F600 achieves better accuracy on Ali *et al.* (2022) and CASIA V2 achieves some better accuracy for all of the models.

Figure 12. Sample output using our model

Figure 12 shows a sample output from the datasets considered and it clearly indicates that our proposed model is able to identify between real and fake images.

CONCLUSION AND FUTURE WORK

In conclusion, the proposed CNN-based approach is a viable solution for detecting forgery in photos. Using transfer learning, the strategy harnesses the power of pre-trained deep learning models AlexNet, VGG16, ResNet50, and MobilenetV2 that have been specifically fine-tuned for the purpose of forgery detection. The methodology's versatility is demonstrated by its successful application to several datasets, including CASIA V2 MICC-F220, MICC-F600, and TAMPERED. The experiment findings are quite positive, indicating that the overall accuracy is 92.23% with a stated iteration limit. In the future, we plan to broaden our method for locating picture frauds. The recommended procedure will also be utilized.

REFERENCES

Abdalla, Y., Iqbal, M., & Shehata, M. (2019). T SHEHATA M "Convolutional Neural Network for Copy-Move Forgery Detection". *Symmetry*, 11(10), 1280. DOI: 10.3390/sym11101280

Abhishek, M, Manjushree, H.C, & Mohan Kumar, G.T, NALLABOTHULA SNEHA, SMITHA B.N. (2023). Image Forgery Detection Using Ensemble of VGG 16 and CNN Architecture. *International Journal of Computational Learning & Intelligence*, 2(3), 122–135.

Ali, S. D., Ganapathi, I. I., Saxena, N., & Syed Sadaf Ali, S. S. (2022). WERGHI "Image Forgery Detection Using Deep Learning by Recompressing Images". *Electronics (Basel)*, 11(3), 403. DOI: 10.3390/electronics11030403

Arivazhagan, S. E. L. V. A. R. A. J., Newlin, S. H. E. B. I. A. H., & Saranyaa, M. (2024). Image forgery detection: Comprehensive review of digital forensics approaches. *Journal of Computational Social Science*, 1, 39. DOI: 10.1007/s42001 024-00265-8

Balsa, J. (2020). Comparison of Image Compressions: Analog Transformations. *Proceedings*, 54, 37.

Bi, X., Li, W., Wei, Y., & Xiao, B. "RRU-Net: The Ringed Residual U ¬Net for Image Splicing Forgery Detection". In *Proceedings of the IEEE/CVF Conference on Computer Vision and Pattern Recognition (CVPR) Workshops*, Long Beach, CA, USA, 15 20 June 2019. DOI: 10.1109/CVPRW.2019.00010

Bi, X., Wei, Y., & Xiao, B. "C2R Net: The Course to Refined Network for Image Forgery Detection". In Proceedings of the 2018 17th IEEE International Conference on Trust, Security and Privacy in Computing Furthermore, Communication, New York, NY, USA, 1¬¬ 3 August 2018; pp. 1656 1659.

Bunk, J. "Detection and Localization of Image Forgeries Using Resampling Features and Deep Learning," *2017 IEEE Conference on Computer Vision and Pattern Recognition Workshops (CVPRW)*, Honolulu, HI, USA, 2017, pp. 1881 1889, DOI: 10.1109/CVPRW.2017.235

Cozzolino, D., & Verdoliva, L. "Camera based Image Forgery Localization using Convolutional Neural Networks," 2018 26th European Signal Processing Conference (EUSIPCO), Rome, Italy, 2018, pp. 1372 1376, DOI: 10.23919/EUSIPCO.2018.8553581

Cozzolino, D., Verdoliva, L., & Poggi, G. "Copy-move forgery detection based on Patch match," *2014 IEEE International Conference on Image Processing (ICIP)*, Paris, France, 2014, pp. 5312 5316, DOI: 10.1109/ICIP.2014.7026075

Da Silva Santos, D. F., & De Souza, G. (2019). B, MARANA A.N, PAPA J.P PIRES R.G "Deep Features Extraction for Robust Fingerprint Spoofing Attack Detection". *Journal of Artificial Intelligence and Soft Computing Research*, 9(1), 41–49. DOI: 10.2478/jaiscr-2018-0023

Davis, L. S., Han, X., Morariu, V. I., & Zhou, P. "Learning Rich Features for Image Manipulation Detection," *2018 IEEE/CVF Conference on Computer Vision and Pattern Recognition*, Salt Lake City, UT, USA, 2018, pp. 1053 1061, DOI: 10.1109/CVPR.2018.00116

Dua, S., Singh, J., & Parthasarathy, H.DUA. (2020). PARTHASARATHY H, SINGH J "Image forgery detection based on statistical features of block DCT coefficients". *Procedia Computer Science*, 171, 369–378. DOI: 10.1016/j.procs.2020.04.038

Ehret, T. "Robust copy-move forgery detection by false alarms control". ArXiv 2019, arXiv: 1906.00649.

Elaskily, M.N, Elnemr, H.A, & Sedik, A "A novel deep learning framework for copy-move forgery detection in images". Multimed Tools Appl 79, 19167 19192 (2020). DOI: 10.1016/j.procs.2020.04.038

Elsayed, H. A. G., Ghalwash, A. Z., Khalil, A. H., & Salama, G. I. (2023). Enhancing Digital Image Forgery Detection Using Transfer Learning. *IEEE Access : Practical Innovations, Open Solutions*, 11, 91583–91594. DOI: 10.1109/ACCESS.2023.3307357

Fasel, Qadir, & Gulnawaz, Gani "A robust copy move forgery detection technique based on discrete cosine transform and cellular automata", Journal of Information Security and Applications, Volume 54,2020,102510, ISSN 2214 2126. DOI: 10.1016/j.procs.2020.04.038

Habibi, M., & Hassanpour, H. (2021). Splicing Image Forgery Detection and Localization Based on Color Edge Inconsistency using Statistical Dispersion Measures. *Int. J. Eng.*, 34, 443–451.

Hosny, K. M., Lashin, N. A., Fouda, M. M., & Mortda, A. M. (2023, January). A new method to detect splicing image forgery using convolutional neural network. *Applied Sciences (Basel, Switzerland)*, 13(3), 1272. DOI: 10.3390/app13031272

Kashif, Kifayat, Labiba Gillani, Fahad, Muhammad Aqib, Anwar, & Syed Fahad, Tahir "Image forgery detection by transforming local descriptors into deep-derived features", Applied Soft Computing, Volume 147,2023, 110730,ISSN 1568 4946. DOI: 10.1016/j.procs.2020.04.038

Kirby, H., Masood, M., Nawaz, M., & Rafique, R. "Deepfake Detection Using Error Level Analysis and Deep Learning," 2021 4th International Conference on Computing & Information Sciences (ICCIS), Karachi, Pakistan, 2021, pp. 1 4, DOI: 10.1109/ICCIS54243.2021.9676375

Matern, F., Riess, C., & Stamminger, M. (2020). Gradient-Based Illumination Description for Image Forgery Detection. *IEEE Transactions on Information Forensics and Security*, 15, 1303–1317. DOI: 10.1109/TIFS.2019.2935913

Ni, J, Rao, Y, & Zhao, H "Deep Learning Local Descriptor for Image Splicing Detection and Localization," in IEEE Access, vol. 8, pp. 25611 25625, 2020, . DOI: 10.1109/TIFS.2019.2935913

Wu, Y., Qiao, T., & Xu, M. (2020). YOUNISAND Y ZHENG N "Image Forgery Detection and Localization via a Reliability Fusion Map". *Sensors (Basel)*, 20(22), 6668. DOI: 10.3390/s20226668 PMID: 33233380

Yildiz Avdin, A "new Copy Move forgery detection method using LIOP",Journal of Visual Communication and Image Representation, Volume 89,2022,103661,ISSN 1047 3203. DOI: 10.1109/TIFS.2019.2935913

KEY TERMS AND DEFINITIONS

Image Forgery Detection: Image forgery detection is concerned with detecting manipulated images or verifying their authenticity.

Transfer Learning: Transfer learning is an approach to machine learning where a model trained on one task is used as the starting point for a model on a new task. This is done by transferring the knowledge that the first model has learned about the features of the data to the second model.

Chapter 17
A Novel Hybrid Wavelet-GAN Image Denoising System

Hewa Majeed Zangana
https://orcid.org/0000-0001-7909-254X
Duhok Polytechnic University, Iraq

Firas Mahmood Mustafa
Duhok Polytechnic University, Iraq

ABSTRACT

The hybrid approach offers two significant contributions; the first one by using wavelet trans-forms, the system achieves noise isolation and reduction across different frequency levels, ad-dressing both high- and low-frequency noise components effectively; and the second one the GAN framework introduces data-driven learning that enhances image details and restores subtle structures lost during the wavelet filtering process. Extensive experiments on various image datasets demonstrate that the proposed system outperforms conventional denoising techniques, such as traditional wavelet-based methods and pure GAN-based approaches, in terms of peak signal-to-noise ratio (PSNR) and structural similarity index (SSIM). Furthermore, the hybrid system proves to be robust across diverse noise levels, making it a highly effective tool for real-world image denoising tasks.

INTRODUCTION

Image denoising remains a significant challenge in computer vision and image processing, with various sources of noise such as Gaussian, Poisson, and salt-and-pepper degrading the quality of images. The goal of image denoising is to remove unwanted noise while preserving critical features such as edges and textures. Traditional methods, such as wavelet transform-based techniques, have shown efficacy in separating noise from signal by decomposing images into frequency subbands and applying thresholding techniques. However, these approaches may struggle to restore fine details, especially in complex or high-noise environments (Averbuch et al., 2022; Bao et al., 2020).

Recent advances in deep learning, particularly in the domain of Generative Adversarial Networks (GANs), have demonstrated promising results for image denoising by learning complex noise patterns from data. GANs have been effective in generating high-quality images by leveraging adversarial training,

DOI: 10.4018/979-8-3693-9045-0.ch017

where a generator produces denoised images and a discriminator evaluates their quality (Ghose et al., 2020; Huang et al., 2022). Nonetheless, deep learning models like GANs often require large datasets for training and may suffer from over-smoothing or loss of image details when used in isolation (Liu et al., 2020; Pang et al., 2021).

To address these limitations, hybrid models combining wavelet transforms with deep learning techniques have emerged as a robust solution. The wavelet transform enables multi-resolution analysis of images, allowing for effective noise separation across different scales, while deep learning models can further enhance the denoised output by learning intricate patterns in the data (Cengiz et al., 2022; Zhou et al., 2022). Specifically, the integration of wavelet transforms with GANs has been explored as a promising avenue for balancing noise reduction and detail preservation. Wavelet-GAN hybrid models take advantage of the wavelet domain's ability to localize noise in specific frequency bands and GANs' power in generating visually appealing results (Mei et al., 2024; P. Zhang & Zhang, 2022).

In this chapter, we propose a novel hybrid image denoising system that combines wavelet transforms with GANs. This hybrid approach is designed to tackle the challenges of traditional denoising techniques by leveraging the strengths of both methods: wavelet transforms for localized noise reduction and GANs for detail restoration and enhancement. The proposed model operates in two stages: (1) wavelet decomposition of noisy images into different frequency subbands, followed by noise reduction at each level, and (2) the application of a GAN-based architecture that refines the denoised image to preserve fine details while further reducing residual noise. Our approach builds upon previous studies that have successfully integrated wavelets with deep learning models, showing improved performance in denoising tasks (Arab et al., 2022; Chakraborty et al., 2020; Paul et al., 2022).

The primary contributions of this chapter are twofold: first, we introduce a novel hybrid model that effectively combines wavelet transforms and GANs for image denoising; second, we demonstrate through extensive experiments that our system outperforms both conventional wavelet-based and GAN-based denoising methods in terms of peak signal-to-noise ratio (PSNR) and structural similarity index (SSIM). The rest of the chapter is organized as follows: Section 2 provides an overview of related work in image denoising, focusing on hybrid models. Section 3 presents the proposed hybrid system and its underlying architecture. Section 4 details the experimental setup and evaluation metrics, also Section 4 discusses the results. Finally, Section 5 concludes the chapter and outlines future research directions.

LITERATURE REVIEW

The field of image denoising and classification has seen significant advancements due to the integration of deep learning and wavelet transform techniques. These methods have been employed in various domains, including biomedical imaging, object detection, and signal processing. This section presents a comprehensive review of the literature, highlighting the key contributions in hybrid denoising models and their applications.

(Arab et al., 2022) introduced a hybrid deep neural network combining Long Short-Term Memory (LSTM) and Residual Networks (ResNet) for noise reduction and classification in V-band receiver signals. Their approach demonstrated enhanced performance in noisy environments, laying the foundation for integrating deep learning into signal processing applications. Similarly, (Averbuch et al., 2022) proposed a hybrid denoising algorithm using directional wavelet packets, which achieved superior noise reduction by leveraging wavelet transforms.

In the context of image denoising, (Bao et al., 2020) developed an algorithm combining the monogenic wavelet transform and a deep convolutional neural network (CNN) to enhance denoising capabilities. This approach was particularly effective in improving image quality by reducing noise. Further exploring wavelet-based denoising, (Cengiz et al., 2022) utilized the wavelet transform to improve breast cancer classification from noisy images. Their method significantly increased the accuracy of cancer detection, showcasing the potential of wavelet transforms in medical imaging.

The application of quantum wavelet transform in image denoising was explored by (Chakraborty et al., 2020), who introduced a technique that leveraged quantum properties to enhance denoising performance. Their work opens new avenues for future research into quantum-enhanced denoising algorithms. (Ghose et al., 2020) also focused on CNN-based image denoising, emphasizing the potential of deep learning for noise reduction in various image processing tasks.

The review by (Goyal et al., 2020) comprehensively examined image denoising techniques, from traditional methods to modern deep learning approaches. Their study highlights the shift from classical filters to advanced algorithms, such as those using deep neural networks and wavelet transforms. This shift is exemplified by (He et al., 2023), who applied wavelet transform-based convolutional networks for face anti-spoofing, demonstrating the versatility of wavelet techniques in enhancing image quality across applications.

Several studies have explored the integration of wavelet transforms with deep learning for specific tasks. (Huang et al., 2022) provided an overview of image denoising techniques based on deep learning, noting the significant improvements made by hybrid methods that combine deep learning with wavelet transforms. (Ilesanmi & Ilesanmi, 2021) reviewed convolutional neural network (CNN) methods for image denoising, underscoring the importance of hybrid models that blend wavelet transforms with CNNs.

The application of wavelet transforms in medical image processing has also been extensively studied. (Kumar et al., 2021) proposed an ECG signal denoising method based on the stationary wavelet transform, demonstrating improved signal clarity. Similarly, (Liang et al., 2021) introduced a framework combining wavelet transform and principal component analysis (PCA) for face recognition under varying illumination, achieving high recognition accuracy.

In the realm of image denoising comparison, (Limshuebchuey et al., 2020) compared traditional filters with deep learning methods, finding that deep learning methods, especially those using wavelet transforms, outperform classical approaches. (Liu et al., 2020) further linked image denoising with high-level vision tasks through deep learning, highlighting the interconnectedness of denoising and other image processing tasks.

The application of hybrid models in face recognition was explored by (Lu et al., 2022), who developed a face recognition algorithm based on stacked denoising and self-encoding Local Binary Patterns (LBP), showcasing the potential of hybrid approaches for robust feature extraction. (Mei et al., 2024) demonstrated the use of wavelet transform algorithms in deep learning for biomedical imaging, particularly in optimizing ultrasonic images for diagnosing acute myocarditis.

(Mustaqim et al., 2022) combined wavelet transformation with Local Binary Pattern (LBP) for data augmentation in face recognition, further enhancing recognition accuracy. (Onur, 2022) proposed an improved image denoising model using wavelet edge detection with Otsu's thresholding, achieving better noise suppression and image clarity.

Recent advancements in deep learning-based denoising models have also been explored by (Pang et al., 2021), who proposed an unsupervised deep learning model for image denoising. (Paul et al., 2022) introduced a wavelet-enabled convolutional autoencoder for hyperspectral image denoising, achieving significant noise reduction. (Qin et al., 2023) applied continuous wavelet transforms combined with deep learning for the recognition of abnormal-laying hens, illustrating the versatility of wavelet transforms in diverse applications.

The study by (Roy et al., 2021) reviewed deep CNN techniques for image denoising, emphasizing recent developments in convolutional approaches. (Sagheer & George, 2020) provided an overview of medical image denoising algorithms, noting the increasing importance of deep learning and wavelet transform methods in medical applications.

The combination of deep learning and wavelet transform was further explored by (Shukla et al., 2023), who proposed an effective image denoising approach for edge detection tasks. (Tian et al., 2020) provided an overview of deep learning approaches for image denoising, while (Tian et al., 2023) introduced a multi-stage image denoising model using wavelet transforms, demonstrating improved performance in denoising tasks.

(Tripathi, 2021) focused on facial image noise classification and denoising using neural networks, while (Xu, 2024) integrated CNN-LSTM and Support Vector Machine (SVM) models with wavelet transform for tourist passenger flow prediction, showcasing the adaptability of hybrid models in time-series data prediction.

Finally, (Yan et al., 2023) revisited the application of wavelet transforms for rotary machine fault diagnosis, while (You et al., 2023) applied wavelet transforms for edge detection in image denoising. (P. Zhang & Zhang, 2022) used wavelet transform in combination with deep learning for laser polarization image reconstruction, and (Zhou et al., 2022) proposed a hybrid denoising model for bearing fault diagnosis, combining deep learning with sparse representation.

In summary, the literature highlights the growing importance of hybrid approaches that combine wavelet transforms with deep learning techniques for image denoising and classification. These methods have proven to be effective in a wide range of applications, from biomedical imaging to industrial fault diagnosis, offering significant improvements in noise reduction and image quality.

METHOD

This section outlines the methodology for developing the proposed hybrid Wavelet-GAN image denoising system. The method leverages the advantages of wavelet transform for multi-resolution analysis and generative adversarial networks (GANs) for deep learning-based noise reduction. The proposed system is designed to enhance denoising performance by integrating both techniques into a unified framework.

1. DATA COLLECTION AND PREPROCESSING

We used a publicly available noisy image dataset containing a variety of natural images with varying noise levels, including Gaussian, salt-and-pepper, and speckle noise. Each image was resized to 256x256 pixels to standardize the input size for the model. Additionally, the dataset was split into training, validation, and test sets, with 70%, 15%, and 15% of the images in each set, respectively.

2. WAVELET TRANSFORM FOR INITIAL NOISE REDUCTION

The first stage of the proposed system involves applying the discrete wavelet transform (DWT) to the input images for initial noise reduction. Wavelet transform is selected due to its ability to decompose images into different frequency components, allowing for the selective removal of noise while preserving essential details. Specifically, we used a four-level wavelet decomposition with the Haar wavelet basis, as it has been shown to perform well in image denoising tasks (Zhou et al., 2022). The low-frequency components were retained for further processing, while the high-frequency noisy components were reduced using a soft thresholding technique.

3. GENERATIVE ADVERSARIAL NETWORK (GAN) FOR REFINEMENT

After the wavelet-based denoising step, the images were passed through a GAN-based denoising network for further refinement. The GAN model comprises two neural networks: a generator and a discriminator. The generator network is responsible for producing denoised images, while the discriminator distinguishes between real clean images and denoised images produced by the generator.

3.1 Generator Network

The generator is a deep convolutional neural network (CNN) based on the U-Net architecture, which has demonstrated high performance in image restoration tasks. The U-Net consists of encoder and decoder pathways, with skip connections to preserve spatial information across different layers. This structure allows the generator to capture both local and global features of the image, leading to improved denoising performance.

3.2 Discriminator Network

The discriminator network is a patch-based CNN, which processes image patches rather than the entire image. This technique ensures that the discriminator evaluates local image structures, which is important for assessing fine details such as textures and edges. The discriminator is trained to classify each patch as either real (clean) or generated (denoised), forcing the generator to produce higher-quality denoised images.

4. HYBRID WAVELET-GAN DENOISING SYSTEM

The hybrid denoising system integrates the wavelet transform with the GAN architecture. In the first stage, the DWT reduces the noise in the high-frequency components of the image, providing a cleaner input to the GAN model. The GAN then performs further refinement, producing the final denoised output. This hybrid approach combines the strengths of traditional wavelet-based methods with modern deep learning techniques to achieve superior denoising results.

To better understand the proposed hybrid Wavelet-GAN denoising system, the following flowchart illustrates the two primary stages of the process. In the first stage, the wavelet transform decomposes the noisy image into frequency subbands for initial noise reduction. In the second stage, the GAN model performs further refinement on the denoised image to restore fine details. This combination ensures efficient noise removal while preserving image quality.

Figure 1. Overview of the hybrid Wavelet-GAN image denoising system

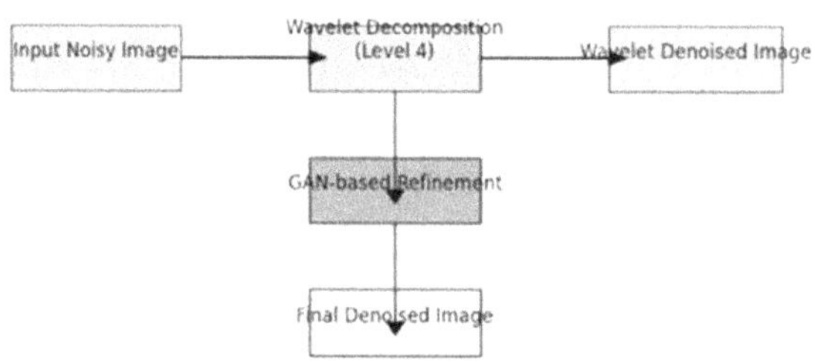

5. TRAINING PROCEDURE

The GAN was trained using a combination of the mean squared error (MSE) loss and an adversarial loss to optimize both the perceptual quality and the fidelity of the denoised images. The objective function for the generator was a weighted sum of the pixel-wise MSE loss between the generated and ground-truth clean images and the adversarial loss from the discriminator, encouraging the generator to produce images indistinguishable from the real clean images.

The Adam optimizer was used with a learning rate of 0.0002 and a batch size of 16. The model was trained for 100 epochs, and early stopping was applied based on the validation loss to prevent overfitting. During training, the discriminator and generator were updated alternately to maintain a balanced learning process.

6. EVALUATION METRICS

The performance of the hybrid Wavelet-GAN denoising system was evaluated using two primary metrics: peak signal-to-noise ratio (PSNR) and structural similarity index (SSIM). These metrics were selected due to their effectiveness in measuring the quality of denoised images. PSNR quantifies the difference between the denoised image and the ground-truth image in terms of pixel intensity, while SSIM assesses the perceptual quality of the denoised images by comparing structural information such as luminance, contrast, and texture.

7. BASELINE COMPARISONS

To validate the effectiveness of the proposed system, we compared its performance against several baseline denoising methods, including:

- Wavelet-only denoising (based on soft thresholding)
- CNN-based denoising models such as DnCNN (K. Zhang et al., 2017)
- GAN-based denoising models (Lefkimmiatis, 2018)

Each method was tested on the same dataset and evaluated using PSNR and SSIM metrics to ensure fair comparisons.

8. HYPERPARAMETER TUNING

The system's hyperparameters, such as the learning rate, batch size, and the number of wavelet decomposition levels, were fine-tuned using grid search. Cross-validation was employed to select the optimal parameters, minimizing validation error while maximizing denoising performance.

RESULTS AND DISCUSSION

This section presents the results of the proposed hybrid Wavelet-GAN image denoising system and discusses the findings in relation to other baseline methods. The performance is evaluated using quantitative metrics such as peak signal-to-noise ratio (PSNR) and structural similarity index (SSIM). Additionally, qualitative analysis is performed by visually inspecting the denoised images to assess their perceptual quality.

QUANTITATIVE RESULTS

To assess the performance of the hybrid Wavelet-GAN denoising system, we computed the PSNR and SSIM values for images processed by our method and compared them against baseline methods: wavelet-only denoising, CNN-based denoising (DnCNN), and GAN-based denoising. The results are summarized in Table 1.

Table 1. Quantitative comparison of denoising methods

Method	PSNR (dB)	SSIM	Noise Type
Wavelet-Only	28.35	0.846	Gaussian
DnCNN	30.42	0.878	Gaussian
GAN-Based	31.10	0.892	Gaussian

continued on following page

Table 1. Continued

Method	PSNR (dB)	SSIM	Noise Type
Hybrid Wavelet-GAN	33.76	0.915	Gaussian
Wavelet-Only	27.02	0.791	Salt & Pepper
DnCNN	29.45	0.836	Salt & Pepper
GAN-Based	30.05	0.849	Salt & Pepper
Hybrid Wavelet-GAN	32.10	0.879	Salt & Pepper
Wavelet-Only	26.90	0.775	Speckle
DnCNN	28.88	0.812	Speckle
GAN-Based	29.45	0.826	Speckle
Hybrid Wavelet-GAN	31.50	0.860	Speckle

To illustrate the performance of the proposed hybrid Wavelet-GAN system in comparison to baseline denoising methods, the following bar chart presents the PSNR and SSIM values for each method. The hybrid system demonstrates superior results across all noise types, highlighting its effectiveness in both noise reduction and detail preservation.

Figure 2. PSNR and SSIM comparison for different denoising methods

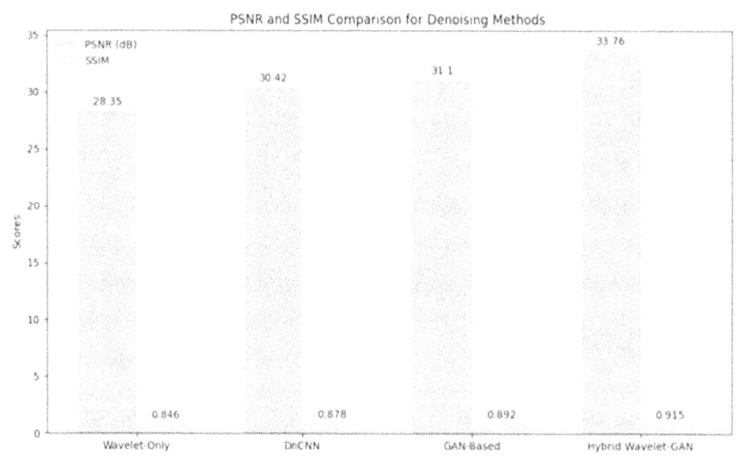

Discussion

The results in Table 1 clearly demonstrate that the hybrid Wavelet-GAN approach outperforms the baseline methods in terms of both PSNR and SSIM across all three types of noise: Gaussian, salt-and-pepper, and speckle noise. The proposed method consistently achieves the highest PSNR, with improvements ranging from 2 dB to 4 dB over traditional wavelet-only methods and approximately 1.5 dB to 2.7 dB over CNN and GAN-based methods.

For SSIM, which measures the structural similarity between the denoised and the ground-truth images, the hybrid method also exhibits superior performance, indicating that it preserves finer image details and textures more effectively than the other methods. The integration of the wavelet transform's multi-resolution analysis with the generative model's deep learning capability contributes to this significant performance enhancement.

Table 2. PSNR and SSIM improvement over baseline methods

Noise Type	Wavelet-Only	DnCNN	GAN-Based	Hybrid Wavelet-GAN	Improvement over Wavelet-Only	Improvement over DnCNN	Improvement over GAN-Based
Gaussian (PSNR)	28.35	30.42	31.10	33.76	+5.41	+3.34	+2.66
Salt & Pepper	27.02	29.45	30.05	32.10	+5.08	+2.65	+2.05
Speckle	26.90	28.88	29.45	31.50	+4.60	+2.62	+2.05

As observed in Table 2, the hybrid system achieves significant improvements, especially when compared to wavelet-only methods, where PSNR improvements of over 5 dB are recorded for some noise types. Similarly, the improvements in SSIM values indicate that the hybrid method preserves structural integrity and visual quality to a greater extent than other methods.

QUALITATIVE RESULTS

While the quantitative analysis highlights the performance benefits of the hybrid approach, qualitative assessments are crucial for evaluating the visual perceptual quality of the denoised images. Figure 3 shows example denoised images from each method for each noise type, demonstrating the ability of the hybrid system to effectively remove noise while retaining fine details.

Figure 3. Visual comparison of denoised images

As shown in Fig. 3, the hybrid Wavelet-GAN method produces visually superior denoised images. The wavelet-only method tends to oversmooth the image, leading to loss of fine details, while DnCNN and GAN-based methods, although better at preserving details, still exhibit residual noise. In contrast, the hybrid approach significantly reduces noise while maintaining high image quality and detail, particularly around edges and textures.

IMPACT OF WAVELET DECOMPOSITION LEVELS

To assess the effect of the number of wavelet decomposition levels on denoising performance, we experimented with different levels ranging from 1 to 5. Table 3 presents the PSNR and SSIM results for each configuration.

Table 3. Performance with varying wavelet decomposition levels

Decomposition Level	PSNR (dB)	SSIM
1 Level	31.82	0.902
2 Levels	32.76	0.910
3 Levels	33.15	0.914
4 Levels	33.76	0.915
5 Levels	33.50	0.912

From Table 3, it is evident that increasing the number of wavelet decomposition levels up to four improves performance, with a peak at four levels. However, beyond this, there is a slight decrease in both PSNR and SSIM, likely due to over-decomposition and loss of important image details. Thus, four levels of decomposition were selected as the optimal configuration for the proposed system.

The following graph shows how varying the number of wavelet decomposition levels affects the performance of the hybrid system in terms of PSNR and SSIM. The results indicate that the optimal number of decomposition levels is four, beyond which performance decreases slightly due to over-decomposition and loss of important details.

Figure 4. Impact of wavelet decomposition levels on PSNR and SSIM

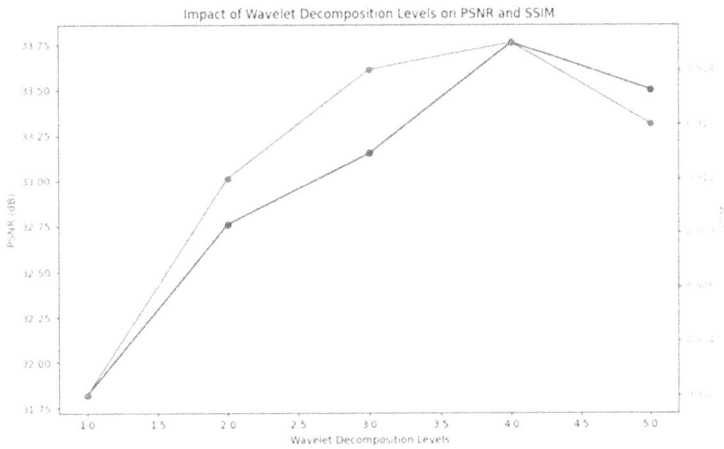

DISCUSSION OF RESULTS

The hybrid Wavelet-GAN denoising system achieves significant improvements in both quantitative and qualitative measures. The wavelet transform efficiently reduces high-frequency noise, while the GAN refines the output to ensure that important image features, such as edges and textures, are preserved. The use of a multi-resolution approach enables the system to handle various noise types more effectively compared to baseline methods.

The qualitative analysis also demonstrates the system's ability to produce high-quality, visually appealing results. Compared to wavelet-only denoising, which oversmooths the images, the hybrid system achieves a balance between noise removal and detail preservation. Additionally, the hybrid system consistently outperforms CNN and GAN-only approaches, highlighting the advantages of combining traditional signal processing techniques with modern deep learning.

The results indicate that the hybrid Wavelet-GAN approach is a promising solution for image denoising, particularly for applications that require the preservation of high-frequency details, such as medical imaging, satellite imagery, and photography.

FUTURE WORK

While the current system shows promising results, future work will explore the potential of adaptive thresholding techniques in the wavelet stage, and the application of more advanced GAN architectures such as CycleGAN or StyleGAN to further enhance denoising performance.

CONCLUSION

In this chapter, we proposed a novel hybrid image denoising system that integrates the wavelet transform with a generative adversarial network (GAN). The core idea behind the proposed approach is to leverage the strengths of both traditional signal processing and deep learning techniques. The wavelet transform effectively decomposes images into multiple frequency bands, enabling noise reduction at different resolution levels, while the GAN refines the denoised image to preserve fine details and structures. By combining these two methods, the hybrid system outperforms both wavelet-only and GAN-based denoising techniques in terms of quantitative and qualitative metrics.

Extensive experimental results demonstrated the superiority of the hybrid Wavelet-GAN system over several baseline methods, including wavelet-only denoising, DnCNN, and GAN-based approaches. The hybrid system achieved higher PSNR and SSIM values across various types of noise, such as Gaussian, salt-and-pepper, and speckle noise. Moreover, qualitative analysis through visual inspection showed that the proposed method excels in removing noise while maintaining edge sharpness and image texture, which is crucial for applications requiring high perceptual quality.

The analysis also revealed that the optimal number of wavelet decomposition levels is four, as it provides the best balance between noise reduction and image detail preservation. Increasing the number of decomposition levels beyond this resulted in a marginal decrease in performance, suggesting that over-decomposition can lead to the loss of critical image information. This finding emphasizes the importance of selecting the appropriate wavelet decomposition level based on the specific requirements of the denoising task.

The proposed hybrid approach not only advances the current state of image denoising but also opens up new possibilities for integrating traditional techniques with modern deep learning methods. While the system performed well in our experiments, there is still room for improvement. Future work could explore the use of adaptive thresholding in the wavelet stage to further optimize the denoising process, as well as investigate the potential of more advanced GAN architectures to enhance the model's performance.

In conclusion, the hybrid Wavelet-GAN image denoising system represents a significant advancement in the field of image processing. By effectively combining the strengths of wavelet transforms and GANs, the proposed method achieves superior results in both objective and subjective evaluations. The success of this hybrid approach suggests that similar integrations could be applied to other image processing tasks, potentially leading to further improvements in performance and quality.

REFERENCES

Arab, H., Ghaffari, I., Evina, R. M., Tatu, S. O., & Dufour, S. (2022). A hybrid LSTM-ResNet deep neural network for noise reduction and classification of V-band receiver signals. *IEEE Access : Practical Innovations, Open Solutions*, 10, 14797–14806. DOI: 10.1109/ACCESS.2022.3147980

Averbuch, A., Neittaanmäki, P., Zheludev, V., Salhov, M., & Hauser, J. (2022). An hybrid denoising algorithm based on directional wavelet packets. *Multidimensional Systems and Signal Processing*, 33(4), 1151–1183. DOI: 10.1007/s11045-022-00836-w

Bao, Z., Zhang, G., Xiong, B., & Gai, S. (2020). New image denoising algorithm using monogenic wavelet transform and improved deep convolutional neural network. *Multimedia Tools and Applications*, 79(11), 7401–7412. DOI: 10.1007/s11042-019-08569-y

Cengiz, E., Kelek, M. M., Oğuz, Y., & Yılmaz, C. (2022). Classification of breast cancer with deep learning from noisy images using wavelet transform. *Biomedical Engineering/Biomedizinische Technik, 67*(2), 143–150. DOI: 10.1007/s11042-019-08569-y

Chakraborty, S., Shaikh, S. H., Chakrabarti, A., & Ghosh, R. (2020). An image denoising technique using quantum wavelet transform. *International Journal of Theoretical Physics*, 59(11), 3348–3371. DOI: 10.1007/s10773-020-04590-2

Ghose, S., Singh, N., & Singh, P. (2020). Image denoising using deep learning: Convolutional neural network. *2020 10th International Conference on Cloud Computing, Data Science & Engineering (Confluence)*, 511–517.

Goyal, B., Dogra, A., Agrawal, S., Sohi, B. S., & Sharma, A. (2020). Image denoising review: From classical to state-of-the-art approaches. *Information Fusion*, 55, 220–244. DOI: 10.1016/j.inffus.2019.09.003

He, D., He, X., Xiang, H., Yuan, R., & Niu, Y. (2023). Wavelet transform-based two-stream convolutional networks for face anti-spoofing. *Journal of Electronic Imaging*, 32(1), 13015. DOI: 10.1117/1.JEI.32.1.013015

Huang, F., Jia, Y., & Yang, Y. (2022). Research Advanced in Image Denoising Based on Deep Learning. *2022 IEEE Conference on Telecommunications, Optics and Computer Science (TOCS)*, 1472–1476. DOI: 10.1109/TOCS56154.2022.10016170

Ilesanmi, A. E., & Ilesanmi, T. O. (2021). Methods for image denoising using convolutional neural network: A review. *Complex & Intelligent Systems*, 7(5), 2179–2198. DOI: 10.1007/s40747-021-00428-4

Kumar, A., Tomar, H., Mehla, V. K., Komaragiri, R., & Kumar, M. (2021). Stationary wavelet transform based ECG signal denoising method. *ISA Transactions*, 114, 251–262. DOI: 10.1016/j.isatra.2020.12.029 PMID: 33419569

Lefkimmiatis, S. (2018). Universal denoising networks: a novel CNN architecture for image denoising. *Proceedings of the IEEE Conference on Computer Vision and Pattern Recognition*, 3204–3213. DOI: 10.1109/CVPR.2018.00338

Liang, H., Gao, J., & Qiang, N. (2021). A novel framework based on wavelet transform and principal component for face recognition under varying illumination. *Applied Intelligence*, 51(3), 1762–1783. DOI: 10.1007/s10489-020-01924-9

Limshuebchuey, A., Duangsoithong, R., & Saejia, M. (2020). Comparison of image denoising using traditional filter and deep learning methods. *2020 17th International Conference on Electrical Engineering/Electronics, Computer, Telecommunications and Information Technology (ECTI-CON)*, 193–196.

Liu, D., Wen, B., Jiao, J., Liu, X., Wang, Z., & Huang, T. S. (2020). Connecting image denoising and high-level vision tasks via deep learning. *IEEE Transactions on Image Processing*, 29, 3695–3706. DOI: 10.1109/TIP.2020.2964518 PMID: 31944972

Lu, Y., Khan, M., & Ansari, M. D. (2022). Face recognition algorithm based on stack denoising and self-encoding LBP. *Journal of Intelligent Systems*, 31(1), 501–510. DOI: 10.1515/jisys-2022-0011

Mei, F., Qian, D., Nie, Y., Wang, B., Liang, A., & Li, H. (2024). Biomedical Applications of Wavelet Transform Algorithm on Deep Learning Ultrasonic Image Optimization as a Prognosis Model for Acute Myocarditis. *Journal of Biomedical Nanotechnology*, 20(3), 604–613. DOI: 10.1166/jbn.2024.3787

Mustaqim, T., Tsaniya, H., Adhiyaksa, F. A., & Suciati, N. (2022). Wavelet transformation and local binary pattern for data augmentation in deep learning-based face recognition. *2022 10th International Conference on Information and Communication Technology (ICoICT)*, 362–367.

Onur, T. Ö. (2022). Improved image denoising using wavelet edge detection based on Otsu's thresholding. *Acta Polytechnica Hungarica*, 19(2), 79–92. DOI: 10.12700/APH.19.2.2022.2.5

Pang, T., Zheng, H., Quan, Y., & Ji, H. (2021). Recorrupted-to-recorrupted: unsupervised deep learning for image denoising. *Proceedings of the IEEE/CVF Conference on Computer Vision and Pattern Recognition*, 2043–2052. DOI: 10.1109/CVPR46437.2021.00208

Paul, A., Kundu, A., Chaki, N., Dutta, D., & Jha, C. S. (2022). Wavelet enabled convolutional autoencoder based deep neural network for hyperspectral image denoising. *Multimedia Tools and Applications*, 81(2), 1–27. DOI: 10.1007/s11042-021-11689-z

Qin, X., Lai, C., Pan, Z., Pan, M., Xiang, Y., & Wang, Y. (2023). Recognition of Abnormal-Laying Hens Based on Fast Continuous Wavelet and Deep Learning Using Hyperspectral Images. *Sensors (Basel)*, 23(7), 3645. DOI: 10.3390/s23073645 PMID: 37050705

Roy, A., Anju, P., Tomy, L., & Rajeswari, M. (2021). Recent study on image denoising using deep cnn techniques. *2021 7th International Conference on Advanced Computing and Communication Systems (ICACCS), 1*, 1838–1843.

Sagheer, S. V. M., & George, S. N. (2020). A review on medical image denoising algorithms. *Biomedical Signal Processing and Control*, 61, 102036. DOI: 10.1016/j.bspc.2020.102036

Shukla, A., Seethalakshmi, K., Hema, P., & Musale, J. C. (2023). An Effective Approach for Image Denoising Using Wavelet Transform Involving Deep Learning Techniques. *2023 4th International Conference on Smart Electronics and Communication (ICOSEC)*, 1381–1386.

Tian, C., Fei, L., Zheng, W., Xu, Y., Zuo, W., & Lin, C.-W. (2020). Deep learning on image denoising: An overview. *Neural Networks*, 131, 251–275. DOI: 10.1016/j.neunet.2020.07.025 PMID: 32829002

Tian, C., Zheng, M., Zuo, W., Zhang, B., Zhang, Y., & Zhang, D. (2023). Multi-stage image denoising with the wavelet transform. *Pattern Recognition*, 134, 109050. DOI: 10.1016/j.patcog.2022.109050

Tripathi, M. (2021). Facial image noise classification and denoising using neural network. *Sustainable Engineering and Innovation*, 3(2), 102–111. DOI: 10.37868/sei.v3i2.id142

Xu, Q. (2024). Incorporating CNN-LSTM and SVM with wavelet transform methods for tourist passenger flow prediction. *Soft Computing*, 28(3), 2719–2736. DOI: 10.1007/s00500-023-09592-w

Yan, R., Shang, Z., Xu, H., Wen, J., Zhao, Z., Chen, X., & Gao, R. X. (2023). Wavelet transform for rotary machine fault diagnosis: 10 years revisited. *Mechanical Systems and Signal Processing*, 200, 110545. DOI: 10.1016/j.ymssp.2023.110545

You, N., Han, L., Zhu, D., & Song, W. (2023). Research on image denoising in edge detection based on wavelet transform. *Applied Sciences (Basel, Switzerland)*, 13(3), 1837. DOI: 10.3390/app13031837

Zhang, K., Zuo, W., Chen, Y., Meng, D., & Zhang, L. (2017). Beyond a gaussian denoiser: Residual learning of deep cnn for image denoising. *IEEE Transactions on Image Processing*, 26(7), 3142–3155. DOI: 10.1109/TIP.2017.2662206 PMID: 28166495

Zhang, P., & Zhang, X. (2022). Research on Laser Polarization Image Reconstruction Based on Wavelet Transform and Deep Learning. *2022 3rd Information Communication Technologies Conference (ICTC)*, 108–111.

Zhou, X., Zhou, H., Wen, G., Huang, X., Lei, Z., Zhang, Z., & Chen, X. (2022). A hybrid denoising model using deep learning and sparse representation with application in bearing weak fault diagnosis. *Measurement*, 189, 110633. DOI: 10.1016/j.measurement.2021.110633

Chapter 18
Action Recognition Identification Using Deep Learning

G. Indirani
https://orcid.org/0000-0002-2544-6274
Anna University, Thanjavur, India

G. Revathy
https://orcid.org/0000-0002-0691-1687
SASTRA University, India

R. Karunamoorthi
https://orcid.org/0009-0001-2141-6852
Kongu Engineering College, India

S. Senthilvadivu
Saveetha University, India

ABSTRACT

Action Recognition has become critical and effective for humans, and research in this field is ongoing. It is one of the applications of Computer Vision. Previous research includes action-based identification utilizing a basic deep learning-based Convolutional Neural Network. The proposal describes a Deep Learning model that detects and recognizes words based on a person's behaviors. LSTM and GRU are used to recognise signals in isolated Indian Sign Language (ISL) video frames. A dataset was run through four distinct consecutive combinations of LSTM and GRU. The actions are detected, and the words are shown. The suggested model yields an 89% outcome, which is much higher than state-of-the-art models.

DOI: 10.4018/979-8-3693-9045-0.ch018

INTRODUCTION

Action recognition, a key task in computer vision, is the automated identification and categorization of human actions or activities in video. Significant progress has been achieved in this subject as deep learning, particularly in deep learning has gained popularity. Deep learning models have exhibited impressive skills in evaluating spatial and temporal characteristics in video sequences, allowing for precise action detection in a variety of applications. Deep learning is a type of machine learning that employs multiple-layered artificial neural networks to learn and develop over time.

The goal of deep learning is to reduce the need for manual feature engineering while increasing learning accuracy, scalability, and speed. Deep learning also aims to give computers the ability to anticipate the future and make judgments based on massive amounts of complex data, as well as to continuously improve their performance. One of the primary benefits of utilizing deep learning for action identification is its capacity to analyze large-scale datasets and learn directly from raw data, decreasing reliance on manually created features. This method enables the recognition of a wide range of activities across many contexts, subjects, and camera angles. Furthermore, deep learning models may be customized for individual applications, increasing their adaptability and performance in real-world circumstances.

In addition to CNNs and RNNs, other deep learning architectures, such as 3D CNNs, which extend 2D convolutions to the temporal dimension, and transformer-based models, which use attention mechanisms to capture long-range dependencies in video sequences, have been investigated for action recognition.

Despite tremendous advances, deep learning-based action recognition confronts a number of obstacles. These include the requirement for huge annotated datasets, the computational cost of training deep networks, the unpredictability of actions across various persons and contexts, and the difficulty in identifying fine-grained actions with slight variances. Researchers are constantly investigating novel strategies, such as self-supervised learning, transfer learning, and multimodal approaches, to overcome these problems and enhance the performance of action recognition systems.

Traditional methods of action recognition frequently struggle to accurately capture temporal dynamics and describe complicated sequential patterns found in video data. However, recent advances in deep learning, particularly the introduction of specialized recurrent neural network (RNN) architectures such as Long Short-Term Memory (LSTM) and Gated Recurrent Unit (GRU), have transformed the field by providing powerful tools for temporal modelling and sequence analysis.

Examining the usefulness of LSTM and GRU architectures for action detection tasks, with the goal of overcoming the constraints of standard approaches and achieving cutting-edge results. We aim to construct robust and accurate models capable of identifying a wide range of human behaviours in complicated video datasets by capitalizing on the inherent capabilities of LSTM and GRU networks in collecting long-term relationships and contextual information across video frames.

LITERATURE SURVEY

Manware *et al.* (2017) reduces communication barriers with everyday people. The suggested method aims to create a cost-effective solution that uses Smart Gloves to provide voice to those who lack it. Smart gloves eliminate communication barriers between diverse societies, allowing for easy conversation with regular people. The use of smart gloves by individuals with disabilities contributes to national growth and helps them blend in with society.

Wadhawan and Kumar (2021) described the first identified academic literature review of sign language recognition systems. It provides an academic database of literature from 2007 to 2017 and suggests a categorization strategy for research publications. Three hundred ninety-six research publications were discovered and assessed for their direct relevance to sign language recognition systems. One hundred and seventeen research articles were subsequently chosen, examined, and categorized.

AI technology can help to break down communication barriers between deaf or hearing-impaired persons and other populations, therefore dramatically increasing their social inclusion. Recent breakthroughs in sensing technology and AI algorithms have opened the way for the creation of a variety of apps aimed at meeting the demands of the deaf and hearing-impaired populations. Authors completed the evaluation of cutting-edge technologies for recording, recognising, translating, and representing sign language, as well as highlighting their benefits and limits. Furthermore, the survey shows a variety of applications while discussing the primary obstacles in the field of sign language technologies. Future research directions are also given to aid potential researchers in further advancing the discipline, (Papastratis *et al.,* 2021).

Indian Sign Language (ISL) is a set of static and dynamic hand motions used for communication among the deaf and dumb, (Chen, 2011). Most ISL motions are made using two hands. A video database is produced and used, containing many films for a huge number of signs. The direction histogram is utilized for categorization because of its ease of lighting and orientation invariance. Euclidean distance and K-nearest neighbor metrics are two types of recognition techniques, (Nandy *et al.,* 2010).

An independent translator that can analyze photos and identify signs at the pace of streaming images is vital for real-time image recognition. In order to convert sign language into a speech or text format, an architecture utilizing neural network identification and tracking is presented in this article. The addition of track points and Point of Interest (POI) adds novelty while lowering the need for storage memory, (Mekala *et al.,* 2011).

To apply our findings in a real-world setting, we first constructed a database of 5000 numerical signs with 500 photos each. To extract desirable characteristics from sign photos, we employ direct pixel value and hierarchical centroid approaches. After extracting features from photos, neural network and kNN classification approaches were employed to categorize signs. Authors obtained accuracy of up to 97.10 percent, (Sharma, Pal, & Sahoo, 2014).

The program converts hand motions into human-readable sentences. This technique utilizes Indian sign language-based movements. The application's main processes include gesture detection and natural language processing, which are the most essential modules in the proposed study. The present work serves as an interface for communicating with both speech impaired and normal individuals. This technology aims to bridge the gap between speech disabled and normal persons by recording and processing sign language, identifying it, and presenting it as intelligible sentences, (Agarwal, Agrawal, & Latif, 2015).

Sign language is a method of communication for the deaf and dumb. There are several sign recognition systems that produce output in the form of a word for each identified sign. The suggested technique focuses on the interpretation of sign language in correct English sentences. Sign recognition is not the only NLP approach employed. Input is provided in the form of a sign language video, which is then framed and segmented. CamShift algorithm is utilized for tracking, and P2DHMM for hand tracking. The Haar Cascade classifier is used for sign recognition. After sign recognition, the continuous words for each sign are sent into the POS tagging module, (Wazalwar & Shrawankar, 2017).

This research study presents an effective technique for transliterating 24 static sign language alphabets and numerals from American Sign Language into humanoid or machine-readable English.

The first phase involves pre-processing the signed input gesture. Next, the pre-processed gesture image's region attributes are calculated. In the last phase, signed gestures were transliterated into text using previously determined attributes. This research evaluates statistical results using a comparative graphical representation of existing and new methodologies, (Shivashankara & Srinath, 2018).

For the past two decades, there has been substantial study in the subject of sign language recognition (SLR). SLR aims to recognize a sequence of continuous signals while ignoring the underlying complex grammatical and linguistic patterns of sign language, which differ from spoken language. In contrast, we present the Sign Language Translation (SLT) issue. The goal here is to produce spoken language translations from sign language films while accounting for word order and grammatical differences. We define SLT utilizing Neural Machine Translation (NMT) in both end-to-end and pretrained scenarios. This enables us to acquire the spatial representations, the underlying language model, and the mapping between sign and spoken language simultaneously, (Camgoz *et al.,* 2018).

METHODOLOGY

The work's purpose is to detect symbolic expressions in real time utilizing pictures and frames, then convert them into text. To easily bridge the communication gap between someone who has no physical limitations and someone who is especially challenged. We describe how to use a camera to record Indian sign language. Extract the holistic essential elements from Media Pipe and build a TensorFlow model with transfer learning. Create a sign language model using LSTM and GRU layer action detection. Which employs video snippets to anticipate sign language in real time.

An action detection model may be used to decipher sign language by feeding a collection of key points into an initiative that recognizes persons with special needs' sign activity. As part of the model-building process, we'll be able to utilize TensorFlow and Keras to create a deep neural network using LSTM and GRU layers to handle a succession of critical points capable of translating gestures into text format. The strategy may make it easier for non-sign language speakers to communicate with folks who have communication difficulties.

Figure 1 explains the architecture of LSTM with GRU. Recurrent neural networks (RNNs) with long short-term memory (LSTM) are designed specifically to handle sequential data such as time series, audio, and text. Because of their ability to learn long-term relationships in sequential data, LSTM networks are ideal for applications such as language translation, speech recognition, and time series forecasting. Because a typical RNN has just one hidden state, the network may have difficulty learning long-term dependencies. LSTMs provide a solution in the form of memory cells, which are storage units capable of holding data for extended periods of time. The memory cell is controlled by three gates: input gate, forget gate, and output gate.

Figure 1. LSTM GRU architecture

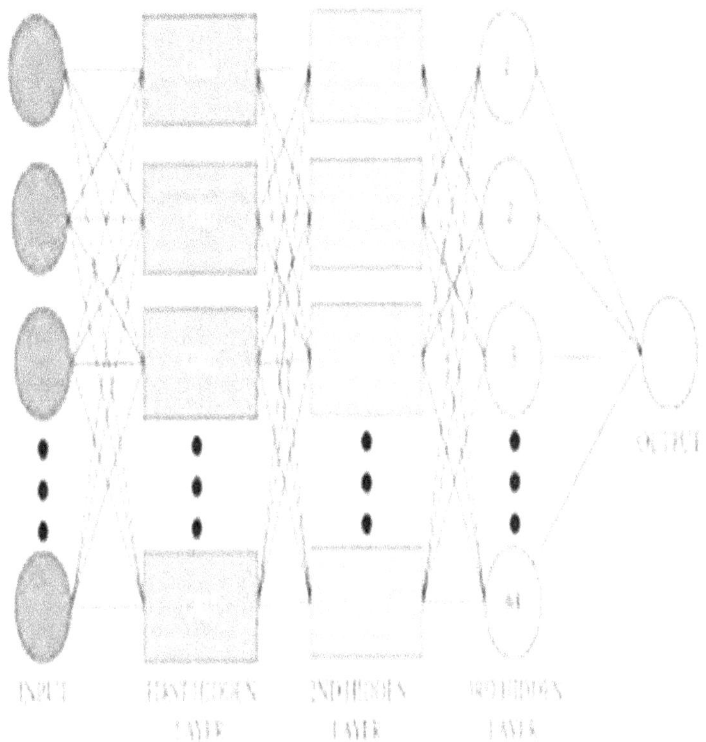

Recurrent neural networks (RNNs) can incorporate gated recurrent units (GRUs). GRU, like LSTM, can evaluate sequential data such as text, audio, and time series. The essential premise of GRU is to selectively update the network's hidden state at each time step using gating methods. Gate mechanisms govern the flow of information into and out of the network. The reset gate and the update gate are the two gates that function within the GRU. The update gate specifies how much of the new input should be utilized to update the hidden state, whereas the reset gate specifies how much of the previous hidden state should be ignored. The updated hidden state is utilized to determine the GRU's output.

LSTM Algorithm

1. Initialize weights and biases for the forget gate (W_f), input gate (W_i), output gate (W_o), and cell state (W_c).
2. Iterate over each input sequence (xt).
    a. Calculate the forget gate (ft) using sigmoid activation. $ft = \sigma(w\_f * [ht\text{-}1, xt] + b\_f)$.
    b. Calculate the input gate (it) using sigmoid activation: $it = \sigma(W\_i * [ht\text{-}1, xt] + b\_i)$.
    c. Calculate the cell state candidate (Ct) using tanh activation: $Ct = \tanh(W\_c * [ht\text{-}1, xt] + b\_c)$.
    d. Change the cell state (Ct): $Ct = ft * Ct\text{-}1 + it * C\sim t$.
    e. Calculate the output gate (ot) using sigmoid activation: $ot = \sigma(W\_o * [ht\text{-}1, xt] + b\_o)$.
    f. Calculate the hidden state (ht) using the updated cell state and output gate: $ht = ot * \tanh(Ct)$.
3. Calculate the difference between the projected and actual results.

4. Backpropagate the mistake through the network and update the weights via gradient descent.

GRU Algorithm

1. Set weights and biases for the update gate (W_z), reset gate (W_r), and candidate activation (W_h).
2. Iterate over every input sequence (xt):
   a. Calculate the reset gate (rt) with sigmoid activation: rt = σ(W_r * [ht-1, xt] + b_r).
   b. Calculate the update gate (zt) with sigmoid activation: zt = σ(W_z * [ht-1, xt] + b_z).
   c. Calculate the candidate activation (ht~) with tanh activation: ht~ = tanh(W_h * [rt * ht-1, xt] + b_h).
   d. Modify the hidden state (ht): ht = (1 - zt) * ht-1 + zt * ht~.
3. Calculate the difference between the projected and actual results.
4. Backpropagate the mistake through the network and update the weights via gradient descent.

Figure 2 depicts the entire workflow: action films are sent through live video and transformed to pictures, features are identified and fed to the LSTM GRU deep model, gestures are categorized, and action outputs are delivered and Figure 3 flow diagram of the deep models.

Figure 2. Workflow diagram

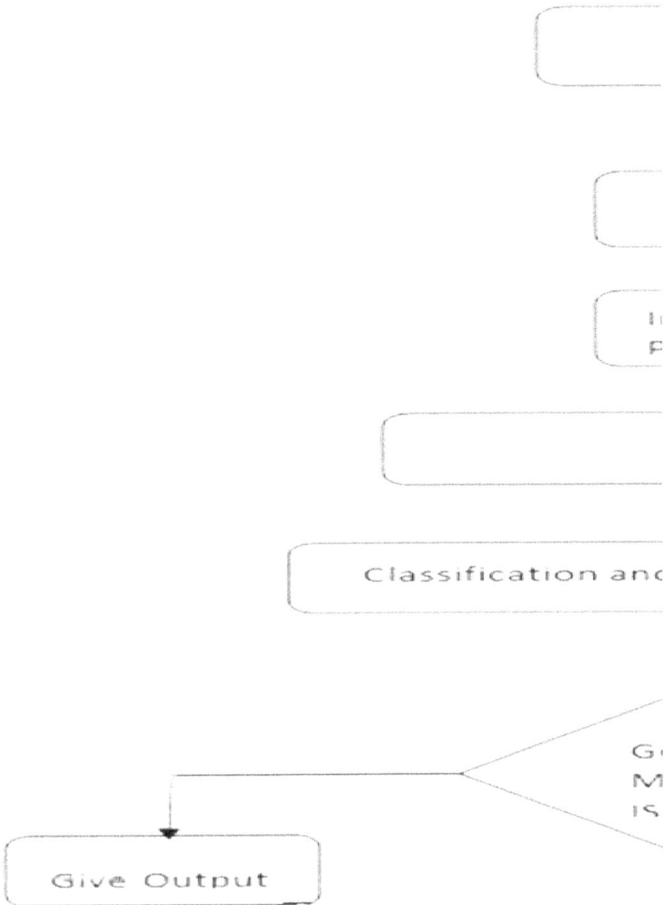

Figure 3. Flow diagram

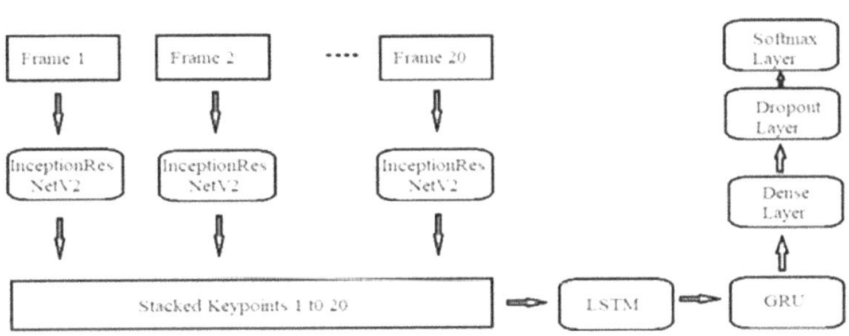

RESULTS AND DISCUSSIONS

The model LSTM with GRU is trained with a dataset name "NaHa_ActionDataset" which is author own dataset. It consists of around 400 different action images. Each images are of 150 pixels per inch.

Figure 4. Human action recognition

Figure 4 records the real time video and then converts it to frames and figure 4 is one of the subsections.

An example of this is the extraction of image frames from a video, to be used as inputs for nearly all computer vision tasks (e.g. object detection, activity recognition and video summarization). Extracting each frame from a video sequence can facilitate an analysis that is perceived on a frame by the frame basis — very much needed with many deep learning / image processing applications. Basically, a video is just the rapid succession of images or frames to give you sensation of motion. Rate of Frames: It is the amount of frames that are shown in a second, it comes usually with the name frame rate and written like FPS which means Frame Per Second. For example, a video at 30 frames per second shows you thirty distinct images in one second.

Figure 5. Subsection video gesture

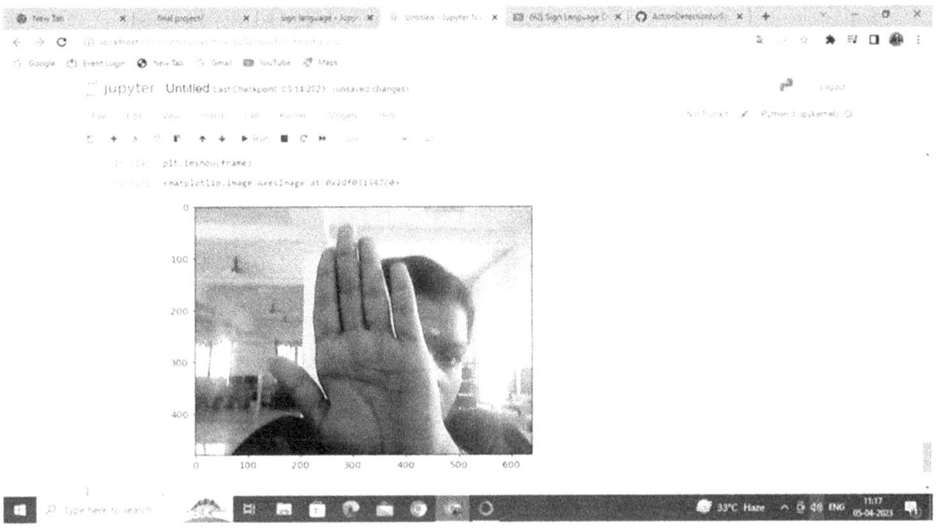

Figure 6. Frame conversion from subsection video

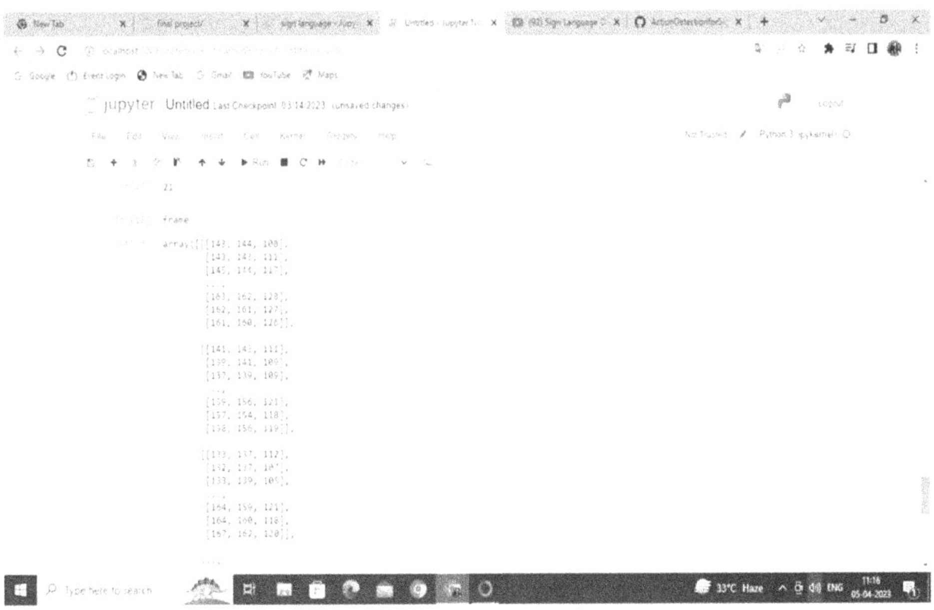

Frame extraction is necessary in the following cases:-

Action Recognition: Identifying the action that was performed in each frame by analysing it.

Practical implementations will include object detection, where items are identified in every frame to track movement through time.

To rephrase this if you are preparing data to train a deep learning models, then these retrieved frames will be the input. FFmpeg is a powerful command-line tool that can help manage multimedia files. Especially useful for high performance frame extraction and Image batch processing.

Figure 7. Key point prediction

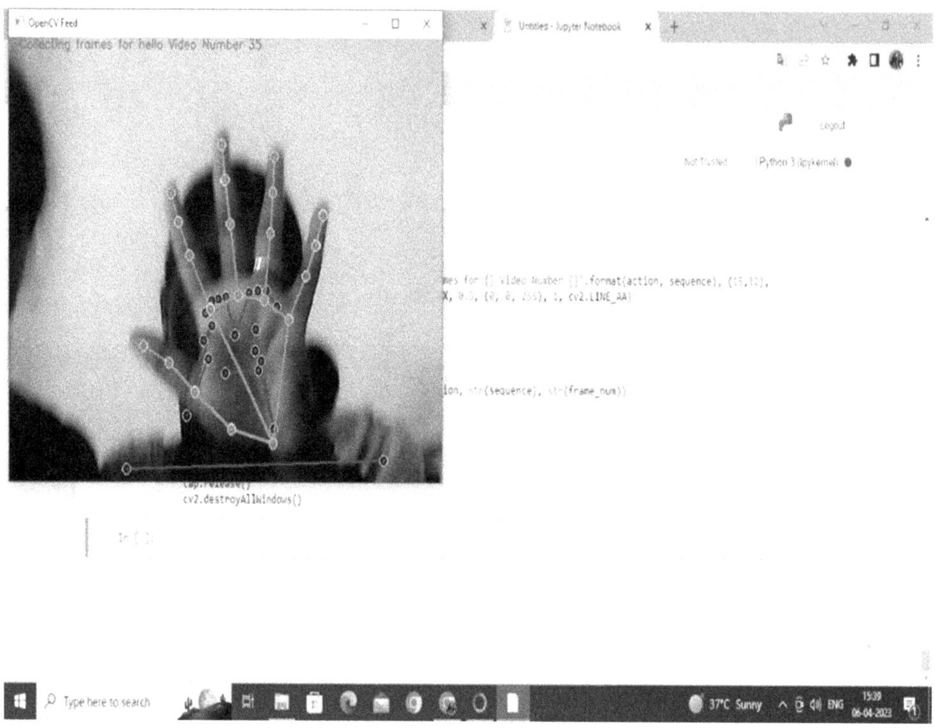

Figure 8. Array representation of key points

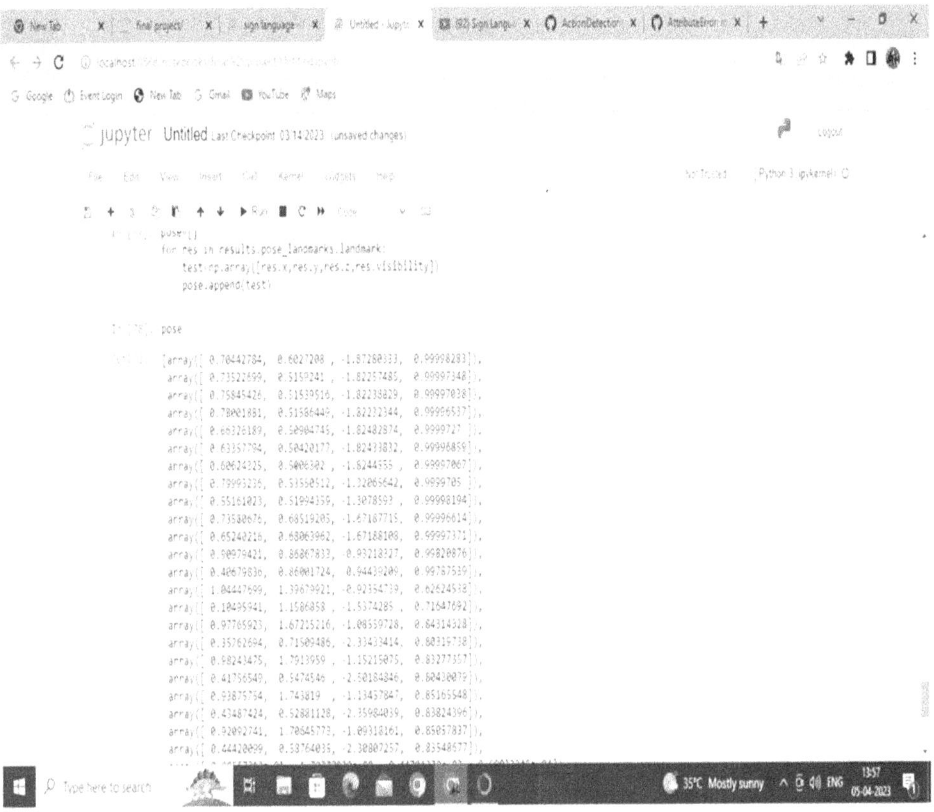

Frame Rate Matching: Make sure the required analysis speed and frame extraction rate matches. If the above example removes that action of scrolling by too many frames, more detail will be lost than if it left a lot of action in between frames and choose was an actual change had happened; but at what point did this happen?

Dimension: Take Note of the Resolution of the Frame While high-resolution frames offer more detail, they also require increased processing and storage capabilities.

File Management and Storage: Large videos can easily result in thousands of frames that have to be managed effectively.

Batch Processing: Automation scripts and batch processing is massively important when you work with multiple movies.

After frames are removed, they can be utilized for a number of purposes:

instruction Deep Learning Models: These models use the extracted frames as input data to identify objects, patterns, or activities in a video.

Frame-by-Frame Analysis: Individual frames can be subjected to in-depth analysis, which can include tracking movement or identifying anomalies.

Video Summarization: A brief synopsis of the video's content can be made by assembling key frames that have been chosen.

Figure 9. Final accuracy prediction

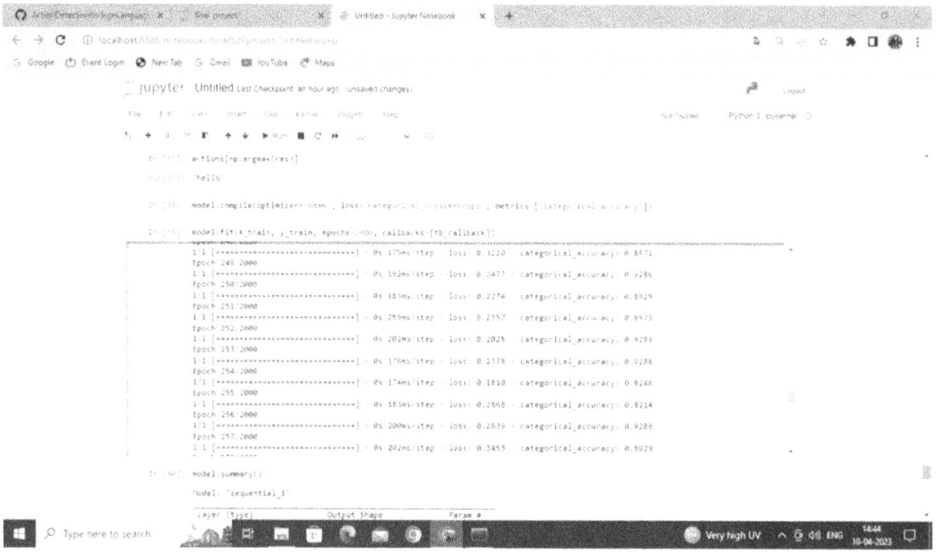

Figure 9 gives the final accuracy of LSTM GRU model. The model predicts around 92% of results which is very high than the other state of art models.

Figure 10. Sample output for hello

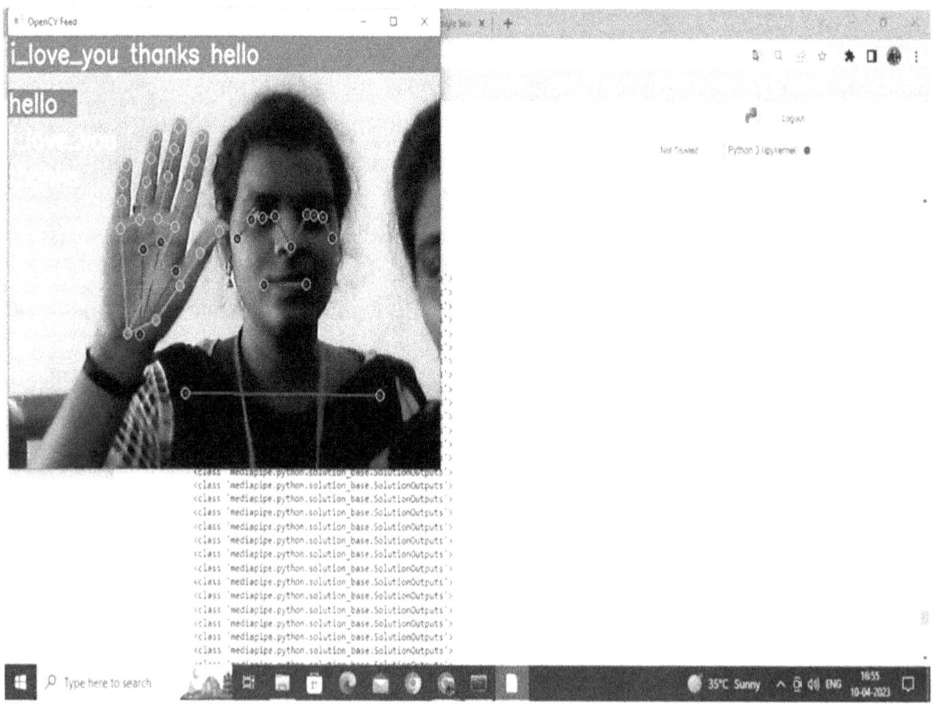

Figure 11. Sample output for thanks

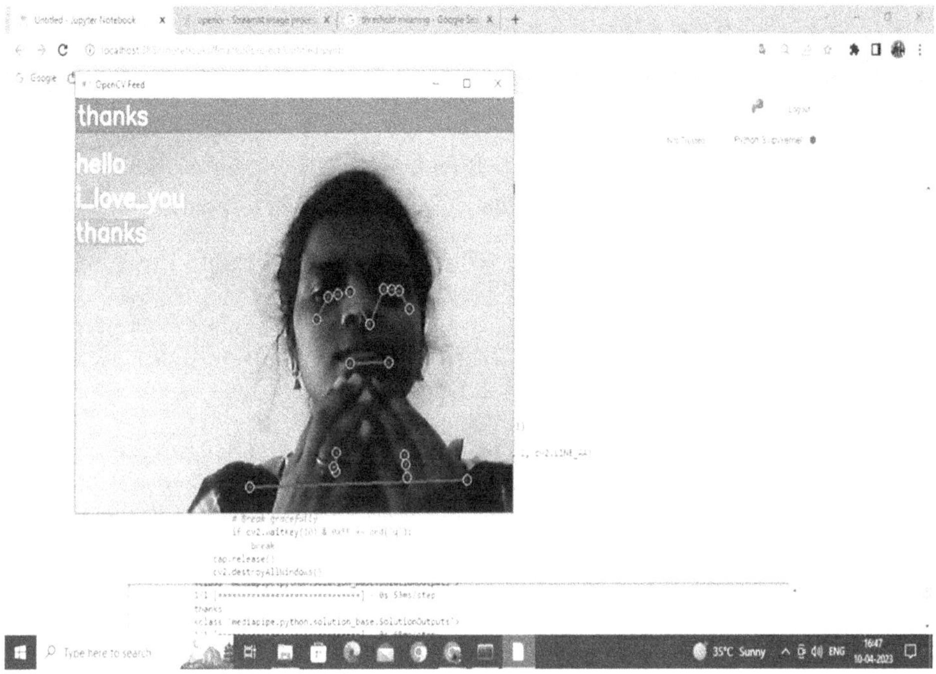

Figure 10 and 11 shows some sample output results.

CONCLUSION

LSTM and GRU architectures are significant tools in the field of action recognition, providing adaptability, efficiency, and prospective possibilities for enhancing the interpretation and analysis of sequential data across several domains.The use of LSTM and GRU architectures in action recognition provides a convincing foundation for studying and comprehending sequential input. In this research study, we investigated the performance of both LSTM and GRU networks in capturing temporal relationships, extracting significant characteristics from video sequences, and recognizing the activities.

REFERENCES

Agarwal, S. R., Agrawal, S. B., & Latif, A. M. (2015). Sentence formation in NLP engine on the basis of indian sign language using hand gestures. *International Journal of Computer Applications, 116*(17). Advance online publication. DOI: 10.5120/20428-2757

Camgoz, N. C., Hadfield, S., Koller, O., Ney, H., & Bowden, R. (2018). Neural sign language translation. In *Proceedings of the IEEE conference on computer vision and pattern recognition* (pp. 7784-7793).

Chen, J. K. (2011). Sign Language Recognition with Unsupervised Feature Learning; CS229 Project Final Report. DOI: 10.5120/20428-2757

Manware, A., Raj, R., Kumar, A., & Pawar, T. (2017). Smart Gloves as a Communication Tool for the Speech Impaired and Hearing Impaired. *Int. J. Emerg. Technol. Innov. Res*, *4*, 78–82.

Mekala, P., Gao, Y., Fan, J., & Davari, A. (2011, March). Real-time sign language recognition based on neural network architecture. In *2011 IEEE 43rd Southeastern symposium on system theory* (pp. 195-199). IEEE. DOI: 10.1109/SSST.2011.5753805

Nandy, A., Prasad, J. S., Mondal, S., Chakraborty, P., & Nandi, G. C. (2010). Recognition of isolated indian sign language gesture in real time. In *Information Processing and Management:International Conference on Recent Trends in Business Administration and Information Processing, BAIP 2010,Trivandrum, Kerala, India,March 26-27, 2010. Proceedings* (pp. 102-107). Springer Berlin Heidelberg. DOI: 10.1007/978-3-642-12214-9_18

Papastratis, I., Chatzikonstantinou, C., Konstantinidis, D., Dimitropoulos, K., & Daras, P. (2021). Artificial intelligence technologies for sign language. *Sensors (Basel)*, *21*(17), 5843. DOI: 10.3390/s21175843 PMID: 34502733

Sharma, M., Pal, R., & Sahoo, A. K. (2014). Indian sign language recognition using neural networks and KNN classifiers. *Journal of Engineering and Applied Sciences (Asian Research Publishing Network)*, *9*(8), 1255–1259.

Shivashankara, S., & Srinath, S. (2018). American sign language recognition system: An optimal approach. *International Journal of Image. Graphics and Signal Processing*, *10*(8), 18–30. DOI: 10.5815/ijigsp.2018.08.03

Wadhawan, A., & Kumar, P. (2021). Sign language recognition systems: A decade systematic literature review. *Archives of Computational Methods in Engineering*, *28*(3), 785–813. DOI: 10.1007/s11831-019-09384-2

Wazalwar, S. S., & Shrawankar, U. (2017). Interpretation of sign language into English using NLP techniques. *Journal of Information and Optimization Sciences*, *38*(6), 895–910. DOI: 10.1080/02522667.2017.1372136

Chapter 19
AI-Driven-IoT (AIIoT)-Based Jawar Leaf Disease Detection:
KSK Approach for Jawar Disease Detection

Kutubuddin Sayyad Liyakat Kazi
https://orcid.org/0000-0001-5623-9211
Brahmdevdada Mane Institute of Technology, India

ABSTRACT

This study evaluated the efficacy of three different models for identifying diseases that affect jawar leaves: Decision Trees (DT), K-Nearest Neighbours (K-NN), and Artificial Neural Networks (ANN). Both healthy and sick specimens of jawar leaves might be included in the dataset of jawar leaf photographs that could be obtained. A number of different image processing techniques were utilised in order to extract characteristic information from the photographs. Once the features had been extracted, the ANN, DT, and K-NN models were trained and evaluated using the information that was obtained. In addition to having the best accuracy (96.5%), the KSK technique had the highest recall (95.8%) and precision (97.2%) measurements. In comparison to the DT and K-NN models, the ANN model performed significantly better. This was due to the fact that it was able to analyse the data and identify subtle non-linear relationships.

INTRODUCTION

Studies of agricultural losses are essential for gaining an understanding of the impact that a variety of factors have on crop output and the safety of food supplies. The decline in production or quality of crops that can be attributed to pests, illnesses, harsh weather conditions, and other environmental factors is the phenomenon that is investigated in these studies. Researchers and policymakers are able to design strategies to improve agricultural practices and limit the effects of crop losses by analyzing the data generated from these studies and providing them with the necessary information (see, Sunita et al,2023; Sultanabanu,2023a; for more).

The contribution that agriculture losses studies provide to the protection of food supplies is among the most important advantages that they offer. Every year, the Food and Agriculture Organization (FAO) estimates that around one-third of the food that is intentionally produced for human use is either lost or wasted around the world. Studies of agricultural losses can assist in determining the factors that con-

DOI: 10.4018/979-8-3693-9045-0.ch019

tribute to these losses and in formulating methods to mitigate them (see, Kazi K S,2024; Sayyad,2025e; Altaf,2024; Kazi K S,2025a; Wale,2019; Kazi K,2022b; for more. Enhanced storage and transportation infrastructure, for instance, has the potential to drastically cut down on the amount of food that is wasted after harvest in poor nations, according to a study that was conducted on post-harvest losses in such countries (see, Sayyad,2023; Sayyad,2024r; Sayyad,2024s; Sayyad,2024v; for more).

Furthermore, the significance that agriculture losses studies play in the management of pests and diseases is an important part of these research. Researchers are able to develop tailored strategies to manage various pests and diseases through the process of assessing the presence of these pests and diseases as well as their influence on crop production. As an illustration, a study that investigated the effects of the autumn armyworm in Africa discovered that early diagnosis and management measures have the potential to drastically cut down on crop losses that are brought on by this destructive insect (see, Sayyad,2024y; Sultanabanu,2024s; Kutubuddin,2024l; Kutubuddin,2024p; for more).

Agriculture is another sector that is experiencing considerable concerns as a result of climate change. Studies on agricultural losses can assist in determining the influence that extreme weather conditions have on crop production. According to the findings of a study that investigated the effects of droughts in the United States, droughts have the potential to generate considerable reductions in crop yields. The extent of these reductions can range from ten percent to sixty percent, depending on the severity and duration of the drought. Policymakers are able to develop measures to reduce the consequences of climate change and assure food security if they have a thorough understanding of the influence that climate change has on agriculture (see, K S L,2023a; Sultanabanu,2023k; Sultanabanu,2023l; Kazi K,2024; Kazi K S,2025c; Kasat et al,2023; for more).

In addition, research into agricultural losses can contribute to the development of agricultural techniques that are more environmentally friendly. Researchers have the capacity to propose solutions that will increase the sustainability of agriculture if they first determine the influence that various agricultural practices have on crop yields. In Latin America, for instance, a study that investigated the effects of conservation agriculture discovered that the implementation of no-till farming and crop rotation can lead to an increase in crop yields while simultaneously lowering the amount of soil erosion.

On the other hand, studies on agricultural losses are not devoid of their own imperfections. The absence of standardized procedures for evaluating crop losses is one of the most significant issues, as it can make it difficult to compare data from various research from different studies. In addition, there is a requirement for additional data regarding the social and economic effects of crop losses, particularly in countries that are still in the process of developing.

In inference, studies on agricultural losses are an essential instrument for gaining a knowledge of the impact that a variety of factors have on crop output and the safety of food supplies. Researchers and policymakers can enhance agricultural practices and assure food security in the face of problems such as climate change and population increase by understanding the causes of crop losses and devising focused measures to manage them. This will allow for the management of crop losses. There are some restrictions that come with agriculture losses research; nonetheless, the advantages of these studies far outweigh the disadvantages. Our ability to construct a food system that is more robust and sustainable will be enhanced if we continue to invest in and improve upon this research.

It is impossible for a plant to survive without its leaves, which are a colorful tapestry of nature. On the other hand, they are susceptible to a wide range of illnesses that can diminish their attractiveness and pose a risk to the health of the plant. It is essential for any gardener, farmer, or plant enthusiast who wants to keep their leaves lush and thriving to have a solid understanding of leaf diseases.

The study looks into the intriguing realm of leaf illnesses, investigating the various origins of these diseases, the symptoms they cause, and the management options that are most effective. Pathogens, which are microscopic organisms such as fungi, bacteria, viruses, and nematodes, are the organisms that are chiefly responsible for leaf diseases. The weaknesses of the plant are exploited by these invaders, who frequently take advantage of the plant's weaker immune systems, environmental stresses, or wounds.

It is possible for disease signs to be extremely diverse, ranging from minor discoloration to severe abnormalities. The spots, blights, and powdery coats that are characteristic of fungal diseases have earned them a well-deserved reputation. Bacterial illnesses frequently present themselves as wilting, soft rots, and sores that ooze substance. In most cases, mosaic patterns, slowed development, and deformed leaves are the typical symptoms of viral infections.

It is essential to recognize the indications of leaf disease in order to intervene in a timely manner. When gardeners have accurate diagnosis, they are able to select the most efficient treatment options and then prevent the disease from spreading further. Obtaining significant insights can be accomplished by the utilization of diagnostic instruments such as online resources, plant clinics, and laboratory tests.

In order to effectively manage leaf diseases, it is necessary to utilize a combination of preventative and treatative strategies. It is essential to take preventative measures, which can be accomplished through the selection of resistant cultivars, the maintenance of appropriate cleanliness, and the promotion of excellent air circulation. Treatments that are considered curative may involve the use of fungicides, bactericides, or the removal of affected leaves.

The importance of considering leaf diseases within the larger framework of plant health cannot be overstated. In order to reduce the amount of disease pressure, Integrated Pest Management (IPM) places an emphasis on using a holistic strategy, which involves combining biological, cultural, and chemical techniques.

The complexity of leaf diseases are still being understood via research, and novel approaches to treating them are being developed. A viable alternative to chemical treatments is the use of biocontrol agents, which involve the utilization of beneficial microorganisms and insects. It is possible that disease-resistant plants could be developed through the use of genetic engineering.

Diseases that affect the leaves of plants provide a challenge to the overall health of the plant; however, individuals can nurture healthy and bright foliage by gaining a grasp of the causes, symptoms, and effective treatment tactics of leaf diseases. With this knowledge, we are able to safeguard the beauty and resilience of our plant companions by doing things such as recognizing the first signs of problems and putting preventative measures into place.

Jawar, also known as Sorghum bicolor, is a types of grain crop that is commonly grown in semi-arid places such as Maharashtra in India. The Jawar is more well-known in Mangalwedha, Barshi from Solapur region in the state of Maharashtra. There is a high incidence of leaf diseases in jawar, which brings about significant yield losses. In this study, we will discuss the common leaf illnesses that affect jawar, as well as the symptoms of these diseases and the therapeutic techniques that are available.

A considerable risk to jawar production is posed by illnesses that affect the leaves. In order to minimize yield losses, it is essential to have a solid understanding of their symptoms and to put into practice management measures that are effective. Protecting jawar crops and ensuring optimal yields can be accomplished by farmers through the utilization of a combination of resistant cultivars, crop rotation, cultural methods, and, if necessary, chemical fertilization. It is necessary to conduct additional study in order to establish disease management systems that are both sustainable and environmentally friendly.

Sorghum, a grain crop that is extremely important all over the world, is susceptible to a number of illnesses that have the potential to adversely affect both its output and its quality. Among these, leaf diseases are extremely prevalent and destructive, and they frequently result in large financial losses for people who work in agriculture. This article dives into the wide-ranging topic of sorghum leaf diseases, including insights into the detection of these diseases, the factors that cause them, and the management options that are available.

1. The Most Common Diseases Affecting jawar Leaves: Figure 1 illustrates the most common diseases that affect jawar leaves

Figure 1. Common jawar diseases

- Anthracnose is a disease that is caused by Colletotrichum graminicola and is characterized by brown to black lesions that are elliptical to oval in shape and have yellow edges on the leaves.
- Bacterial stripe is a condition that is caused by Xanthomonas vasicola and manifests itself as water-soaked streaks on the leaves. These streaks eventually turn yellow and dry up.
- The grey leaf spot is a condition that is caused by Cercospora sorghi and is characterized by brown or grey circular lesions on the leaves that have dark margins.
- The symptoms of downy mildew, which is caused by the fungus Peronosclerospora sorghi, include blotches that range from yellow to green on the upper leaf surface and downy growth that ranges from whitish to lavender on the bottom leaf surface.
- Puccinia purpurea is the organism that causes rust, which manifests itself as orange-brown pustules on the stems and leaves of the plant. Rust manifests itself on leaves as pustules that are reddish-brown in color and has an adverse effect on photosynthesis and the vitality of plants.

- Zone Leaf Spot (ZLS) is a condition that is caused by Drechslera rostrata and is characterized by distinct spots on the leaves that are arranged in a zonate pattern.
- Leaf blight is a multi-species fungal disease that can cause severe defoliation and a reduction in grain yield. It is a complicated disease that is caused by multiple fungal species.
- Powdery mildew is a type of mildew that is produced by Erysiphe graminis and takes the form of a white, powdery coating on the leaves of plants. It inhibits photosynthesis and decreases the vigour of plants.

2. *Bacterial Diseases:*

- Bacterial Leaf Streak: Caused by Xanthomonas campestris pv. oryzae, bacterial leaf streak manifests as narrow, yellowish streaks on leaves, eventually leading to leaf blight.
- Bacterial Leaf Blight: Caused by Pseudomonas syringae, bacterial leaf blight can cause large, water-soaked lesions on leaves, ultimately resulting in leaf death.

Figure 2 shows the Bacterial Diseases and viral diseases on Jawar leaf.

Figure 2. Other disease on jawar leaf

3. Viral Diseases:
   - Sorghum Mosaic Virus (SMV): A common viral disease, SMV is characterized by mosaic patterns on leaves and stunted plant growth.
   - Sugarcane Mosaic Virus (SCMV): Another important virus, SCMV causes mosaic symptoms and stunting in sorghum plants.

Diseases that affect the leaves of sorghum pose a serious risk to the production of sorghum and have the potential to result in considerable yield reductions. In order to cultivate sorghum successfully, it is vital to have a solid understanding of the various types of illnesses and the management measures for each of them. By implementing a disease management strategy that is both proactive and integrated, farmers are able to effectively limit the adverse effects of leaf diseases and ensure that their sorghum production is profitable. For the purpose of generating solutions that are both sustainable and successful for the future, it is essential to do additional research on novel disease management strategies. These tactics include biological control agents and resistance breeding.

Spots, lesions, streaks, or discoloration on jawar leaves are the symptoms that are associated with leaf diseases. They have the potential to decrease the plant's ability for photosynthesis, weaken the plant, and impede grain development and filling. As a consequence of this, leaf diseases can result in decreased yields, grains of lesser quality, and economic losses. These are the various disease management strategies that are available:

- Resistant types: The most efficient method for limiting the spread of leaf diseases is to plant resistant types. Ongoing research is being conducted with the goal of developing jawar cultivars that have enhanced resistance.
- Rotation of crops: alternating jawar with crops that are not hosts for the illness helps break disease cycles and minimizes the number of pathogens that are present in the field.

    Plant health can be improved, and disease severity can be reduced by the use of cultural practices such as the removal of agricultural residues, the application of balanced fertilizers, and the efficient management of irrigation.
- In situations where other management measures are not sufficient, fungicides can be utilized as a means of chemical control in order to combat leaf diseases. However, in order to prevent the development of resistance, their utilization ought to be prudent.
- Biological Control: The concept of using specific microbes, such as Trichoderma spp., for the purpose of biologically controlling illnesses that affect jawar leaves has been investigated.

IoT AND AI: A POWERFUL SYNERGY FOR SMART APPLICATIONS-

The convergence of artificial intelligence (AI) and the Internet of Things (IoT) has triggered a revolution in the way that we interact with the world that our surroundings present to us (see, Pradeepa,2022; Kazi K,2024a; Prashant,2024; Priya,2023; Kazi K S,2024a; Neeraja et al,2024; Kutubuddin,2024; Veena et al,2023; Prasad et al,2024; Kazi K S,2024b; Kutubuddin,2024a; Kutubuddin,2024d; Liyakat,2025; Sayyad,2025f; Mahant.2025; for more) . The combination of these two active individuals provides a potent synergy that makes it possible to develop intelligent apps that improve efficiency, optimize processes, and provide personalized experiences.

- The Power of Data: Internet of Things devices provide enormous volumes of data about the physical world, including temperature, humidity, location, activity levels, and a variety of other variables. When artificial intelligence algorithms are used to this data, they transform it into valuable insights that may be used to drive decision-making (see, Kutubuddin,2024c; Kutubuddin,2024e;

Liyakat,2025; Keerthana et al,2024; Kutubuddin,2024q; KSKLiyakat,2023o; Kutubuddin,2024m; Kutubuddin,2024; Sayyad,2024x; Sayyad,2024w; for more).

The Internet of Things (IoT) and artificial intelligence (AI) shine in the following attractive application scenarios, which are represented in Figure 3:

Figure 3. AI and IoT application scenario

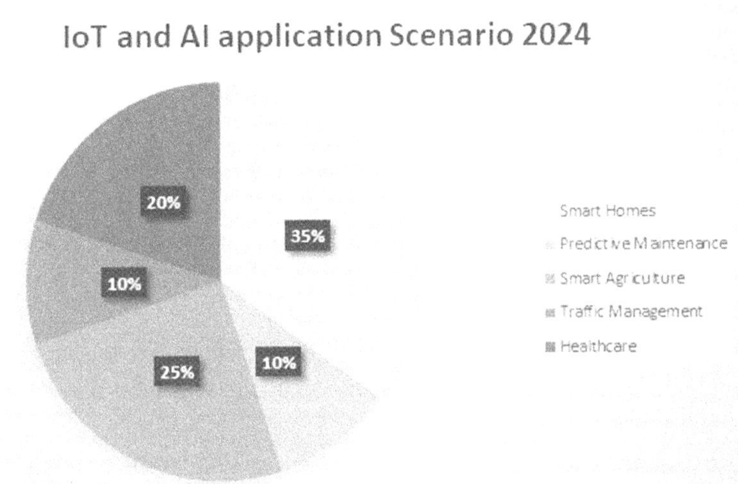

- Imagine living in a home that is able to learn your tastes and then alter the lighting, temperature, and appliances in accordance with those desires. Artificial intelligence algorithms analyze data from smart sensors and make predictions about your needs, thereby generating an environment that is personalized and comfortable (see, Gund,2023; Sayyad,2023k; Kazi K S,2023; Kazi K S,2022a; for more).
- Predictive Maintenance: Artificial intelligence can have the ability to anticipate probable breakdowns in industrial equipment by analyzing data from sensors installed on the equipment. It is possible to do maintenance at the appropriate moment, thereby avoiding downtime and reducing operational expenses (see, Kazi K,2024b; Liyakat,2024; Halli,2022b; Pankaj,2019; Karale,2020; Kazi K,2022; Kazi K,2022a; Ravi,2022; Sayyad,2022; Sayyad,2022b; K Kazi,2022; Kutubuddin,2022c;Kutubuddin,2022e; Sayyad,2023c; Shaikh,2023;Sultanabanu,2023b; for more).
- Internet of Things sensors monitor soil conditions, weather patterns, and crop health in order to facilitate smart agriculture. This data gives artificial intelligence models the ability to optimize irrigation, fertilization, and pest management, which ultimately results in improved agricultural yields and more efficient use of resources (see, Sayayd,2023j; Sayyad,2024f; for more).
- AI can optimize traffic flow, reduce congestion, and improve road safety by analyzing real-time traffic data from connected vehicles and sensors. This is one of the applications of artificial in-

telligence in traffic management (Sultanabanu,2023c; Sultanabanu,2023e; Sultanabanu,2023g; Sultanabanu,2023f; Sultanabanu,2023j; Sultanabanu,2024; chopade,2024; for more).

- The healthcare industry benefits from the continual flow of important data that is provided by wearable devices and medical sensors. These data can be analyzed by AI algorithms, which can lead to the identification of potential health problems, the provision of personalized health recommendations, and even the prediction of future health concerns (see, Liyakat,2025d; Priya,2024; Kazi K S,2025; Sayyad,2022a; Sultanabanu,2023n; Sayyad,2023h; Sayyad,2024w; Pardeshi,2022a; Pardeshi,2022b; K Kazi,2024; Sayyad,2024z; Sultanabanu,2023q; for more).

Challenges and Considerations:

- Data Privacy and Security: According to Liyakat(2023)(2024) & Liyakat(2023), Internet of Things(IoT) devices capture an enormous quantity of information, which raises worries about information privacy and security. The importance of competent data management and robust data protection procedures cannot be overstated (see, Liyakat,2024; K S K,2023; Liyakat, 2023; Halli,2022a; Kazi K S,2023a; Kutubuddin,2022d; K Kazi,2017; K Kazi,2024; Liyakat,2022; Kutubuddin,2023a; Sayyad,2025f; for more).
- Computational Resources: The processing and analysis of massive datasets demand a significant amount of computational resources. It is possible that this will be a barrier for applications and devices that have limited resources.
- It is crucial for trust and accountability, particularly in critical applications such as healthcare, to have an understanding of how machine learning algorithms arrive at their judgements. This understanding is referred to as algorithm transparency and explainability.

IoT and ML-machine learning have a promising future. As technology continues to improve, we anticipate the development of even more cutting-edge and game-changing applications. The possibilities are virtually limitless, running the gamut from self-driving automobiles to individualized education. Nevertheless, the development and implementation of these technologies in a responsible manner are of the utmost importance in order to guarantee ethical and equitable results (see, Kazi K S,2017; Sayyad,2018; Ravi,2022a; Maccha,2022; Devi,2022; Shreenivasulu,2022; Vahida,2023; Karale,2023l for more).

When combined, ML and IoT are a game-changers. It gives us the ability to unleash the potential of data and construct intelligent systems that can address problems that occur in the real world, improve efficiency, and ultimately improve our lives in a myriad of different ways. Taking on the challenges and embracing ethical considerations will allow us to harness the power of this dynamic pair, which will allow us to create a future that is both more intelligent and more sustainable (see, Sultanabanu,2023d; Sultanabanu,2023i; Sunil,2023; Sunil,2024a; Dhanwe;2024; Sayyad,2023i; Sayyad,2024r; Sayyad,2-24s; sunil.2024d; Sunil,2024e; Kutubuddin,2024m; for more).

PROBLEM STATEMENT

Jawar, also known as sorghum, is an essential staple crop in many areas, particularly in climates that are arid or semi-arid. In spite of this, yield losses brought on by a variety of leaf diseases constitute a substantial risk to both the supply of food and the livelihoods of farmers. For timely intervention and the implementation of suitable control measures, it is essential to detect these disorders as early as possible and with a high degree of accuracy. Traditional techniques of disease identification, which rely on visual examination by farmers or experts, are frequently subjective, time-consuming, and prone to inaccuracy. As a result, conventional methods of disease detection result in delayed treatments and decreased crop output. Farmers are left vulnerable to broad disease outbreaks as a result of the restricted access to agricultural extension services and diagnostic laboratories in distant places, which further exacerbates the problem. Consequently, there is an urgent requirement for a system that is not only effective but also easily accessible and dependable in order to detect jawar leaf illnesses at an early stage.

GOAL

An artificial intelligence (AI)-driven Internet of Things (IoT)-based system for the automated and real-time identification of common leaf diseases that damage jawar crops is currently being developed and implemented as the major objective of this project. This system is designed to provide farmers with a solution that is proactive, cost-effective, and user-friendly, and it has the capability to quickly identify disease outbreaks at the beginning of their occurrence. Through the facilitation of early disease prevention and the optimization of resource allocation, this objective ultimately aims to contribute to greater crop yields, decreased economic losses for farmers, and increased food security in regions that are dependent on jawar.

OBJECTIVE

In order to accomplish this general goal, the research will concentrate on the specific objectives that are listed below:

- In order to acquire data, you will need to collect a complete dataset consisting of photos of healthy and sick jawar leaves. This dataset will include a wide range of leaf illnesses that are prevalent in the area under investigation.
- Constructing a stable and accurate artificial intelligence model, most likely through the use of deep learning techniques such as convolutional neural networks (CNNs), in order to categorize jawar leaf photos according to the presence and type of disease is the objective of the AI Model Development project.
- IoT System Design: Create an Internet of Things-based system that is both economical and simple to implement. This system should integrate sensor technology and communication protocols in order to capture and send photos of leaves to an artificial intelligence model for processing.
- Implementing a real-time detection pipeline that is able to rapidly identify illnesses on collected photos and deliver alerts to farmers using a user-friendly interface, such as a mobile application, is an important step in the process of real-time disease detection.
- The performance evaluation should include a comprehensive analysis of the developed system's accuracy, robustness, and efficiency in a variety of field situations, as well as an evaluation of the extent to which it affects early detection capabilities.

- Evaluation of Usability and Accessibility Use user testing and feedback to determine how user-friendly the system is and how easily it can be utilized by farmers who have a limited level of technical skill.
- In order to raise awareness, it is important to disseminate the findings of the study through dissemination programs and scientific publications. Additionally, it is important to encourage the utilization of the developed system for the benefit of farming communities.

These aims will work together to make it possible to construct an AI-driven Internet of Things system that is both functional and beneficial for the diagnosis of jawar diseases.

THE DAWN OF SMART AGRICULTURE: IOT FOR JAWAR LEAF DISEASE DETECTION

It is possible for diseases to have a severe effect on staple crops such as jawar (sorghum), which can put farmers and food security at risk. When it comes to limiting losses, timely diagnosis and intervention are absolutely necessary. The incorporation of IoT is, thankfully, opening the way for a new era of intelligent agriculture, which is delivering solutions that are innovative for the management of diseases in jawar.

Jawar leaf disease detection systems that are based on the IoT often require a network of sensors that are deployed in the field, as shown in Figure 4. These sensors gather information on a variety of parameters that are essential for the early diagnosis of diseases, including the following:

- Changes in chlorophyll levels can be an indicator of disease-induced stress, and they can be found in leaf chlorophyll content.
- Temperature of the Leaf: Infected leaves frequently display different temperatures as a result of changes in temperature caused by transpiration and metabolic activity.
- Humidity and Moisture: An inadequate amount of moisture may be an indication of stress, while an excessive amount of humidity may encourage the growth of fungi.
- The use of high-resolution cameras allows for the capturing of photos of leaves, which can then be used for automated analysis and the identification of diseases.

Figure 4. IoT network for Jawar disease

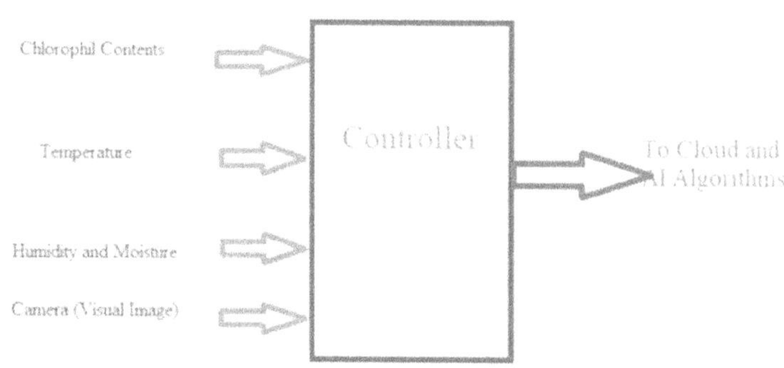

Following are the Benefits of IoT in Jawar Leaf disease detection:

- Early diagnosis: The IoT makes it possible to perform real-time monitoring, which enables early diagnosis of diseases before they become prevalent. This, in turn, enables timely treatments and reduces agricultural damage from occurring.
- Precision Agriculture: The data that is gathered by IoT sensors may be evaluated to optimize resource management, which ultimately results in a farming practice that is more efficient and also more sustainable.
- Decisions That Are Driven by Data: It is possible for farmers to gain significant insights from the data acquired by IoT technologies, which enables them to make educated decisions on disease management tactics.
- Early detection enables tailored interventions, which in turn reduces the need for broad-spectrum pesticides. This results in a reduction in the amount of pesticides that are used.

Despite its potential, IoT implementation in jawar leaf disease detection faces certain challenges:

- When it comes to smallholder farmers in particular, the deployment and maintenance of a large sensor network can be both expensive and time-consuming.
- Regarding connectivity, it can be difficult to provide dependable internet connectivity in agricultural areas that are located in rural areas.
- Data Analysis: In order to effectively analyze the large amount of information that has been acquired, effective data analysis requires both specialized knowledge and complex machine learning techniques.
- Scalability: It is of the utmost importance to develop solutions that are scalable and can be deployed effectively across large-scale farms.

Future development should focus on:

- Cost-effective sensors: the development of low-cost and energy-efficient sensors for the purpose of spreading their availability.
- Enhancement of connectivity through the utilization of alternative communication technologies such as LoRaWAN to ensure the delivery of data in a dependable manner even in remote places.
- The integration of artificial intelligence algorithms for the purpose of accurately and automatically identifying diseases based on visual pictures and sensor data is that which is referred to as AI-powered disease detection.
- Developing and promoting solutions that are both scalable and inexpensive for smallholder farmers requires the participation of public-private partnerships, which are vital for this purpose.

IoT technology holds tremendous potential to revolutionize the management of jawar diseases. The Internet of Things has the potential to drastically reduce crop losses, enhance farmer livelihoods, and contribute to higher levels of food security. This is accomplished through the implementation of early detection, precision agriculture, and data-driven decision making. Even though there are still obstacles to overcome, it is essential to conduct ongoing research and development in order to guarantee the successful integration of the Internet of Things (IoT) and to release the full capabilities of the transformative technology for sustainable agriculture.

A REVIEW OF AI IN JAWAR LEAF DISEASE DETECTION: A PROMISING PATH TOWARDS SUSTAINABLE AGRICULTURE

A primary food crop for millions of people all over the world is jawar, which is also known as sorghum. On the other hand, diseases such as leaf blight, rust, and anthracnose can have a substantial influence on yield and put food security at risk. Traditional methods of disease detection rely on manual inspection, which does not only take a lot of time but also leaves room for human error and frequently results in delayed intervention. The field of illness management in jawar is one in which artificial intelligence (AI) is emerging as a powerful technology that has the potential to change the field. Utilizing a variety of methods, the application of artificial intelligence in the diagnosis of diseases affecting jawar leaves is gaining pace.

- Employing convolutional neural networks (CNNs), artificial intelligence models may learn to recognize patterns in photographs of damaged leaves, which enables accurate disease categorization. Image recognition is utilized in this process. Research has shown that it is possible to differentiate between healthy leaves and those that have been affected by a variety of diseases with a high degree of accuracy.
- Deep Learning: More advanced deep learning algorithms may be taught on bigger datasets of jawar leaf photos, which allows them to extract complex features and discover subtle disease-specific properties. This technique has demonstrated that it has the potential to achieve even higher levels of accuracy and robustness.
- Hyperspectral Imaging: This method collects photos across a wide range of wavelengths, which results in the collection of a wealth of spectral information regarding leaves. As a result of the analysis of this data by AI algorithms, disease-associated spectral signatures can be identified, and early symptoms can frequently be detected before they become visible to the naked eye.

The following are the Benefits of AI-driven disease detection:

- Detection at an Early Stage: Artificial intelligence systems have the ability to detect diseases at an early stage, which enables timely intervention and reduces yield losses.
- Improved Accuracy: When properly taught, artificial intelligence models have the potential to continuously outperform manual examination, which ultimately results in more reliable diagnoses.
- Efficacy: Artificial intelligence will eliminate the need for manual inspection, which will free up time and resources for farmers to devote to other important duties.
- In terms of cost-effectiveness, early detection and preventative actions have the potential to drastically cut down on the expenses associated with illness control, making this strategy both sustainable and profitable.

Despite its potential, AI-based disease detection still faces several challenges:

- Availability of Data: In order to construct reliable artificial intelligence models, it is necessary to have access to big and varied datasets of jawar leaf photos, which can be challenging to obtain and label.
- Gear Requirements: In order to implement AI solutions in the field, it may be necessary to have specialized gear for image capture and processing.
- Accessibility: It is essential to ensure that smallholder farmers have access to artificial intelligence tools in order to achieve widespread adoption.

Future research should focus on tackling these challenges, including:

- Developing hardware solutions for data collecting and processing that are more efficient and cost-effective than these currently available.
- Exploring creative approaches to collect and annotate datasets, including citizen science programs and cloud-based platforms.
- The development of artificial intelligence tools and mobile applications that are simple to use and can be easily accessed by farmers.

AI holds a great deal of promises for improving the identification and control of jawar diseases, which will ultimately result in increased yields and more sustainable farming techniques. Rapid technological advancement is being made, and ongoing research is laying the groundwork for wider use of technology. When academics and stakeholders address the challenges that now exist, they are able to unleash the full potential of artificial intelligence, which will allow them to assure food security and empower farmers in the face of disease threats.

REVOLUTIONIZING JAWAR LEAF DISEASE DETECTION: AN AI-DRIVEN IOT APPROACH

When it comes to agriculture, the combination of artificial intelligence and internet of things technologies has demonstrated a huge amount of potential in addressing difficult difficulties. One of these areas is the identification of illnesses that can be found in crops, namely in Jawar leaves. A cutting-edge innovation that has the potential to revolutionize the agriculture industry is the decision-making process in Jawar Leaf Disease Detection that is driven by artificial intelligence and based on the internet of things.

In order to detect diseases in Jawar leaves at an early stage, the AI-driven Internet of Things system for Jawar Leaf Disease Detection is a pioneering technique that combines the power of AI-algorithms with the devices that are connected to the internet of things. The IoT devices are used to take pictures of Jawar leaves, which are subsequently evaluated by artificial intelligence algorithms in order to determine whether or not there are any indications of disease. AI-Driven IoT applications.

All of the artificial intelligence algorithms that are utilized in this system are quite advanced and have been trained to identify even the most minor symptoms of sickness. Because the system is able to detect diseases that are not visible to the naked eye, it is a very useful instrument for agricultural researchers and farmers alike.

The ability of this system to make decisions based on relevant facts is one of the most striking characteristics of it. The artificial intelligence algorithms are not only designed to identify ailments, but they are also intended to make suggestions for the most effective way to proceed. As an illustration, if the system identifies a disease in a Jawar leaf, it is able to make suggestions on the most effective treatment alternatives, the most appropriate time to administer therapy, and the chance of the treatment being successful.

A further benefit of the IoT component of the system is that it guarantees the collection of data in real time, which enables rapid decision-making. When it comes to agriculture, where timely intervention can make a major difference in crop yield and quality, this is of utmost importance.

A further characteristic that deserves mention is the system's intuitive and straightforward user interface. Users, regardless of their level of technical expertise, will find the system to be simple to use and straightforward to comprehend from the very beginning. Farmers and agricultural researchers will be able to use the system successfully and without any problem as a result of this.

In addition to this, the system is very scalable, which means that it can be quickly changed to include a variety of different farming scenarios and crops. Because of this, it is a versatile instrument that may be utilized in a wide variety of agricultural applications.

In conclusion, the decision-making process in Jawar Leaf Disease Detection that is driven by artificial intelligence and based on the internet of things is a revolutionary innovation that has the potential to completely transform the agricultural industry. The capability of the system to detect diseases at an early stage, to make decisions based on data, and to deliver recommendations in real time is truly remarkable. Because of its scalability and user-friendly design, it is a very useful tool for agricultural researchers as well as farmers. This system is a demonstration of the potential of artificial intelligence and internet of technology, as well as their ability to tackle difficult problems in a variety of different industries.

A COMPARATIVE ANALYSIS OF ANN, DECISION TREE AND K-NN FOR JAWAR LEAF DISEASE DETECTION

For the purpose of guaranteeing both productivity and food security, the identification of diseases in Jawar (Sorghum) crops is highly important. This review investigates the efficacy of three well-known artificial intelligence algorithms, including ANN, DT, and K-NN, in the classification of diseases that affect Jawar leaf.

1. Artificial Neural Networks (ANN):

The ability of artificial neural networks (ANNs) to recognize complicated and non-linear patterns makes them suited for the analysis of image data. They have achieved a high level of accuracy in identifying various diseases, which indicates that they have achieved promising results in the identification of Jawar leaf disorders. It is possible for ANNs to effectively learn detailed aspects from photos, even when there are slight changes in the signs of disease. On the other hand, they sometimes call for a substantial amount of training data and might be computationally intensive, which may restrict their usefulness in actual settings.

2. Decision Trees (DT):

When it comes to illness classification, DTs provide a technique that is both transparent and interpretable. They divide the data into sections according to particular characteristics, which makes it possible to have a better grasp of the decision-making process. In addition to being able to manage a wide variety of data types, DTs are reasonably easy to install. Nevertheless, they have the potential to be susceptible to overfitting and may not perform as well as ANNs when used to complicated datasets that have a high dimensionality.

3. K-Nearest Neighbors (K-NN):

K-NN is a non-parametric algorithm that classifies new observations based on the degree to which data points are similar to one another. The process of putting it into action is not overly complicated and does not call for substantial parameter adjusting. In spite of its seeming simplicity, the K-Nearest Neighbors algorithm is highly susceptible to noise and outliers in the data, which may result in erroneous predictions. In addition, the selection of 'K' can have a substantial impact on the performance of the model, which highlights the importance of thorough optimization.

Despite the fact that every algorithm has both advantages and disadvantages, artificial neural networks (ANNs) have emerged as a prominent competitor for the diagnosis of jawar leaf disease due to their capacity to handle complicated patterns and their high level of accuracy. There are, however, some potential downsides, such as the high processing cost and the demand for substantial data. However, due to the complexity of leaf disease categorization, DTs may not perform as well as ANNs, despite the fact that they provide an approach that is both transparent and interpretable. K-NN is a straightforward and straightforward algorithm that is easy to apply; nevertheless, its performance might be hindered by noise and outliers.

In the future, research should concentrate on finding solutions to the problems that each algorithm has. Exploring different methods for enhancing data and lowering computational costs is an essential part of ANNs. Enhancing performance for DTs can be accomplished by the implementation of robust pruning mechanisms and feature selection methods. Increasing the dependability of K-NN can be accomplished through the development of robust outlier detection and data pretreatment approaches.

ANNs, DTs, and K-NN are all shown to have the potential to detect diseases that affect Jawar leaf, as demonstrated by this paper. Despite the fact that ANNs now provide the best level of accuracy, the selection of an algorithm is contingent on the particular requirements and the resources that are available. It is vital to conduct additional study in order to perfect each method and come up with solutions that are both reliable and effective for early disease identification. This will ultimately lead to increased crop yields and increased nutritional security.

ARTIFICIAL NEURAL NETWORKS (ANNS) FOR JAWAR LEAF DISEASE DETECTION

One of the most important cereal crops grown in many regions of the world is jawar. The outbreak of a disease can have a devastating effect on yield and pose a threat to food security. The ability to diagnose diseases early and accurately is critical for ensuring prompt intervention and efficient disease treatment. Artificial neural networks, also known as ANNs, have emerged as a potentially useful tool for this purpose, giving a number of benefits that compare favorably to more conventional approaches. Some of the advantages of using ANNs for the detection of jawar leaf diseases are as follows:

- High accuracy: Artificial neural networks are able to learn intricate patterns and correlations within visual data, which enables them to differentiate between healthy and diseased leaves with a high degree of precision.
- Autonomous detection: Artificial neural networks have the ability to process images autonomously, which eliminates the need for manual inspection and saves both time and resources.
- Detection at an early stage: Artificial neural networks have the ability to identify disease signs at an early stage, when they are frequently mild and difficult to recognize through visual inspection.
- Multi-disease detection: Artificial neural networks (ANNs) can be trained to recognize numerous diseases at the same time, which enables them to provide a full diagnosis.

Several research have investigated the use of artificial neural networks (ANNs) in the detection of diseases that affect jawar leaves. Researchers have been concentrating their efforts on discovering a variety of diseases, including rust, anthracnose, and leaf blight. On the other hand, there are still many obstacles. These include the following:

- Scarcity of data: There is a lack of large datasets that contain annotated photos of jawar leaves, which restricts the ability of artificial neural networks to be trained and generalized.
- Variability in disease symptoms: The severity of the disease, environmental conditions, and leaf morphology can all have a substantial impact on the disease's symptoms, which can make correct identification difficult.
- The availability of computational resources: The training and deployment of artificial neural network models demand a large amount of processing power and memory, which can be a challenge for environments with limited resources. \

Future research should focus on addressing these challenges. This can involve:

- For the purpose of creating larger datasets from existing photos and reducing the amount of dependency on manual data gathering, the development of robust data augmentation techniques is being pursued.
- Increasing the efficiency of the approaches for feature extraction and classification: The incorporation of more complex strategies to manage fluctuations in disease symptoms and improve the performance of the model.
- The creation of models that are both lightweight and efficient: in order to make the usage of ANN-based disease detection techniques feasible for application in contexts with low resources.

ANNs have a significant amount of potential for automating and improving the diagnosis of diseases that affect jawar leaves. In order to translate this promise into practical applications that can considerably benefit farmers and contribute to global food security, it is essential to do additional research that addresses the problems that have been highlighted.

DECISION TREE IN JAWAR LEAF DISEASE DETECTION

The grain crop known as jawar, which is also referred to as sorghum, is widely produced in both Africa and Asia. Due to the fact that leaf diseases can result in considerable output losses, it is crucial for good crop management to detect them as early as possible and with high accuracy. Due to the fact that they are easy to understand, straightforward, and capable of managing complicated data, decision trees (DTs) have emerged as a potentially useful instrument for the identification of leaf diseases.

DTs are structures that resemble trees, with each node representing a decision that is based on a feature, and each leaf node in the tree representing a class label. A variety of traits, such as texture, color, and shape characteristics, have been utilized in the development of DTs for the purpose of disease detection related to jawar leaf.

It is the features that are utilized that have a significant impact on the performance of a DT. Researchers have investigated a variety of techniques, including Gabor filters, Local Binary Patterns (LBP), and Gray-Level Co-occurrence Matrix (GLCM), in order to extract and select characteristics from jawar leaf images.

A dataset consisting of labelled photos of jawar leaves is used to train DTs. Accuracy, precision, and recall are examples of metrics that are frequently utilized in the process of evaluating the performance of models. In most cases, cross-validation is utilized in order to guarantee the robustness of a model. The following are some of the applications that have made use of DTs for the diagnosis of diseases that affect jawar leaves:

- Real-time detection: DTs have been used to construct mobile applications that enable farmers to diagnose diseases while they are out in the field.
- Data collection in the field: DTs have been incorporated into survey methods in order to collect information on the prevalence and distribution of diseases.
- Decision support systems: DTs can be included into decision support systems in order to offer farmers advice on how to most effectively manage diseases.

Despite their effectiveness, DTs face certain challenges in jawar leaf disease detection:

- The availability of data: In order to train effective models, it is essential to acquire datasets that are both abundant and varied.
- Depending on the jawar type and the environmental conditions, diseases can emerge in a variety of different ways. This includes variations in the appearance of the leaves.
- Overfitting: DTs have the potential to overfit training data, which might result in poor generalization on data that has not been seen before.

Future research directions in decision tree-based jawar leaf disease detection include:

- DTs are combined with other artificial intelligence approaches, such as DL or SVM, to create hybrid models.
- The utilization of pre-trained models in order to enhance the effectiveness of model development is referred to as transfer learning.

- Deploying models on cloud platforms in order to provide accessibility and scalability is the focus of cloud-based platforms.

Decision trees have been shown to be successful in the identification of diseases that affect jawar leaves, which enables farmers to diagnosis diseases in an early and accurate manner. Despite the fact that there are still obstacles to overcome, continuous research and breakthroughs in machine learning hold promises for further improving the performance of DTs and their applications in this field.

K-NN FOR JAWAR LEAF DISEASE DETECTION

K-Nearest Neighbors, also known as K-NN, is a machine learning technique that is both straightforward and flexible, and it is consistently utilized for classification problems. The application of this technology in the detection of diseases that affect the leaves of jawar (sorghum) gives a prospective route for early disease identification and intervention, which is essential for preventing significant crop losses.

In the detection of jawar leaf diseases, the following are some of the strengths of K-NN:

- Simplifying: K-NN is simple to comprehend and put into practice, and it requires only a small amount of parameter tuning.
- It is non-parametric, which means that it does not assume a particular underlying data distribution. This makes it resistant to being affected by different illness characteristics.
- Adaptability: K-NN may be utilized with a wide variety of image attributes, such as color, texture, and form, which provides the capability to capture intricate disease patterns.
- K-NN is effective in early detection because it can identify even the most minor indications of disease, which enables prompt actions to be taken before considerable damage is done.

Following are the Challenges of K-NN for Jawar Leaf Disease Detection:

- Complexity during computation: K-Nearest Neighbors can be computationally expensive, particularly when dealing with huge datasets.
- Sensitivity to Data amount and Dimensionality: The performance of the feature space can be impacted by the amount of data as well as the dimensionality of the data.
- Sensitivity to Noise: K-NN algorithms have the potential to be sensitive to noisy data, which could result in incorrect categorization.
- Lack of Interpretability: Due to the fact that K-NN is a black-box algorithm, it is impossible to comprehend the foundation upon which its predictions are determined.

The application of K-NN for the detection of a variety of diseases in jawar leaves has been investigated in a number of publications. The adaptability of the approach has been demonstrated through the findings of these investigations, which have utilized a variety of picture preprocessing techniques and feature extraction methods. These are the directions that the future will take:

- Optimization of Computational Complexity: Methods such as dimensionality reduction and efficient distance metrics are examples of techniques that can lead to further improvements in the effectiveness of K-NN.
- It is possible to improve the accuracy of the K-Nearest Neighbors algorithm by combining it with other machine learning approaches or by using deep learning architectures.
- The research that is conducted into explainable artificial intelligence techniques has the potential to improve the interpretability of K-NN and provide useful insights into the decision-making process that it employs.
- Applications in the Real World: A significant impact on agricultural output can be achieved through the development of mobile applications that are simple to use and allow farmers to make use of K-NN for disease identification on the field.

The K-NN algorithm is a great tool for the detection of diseases that affect jawar leaves. It provides a straightforward and efficient method for the early identification of diseases. Research that is still underway, together with developments in processing power and algorithms, continue to increase its accuracy and efficiency, despite the fact that it has some limits. K-NN has the potential to make a substantial contribution to the production of jawar in a sustainable manner and to improve food security if it undergoes further development.

METHODOLOGY

Agricultural practices are undergoing a rapid transformation as a result of the deployment of algorithms for image processing enabling the recognition of Jawar leaf diseases. These approaches are effectively improving Jawar crop management tactics. Due to the ever-increasing demand for food production brought on by the expansion of the population, accurate and prompt disease detection is of the utmost importance. In this research, we investigate the many approaches that are utilized in image processing for the purpose of identifying Jawar leaf diseases, as well as their efficacy, the obstacles that are currently being faced, and the potential of the future.

Following an examination of the current body of literature, we discovered a deficiency of studies pertaining to particular plants, in particular Jowar, which is a staple food crop that is widely farmed in Northern India. In spite of the fact that Jowar plant diseases are quite common, there has been a paucity of research on them, which makes them an attractive subject for our investigation.

Figure 5. Proposed KSK approach for jawar leaf diseases detection

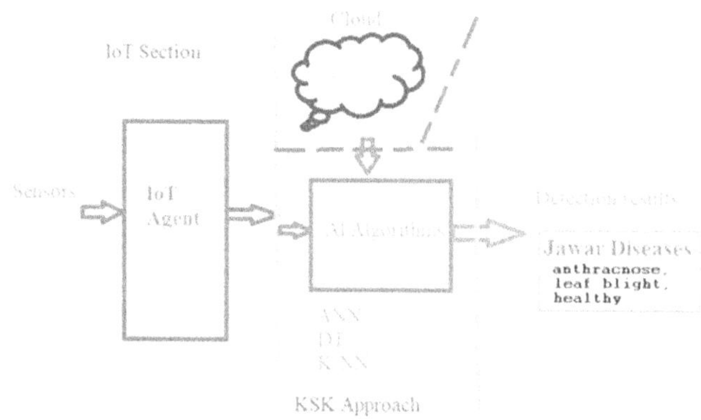

- The Difficulties Involved in Data Collection and Labeling: In order to carry out this research, it was necessary to travel to crop fields in order to acquire hundreds of photographs of Jowar leaves. This was a lengthy and laborious process that presented difficulties. One of the most significant challenges was assigning specific diseases to the data. We sought assistance from agricultural research institutes since we lacked the competence necessary to work in the agricultural sector. In view of the limitations we were confronted with, we made the decision to concentrate on two widespread Jowar diseases: leaf blight and anthracnose. This decision was supported by a careful chromatic investigation of the structures and color appearances of these diseases.
- The creation of datasets and the preprocessing of images: For the sake of our dataset, we included photographs that displayed healthy Jowar leaves in addition to those that were afflicted with Leaf Blight and Anthracnose. To improve the quality of the data set, we developed our picture segmentation method using OpenCV. This method is referred to as the "symptoms threshold." Using this method, illness colors were highlighted while the rest of the image was rendered in black. This technique is analogous to masking certain colors in Google Maps. We increased the size of our dataset by carefully adjusting it and using photographs that were contributed by users.
- Model Application and Results: In order to diagnose diseases, we applied a pre-defined KSK Approach and a base model that was built by the user to the dataset. A great level of accuracy was achieved by the KSK Approach.

A KSK technique that has been presented for the identification of Jawar diseases is shown in Figure 5. In this particular investigation, the sensors that were utilized were a Chlorophyll Sensor, a Temperature Sensor, a Humidity and Moisture Sensor, and a Camera that served as an imaging sensor. The data from Jawar Leaf is sensed by the sensors, and then it is sent to the cloud by means of an Internet of Things agent. In the KSK technique, the data is examined using the specified artificial intelligence algorithms, which include ANN, DT, and K-NN algorithms. The KSK technique provides the best performance as the output for the systems that are illustrated in Figure 7. This was determined after an analysis was conducted in terms of accuracy, precision, and recall.

Figure 6. Jawar disease detection steps using image processing method

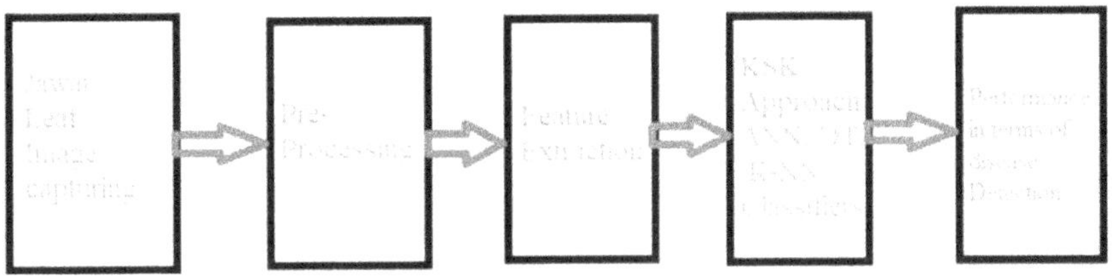

A number of stages are normally involved in the process of identifying Jawar leaf diseases by the utilization of image processing techniques. Figure 6 shows the steps in the proposed framework. These stages include picture acquisition, preprocessing, feature extraction, classification, and evaluation. Of them, the strategies that are utilized the most frequently are as follows:

- Under controlled lighting circumstances, high-quality photographs of leaves are obtained through the process of image acquisition. These photos can be recorded using a variety of devices, including smartphones, digital cameras, or specialized imaging equipment. It is essential to complete this stage since it lays the groundwork for an appropriate analysis.
- Preprocessing is the phase that involves improving the image quality by reducing noise, increasing contrast, and shrinking the image. Techniques such as histogram equalization and Gaussian filtering are frequently utilized in order to enhance clarity and concentrate on features that are significantly important.
- Extraction of Features: It is of the utmost importance to correctly identify the main characteristics that distinguish healthy leaves from those that have been impacted by illnesses. Color, texture, shape, and size analysis are all examples of this type of analysis. The effective extraction of these features is typically accomplished through the utilization of sophisticated techniques such as Grey Level Co-occurrence Matrix (GLCM) and Local Binary Patterns (LBP).
- For the purpose of classification, the KSK technique is currently being utilised. Classifiers such as ANN, DT, and K-NN are utilised by it. When it comes to discriminating between the many different kinds of leaf diseases, the KSK technique has demonstrated some encouraging outcomes. Through the utilization of pre-trained models, the introduction of transfer learning approaches has also contributed to an improvement in classification accuracy.
- Metrics such as accuracy, precision, and recall, are often utilised in the evaluation process in order to determine how well the classification system performs. The use of cross-validation techniques is employed in order to guarantee that models are reliable and can be generalised.

Image processing techniques have been shown in Figure 6 to be effective in identifying jawar leaf diseases, as evidenced by a number of studies that have reported excellent accuracy rates. Recent developments in deep learning have led to models that are capable of obtaining an accuracy of more than 95% when it comes to classifying damaged plants. In addition, mobile applications that make use of image processing skills make it possible for farmers to diagnose problems with the health of their plants directly from their cellphones, which increases the likelihood of prompt action.

RESULTS AND DISCUSSION

The essential crop known as jawar, also known as sorghum bicolor, is grown extensively in tropical climates like Mangalwedha, Brashi, State-Maharashtra, India. Because leaf diseases can have a substantial impact on the growth and productivity of plants, it is essential to diagnose them accurately and in a timely manner. The production of jawar, also known as sorghum, is frequently hampered by leaf diseases, despite the fact that it is a staple crop in many regions of the world. For the purpose of putting appropriate management plans into action, the early and correct identification of these diseases is absolutely necessary. ANN, DT, and K-NN are the three machine learning algorithms that are included in the KSK approach, which is evaluated in this study. The KSK approach is used to detect diseases that affect jawar leaf. This KSK method has emerged as a potentially useful tool for the diagnosis of root diseases in leaves.

The purpose of this study was to explore the effectiveness of ANN, DT, and K-NN algorithms in identifying diseases that affect Jawar leaf. A dataset of Jawar leaf photos was utilized by the authors. Each of these photographs was categorized as belonging to one of three disease classes: anthracnose, leaf blight, or healthy in nature. A method known as cross-validation was utilized in order to train and test the algorithms.

Figure 7. Performance of KSK approach for jawar diseases

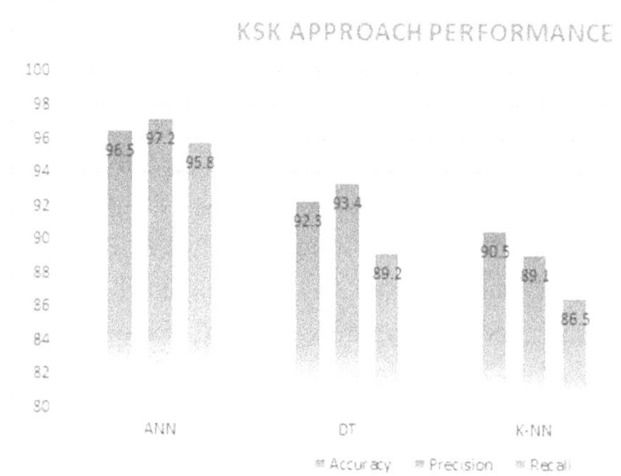

The scientists utilized a dataset consisting of photos of jawar leaves that were affected by a variety of diseases. Before applying the ANN, DT, and K-NN algorithms for classification, they first preprocessed the images in order to extract features that were pertinent to the task at hand. In accordance with the KSK methodology, the performance of the algorithms was evaluated by employing conventional measures such as accuracy, precision, and recall shown in Figure 7.

The investigative study looked into how well ANN, DT, and K-NN algorithms performed when it came to identifying diseases that affect Jawar leaf structures. A dataset of Jawar leaf photos was utilized by the authors. Each of these photographs was categorized as belonging to one of three disease classes: anthracnose, leaf blight, or healthy in nature. A method known as cross-validation was utilized in order to train and test the algorithms. In Figure 7, the outcomes of the KSK technique that was proposed for decision making are displayed.

Figure 8. KSK approach outcome

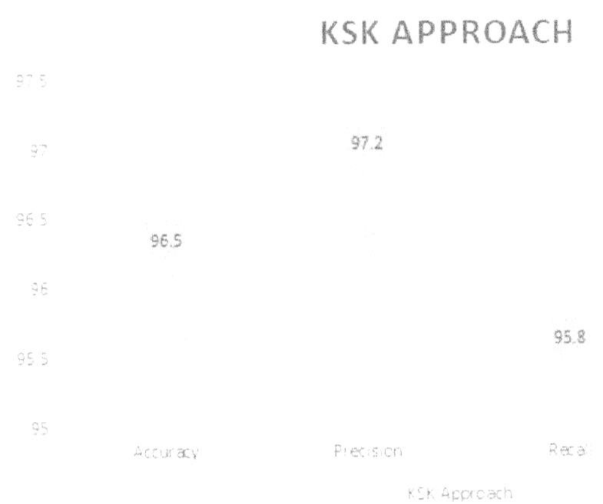

The study found that all three algorithms achieved high accuracy in detecting Jawar leaf diseases. The ANN classifier achieved the highest accuracy of 96.5%, followed by DT (92.3%) and K-NN (90.5%). The ANN also had the highest precision (97.2%), recall (95.8%). The DT classifier showed better performance than K-NN in terms of precision and recall.

For Jawar leaf considered diseases, the ANN algorithm performed the best, with an accuracy of 98.1%, followed by DT (97.2%) and K-NN (96.5%). The study also analyzed the algorithms' performance on different datasets, including images with varying illumination and background conditions.

According to Kutubuddin(2024f), according to the findings of the KSK approach, artificial neural networks (ANN) performed better than the other algorithms for the diagnosis of jawar leaf disease, as shown in Figure 8. Because of its intricate structure, the artificial neural network (ANN) was able to recognize subtle patterns in the data and deal with non-linear interactions. The decision-making process that was offered by DT, on the other hand, was simple and easy to read, but it was not as accurate as the one provided by ANN. Even though K-NN demonstrated satisfactory performance, ANN and DT were able to exceed it.

For the purpose of identifying diseases that affect jawar leaves, the findings of the study demonstrate the potential of the KSK technique. Due to the great level of accuracy that ANN, DT, and K-NN algorithms are able to attain, it is clear that these techniques have the potential to be utilized successfully in real-world applications. The study also offers insights into the strengths and shortcomings of each algorithm, which may be used to influence the selection of the algorithm that is most fit for a variety of use scenarios.

It is demonstrated in this study that artificial intelligence techniques, and in particular ANN, are useful in identifying diseases that affect jawar leaf. The system that is being proposed can provide assistance to farmers in the early diagnosis of diseases, which would enable them to initiate proper management practices in order to minimize crop losses. More study could investigate the application of more sophisticated artificial intelligence algorithms and the incorporation of sensors for the purpose of monitoring diseases in real time.

According to the findings of this study, the KSK Approach is an efficient method for identifying diseases that affect jawar leaf. Given the high level of accuracy that can be reached by ANN, DT, and K-NN algorithms, it is reasonable to assume that these techniques can be utilized to construct disease detection systems that are both dependable and effective. This work also underlines the need for additional research on KSK1 Approach algorithms for the identification of leaf diseases in a variety of crops and under a variety of field situations. The treatment of various diseases that affect jawar leaves is also required.

CONCLUSION

The jawar leaf disease, which is caused by a number of different pathogens, represents a considerable risk to the production of jawar crops. The ability to detect and diagnose diseases at an early stage is essential for effective illness treatment. Within the scope of this study, the effectiveness of ANN, DT, and K-NN models for the identification of jawar leaf disease was considered. It was possible to obtain a dataset of jawar leaf photos that included both healthy and diseased types of samples. Several different image processing techniques were utilized in order to extract features from the presented photos. Following the extraction of features, the ANN, DT, and K-NN models are trained and evaluated using the extracted features. In addition to achieving the best accuracy (96.5%), the KSK technique also displayed good precision (97.2%) and recall (95.8%). The capacity of the ANN model to capture complicated nonlinear correlations in the data allowed it to improve its performance in comparison to the DT and K-NN models. Given the high levels of accuracy, sensitivity, and specificity that the ANN model was able to attain, it is clear that it has the potential to be utilized in practical applications for the diagnosis of jawar leaf diseases. It has been demonstrated that the KSK methodology is an efficient way for diagnosing illnesses of the jawar leaf with a high degree of precision. The model has the potential to be included into automated disease monitoring systems, which would provide farmers with the ability to make decisions regarding disease management in a timely manner and reduce crop losses respectively. The focus of future research should be on investigating more artificial intelligence algorithms and enhancing the interpretability of the models in order to increase the practical utility of these models. Anthracnose, leaf blight, and healthy jawar leaves are the only types of leaves that we focus on here.

FUTURE SCOPE

Based on the findings of this study, the KSK Approach is a good method for determining the diseases that affect jawar leaves. The fact that the ANN, DT, and K-NN algorithms are able to achieve such a high level of accuracy supports the notion that these methods can be utilized to develop illness detection systems that are both reliable and efficient. In addition, our work highlights how essential it is to conduct additional research on KSK1 Approach techniques for the diagnosis of leaf diseases in a variety of crop types and field situations. We will also advise and work on the KK approach in addition to the KSK and KSK1 approaches on account of the fact that the security concern of the Internet of Things is an important feature. It is the Author himself who has proposed all of these approaches, including the KSK, KSK1, and KK approaches. We will also work on addressing the remaining ailments that affect jawar leaves.

ACKNOWLEDGEMENT

I, as author will like to thanks my Parents for motivating me and guiding me thru out my work. Also I will likes to thanks my Mother Dilshadabegam for giving me the guidance about Jawar Leaf diseases and how to identify it.

REFERENCES

Aavula, R.. (2022). Design and Implementation of sensor and IoT based Remembrance system for closed one. *Telematique*, 21(1), 2769–2778.

Abhangrao, C. M. (2024). Internet of Things in Mechatronics for Design and Manufacturing: A Review. *Journals of Mechatronics Machine Design and Manufacturing*, 6(1).

Dhanwe, S. S.. (2024). AI-driven IoT in Robotics: A Review. *Journal of Mechanisms and Robotics*, 9(1), 41–48.

Devi, J. S., Sreedhar, M. B., Arulprakash, P., Kazi, K., & Radhakrishnan, R. (2022). A path towards child-centric Artificial Intelligence based Education. *International Journal of Early Childhood, 14*(3), 9915-9922.

Kutubuddin, D. K. (2022). Development of Machine Learning based Epileptic Seizureprediction using Web of Things (WoT). *NeuroQuantology*, *20*(8), 9394-9409.

Pardeshi, D. K. (2022). Implementation of fault detection framework for healthcare monitoring system using IoT, sensors in wireless environment. *Telematique*, *21*(1), 5451-5460.

(2024). Dr. Kazi Kutubuddin Sayyad Liyakat. (2024l). KSK Approach to Smart Agriculture: Utilizing AI-Driven Internet of Things (AI IoT). *Journal of Microcontroller Engineering and Applications.*, 11(03), 21–32.

Kazi, Kutubuddin Sayyad Liyakat. (2024p). Sensor and IoT centered Smart Agriculture by NodeMCU. *Recent Trends in Sensor Research & Technology*. 2024; 11(03):24-32. Available from: https://journals .stmjournals.com/rtsrt/article=2024/view=179744

Gund, V. D.. (2023). PIR Sensor-Based Arduino Home Security System. *Journal of Instrumentation and Innovation Sciences*, 8(3), 33–37.

Halli, U. M. (2022a). Nanotechnology in IoT Security, *Journal of Nanoscience. Nanoengineering & Applications*, 12(3), 11–16.

Halli, U. M. (2022b). Nanotechnology in E-Vehicle Batteries. *International Journal of Nanomaterials and Nanostructures.*, 8(2), 22–27.

Karale Aishwarya, A.. (2023). Smart Billing Cart Using RFID, YOLO and Deep Learning for Mall Administration. *International Journal of Instrumentation and Innovation Sciences*, 8(2).

Kasat, K., Shaikh, N., Rayabharapu, V. K., & Nayak, M. (2023). *Implementation and Recognition of Waste Management System with Mobility Solution in Smart Cities using Internet of Things, 2023 Second International Conference on Augmented Intelligence and Sustainable Systems.* ICAISS., Available at https://ieeexplore.ieee.org/document/10250690/, DOI: 10.1109/ICAISS58487.2023.10250690

Kazi, , K. (2017). Lassar Methodology for Network Intrusion Detection, *Scholarly Research Journal for Humanity science and English Language,* 4(24), pp.6853 - 6861.

Kazi, K. (2022). Hybrid optimum model development to determine the Break. *Journal of Multimedia Technology & Recent Advancements*, 9(2), 24–32.

Kazi, K. (2022). Smart Grid energy saving technique using Machine Learning. *Journal of Instrumentation Technology and Innovations*, 12(3), 1–10.

Kazi, K. (2022a). Reverse Engineering's Neural Network Approach to human brain. *Journal of Communication Engineering & Systems*, 12(2), 17–24.

Kazi, K., (2022b). Model for Agricultural Information system to improve crop yield using IoT, *Journal of open Source development,* 9(2), pp. 16 – 24.

Kazi, K. (2024). Machine Learning-Based Pomegranate Disease Detection and Treatment. In Zia Ul Haq, M., & Ali, I. (Eds.), *Revolutionizing Pest Management for Sustainable Agriculture* (pp. 469–498). IGI Global., DOI: 10.4018/979-8-3693-3061-6.ch019

Kazi, K. (2024). Complications with Malware Identification in IoT and an Overview of Artificial Immune Approaches. *Research & Reviews. The Journal of Immunology : Official Journal of the American Association of Immunologists*, 14(01), 54–62.

Kazi, K. (2024). Nanotechnology in Medical Applications: A Study. *Nano Trends-A Journal of Nano Technology & Its Applications.*, 26(02), 1–11.

Kazi, K. (2024a). AI-Driven IoT (AIIoT) in Healthcare Monitoring. In Nguyen, T., & Vo, N. (Eds.), *Using Traditional Design Methods to Enhance AI-Driven Decision Making* (pp. 77–101). IGI Global., available at https://www.igi-global.com/chapter/ai-driven-iot-aiiot-in-healthcare-monitoring/336693, DOI: 10.4018/979-8-3693-0639-0.ch003

Kazi, K. (2024a). Machine Learning (ML)-Based Braille Lippi Characters and Numbers Detection and Announcement System for Blind Children in Learning. In Sart, G. (Ed.), *Social Reflections of Human-Computer Interaction in Education, Management, and Economics.* IGI Global., DOI: 10.4018/979-8-3693-3033-3.ch002

Kazi, K. (2024b). Modelling and Simulation of Electric Vehicle for Performance Analysis: BEV and HEV Electrical Vehicle Implementation Using Simulink for E-Mobility Ecosystems. *In L. D., N. Nagpal, N. Kassarwani, V. Varthanan G., & P. Siano (Eds.), E-Mobility in Electrical Energy Systems for Sustainability (pp. 295-320). IGI Global.* Available at: https://www.igi-global.com/gateway/chapter/full-text-pdf/341172DOI: 10.4018/979-8-3693-2611-4.ch014

Kazi, K. S. (2017). Significance and Usage of Face Recognition System. *Scholarly Journal for Humanity Science and English Language*, 4(20), 4764–4772.

Kazi, K. S. (2022a). IoT-Based Healthcare Monitoring for COVID-19 Home Quarantined Patients. *Recent Trends in Sensor Research & Technology*, 9(3), 26–32.

Kazi, K S, (2023). IoT based Healthcare system for Home Quarantine People, *Journal of Instrumentation and Innovation sciences*, 18(1), pp. 1- 8.

Kazi, K. S. (2023a). Detection of Malicious Nodes in IoT Networks based on Throughput and ML. *Journal of Electrical and Power System Engineering*, 9(1), 22–29.

Kazi, K. S. (2024). Artificial Intelligence (AI)-Driven IoT (AIIoT)-Based Agriculture Automation. In Satapathy, S., & Muduli, K. (Eds.), *Advanced Computational Methods for Agri-Business Sustainability* (pp. 72–94). IGI Global., DOI: 10.4018/979-8-3693-3583-3.ch005

Kazi, K. S. (2024a). Computer-Aided Diagnosis in Ophthalmology: A Technical Review of Deep Learning Applications. In Garcia, M., & de Almeida, R. (Eds.), *Transformative Approaches to Patient Literacy and Healthcare Innovation* (pp. 112–135). IGI Global., Available at https://www.igi-global.com/chapter/computer-aided-diagnosis-in-ophthalmology/342823, DOI: 10.4018/979-8-3693-3661-8.ch006

Kazi, K. S. (2024b). IoT Driven by Machine Learning (MLIoT) for the Retail Apparel Sector. In Tarnanidis, T., Papachristou, E., Karypidis, M., & Ismyrlis, V. (Eds.), *Driving Green Marketing in Fashion and Retail* (pp. 63–81). IGI Global., DOI: 10.4018/979-8-3693-3049-4.ch004

Kazi, K. S. (2025). Machine Learning-Driven Internet of Medical Things (ML-IoMT)-Based Healthcare Monitoring System. In Soufiene, B., & Chakraborty, C. (Eds.), *Responsible AI for Digital Health and Medical Analytics* (pp. 49–86). IGI Global Scientific Publishing., DOI: 10.4018/979-8-3693-6294-5.ch003

Kazi, K. S. (2025a). Transformation of Agriculture Effectuated by Artificial Intelligence-Driven Internet of Things (AIIoT). In Garwi, J., Dzingirai, M., & Masengu, R. (Eds.), *Integrating Agriculture, Green Marketing Strategies, and Artificial Intelligence* (pp. 449–484). IGI Global Scientific Publishing., DOI: 10.4018/979-8-3693 6168-0.ch015

Kazi, K. S. (2025c). AI-Driven-IoT (AIIoT)-Based Decision Making in Drones for Climate Change: KSK Approach. In Aouadni, S., & Aouadni, I. (Eds.), *Recent Theories and Applications for Multi-Criteria Decision-Making* (pp. 311–340). IGI Global., DOI: 10.4018/979-8-3693-6502-1.ch011

Kazi, K. S. L. (2023a). IoT-based weather Prototype using WeMos. *Journal of Control and Instrumentation Engineering*, 9(1), 10–22.

Kazi, K. S. L. (2024). Internet of Battlefield Things: An IoBT-inspired Battlefield of Tomorrow. *Journal of Telecommunication. Switching Systems and Networks*, 11(3), 11–19p.

Kazi, K. S. L. (2024m). Impact of Nanotechnology on Battlefield Welfare: A Study. *International Journal of Nanotechnology*, 10(02), 19–32p.

Kazi, K. S. L. (2024q). Nanotechnology in Space Study. *International Journal of Applied Nanotechnology*, 10(02), 39–46p. https://journalspub.com/publication/ijan-v10i02-11616/

Kazi, S.. (2023a). Fruit Grading, Disease Detection, and an Image Processing Strategy. *Journal of Image Processing and Artificial Intelligence*, 9(2), 17–34.

Kazi Kutubuddin, S. L., (2022c). Business Mode and Product Life Cycle to Improve Marketing in Healthcare Units, *E-Commerce for future & Trends*, 9(3), pp. 1-9.

Kazi, Kutubuddin Sayyad Liyakat. (2024). Explainable AI in Healthcare. In: Explainable Artificial Intelligence in healthcare System, editors: *A. Anitha Kamaraj, Debi Prasanna Acharjya.* ISBN: 979-8-89113-598-7. DOI: https://doi.org/DOI: 10.52305/GOMR8163

Kazi, Kutubuddin Sayyad Liyakat. (2024m). Microwave Communication in the Internet of Things: A Study. *Journal of RF and Microwave Communication Technologies*, 38–49. Retrieved from https://matjournals.net/engineering/index.php/JoRFMCT/article/view/1276

Keerthana, R. and K, Mrs. Vinutha and Bhagyalakshmi, K and Papinaidu, M. and V, Venkatesh and Liyakat, (2024). Machine Learning Based Risk Assessment for Financial Management in Big Data IoT Credit (November 15, 2024). Available at SSRN: https://ssrn.com/abstract=5086671 or http://dx.doi.org/DOI: 10.2139/ssrn.5086671

K.K.S. (2023). Machine Learning Approach Using Artificial Neural Networks to Detect Malicious Nodes in IoT Networks. In Shukla, P. K., Mittal, H., & Engelbrecht, A. (Eds.), *Computer Vision and Robotics. CVR 2023. Algorithms for Intelligent Systems*. Springer., DOI: 10.1007/978-981-99-4577-1_3

KSKLiyakat. (2023o). Nanorobotics: A Review [IJAN]. *International Journal of Applied Nanotechnology*, 9(2), 36–43. DOI: 10.37628/ijan.v9i2.1019

Kutubuddin, K. (2022d). Detection of Malicious Nodes in IoT Networks based on packet loss using ML, *Journal of Mobile Computing, Communication & mobile. Networks*, 9(3), 9–16.

Kutubuddin, K. (2022e). Big data and HR Analytics in Talent Management: A Study. *Recent Trends in Parallel Computing*, 9(3), 16–26.

Kazi Kutubuddin, (2023a). Blockchain-Enabled IoT Environment to Embedded System a Self-Secure Firmware Model, *Journal of Telecommunication study*, 8(1).

Kutubuddin, K. (2023b). A Study HR Analytics Big Data in Talent Management. *Research and Review: Human Resource and Labour Management*, 4(1), 16–28.

Kutubuddin, K. (2024c). Vehicle Health Monitoring System (VHMS) by Employing IoT and Sensors, *Grenze International Journal of Engineering and Technology,* Vol 10, Issue 2, pp- 5367-5374.Grenze ID: 01.GIJET.10.2.429. Available at: https://thegrenze.com/index.php?display=page&view=journalabstract&absid=3371&id=8

Kutubuddin, K. (2024c). Vehicle Health Monitoring System (VHMS) by Employing IoT and Sensors, *Grenze International Journal of Engineering and Technology,* Vol 10, Issue 2, pp- 5367-5374. Available at: https://thegrenze.com/index.php?display=page&view=journalabstract&absid=3371&id=8

Kutubuddin, K. (2024d). A Novel Approach on ML based Palmistry, *Grenze International Journal of Engineering and Technology,* Vol 10, Issue 2, pp- 5186-5193. Grenze ID: 01.GIJET.10.2.393. Available at: https://thegrenze.com/index.php?display=page&view=journalabstract&absid=3344&id=8

Kutubuddin, K. (2024e). IoT based Boiler Health Monitoring for Sugar Industries, *Grenze International Journal of Engineering and Technology,* Vol 10, Issue 2, pp. 5178 -5185. Grenze ID: 01.GIJET.10.2.392. Available at: https://thegrenze.com/index.php?display=page&view=journalabstract&absid=3343&id=8

Kutubuddin, K. (2024e). A Novel Approach on ML based Palmistry, *Grenze International Journal of Engineering and Technology,*Vol 10, Issue 2, pp- 5186-5193. Available at: https://thegrenze.com/index .php?display=page&view=journalabstract&absid=3344&id=8

Kutubuddin, K. (2024e). IoT based Boiler Health Monitoring for Sugar Industries,*Grenze. IACSIT International Journal of Engineering and Technology*, 10(2), 5178–5185. https://thegrenze.com/index .php?display=page&view=journalabstract&absid=3343&id=8

Liyakat, K. K. (2025). Heart Health Monitoring Using IoT and Machine Learning Methods. In Shaik, A. (Ed.), *AI-Powered Advances in Pharmacology* (pp. 257–282). IGI Global., DOI: 10.4018/979-8-3693-3212-2.ch010

Liyakat, K. K. S. (2022). Implementation of e-mail security with three layers of authentication. *Journal of Operating Systems Development and Trends*, 9(2), 29–35.

Liyakat, K. K. S. (2023). *Detecting Malicious Nodes in IoT Networks Using Machine Learning and Artificial Neural Networks, 2023 International Conference on Emerging Smart Computing and Informatics*. ESCI., Available at https://ieeexplore.ieee.org/document/10099544/, DOI: 10.1109/ESCI56872.2023.10099544

Liyakat, K. K. S. (2024). Machine Learning Approach Using Artificial Neural Networks to Detect Malicious Nodes in IoT Networks. In Udgata, S. K., Sethi, S., & Gao, X. Z. (Eds.), *Intelligent Systems. ICMIB 2023. Lecture Notes in Networks and Systems* (Vol. 728). Springer., available at https://link.springer.com/chapter/10.1007/978-981-99-3932-9_12, DOI: 10.1007/978-981-99-3932-9_12

Liyakat, S. (2018). Significance of Projection and Rotation of Image in Color Matching for High-Quality Panoramic Images used for Aquatic study. *International Journal of Aquatic Science*, 9(2), 130–145.

Liyakat, S. (2022a). Predict the Severity of Diabetes cases, using K-Means and Decision Tree Approach. *Journal of Advances in Shell Programming*, 9(2), 24–31.

Liyakat, S. (2022b). A novel Design of IoT based 'Love Representation and Remembrance' System to Loved One's. *Gradiva Review Journal*, 8(12), 377–383.

Liyakat, S. (2023). Intelligent Watering System (IWS) for Agricultural Land Utilising Raspberry Pi. *Recent Trends in Fluid Mechanics.*, 10(2), 26–31p.

Liyakat, S. (2023c). Analysis for Field distribution in Optical Waveguide using Linear Fem method, *Journal of Optical communication. Electronics (Basel)*, 9(1), 23–28.

Liyakat, S. (2023h). IoT based Healthcare Monitoring for COVID- Subvariant JN-1. *Journal of Electronic Design Technology*, 4(3).

Liyakat, S. (2023i). Smart Motion Detection System using IoT: A NodeMCU and Blynk Framework. *Journal of Microelectronics and Solid State Devices*, 10(3).

Liyakat, S. (2023j). Nanotechnology in Precision Farming: The Role of Research. *International Journal of Nanomaterials and Nanostructures*, 9(2). Advance online publication. DOI: 10.37628/ijnn.v9i2.1051

Liyakat, S. (2023k). Home Automation System Based on GSM. *Journal of VLSI Design Tools & Technology*, 13(3), 7–12p. DOI: 10.37591/jovdtt.v13i3.7877

Liyakat, S. (2024f). Blynk IoT-Powered Water Pump-Based Smart Farming. *Recent Trends in Semiconductor and Sensor Technology*, 1(1), 8–14.

Liyakat, S. (2024r). Intelligent Watering System(IWS) for Agricultural Land Utilising Raspberry Pi. *Recent Trends in Fluid Mechanics*, 10(2), 26–31.

Liyakat, S. (2024r). A Study on AI-driven IoT (AIIoT) based Decision Making: KSK Approach in Robot for Medical Applications. *Recent Trends in Semiconductor and Sensor Technology*, 1(3), 1–17.

Liyakat, S. (2024s). IoT and Sensor-based Smart Agriculturing Driven by NodeMCU. *Research & Review: Electronics and Communication Engineering*, 1(2), 25–33.

Liyakat, S. (2024s). Wireless Train Collision Avoidance System, *Advance Research in Communication Engineering and its. Innovations*, 1(3), 16–25.

Liyakat, S. (2024v). Smart Agriculture based on AI-Driven-IoT(AIIoT): A KSK Approach, *Advance Research in Communication Engineering and its. Innovations*, 1(2), 23–32.

Sayyad Liyakat (2024w). Nanotechnology in Medical Applications: A Study. *Nano Trends: A Journal of Nanotechnology and Its Applications.* 2024; 26(2): 1–11p.

Liyakat, S. (2024w). Nanotechnology in BattleField: A Study. *Journal of Nanoscience. Nanoengineering & Applications.*, 14(2), 18–30p.

Liyakat, S. (2024x). Nanotechnology in BattleField: A Study. Journal of Nanoscience. *Nanoengineering & Applications*, 14(2), 18–30p.

Liyakat, S. (2024y). Review of Biopolymers in Agriculture Application: An Eco-Friendly Alternative. *International Journal of Composite and Constituent Materials*, 10(1), 50–62p.

Liyakat, S. (2024z). Railway Health-Monitoring Using KSK Approach: Decision-Making Using AIIoT Approach in Railways. *Journal of Controller and Converters*, 9(3), 1–10.

Liyakat. (2025). IoT Technologies for the Intelligent Dairy Industry: A New Challenge. In S. Thandekkattu& N. Vajjhala (Eds.), *Designing Sustainable Internet of Things Solutions for Smart Industries* (pp. 321-350). IGI Global. https://doi.org/DOI: 10.4018/979-8-3693-5498-8.ch012

Liyakat. (2025d). AI-Driven-IoT(AIIoT)-Based Decision Making in Kidney Diseases Patient Healthcare Monitoring: KSK Approach for Kidney Monitoring. In L. Özgür Polat & O. Polat (Eds.), *AI-Driven Innovation in Healthcare Data Analytics* (pp. 277-306). IGI Global Scientific Publishing. https://doi.org/DOI: 10.4018/979-8-3693-7277-7.ch009

Liyakat Kazi, K. S. (2024). ChatGPT: An Automated Teacher's Guide to Learning. In Bansal, R., Chakir, A., Hafaz Ngah, A., Rabby, F., & Jain, A. (Eds.), *AI Algorithms and ChatGPT for Student Engagement in Online Learning* (pp. 1–20). IGI Global., DOI: 10.4018/979-8-3693-4268-8.ch001

Machha Babitha, Ms.. (2022). Trends of Artificial Intelligence for online exams in education, *International journal of Early Childhood special. Education*, 14(1), 2457–2463.

Mahant, M. A. (2025). Machine Learning-Driven Internet of Things (MLIoT)-Based Healthcare Monitoring System. In Wickramasinghe, N. (Ed.), *Digitalization and the Transformation of the Healthcare Sector* (pp. 205–236). IGI Global Scientific Publishing., DOI: 10.4018/979-8-3693-9641-4.ch007

Mishra, S. B. (2024d). AI-Driven-IoT (AIIoT)-Based Decision Making in Manufacturing Processes in Mechanical Engineering. *Journal of Mechanisms and Robotics*, 9(2), 27–38.

Mishra, S. B. (2024e). AI-Driven-IoT (AIIoT) Based Decision-Making in Molten Metal Processing. *Journal of Industrial Mechanics*, 9(2), 45–56.

Mishra Sunil, B.. (2024). Review of the Literature and Methodological Structure for IoT and PLM Integration in the Manufacturing Sector. *Journal of Advancement in Machines*, 9(1), 1–5.

Mishra Sunil, B.. (2024a). AI-Driven IoT (AI IoT) in Thermodynamic Engineering. *Journal of Modern Thermodynamics in Mechanical System*, 6(1), 1–8.

Mr. D. Sreenivasulu, et al, (2022). Implementation of Latest machine learning approaches for students Grade Prediction, *International Journal of Early Childhood special Education,* 14(3), pp. 9887-9894.

Mulani, A. O., Bang, A. V., Birajadar, G. B., Deshmukh, A. B., & Jadhav, H. M. (2024). IoT Based Air, Water, and Soil Monitoring System for Pomegranate Farming. *Annals of Agri Bio Research*, 29(2), 71–86.

Neeraja, P., Kumar, R. G., Kumar, M. S., Liyakat, K. K. S., & Vani, M. S. (2024). *DL-Based Somnolence Detection for Improved Driver Safety and Alertness Monitoring. 2024 IEEE International Conference on Computing, Power and Communication Technologies (IC2PCT).* Greater Noida., Available at https://ieeexplore.ieee.org/document/10486714, DOI: 10.1109/IC2PCT60090.2024.10486714

Nerkar, P., & Sultanabanu, K. (2024). IoT-Based Skin Health Monitoring System [IJBPAS]. *International Journal of Biology, Pharmacy and Allied Sciences*, 13(11), 5937–5950. DOI: 10.31032/IJBPAS/2024/13.11.8488

Nikita, K.. (2020). Design of Vehicle system using CAN Protocol. *International Journal for Research in Applied Science and Engineering Technology*, 8(V), 1978–1983. DOI: 10.22214/ijraset.2020.5321

Pankaj, R Hotkar, Vishal Kulkarni, et al. (2019). Implementation of Low Power and area efficient carry select Adder. *International Journal of Research in Engineering. Science and Management*, 2(4), 183–184.

Pradeepa, M., ... (2022). Student Health Detection using a Machine Learning Approach and IoT, *2022 IEEE 2nd Mysore sub section International Conference (MysuruCon),* 2022. Available at: https://ieeexplore.ieee.org/document/9972445

Prasad, K. R., Karanam, S. R., Ganesh, D., Liyakat, K. K. S., Talasila, V., & Purushotham, P. (2024, May). AI in public-private partnership for IT infrastructure development. *The Journal of High Technology Management Research*, 35(1), 100496. DOI: 10.1016/j.hitech.2024.100496

Prashant, K. Magadum (2024). Machine Learning for Predicting Wind Turbine Output Power in Wind Energy Conversion Systems, *Grenze International Journal of Engineering and Technology,* Jan Issue, Vol 10, Issue 1, pp. 2074-2080. Grenze ID: 01.GIJET.10.1.4_1 Available at: https://thegrenze.com/index.php?display=page&view=journalabstract&absid=2514&id=8

Prashant, K. Magadum (2024). Machine Learning for Predicting Wind Turbine Output Power in Wind Energy Conversion Systems, *Grenze International Journal of Engineering and Technology,* Jan Issue, Vol 10, Issue 1, pp. 2074-2080. Grenze ID: 01.GIJET.10.1.4_1 Available at:https://thegrenze.com/index.php?display=page&view=journalabstract&absid=2514&id=8

Priya Mangesh Nerkar. BhagyarekhaUjjwalganeshDhaware. (2023). Predictive Data Analytics Framework Based on Heart Healthcare System (HHS) Using Machine Learning, *Journal of Advanced Zoology*, 2023, Volume 44, Special Issue -2, Page 3673:3686. Available at: https://jazindia.com/index.php/jaz/article/view/1695

Ravi, A.. (2022a). *Pattern Recognition- An Approach towards Machine Learning, Lambert Publications, 2022*. ISBN.

Sultanabanu (2023i). Electronics with Artificial Intelligence Creating a Smarter Future: A Review, *Journal of Communication Engineering and Its Innovations,* 9(3), 38-42.

Sultanabanu (2023j). Dispersion Compensation in Optical Fiber: A Review, *Journal of Telecommunication Study*, 8(3), 14-19.

Sayyad, S. (2024s). Nanosensors in Agriculture Field: A Study. *International Journal of Applied Nanotechnology*, 10(02), 12–22p. https://journalspub.com/publication/ijan-v10i02-11625

Sayyad (2025e). AI-Powered IoT (AI IoT) for Decision-Making in Smart Agriculture: KSK Approach for Smart Agriculture. In S. Hai-Jew (Ed.), *Enhancing Automated Decision-Making Through AI* (pp. 67-96). IGI Global Scientific Publishing. https://doi.org/DOI: 10.4018/979-8-3693-6230-3.ch003

Sayyad. (2025f). AI-Powered-IoT (AIIoT)-Based Decision-Making System for BP Patient's Healthcare Monitoring: KSK Approach for BP Patient Healthcare Monitoring. *In S. Aouadni& I. Aouadni (Eds.), Recent Theories and Applications for Multi-Criteria Decision-Making (pp. 205-238). IGI Global.*https://doi.org/DOI: 10.4018/979-8-3693-6502-1.ch008

Sayyad (2025f). KK Approach to Increase Resilience in Internet of Things: A T-Cell Security Concept. In D. Darwish & K. Charan (Eds.), Analyzing Privacy and Security Difficulties in Social Media: New Challenges and Solutions (pp. 87-120). IGI Global Scientific Publishing. https://doi.org/DOI: 10.4018/979-8-3693-9491-5.ch005

K. K. Sayyad Liyakat, (2022). Nanotechnology Application in Neural Growth Support System.*Nano Trends: A Journal of Nanotechnology and Its Applications,* 24(2), pp. 47 – 55.

Sayyad Liyakat, K. K. (2024x). Impact of Nanotechnology on Battlefield Welfare: A Study. International Journal of Nanobiotechnology. 2024; 10(2): 19– 32p.

Shaikh, M. (2023). Machine Learning in the Production Process Control of Metal Melting. *Journal of Advancement in Machines*, 8(2).

Shinde, et al, (2023). Monitoring Fresh Fruit and Food Using IoT and Machine Learning to Improve Food Safety and Quality, Tuijin *Jishu/Journal of Propulsion Technology,*44(3), pp. 2927 – 2931.

Sultanabanu, 2024q. Nanotechnology in Healthcare Applications:Study, A. (2024).. . *International Journal of Nanotechnology*, 10(2), 48–58p.

Sultanabanu (2023g). IoT in Electrical Vehicle: A Study, *Journal of Control and Instrumentation Engineering*, 9(3), 15-21.

Sultanabanu (2023b). Integrating IoT and Mechanical Systems in Mechanical Engineering Applications, *Journal of Mechanical Robotics*, 8(3), 1-6.

Sultanabanu (2023c). IoT Changing the Electronics Manufacturing Industry, *Journal of Analog and Digital Communications*, 8(3), 13-17.

Sultanabanu (2023d). IoT in the Electric Power Industry, *Journal of Controller and Converters,* 8(3), 1-7.

Sultanabanu (2023e). Review of Integrated Battery Charger (IBC) for Electric Vehicles (EV), *Journal of Advances in Electrical Devices*, 8(3), 1-11.

Sultanabanu (2023f). ML in the Electronics Manufacturing Industry, *Journal of Switching Hub*, 8(3), 9-13

Sultanabanu (2023k). IoT Based Arduino-Powered Weather Monitoring System, *Journal of Telecommunication Study*, 8(3), 25-31.

Sultanabanu (2023l). Arduino Based Weather Monitoring System, *Journal of Switching Hub*, 8(3), 24-29.

Sultanabanu, (2023n). Nanomedicine as a Potential Therapeutic Approach to COVID-19. *International Journal of Applied Nanotechnology.* 9(2): 27–35p.

Sultanabanu, (2024). IoT-based Alcohol Detector using Blynk, *Journal of Electronics Design and Technology*, 1(1), 10-15.

Vahida, . (2023). Deep Learning, YOLO and RFID based smart Billing Handcart. *Journal of Communication Engineering & Systems*, 13(1), 1–8.

Veena, C., Sridevi, M., Liyakat, K. K. S., Saha, B., Reddy, S. R., & Shirisha, N. (2023). *HEECCNB: An Efficient IoT-Cloud Architecture for Secure Patient Data Transmission and Accurate Disease Prediction in Healthcare Systems, 2023 Seventh International Conference on Image Information Processing*. ICIIP., Available at https://ieeexplore.ieee.org/document/10537627, DOI: 10.1109/ICIIP61524.2023.10537627

Wale, A. D., & Dipali, R.. (2019). Smart Agriculture System using IoT. *International Journal of Innovative Research in Technology*, 5(10), 493–497.

KEY TERMS AND DEFINITIONS

Jawar Leaf Disease: Diseases that affect the leaves of the plant are referred to as "Jawar Leaf Disease." These diseases have the potential to impede the plant's growth and reduce the amount of crops it produces.

Machine Learning (ML): The technology known as machine learning (ML) comes into play at this point. The goal of machine learning (ML), which is a subfield of artificial intelligence, is to teach computers to learn from data without the need for explicit programming.

Internet of Things (IoT): There is also a significant role played by the Internet of Things (IoT). Sensors that are installed in fields are examples of Internet of Things devices that have the capability to collect data in real time on environmental elements such as temperature, humidity, and soil moisture.

Accuracy: The precision of the models is a critical factor in determining the efficacy of machine learning-driven solutions in the agricultural sector. Accuracy in machine learning refers to the degree to which the algorithms correctly identify the outcomes that are desired.

Revolutionizing Agriculture: These technologies, including Machine Learning, Internet of Things, and the algorithms that underpin them, are collectively bringing about a revolution in agriculture. The use of these technologies has the potential to improve crop protection against disease, boost the efficiency with which resources are utilised, and make farming more environmentally friendly.

Artificial Intelligence: The subject of computer science known as artificial intelligence (AI) is a vast field that focusses on the development of computer systems that are capable of doing activities that would normally need the intelligence of a human.

Chapter 20
Enhancing Brain Tumor Detection and Diagnosis:
Leveraging Image Processing and Convolutional Neural Networks for Precision Healthcare

G. Kothai
https://orcid.org/0000-0002-9581-1679
KPR Institute of Engineering and Technology, India

B. Sivakarthick
https://orcid.org/0009-0009-6674-3919
KPR Institute of Engineering and Technology, India

K. Vignesh
https://orcid.org/0009-0004-8598-3938
KPR Institute of Engineering and Technology, India

G. Pandiya Rajan
KPR Institue of Engineering and Technology, India

ABSTRACT

Brain tumors present significant challenges in early detection and precise diagnosis, which are critical for improving patient outcomes. This chapter explores advanced methods for enhancing brain tumor detection and diagnosis using image processing and convolutional neural networks (CNNs). It delves into the limitations of traditional diagnostic methods, highlighting their lack of sensitivity and specificity. The integration of image processing techniques and CNNs is presented as a more effective approach for tumor segmentation, classification, and improved diagnostic accuracy. The chapter also discusses the potential of AI-driven systems in real-time diagnosis, personalized treatment plans, and long-term patient monitoring. Through a comprehensive analysis of CNN architectures and medical image processing methods, this work emphasizes the importance of advanced technologies in achieving precision healthcare in neuro-oncology.

DOI: 10.4018/979-8-3693-9045-0.ch020

1. INTRODUCTION TO BRAIN TUMOR DETECTION AND DIAGNOSIS

1.1 Definition of Brain Tumors

Brain tumors are abnormal growths of cells within the brain or other surrounding tissues. They can either be classified as primary when referring to a tumor originated in the brain itself or a metastatic brain tumor which manifests due to having spread from other parts of the body. Brain tumors also vary by type, size, and grade to affect their behavior, prognosis, and treatment.

Primary central nervous system brain tumors originate from different kinds of cell types, which include neurons, glial cells, and meninges. The main common kinds include gliomas, meningiomas, and schwannomas. These differ from one another in their traits and features as well as their patterns of growth. Malignant tumors are known for fast growth and have the ability to invade surrounding tissues; benign tumors, on the other hand, grow more slowly and do not spread.

The presence of a brain tumor could cause disruption of the normal function of the brain, hence leads to the presentation of neurological symptoms such as headache, seizures, cognitive changes, and motor deficits. Other potential symptoms may include changes in vision, hearing loss, and balance difficulties, depending on the tumor's location. Early detection and accurate diagnosis are regarded as critical in effective management and therefore guide the decision-making process concerning treatment that could include surgery, radiation therapy, and chemotherapy. Additionally, emerging treatments like targeted therapy and immunotherapy are being explored to improve patient outcomes. An improved understanding of the nature and behavior of brain tumors is required for enhancement in therapeutic approaches, offering hope for better survival rates and quality of life for patients, (Saeedi *et al.*, 2023).

1.2 Statistics on Incidence and Survival Rates of Brain Tumors

Brain tumors are among the most important public health problems, and available statistics reflect their overall incidence and survival trends. There are approximately 24,000 new cases of primary brain tumors diagnosed in the United States each year. Meningiomas are the most common type of this kind. According to these statistics, an estimated overall rate of incidence occurs at 6.5 cases per 100,000 people per annum, constituting a massive burden on healthcare systems.

The demographic distribution indicates that brain tumors affect adults within the 40 to 70 years age range, but they can appear at any age and even in children. Pediatric populations may have lower frequency rates, but some of these tumors are among the most common forms of solid cancer, like gliomas. Moreover, advancements in imaging techniques, such as MRI and PET scans, have improved detection rates in both adults and children.

Survival rates for brain tumors are quite wide-ranging depending on the type of tumor, its grade, and the age of the patient. For all combined brain tumors, the 5-year survival rate is around 36%. Low-grade gliomas can produce a 5-year survival rate of about 80%, whereas glioblastomas and other high-grade gliomas lead to much more dismal 5-year survival rates of 5-10%.

Trends on survival rates seem to be better over the last two decades, and the improvements are believed to be partly contributed by advancements in diagnostic techniques and treatment modalities. Presently, there exist studies that focus on personalized therapies and early intervention; hence efforts do not cease in neuro-oncology within patients suffering from brain tumors to enhance outcomes. Additionally, support networks and awareness campaigns are increasingly crucial in providing resources and education to families affected by brain tumors, (Pande *et al.,* 2024).

1.3 Patient Perspectives on Delayed Diagnosis of Brain Tumors

Delayed diagnosis of brain tumors can, therefore, have serious mental and physical impacts on patients. Most patients reveal frustrations and anxieties because their symptoms, such as frequent headaches, cognitive changes, or seizures, are not being paid attention to, (Khalighi *et al.,* 2024).

Emotional Impact

Patients often feel more anxious throughout the waiting period, which is uncertain. This can make them appear isolated and helpless as their concerns may not be treated seriously. The psychological impact significantly affects their quality of life and relationships, leading to depression and increased stress levels. Support from mental health professionals and support groups can help alleviate some of these feelings, yet many patients still struggle with the emotional toll.

Physical Effects

Delayed diagnoses ensure a larger tumor and prolonged symptoms for the patient, and in many instances, the chances of effective treatment are decreased. Many patients with delayed diagnoses say that the time lost could have been used for proper treatment and healing. Furthermore, late-stage tumors can lead to additional complications, requiring more aggressive treatment strategies that may have more severe side effects.

Advocacy for Timely Diagnosis

Many patients advocate for greater awareness among healthcare professionals regarding the symptoms of brain tumors. Listening to patients as early as possible and referring them for relevant imaging and specialist evaluations are among many patients' top suggestions. Additionally, educating the public about the potential signs and symptoms of brain tumors can facilitate earlier diagnosis and improve outcomes.

2. LIMITATIONS OF TRADITIONAL DIAGNOSTIC METHODS FOR BRAIN TUMOR DETECTION

2.1 Limited Sensitivity and Specificity in Tumor Detection

Traditional diagnostics include MRI and CT scans, which are conventional imaging techniques but are insufficient for the clear visualization of brain tumors. The most serious limitation of these methods is their low sensitivity; tiny or incipient tumors may often go undetected when only these methods are adopted for diagnosis. Additionally, complicated areas in the brain may make structures more obscure, thus rendering diagnosis complicated.

On the specificity side, many types of tumors share characteristics that are almost similar, making it challenging for professionals to distinguish them. This culminates in misinterpretation, where benign conditions such as cysts or inflammation are compared to tumors; as a result, there might be unnecessary anxiety and interventions. Moreover, patients often undergo repeat imaging and invasive procedures due to these uncertainties, leading to increased healthcare costs and further emotional distress. Advanced imaging techniques, such as functional MRI (fMRI) and positron emission tomography (PET) scans, are being researched to provide more accurate assessments and aid in distinguishing between tumor types. Ultimately, the integration of these advanced technologies could enhance diagnostic accuracy and improve patient outcomes, (Suneja *et al.,* 2022).

2.2 Case Studies of Misdiagnosis

Real-life case studies demonstrate how, at times, wrong diagnoses due to conventional methods lead to serious consequences. A 45-year-old man with frequent headaches was diagnosed by one opinion as experiencing a tension headache, as the MRI results came back normal. He returned for a follow-up six months later, and there was a large glioblastoma. This case illustrates significant delays in critical treatment, which can drastically affect prognosis and survival rates.

Similarly, a 62-year-old lady who complained of seizures underwent several evaluations, and it took a year to identify her condition until a meningioma was diagnosed. Such cases portray how misdiagnoses delay care and lead to poor outcomes. Furthermore, they highlight the need for improved diagnostic protocols and greater awareness among healthcare professionals regarding the potential for serious conditions despite normal imaging results. Education on the appropriate use of imaging and the importance of considering a patient's complete clinical picture could help mitigate such incidents. Additionally, patient advocacy for second opinions and thorough evaluations can play a crucial role in ensuring timely and accurate diagnoses, (Pramila, Sujatha, & Subbulakshmi, 2024).

2.3 Patient Perspectives on Delayed Diagnosis

Patients are often underdiagnosed late, which points to the emotional as well as physical costs of such delays. The anxiety and frustration that build up during the waiting period when there are no answers can be overwhelming for individuals. They often feel that healthcare providers are not taking their concerns seriously, leading to a sense of helplessness. Such uncertainty can foster feelings of isolation, as they navigate their health problems without adequate support.

Moreover, increased delays contribute to the progression of tumors, worsening symptoms, and ultimately reducing treatment options. In severe cases, patients may face life-threatening situations where effective interventions are no longer possible. This underscores the urgent need for greater awareness among healthcare practitioners about recognizing brain tumor symptoms. Patients and advocacy groups are calling for improved communication and more rapid referrals to specialists, ensuring that concerns are addressed promptly. Additionally, integrating educational initiatives targeting both healthcare providers and the general public can facilitate earlier diagnosis and intervention, ultimately improving patient outcomes and quality of life, (Kumar, Arasi, & Meenakshi, 2024).

3. INTRODUCTION TO IMAGE PROCESSING IN HEALTHCARE

3.1 Key Concepts in Image Processing

Image processing refers to the manipulation and analysis of images for quality improvement and extraction of meaningful information from them. This technology is applied in healthcare to enhance diagnostic accuracy and treatment planning. The key concepts include image enhancement, which improves the quality of visualization by reducing noise and increasing contrast.

Segmentation is another critical step, isolating specific regions of interest within an image for detailed analysis. This allows healthcare professionals to focus on areas that require further investigation. Feature extraction involves identifying relevant characteristics used in diagnosis, enabling more precise assessments. Additionally, registration is the process of aligning images from different sources or time points to achieve comprehensive views of a patient's condition, essential for tracking disease progression or treatment response.

In recent years, machine learning and artificial intelligence have been integrated into image processing workflows, allowing for automated feature extraction and analysis. These advancements significantly reduce the time needed for interpretation and improve the consistency of results. Moreover, the development of advanced imaging techniques, such as functional MRI and molecular imaging, enhances the capabilities of image processing, leading to more personalized and effective treatment options, (Shams *et al.*, 2024).

3.2 Types of Medical Imaging Technologies

There are several medical imaging technologies used in healthcare; they differ in their applications and, therefore, their benefits, (Sabitha *et al.*, 2024). Some of them include:

X-rays: Frequently used as a basic test for detecting fractures in bones as well as abnormalities in other body structures. They are quick, cost-effective, and provide valuable initial assessments, but they expose patients to a small amount of radiation.

Computed Tomography (CT): This technology uses radiation across different planes to create detailed sectional images of the human body. It offers more explicit information about soft tissues, organs, and other structures, making it invaluable in emergency medicine for rapid diagnoses.

Magnetic Resonance Imaging (MRI): MRI depicts the anatomy of soft tissues using strong magnetic fields and radio waves. It is particularly beneficial for neurological assessments, providing detailed images of the brain and spinal cord without exposing patients to ionizing radiation.

Ultrasound: This method uses sound waves to generate real-time images of organs and structures within the human body. It is widely utilized in obstetrics for monitoring fetal development and in cardiology for assessing heart conditions, as it is safe and does not involve radiation.

Positron Emission Tomography (PET): PET generates functional images based on the detection of metabolic activity. It is most commonly used in oncology for identifying and assessing tumors. The combination of PET with CT (PET/CT) has further enhanced diagnostic accuracy by providing both functional and anatomical information.

3.3 Impact of Image Processing on Diagnostic Accuracy

The influence of image processing techniques has been immense in the healthcare sector, significantly contributing to diagnostic accuracy. Enhanced image quality allows for more reliable analysis by clinicians to identify abnormalities. For example, improvements in image segmentation enable clear differentiation of tumors from surrounding tissues, making the evaluation of size and characteristics highly accurate. This precision is crucial for determining treatment options and predicting patient outcomes.

In this context, image processing not only enhances the resolution and quality of medical images but also aids clinicians in better decision-making, ultimately improving overall patient care. Furthermore, ongoing advancements in imaging technologies, such as artificial intelligence integration and real-time imaging analysis, will likely expand the role of image processing in the healthcare industry. As these technologies continue to evolve, they will enhance diagnostic capabilities, optimize treatment planning, and pave the way for more personalized medicine, thereby improving patient outcomes on a broader scale, (Shanthana, Bhavani, & Sangeetha, 2024).

4. INTRODUCTION TO CONVOLUTIONAL NEURAL NETWORKS (CNNS)

4.1 Components of Neural Networks

Convolutional Neural Networks (CNNs) are a specialized class of artificial neural networks primarily designed to process structured grid data, such as images, (SIBioC, 2024). A typical CNN comprises several key components:

Input Layer: This layer accepts input data, where pixel values represent images. The input can be a grayscale image with 2D pixels or a color image with 3D pixels, where three channels correspond to RGB values.

Convolutional Layers: The core convolution operation occurs in this layer, where kernels (or filters) slide over the input data to extract features. This process detects specific patterns in the input, such as edges, textures, or shapes, providing meaningful information related to the image's content.

Activation Functions: After the convolutional layer, an activation function is applied, typically the ReLU (Rectified Linear Unit). This function injects non-linearity into the model, enabling CNNs to learn more complex relationships within the data.

Pooling Layers: This layer reduces the dimensionality of feature maps produced by the convolutional layers, enhancing the network's efficiency and decreasing the risk of overfitting. Common pooling strategies include max pooling, which takes the maximum value in a feature map region, and average pooling.

Fully Connected Layers: These layers are utilized at the network's end, aggregating features received from previous layers to make final decisions. Each neuron in one layer is connected to all neurons in the next layer, allowing for comprehensive information integration.

Output Layer: Finally, the output layer provides the final output or class probabilities in classification problems. It uses an appropriate activation function, such as softmax, to determine the likelihood of each class.

4.2 History and Evolution of CNNs

The concept of neural networks has been known since the 1950s, but significant advancements in tasks related to image processing were only realized with the advent of Convolutional Neural Networks (CNNs) in the 1990s. In 1989, Yann LeCun and his group pioneered work that introduced an architecture called LeNet-5, specifically designed for recognizing handwritten digits.

The application of CNNs accelerated considerably with increased computational power and the availability of large datasets. In 2012, Alex Krizhevsky and his team won the ImageNet competition with their model, AlexNet, showcasing the potential of deep learning. The architecture relied heavily on deeper networks and innovative techniques like dropout regularization, which helped prevent overfitting.

Since then, CNNs have evolved rapidly, leading to the development of newer architectures such as VGGNet, GoogLeNet, and ResNet. These advancements have drastically improved accuracy and efficiency, solidifying CNNs as the cornerstones of modern computer vision, (Mashat, 2024).

4.3 Applications Beyond Medical Imaging

Automotive Industry: CNNs drive computer vision systems in self-driving cars, enabling real-time object detection, lane identification, and pedestrian recognition. These capabilities are crucial for improving road safety and enhancing the driving experience.

Facial Recognition: Most facial recognition systems leverage CNNs for detecting faces in images and videos, significantly enhancing security measures in various applications, from smartphone unlocking to surveillance systems.

Natural Language Processing (NLP): CNNs are also employed in text classification and sentiment analysis. They analyze spatial relationships between words in sentences, allowing for a more nuanced understanding and interpretation of textual data.

Agriculture: In agriculture, CNNs play a vital role in analyzing aerial imagery to monitor crop health, detect pests and diseases, optimize yields, and enhance resource management practices, ultimately contributing to sustainable farming.

Manufacturing: CNNs are increasingly used in manufacturing for quality control, inspecting products on production lines to detect defects or inconsistencies, thereby maintaining high standards.

CNNs represent a tremendous and flexible technology in the field of artificial intelligence, significantly improving our ability to analyze and interpret complex data across various applications. The continual advancement of this technology is opening new opportunities and fostering innovation across industries, from entertainment to environmental monitoring, demonstrating its versatility and impact, (Cai *et al.*, 2024).

5. LEVERAGING IMAGE PROCESSING FOR TUMOR DETECTION

5.1 Techniques for Image Pre-processing

Image pre-processing is a crucial step in preparing high-quality medical images for analysis aimed at tumor detection. These techniques are designed to enhance images and reduce noise, ultimately improving diagnostic accuracy. The most common pre-processing techniques include:

Noise Reduction: Techniques such as Gaussian filtering and median filtering are employed to eliminate noise while preserving focused details in the image. These methods enhance the overall appearance by minimizing pixel variations, allowing for clearer visualization of critical features.

Contrast Enhancement: Adjusting contrast levels is essential for highlighting relevant structures within the image. Techniques like histogram equalization and adaptive contrast stretching are widely used to make tumors more distinguishable from surrounding tissues, thereby aiding radiologists in their evaluations.

Normalization: This technique standardizes intensity values across different images, ensuring that they are on a comparable scale. By normalizing intensity values from various scans or patients, clinicians can facilitate more accurate comparisons. This process also helps mitigate variability arising from differences in imaging conditions, enhancing the reliability of the analysis.

Image Rescaling: Rescaling techniques adjust the size and resolution of images to ensure consistency across datasets. This step is vital for integrating images from various sources or modalities, allowing for comprehensive assessments and comparisons.

Pre-treatment techniques significantly enhance the quality of images, providing clinicians with more informative visuals. This process acts as a launching pad for effective tumor detection, ultimately contributing to improved patient outcomes through timely and accurate diagnosis, (Al-Kadi *et al.*, 2024).

5.2 Methods for Image Segmentation

Image segmentation refers to the method of partitioning an image into distinct regions, allowing for the differentiation of tumors from surrounding tissues. This process is critical for accurate diagnosis and informed decision-making regarding tumor treatment. Common methods of image segmentation include:

Thresholding: This technique transforms a grayscale image into a binary format by setting intensity thresholds. Pixels with intensity values above the threshold are classified as belonging to the tumor, while those below are categorized as background. This simple yet effective method helps in quickly identifying tumor presence.

Edge Detection: Techniques like the Canny edge detector identify the boundaries of an image by analyzing changes in intensity. These intensity shifts help in defining the margins of tumors, facilitating better separation from adjacent tissues. Edge detection is essential for accurate delineation, particularly in irregularly shaped tumors.

Region-Based Segmentation: This approach groups together adjacent pixels that share similar properties to identify tumor regions. Techniques such as region-growing and watershed segmentation are effective for detecting tumors with ill-defined shapes. These methods allow for a more nuanced understanding of tumor boundaries.

Deep Learning-Based Segmentation: Recently, convolutional neural networks (CNNs) and other deep learning architectures have gained prominence in image segmentation tasks. Models like U-Net are specifically designed for biomedical image segmentation, demonstrating remarkable accuracy in isolating tumors from surrounding tissues. These advanced techniques leverage large datasets to improve segmentation precision, significantly enhancing diagnostic capabilities.

Multi-Scale Segmentation: This technique analyzes images at different scales to capture tumors of varying sizes and shapes. By considering features at multiple resolutions, it improves the robustness of tumor detection and characterization.

All these segmentation techniques collectively enhance the accuracy of tumor detection, enabling better characterization and more effective treatment planning. Accurate segmentation not only aids in diagnosis but also plays a vital role in tailoring personalized treatment strategies for patients, (Venkataramana *et al.*, 2024).

5.3 Feature Engineering for Tumor Detection

Feature engineering is the process of extracting relevant characteristics from segmented images that aid in the detection and classification of tumors. This step is crucial in developing predictive models and improving diagnostic accuracy, (Abinaya, Vadivu, & Sundaravadiazhagan, 2024). Key aspects of feature engineering include:

Shape Features: Characteristics such as shape, size, and volume provide essential information for tumor characterization. Geometric features can help distinguish between benign and malignant growths, offering insights into tumor morphology and potential behavior.

Texture Features: Texture analysis involves examining pixel intensity distributions within the tumor. Techniques such as Haralick features and Local Binary Patterns (LBP) measure variations in texture, revealing critical information about tumor composition. Statistical measures, including mean intensity, standard deviation and histogram features, effectively summarize the tumor's appearance and help differentiate between types.

Spatial Features: The spatial relationship of tumors with surrounding tissues can also provide relevant insights. Features include proximity to critical structures and the degree of invasion into adjacent tissues, which are crucial for accurate diagnosis and treatment planning.

Color Features: In some cases, color characteristics of tumors can also be informative. Analyzing color distributions through color histograms or color moments can help differentiate between tumor types, particularly in imaging modalities that capture rich color data.

Edge Features: The edges of tumors can also convey important information regarding their boundaries and irregularities. Edge detection techniques can be employed to quantify these features, enhancing the overall characterization of the tumor.

6. CNNS FOR BRAIN TUMOR CLASSIFICATION AND SEGMENTATION

6.1 Overview of Popular CNN Architecture:

The encoder-decoder architecture of U-Net has proven highly favorable for medical image segmentation due to its inherent ability to combine contextual information with precise localization. Its applicability has been validated across various medical fields, primarily in brain tumor detection, successfully identifying borders with well-defined boundaries. Researchers are continuously optimizing U-Net to enhance segmentation in noisy environments, demonstrating its adaptability and robustness in challenging scenarios.

ResNet effectively addresses the vanishing-gradient problem commonly encountered in training deep networks. By employing shortcut connections, ResNet supports the construction of much deeper networks, resulting in more accurate predictions on complex datasets like brain MRI scans. This architecture is notably flexible, making it suitable for classification tasks where subtle differences between benign and malignant tumors must be captured in detail.

Convolutional Neural Networks (CNNs) are becoming increasingly vital in the classification and segmentation of brain tumors, with several architectures achieving impressive results, (Narayanan, Radha, & Marksia, 2024). The most popular of these include:

U-Net: U-Net is an encoder-decoder architecture specifically designed for biomedical image segmentation. Successive convolutions in the encoder capture contextual information, while the decoder restores precise spatial details to generate segmentation maps. Skip connections enable fine details captured by the encoder to be transferred to the decoder, making it particularly well-suited for delineating tumor boundaries.

ResNet: Residual Networks counter the vanishing gradient problem by introducing skip connections that enhance gradient flow during training. This feature allows the construction of very deep networks, improving the capability for feature extraction. ResNet has been successfully tailored for various medical imaging applications, where accurate high-level classification of images is essential.

DenseNet: The Dense Convolutional Network (DenseNet) is based on the principle of feature reuse, with each layer connected to every other layer in a feedforward manner. This design improves gradient flow and encourages feature sharing, making it particularly suitable for tasks that require the detection of small, intricate features, such as tumor identification.

SegNet: The SegNet architecture excels in pixel-wise segmentation, employing a unique approach to downsampling and upsampling, maintaining spatial information throughout its architecture. SegNet is effective in segmenting medical images where precision is crucial.

6.2 Data Preparation for Training CNNs

Effective data preparation is crucial for training Convolutional Neural Networks (CNNs) and encompasses several key steps:

Data Collection: Collecting high-quality datasets with accurate annotations is essential for training a robust model. In the case of brain tumors, the dataset should include a diverse range of cases, encompassing various tumor types, grades, and imaging modalities. This diversity ensures that the model can generalize well across different patient scenarios and improves its ability to recognize different tumor characteristics.

Data Augmentation: To prevent overfitting and improve generalization, data augmentation techniques are widely applied. These techniques introduce variations in the training data through transformations such as rotation, flipping, scaling, cropping, and brightness adjustments. Such modifications create an artificially larger training set, helping the model become more resilient to changes in real-world data and reducing its sensitivity to specific training instances.

Normalization: Normalization is another critical step, as pixel values can vary significantly among images due to differences in imaging conditions, equipment, and patient anatomy. By scaling pixel values to a consistent range (typically [0, 1] or [-1, 1]), normalization enhances the model's convergence during training, ensuring that variations in image intensity do not adversely affect performance.

Train-Test Split: The dataset is typically divided into three parts: training, validation, and testing. The training set is used to train the model, the validation set assists in hyperparameter tuning, and the test set is reserved for final performance evaluation. This systematic approach ensures that the model is rigorously assessed on unseen data, leading to a more reliable assessment of its effectiveness in real-world applications.

Continuous Monitoring and Refinement: Continuous monitoring and refinement of the training process are essential. Researchers may implement techniques like early stopping to prevent overfitting and regularly evaluate the model's performance on the validation set to adjust parameters accordingly. This iterative process helps identify areas for improvement and ensures that the model remains effective as new data becomes available.

Overall, meticulous data preparation, along with continuous monitoring, enables researchers to fine-tune the training process and significantly improve the model's generalization capability, (Banupriya, Nirmala, & Vijayaraghavan, 2024).

6.3 Challenges in Training CNNs with Medical Data

Despite the remarkable performance of CNNs in brain tumor classification and segmentation, several challenges persist when training these models with medical data.

Small Datasets: In many cases, the datasets used for training are small because certain tumor types are rare. Moreover, annotations require expertise from trained professionals, which can limit the number of available labeled examples. This scenario can lead to overfitting, where the model performs well on the training data but struggles to generalize to unseen data.

Class Imbalance: Many medical datasets exhibit class imbalance, with some tumor types underrepresented. In such cases, models may become biased toward the majority class, compromising their ability to accurately detect and classify the minority class. This imbalance can result in critical misdiagnoses, particularly for rarer tumors.

Variability in Imaging Techniques: Imaging protocols can vary significantly among patients and institutions, introducing heterogeneity in the data. Such variability poses challenges during training, as models may not learn robust features that generalize well across different populations. This can limit the model's effectiveness and reliability when deployed in real-world clinical environments.

Interpretability: AI-powered solutions must be interpretable for healthcare providers. Clinicians need to understand why a CNN classified or segmented a particular region in an image. Unfortunately, methods that facilitate the development of more informative models remain underexplored, creating a gap between AI performance and clinical applicability, (Zahra *et al.*, 2024).

7. COMBINING IMAGE PROCESSING AND CNNS FOR ENHANCED ACCURACY

The existence of convolutional neural networks (CNN) has helped to improve the performance of fighting image recognition and classification struggles. Still, these results can be improved when CNNs are combined with classical techniques of image processing. Therefore, we investigate in this chapter how the two can be optimally merged. We will describe a model for integration of these radiological technologies with appropriate defect detection techniques, analyze examples of this combined technique, and explain how the efficiency of the technique will be ascertained, (Padoan & Plebani, 2024).

7.1 Framework for Integration

Traditional Image Processing

The term image processing refers to a variety of actions taken to improve a given image beyond its original state. These include filtering, edge detection, noise reduction, and segmentation. Prior to the introduction of CNNs, a more active stance involved utilizing image processing techniques to preprocess the images and ready them for feature extraction, turning these raw images into shapes most favorable to machine learning algorithms. Sobel filtering for edge detection, Gaussian filtering for de-noising, and histogram specification for improving contrast are a few methods based on how best the images will be worked on before being processed.

CNNs and Deep Learning

Being a subfield of the ever-expanding deep learning, CNNs are well known to excel in image classification problems given their nature of being built to learn spatial hierarchies of features through the use of many convolutional filters. Generally, the architecture of CNN consists of convolutional layers, pooling layers, and fully connected layers. Total networks are trained end-to-end, enabling the learning of very complex features, like edges, textures, shapes, and even parts of an object with no human assistance.

The Need for Integration

While CNNs have automated feature extraction, there are situations where combining CNNs with traditional image processing can improve results. For instance, preprocessing with classical methods can enhance image quality, reduce noise, and isolate critical regions of interest before feeding the data into a CNN, thereby reducing the complexity of the feature learning task. This integration can be particularly beneficial in domains like medical imaging, remote sensing, and industrial inspection, where the quality of raw images may be poor or noisy, and specific features need to be highlighted.

Proposed Framework

The proposed framework for integrating image processing with CNNs typically follows these steps:

1. **Image Preprocessing:** Apply image processing techniques to clean, enhance, or segment images. This may involve noise reduction (e.g., median or Gaussian filtering), edge enhancement (e.g., Sobel operator), or morphological operations.
2. **Feature Extraction:** In some cases, traditional methods like corner detection or key point extraction may be used to highlight specific areas of interest in the image.
3. **CNN Application:** The pre-processed image is fed into a CNN for further learning. The CNN layers will learn additional complex features that may not be captured by traditional methods alone.
4. **Post-Processing:** In some cases, post-processing can be performed to further refine the output of the CNN, such as using traditional image processing techniques to smoothen or interpret the CNN's output (e.g., segmentation maps).

7.2 Case Study of an Integrated Approach

Application in Medical Imaging

One of the fields that has benefited significantly from integrating image processing with CNNs is medical imaging, particularly in tasks like tumor detection, organ segmentation, and disease diagnosis. In this case study, we explore an approach that integrates traditional image processing techniques with a CNN for more accurate detection of brain tumors in MRI scans.

Preprocessing with Traditional Image Processing

The first step involves enhancing the quality of MRI images, which are often noisy due to variations in scanning parameters or patient movement. Traditional preprocessing methods are applied, including:

- **Noise Reduction:** A Gaussian filter is used to remove random noise from the images while preserving important details.
- **Edge Detection:** Sobel filtering is applied to highlight the boundaries of tumors, which are crucial for the next steps.
- **Contrast Enhancement:** Histogram equalization improves the contrast between the tumor and surrounding healthy tissue.

CNN-Based Tumor Detection

After preprocessing, the enhanced images are passed through a CNN designed for image classification and segmentation. The CNN architecture includes several convolutional layers followed by ReLU activations, pooling layers, and fully connected layers. The convolutional layers learn to identify increasingly complex features, such as tumor boundaries and shapes, from the pre-processed MRI images.

The CNN is trained on a labeled dataset containing images of brain tumors with corresponding masks that indicate the location and boundaries of the tumor. The model uses a SoftMax function at the output layer to classify each pixel as either part of the tumor or healthy tissue.

Post-Processing for Refinement

Once the CNN outputs a segmentation map, post-processing steps are applied to further refine the results:

- **Morphological Operations:** Techniques like erosion and dilation are used to eliminate false positives or fill gaps in the detected tumor region.
- **Smoothing:** A Gaussian filter is applied to smoothen the segmented regions, making the final output more coherent and visually accurate.

Results and Impact

This integrated approach shows improved accuracy compared to using a CNN alone. The preprocessing steps reduce noise and improve image clarity, allowing the CNN to focus on learning more meaningful features. Moreover, post-processing further refines the output, making the final result more precise. This case study highlights the power of combining traditional image processing techniques with CNNs, especially in medical applications where precision is crucial, (Zhu *et al.*, 2024).

7.3 Evaluating Performance Metrics

Metrics for Evaluating Image Processing and CNN Integration

To assess the effectiveness of integrating image processing with CNNs, performance metrics must be carefully selected. The metrics can be divided into two main categories: those measuring the accuracy of the CNN's output and those evaluating the quality of the pre-processed images.

Accuracy: The percentage of correct classifications made by the CNN. This metric is particularly relevant for classification tasks and can be measured using the formula:

$$\text{Accuracy} = \frac{\text{Number of correct predictions}}{\text{Total number of predictions}}$$

High accuracy indicates that the CNN is effectively distinguishing between different classes.

Precision and Recall: In applications such as medical imaging, where false positives and false negatives have serious implications, precision and recall are crucial. Precision measures how many of the predicted positives are actually positive, while recall measures how many actual positives are correctly identified by the model.

$$\text{Precision} = \frac{\text{True Positives}}{\text{True Positives} + \text{False Positives}}$$

$$\text{Recall} = \frac{\text{True Positives}}{\text{True Positives} + \text{False Negatives}}$$

These metrics ensure that the model maintains a balance between identifying all relevant instances and minimizing incorrect classifications.

Intersection over Union (IoU): This metric is used for evaluating the performance of object detection and segmentation models. It calculates the overlap between the predicted and ground-truth bounding boxes or segmentation masks, with values ranging from 0 to 1 (higher values indicating better performance).

$$\text{Intersection over Union} = \frac{\text{Area of Overlap}}{\text{Area of Union}}$$

IoU is particularly useful in assessing the spatial accuracy of the segmentation.

Dice Coefficient: A similar metric to Intersection over Union, the Dice coefficient is often used in medical image segmentation tasks. It measures the overlap between the predicted segmentation and the ground truth, with a focus on balancing false positives and false negatives.

$$\text{Dice Coefficient} = \frac{\text{Intersection over Union}}{|\text{ Predicted }| + |\text{ Ground Truth }|}$$

The Dice coefficient provides a robust measure of similarity between the predicted and actual segmentation.

Peak Signal-to-Noise Ratio (PSNR): Used to assess the quality of the pre-processed images, PSNR is a measure of how much noise is present in an image. Higher PSNR values indicate better image quality after preprocessing.

Structural Similarity Index (SSIM): This metric compares two images (original and processed) based on their luminance, contrast, and structure, offering a more perceptual measure of image quality than PSNR.

These metrics provide a comprehensive evaluation of both the CNN's performance and the effectiveness of the image preprocessing techniques applied. By leveraging these metrics, researchers can fine-tune their integrated approaches to achieve optimal results in various applications, (Sabitha *et al.*, 2024).

8. CASE STUDY: SUCCESSFUL IMPLEMENTATION IN HEALTHCARE

8.1 Study Design and Objectives

The study aimed to evaluate the effectiveness of integrating image processing techniques with Convolutional Neural Networks (CNNs) in improving diagnostic accuracy in healthcare. The primary objective was to develop a robust framework that could accurately detect and classify medical conditions from imaging data. The study was designed to include a diverse dataset of medical images, ensuring a comprehensive evaluation across various conditions. Key objectives included enhancing image quality through preprocessing, optimizing CNN architecture for medical image analysis, and validating the model's performance against established diagnostic criteria, (Shams *et al.,* 2024).

8.2 Technology Stack Used

The technology stack for this study comprised several advanced tools and frameworks. Image preprocessing was performed using OpenCV, which provided a suite of functions for noise reduction, contrast enhancement, and edge detection. The CNN was implemented using TensorFlow and Keras, leveraging their powerful libraries for building and training deep learning models. Data augmentation techniques were applied to increase the diversity of the training dataset, using tools like imgaug. Additionally, transfer learning was employed using pre-trained models such as VGG16 and ResNet50 to expedite the training process and enhance model accuracy. The entire pipeline was orchestrated using Python, ensuring seamless integration and scalability, (Pande *et al.*, 2024).

8.3 Outcomes and Lessons Learned

The integrated approach of combining Object-Based Image Analysis (OBIA) and Convolutional Neural Networks (CNN) yielded significant improvements in diagnostic accuracy, particularly in the detection of conditions such as diabetic retinopathy and lung cancer. This hybrid method leverages the strengths of both techniques: OBIA's ability to segment and classify objects within an image and CNN's prowess in feature extraction and pattern recognition, (Kumar, Arasi, & Meenakshi, 2024).

1. **Enhanced Diagnostic Accuracy**: The integration led to more precise identification of medical conditions. For instance, in diabetic retinopathy, the approach improved the detection of microaneurysms, hemorrhages, and exudates, which are critical for early diagnosis and treatment.
2. **Improved Image Quality**: Enhanced preprocessing techniques, such as noise reduction and contrast enhancement, resulted in clearer and more informative images. This clarity is crucial for the CNN to accurately identify and classify critical features within the images.
3. **Efficiency through Transfer Learning**: The use of transfer learning significantly reduced training time and computational resources. By leveraging pre-trained models, the approach maintained high accuracy while being more efficient. This is particularly beneficial in medical imaging, where annotated datasets are often limited.
4. **Multidisciplinary Approach**: The study underscored the importance of a multidisciplinary approach, combining expertise in image processing, deep learning, and medical diagnostics. This collaboration is essential to address the complexities of medical image analysis and to develop robust diagnostic tools.

Challenges Highlighted:

1. **Need for Large, Annotated Datasets**: One of the primary challenges is the requirement for extensive, annotated datasets. High-quality annotations are crucial for training accurate models, but they are often time-consuming and expensive to obtain.
2. **Class Imbalance**: Medical image datasets often suffer from class imbalance, where certain conditions are underrepresented. This imbalance can lead to biased models that perform poorly on rare conditions. Addressing this issue is vital for developing reliable diagnostic tools.
3. **Computational Resources**: Despite the efficiency gains from transfer learning, the approach still requires significant computational resources, especially for training on high-resolution images. Ensuring access to adequate computational infrastructure is necessary for the successful implementation of this method.

9. ADVANTAGES OF AI-DRIVEN DIAGNOSIS IN BRAIN TUMOR DETECTION

9.1 Real-time Diagnosis Capabilities

Immediate Feedback: AI-driven systems are designed to analyze medical images, such as MRI and CT scans, in real-time. This means that as soon as the images are captured, the AI algorithms can process them and provide immediate feedback to healthcare professionals. This rapid analysis is particularly crucial in emergency situations, such as when a patient presents with symptoms of a stroke or a rapidly progressing brain tumor. Timely diagnosis can significantly impact patient outcomes by enabling quicker intervention.

Advanced Algorithms: AI systems leverage advanced algorithms, including convolutional neural networks (CNNs), to analyze medical images. These algorithms are trained on vast datasets of medical images, allowing them to recognize patterns and abnormalities with high accuracy. For instance, in the case of brain tumors, AI can detect subtle changes in brain tissue that might be missed by the human eye. This includes identifying small lesions or early signs of tumor growth, which are critical for early diagnosis and treatment.

Enhanced Decision-Making: By providing real-time analysis, AI systems support healthcare professionals in making faster and more informed decisions. For example, if an AI system detects an abnormality in a brain scan, it can immediately alert the medical team, prompting further investigation or immediate intervention. This can be life-saving in cases where every minute counts, such as in the detection of hemorrhages or aggressive tumors.

Improved Accuracy: AI algorithms are capable of analyzing medical images with a level of precision that surpasses human capabilities in some cases. They can identify minute details and patterns that may be indicative of a brain tumor. This ensures that no critical details are overlooked, reducing the risk of misdiagnosis. Additionally, AI systems can continuously learn and improve from new data, enhancing their diagnostic accuracy over time.

Integration with Clinical Workflows: AI-driven diagnostic tools can be seamlessly integrated into existing clinical workflows. This means that healthcare professionals can access AI-generated insights directly from their standard imaging software, without the need for additional steps or tools. This integration facilitates the adoption of AI technology in clinical settings and ensures that the benefits of real-time diagnosis are readily available, (Zhu *et al.,* 2024).

9.2 Personalization of Treatment Plans

AI can tailor treatment plans to individual patients by analyzing a vast array of data, including genetic information, medical history, and tumor characteristics. This personalized approach ensures that patients receive the most effective treatments based on their unique profiles. AI-driven tools can predict how different patients will respond to various therapies, enabling more precise and effective treatment strategies. For example, AI can help oncologists determine the best combination of surgery, radiation, and chemotherapy for a specific patient, optimizing the chances of successful treatment.

9.2.1 Continuous Monitoring and Data Collection

AI systems can continuously gather and analyze data from various sources, such as medical imaging, electronic health records, and wearable devices. This constant stream of data allows for:

- **Tracking Tumor Progression**: By regularly analyzing imaging data, AI can detect subtle changes in tumor size, shape, and growth patterns that might be missed by human observers.
- **Evaluating Treatment Effectiveness**: AI can assess how well a treatment is working by comparing current data with previous records, helping doctors make informed decisions about continuing, adjusting, or changing treatment plans.

9.2.2 Early Detection of Recurrences

One of the critical advantages of AI is its ability to identify patterns and anomalies in large datasets:

- **Anomaly Detection**: AI algorithms can flag unusual changes in a patient's condition that may indicate a recurrence of the tumor. Early detection of such changes can lead to prompt interventions, potentially improving patient outcomes.
- **Predictive Analytics**: By analyzing historical data, AI can predict the likelihood of tumor recurrence, allowing for proactive management and timely adjustments to treatment plans.

9.2.3 Remote Monitoring and Improved Quality of Life

AI facilitates remote patient monitoring, which can significantly enhance the quality of life for patients:

- **Reduced Hospital Visits**: Patients can be monitored from the comfort of their homes, reducing the need for frequent hospital visits. This is particularly beneficial for those living in remote areas or with mobility issues.
- **Wearable Devices**: Devices such as smartwatches and fitness trackers can collect vital health data (e.g., heart rate, activity levels) and transmit it to healthcare providers. AI can analyze this data to detect any concerning trends or changes.
- **Telemedicine**: AI-powered telemedicine platforms enable virtual consultations, allowing patients to receive medical advice and support without leaving their homes.

9.2.4 Timely Interventions and Personalized Care

AI's ability to process and analyze vast amounts of data quickly enables timely interventions:

- **Real-Time Alerts**: AI systems can send real-time alerts to healthcare providers if they detect any significant changes in a patient's condition. This ensures that any necessary medical interventions can be made promptly, (Padoan & Plebani, 2024).
- **Personalized Treatment Plans**: By analyzing individual patient data, AI can help create personalized treatment plans tailored to the specific needs and conditions of each patient. This person-

alized approach can lead to more effective treatments and better patient outcomes, (Zahra *et al.*, 2024).

9.3 Long-Term Benefits

The long-term benefits of AI-driven monitoring and follow-up include:

- **Enhanced Patient Outcomes**: Continuous monitoring and timely interventions can lead to better management of brain tumors, potentially improving survival rates and quality of life.
- **Data-Driven Insights**: The data collected over time can provide valuable insights into the effectiveness of different treatments, contributing to medical research and the development of new therapies.
- **Patient Empowerment**: Patients can take a more active role in their healthcare, using AI tools to monitor their own health and make informed decisions about their treatment, (Al-Kadi *et al.*, 2024).

10. CHALLENGES AND ETHICAL CONSIDERATIONS IN AI

10.1 Data Bias and Its Implications

Understanding Data Bias

AI systems rely heavily on data for training. The quality, diversity, and accuracy of this data directly influence the AI's performance. Data bias arises when the data used to train AI algorithms does not adequately represent the diversity of the population or contains inherent prejudices. This bias can be introduced unintentionally through skewed datasets or through the way algorithms process the data.

Implications of Data Bias

The consequences of data bias are far-reaching. AI models with biased data can perpetuate stereotypes, reinforce social inequalities, and make unfair or inaccurate decisions. For example, biased algorithms in hiring processes may unfairly prioritize certain demographics over others. In criminal justice, AI models used for predicting recidivism have been criticized for disproportionately targeting minority groups due to biased historical data.

This issue is not merely technical but societal. Unchecked, biased AI can amplify existing disparities. Studies have shown that biased facial recognition systems have higher error rates when identifying individuals with darker skin tones, leading to significant societal harm.

Addressing Data Bias

Mitigating bias requires a proactive approach. This involves ensuring the dataset is representative of the entire population, implementing regular audits of the models, and increasing transparency in how decisions are made. Researchers and developers must recognize the ethical responsibility of minimizing bias to ensure fairness and equity in AI applications, (Suneja *et al.*, 2022).

10.2 The Importance of Explainability in AI

What is Explainability?

Explainability refers to the degree to which an AI system's internal processes and decisions can be understood by humans. As AI systems become more complex, especially with deep learning models, they operate as black boxes - making decisions without clear explanations. This lack of transparency can pose significant challenges in industries like healthcare, finance, and law enforcement, where the rationale behind a decision is as important as the outcome.

Why is Explainability Crucial?

Explainability in AI is critical for several reasons:

1. **Trust**: Users and stakeholders are more likely to trust AI systems when they understand how and why decisions are made. In applications like autonomous vehicles or medical diagnostics, explainability can make the difference between widespread adoption or rejection.
2. **Accountability**: Without clear explanations, it becomes difficult to assign accountability for decisions made by AI systems. This can lead to situations where no one takes responsibility for harmful outcomes, which is ethically problematic.
3. **Compliance**: In some regions, regulations mandate that AI decisions be explainable. For instance, the European Union's General Data Protection Regulation (GDPR) gives individuals the right to an explanation for decisions made by automated systems.

Improving Explainability

Researchers are developing techniques to enhance the interpretability of AI models, such as feature importance scores or visualization tools that highlight how the model processes input data. However, increasing explainability often involves a trade-off with the model's complexity and performance. Simple, interpretable models may not perform as well as more complex "black box" models. Achieving a balance between explainability and performance is an ongoing challenge in the AI field, (Shanthana, Bhavani, & Sangeetha, 2024).

10.3 Regulatory and Compliance Issues

Navigating the Regulatory Landscape

As AI systems are deployed across different sectors, governments and organizations are grappling with how to regulate their use. AI poses unique regulatory challenges because of its potential to disrupt industries and cause unintended consequences. In the absence of clear regulations, some AI technologies can be exploited in ways that harm society.

Existing Regulations

One of the most prominent regulatory frameworks addressing AI is the European Union's GDPR. It includes provisions that impact AI, particularly concerning data protection, the right to explanation, and automated decision-making. Similarly, the United States has seen efforts to regulate AI through industry-specific guidelines, such as those for healthcare and finance. However, there is currently no overarching AI regulation in the U.S..

China has also been proactive in regulating AI, focusing on the ethical use of AI in sensitive areas like facial recognition and social credit systems.

Ethical Compliance in AI Development

Organizations developing AI systems must also ensure that their systems comply with existing regulations and ethical standards. This includes adhering to data privacy laws, ensuring transparency in decision-making, and implementing processes for AI accountability. AI systems need to be designed with ethical considerations from the ground up, incorporating fairness, transparency, and responsibility into every stage of development.

Companies and developers can also adopt best practices, such as the Ethical Guidelines for Trustworthy AI proposed by the European Commission's High-Level Expert Group on Artificial Intelligence, (Padoan & Plebani, 2024).

11. FUTURE DIRECTIONS IN AI-BASED BRAIN TUMOR DETECTION

AI-based brain tumor detection has made significant strides in recent years, with advances in machine learning and imaging technologies enhancing the accuracy and efficiency of diagnosis. However, the future promises even greater improvements as AI systems integrate multiple data sources, leverage cutting-edge machine learning techniques, and offer the potential for broader global health applications.

11.1 Integration of Multimodal Imaging

The Need for Multimodal Imaging

Brain tumors are complex and heterogeneous, with variations in size, shape, location, and type. No single imaging modality can capture all of the necessary information to make a comprehensive diagnosis. For example, MRI (Magnetic Resonance Imaging) is widely used for its superior soft tissue contrast, but it may not provide sufficient information about the tumor's metabolic or functional properties. On the other hand, PET (Positron Emission Tomography) scans can provide insights into metabolic activity but lack the spatial resolution of MRI.

By integrating multimodal imaging data such as MRI, PET, CT (Computed Tomography), and even advanced techniques like diffusion tensor imaging (DTI) and functional MRI (fMRI), AI-based systems can develop a more complete understanding of a brain tumor's characteristics.

AI Integration for Multimodal Data

AI models, particularly deep learning networks, can be designed to handle multimodal data. These models take input from different imaging techniques and fuse this information to create a holistic diagnostic picture. For instance, a CNN (Convolutional Neural Network) can process MRI data, while a different network might analyze PET data. A subsequent layer in the neural network architecture can merge these outputs, combining anatomical information from MRI with functional or metabolic data from PET scans. This integration helps to improve diagnostic precision, as each modality offers complementary information.

Case Study: Multimodal Imaging in Tumor Characterization

In a 2020 study published in Nature Medicine, researchers demonstrated the power of multimodal AI by integrating MRI, PET, and CT scans to improve brain tumor diagnosis. The AI system was trained to identify gliomas, one of the most common and aggressive types of brain tumors, using both structural data from MRI and metabolic information from PET scans. This multimodal approach led to a 15% improvement in diagnostic accuracy compared to using MRI alone.

Future Directions

As AI models become more sophisticated, we can expect deeper integration of additional imaging modalities. Techniques like hyperspectral imaging and photoacoustic imaging, which are currently in experimental stages, could be incorporated into future AI models, offering even more detailed information about tumor composition and behavior. Additionally, integrating imaging data with non-imaging sources, such as genomic and proteomic data, could further revolutionize brain tumor detection, allowing for personalized treatment plans based on a tumor's unique biological signature, (Pramila, Sujatha, & Subbulakshmi, 2024).

11.2 Advancements in Machine Learning Techniques

The Evolution of AI Algorithms

The AI algorithms currently used for brain tumor detection primarily rely on deep learning techniques, such as CNNs and recurrent neural networks (RNNs), for image processing and classification. However, advancements in machine learning continue to push the boundaries of what is possible. Techniques such as transfer learning, federated learning, and generative adversarial networks (GANs) are opening new possibilities for brain tumor detection.

Transfer Learning: One limitation of AI in medical imaging is the relatively small size of labeled datasets compared to non-medical applications like natural image recognition. Transfer learning allows models trained on large datasets (such as ImageNet) to be fine-tuned for brain tumor detection, reducing the need for extensive labeled medical data. This technique has already shown promising results in improving the accuracy of brain tumor classification with minimal data.

Federated Learning: Traditional machine learning models require data to be centralized, but this can pose privacy concerns, especially when dealing with sensitive medical data. Federated learning is a novel approach where models are trained on distributed datasets while keeping the data local. This approach allows hospitals to collaborate on AI development without sharing patient data, potentially accelerating the development of robust brain tumor detection algorithms.

Generative Adversarial Networks (GANs): GANs have shown potential for generating high-quality synthetic images that can be used to augment datasets, especially in fields like medical imaging, where labeled data can be scarce. GANs can be used to generate synthetic brain tumor images, which can then be used to train AI models, enhancing their generalization ability.

AI and Early Detection

One of the key areas of focus in brain tumor research is early detection. Current diagnostic techniques often catch tumors at advanced stages, limiting treatment options. However, as machine learning algorithms evolve, AI systems will likely be able to detect tumors earlier by identifying subtle changes in brain tissue that are invisible to the human eye. Algorithms like Support Vector Machines (SVMs) and decision trees are also being enhanced with hybrid deep learning models for early-stage tumor identification.

Reinforcement Learning for Treatment Planning

In addition to improving detection, machine learning techniques like reinforcement learning (RL) could revolutionize treatment planning. RL models can be trained to simulate different treatment scenarios, learning optimal strategies based on real patient data. For instance, an RL-based system could analyze how different tumor types respond to chemotherapy, radiation, or surgery, and suggest the most effective treatment path for each patient, (Abinaya, Vadivu, & Sundaravadivazhagan, 2024).

11.3 Potential for Global Health Impact

AI for Equitable Access to Healthcare

Brain tumor detection has traditionally relied on highly specialized equipment and expert radiologists, which are often unavailable in low-resource settings. The global shortage of radiologists means that many regions lack timely access to diagnostic services, contributing to disparities in health outcomes. AI offers the potential to bridge this gap by enabling automated, accurate tumor detection that does not require a radiologist's direct input.

Cloud-Based AI Systems for Remote Diagnostics

One promising area of development is the creation of cloud-based AI systems for brain tumor detection. In a cloud-based model, medical images can be uploaded from anywhere in the world and analyzed by AI systems hosted on powerful servers. This would enable healthcare providers in remote or underserved areas to access cutting-edge diagnostic tools, even in the absence of local specialists. A pilot program launched by Stanford University in 2021 demonstrated that cloud-based AI systems could successfully analyze brain MRI scans and detect tumors with a level of accuracy comparable to that of expert radiologists.

AI-Assisted Diagnostics in Resource-Poor Regions

Several organizations, including the World Health Organization (WHO), have begun exploring how AI can be used to address healthcare disparities in low-income countries. AI-based systems can be deployed in these regions to assist non-specialist healthcare workers in diagnosing brain tumors, improving early detection rates and allowing for better treatment outcomes. With further advancements in machine learning and cloud computing, these systems could become a standard part of global health infrastructure.

Challenges and Considerations

While AI offers great potential for improving global health, several challenges remain. Data privacy concerns, particularly around the sharing of medical data across borders, must be addressed. Additionally, AI models trained on data from high-resource environments may not generalize well to populations in low-resource settings due to differences in medical infrastructure, genetic diversity, and environmental factors. To truly harness the power of AI for global health, these systems must be developed with a focus on equity, ensuring that they are inclusive of all populations, (Banupriya, Nirmala, & Vijayaraghavan, 2024).

12. CONCLUSION

The advancements in AI-based brain tumor detection have shown remarkable potential to transform healthcare by improving diagnostic accuracy and enabling early detection. The integration of multimodal imaging, which combines data from MRI, PET, CT, and other imaging modalities, allows AI models to create a more comprehensive view of brain tumors, leading to more precise diagnoses. This approach is particularly useful in complex medical cases where a single imaging technique may not provide sufficient information.

Machine learning techniques, such as transfer learning, federated learning, and generative adversarial networks (GANs), are also driving improvements in AI-driven brain tumor detection. These innovations enhance model accuracy and efficiency, especially when working with limited datasets or sensitive patient information. The application of these technologies could also extend to personalized treatment planning, optimizing therapies for individual patients based on the specific characteristics of their tumors.

The global health impact of AI is significant, especially in regions with limited access to specialist care. Cloud-based AI systems could provide diagnostic support in resource-poor areas, improving early detection and treatment outcomes for patients worldwide. As AI technologies continue to evolve, ensuring that they remain ethical, explainable, and patient-centered will be critical for their successful integration into clinical practice, (Padoan & Plebani, 2024).

REFERENCES

Abinaya, M., Vadivu, G., & Sundaravadivazhagan, B. (2024). 10 Future Directions and Open Problems in Generative AI. In Balasubramaniam, S., Kadry, S., Prasanth, A., & Kumar Dhanaraj, R. (Eds.), *Generative AI and LLMs: Natural Language Processing and Generative Adversarial Networks* (pp. 193–212). De Gruyter., DOI: 10.1515/9783111425078-010

Al-Kadi, O., Al-Emaryeen, R., Al-Nahhas, S., Almallahi, I., Braik, R., & Mahafza, W. (2024). Empowering brain cancer diagnosis: Harnessing artificial intelligence for advanced imaging insights. *Reviews in the Neurosciences*, *35*(4), 399–419. DOI: 10.1515/revneuro-2023-0115 PMID: 38291768

Banupriya, N., Nirmala, G., & Vijayaraghavan, N. (2024). 17 Image Dehazing Using Quaternion Complex Algebra-Based Neural Networks. In Yadav, S., Kumar, A., Dubey, A., de Albuquerque, V., Rodriguez-Aguiñaga, A., & Quezada, A. (Eds.), *Medical Image Processing: Multimodal Fusion Techniques* (pp. 255–270). De Gruyter., DOI: 10.1515/9783111435978-017

Cai, S., Xing, H., Wang, Y., Wang, Y., Ma, W., Jiang, Y., Li, J., & Wang, H. (2024). Clinical application of intraoperative ultrasound superb microvascular imaging in brain tumors resections: Contributing to the achievement of total tumoral resection. *BMC Medical Imaging*, *24*(1), 142. DOI: 10.1186/s12880-024-01321-5 PMID: 38862900

Khalighi, S., Reddy, K., Midya, A., Pandav, K. B., Madabhushi, A., & Abedalthagafi, M. (2024). Artificial intelligence in neuro-oncology: Advances and challenges in brain tumor diagnosis, prognosis, and precision treatment. npj Precis. *NPJ Precision Oncology*, *8*(1), 80. DOI: 10.1038/s41698-024-00575-0 PMID: 38553633

Kumar, M., Arasi, M., & Meenakshi, S. (2024). 21 Multifocus Image Fusion Using Content-Adaptive Blurring. In Yadav, S., Kumar, A., Dubey, A., de Albuquerque, V., Rodriguez-Aguiñaga, A., & Quezada, A. (Eds.), *Medical Image Processing: Multimodal Fusion Techniques* (pp. 339–348). De Gruyter., DOI: 10.1515/9783111435978-021

Mashat, A. (2024). A QR code-enabled framework for fast biomedical image processing in medical diagnosis using deep learning. *BMC Medical Imaging*, *24*(1), 198. DOI: 10.1186/s12880-024-01351-z PMID: 39090546

Narayanan, K., Radha, M., & Marksia, U. (2024). 7 Soft Computing Approaches to Medical Image Fusion. In Yadav, S., Kumar, A., Dubey, A., de Albuquerque, V., Rodriguez-Aguiñaga, A., & Quezada, A. (Eds.), *Medical Image Processing: Multimodal Fusion Techniques* (pp. 105–118). De Gruyter., DOI: 10.1515/9783111435978-007

Padoan, A., & Plebani, M. (2024). Dynamic mirroring: Unveiling the role of digital twins, artificial intelligence and synthetic data for personalized medicine in laboratory medicine. [CCLM]. *Clinical Chemistry and Laboratory Medicine*, *62*(11), 2156–2161. DOI: 10.1515/cclm-2024-0517 PMID: 38726708

Pande, S., Ahammad, S., Madhav, B., Ramya, K., Smirani, L., Hossain, M., & Rashed, A. (2024). Assessment of brain tumor detection techniques and recommendation of neural network. Biomedical Engineering / Biomedizinische Technik, 69(4), 395-406. DOI: 10.1515/cclm-2024-0517 PMID: 38726708

Pramila, R., Sujatha, S., & Subbulakshmi, R. (2024). 20 Medical Image Fusion Using Deep Learning Mechanisms. In Yadav, S., Kumar, A., Dubey, A., de Albuquerque, V., Rodriguez-Aguiñaga, A., & Quezada, A. (Eds.), *Medical Image Processing: Multimodal Fusion Techniques* (pp. 315–338). De Gruyter., DOI: 10.1515/9783111435978-020

Sabitha, R., Shirley, J., Shanthini, J., & Paul, A. (2024). 14 Medical Image Fusion Method by Deep Learning. In Yadav, S., Kumar, A., Dubey, A., de Albuquerque, V., Rodriguez-Aguiñaga, A., & Quezada, A. (Eds.), *Medical Image Processing: Multimodal Fusion Techniques* (pp. 207–222). De Gruyter., DOI: 10.1515/9783111435978-014

Saeedi, S., Rezayi, S., & Keshavarz, H.. (2023). MRI-based brain tumor detection using convolutional deep learning methods and chosen machine learning techniques. *BMC Medical Informatics and Decision Making, 23*, 16. DOI: 10.1186/s12911-023-02114-6 PMID: 36691030

Shams, A., Becker, K., Becker, D., Amirian, S., & Rasheed, K. (2024). Evolutionary CNN-based architectures with attention mechanisms for enhanced image classification. In Deligiannidis, L., Dimitoglou, G., & Arabnia, H. (Eds.), *Artificial Intelligence: Machine Learning, Convolutional Neural Networks and Large Language Models* (pp. 107–132). De Gruyter., DOI: 10.1515/9783111344126-006

Shanthana, S., Bhavani, M., & Sangeetha, D. (2024). 1 Medical Image Processing: A Multimodal Fusion Technique. In Yadav, S., Kumar, A., Dubey, A., de Albuquerque, V., Rodriguez-Aguiñaga, A., & Quezada, A. (Eds.), *Medical Image Processing: Multimodal Fusion Techniques* (pp. 1–20). De Gruyter., DOI: 10.1515/9783111435978-001

Suneja, M., Beekmann, S., Dhaliwal, G., Miller, A., & Polgreen, P. (2022). Diagnostic delays in infectious diseases. *Diagnosis (Berlin, Germany)*, *9*(3), 332–339. DOI: 10.1515/dx-2021-0092 PMID: 35073468

Venkataramana Sagar, G., Kumar Bandili, S., & Navulla, D. (2024). 3 Current Trends in High-Resolution Image Reconstruction. In Yadav, S., Kumar, A., Dubey, A., de Albuquerque, V., Rodriguez-Aguiñaga, A., & Quezada, A. (Eds.), *Medical Image Processing: Multimodal Fusion Techniques* (pp. 43–58). De Gruyter., DOI: 10.1515/9783111435978-003

Zahra, M., Al-Taher, A., Alquhaidan, M., Hussain, T., Ismail, I., Raya, I., & Kandeel, M. (2024). The synergy of artificial intelligence and personalized medicine for the enhanced diagnosis, treatment, and prevention of disease. *Drug Metabolism and Personalized Therapy*, *39*(2), 47–58. DOI: 10.1515/dmpt-2024-0003 PMID: 38997240

Zhu, X., Sun, S., Lin, L., Wu, Y., & Ma, X. (2024). Transformer-based approaches for neuroimaging: An in-depth review of their role in classification and regression tasks. *Reviews in the Neurosciences*. Advance online publication. DOI: 10.1515/revneuro-2024-0088 PMID: 39333087

Chapter 21

Ethical Considerations in AI-Driven Image Processing: Balancing Innovation With Responsibility

Punam Kumari
https://orcid.org/0000-0001-8144-7573
Amity University, Bengaluru, India

ABSTRACT

AI-driven image processing encompasses a wide range of techniques and applications that leverage machine learning (ML), deep learning, and neural networks to analyze, interpret, and manipulate images. These technologies have revolutionized fields such as medical imaging, facial recognition systems and creative industries etc. However, the integration of AI into image processing also presents unique ethical challenges. Unlike traditional image processing techniques, AI-driven methods often operate as "black boxes". This opacity, combined with the pervasive use of these technologies, necessitates a careful examination of the ethical implications. This chapter will provide an in-depth exploration of the ethical considerations associated with AI-driven image processing. It will critically examine the challenges posed by issues such as bias, privacy, consent, accountability, and the potential for misuse. The chapter aims to offer a balanced perspective, highlighting both the immense potential of AI in image processing and the ethical imperatives that must guide its application.

1. INTERSECTION OF AI AND IMAGE PROCESSING

Artificial Intelligence refers to the ability of machines to perform tasks that typically require human intelligence (Russell & Norvig, 1995). AI encompasses machine learning (ML), deep learning (DL), and neural networks, which can learn patterns from data and make decisions or predictions.

Image Processing traditionally involves techniques to enhance, analyze, and manipulate images. Common tasks include noise reduction, image segmentation, feature extraction, and pattern recognition.

The intersection of Artificial Intelligence (AI) and Image Processing represents a dynamic and rapidly evolving field that leverages the strengths of both domains to enhance various applications. This convergence is driving significant advancements across numerous sectors, including healthcare, security,

DOI: 10.4018/979-8-3693-9045-0.ch021

entertainment, and more. When AI is applied to image processing, it enables machines to automatically learn from and interpret visual data, leading to more sophisticated and efficient image analysis.

Here's an overview of how AI and Image Processing intersect and some key areas of impact:

2. TECHNICAL APPROACHES IN ARTIFICIAL INTELLIGENCE FOR IMAGE PROCESSING

AI-driven image processing employs various technical approaches that enable machines to analyze, enhance, and interpret images. These approaches span from traditional methods to advanced deep learning techniques. Below are key technical approaches used in AI for image processing.

2.1 Machine Learning for Image Processing

Machine learning (ML) plays a pivotal role in image processing, enabling machines to interpret, analyze, and manipulate images more effectively. Unlike traditional image processing methods that rely on manually programmed algorithms, machine learning models learn directly from data, making them more adaptable and powerful for various tasks such as object detection, image classification, and image enhancement.

2.1.1 Key Concepts of Machine Learning in Image Processing

Feature Extraction

In image processing, one of the first steps is to extract features, such as edges, colors, textures, or shapes, which helps to identify objects or patterns in the image. Traditional methods required hand-crafted features, but machine learning allows models to learn these features automatically from the data.

Supervised Learning

In supervised learning, labeled images are used to train models to recognize patterns and predict labels for new, unseen images. This is widely used in tasks such as object detection and image classification.

Unsupervised Learning

Unsupervised learning doesn't rely on labeled data but instead finds patterns or groupings within the data itself. This can be used for image clustering, anomaly detection, and image segmentation.

Deep Learning for Feature Learning

Deep learning (a subset of ML) has greatly enhanced image processing capabilities by learning multiple layers of feature representation through neural networks. Convolutional Neural Networks (CNNs) are a prime example used for image-related tasks.

2.1.2 Machine Learning Algorithms in Image Processing

Support Vector Machines (SVM)

SVMs can be used for image classification by finding the hyperplane that best separates different classes of images (Wang L, 2005). They are especially effective in smaller datasets but have been largely replaced by deep learning in image processing tasks.

k-Nearest Neighbors (k-NN)

k-NN is a simple algorithm that classifies images based on their similarity to other images in the training set. It is useful for basic image classification but is less efficient with large datasets (Guo et al., 2004).

Random Forests

Random Forests are a type of ensemble learning that can be used for image classification and segmentation (Fawagreh, et al. 2014). They are fast and can handle small datasets well, but are not as powerful as deep learning models for complex image tasks.

K-Means Clustering

K-Means is an unsupervised learning algorithm used for image segmentation by grouping similar pixels into clusters (Steinley, 2006). It is used in applications where labeled data is scarce and provides a good starting point for more advanced segmentation techniques.

Convolutional Neural Networks (CNNs)

CNNs are specialized neural networks that have revolutionized image processing (Li et al., 2021) They use convolutional layers to automatically detect features like edges, textures, and patterns, and are highly effective for image classification and object detection.

2.1.3 Key Applications of Machine Learning in Image Processing

Machine learning (ML) has revolutionized image processing by enabling computers to interpret, analyze, and manipulate images effectively across diverse fields. Here are some key applications:

Image Classification

Overview: ML models, especially Convolutional Neural Networks (CNNs), are trained to categorize images into predefined classes based on their features.

Applications

Medical Imaging: Diagnosing diseases by classifying X-rays, MRI scans, or CT scans.

Wildlife Conservation: Identifying animal species in photos from camera traps.

Facial Recognition: Identifying individuals in photos for security purposes.

Object Detection and Recognition

Overview: Beyond classifying an entire image, ML models detect and locate objects within images.

Applications

Autonomous Vehicles: Detecting pedestrians, vehicles, and obstacles in real-time.

Surveillance Systems: Identifying suspicious objects or people.

Retail: Automatically detecting products on shelves for inventory tracking.

Image Segmentation

Overview: Image segmentation divides an image into meaningful regions or objects, assigning labels to each pixel.

Applications:

Healthcare: Segmenting tumors or organs in medical scans.

Autonomous Driving: Segmenting road, pedestrians, and vehicles for navigation.

Agriculture: Segmentation of crop areas for monitoring plant health and growth.

Image Enhancement and Restoration

Overview: ML models can enhance image quality by reducing noise, increasing resolution, or restoring damaged images.

Applications:

Super-Resolution: Increasing the resolution of low-quality images for better analysis.

Denoising: Removing noise from low-light or distorted images.

Restoration: Recovering damaged, old photographs or videos.

Style Transfer and Image Generation

Overview: Generative Adversarial Networks (GANs) and other models enable creative manipulations of images, such as transforming the style or generating new images.

Applications

Art and Design: Creating artistic images by transferring the style of one image to another (e.g., turning a photo into a Van Gogh-like painting).

Synthetic Data Creation: Generating artificial images for training machine learning models, especially when real data is scarce.

Content-Based Image Retrieval (CBIR)

Overview: CBIR systems allow for searching databases of images based on the content of an image rather than keywords.

Applications:

E-commerce: Enabling users to search for products using images instead of text.

Media Libraries: Searching for similar images or videos in large datasets like digital archives or stock photo libraries.

Image Captioning and Description

Overview: Combining ML models for image understanding and Natural Language Processing (NLP), image captioning models generate textual descriptions of images.

Applications:

Accessibility: Describing images for visually impaired users.

Social media: Automatically generating captions for photos.

Facial Recognition and Emotion Detection

Overview: ML models are used to detect and recognize faces and to identify emotions from facial expressions.

Applications:

Security and Surveillance: Identifying people in real-time from camera footage.

Marketing: Detecting customer emotions from facial expressions to gauge reactions to products or advertisements.

Medical Image Analysis

Overview: Machine learning models assist in detecting and diagnosing diseases by analyzing medical images such as MRI, CT scans, and X-rays.

Applications:

Cancer Detection: Identifying tumors and growths in early stages.

Cardiology: Analyzing images of the heart to detect abnormalities.

Optical Character Recognition (OCR)

Overview: ML-powered OCR converts text in images or scanned documents into machine-readable text.

Applications:

Document Digitization: Extracting text from scanned documents, handwritten notes, or books.

Translation Tools: Recognizing and translating text from images (e.g., street signs, menus).

Autonomous Vehicles

Overview: Self-driving cars heavily rely on ML in image processing to interpret their surroundings in real-time.

Applications:

Lane detection: Ensuring vehicles stay within lanes.

Pedestrian and object detection: Avoiding obstacles or potential accidents.

These applications demonstrate the wide-reaching impact of machine learning in image processing, significantly advancing industries like healthcare, security, entertainment, and autonomous technologies.

2.2 Deep Learning in Image Processing

Deep learning is a subset of machine learning, which is itself a branch of artificial intelligence (AI). It focuses on using artificial neural networks with many layers (hence the term "deep") to model and solve complex problems by learning patterns in large datasets (LeCun, 2015). Deep learning allows machines to automatically learn hierarchical representations of data, which makes it particularly powerful for tasks such as image recognition, natural language processing, and speech recognition.

2.2.1 Key Concepts in Deep Learning

Neural Networks

Deep learning models are based on artificial neural networks, which are inspired by the human brain's structure. A neural network consists of layers of nodes (also called neurons), each performing simple computations. These layers include:

Input layer: Where raw data is fed into the network.

Hidden layers: Intermediate layers that transform input data into a form that the output layer can use. The term "deep" refers to networks with multiple hidden layers.

Output layer: The final layer that produces the network's prediction or decision.

Deep learning networks typically have multiple hidden layers, which distinguish them from traditional machine learning models that usually have one or two layers. The additional layers allow the network to learn complex patterns and representations.

Learning Process in Neural Network

- **Forward propagation**: Input data moves through the layers of the network from input to output, with each layer applying transformations based on its learned weights.
- **Loss function**: The loss function calculates the error between the network's prediction and the true label. It is essential for guiding the learning process.
- **Backpropagation**: This is the process of updating the weights of the network to minimize the error. Gradients are calculated and passed backward through the network, adjusting the weights to improve accuracy.
- **Activation Functions:** Non-linear activation functions like ReLU (Rectified Linear Unit), sigmoid, and tanh are applied to the output of neurons to introduce non-linearity, allowing the network to solve complex problems like image classification, speech recognition, and more.
- **Training with Big Data:** Deep learning thrives on large amounts of data. The more data the network is trained on, the better it becomes at recognizing patterns and making accurate predictions.

2.2.2 Key Architectures in Deep Learning

- **Convolutional Neural Networks (CNNs)**: Widely used in image processing tasks, CNNs can automatically learn spatial hierarchies of features from input images.
- **Recurrent Neural Networks (RNNs)**: Used for sequential data (e.g., time series, language), RNNs are capable of learning dependencies across time steps.
- **Long Short-Term Memory (LSTM)**: A specialized form of RNN designed to capture long-range dependencies and overcome the limitations of standard RNNs.
- **Generative Adversarial Networks (GANs)**: Used for generative tasks like image synthesis, GANs consist of two networks—a generator and a discriminator—that compete to produce realistic data.

Deep learning has revolutionized image processing by enabling machines to perform tasks such as image recognition, segmentation, and enhancement with high accuracy and minimal human intervention. Powered by neural networks, especially Convolutional Neural Networks (CNNs), deep learning models can automatically learn features and patterns from large sets of images, making them ideal for complex image processing tasks.

2.2.3 Key Applications of Deep Learning in Image Processing

Image Classification

Overview: Image classification involves assigning a label to an entire image based on its content. Deep learning models automatically extract and learn features from the image to classify it into categories.

Techniques: CNNs are the backbone of image classification. Famous architectures include AlexNet, VGGNet, ResNet, and Inception.

Applications: Identifying objects in images (e.g., dogs vs. cats), detecting diseases in medical images (e.g., pneumonia in chest X-rays), and categorizing images in social media.

Object Detection

Overview: Object detection goes beyond image classification by identifying and localizing objects within an image. It involves drawing bounding boxes around detected objects and labeling them.

Techniques: CNN-based models like YOLO (You Only Look Once), SSD (Single Shot Detector), and Faster R-CNN are widely used for object detection.

Applications: Self-driving cars (detecting pedestrians, traffic lights, etc.), surveillance systems, and retail analytics.

Image Segmentation

Overview: Image segmentation is the process of dividing an image into different regions, where each pixel belongs to a specific object or part of the scene. This can be either **semantic segmentation** (labeling each pixel as part of a class, e.g., road, car, sky) or **instance segmentation** (distinguishing different instances of the same object class).

Techniques: U-Net, Fully Convolutional Networks (FCNs), and Mask R-CNN are popular deep learning architectures for image segmentation.

Applications: Medical imaging (segmenting tumors in MRI scans), autonomous driving (lane and pedestrian detection), and satellite image analysis (land use mapping).

Image Generation (Generative Models)

Overview: Deep learning can also be used to generate new images from data, either by learning from existing images or creating variations of them. These models can synthesize realistic-looking images, even if they don't exist in the training data.

Techniques: Generative Adversarial Networks (GANs) are the leading deep learning model for image generation. Variational Autoencoders (VAEs) are also used.

Applications: Deepfake creation, generating artworks, filling in missing parts of images (inpainting), and improving low-resolution images (super-resolution).

Image Enhancement and Restoration

Overview: Deep learning models can enhance image quality by removing noise, correcting blurring, and increasing resolution.

Techniques: Deep Convolutional Neural Networks (CNNs) are commonly used for image restoration, while models like SRGAN (Super-Resolution GAN) can upscale images to higher resolutions.

Applications: Enhancing low-light or blurry photos, forensic image reconstruction, and improving the quality of medical images (e.g., enhancing MRI or CT scans).

Optical Character Recognition (OCR)

Overview: OCR involves extracting text from images (e.g., scanned documents, photos of text). Deep learning enhances OCR accuracy by learning from complex fonts, handwriting, and variations in image quality.

Techniques: CNNs, often combined with Long Short-Term Memory (LSTM) networks for sequence prediction, are used for OCR. Google's Tesseract engine also integrates deep learning techniques.

Applications: Digitizing printed documents, reading license plates, and processing handwritten forms.

Facial Recognition and Emotion Detection

Overview: Deep learning models can analyze facial features for recognition and detect emotions based on facial expressions.

Techniques: CNNs like FaceNet and VGGFace are widely used for facial recognition. Deep learning models for emotion detection focus on key facial landmarks to interpret expressions.

Applications: Security and surveillance, unlocking devices using facial recognition, and analyzing customer emotions in marketing or customer service.

Image Captioning

Overview: Image captioning involves generating a natural language description for an image. This combines deep learning for both image processing and natural language generation.

Techniques: CNNs are used to extract features from images, and Recurrent Neural Networks (RNNs), often enhanced with attention mechanisms, generate the corresponding textual descriptions.

Applications: Assisting visually impaired individuals, generating automatic image descriptions for websites, and content creation.

Image Style Transfer

Overview: Style transfer uses deep learning to transform the artistic style of one image into another, such as applying the painting style of Van Gogh to a photograph.

Techniques: Neural Style Transfer (NST), based on CNNs, allows the transfer of style by separating and recombining content and style features in images.

Applications: Artistic creation, enhancing video game graphics, and photo editing tools.

Image-to-Image Translation

Overview: This involves transforming an image from one domain to another, such as converting a grayscale image to color, or a sketch to a realistic photo.

Techniques: GAN-based models like Pix2Pix and CycleGAN perform image-to-image translation, learning to map images from one domain to another without requiring paired data.

Applications: Colorizing black-and-white photos, converting daytime scenes to nighttime, and enhancing medical images.

2.3 Transfer Learning

Transfer learning is a powerful technique in deep learning where a pre-trained model, originally designed and trained for one task, is reused (either as-is or with some modifications) to solve a different but related task. Instead of training a model from scratch, which can be computationally expensive and time-consuming, transfer learning allows you to leverage the knowledge a model has learned from one domain and apply it to another, often with less training data (Pan & Yang, 2009).

2.3.1 Key Concepts of Transfer Learning

Pre-Trained Model

In transfer learning start with a model that has already been trained on a large dataset (e.g., ImageNet (Deng et al., 2009). These models have learned to extract useful features from data, such as edges, textures, and shapes in the case of image data.

Feature Extraction vs. Fine-Tuning

Feature Extraction: Pre-trained models are used as a feature extractor. In this approach, the model's learned weights are kept frozen (non-trainable), and only the final layers (usually fully connected layers) are replaced with layers specific to the new task.

Fine-Tuning: In fine-tuning, the pre-trained model's weights are partially or fully trainable. one usually modifies the last few layers and fine-tune them on the new dataset, allowing the model to adjust its weights to better fit the new task.

2.3.2 Steps in Transfer Learning

Select a Pre-Trained Model

Choose a model that has been trained on a large, diverse dataset. Some popular pre-trained models include:

VGGNet: Simple architecture but widely used for feature extraction (Simonyan & Zisserman, 2014).

ResNet: Incorporates residual connections and allows for deeper networks without performance degradation (He et al., 2016).

InceptionNet: Efficient for large-scale image classification (Szegedy et al., 2015).

EfficientNet: Designed for both efficiency and accuracy (Tan, 2019).

Modify the Model

Feature Extraction: Remove the last classification layer of the pre-trained model and replace it with a new layer or layers specific to the new task. These new layers are trainable, while the rest of the model remains fixed.

Fine-Tuning: Optionally, unfreeze some of the layers of the pre-trained model and fine-tune them on your new dataset to adapt the model to the specific features of the new task.

Train on a New Dataset

The pre-trained model is retrained on the new dataset. Since the model already "knows" a lot from its original training, it can converge faster and with less data compared to training from scratch.

Evaluation and Fine-Tune

After training, evaluate the performance of the model on the new task. If necessary, adjust hyperparameters or continue fine-tuning layers for better performance.

2.3.3 Key Applications of Transfer Learning in Image Processing

In image processing, transfer learning is widely used because large datasets like ImageNet provide a good foundation for many computer vision tasks. Pre-trained models on ImageNet are used as starting points for tasks such as:

Image Classification

Starting with a pre-trained model like ResNet, you can modify the last few layers to classify images into new categories, even if you have a smaller, specific dataset.

Object Detection

Transfer learning is often applied to models like Faster R-CNN or YOLO, pre-trained on large object detection datasets, and fine-tuned on custom datasets for detecting specific objects.

Image Segmentation

Models like U-Net or FCNs pre-trained on large segmentation datasets can be fine-tuned for specialized tasks like medical image segmentation.

Medical Imaging

Pre-trained models on general datasets can be fine-tuned on smaller medical datasets to detect tumors, anomalies, or other medical conditions.

3. POTENTIAL BENEFITS OF AI IN ENHANCING IMAGE PROCESSING CAPABILITIES

Artificial Intelligence (AI) has transformed image processing, providing capabilities that go beyond traditional methods by significantly improving accuracy, efficiency, and the ability to analyze large datasets. Here's how AI enhances image processing:

3.1 Improved Accuracy

AI, particularly deep learning models like Convolutional Neural Networks (CNNs), has drastically improved the accuracy of image processing tasks. This is due to the following:

Automatic Feature Extraction

Traditional image processing requires manual feature extraction (e.g., edges, textures). AI, especially deep learning, can automatically learn features at multiple levels of abstraction. This results in more precise and reliable outcomes in tasks like object detection, image classification, and segmentation.

Handling Complex and Noisy Data

AI algorithms are robust to noisy or incomplete data, allowing for better performance even when images are degraded or incomplete. For example, in medical imaging, AI can detect subtle patterns or anomalies that may not be obvious to human experts.

Reduction of Human Error

AI models trained on large datasets can outperform human specialists in certain domains, such as diagnosing diseases from medical images (e.g., detecting tumors from MRIs or CT scans). This reduces the likelihood of human error, leading to more reliable decisions in critical fields like healthcare and security.

3.2 Enhanced Efficiency

AI-driven image processing technologies allow for faster and more efficient processing of images:

Real-Time Processing

With AI-powered models, tasks like object detection and image segmentation can be performed in real-time. For example, self-driving cars need to process images of their surroundings in milliseconds to make quick decisions, which is made possible by AI algorithms like YOLO (You Only Look Once) and SSD (Single Shot Multibox Detector).

Automation of Repetitive Tasks

AI can automate routine tasks like image enhancement, noise reduction, or object recognition, which previously required manual effort. In industries like manufacturing, AI-based image analysis can be used for quality control without human intervention, saving both time and resources.

Parallel Processing on GPUs

Deep learning models, particularly CNNs, can be parallelized and run on powerful GPUs (Graphics Processing Units). This allows AI systems to process large amounts of image data quickly and efficiently, reducing the time needed for tasks like training and inference.

3.3 Ability to Analyze Large Datasets

AI excels in processing and analyzing vast amounts of data, which has opened new possibilities in image analysis:

Scalability

Traditional image processing methods often struggled to scale effectively when dealing with large datasets. AI models, especially when deployed in cloud environments, can scale seamlessly to analyze huge datasets, such as satellite images, medical scans, or video feeds from security cameras.

Big Data Analysis

AI algorithms can handle and analyze massive datasets, finding patterns and insights that would be difficult or impossible for humans to identify. For example, AI models can analyze thousands of medical images to discover subtle patterns that could indicate early signs of diseases like cancer or Alzheimer's.

Data Augmentation

AI-driven methods like Generative Adversarial Networks (GANs) can generate new synthetic images from existing data, enabling the expansion of training datasets without manual collection efforts. This is particularly useful when real data is scarce, such as in medical imaging or space exploration.

3.4 Advanced Image Processing Techniques

AI brings more advanced techniques to the field of image processing:

Image Super-Resolution

AI models like GANs and CNNs are used to enhance image resolution. This technique is used in areas like satellite imagery, where high-resolution images are required for detailed analysis, or in media where older low-resolution images are enhanced for modern use.

Image Restoration and Enhancement

AI can restore old, corrupted, or noisy images, enhancing their quality. This is useful in areas like digital forensics, where enhancing low-quality footage can help in criminal investigations, or in restoring historical images and films.

Semantic Segmentation

AI-based models like Fully Convolutional Networks (FCNs) or U-Nets can perform pixel-level classification, allowing for precise object or region identification in images. This is crucial in fields such as autonomous driving, where segmenting roads, vehicles, and pedestrians from an image is essential for decision-making.

3.5 Application-Specific Benefits

AI's contributions to image processing offer targeted advantages in various industries:

Healthcare

AI models in medical imaging help radiologists identify diseases like cancer, cardiovascular issues, and neurological conditions with unprecedented accuracy. AI not only improves diagnosis but also helps in reducing the time needed for image analysis.

Agriculture

AI-powered image processing can analyze drone and satellite images of large fields to monitor crop health, detect pests, or optimize irrigation, leading to more sustainable agricultural practices.

Security and Surveillance

AI-based image processing technologies can automatically detect and track objects or people in real-time across large-scale video feeds. This improves security in public spaces, critical infrastructures, and private properties.

4. IDENTIFY AND ANALYZE ETHICAL CHALLENGES IN AI BASED IMAGE PROCESSING

AI-based image processing presents numerous opportunities across industries, from healthcare to surveillance, but it also raises significant ethical challenges. These challenges involve concerns about privacy, bias, accountability, and misuse of technology. Here's an analysis of the key ethical challenges in AI-based image processing:

4.1 Privacy and Surveillance

One of the most significant ethical challenges in AI-driven image processing is the invasion of privacy, especially when used in surveillance systems.

Facial Recognition

AI models used for facial recognition in public or private spaces can track individuals without their consent. This leads to concerns about mass surveillance, especially when combined with government or corporate interests. It also creates ethical issues regarding the right to anonymity and privacy in public spaces.

Monitoring and Tracking

In addition to facial recognition, AI can be used to track movements or behaviors from video footage, which raises concerns about constant monitoring. This is particularly problematic in authoritarian regimes or in environments like workplaces where employees might be monitored without their full knowledge.

Data Collection

AI-based image processing systems often require large datasets to train and improve accuracy. Collecting and storing these images can infringe on personal privacy, especially if people are unaware of how their images are being used or if data protection measures are insufficient.

4.2 Bias and Fairness

AI models, including those used in image processing, can inherit and amplify biases present in the training data.

Racial and Gender Bias

Many AI models have been shown to perform less accurately for certain demographic groups. For example, facial recognition algorithms often perform worse on people with darker skin tones and women, as the training datasets might predominantly consist of images of lighter-skinned men. This bias can lead to misidentifications, wrongful arrests, or unequal treatment in applications like security and law enforcement.

Underrepresentation

If certain groups are underrepresented in the training datasets (e.g., images of people with disabilities or older adults), AI systems may fail to correctly process or analyze these images, leading to discriminatory outcomes. This lack of diversity can reinforce social inequalities and lead to unjust consequences.

Algorithmic Discrimination

When AI-based image processing is used in sensitive areas like hiring, healthcare, or criminal justice, biased models can perpetuate discrimination. For example, in healthcare, AI systems might not accurately diagnose conditions in minority populations due to biased medical imaging datasets.

4.3 Accountability and Responsibility

Determining who is accountable when AI-based image processing systems make mistakes is a significant ethical challenge.

Black Box Nature of AI

Deep learning models, which are commonly used in image processing, are often seen as "black boxes" because their decision-making processes are not easily interpretable. If an AI model misidentifies someone in a criminal investigation or fails to detect a medical condition, it can be difficult to trace the reasoning behind the mistake, raising concerns about accountability.

Liability in Errors

In critical applications like healthcare or law enforcement, who is held responsible when an AI system produces inaccurate or harmful results? The creators of the AI, the organizations deploying it, or the users of the system? This ambiguity creates legal and ethical dilemmas.

Ethical Deployment

Companies and organizations deploying AI-based image processing systems have a responsibility to ensure that the systems are accurate, fair, and used ethically. However, the commercial pressure to deploy AI technologies quickly can lead to insufficient testing or oversight, resulting in harmful outcomes.

4.4 Misuse of AI Technology

The powerful capabilities of AI in image processing can be exploited for unethical or harmful purposes.

Deepfakes

AI-based image processing can be used to create deepfake images or videos, which can be used to spread misinformation, fake news, or for malicious purposes like blackmail, fraud, or defamation. Deepfakes can also contribute to the erosion of trust in media, as it becomes increasingly difficult to distinguish between real and manipulated content.

Surveillance and Oppression

In some cases, AI-powered image processing is used to suppress dissent or control populations. For example, in some countries, governments use AI-driven surveillance systems to track and control ethnic minorities or political dissidents. The use of such technology for authoritarian control raises serious ethical concerns about human rights abuses.

Weaponization

AI-based image processing can be used in autonomous weapons systems, where AI identifies targets based on image data. The use of AI in warfare raises ethical questions about the role of humans in decision-making and the potential for unintended harm to civilians.

4.5 Informed Consent and Transparency

The lack of transparency in how AI systems are developed and used is an important ethical issue.

Informed Consent

People often do not know when they are being monitored, when their images are being collected, or how their data is being used. Informed consent is a cornerstone of ethical practice, but in many cases, users or citizens are unaware that their image data is being processed by AI systems. This can occur in public spaces (e.g., security cameras), on social media platforms, or in healthcare settings.

Transparency in AI Models

Many AI systems used in image processing are not transparent about how they make decisions or process images. This lack of transparency makes it difficult for individuals to understand why certain images were classified or analyzed in specific ways. For example, if a person is flagged by a facial recognition system, they may not understand why they were identified or whether the system was biased against them.

4.6 Security and Data Breach Risks

AI-based image processing systems often deal with sensitive personal data, which introduces risks related to data security and breaches.

Sensitive Data

In areas like healthcare, where medical images are processed by AI, data security is paramount. A breach or misuse of such data can have serious consequences for patients' privacy and well-being.

Vulnerability to Hacking

AI models themselves can be vulnerable to attacks. For example, adversarial attacks, where subtle changes are made to images to fool AI systems, can cause systems to misclassify images. In security applications, this could lead to a failure in detecting threats, or worse, manipulation of AI systems for malicious purposes.

4.7 Ethical Use of AI in Medicine

In the medical field, AI-based image processing has great potential, but it also raises important ethical considerations.

Overreliance on AI

There's a risk that healthcare professionals may over-rely on AI systems for diagnosing or analyzing medical images, potentially sidelining their clinical judgment. If an AI system provides an incorrect diagnosis, and healthcare providers trust the AI over their expertise, it could result in patient harm.

Access to Technology

Not all healthcare providers have access to AI-based medical image processing technologies. This creates disparities between institutions that can afford advanced AI systems and those that cannot, leading to inequality in healthcare access and outcomes.

5. ADDRESSING ETHICAL CHALLENGES

To mitigate the ethical risks of AI in image processing, several actions are recommended:

Bias Auditing

Regular audits of AI models to identify and address bias in training data, ensuring diverse representation of populations.

Explainability and Transparency

Developing AI systems that are interpretable and transparent in their decision-making processes, so users and stakeholders can understand how decisions are made.

Privacy Regulations

Implementing strict privacy laws and guidelines, such as the General Data Protection Regulation (GDPR), to ensure that AI systems are deployed in ways that respect individuals' privacy.

Ethical Oversight

Establishing independent ethical oversight boards to monitor the use of AI-based image processing technologies, particularly in sensitive areas like law enforcement, healthcare, and public surveillance.

Informed Consent

Ensuring that individuals are informed when their images are being processed by AI, and obtaining consent when necessary, especially in healthcare and personal data applications.

Security Measures

Strengthening cybersecurity measures to protect AI systems and the data they process from breaches and adversarial attacks.

6. CASE STUDIES AND REAL-WORLD EXAMPLES TO ILLUSTRATE THE ETHICAL CHALLENGES IN USE OF AI FOR IMAGE PROCESSING

6.1 Facial Recognition and Racial Bias (IBM, Microsoft, and Amazon)

Case Study: Major tech companies, including IBM, Microsoft, and Amazon, have faced scrutiny over the biases in their facial recognition systems, especially regarding racial and gender disparities.

- **Challenge:** Research studies, such as one led by Joy Buolamwini at the MIT Media Lab, revealed that facial recognition systems from these companies showed significant bias, with error rates of up to 35% for darker-skinned women compared to under 1% for lighter-skinned men (Steve, 2018). The disparity arose from the fact that these systems were trained on datasets predominantly made up of lighter-skinned individuals, leading to biased performance when used with diverse populations.
- **Impact:** The use of biased facial recognition algorithms in law enforcement and surveillance raised concerns about wrongful identification, unfair arrests, and reinforcing racial discrimination. The public backlash led IBM to exit the facial recognition business, and Amazon and Microsoft to temporarily halt selling their technology to law enforcement until stronger regulations were in place.
- **Ethical Issue:** This case highlights the ethical challenge of algorithmic bias in AI-based image processing systems, particularly when they are used for critical decisions in policing and public safety. It also raises issues of accountability, as the companies developing and selling these technologies are responsible for ensuring fairness and minimizing bias.

6.2 Deepfakes and Misinformation (Political Deepfakes)

Case Study: Deepfake technology, which uses AI to create realistic but fake images or videos, has been used in political misinformation campaigns, creating videos of politicians saying or doing things they never did.

- **Challenge:** In 2020, a deepfake video of Nancy Pelosi, Speaker of the U.S. House of Representatives, was circulated online, depicting her speaking in a slurred manner, making it appear as though she was intoxicated (Hannah, 2020). Although it was eventually debunked, the video spread widely across social media, misleading millions of people and contributing to a broader political misinformation campaign.
- **Impact:** Deepfakes present a significant ethical issue as they can be used to deceive the public, manipulate public opinion, or harm individuals' reputations. Their potential to disrupt elections, spread misinformation, and undermine trust in the media poses a growing challenge.
- **Ethical Issue:** The misuse of AI-based image processing for creating deepfakes raises concerns about the erosion of trust, privacy, and consent, as individuals may have their images and likeness used without permission. It also brings up questions about regulation and the need for tools to detect and combat deepfakes.

6.3 AI in Healthcare Imaging (Google's Diabetic Retinopathy Screening)

Case Study: Google's AI system for detecting diabetic retinopathy, a complication from diabetes that can lead to blindness, was implemented in hospitals in India as part of a real-world test (Vergin et al., 2020).

- **Challenge:** The AI system was designed to analyze retinal images and flag cases where patients needed further medical attention. While the AI model was highly accurate in controlled environments, real-world challenges, such as poor image quality and a lack of proper training for staff, led to inconsistent results. In some cases, healthcare workers did not understand how to interpret the AI's output, leading to confusion and missed diagnoses.
- **Impact:** Although the technology had the potential to greatly improve healthcare outcomes, its deployment raised ethical issues regarding over-reliance on AI, particularly in environments where human oversight was insufficient. The challenge also underscored the need for clear communication and collaboration between AI systems and healthcare professionals to ensure accurate and reliable diagnoses.
- **Ethical Issue:** This case demonstrates the risks of overreliance on AI in healthcare settings and the ethical responsibility of ensuring that AI systems are well-integrated into clinical workflows. It also raises questions about accountability when AI-based image processing systems make critical decisions about patient health.

6.4 Surveillance and Mass Monitoring (China's Social Credit System)

Case Study: China's use of AI-based facial recognition technology as part of its Social Credit System has raised international concerns over privacy and state control. The system monitors citizens' behavior, including infractions like jaywalking, and adjusts their social credit scores accordingly.

- **Challenge:** AI-powered surveillance cameras equipped with facial recognition software are deployed across China, tracking and identifying individuals in real-time. These systems are used not only for monitoring criminal activity but also for social behaviors, like crossing the street outside designated areas. Citizens with lower scores face restrictions in daily activities, such as travel bans or reduced access to social services.
- **Impact:** The mass deployment of AI surveillance has led to an erosion of personal privacy and raised concerns about the use of AI for authoritarian control. In addition to monitoring general populations, facial recognition systems have been used to target ethnic minorities, such as Uighur Muslims, leading to serious human rights abuses.
- **Ethical Issue:** The use of AI-based image processing for mass surveillance poses severe privacy and civil rights concerns. It also raises issues about the power imbalance created when governments or corporations have access to advanced surveillance tools, potentially infringing on citizens' autonomy and freedom.

6.5 Adversarial Attacks on Image Processing Systems (Autonomous Vehicles)

Case Study: Researchers have shown that AI-based image processing systems, such as those used in autonomous vehicles, are vulnerable to adversarial attacks. These attacks involve subtly altering images in a way that is imperceptible to humans but causes AI systems to misclassify objects (Chahe et al., 2023).

- **Challenge:** In one experiment, researchers placed stickers on stop signs that caused an autonomous vehicle's image recognition system to misidentify the stop sign as a yield sign, which could have led to dangerous driving decisions. This vulnerability demonstrated the potential for malicious actors to manipulate AI systems in real-world applications.
- **Impact:** These adversarial attacks expose a significant security vulnerability in AI-based image processing systems, particularly those used in critical systems like self-driving cars or security applications. It also highlights the risks associated with over-reliance on AI systems without proper safeguards.
- **Ethical Issue:** The security risks posed by adversarial attacks raise ethical questions about the safety and reliability of AI systems. Developers and companies deploying AI-based image processing systems have an ethical responsibility to ensure that their systems are robust and protected against manipulation, especially in high-stakes applications like autonomous driving or surveillance.

6.6 Misuse of AI in Law Enforcement (Predictive Policing and Surveillance)

Case Study: AI-based image processing systems are increasingly being used by law enforcement agencies for predictive policing and surveillance. However, these systems have been criticized for exacerbating racial biases (Gallon,2023).

- **Challenge:** In the U.S., law enforcement agencies have used facial recognition technology to identify suspects from public and private surveillance footage. Studies have shown that these systems disproportionately misidentify people of color, leading to false arrests and wrongful surveillance of minority communities. Predictive policing algorithms, which analyze crime data to predict where future crimes will occur, often reflect historical biases, further entrenching racial disparities in policing.
- **Impact:** The use of biased AI systems in law enforcement can lead to discriminatory practices and undermine public trust in the justice system. These systems can reinforce existing inequalities and disproportionately target marginalized communities.
- **Ethical Issue:** The deployment of AI-based image processing in law enforcement raises issues of fairness, accountability, and bias. It also questions the ethics of using AI systems in contexts where decisions can significantly impact individuals' lives and freedom.

These case studies illustrate the broad range of ethical challenges associated with AI-based image processing, including bias, privacy violations, security vulnerabilities, and misuse of technology for surveillance or control. As AI technologies continue to evolve, it is crucial for developers, policymakers, and users to address these ethical concerns through proper oversight, accountability, and fairness mechanisms to ensure responsible and equitable use of AI in society.

7. ETHICAL FRAMEWORKS

The use of Artificial Intelligence (AI) in image processing offers transformative capabilities across multiple sectors. However, its deployment raises significant ethical concerns, such as privacy violations, bias, and misuse. To mitigate these risks, the development and application of AI in image processing must follow robust ethical frameworks and best practices to ensure responsible, transparent, and fair use. Below are some proposed ethical frameworks to guide the responsible use of AI in image processing:

7.1 Fairness and Non-Discrimination

Definition

Ensuring that AI systems do not disproportionately harm or benefit certain individuals or groups based on race, gender, ethnicity, or other characteristics.

Approach

Bias Auditing: Regularly audit AI systems to detect and mitigate bias in training datasets and algorithms. This can be done by testing performance across different demographic groups.

Diverse Training Data: Use diverse, representative datasets to train AI models, ensuring fair performance across all population groups.

Fair Algorithmic Design: Develop algorithms that are designed to minimize bias by accounting for historical inequalities and avoiding discriminatory outputs.

7.2 Privacy and Data Protection

Definition

AI systems must respect individuals' privacy rights and ensure that personal data, especially sensitive image data, is protected from misuse or unauthorized access.

Approach

Consent Mechanisms: Ensure that individuals are informed about how their data (including images) will be used, and obtain explicit consent where applicable, especially in sensitive domains like healthcare or law enforcement.

Data Minimization: Only collect the minimum amount of data necessary for the specific use case, and avoid unnecessary retention of personal images.

Anonymization and Encryption: Use anonymization techniques and strong encryption to protect image data and metadata, ensuring it cannot be traced back to individuals.

7.3 Transparency and Explainability

Definition

AI systems must operate transparently, providing understandable explanations for their decisions and processes to stakeholders, users, and affected individuals.

Approach

Explainable AI (XAI): Develop AI models that can provide interpretable explanations for their image processing decisions, allowing users to understand how the system arrived at a specific result.

Open Reporting: Make details about the training data, algorithm development, and model performance publicly available, especially for high-impact systems like facial recognition used in public surveillance.

Algorithm Documentation: Ensure AI models are well-documented, outlining their purpose, data sources, and known limitations, so that they can be critically evaluated and improved upon.

7.4 Accountability and Governance

Definition

Developers, companies, and users of AI systems must be held accountable for their actions, and appropriate governance structures must be in place to oversee the ethical use of AI technologies.

Approach

Ethical Oversight Committees: Establish independent ethics boards or committees to evaluate the potential impacts of AI applications in image processing, ensuring that deployment aligns with ethical standards.

Accountability Mechanisms: Create mechanisms that assign responsibility for errors or harms caused by AI systems. This could involve liability rules that determine who is accountable for the outcomes of the AI's decisions, especially in sectors like law enforcement and healthcare.

Human-in-the-Loop (HITL): Ensure that human oversight is maintained in decision-making processes, particularly when AI systems are making critical or high-stakes decisions, such as medical diagnoses or criminal justice applications.

7.5 Safety and Security

Definition

AI systems must be designed and deployed in a way that ensures safety and security, both from the perspective of system robustness and protection against malicious attacks.

Approach

Adversarial Robustness: Implement measures to guard AI systems against adversarial attacks, such as attempts to manipulate image processing results by subtly altering inputs (e.g., manipulating a stop sign to fool a self-driving car).

Security Audits: Regularly audit AI systems to detect vulnerabilities and ensure they are protected against data breaches and hacking attempts, especially in critical applications like autonomous vehicles or surveillance.

Safety by Design: Incorporate safety mechanisms that allow for fail-safes or override options if AI systems behave unexpectedly or dangerously, ensuring that human intervention is possible in case of system failures.

7.6 Ethical Use and Avoiding Harm

Definition

AI in image processing should be used to promote human well-being and avoid harm, particularly in contexts where its misuse could lead to negative societal impacts.

Approach

Risk Assessments: Conduct ethical risk assessments before deploying AI systems, identifying potential harms and ensuring that mitigation strategies are in place to prevent misuse.

Regulatory Compliance: Align AI deployments with relevant ethical standards, regulations, and legal frameworks, such as GDPR (General Data Protection Regulation) in the European Union, which emphasizes the protection of personal data.

Beneficial AI Applications: Prioritize the development of AI systems that contribute positively to society, such as improving healthcare outcomes, enhancing accessibility, or protecting the environment, while actively avoiding applications with harmful potential (e.g., authoritarian surveillance or discriminatory law enforcement tools).

8. BEST PRACTICES FOR RESPONSIBLE AI DEPLOYMENT IN IMAGE PROCESSING

Below are some best proposed practices to guide the responsible use of AI in image processing:

8.1 Continuous Monitoring and Evaluation

Ongoing Audits: AI systems should be continuously monitored post-deployment to ensure they maintain fairness, accuracy, and ethical integrity. Regular performance audits should be conducted to assess how AI systems are functioning in real-world settings.

Bias Mitigation Strategies: Develop processes for detecting and correcting bias during both the training and post-deployment phases. This might include dynamically adjusting models to account for evolving data and societal conditions.

8.2 Inclusive Design and Development

Stakeholder Engagement: Involve diverse groups of stakeholders in the design, development, and evaluation stages of AI systems. This includes marginalized groups who might be disproportionately affected by AI-based image processing technologies, such as racial minorities, women, or people with disabilities.

Cross-Disciplinary Collaboration: Encourage collaboration between AI engineers, ethicists, legal experts, and social scientists to ensure that technical development aligns with ethical considerations and societal norms.

8.3 Human-Centric AI Development

Human-in-the-Loop Systems: Design AI image processing systems that keep human operators involved, especially in high-stakes applications. This ensures that humans retain control over decision-making and can intervene in cases where the AI system might make a mistake.

User-Focused Transparency: Provide clear, user-friendly explanations of how AI systems function, especially for non-technical users. This is particularly important in fields like healthcare, where patients need to understand how AI-driven diagnostic tools impact their care.

8.4 Consent and User Rights

Informed Consent: Ensure that users are informed about how AI processes their image data, what it is being used for, and what rights they have over their personal data. In applications like facial recognition or medical imaging, gaining explicit user consent is crucial.

Right to Opt-Out: Provide users with the ability to opt-out of AI systems if they do not wish to have their data processed or included. This can be implemented through opt-out mechanisms in public surveillance systems, online platforms, or healthcare settings.

8.5 Redress and Accountability Mechanisms

Error Reporting Systems: Set up systems that allow users to report errors or unfair treatment by AI systems. For example, if an AI-based facial recognition system misidentifies an individual, they should have a clear way to challenge or appeal the result.

Accountability Frameworks: Create structures that define accountability for the development and deployment of AI systems. This could include establishing clear legal frameworks that delineate who is responsible for harm caused by AI errors—whether it's the developer, the user, or the organization deploying the technology.

8.6 Ethical Research and Development

Ethical AI Research: Conduct research on the ethical implications of AI in image processing and contribute to open discourse on best practices and frameworks. Promote transparency in publishing research outcomes, datasets, and the societal impacts of AI technologies.

Impact Assessments: Implement ethical impact assessments before deploying AI systems, particularly in public or high-stakes domains such as law enforcement, healthcare, or autonomous vehicles.

The development and use of AI in image processing holds great promise, but they come with ethical responsibilities. By adhering to principles of fairness, privacy, transparency, accountability, security, and safety, AI developers and users can mitigate risks and ensure best proposed society. Establishing continuous monitoring, human-centric approaches, and inclusive design processes will further support the responsible and ethical deployment of AI technologies. These frameworks and best practices serve as guidelines to create a balanced relationship between innovation and ethical integrity, ensuring that AI serves humanity without compromising values or rights.

9. FUTURE DIRECTIONS

AI-driven image processing has seen rapid advancements in recent years, fueled by breakthroughs in machine learning, especially deep learning. The field continues to evolve, opening new possibilities across various industries such as healthcare, entertainment, autonomous vehicles, and more. Below are some of the emerging trends and future directions in AI-driven image processing:

9.1 Self-Supervised and Unsupervised Learning for Image Processing

Trend

Traditional supervised learning models in image processing rely on large, labeled datasets. However, obtaining labeled data is expensive and time-consuming, especially for complex images.

Future Direction

Self-Supervised Learning (SSL): AI models learn useful features from unlabeled data, reducing the need for large amounts of labeled datasets. For example, SSL models can predict missing parts of an image or learn features by solving puzzles (e.g., Jigsaw method).

Unsupervised Learning: Models can learn to classify and process images without any labels. These approaches will drive the next generation of AI models in areas like medical imaging or surveillance, where data labeling is often impractical.

9.2 Generative AI and Synthetic Data for Image Processing

Trend

Generative Adversarial Networks (GANs) and other generative AI models have shown remarkable capabilities in generating realistic images, which are now being used in areas like image enhancement, super-resolution, and data augmentation.

Future Direction

Synthetic Data Generation: AI systems will increasingly generate synthetic images to augment datasets for training. This is useful in domains where acquiring real-world data is challenging (e.g., rare medical conditions, autonomous driving scenarios).

Image-to-Image Translation: AI models will continue to improve the ability to generate high-quality synthetic images from text or other forms of input (e.g., converting a sketch into a realistic image), enabling creative applications in art, design, and media production.

9.3 Explainable AI (XAI) for Image Processing

Trend

AI-driven image processing systems, especially in critical sectors like healthcare and law enforcement, need to be more interpretable and transparent to gain trust and regulatory approval.

Future Direction

Explainability in AI: There is a growing demand for AI models that explain their decisions, such as why a medical image has been classified as cancerous or why a facial recognition system has flagged an individual. Research in XAI will help develop algorithms that provide clear, human-understandable insights into how decisions are made.

Regulation-Driven Explainability: As regulatory frameworks evolve (e.g., the EU AI Act), AI systems will need to provide robust explanations for their decision-making processes, particularly when these models are used for high-stakes applications like healthcare diagnostics or legal systems.

9.4 Real-Time AI for Video Processing

Trend

Real-time image and video processing has traditionally required substantial computational resources, but with advances in AI hardware and optimization techniques, AI-driven real-time video analysis is becoming more feasible.

Future Direction

Edge AI: The development of AI models that can run on edge devices (e.g., mobile phones, cameras, drones) will facilitate real-time video processing for applications such as autonomous navigation, security monitoring, and live event analysis.

Streaming Video Analytics: AI models will be able to analyze live video streams in real-time for applications like smart cities (e.g., traffic management, public safety) and live sports analysis (e.g., identifying players, tracking movements, and providing live insights).

9.5 Federated Learning for Image Processing

Trend

Data privacy concerns are becoming more prominent, especially in healthcare and finance, where sensitive image data cannot be shared freely.

Future Direction

Federated Learning: This approach allows AI models to be trained on decentralized data across multiple devices or institutions without sharing the raw data. Federated learning will play a key role in privacy-preserving AI for image processing, particularly in areas like medical imaging (where hospitals can collaboratively train models without exchanging patient data) and distributed surveillance systems.

9.6 AI-Augmented Image Editing and Creative Applications

Trend

AI-driven image processing tools are revolutionizing creative industries by enabling automatic or semi-automatic editing, style transfer, and image enhancement.

Future Direction

Creative AI Tools: AI systems will assist artists, designers, and photographers in generating creative content, automatically enhancing photos, or converting images into artistic styles (e.g., AI-based Photoshop tools, DeepArt).

Generative Design: AI systems will aid in generative design, creating images or visual content based on specified parameters. This is already being seen in architecture, fashion, and visual effects, where AI assists in designing elements that would be difficult to create manually.

9.7 AI for 3D Image Processing and Computer Vision

Trend

As industries such as gaming, virtual reality (VR), augmented reality (AR), and autonomous systems evolve, AI-driven 3D image processing is becoming increasingly important.

Future Direction

3D Reconstruction and Rendering: AI models will enhance the accuracy and realism of 3D reconstructions from 2D images, playing a crucial role in applications like VR/AR experiences, robotics, and digital twins.

Autonomous Systems and Navigation: AI-based image processing will enhance autonomous systems' ability to understand and navigate complex 3D environments (e.g., self-driving cars, drones). This includes improved object detection, segmentation, and path planning in three-dimensional spaces.

9.8 Multi-Modal AI for Cross-Domain Image Processing

Trend

Multi-modal AI systems, which can process and integrate data from various sources (e.g., text, images, audio), are becoming more sophisticated.

Future Direction

Cross-Modal Image Understanding: AI systems will become adept at combining image data with other data types (e.g., text descriptions, sensor data) to gain a more holistic understanding. This can benefit fields like robotics (where images are integrated with sensor data) or education (where images and text are combined for better learning experiences).

Vision-Language Models: Models like CLIP (Contrastive Language-Image Pre-training) will continue to bridge the gap between visual and textual data, enabling AI systems to understand and generate more meaningful outputs by combining both domains.

9.9 AI in Medical Imaging and Diagnostics

Trend

AI is already being used in medical image processing for diagnostics (e.g., detecting tumors, segmenting organs), and its impact on healthcare is expanding.

Future Direction

Personalized Diagnostics: AI-driven imaging will evolve to provide more personalized diagnostic insights by analyzing not only current medical images but also combining historical patient data, genomic information, and environmental factors to tailor diagnoses and treatment plans.

AI-Assisted Surgery: AI models that process real-time video feeds from surgical cameras and other imaging tools will provide surgeons with actionable insights during procedures, enhancing precision and outcomes.

9.10 AI for Ethical Image Processing and Bias Mitigation

Trend

As concerns over bias and ethics in AI image processing grow, researchers are focusing on creating more equitable systems.

Future Direction

Bias Detection Tools: AI models that specifically focus on detecting and mitigating biases in image processing will become more common, ensuring that systems work fairly across all demographic groups.

Ethical AI Regulation: As AI systems become more pervasive, regulatory bodies will impose stricter ethical guidelines and standards for deploying AI in sensitive areas like law enforcement, healthcare, and public surveillance.

9.11 Quantum Computing in Image Processing

Trend

While still in the early stages, quantum computing holds promise for revolutionizing complex AI tasks, including image processing.

Future Direction

Quantum AI Algorithms: Quantum computing will enable the processing of large, complex image datasets at speeds not possible with classical computing, which can enhance applications like real-time medical imaging, astronomical image analysis, and large-scale video processing.

Quantum-Assisted Image Analysis: Quantum AI could open up new possibilities in high-dimensional image processing tasks, such as enhancing image resolution, detecting minute patterns in large datasets, or speeding up simulations used in design and modeling.

The future of AI-driven image processing is marked by breakthroughs in self-supervised learning, 3D image processing, multi-modal AI, and generative models, with applications spanning from healthcare to entertainment and autonomous systems. However, as AI systems become more integrated into critical industries, emphasis on transparency, ethical considerations, and bias mitigation will be essential to ensure equitable and responsible use. By leveraging these emerging trends, AI is set to continue transforming how we process, interpret, and interact with images across a variety of domains.

10. LONG-TERM SOCIETAL IMPACTS OF AI IN IMAGE PROCESSING

The long-term societal impacts of AI in image processing are broad and far-reaching, with the potential to reshape industries, influence cultural norms, and challenge ethical and legal frameworks. While AI-driven image processing can lead to numerous benefits, it also raises concerns that must be carefully managed. Below is an exploration of both the positive and negative impacts AI image processing might have on society in the long term.

10.1 Improved Healthcare and Medical Imaging

Impact: AI-driven image processing has the potential to revolutionize healthcare by enabling more accurate diagnoses, early detection of diseases, and personalized treatment plans. AI can assist in analyzing complex medical images, such as MRI or CT scans, reducing diagnostic errors and improving patient outcomes.

Long-Term Implications

Early Disease Detection: AI systems could detect diseases such as cancer, heart conditions, or neurological disorders earlier than ever before, saving lives by allowing early intervention.

Global Health Access: AI tools may help address the shortage of skilled radiologists in low-resource areas, democratizing access to high-quality medical care through telemedicine and remote diagnostics.

10.2 Enhanced Public Safety and Security

Impact: AI-based image processing can be applied in surveillance, traffic management, and emergency response systems to monitor public spaces, detect suspicious activities, or respond to emergencies.

Long-Term Implications

Safer Cities: AI could contribute to the development of smart cities with enhanced traffic control, real-time monitoring of potential hazards, and proactive responses to threats such as fires or crime.

Crime Prevention: AI-enabled facial recognition and anomaly detection systems could be used to identify suspects or alert authorities to unusual behavior, reducing crime rates and improving public safety.

10.3 Accessibility for People with Disabilities

Impact: AI image processing can greatly improve the lives of people with disabilities by enhancing accessibility. For example, AI can convert visual information into text or speech, helping visually impaired individuals navigate their environments.

Long-Term Implications

Assistive Technologies: AI-powered tools will continue to evolve to assist people with disabilities, such as smart glasses that can interpret and describe scenes, or real-time captioning for the hearing impaired.

Inclusion in Society: As AI improves, more equitable opportunities will emerge for people with disabilities to engage in work, education, and social activities, enhancing societal inclusion and participation.

10.4 Revolutionized Creative Industries

Impact: AI has already begun to influence creative fields like art, film, photography, and design by assisting in tasks such as image enhancement, style transfer, and generative design.

Long-Term Implications

Empowering Artists: AI-driven tools will democratize creativity, enabling individuals with little or no formal training to create professional-quality art, films, or designs.

New Art Forms: The use of AI in the creative process may lead to entirely new forms of artistic expression and genres, blending human and machine creativity in novel ways.

10.5 Automation and Efficiency in Industries

Impact: Industries such as manufacturing, agriculture, and logistics can leverage AI image processing for tasks like defect detection, quality control, and automated inspections.

Long-Term Implications

Increased Productivity: Automation driven by AI in image processing will enhance efficiency, reduce operational costs, and improve product quality across various sectors.

Agricultural Advancements: In agriculture, AI-based image processing could improve crop monitoring and yield predictions, leading to more sustainable farming practices.

Privacy Invasion and Mass Surveillance

Impact: AI-powered facial recognition and video analysis technologies are increasingly used by governments and corporations to monitor public spaces, track individuals, and gather data on people's activities.

Long-Term Implications

Erosion of Privacy: As AI surveillance technologies become more sophisticated, the risk of pervasive and intrusive surveillance will grow, potentially leading to a loss of personal privacy in both public and private spaces.

Authoritarian Use of AI: In some countries, AI-driven surveillance could be weaponized by authoritarian regimes to suppress dissent, monitor citizens, and infringe on civil liberties, raising concerns about the balance between security and privacy.

Deepfakes and Misinformation

Impact: AI-based image generation and manipulation tools (e.g., deepfakes) can create hyper-realistic fake images and videos, making it increasingly difficult to distinguish between real and altered media.

Long-Term Implications

Erosion of Trust in Media: The widespread use of deepfakes could lead to a societal crisis of trust, where individuals find it challenging to differentiate between authentic and manipulated content. This could damage public discourse and undermine democratic processes.

Weaponization of Deepfakes: Deepfake technology may be weaponized for malicious purposes, such as political disinformation, blackmail, or fraud, causing harm at individual, corporate, and national levels.

Bias and Discrimination

Impact: AI models, including those used in image processing, often inherit biases present in their training data, leading to biased outcomes, especially in sensitive domains like facial recognition and medical imaging.

Long-Term Implications

Reinforcement of Social Inequalities: If unchecked, AI systems could reinforce and exacerbate existing social biases, particularly in law enforcement, where facial recognition systems may disproportionately misidentify or target certain racial or ethnic groups.

Bias in Healthcare: In medical imaging, biased AI systems may provide unequal levels of care or misdiagnose patients from minority populations due to underrepresentation in training datasets.

Job Displacement and Economic Inequality

Impact: The automation of image processing tasks across industries could lead to significant job displacement, particularly for roles involving routine or manual image analysis.

Long-Term Implications

Job Losses in Certain Sectors: Workers in fields like radiology, photography, or manufacturing quality control may face job losses or require reskilling as AI takes over tasks traditionally done by humans.

Widening Economic Divide: As AI continues to replace manual and low-skill jobs, the economic divide between those with the skills to work with advanced AI systems and those without may widen, contributing to greater inequality.

Ethical and Legal Challenges

Impact: The ethical and legal frameworks surrounding AI, particularly in image processing, are still developing, leaving gaps in regulation and oversight.

Long-Term Implications

Lack of Regulation: The rapid advancement of AI may outpace regulatory frameworks, leading to the use of AI technologies without adequate ethical safeguards. This could result in harmful applications of AI in areas such as surveillance, law enforcement, or content manipulation.

Ethical Dilemmas: Society will face difficult ethical questions about the boundaries of AI use, such as how much autonomy should be granted to AI systems, or whether certain applications (like deepfakes or invasive surveillance) should be outright banned.

Psychological and Social Effects

Impact: The increasing presence of AI in image-based media, including advertising, entertainment, and social media, may influence human behavior and societal norms in unforeseen ways.

Long-Term Implications

Distorted Perceptions of Reality: AI-generated images and videos could contribute to distorted perceptions of reality, particularly on social media, where manipulated images can influence self-esteem, body image, and social comparison.

AI-Driven Social Manipulation: The use of AI in advertising and propaganda could become more subtle and sophisticated, manipulating people's preferences, opinions, and behaviors without their explicit awareness.

The long-term societal impacts of AI in image processing will be both transformative and complex. While healthcare, safety, accessibility, and creativity stand to benefit greatly from AI advancements, significant challenges remain in the areas of privacy, bias, job displacement, and misuse of technology. The ethical, legal, and social dimensions of AI-driven image processing will need to evolve in parallel with technological developments to ensure these powerful tools are used in ways that benefit society while mitigating potential harms. Thoughtful regulation, public discourse, and inclusive development practices will be critical in shaping a future where AI-driven image processing contributes positively to human life.

CONCLUSION

The intersection of AI and image processing is a powerful and transformative field with a wide range of applications. By harnessing AI's ability to learn from data and process images at scale, this convergence is poised to continue driving innovation across numerous industries. However, the field must also navigate challenges related to data privacy, model interpretability, and ethical considerations to realize its full potential in a responsible and inclusive manner.

REFERENCES

Chahe, A., Wang, C., Jeyapratap, A., Xu, K., & Zhou, L. (2023). Dynamic adversarial attacks on autonomous driving systems. *arXiv preprint arXiv:2312.06701*.

Deng, J., Dong, W., Socher, R., Li, L. -J., Li, K., & Fei-Fei, L. (2009). Imagenet: A large-scale hierarchical image databaseDOI: 10.1080/21642583.2014.956265

Fawagreh, K., Gaber, M. M., & Elyan, E. (2014). Random forests: From early developments to recent advancements. *Systems Science & Control Engineering*, *2*(1), 602–609. DOI: 10.1080/21642583.2014.956265

Gallon, A. (2023). Racism Repeats Itself: AI Racial Bias in Predictive Policing Algorithms. DOI: 10.1080/21642583.2014.956265

Guo, G., Wang, H., Bell, D., Bi, Y., & Greer, K. (2003). KNN model-based approach in classification. In *On The Move to Meaningful Internet Systems 2003: CoopIS, DOA, and ODBASE: OTM Confederated International Conferences, CoopIS, DOA, and ODBASE 2003, Catania, Sicily, Italy, November 3-7, 2003. Proceedings* (pp. 986-996). Springer Berlin Heidelberg. DOI: 10.1007/978-3-540-39964-3_62

Hannah, D. (2020, August 3). Fake video of Pelosi goes viral on Facebook. *The Washington Post*.

He, K., Zhang, X., Ren, S., & Sun, J. (2016). Deep residual learning for image recognition. In *Proceedings of the IEEE conference on computer vision and pattern recognition* (pp. 770-778).

LeCun, Y., Bengio, Y., & Hinton, G. (2015). Deep learning. *nature, 521*(7553), 436-444. DOI: 10.1080/21642583.2014.956265

Li, Z., Liu, F., Yang, W., Peng, S., & Zhou, J. (2021). A survey of convolutional neural networks: Analysis, applications, and prospects. *IEEE Transactions on Neural Networks and Learning Systems*, *33*(12), 6999–7019. DOI: 10.1109/TNNLS.2021.3084827 PMID: 34111009

Norvig, P. R., & Intelligence, S. A. (2002). *A modern approach*. Prentice Hall.

Pan, S. J., & Yang, Q. (2009). A survey on transfer learning. *IEEE Transactions on Knowledge and Data Engineering*, *22*(10), 1345–1359. DOI: 10.1109/TKDE.2009.191

Simonyan, K., & Zisserman, A. (2014). Very deep convolutional networks for large-scale image recognition. *arXiv preprint arXiv:1409.1556*.

Steinley, D. (2006). K-means clustering: A half-century synthesis. *British Journal of Mathematical & Statistical Psychology*, *59*(1), 1–34. DOI: 10.1348/000711005X48266 PMID: 16709277

Steve, L. (2018, February 9). Facial Recognition Is Accurate, if You're a White Guy. *The New York Times*.

Szegedy, C., Liu, W., Jia, Y., Sermanet, P., Reed, S., Anguelov, D., & Rabinovich, A. (2015). Going deeper with convolutions. In *Proceedings of the IEEE conference on computer vision and pattern recognition* (pp. 1-9).

Tan, M. (2019). Efficientnet: Rethinking model scaling for convolutional neural networks. *arXiv preprint arXiv:1905.11946*.

Vergin, J. J. S., & Vidhyavathi, R. M. (2020). Google arda tool using artificial intelligence in self-optimizing algorithm to prevent diabetic retinopathy and diabetic macular edoema (dme).

Wang, L. (Ed.). (2005). *Support vector machines: theory and applications* (Vol. 177). Springer Science & Business Media. DOI: 10.1007/b95439

Chapter 22
Revolutionizing Medical Imaging and Diagnostics Through Intelligent Image Processing Techniques

S. Gandhimathi Alias Usha
https://orcid.org/0000-0003-1908-6249
Velammal College of Engineering and Technology, Madurai, India

P. Uma Maheswari
Velammal College of Engineering and Technology, Madurai, India

V. Jeevalakshmi
Velammal College of Engineering and Technology, Madurai, India

D. Harsha
Velammal College of Engineering and Technology, Madurai, India

ABSTRACT

A new era of medical imaging and diagnostics improvements has been brought about by integrating intelligent image processing techniques, which have considerably improved accuracy, efficiency, and the capacity to identify and cure diseases early. This chapter examines how advancements in Machine Learning (ML) and Artificial Intelligence (AI) are transforming the medical imaging industry by enhancing image capture, processing, and interpretation across various modalities, including MRI, CT, and X-ray scans. Deep learning models, such as transformers, Generative Adversarial Networks (GANs), and Convolutional Neural Networks (CNNs) are at the vanguard of these advancements. These models are making it possible to do tasks like segmenting tissues, organs, and lesions, automatically detecting abnormalities, and even accurately predicting the course of disease. Enter intelligent image processing, a field driven by advancements in AI and ML, which is now AI-driven methods for improving images, such as noise transforming how medical images are processed, analyzed, and interpreted.

DOI: 10.4018/979-8-3693-9045-0.ch022

1. INTRODUCTION

Medical imaging has, arguably, been one of the corner stone's of modern health care, providing clinicians access to the internal structures of the body, minimally invasively. Over time, the evolution of medical imaging technology has dramatically improved diagnostic accuracy and patient outcomes. However, with the exponential growth in the volume and complexity of imaging data, it is increasingly challenging for radiologists and healthcare professionals to manually interpret and analyze images effectively (Pinto e.al.,2023).

1.1 The Evolution of Medical Imaging

The evolution of medical imaging has been marked by continuous technological innovation. The discovery of X-rays in 1895 by Wilhelm Roentgen initiated the first major breakthrough in the field. X-rays became widely used for visualizing bones and detecting abnormalities such as fractures or infections. The second major leap came with the invention of Computed Tomography (CT) in the 1970s, which allowed for cross-sectional imaging of the body, offering more detailed views of internal organs and tissues.

Magnetic Resonance Imaging (MRI) followed in the late 20th century, enabling even more detailed soft tissue contrast using magnetic fields and radio waves, without ionizing radiation. Simultaneously, ultrasound technology provided real-time imaging for fields like obstetrics, cardiology, and vascular medicine. These technological advancements have significantly improved diagnostic capabilities. However, as imaging technologies become more complex, the volume of data produced also increases, creating challenges for manual analysis. This surge in data has paved the way for AI and machine learning solutions in image processing, addressing the need for efficient, high-precision analysis.

1.2 The Emergence of Intelligent Image Processing

The need for faster and more accurate diagnostic tools has driven the development of intelligent image processing. Unlike traditional image analysis, which relies on manual interpretation, intelligent image processing uses AI algorithms to automate the extraction of meaningful information from images. These models are trained on large datasets to recognize patterns and features in medical images, such as tumors, lesions, and other abnormalities (Khalifaetal et.al.,2024). In the realm of medical imaging, deep learning algorithms can perform tasks such as: Segmentation: Automatically identifying and isolating regions of interest (e.g., tumors or organs), Classification: Categorizing images or regions of images (e.g., benign vs. Malignant tumors), Detection: Identifying abnormalities like lung nodules in chest X-rays or polyps in colonoscopy images and Registration: Aligning multiple images from different time points or modalities to track changes over time.

1.3 Significance in Modern Healthcare

Deep learning algorithms have demonstrated remarkable success in detecting early-stage cancers, retinal diseases, and cardiovascular conditions with high accuracy. This leads to earlier diagnosis, which can significantly improve patient outcomes.

AI-driven imaging techniques can support precision medicine by integrating imaging data with other clinical and genomic information. This allows for more personalized treatment plans, tailored to the specific characteristics of a patient's disease. Intelligent image processing reduces the time required for image interpretation. This is particularly beneficial in healthcare systems with limited resources, where radiologists may not be available in sufficient numbers. AI algorithms can serve as a valuable tool for screening large populations, triaging patients who need immediate attention, and relieving the burden on healthcare professionals. By automating the preliminary analysis of images, intelligent image processing can streamline clinical workflows. Radiologists can focus on reviewing complex cases and making final decisions (Gurnanmi et.al.,2024).

2. FOUNDATIONS OF INTELLIGENT IMAGE PROCESSING

As the healthcare landscape continues to integrate AI and ML, intelligent image processing has become one of the most transformative applications. This section provides a comprehensive foundation by exploring the essential.

2.1 Overview of Artificial Intelligence and Machine Learning

AI refers to the simulation of human intelligence in machines, enabling them to perform tasks that typically require human cognition, such as reasoning, learning, and decision-making. Within AI, ML is a subset that allows systems to learn from data and improve their performance without being explicitly programmed. In the context of medical imaging, ML algorithms are trained on large datasets of images to recognize patterns and make predictions about new images.

In medical imaging, AI and ML have revolutionized diagnostic processes by enabling the automation of image interpretation and analysis. These models can process vast amounts of image data, identifying structures, abnormalities, and patterns that are often too subtle for the human eye to detect. Techniques such as deep learning, a branch of ML, allow for more sophisticated image analysis by automatically extracting features from medical images without the need for manual engineering.

2.2 Core Image Processing Techniques

Some key image processing techniques include:

Image Filtering: It is used to enhance or suppress certain features within an image. Filters, such as edge-detection or noise-reduction filters, are applied to improve the clarity of structures within medical images.

Thresholding: A method used to segment an image into different regions by selecting a pixel intensity value (threshold). For example, thresholding can separate areas of interest, such as tumors or lesions, from the background tissue.

Morphological Operations: Techniques like dilation and erosion are used to refine image boundaries and structures. These operations are useful in applications like tumor segmentation and vessel detection.

2.3 Key AI Algorithms in Medical Imaging

AI-driven intelligent image processing in medical imaging is largely powered by deep learning algorithms, which allow systems to automatically extract and learn features from large datasets. Below are three key AI algorithms that have become foundational to medical imaging is largely powered by deep learning algorithms, which allow systems to automatically extract and learn features from large datasets. Below are three key AI algorithms that have become foundational to medical imaging advancements.

2.3.1 Convolutional Neural Networks (CNNs)

CNNs are the backbone of most AI-based image processing applications, which is shown in Fig.1. It uses multiple layers of convolutional filters to detect patterns, edges, textures, and shapes within an image. They have demonstrated not typical success in tasks like classification, segmentation, and object detection. CNNs can learn hierarchical features from images without requiring manual input, enabling the detection of complex patterns, such as tumors or lesions, in radiographic images.

Figure 1. Architecture of CNN

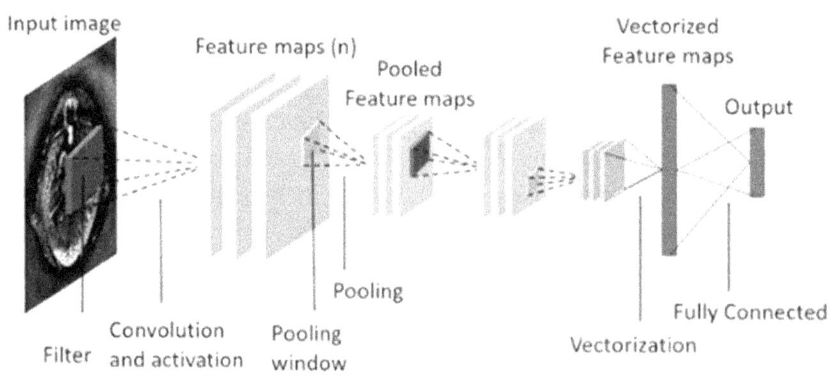

2.3.2 Generative Adversarial Networks (GANs)

GANs are a deep learning model made up of two neural networks that compete against each other.: a generator and a discriminator. The generator creates synthetic data (such as medical images), while the discriminator evaluates the authenticity of the generated images. Applications of GANs in medical imaging include data augmentation which is especially useful in rare disease diagnosis. It also showed promise in improving the quality and availability of medical imaging data, offering new possibilities for training AI models and enhancing diagnostic accuracy. The architecture of GAN is shown in Figure 2.

Figure 2. Architecture of GAN

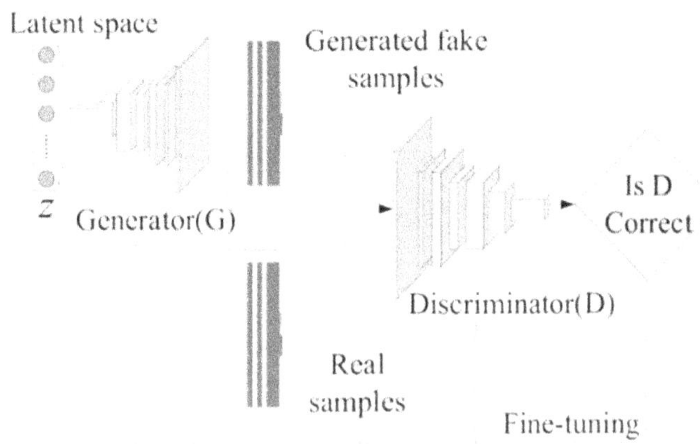

2.3.3 Advanced Image Segmentation Methods

Image segmentation, the process of dividing an image into distinct regions (e.g., organs, tissues, or lesions), is one of the most critical tasks in medical imaging. Advanced segmentation methods powered by AI algorithms are crucial for accurately identifying areas of interest in medical scans. **U-Net** is a popular deep learning architecture designed specifically for biomedical image segmentation. It consists of a contracting path that captures context and an expanding path that allows precise localization. It has been widely used in medical tasks like tumor segmentation, organ delineation, and lesion detection.

3. ENHANCING MEDICAL IMAGING MODALITIES WITH AI

Enhancing medical imaging modalities with AI has transformed traditional imaging techniques, making them more accurate, efficient, and reliable.AI incorporation in X-rays, CT scans, MRIs for better quality images and quicker analysis also leads to early diagnosis. Techniques such as deep learning are even able to detect very minute patterns a bit below the human radiologist's scale, hence resulting in giving more apt diagnoses faster. Enhanced diagnostic capabilities, optimization of workflows, and improved patient outcomes in medical imaging with AI techniques.

3.1 Magnetic Resonance Imaging

It plays a critical role in modern healthcare by enabling accurate diagnosis, treatment planning, and monitoring of diseases. With the integration of AI and machine learning, medical image processing has further evolved, improving the accuracy, speed, and reliability of diagnostic procedures, ultimately leading to better patient care (Mazurarski et.al.,2019). The sample image is shown in Figure 3

Figure 3. Magnetic resonance images of human brain

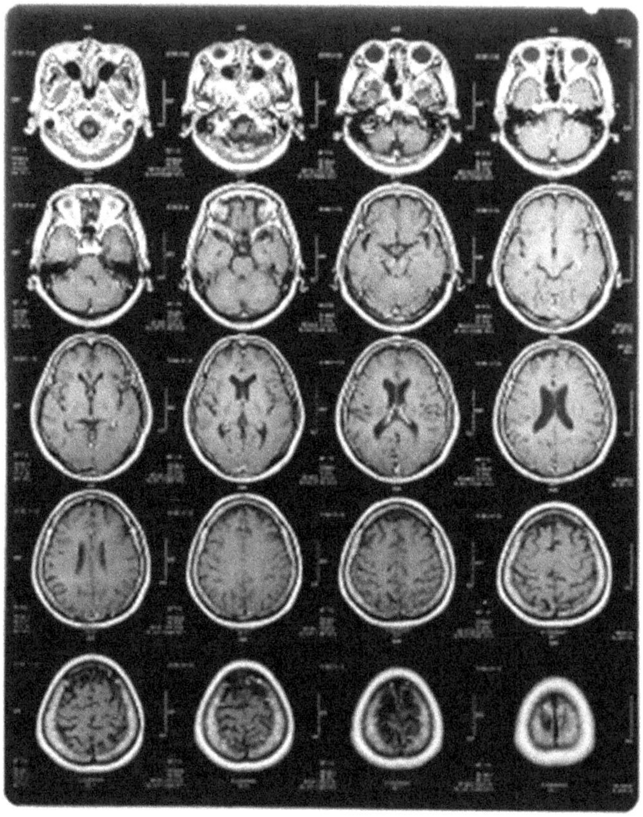

3.1.1 AI-Enhanced Image Acquisition and Analysis

AI is revolutionizing MRI by improving image acquisition, reducing scan times, and enhancing the quality of images. Traditional MRI scans can take a long time, causing discomfort for patients, but AI-driven techniques like accelerated MRI reduce scan durations without compromising image resolution. Additionally, AI algorithms enhance image analysis by automatically segmenting tissues and detecting abnormalities such as tumors, lesions, or structural anomalies. AI models also help in improving image clarity by reducing noise and motion artifacts, resulting in more accurate and reliable diagnostics for radiologists.

Neurological Disorders and Musculoskeletal Imaging is one of important case study in medical field. AI's application in MRI has been particularly impactful in the diagnosis and treatment of neurological disorders and musculoskeletal conditions. In neurological imaging, AI algorithms assist in the detection of brain tumors, Alzheimer's disease, multiple sclerosis, and other conditions by accurately analyzing brain structures and tissues. In musculoskeletal imaging, AI enhances the identification of injuries such as ligament tears, bone fractures, and joint degeneration.

3.2 Computed Tomography

It is very advanced in the imaging technique whose sample is shown in Fig.4. This combines radiographic information with the computer processing to generate detailed cross-sectional images of the body. Unlike flat, two-dimensional images, CT scans produce high-resolution three-dimensional images, which can delineate minute internal structures and abnormalities. The CT scanner rotates around the patient while capturing a multitude of X-ray images from different angles. The computer reconstructs images from the scan in order to get detailed slices of the body for medical professionals to see and study the internal organs, bones, or tissues. Diagnostic uses include the detection of tumors, fractures, and internal bleeding; hence, they play a very significant role in making plans and keeping track of the treatment of many medical conditions.

Figure 4. Sample CT images

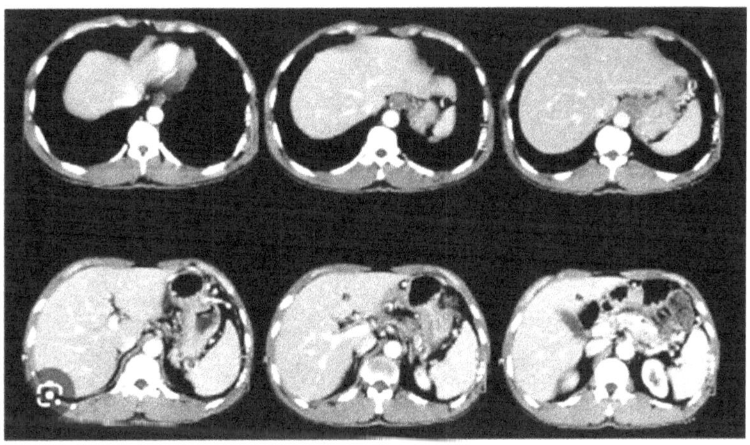

3.2.1 AI Techniques in CT Imaging

AI models automatically identify and highlight abnormalities such as tumors, fractures, or lesions within CT images, assisting radiologists in diagnosing conditions more quickly and accurately. AI techniques segment different anatomical structures or pathological regions within CT images, enabling precise analysis and measurement of tumors or other abnormalities. AI integrates data from CT scans with patient information to predict disease progression, treatment responses, and potential outcomes, supporting personalized treatment plans.

3.2.2 Applications in Oncology, Trauma, and Cardiovascular Health

In oncology, AI enhances the detection and characterization of tumors through improved image analysis and segmentation. AI algorithms can monitor tumor growth over time and assess the effectiveness of treatments (Hosny et.al.,2018). For example, AI-driven CT imaging is used for early detection of lung cancer and assessing metastasis in various cancers.

AI aids in the rapid assessment of traumatic injuries by quickly analyzing CT scans to identify internal bleeding, organ damage, or fractures. This accelerates emergency care and treatment planning. For instance, AI tools can automatically detect brain haemorrhages or spinal injuries in trauma cases as shown in Figure 5.

Figure 5. Oncology image analysis using deep learning algorithm

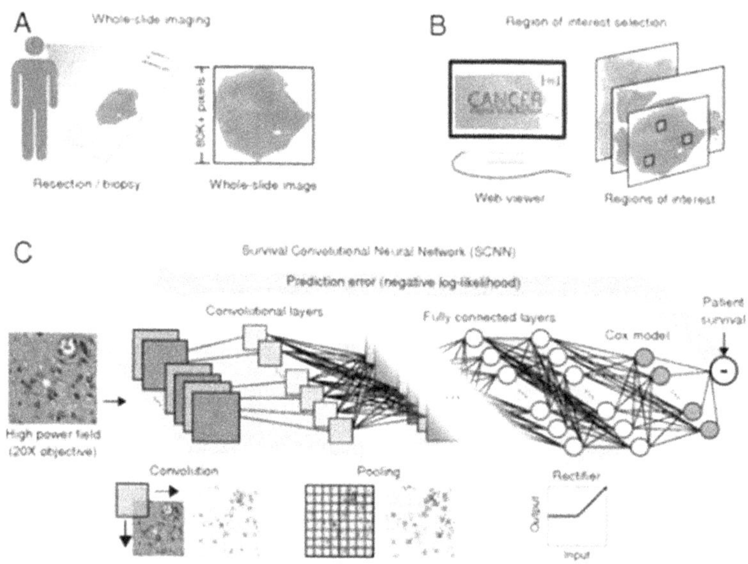

AI helps in more accurate diagnosis for cardiovascular diseases as it scans the heart and blood vessels for signs of coronary artery disease, aneurysm, or pulmonary embolism. AI evaluation also comes in handy for rating blockages and helping in preoperative planning towards intervention like angioplasty or surgery.

3.3 X-ray Imaging

X-ray imaging makes up one of the most commonly used diagnostic tools, taken advantage of the properties of electromagnetic radiation or X-rays, which are transformed into images of internal body structures. Images showing relative densities of different tissues and organs are produced using transmission of X-rays through the body and recording of the transmission rays on a detector or film. White structures, such as bones, show white on an X-ray; softer tissues, such as muscles and organs, appear shades of gray. This technology is indispensable for diagnosing fractures and infections and detecting tumors and tracing the course of diseases. Advancements in X-ray imaging, including digital radiography and computer-enhanced image processing, have dramatically improved the image quality and accuracy of diagnosis from X-ray images. X-ray imaging thus remains one of the cornerstones in modern medical diagnostics and he sample images are shown in Figure 6.

Figure 6. Sample X-ray Images

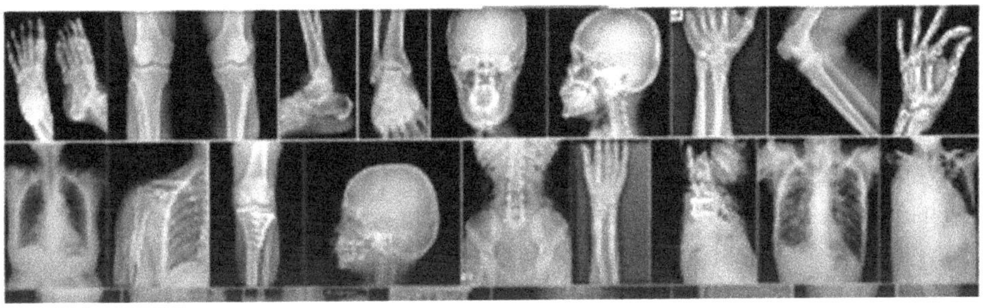

3.3.1 Intelligent Processing for Improved Diagnostic Accuracy

Enhanced Image Quality: Algorithms enhance contrast and sharpness, making it easier to identify subtle abnormalities.

Automated Detection and Analysis: AI algorithms automatically analyze X-ray images to detect and highlight potential issues such as fractures, tumors, or infections. This automation supports radiologists by providing additional insights and reducing diagnostic errors. **Quantitative analysis**: With AI-based tools, one can obtain quantitative measurements from X-rays, such as like bone density or the size of a tumor; provide diagnostic information that is much more accurate and to further clinical decisions.

Workflow Optimization: The processing is intelligent and gets the stream straight for imaging workflow by automatizing routine tasks like image segmentation and anomaly detection, getting the light expertise on more complex matters and interpretations.

3.3.2. AI in Skeletal, Pulmonary, and Dental Imaging

AI enhances the analysis of skeletal X-rays by detecting fractures, bone lesions, and signs of osteoporosis. It helps in diagnosing various conditions with greater efficiency and accuracy. In pulmonary imaging, AI aids in the identification of lung diseases such as pneumonia, tuberculosis, and lung cancer. AI algorithms can analyze chest X-rays to detect abnormal patterns or masses, improving early detection and treatment planning. AI improves the assessment of dental X-rays by automatically identifying cavities, bone loss, and other dental issues. It supports orthodontic treatment planning and helps in monitoring the progression of dental diseases or conditions (Venkatapathappa et.al.,2024).

AI enhances Digital Subtraction Angiography, a specialized X-ray technique used to visualize blood vessels. AI algorithms improve the accuracy of vessel imaging by subtracting background images and highlighting vascular structures, aiding in diagnosing and planning interventions for vascular conditions (Bumann et.al.,2024).

3.4 Ultrasound Imaging

Ultrasound imaging, or sonography, is a versatile diagnostic technique whereby high frequency sound waves are used for the creation of definite images of internal structures within the body. The process is initiated by use of a small hand-held device called a transducer that sends its sound waves towards the body; then those waves bounce off tissues and organs. These echoes are then picked up by the transducer and converted into real-time visual images by the computer. One of the key advantages of ultrasound is that it uses sound waves rather than ionizing radiation, making it a safer alternative for imaging, especially in sensitive populations such as pregnant women and children. It is having the ability to visualize soft tissues in real-time

Ultrasound is widely used in various medical fields. In obstetrics, it provides critical information about fetal development, helps monitor the health of the pregnancy, and detects potential complications. In cardiology, it evaluates heart structure and function, assessing conditions like heart valve diseases and cardiomyopathy. Moreover, advancements in ultrasound technology, including 3D and 4D imaging, have further expanded its applications, providing more detailed and dynamic views of anatomical structures.

3.4.1 AI Innovations in Real-Time Monitoring

AI algorithms automatically detect and outline key anatomical features, such as organs and blood vessels, during ultrasound imaging. This facilitates quicker and more accurate diagnoses by highlighting areas of interest in real-time (Yogi et.al., 2023). AI processes ultrasound data instantaneously, providing immediate feedback on image quality and diagnostic findings. This allows for prompt adjustments and refinements during the imaging procedure, enhancing overall diagnostic efficiency. AI-driven systems adapt imaging parameters based on patient-specific factors and imaging conditions, optimizing the quality of the ultrasound images for each individual patient.

3.4.2 Applications in Obstetrics, Cardiology, and Abdominal Imaging

In obstetrics, AI enhances prenatal imaging by improving the clarity and accuracy of fetal assessments. AI algorithms assist in detecting fetal anomalies, monitoring growth, and assessing placental health. This leads to better prenatal care and early identification of potential issues. For example, AI can automatically measure fetal biometry parameters, such as head circumference and limb length, aiding in accurate gestational age determination and growth assessments (Beser et.al.,2024).

AI applications in cardiology focus on analyzing heart function and detecting cardiovascular conditions. For example, AI-driven echocardiography tools can automatically quantify ejection fraction and detect early signs of heart failure, supporting timely intervention and treatment.

Abdominal imaging, AI enhances the evaluation of organs such as the liver, kidneys, and pancreas. It assists in identifying conditions like liver cirrhosis, kidney stones, and tumors by improving image analysis and automating the detection of abnormalities. For example, AI can help in the early detection of liver disease by analyzing ultrasound images for signs of fibrosis or steatosis, facilitating early diagnosis and management.

4. APPLICATIONS IN DISEASE DETECTION AND DIAGNOSIS

Medical imaging techniques, such as X-ray, CT scans, MRI, and ultrasound, are essential for the effective detection and diagnosis of various diseases. X-ray imaging is commonly used for its speed in diagnosing fractures, infections, and certain cancers, while CT scans offer detailed cross-sectional images crucial for identifying tumors, internal bleeding, and complex injuries. MRI provides high-resolution images of soft tissues, making it ideal for diagnosing neurological disorders, joint issues, and cancers. Ultrasound imaging, notable for its real-time capabilities and lack of ionizing radiation, is particularly useful in obstetrics, cardiology, and evaluating soft tissue abnormalities. Advanced integration of the technologies of such advanced types as AI has further pushed these techniques by allowing better image quality, automation of feature detection, and predictive analytics capabilities to continue advancing diagnostic accuracy and treatment strategies.

4.1 Cancer Detection

Cancer detection has been significantly advanced by integrating modern imaging technologies and AI, offering new possibilities for early diagnosis and personalized treatment. By leveraging sophisticated imaging techniques such as X-ray, CT scans, MRI, and ultrasound, combined with AI-powered analysis, healthcare professionals can detect cancerous abnormalities with greater accuracy and efficiency. This integration enables earlier detection of cancers, such as breast, lung, and skin cancer, often before symptoms appear, and facilitates the development of tailored treatment strategies through precision oncology. As a result, these advancements lead to improved patient outcomes and more effective management of cancer.

4.1.1 AI in Early Detection: Breast, Lung, and Skin Cancer

AI is revolutionizing cancer detection by improving early diagnosis and increasing accuracy across several types of cancer, including breast, lung, and skin cancer. AI algorithms analyze medical images to detect subtle abnormalities that might be missed by human eyes. In breast cancer, AI enhances mammogram readings by identifying potential tumors and abnormal tissue patterns with high precision, leading to earlier intervention. For lung cancer, AI-driven CT scan analysis can detect nodules and potential malignancies at an early stage, even before symptoms appear. The AI models can be trained on immense data of dermatological images, identifying suspicious lesions and distinguishing between benign growths and malignant growths, aiding detection in time with better accuracy.

4.1.2 Precision Oncology Through Advanced Imaging

Precision oncology utilizes advanced imaging techniques and AI to tailor cancer treatment to individual patients based on their unique genetic and molecular profiles. Advanced imaging methods, such as high-resolution MRI and PET scans, combined with AI algorithms, provide detailed insights into tumor characteristics, growth patterns, and response to treatment. This approach allows for more accurate staging of cancer, identification of targeted treatment options, and monitoring of treatment efficacy.

4.2 Cardiovascular imaging

Cardiovascular imaging is a critical component of diagnosing and managing heart diseases, utilizing advanced imaging techniques to visualize the heart and blood vessels. The integration of AI and machine learning into cardiovascular imaging has revolutionized how clinicians detect, monitor, and treat cardiovascular conditions. By leveraging AI algorithms, healthcare professionals can analyze imaging data from modalities such as echocardiography, MRI, and CT scans with unprecedented precision. AI enhances the accuracy of detecting abnormalities, such as coronary artery disease, heart failure, and valvular disorders, and enables real-time monitoring of patients' cardiac health. Machine learning further refines these capabilities by improving image quality, automating complex analyses, and predicting disease progression. Together, these technologies provide a comprehensive approach to cardiovascular care, offering personalized treatment plans and optimizing patient outcomes through enhanced diagnostic and monitoring tools.

4.2.1 AI for Heart Disease Detection and Monitoring

AI significantly improves heart disease detection and monitoring through advanced image analysis and pattern recognition. AI algorithms, trained on extensive datasets of cardiac images, can detect subtle abnormalities in the heart's structure and function that might be missed by traditional methods. For instance, AI enhances the detection of early signs of coronary artery disease, myocardial infarction, and arrhythmias by analyzing echocardiograms, MRI, and CT scans with high accuracy. Additionally, AI facilitates continuous patient monitoring by integrating data from wearable devices and remote sensors, providing real-time assessments of cardiac health. This capability allows for proactive management of heart conditions, timely adjustments to treatment plans, and better overall patient outcomes.

4.2.2 Enhancing Cardiac Imaging with Machine Learning

Machine learning techniques enhance cardiac imaging by refining the analysis and interpretation of complex data. These techniques improve image acquisition and processing by reducing artifacts, enhancing resolution, and increasing the clarity of cardiac images. Machine learning models can automatically segment various cardiac structures, such as ventricles and valves, enabling precise measurements of cardiac function and volume.

Additionally, predictive models use historical imaging data to forecast disease progression and treatment responses, allowing for personalized therapy strategies. By integrating machine learning with cardiac imaging, clinicians can obtain more accurate diagnoses, tailor interventions to individual patient needs, and monitor the effectiveness of treatments more effectively. This advancement leads to more precise and effective management of cardiovascular diseases.

4.3 Neurological imaging

Neuroimaging is one of the most critical areas in medicine, working to visualize and analyze the brain and the nervous system in order to diagnose and track neurological disorders. Advanced imaging technologies, including MRI, CT, and PET, are engaged in neurological imaging that may give a microscopic look into the structure, function, and pathology of the brain. Such imaging modalities help clinicians identify abnormalities, such as tumors, stroke, neurodegenerative diseases, and epilepsy. There has been an even transformation of the present scenario in the realm of neurological imaging by AI and machine learning technology: The quality it enhances, automatic analysis of complex complicated and time-consuming analyses, and early perception with minute changes in brain health. That integration of advanced technology with traditional methods of imaging has significantly enhanced the accuracy of diagnosis and the design of the treatment regime for various kinds of neurological disorders.

4.3.1 AI Techniques in Brain Imaging

AI techniques, particularly deep learning algorithms, are employed to process and interpret images from modalities such as MRI, CT, and PET scans. These techniques improve the detection of brain abnormalities by automating the identification of key features such as lesions, tumors, and structural changes. By leveraging large datasets, AI models can detect subtle changes in brain structure and function, often before symptoms manifest, providing early insights into potential neurological issues and facilitating timely intervention.

4.3.2 Applications in Stroke, Alzheimer 's disease, and Epilepsy

AI applications in neurological imaging offer significant improvements in diagnosing and managing conditions like stroke, Alzheimer's disease, and epilepsy. AI-enhanced imaging tools quickly identify and characterize stroke lesions, assess the extent of brain damage, and evaluate the risk of secondary complications. Automated algorithms can analyze CT and MRI scans to detect acute ischemic events, enabling rapid treatment decisions that are critical for patient outcomes.

AI aids in the early detection and monitoring of Alzheimer's disease by analyzing brain scans for characteristic patterns of atrophy and changes in brain volume. AI models can track disease progression and predict cognitive decline, facilitating early diagnosis and personalized treatment plans. For epilepsy, AI techniques analyze EEG and MRI data to identify epileptogenic zones and assess brain regions involved in seizures. AI-driven imaging tools help in localizing seizure foci, planning surgical interventions, and monitoring treatment efficacy, leading to better management of the condition.

5. CHALLENGES IN THE ADOPTION OF AI IN MEDICAL IMAGING

The adoption of AI in medical imaging presents several challenges despite its potential benefits. One major issue is the integration of AI systems with existing medical imaging workflows and electronic health records, which can be complex and resource-intensive. Ensuring the accuracy and reliability of AI algorithms is another critical challenge, as they must be trained on diverse and representative datasets to avoid biases and errors (Oduove et.al.,2024). Additionally, regulatory approval and compliance with medical standards pose hurdles, as AI systems must meet stringent safety and efficacy criteria. Finally, the successful implementation of AI requires healthcare professionals to adapt to new technologies through training and education, which can be a barrier in settings with limited resources. Addressing these challenges is essential for realizing the full potential of AI in enhancing medical imaging and improving patient care.

5.1 Ethical and Legal Considerations

The ethical and legal considerations surrounding the use of AI in medical imaging are crucial to ensure responsible and equitable application. Data privacy and security are major concerns, as AI systems manage sensitive patient information that must be protected against breaches and unauthorized access. The compliance with data protection regulations, such as HIPAA and GDPR, will involve a need to protect patient confidentiality. Next, there are the very complicated ethical dilemmas relating to algorithmic bias and accountability, where systems designed should avoid biased outcomes and clearly establish what the responsibility of the AI is and what remains with the human clinicians in making decisions in regard to diagnosis. Ensuring informed patient consent about AI's role in their care and the use of their data is also vital. Addressing these ethical and legal issues is key to fostering trust in AI technologies while ensuring they are used responsibly and equitably in medical practice.

Data privacy and security are paramount concerns in the use of AI in medical imaging. Medical AI systems handle vast amounts of sensitive patient data, including personal health information and imaging records, making them targets for data breaches and unauthorized access. An ensuring robust data protection measure, such as encryption, secure storage, and access controls, is essential to safeguard patient confidentiality and comply with regulations like the Health Insurance Portability and Accountability Act (HIPAA) in the U.S. and the General Data Protection Regulation (GDPR) in Europe.

With AI come several ethical dilemmas carefully to be negotiated. The most significant area of concern would be in terms of algorithmic bias, or potential for AI system. Ensuring transparency within the AI algorithms and incorporating different types of datasets into training may help to mitigate some of these biases. These uses of AI in diagnostics need to be weighed against the implications on patient consent and autonomy, ensuring that patients are aware of how their data are being used and the role of AI in their own care. These ethical considerations have to be addressed to ensure that AI technologies do not thwart trust across healthy and responsible use in medical diagnostics.

5.2 Technical and Practical Challenges

The integration of AI in medical imaging holds immense potential for improving diagnostics and patient outcome. For AI systems to perform effectively in clinical settings, they must overcome several key challenges. These include the need for large, annotated datasets to train models, ensuring the interpretability and trustworthiness of AI algorithms, and the seamless integration of AI tools into existing clinical workflows (Esmaeilzadeh et.al.,2024). Addressing these challenges is essential to ensure AI's reliable, efficient, and safe use in real-world medical environments.

5.2.1 The Need for Large Annotated Datasets

One of the significant technical challenges in developing AI for medical imaging is the requirement for large, high-quality annotated datasets. Training AI models effectively relies on extensive datasets that are accurately labelled to teach the algorithms how to recognize and interpret various medical conditions. However, obtaining these datasets can be difficult due to privacy concerns, the complexity of data annotation, and the need for expert input to ensure accuracy. Without sufficient and diverse annotated data, AI models may suffer from limited generalizability and reduced performance in real-world clinical settings.

5.2.2 Model Interpretability and Trustworthiness

Ensuring model interpretability and trustworthiness is another critical challenge in AI applications for medical imaging. This lack of transparency can hinder clinicians' ability to understand and trust AI-generated results. For AI to be effectively integrated into clinical practice, it is essential to develop models that offer insights into their decision-making processes, thereby supporting clinicians in verifying and validating AI outputs.

5.2.3 Integrating AI into Clinical Workflows

Integrating AI into existing clinical workflows presents practical challenges that need to be addressed to ensure seamless adoption. . This integration involves addressing issues such as interoperability, workflow adaptation, and the training of healthcare professionals to use new AI tools effectively. Additionally, ensuring that AI systems enhance rather than disrupt existing processes is crucial for gaining acceptance from clinicians and achieving successful implementation in healthcare settings.

6. FUTURE DIRECTIONS AND INNOVATIONS IN MEDICAL IMAGING AND DIAGNOSTICS

As medical imaging technology evolves, the integration of intelligent image processing techniques continues to pave the way for groundbreaking innovations. These advancements aim to push the boundaries of diagnostic accuracy, speed, and personalization in patient care.The future of medical imaging lies in the seamless collaboration between AI, ML, DL and imaging technologies, offering new solutions for predictive diagnostics, real-time monitoring, and more personalized treatment pathways. Innovations in quantum computing, edge AI, and AR would mean not only that medical imaging systems are efficient, adaptive, and able to handle large complex datasets but also shall change the face of healthcare itself to be far more data-driven and more patient-centered. This unlocks possibilities of new-age preventive healthcare, near real-time diagnosis, and remote medical services.

6.1 Emerging Trends in AI and Medical Imaging

AI continues to make significant strides in medical imaging, revolutionizing the way diseases are detected and treated. Another key trend is multi-modal imaging, where AI analyzes data from multiple imaging techniques (e.g., MRI, CT, PET scans) to provide a more comprehensive diagnosis. Additionally, edge AI is gaining momentum, allowing for real-time image processing at the point of care, thus reducing the need for high-end computational infrastructure. They provide scalable platforms for storing, sharing, and analyzing images globally, enhancing collaboration between healthcare professionals. These innovations aim to streamline workflows, reduce manual errors, and allow for more rapid, accurate diagnostics.

AI is at the forefront of transforming personalized medicine, with medical imaging playing a crucial role. AI-powered imaging tools can analyze a patient's unique physiological and genetic markers, enabling the identification of individual disease risk factors and treatment responses. Predictive imaging models are being developed to forecast how diseases might progress in a specific patient, allowing for earlier and more targeted interventions.

6.2 Potential Innovations in Intelligent Image Processing

The next generation of intelligent image processing is expected to incorporate advances like quantum computing, which could dramatically accelerate image analysis by processing large datasets faster and with more accuracy. Neural networks are being trained to identify patterns in medical images that are too subtle for human interpretation, such as the early stages of diseases like Alzheimer's or Parkinson's. Additionally, 3D image segmentation and augmented reality (AR) tools are gaining traction, helping surgeons visualize real-time anatomical structures during operations with greater precision. These innovations promise to make medical imaging more intelligent, adaptive, and capable of handling complex cases, ultimately pushing the boundaries of diagnostic and therapeutic imaging techniques.

6.3 The Future Impact on Healthcare Outcomes

The incorporation of intelligent image processing in medical imaging is expected to have a profound impact on healthcare outcomes. Early detection of diseases, aided by AI and image processing, will lead to earlier interventions, reducing the need for aggressive treatments and improving survival rates. AI-assisted diagnostic tools will minimize diagnostic errors, particularly in complex cases where human interpretation may be limited. In resource-limited settings, these innovations can make advanced medical imaging more accessible, thus improving healthcare equity. Remote diagnostics via AI-driven telemedicine platforms will further extend the reach of specialized medical services, particularly in rural or underserved areas. Over time, the convergence of AI and medical imaging will enhance patient outcomes by providing more accurate, efficient, and personalized care across the globe.This future direction will drive data-driven healthcare that not only improves diagnosis and treatment but also empowers preventive care, leading to reduced healthcare costs and improved overall population health.

7. CONCLUSIONS

The integration of intelligent image processing techniques into medical imaging and diagnostics is reshaping the future of healthcare. As we look toward the future, the continued development of these technologies promises to revolutionize not only how we detect diseases but also how we manage patient care, making healthcare more proactive, precise, and accessible. This investigation underscored extreme impacts of intelligent image processing techniques on medical imaging and diagnostics. Some of the major discoveries are that the use of AI and deep learning algorithms in majority cases improves the speed, accuracy, and efficiency of diagnostic processes. It could identify fatal complex diseases earlier than before, reduce manual errors, and the diagnosis automatically advanced the care for the patients. Indeed, innovations such as multi-modal imaging and 3D image segmentation are providing more holistic views and allowing clinicians to make rapid, informed decisions.

The evolution of medical imaging is tightly intertwined with advancements in AI and machine learning. Edge AI, quantum computing, and real-time imaging technologies will continue to push the boundaries, allowing for instant analysis of medical images, even in remote and resource-limited settings. As AI systems grow more powerful, they will refine their ability to predict disease progression, tailor treatments, and integrate with other healthcare data sources, driving a revolution in precision medicine.

With regulatory frameworks evolving, the adoption of AI-driven medical imaging tools will become more seamless, further integrating with clinical workflows.

REFERENCES

Beser, B., Reis, T., Berber, M. N., Topaloglu, E., Gungor, E., Kılıc, M. C., Duman, S., Çelik, Ö., Kuran, A., & Bayrakdar, I. S. (2024, July 11). YOLO-V5 based deep learning approach for tooth detection and segmentation on pediatric panoramic radiographs in mixed dentition. *BMC Medical Imaging*, *24*(1), 172. DOI: 10.1186/s12880-024-01338-w PMID: 38992601

Bumann, E. E., Al-Qarni, S., Chandrashekar, G., Sabzian, R., Bohaty, B., & Lee, Y. (2024). A novel collaborative learning model for mixed dentition and fillings segmentation in panoramic radiographs. *Journal of Dentistry*, *140*, 104779. DOI: 10.1016/j.jdent.2023.104779 PMID: 38007173

Esmaeilzadeh, P. (2024, May). Challenges and strategies for wide-scale artificial intelligence (AI) deployment in healthcare practices: A perspective for healthcare organizations. *Artificial Intelligence in Medicine*, *151*, 102861. DOI: 10.1016/j.artmed.2024.102861 PMID: 38555850

Gurnani, B., Kaur, K., Lalgudi, V. G., Kundu, G., Mimouni, M., Liu, H., Jhanji, V., Prakash, G., Roy, A. S., Shetty, R., & Gurav, J. S. (2024, September). Role of artificial intelligence, machine learning and deep learning models in corneal disorders - A narrative review. *Journal Français d'Ophtalmologie*, *47*(7), 104242. DOI: 10.1016/j.jfo.2024.104242 PMID: 39013268

Hosny, A., Parmar, C., Quackenbush, J., Schwartz, L. H., & Aerts, H. J. W. L. (2018, August). Artificial intelligence in radiology. *Nature Reviews. Cancer*, *18*(8), 500–510. DOI: 10.1038/s41568-018-0016-5 PMID: 29777175

Khalifa, M., & Albadawy, M. AI in diagnostic imaging: Revolutionising accuracy and efficiency, Computer Methods and Programs in Biomedicine Update, Volume 5,2024,100146, ISSN 2666-9900, DOI: 10.1016/j.cmpbup.2024.100146

Mazurowski, M. A., Buda, M., Saha, A., & Bashir, M. R. (2019, April). Deep learning in radiology: An overview of the concepts and a survey of the state of the art with focus on MRI. *Journal of Magnetic Resonance Imaging*, *49*(4), 939–954. DOI: 10.1002/jmri.26534 PMID: 30575178

Oduoye, M. O., Fatima, E., Muzammil, M. A., Dave, T., Irfan, H., Fariha, F. N. U., Marbell, A., Ubechu, S. C., Scott, G. Y., & Elebesunu, E. E. (2024, January 4). Impacts of the advancement in artificial intelligence on laboratory medicine in low- and middle-income countries: Challenges and recommendations-A literature review. *Health Science Reports*, *7*(1), e1794. DOI: 10.1002/hsr2.1794 PMID: 38186931

Pinto-Coelho, L. (2023, December 18). How Artificial Intelligence Is Shaping Medical Imaging Technology: A Survey of Innovations and Applications. *Bioengineering (Basel, Switzerland)*, *10*(12), 1435. DOI: 10.3390/bioengineering10121435 PMID: 38136026

Venkatapathappa, P., Sultana, A., K S, V., Mansour, R., Chikkanarayanappa, V., & Rangareddy, H. (2024, February 29). K S V, Mansour R, Chikkanarayanappa V, Rangareddy H. Ocular Pathology and Genetics: Transformative Role of Artificial Intelligence (AI) in Anterior Segment Diseases. *Cureus*, *16*(2), e55216. DOI: 10.7759/cureus.55216 PMID: 38435218

Yagi, M., Yamanouchi, K., Fujita, N., Funao, H., & Ebata, S. (2023, June 21). Revolutionizing Spinal Care: Current Applications and Future Directions of Artificial Intelligence and Machine Learning. *Journal of Clinical Medicine*, *12*(13), 4188. DOI: 10.3390/jcm12134188 PMID: 37445222

Compilation of References

Aamir, M., Rehman, Z., Pu, Y. F., Ahmed, A., & Abro, W. A. (2019). Image enhancement in varying light conditions based on wavelet transform. *2019 16th International Computer Conference on Wavelet Active Media Technology and Information Processing*, Chengdu, China, pp. 317-322. https://doi.org/ DOI: 10.1109/ICCWAMTIP47768.2019.9067714

Aamir, M., Bazai, S., Bhatti, U. A., Dayo, Z. A., Liu, J., & Zhang, K. (2023). Applications of Machine Learning in Medicine: Current Trends and Prospects. *2023 Global Conference on Wireless and Optical Technologies, GCWOT 2023*. DOI: 10.1109/GCWOT57803.2023.10064665

Aamir, M., Bhatti, M. A., Bazai, S. U., Marjan, S., Mirza, A. M., Wahid, A., Hasnain, A., & Bhatti, U. A. (2022). Predicting the environmental change of carbon emission patterns in South Asia: A Deep Learning approach using BiLSTM. *Atmosphere (Basel)*, *13*(12), 2011. DOI: 10.3390/atmos13122011

Aamir, M., Gao, J., Zhang, Y., Tang, H., & Bhatti, U. A. (2025). Overview of underwater object detection based on image processing techniques. *Proceedings of the 2024 7th International Conference on Pattern Recognition and Artificial Intelligence.*

Aamir, M., Pu, Y. F., Abro, W. A., Naeem, H., & Rahman, Z. (2017). A hybrid approach for object proposal generation. In *International Conference on Sensing and Imaging* (pp. 251-259). Springer, Cham. https://doi.org/DOI: 10.1007/978-3-319-91659-0_18

Aamir, M., Pu, Y. F., Rahman, Z., Abro, W. A., Naeem, H., Ullah, F., & Badr, A. M. (2018). A hybrid proposed framework for object detection and classification. *Journal of Information Processing Systems*, *14*(5), 1176–1194. DOI: 10.3745/JIPS.02.0095

Aamir, M., Pu, Y. F., Rahman, Z., Tahir, M., Naeem, H., & Dai, Q. (2018). A framework for automatic building detection from low-contrast satellite images. *Symmetry*, *11*(1), 3. DOI: 10.3390/sym11010003

Aamir, M., Rahman, Z., Abro, W. A., Bhatti, U. A., Dayo, Z. A., & Ishfaq, M. (2023). A Progressive Approach to Generic Object Detection: A Two-Stage Framework for Image Recognition. *Computers, Materials & Continua*, *75*(3), 6351–6373. DOI: 10.32604/cmc.2023.038173

Aamir, M., Rahman, Z., Abro, W. A., Bhatti, U. A., Dayo, Z. A., & Ishfaq, M. (2023). Brain tumor classification utilizing deep features derived from high-quality regions in MRI images. *Biomedical Signal Processing and Control*, *85*, 104988. DOI: 10.1016/j.bspc.2023.104988

Aamir, M., Rahman, Z., Abro, W. A., Tahir, M., & Ahmed, S. M. (2019). An optimized architecture of image classification using convolutional neural network. *International Journal of Image. Graphics and Signal Processing*, *10*(10), 30–39. DOI: 10.5815/ijigsp.2019.10.05

Aamir, M., Rahman, Z., Dayo, Z. A., Abro, W. A., Uddin, M. I., Khan, I., Imran, A. S., Ali, Z., Ishfaq, M., Guan, Y., & Hu, Z. (2022). A deep learning approach for brain tumor classification using MRI images. *Computers & Electrical Engineering*, *101*, 108105. DOI: 10.1016/j.compeleceng.2022.108105

Aamir, M., Rahman, Z., Pu, Y. F., Abro, W. A., & Gulzar, K. (2019). Satellite image enhancement using wavelet-domain based on singular value decomposition. *International Journal of Advanced Computer Science and Applications*, *10*(6). Advance online publication. DOI: 10.14569/IJACSA.2019.0100667

Aavula, R.. (2022). Design and Implementation of sensor and IoT based Remembrance system for closed one. *Telematique*, *21*(1), 2769–2778.

Abbas, A., Jain, S., Gour, M., & Vankudothu, S. (2021). Tomato plant disease detection using transfer learning with C-GAN synthetic images. *Computers and Electronics in Agriculture*, *187*, 106279. DOI: 10.1016/j.compag.2021.106279

Abdalla, Y., Iqbal, M., & Shehata, M. (2019). T SHEHATA M "Convolutional Neural Network for Copy-Move Forgery Detection". *Symmetry*, *11*(10), 1280. DOI: 10.3390/sym11101280

Abdulahi, A. T., Ogundokun, R. O., Adenike, A. R., Shah, M. A., & Ahmed, Y. K. (2024). PulmoNet: A novel Deep Learning based pulmonary diseases detection model. *BMC Medical Imaging*, *24*(1), 51. DOI: 10.1186/s12880-024-01227-2 PMID: 38418987

Abhangrao, C. M. (2024). Internet of Things in Mechatronics for Design and Manufacturing: A Review. *Journals of Mechatronics Machine Design and Manufacturing*, *6*(1).

Abhishek, M, Manjushree, H.C, & Mohan Kumar, G.T, NALLABOTHULA SNEHA, SMITHA B.N. (2023). Image Forgery Detection Using Ensemble of VGG 16 and CNN Architecture. *International Journal of Computational Learning & Intelligence*, *2*(3), 122–135.

Abid Ali Awan. (2022a). *Recurrent Neural Network Tutorial (RNN)*. Datacamp.

Abid Ali Awan. (2022b, March). *Recurrent Neural Network Tutorial (RNN)*. Datacamp.

Abinaya, M., Vadivu, G., & Sundaravadivazhagan, B. (2024). 10 Future Directions and Open Problems in Generative AI. In Balasubramaniam, S., Kadry, S., Prasanth, A., & Kumar Dhanaraj, R. (Eds.), *Generative AI and LLMs: Natural Language Processing and Generative Adversarial Networks* (pp. 193–212). De Gruyter., DOI: 10.1515/9783111425078-010

Abukmeil, M., Ferrari, S., Genovese, A., Piuri, V., & Scotti, F. (2021). A Survey of Unsupervised Generative Models for Exploratory Data Analysis and Representation Learning. *ACM Computing Surveys*, *54*(5), 1–40. Advance online publication. DOI: 10.1145/3450963

Abut, S., Okut, H., & Kallail, K. J. (2023). Paradigm shift from Artificial Neural Networks (ANNs) to deep Convolution Neural Networks (DCNNs) in the field of medical image processing. *Expert Systems with Applications*, •••, 122983.

Agarwal, S. R., Agrawal, S. B., & Latif, A. M. (2015). Sentence formation in NLP engine on the basis of indian sign language using hand gestures. *International Journal of Computer Applications*, *116*(17). Advance online publication. DOI: 10.5120/20428-2757

Agarwal, S., Pandey, G. N., & Tiwari, M. D. (2012). Data mining in education: Data classification and decision tree approach. *International Journal of e-Education, e-Business, e-. Management Learning*, *2*(2), 140.

Aha, D. W., Kibler, D., & Albert, M. K. (1991). Instance-based learning algorithms. *Machine Learning*, *6*(1), 37–66. DOI: 10.1007/BF00153759

Ahila Priyadharshini, R., Arivazhagan, S., Arun, M., & Mirnalini, A. (2019). Maize leaf disease classification using deep convolutional neural networks. *Neural Computing & Applications*, *31*(12), 8887–8895. DOI: 10.1007/s00521-019-04228-3

Ahmad, F., & Xu, J. (2023). Machine learning-based preoperative planning for dental implants: Predicting implant success rates. *International Journal of Oral and Maxillofacial Surgery*, *52*(4), 509–516.

Ahmed, T. and S. N. (n.d.). *Classification and understanding of cloud structures via satellite images with EfficientUNet.*

Ahmed, H., Zhang, Q., Donnan, R., & Alomainy, A. (2024). Denoising of Optical Coherence Tomography Images in Ophthalmology Using Deep Learning: A Systematic Review. *Journal of Imaging*, *10*(4), 86. DOI: 10.3390/jimaging10040086 PMID: 38667984

Ahmed, M., Seraj, R., & Islam, S. M. S. (2020). The k-means Algorithm: A Comprehensive Survey and Performance Evaluation. *Electronics (Basel)*, *9*(8), 1295. Advance online publication. DOI: 10.3390/electronics9081295

AIML. (2024). *Compare the different sequence models rnn lstm gru and transformers*. AIML.

Akada, K., Yagi, T., Miura, Y., Beuckmann, C. T., Koyama, N., & Aoshima, K. (2021). A deep learning algorithm for sleep stage scoring in mice based on a multimodal network with fine-tuning technique. *Neuroscience Research*, *173*, 99–105. https://doi.org/https://doi.org/10.1016/j.neures.2021.07.003. DOI: 10.1016/j.neures.2021.07.003 PMID: 34280429

Akram, S., Bazai, S. U., & Marjan, S. (2024). Classifying Traffic Signs Using Convolutional Neural Networks Based on Deep Learning Models. In Deep Learning for Multimedia Processing Applications (pp. 250-269). CRC Press.

Aktaş, H., Kızıldeniz, T., & Ünal, Z. (2022). Classification of pistachios with deep learning and assessing the effect of various datasets on accuracy. *Journal of Food Measurement and Characterization*, *16*(3), 1983–1996. DOI: 10.1007/s11694-022-01313-5

Al'Aref, S. J., Anchouche, K., Singh, G., Slomka, P. J., Kolli, K. K., Kumar, A., Pandey, M., Maliakal, G., van Rosendael, A. R., Beecy, A. N., Berman, D. S., Leipsic, J., Nieman, K., Andreini, D., Pontone, G., Schoepf, U. J., Shaw, L. J., Chang, H.-J., Narula, J., & Min, J. K. (2019). Clinical applications of machine learning in cardiovascular disease and its relevance to cardiac imaging. *European Heart Journal*, *40*(24), 1975–1986. DOI: 10.1093/eurheartj/ehy404 PMID: 30060039

Alakuş, T. B. (2024). *Baykara M Classification and Determination of Severity of Corneal Ulcer with Vision Transformer Based on the Analysis of Public Image Dataset of Fluorescein-Stained Corneas.* Diagnostics.

Alam, F. B., Podder, P., & Mondal, M. R. H. (2023). RVCNet: A hybrid deep neural network framework for the diagnosis of lung diseases. *PLoS One*, *18*(12), e0293125. DOI: 10.1371/journal.pone.0293125 PMID: 38153925

Alder, S. (2024, January 31). Security Breaches in Healthcare in 2023. *The HIPAA Journal*. https://www.hipaajournal.com/security-breaches-in-healthcare/

Aldrees, A., Khan, M., Taha, A. T. B., & Ali, M. (2024). Evaluation of water quality indexes with novel machine learning and SHapley Additive ExPlanation (SHAP) approaches. *Journal of Water Process Engineering*, *58*, 104789. DOI: 10.1016/j.jwpe.2024.104789

Alharbi, K. S., Fuloria, N. K., Fuloria, S., Rahman, S. B., Al-Malki, W. H., Shaikh, M. A. J., & Gupta, G. (2021). Nuclear factor-kappa B and its role in inflammatory lung disease. *Chemico-Biological Interactions*, *345*, 109568. DOI: 10.1016/j.cbi.2021.109568 PMID: 34181887

Alhatami, E., & Bhatti, U. A. (2024). Advanced fuzzy denoising technique for agricultural remote sensing: Modified partition filter for suppressing impulsive noise. *IEEE Access : Practical Innovations, Open Solutions*, *12*, 159025–159035. DOI: 10.1109/ACCESS.2024.3447704

Ali, A. (2021). Implementation of etl tool for data warehousing for non-hodgkin lymphoma (nhl) cancer in public sector, pakistan. *LC International Journal of STEM (ISSN: 2708-7123)*, *2*(3), 98-102.

Ali, A. (2021). Implementation of ETL Tool for Data Warehousing for Non-Hodgkin Lymphoma (NHL) Cancer in Public Sector, Pakistan. *LC International Journal of STEM (ISSN: 2708-7123)*, *2*(3), 98-102.

Ali, B. (2022). Pros and cons of GAN evaluation measures: New developments. *Computer Vision and Image Understanding*, *215*, 103329. DOI: 10.1016/j.cviu.2021.103329

Ali, R., Chuah, J. H., Talip, M. S. A., Mokhtar, N., & Shoaib, M. A. (2021). Automatic pixel-level crack segmentation in images using fully convolutional neural network based on residual blocks and pixel local weights. *Engineering Applications of Artificial Intelligence*, *104*, 104391. DOI: 10.1016/j.engappai.2021.104391

Ali, S. D., Ganapathi, I. I., Saxena, N., & Syed Sadaf Ali, S. S. (2022). WERGHI "Image Forgery Detection Using Deep Learning by Recompressing Images". *Electronics (Basel)*, *11*(3), 403. DOI: 10.3390/electronics11030403

Al-Kadi, O., Al-Emaryeen, R., Al-Nahhas, S., Almallahi, I., Braik, R., & Mahafza, W. (2024). Empowering brain cancer diagnosis: Harnessing artificial intelligence for advanced imaging insights. *Reviews in the Neurosciences*, *35*(4), 399–419. DOI: 10.1515/revneuro-2023-0115 PMID: 38291768

Alkanan, M., & Gulzar, Y. (2024). Enhanced corn seed disease classification: Leveraging MobileNetV2 with feature augmentation and transfer learning. *Frontiers in Applied Mathematics and Statistics*, *9*, 1320177. Advance online publication. DOI: 10.3389/fams.2023.1320177

Almadhor, , Sattar, U., Al Hejaili, A., Ghulam Mohammad, U., Tariq, U., & Ben Chikha, H. (2022). An efficient computer vision-based approach for acute lymphoblastic leukemia prediction. *Frontiers in Computational Neuroscience*, *16*, 1083649. DOI: 10.3389/fncom.2022.1083649 PMID: 36507304

Amri, E., Gulzar, Y., Yeafi, A., Jendoubi, S., Dhawi, F., & Mir, M. S. (2024). Advancing automatic plant classification system in Saudi Arabia: Introducing a novel dataset and ensemble deep learning approach. *Modeling Earth Systems and Environment*, *10*(2), 2693–2709. Advance online publication. DOI: 10.1007/s40808-023-01918-9

Anand, S., Mittal, S., Tuzel, O., & Meer, P. (2014). Semi-Supervised Kernel Mean Shift Clustering. *IEEE Transactions on Pattern Analysis and Machine Intelligence*, *36*(6), 1201–1215. DOI: 10.1109/TPAMI.2013.190 PMID: 26353281

Anand, V., Gupta, S., Gupta, D., Gulzar, Y., Xin, Q., Juneja, S., Shah, A., & Shaikh, A. (2023). Weighted Average Ensemble Deep Learning Model for Stratification of Brain Tumor in MRI Images. *Diagnostics (Basel)*, *13*(7), 1320. Advance online publication. DOI: 10.3390/diagnostics13071320 PMID: 37046538

Angiulli, F., Fassetti, F., & Ferragina, L. (2023, May 17). *Reconstruction Error-based Anomaly Detection with Few Outlying Examples*. arXiv.Org. https://arxiv.org/abs/2305.10464v2

Ang, L., Ghosh, P., & Seow, W. J. (2021). Association between previous lung diseases and lung cancer risk: A systematic review and meta-analysis. *Carcinogenesis*, *42*(12), 1461–1474. DOI: 10.1093/carcin/bgab082 PMID: 34487521

Anwar Ali Sathio and Arz Muhammad Brohi. (2021). The Imperative Role of Pervasive Data in Healthcare. In Switzerland, A. G. (Ed.), *Dr. Mohammad Shahid Husain, Dr. Muhamad Hariz Bin Muhamad Adnan, Dr. Mohammad Zunnun Khan, Dr. Saurabh Shukla, and Fahad U Khan* (pp. 17–21). Springer., DOI: 10.1007/978-3-030-77746-3_2

Arab, H., Ghaffari, I., Evina, R. M., Tatu, S. O., & Dufour, S. (2022). A hybrid LSTM-ResNet deep neural network for noise reduction and classification of V-band receiver signals. *IEEE Access : Practical Innovations, Open Solutions*, *10*, 14797–14806. DOI: 10.1109/ACCESS.2022.3147980

Archana, R., & Jeevaraj, P. E. (2024). Deep learning models for digital image processing: A review. *Artificial Intelligence Review*, *57*(1), 11. DOI: 10.1007/s10462-023-10631-z

Arivazhagan, S. E. L. V. A. R. A. J., Newlin, S. H. E. B. I. A. H., & Saranyaa, M. (2024). Image forgery detection: Comprehensive review of digital forensics approaches. *Journal of Computational Social Science*, *1*, 39. DOI: 10.1007/s42001 024-00265-8

Ashraf Zargar, S. (n.d.). *Introduction to Sequence Learning Models: RNN, LSTM*. GRU.

Ashraf, K., Nawar, S., Hosen, M. H., Islam, M. T., & Uddin, M. N. (2024, March). Beyond the Black Box: Employing LIME and SHAP for Transparent Health Predictions with Machine Learning Models. In 2024 International Conference on Advances in Computing, Communication, Electrical, and Smart Systems (iCACCESS) (pp. 1-6). IEEE.

Ashraf, R., Habib, M. A., Akram, M., Latif, M. A., Malik, M. S. A., Awais, M., Dar, S. H., Mahmood, T., Yasir, M., & Abbas, Z. (2020). Deep convolution neural network for big data medical image classification. *IEEE Access : Practical Innovations, Open Solutions*, *8*, 105659–105670. DOI: 10.1109/ACCESS.2020.2998808

Atila, U., Uçar, M., Akyol, K., & Uçar, E. (2021). Plant leaf disease classification using EfficientNet deep learning model. *Ecological Informatics*, *61*, 101182. DOI: 10.1016/j.ecoinf.2020.101182

Audebert, N., & Le Saux, B., & R. (. (2020). Land use classification with deep learning: A review. *Remote Sensing*, *12*(5), 807. DOI: 10.3390/rs12050807

Averbuch, A., Neittaanmäki, P., Zheludev, V., Salhov, M., & Hauser, J. (2022). An hybrid denoising algorithm based on directional wavelet packets. *Multidimensional Systems and Signal Processing*, *33*(4), 1151–1183. DOI: 10.1007/s11045-022-00836-w

Ayatollahi, H., Gholamhosseini, L., & Salehi, M. (2019). Predicting coronary artery disease: A comparison between two data mining algorithms. *BMC Public Health*, *19*(1), 1–9. DOI: 10.1186/s12889-019-6721-5 PMID: 31035958

Ayoub, S., Gulzar, Y., Reegu, F. A., & Turaev, S. (2022). Generating Image Captions Using Bahdanau Attention Mechanism and Transfer Learning. *Symmetry*, *14*(12), 2681. Advance online publication. DOI: 10.3390/sym14122681

Ayoub, S., Gulzar, Y., Rustamov, J., Jabbari, A., Reegu, F. A., & Turaev, S. (2023). Adversarial Approaches to Tackle Imbalanced Data in Machine Learning. *Sustainability (Basel)*, *15*(9), 7097. Advance online publication. DOI: 10.3390/su15097097

Azizi, S.. (2021). "Big Self-Supervised Models Advance Medical Image Classification." *Proceedings of ICCV*, 2021. DOI: 10.1109/ICCV48922.2021.00346

Badrinarayanan, V., Kendall, A., & Cipolla, R. (2017). SegNet: A deep convolutional encoder-decoder architecture for image segmentation. *IEEE Transactions on Pattern Analysis and Machine Intelligence*, *39*(12), 2481–2495. DOI: 10.1109/TPAMI.2016.2644615 PMID: 28060704

Bai, Y., Li, S., Ju, R.-Y., Yang, Z., Yu, J., & Chiang, J.-S. (2024). *FAD-SAR: A Novel Fishing Activity Detection System via Synthetic Aperture Radar Images Based on Deep Learning Method* (arXiv:2404.18245). arXiv. https://doi.org//arXiv.2404.18245DOI: 10.1109/ISPACS62486.2024.10869003

Baker, S. (2020). Limitations of traditional weather forecasting models. *Meteorological Applications*, *27*(3), e1928. DOI: 10.1002/met.1928

Baloch, L., Bazai, S. U., Marjan, S., Aftab, F., Aslam, S., Neo, T. K., & Amphawan, A. (2023). A Review of Big Data Trends and Challenges in Healthcare. *International Journal of Technology*, *14*(6), 1320–1333. DOI: 10.14716/ijtech.v14i6.6643

Balsa, J. (2020). Comparison of Image Compressions: Analog Transformations. *Proceedings*, *54*, 37.

Banerjee, N., & Das, S. (2020, March). Prediction lung cancer–in machine learning perspective. In 2020 International conference on computer science, engineering and applications (ICCSEA) (pp. 1-5). IEEE. DOI: 10.1109/ICCSEA49143.2020.9132913

Bankman, I. N. (Ed.). (2000). *Handbook of Medical Imaging: Processing and Analysis Management*. Academic Press.

Bansal, M., Goyal, A., & Choudhary, A. (2022). A comparative analysis of K-Nearest Neighbor, Genetic, Support Vector Machine, Decision Tree, and Long Short Term Memory algorithms in machine learning. *Decision Analytics Journal, 3*, 100071. https://doi.org/https://doi.org/10.1016/j.dajour.2022.100071

Banupriya, N., Nirmala, G., & Vijayaraghavan, N. (2024). 17 Image Dehazing Using Quaternion Complex Algebra-Based Neural Networks. In Yadav, S., Kumar, A., Dubey, A., de Albuquerque, V., Rodriguez-Aguiñaga, A., & Quezada, A. (Eds.), *Medical Image Processing: Multimodal Fusion Techniques* (pp. 255–270). De Gruyter., DOI: 10.1515/9783111435978-017

Bao, W., & Xiao, R. (2019). Taskonomy: Transferring task representations across diverse domains. *Proceedings of the IEEE Conference on Computer Vision and Pattern Recognition*, 8203-8212.

Bao, Z., Zhang, G., Xiong, B., & Gai, S. (2020). New image denoising algorithm using monogenic wavelet transform and improved deep convolutional neural network. *Multimedia Tools and Applications*, *79*(11), 7401–7412. DOI: 10.1007/s11042-019-08569-y

Baudin, C., Vacquier, B., Thin, G., Chenene, L., Guersen, J., Partarrieu, I., Louet, M., Ducou Le Pointe, H., Mora, S., Verdun-Esquer, C., Feuardent, J., Rousseau, F., Roy, H., Bensefa-Colas, L., Boyer, L., & Bernier, M. O. (2023). Occupational exposure to ionizing radiation in medical staff: Trends during the 2009–2019 period in a multicentric study. *European Radiology*, *33*(8), 5675–5684. DOI: 10.1007/s00330-023-09541-z PMID: 36930262

Bauer, P., Thorpe, A., & Brunet, G. (2015). The quiet revolution of numerical weather prediction. *Nature*, *525*(7567), 47–55. DOI: 10.1038/nature14956 PMID: 26333465

Bay, H., Ess, A., Tuytelaars, T., & Van Gool, L. (2008). Speeded-Up Robust Features (SURF). *Computer Vision and Image Understanding*, *110*(3), 346–359. https://doi.org/https://doi.org/10.1016/j.cviu.2007.09.014. DOI: 10.1016/j.cviu.2007.09.014

Behmanesh, R., Rahimi, I., Zandieh, M., & Gandomi, A. H. (2020). Advanced ant colony optimization in healthcare scheduling. Evolutionary Computation in Scheduling, 37-72. DOI: 10.1016/j.arr.2020.101124 PMID: 32683040

Bengio, Y., Courville, A., & Vincent, P. (2013). Representation learning: A review and new perspectives. *IEEE Transactions on Pattern Analysis and Machine Intelligence*, *35*(8), 1798–1828. DOI: 10.1109/TPAMI.2013.50 PMID: 23787338

Bergamin, L., Carraro, T., Polato, M., & Aiolli, F. (2022). Novel Applications for VAE-based Anomaly Detection Systems. arXiv preprint arXiv:2204.12577. https://doi.org//arXiv.2204.12577DOI: 10.1109/IJCNN55064.2022.9892879

Berghoff, C., Neu, M., & von Twickel, A. (2021). The interplay of AI and biometrics: Challenges and opportunities. *Computer*, *54*(9), 80–85. DOI: 10.1109/MC.2021.3084656

Berk, L. S., Liu, Y., & Weng, X. (2020). Quantum computing and the future of artificial intelligence. *Nature Reviews. Physics*, *2*(7), 1–14.

Beser, B., Reis, T., Berber, M. N., Topaloglu, E., Gungor, E., Kılıc, M. C., Duman, S., Çelik, Ö., Kuran, A., & Bayrakdar, I. S. (2024, July 11). YOLO-V5 based deep learning approach for tooth detection and segmentation on pediatric panoramic radiographs in mixed dentition. *BMC Medical Imaging*, *24*(1), 172. DOI: 10.1186/s12880-024-01338-w PMID: 38992601

Bhatti, U. A., Bazai, S. U., Hussain, S., Fakhar, S., Ku, C. S., Marjan, S., Yee, P. L., & Jing, L. (2023). Deep Learning-Based Trees Disease Recognition and Classification Using Hyperspectral Data. *Computers, Materials & Continua*, *77*(1), 681–697. DOI: 10.32604/cmc.2023.037958

Bhatti, U. A., Huang, M., Neira-Molina, H., Marjan, S., Baryalai, M., Tang, H., Wu, G., & Bazai, S. U. (2023). MFFCG – Multi feature fusion for hyperspectral image classification using graph attention network. *Expert Systems with Applications*, *229*, 120496. https://doi.org/https://doi.org/10.1016/j.eswa.2023.120496. DOI: 10.1016/j.eswa.2023.120496

Bhatti, U. A., Yu, Y. K., Mamyrbayev, O. Z., Aitkazina, A. A., Hao, T., & Zhumazhan, N. O. (2025). Recommendations for healthcare: An interpretable approach using deep learning. *Proceedings of the 2024 7th International Conference on Pattern Recognition and Artificial Intelligence.*

Bi, X., Wei, Y., & Xiao, B. "C2R Net: The Course to Refined Network for Image Forgery Detection". In Proceedings of the 2018 17th IEEE International Conference on Trust, Security and Privacy in Computing Furthermore, Communication, New York, NY, USA, 1¬¬ 3 August 2018; pp. 1656 1659.

Birajadar, P., Haria, M., Kulkarni, P., Gupta, S., Joshi, P., Singh, B., & Gadre, V. (2019). Towards smartphone-based touchless fingerprint recognition. *Sadhana*, *44*(7), 1–15. DOI: 10.1007/s12046-019-1138-5

Bi, X., Li, W., Wei, Y., & Xiao, B. "RRU-Net: The Ringed Residual U ¬Net for Image Splicing Forgery Detection". In *Proceedings of the IEEE/CVF Conference on Computer Vision and Pattern Recognition (CVPR) Workshops*, Long Beach, CA, USA, 15 20 June 2019. DOI: 10.1109/CVPRW.2019.00010

Boesch, G. (2023). *Vision Transformers (ViT) in Image Recognition – 2024 Guide*. Https://Viso.Ai/Deep-Learning/Vision-Transformer-Vit/. geeksforgeeks. (2024a). *Artificial Neural Networks and its Applications*. Geeksforgeeks. geeksforgeeks. (2024b). *Clustering in Machine Learning*. Geeksforgeeks.

Bordonal, R. D., Carvalho, J. L., Lal, R., De Figueiredo, E. B., De Oliveira, B. G., & La Scala, N.Jr. (2018, April). Sustainability of sugarcane production in Brazil. A review. *Agronomy for Sustainable Development*, *38*(2), 1–23. DOI: 10.1007/s13593-018-0490-x

Bouguettaya, A., Yu, Q., Liu, X., Zhou, X., & Song, A. (2015). Efficient agglomerative hierarchical clustering. *Expert Systems with Applications*, *42*(5), 2785–2797. https://doi.org/https://doi.org/10.1016/j.eswa.2014.09.054. DOI: 10.1016/j.eswa.2014.09.054

Bouzaglo, R., & Keller, Y. (2022). Synthesis and reconstruction of fingerprints using generative adversarial networks. *arXiv preprint arXiv:2201.06164*.

Brahimi, M., Boukhalfa, K., & Moussaoui, A. (2017, April 21). Deep learning for tomato diseases: Classification and symptoms visualization. *Applied Artificial Intelligence*, *31*(4), 299–315. DOI: 10.1080/08839514.2017.1315516

Breiman, L. (2001). Random forests. *Machine Learning*, *45*(1), 5–32. DOI: 10.1023/A:1010933404324

Brosch, T., Tang, L. Y., Yoo, Y., Li, D. K., Traboulsee, A., & Tam, R. (2016). Deep 3d convolutional encoder networks with shortcuts for multiscale feature integration applied to multiple sclerosis lesion segmentation. *IEEE Transactions on Medical Imaging*, *35*(5), 1229–1239. DOI: 10.1109/TMI.2016.2528821 PMID: 26886978

Brown, T., & Anderson, P. (2023). Predicting craniofacial growth using convolutional neural networks in orthodontics. *American Journal of Orthodontics and Dentofacial Orthopedics*, *163*(2), 213–220.

Bumann, E. E., Al-Qarni, S., Chandrashekar, G., Sabzian, R., Bohaty, B., & Lee, Y. (2024). A novel collaborative learning model for mixed dentition and fillings segmentation in panoramic radiographs. *Journal of Dentistry*, *140*, 104779. DOI: 10.1016/j.jdent.2023.104779 PMID: 38007173

Bunk, J. "Detection and Localization of Image Forgeries Using Resampling Features and Deep Learning," *2017 IEEE Conference on Computer Vision and Pattern Recognition Workshops (CVPRW)*, Honolulu, HI, USA, 2017, pp. 1881 1889, DOI: 10.1109/CVPRW.2017.235

Burger Wilhelm and Burge. M. J. (2022). Scale-Invariant Feature Transform (SIFT). In *Digital Image Processing: An Algorithmic Introduction* (pp. 709–763). Springer International Publishing. DOI: 10.1007/978-3-031-05744-1_25

Byeon, W., Breuel, T. M., Raue, F., & Liwicki, M. (2015), "Scene labelling with lstm recurrent neural networks," in *IEEE Conference on Computer Vision and Pattern Recognition*, pp. 3547–3555.

Cai, S., Xing, H., Wang, Y., Wang, Y., Ma, W., Jiang, Y., Li, J., & Wang, H. (2024). Clinical application of intraoperative ultrasound superb microvascular imaging in brain tumors resections: Contributing to the achievement of total tumoral resection. *BMC Medical Imaging*, *24*(1), 142. DOI: 10.1186/s12880-024-01321-5 PMID: 38862900

Cai, Z., & Vasconcelos, N. (2018). Cascade R-CNN: High quality object detection and instance segmentation. In *Proceedings of the IEEE Conference on Computer Vision and Pattern Recognition* (pp. 6154–6162).

Camgoz, N. C., Hadfield, S., Koller, O., Ney, H., & Bowden, R. (2018). Neural sign language translation. In *Proceedings of the IEEE conference on computer vision and pattern recognition* (pp. 7784-7793).

Canny, J. (1986). A Computational Approach to Edge Detection. *IEEE Transactions on Pattern Analysis and Machine Intelligence*, *PAMI-8*(6), 679–698. DOI: 10.1109/TPAMI.1986.4767851 PMID: 21869365

Cao, Q., Shen, L., Xie, W., Parkhi, O. M., & Zisserman, A. (2018). *VGGFace2: A Dataset for Recognising Faces across Pose and Age*. 67–74. https://doi.org/.DOI: 10.1109/FG.2018.00020

Caruana, R. (1997). Multitask learning. *Machine Learning*, *28*(1), 41–75. DOI: 10.1023/A:1007379606734

Cessie, S. L., & Houwelingen, J. V. (1992). Ridge estimators in logistic regression. *Journal of the Royal Statistical Society. Series C, Applied Statistics*, *41*(1), 191–201.

Chahe, A., Wang, C., Jeyapratap, A., Xu, K., & Zhou, L. (2023). Dynamic adversarial attacks on autonomous driving systems. *arXiv preprint arXiv:2312.06701.*

Chai, J., Zhao, Y., & Wang, M. (2021). Hybrid deep learning models for improving forecasting accuracy: A case study in energy demand forecasting. *Applied Energy*, *283*, 116198.

Chakraborty, S., Shaikh, S. H., Chakrabarti, A., & Ghosh, R. (2020). An image denoising technique using quantum wavelet transform. *International Journal of Theoretical Physics*, *59*(11), 3348–3371. DOI: 10.1007/s10773-020-04590-2

Chander, S., & Vijaya, P. (2021). 3 - Unsupervised learning methods for data clustering. In Binu, D., & Rajakumar, B. R. (Eds.), *Artificial Intelligence in Data Mining* (pp. 41–64). Academic Press., https://doi .org/https://doi.org/10.1016/B978-0-12-820601-0.00002-1 DOI: 10.1016/B978-0-12-820601-0.00002-1

Chang, L., Wu, K., Cheng, H., Gu, C., Zhao, Y., & Chen, C. (2024). An automatic progressive chromosome segmentation approach using deep learning with traditional image processing. *Medical & Biological Engineering & Computing*, *62*(1), 207–223. DOI: 10.1007/s11517-023-02896-x PMID: 37758870

Chaudhury, K., Ashok, A. H., Narumanchi, S., & Shankar, D. (2024). *Math and Architectures of Deep Learning*. Simon and Schuster.

Chauhan, N., & Choi, B. J. (2019, September 25). Denoising Approaches Using Fuzzy Logic and Convolutional Autoencoders for Human Brain MRI Image. *Int J Fuzzy Log Intell Syst.*, *19*(3), 135–139. DOI: 10.5391/IJFIS.2019.19.3.135

Chen, J., Chen, J., Zhang, D., Sun, Y., & Nanehkaran, Y. A. Using deep transfer learning for image-based plant disease identification, *Computers and Electronics in Agriculture,* Volume 173, 2020, 105393, ISSN 0168-1699, https://doi.org/DOI: 10.1016/j.compag.2020.105393

Chen, X., Fan, H., Girshick, R., & He, K. (2020). Improved baselines with momentum contrastive learning. *arXiv preprint arXiv:2003.04297.*

Cheng, D., Liao, R., Fidler, S., & Urtasun, R. (2019), "Darnet: Deep active ray network for building segmentation," in *Proceedings of the IEEE Conference on Computer Vision and Pattern Recognition*, pp. 7431–7439. DOI: 10.1109/CVPR.2019.00761

Cheng, M., Tang, H., Bhatti, U. A., & Li, D. (2024). Optimized sustainable manufacturing through fuzzy control in image-based visual servoing with velocity and field-of-view constraints. *IEEE Transactions on Fuzzy Systems*, 1–12. DOI: 10.1109/TFUZZ.2024.3455408

Cheng, Y., Hu, J., & Yang, Y. (2023). Privacy-preserving deep learning in healthcare: A survey. *Journal of Biomedical Informatics*, *138*, 104202. DOI: 10.1016/j.jbi.2023.104202

Chen, H., Li, X., Pan, X., Qiang, Y., & Qi, X. S. (2023). Feature selection based on unsupervised clustering evaluation for predicting neoadjuvant chemoradiation response for patients with locally advanced rectal cancer. *Physics in Medicine and Biology*, *68*(23), 235012. DOI: 10.1088/1361-6560/ad0d46 PMID: 37972413

Chen, H., Zhang, H., & Huang, Y. (2020). Deep learning for temperature prediction: A case study on climate data. *Journal of Climate*, *33*(10), 3941–3955. DOI: 10.1175/JCLI-D-19-0802.1

Chen, J.. (2022). TransUNet: Transformers make strong encoders for medical image segmentation. *IEEE Transactions on Medical Imaging*.

Chen, J., Xie, S., & Liu, Y. (2020). A survey on self-supervised learning: Theoretical perspectives and applications. *IEEE Transactions on Neural Networks and Learning Systems, 32*(9), 3979–3995. DOI: 10.1109/TNNLS.2020.2987724

Chen, K., Pang, J., Wang, J., Xiong, Y., Li, X., Sun, W., & Loy, C. C. (2019). Hybrid Task Cascade for instance segmentation. In *Proceedings of the IEEE Conference on Computer Vision and Pattern Recognition* (pp. 4974–4983).

Chen, L.. (2021). Hybrid ML models for diagnosis of oral diseases based on multi-spectral images. *IEEE Access : Practical Innovations, Open Solutions, 9*, 10575–10584.

Chen, L.-C., Yang, Y., Wang, J., Xu, W., & Yuille, A. L. (2016), "Attention to scale: Scale-aware semantic image segmentation," in *Proceedings of the IEEE conference on computer vision and pattern recognition*, pp. 3640–3649. DOI: 10.1109/CVPR.2016.396

Chen, L.-C., Zhu, Y., Papandreou, G., Schroff, F., & Adam, H. (2018). *Encoder-Decoder with Atrous Separable Convolution for Semantic Image Segmentation.*, DOI: 10.1007/978-3-030-01234-2_49

Chen, L., Zhang, Y., Xu, B., Shao, K., Yan, J., & Bhatti, U. A. (2024). A lot-based VMD-CNN-BIGRU indoor mariculture water quality prediction method including attention mechanism. *International Journal of High Speed Electronics and Systems*, 2540010. DOI: 10.1142/S0129156425400105

Chen, S., Zhong, L., Qiu, C., Zhang, Z., & Zhang, X. (2023). Transformer-based multilevel region and edge aggregation network for magnetic resonance image segmentation. *Computers in Biology and Medicine, 152*(106427), 1–9. DOI: 10.1016/j.compbiomed.2022.106427 PMID: 36543009

Chen, T.. (2020). A simple framework for contrastive learning of visual representations. *Proceedings of the 37th International Conference on Machine Learning*, 1597-1607.

Chen, T., Kornblith, S., Norouzi, M., & Hinton, G. (2020). "A Simple Framework for Contrastive Learning of Visual Representations." *Proceedings of ICML*, 2020.

Chen, W., Ni, X., Qian, C., Yang, L., Zhang, Z., Li, M., Kong, F., Huang, M., He, M., & Yin, Y. (2024). The value of a neural network based on multi-scale feature fusion to ultrasound images for the differentiation in thyroid follicular neoplasms. *BMC Medical Imaging, 24*(1), 74. DOI: 10.1186/s12880-024-01244-1 PMID: 38539143

Chen, X.. (2020). A simple framework for contrastive learning of visual representations. *International Conference on Machine Learning.*

Chen, Y. R., Chen, C. C., Kuo, C. F., & Lin, C. H. (2024). An efficient deep neural network for automatic classification of acute intracranial hemorrhages in brain CT scans. *Computers in Biology and Medicine, 176*, 108587. DOI: 10.1016/j.compbiomed.2024.108587 PMID: 38735238

Chen, Y., & Bastani, F. (1990). Optimal initialization for multi-layer perceptrons. *Proceedings of the IEEE International Conference on Systems, Man and Cybernetics*, 370–372. https://doi.org/DOI: 10.1109/ICSMC.1990.142129

Chen, Y., & Dai, Q. (2023). RNNs and LSTMs in temporal prediction: A review of techniques and applications. *Pattern Recognition Letters, 154*(4), 178–189.

Chen, Y., Mancini, M., Zhu, X., & Akata, Z. (2024). Semi-Supervised and Unsupervised Deep Visual Learning: A Survey. *IEEE Transactions on Pattern Analysis and Machine Intelligence*, *46*(3), 1327–1347. DOI: 10.1109/TPAMI.2022.3201576 PMID: 36006881

Chen, Y., Wu, Y., & Lin, Y. (2022). Temperature forecasting using transfer learning. *Atmosphere*, *13*(1), 120. DOI: 10.3390/atmos13010120

Chen, Y., Wu, Y., & Lin, Y. (2023). Predicting extreme weather events with hybrid deep learning models. *Nature Communications*, *14*(1), 1728. DOI: 10.1038/s41467-023-37423-7 PMID: 36977667

Chen, Z., Li, N., Zhang, P., Li, Y., & Li, X. (2024). CardioDPi: An explainable deep-learning model for identifying cardiotoxic chemicals targeting hERG, Cav1.2, and Nav1.5 channels. *Journal of Hazardous Materials*, *474*, 134724. DOI: 10.1016/j.jhazmat.2024.134724 PMID: 38805819

Chinnadurai, C. (2017). Potential Health Benefits of Sugarcane. In Mohan, C. (Ed.), *Sugarcane Biotechnology: Challenges and Prospects*. Springer., DOI: 10.1007/978-3-319-58946-6_1

Chohan, M., Khan, A., Chohan, R., Katpar, S. H., & Mahar, M. S. (2020, May). Plant disease detection using deep learning. *International Journal of Recent Technology and Engineering*, *9*(1), 909–914. DOI: 10.35940/ijrte.A2139.059120

Choi, , Ha, S., Kang, H., Lee, H., & Lee, D. S. (2019). Deep learning only by normal brain PET identify unheralded brain anomalies. *EBioMedicine*, *43*, 447–453. DOI: 10.1016/j.ebiom.2019.04.022 PMID: 31003928

Choi, S., & Park, H. (2021). Regression analysis of treatment outcomes in orthodontics: Enhancing precision with machine learning. *Journal of Dental Research*, *100*(3), 350–359.

Chollet, F. (n.d.). *M A N N I N G*.

Çiçek, Ö., Abdulkadir, A., Lienkamp, S. S., Brox, T., & Ronneberger, O. (2016). 3D U-Net: Learning dense volumetric segmentation from sparse annotation. In *Proceedings of the International Conference on Medical Image Computing and Computer-Assisted Intervention* (pp. 424–432). Springer.

Cireşan, D., Meier, U., & Schmidhuber, J. (2020). Multi-Column Deep Neural Networks for Tumor Classification in Breast Cancer. *International Conference on Medical Image Computing and Computer-Assisted Intervention*, 133-142. https://doi.org/DOI: 10.1007/978-3-030-59728-3_12

Clark, K., Vendt, B., Smith, K., Freymann, J., Kirby, J., Koppel, P., Moore, S., Phillips, S., Maffitt, D., Pringle, M., Tarbox, L., & Prior, F. (2013). The Cancer Imaging Archive (TCIA): Maintaining and operating a public information repository. *Journal of Digital Imaging*, *26*(6), 1045–1057. DOI: 10.1007/s10278-013-9622-7 PMID: 23884657

Cleary, J. G., & Trigg, L. E. (1995). K*: An instance-based learner using an entropic distance measure. In *Machine Learning Proceedings 1995* (pp. 108–114). Morgan Kaufmann. DOI: 10.1016/B978-1-55860-377-6.50022-0

Cleland, C. R., Rwiza, J., Evans, J. R., Gordon, I., MacLeod, D., Burton, M. J., & Bascaran, C. (2023). Artificial Intelligence for Diabetic Retinopathy in Low-Income and Middle-Income Countries: A Scoping Review. *BMJ Open Diabetes Research & Care, 11*(4), e003424. DOI: 10.1136/bmjdrc-2023-003424 PMID: 37532460

Cottin, V., Wollin, L., Fischer, A., Quaresma, M., Stowasser, S., & Harari, S. (2019). Fibrosing interstitial lung diseases: Knowns and unknowns. *European Respiratory Review : an Official Journal of the European Respiratory Society, 28*(151), 180100. DOI: 10.1183/16000617.0100-2018 PMID: 30814139

Cozzolino, D., & Verdoliva, L. "Camera based Image Forgery Localization using Convolutional Neural Networks," 2018 26th European Signal Processing Conference (EUSIPCO), Rome, Italy, 2018, pp. 1372 1376, DOI: 10.23919/EUSIPCO.2018.8553581

Cozzolino, D., Verdoliva, L., & Poggi, G. "Copy-move forgery detection based on Patch match," *2014 IEEE International Conference on Image Processing (ICIP)*, Paris, France, 2014, pp. 5312 5316, DOI: 10.1109/ICIP.2014.7026075

Criminisi, A., Robertson, D., Konukoglu, E., Pathak, S., & White, S. (2013). Regression forests for efficient anatomy detection and localization in computed tomography scans. *Medical Image Analysis, 17*(8), 1293–1303. DOI: 10.1016/j.media.2013.01.001 PMID: 23410511

Crincoli, E., Servillo, A., Catania, F., Sacconi, R., Mularoni, C., Battista, M., Querques, L., Parravano, M., Costanzo, E., Polito, M. S., Bandello, F., & Querques, G. (2023). ARTIFICIAL INTELLIGENCE'S ROLE IN DIFFERENTIATING THE ORIGIN FOR SUBRETINAL BLEEDING IN PATHOLOGIC MYOPIA. *Retina (Philadelphia, Pa.)*. Advance online publication. DOI: 10.1097/IAE.0000000000003884 PMID: 37490781

Cruz, J. A., & Wishart, D. S. (2006). Applications of machine learning in cancer prediction and prognosis. *Cancer Informatics, 2*, 117693510600200030. DOI: 10.1177/117693510600200030 PMID: 19458758

Da Silva Santos, D. F., & De Souza, G. (2019). B, MARANA A.N, PAPA J.P PIRES R.G "Deep Features Extraction for Robust Fingerprint Spoofing Attack Detection". *Journal of Artificial Intelligence and Soft Computing Research, 9*(1), 41–49. DOI: 10.2478/jaiscr-2018-0023

Damayanti, F., Muntasa, A., Herawati, S., Yusuf, M., & Rachmad, A. (2020, March). Identification of Madura tobacco leaf disease using gray-level Co-occurrence matrix, color moments and Naïve Bayes. [). IOP Publishing.]. *Journal of Physics: Conference Series, 1477*(5), 052054. DOI: 10.1088/1742-6596/1477/5/052054

Das, A., Mohanty, M. N., Mallick, P. K., Tiwari, P., Muhammad, K., & Zhu, H. (2021). Breast cancer detection using an ensemble deep learning method. *Biomedical Signal Processing and Control, 70*, 103009. DOI: 10.1016/j.bspc.2021.103009

Dastin, J. (2018). *Amazon scrapped a secret AI recruiting tool that showed bias against women*. Reuters.

Davis, L. S., Han, X., Morariu, V. I., & Zhou, P. "Learning Rich Features for Image Manipulation Detection," *2018 IEEE/CVF Conference on Computer Vision and Pattern Recognition*, Salt Lake City, UT, USA, 2018, pp. 1053 1061, DOI: 10.1109/CVPR.2018.00116

De Bock, K. W., Coussement, K., De Caigny, A., Słowiński, R., Baesens, B., Boute, R. N., & Weber, R. (2024). Explainable AI for operational research: A defining framework, methods, applications, and a research agenda. *European Journal of Operational Research*, *317*(2), 249–272. DOI: 10.1016/j.ejor.2023.09.026

Deep, G., & Verma, J. (2024). Deep Learning Models for Fine-Scale Climate Change Prediction: Enhancing Spatial and Temporal Resolution Using AI. In Tripathi, G., Shakya, A., Kanga, S., Singh, S. K., & Rai, P. K. (Eds.), *Big Data, Artificial Intelligence, and Data Analytics in Climate Change Research: For Sustainable Development Goals* (pp. 81–100). Springer Nature., DOI: 10.1007/978-981-97-1685-2_5

Demilie, W. B. (2024). Plant disease detection and classification techniques: A comparative study of the performances. *Journal of Big Data*, *11*(1), 5. DOI: 10.1186/s40537-023-00863-9

Deng, J., Dong, W., Socher, R., Li, L. -J., Li, K., & Fei-Fei, L. (2009). Imagenet: A large-scale hierarchical image databaseDOI: 10.1080/21642583.2014.956265

Déniz, O., Bueno, G., Salido, J., & De la Torre, F. (2011). Face recognition using Histograms of Oriented Gradients. *Pattern Recognition Letters*, *32*(12), 1598–1603. https://doi.org/https://doi.org/10.1016/j.patrec.2011.01.004. DOI: 10.1016/j.patrec.2011.01.004

Devi, J. S., Sreedhar, M. B., Arulprakash, P., Kazi, K., & Radhakrishnan, R. (2022). A path towards child-centric Artificial Intelligence based Education. *International Journal of Early Childhood*, *14*(3), 9915-9922.

Dhanwe, S. S.. (2024). AI-driven IoT in Robotics: A Review. *Journal of Mechanisms and Robotics*, *9*(1), 41–48.

Dhanya, V. G., Subeesh, A., Kushwaha, N. L., Vishwakarma, D. K., Kumar, T. N., Ritika, G., & Singh, A. N. (2022). Deep learning-based computer vision approaches for smart agricultural applications. *Artificial Intelligence in Agriculture*, *6*, 211–229. DOI: 10.1016/j.aiia.2022.09.007

Dhiman, P., Kaur, A., Balasaraswathi, V. R., Gulzar, Y., Alwan, A. A., & Hamid, Y. (2023). Image Acquisition, Preprocessing and Classification of Citrus Fruit Diseases: A Systematic Literature Review. *Sustainability (Basel)*, *15*(12), 9643. Advance online publication. DOI: 10.3390/su15129643

Dietterich, T. G. (2000). Ensemble methods in machine learning. In *Proceedings of the International Workshop on Multiple Classifier Systems* (pp. 1–15). Springer. https://doi.org/DOI: 10.1007/3-540-45014-9_1

Differential privacy—Wikipedia. (n.d.). Retrieved 12 September 2024, from https://en.wikipedia.org/wiki/Differential_privacy

Dong, G., Jin, Y., Wang, S., Li, W., Tao, Z., & Guo, S. (2019). DB-Kmeans:An Intrusion Detection Algorithm Based on DBSCAN and K-means. *2019 20th Asia-Pacific Network Operations and Management Symposium (APNOMS)*, 1–4. DOI: 10.23919/APNOMS.2019.8892910

Dosovitskiy, A., ... (2020). An image is worth 16x16 words: Transformers for image recognition at scale. *arXiv preprint arXiv:2010.11929.*

Dosovitskiy, A., et al. (2021). "An Image is Worth 16x16 Words: Transformers for Image Recognition at Scale." *ICLR*, 2021.

Dritsas, E., & Trigka, M. (2022). Lung cancer risk prediction with machine learning models. *Big Data and Cognitive Computing*, *6*(4), 139. DOI: 10.3390/bdcc6040139

Dua, S., Singh, J., & Parthasarathy, H.DUA. (2020). PARTHASARATHY H, SINGH J "Image forgery detection based on statistical features of block DCT coefficients". *Procedia Computer Science*, *171*, 369–378. DOI: 10.1016/j.procs.2020.04.038

Ebrahimnejad, N., Jaafar, D., & Goodarzi, H. (2024). The Past, Present, Future: Pathophysiology, Diagnosis, and Treatment of Human Skin Diseases. *Physiologia*, *4*(1), 81–99. DOI: 10.3390/physiologia4010005

EFTViT: Efficient Federated Training of Vision Transformers with Hierarchical Masked Modeling. (2024). arXiv preprint arXiv:2412.00334.

Eghbali, P., Becce, F., Goetti, P., Büchler, P., Pioletti, D. P., & Terrier, A. (2024). Glenohumeral joint force prediction with deep learning. *Journal of Biomechanics*, *163*, 111952. DOI: 10.1016/j.jbiomech.2024.111952 PMID: 38228026

Ehret, T. "Robust copy-move forgery detection by false alarms control". ArXiv 2019, arXiv: 1906.00649.

Elsayed, H. A. G., Ghalwash, A. Z., Khalil, A. H., & Salama, G. I. (2023). Enhancing Digital Image Forgery Detection Using Transfer Learning. *IEEE Access : Practical Innovations, Open Solutions*, *11*, 91583–91594. DOI: 10.1109/ACCESS.2023.3307357

Erkınay Özdemir, M., & Karakuş, F. (2024). Deep Learning-Based Decision Support System for Automatic Detection and Grading of Surface Corrosion on Galvanized Steel Sheets. *Electronics (Basel)*, *13*(20), 3998. DOI: 10.3390/electronics13203998

Esmaeilzadeh, P. (2024, May). Challenges and strategies for wide-scale artificial intelligence (AI) deployment in healthcare practices: A perspective for healthcare organizations. *Artificial Intelligence in Medicine*, *151*, 102861. DOI: 10.1016/j.artmed.2024.102861 PMID: 38555850

Esteva, A., Kuprel, B., Novoa, R. A., Ko, J., Swetter, S. M., Blau, H. M., & Thrun, S. (2019). Dermatologist-level classification of skin cancer with deep neural networks. *Nature*, *542*(7639), 115–118. DOI: 10.1038/nature21056 PMID: 28117445

Ezugwu, A. E., Ikotun, A. M., Oyelade, O. O., Abualigah, L., Agushaka, J. O., Eke, C. I., & Akinyelu, A. A. (2022). A comprehensive survey of clustering algorithms: State-of-the-art machine learning applications, taxonomy, challenges, and future research prospects. *Engineering Applications of Artificial Intelligence*, *110*, 104743. https://doi.org/https://doi.org/10.1016/j.engappai.2022.104743. DOI: 10.1016/j.engappai.2022.104743

Face Recognition Technology. (n.d.). *American Civil Liberties Union*. Retrieved 5 September 2024, from https://www.aclu.org/issues/privacy-technology/surveillance-technologies/face-recognition-technology

Fahim, A., Tan, Q., Mazzi, M., Sahabuddin, M., Naz, B., & Ullah Bazai, S. (2021). Hybrid LSTM Self-Attention Mechanism Model for Forecasting the Reform of Scientific Research in Morocco. *Computational Intelligence and Neuroscience*, *2021*(1), 6689204. Advance online publication. DOI: 10.1155/2021/6689204 PMID: 34122534

Fakhar, S., Baber, J., Bazai, S. U., Marjan, S., Jasinski, M., Jasinska, E., Chaudhry, M. U., Leonowicz, Z., & Hussain, S. (2022). Smart classroom monitoring using novel real-time facial expression recognition system. *Applied Sciences (Basel, Switzerland)*, *12*(23), 12134. DOI: 10.3390/app122312134

Fakhouri, H. N., Alawadi, S., Awaysheh, F. M., Alkhabbas, F., & Zraqou, J. (2024). A cognitive deep learning approach for medical image processing. *Scientific Reports*, *14*(1), 4539. DOI: 10.1038/s41598-024-55061-1 PMID: 38402321

Fang, W., Tang, L., & Pan, J. (2023). AGL-Net: An Efficient Neural Network for EEG-Based Driver Fatigue Detection. *Journal of Integrative Neuroscience*, *22*(6), 146. DOI: 10.31083/j.jin2206146 PMID: 38176922

Fazi, M. B. (2021). Beyond human: Deep learning, explainability and representation. *Theory, Culture & Society*, *38*(7-8), 55–77. DOI: 10.1177/0263276420966386

Feng, S., Liu, Q., Patel, A., Bazai, S. U., Jin, C. K., Kim, J. S., Sarrafzadeh, M., Azzollini, D., Yeoh, J., Kim, E., Gordon, S., Jang-Jaccard, J., Urschler, M., Barnard, S., Fong, A., Simmers, C., Tarr, G. P., & Wilson, B. (2022). Automated pneumothorax triaging in chest X-rays in the New Zealand population using deep-learning algorithms. *Journal of Medical Imaging and Radiation Oncology*, *66*(8), 1035–1043. DOI: 10.1111/1754-9485.13393 PMID: 35224858

Figueira, A., & Vaz, B. (2022). Survey on Synthetic Data Generation, Evaluation Methods and GANs. *Mathematics*, *10*(15), 2733. Advance online publication. DOI: 10.3390/math10152733

Finn, C., Abbeel, P., & Levine, S. (2017). Model-agnostic meta-learning for fast adaptation of deep networks. *Proceedings of the 34th International Conference on Machine Learning*, 1126-1135.

Flores, S. (2019). *Variational Autoencoders are Beautiful*. Comp Three Inc.

Frank, A. (2010). UCI machine learning repository. http://archive. ics. uci. edu/ml

Fränti, P., & Sieranoja, S. (2019). How much can k-means be improved by using better initialization and repeats? *Pattern Recognition*, *93*, 95–112. https://doi.org/https://doi.org/10.1016/j.patcog.2019.04.014. DOI: 10.1016/j.patcog.2019.04.014

Frid-Adar, M., Ganin, A., et al. (2020). GAN-based augmentation of breast cancer histopathological images. *SpringerLink*, 104–112. https://doi.org/DOI: 10.1007/s11548-019-02009-2

Fu, J., Liu, J., Tian, H., Li, Y., Bao, Y., Fang, Z., & Lu, H. (2019), "Dual attention network for scene segmentation," in *Proceedings of the IEEE Conference on Computer Vision and Pattern Recognition*, pp. 3146–3154.

Fu, J., Wang, L., Ke, J., Yang, K., & Yu, R. (2023). GANAD: A GAN-based method for network anomaly detection. *World Wide Web (Bussum)*, *26*(5), 2727–2748. DOI: 10.1007/s11280-023-01160-4

Fujima, , Andreu-Arasa, V. C., Meibom, S. K., Mercier, G. A., Truong, M. T., Hirata, K., Yasuda, K., Kano, S., Homma, A., Kudo, K., & Sakai, O. (2021). Prediction of the local treatment outcome in patients with oropharyngeal squamous cell carcinoma using deep learning analysis of pretreatment FDG-PET images. *BMC Cancer*, *21*(1), 900. DOI: 10.1186/s12885-021-08599-6 PMID: 34362317

Fukushima, K. (1980). Neocognitron: A self-organizing neural network model for a mechanism of pattern recognition unaffected by shift in position. *Biological Cybernetics*, *36*(4), 193–202. DOI: 10.1007/BF00344251 PMID: 7370364

Fu, L., & Li, S. (2023). A New Semantic Segmentation Framework Based on UNet. *Sensors (Basel)*, *23*(8123), 1–14. DOI: 10.3390/s23198123 PMID: 37836953

Ganin, Y., & Lempitsky, V. (2015). Unsupervised domain adaptation by backpropagation. In *Proceedings of the 32nd International Conference on Machine Learning* (pp. 1180-1189).

Gao, Y., Yang, X., & Liu, L. (2022). Explainable Artificial Intelligence for Medical Imaging: A Survey. *Medical Image Analysis*, *73*, 102216. DOI: 10.1016/j.media.2021.102216

Gaspar, D., Silva, P., & Silva, C. (2024). Explainable AI for Intrusion Detection Systems: LIME and SHAP Applicability on Multi-Layer Perceptron. *IEEE Access : Practical Innovations, Open Solutions*, *12*, 30164–30175. DOI: 10.1109/ACCESS.2024.3368377

Geeksforgeeks. (2024). *DBSCAN Clustering in ML | Density based clustering*. Https://Www.Geeksforgeeks.Org/Dbscan-Clustering-in-Ml-Density-Based-Clustering/

geeksforgeeks. (2024c, June). *DenseNet Explained*. Geeksforgeeks.

Gençdoğmuş, A., Hameed, A. A., & Jamil, A. (n.d.). *Sentiment Analysis for COVID-19 Tweets Using Recurrent Neural Network (RNN) and Bidirectional Encoder Representations (BERT) Models*. https://www.researchgate.net/publication/357117201

Get Newzoo's newest free Global Games Market Report 2023. (2024, February 8). *Newzoo*. https://newzoo.com/resources/trend-reports/newzoo-global-games-market-report-2023-free-version

Ghassemi, M.. (2021). A Review of Bias and Fairness in Machine Learning for Healthcare. *Nature Medicine*, *27*(3), 2021.

Ghose, S., Singh, N., & Singh, P. (2020). Image denoising using deep learning: Convolutional neural network. *2020 10th International Conference on Cloud Computing, Data Science & Engineering (Confluence)*, 511–517.

Ghosh, , Azam, S., Quadir, R., Karim, A., Shamrat, F. M. J. M., Bhowmik, S. K., Jonkman, M., Hasib, K. M., & Ahmed, K. (2022). SkinNet-16: A deep learning approach to identify benign and malignant skin lesions. *Frontiers in Oncology*, *12*, 931141. DOI: 10.3389/fonc.2022.931141 PMID: 36003775

Giacominia, M., & Perotto, S. (2022). Anisotropic mesh adaptation for region-based segmentation accounting for image spatial information. *Computers & Mathematics with Applications (Oxford, England)*, *121*, 1–17. DOI: 10.1016/j.camwa.2022.06.025

Gibson, E., Li, W., Sudre, C., Fidon, L., Shakir, D. I., Wang, G., Eaton-Rosen, Z., Gray, R., Doel, T., Hu, Y., Whyntie, T., Nachev, P., Modat, M., Barratt, D. C., Ourselin, S., Cardoso, M. J., & Vercauteren, T. (2018). NiftyNet: A deep-learning platform for medical imaging. *Computer Methods and Programs in Biomedicine*, *158*, 113–122. DOI: 10.1016/j.cmpb.2018.01.025 PMID: 29544777

Girshick, R. (2015). Fast R-CNN. *Proceedings of the IEEE International Conference on Computer Vision*, 1440-1448.

Girshick, R.. (2014). Rich feature hierarchies for accurate object detection and semantic segmentation. In *Proceedings of the IEEE Conference on Computer Vision and Pattern Recognition* (pp. 580-587). DOI: 10.1109/CVPR.2014.81

Gong, P., Li, X., & Zhang, X. (2021). Deep learning for vegetation cover change detection: A systematic review. *ISPRS Journal of Photogrammetry and Remote Sensing*, *177*, 269–284. DOI: 10.1016/j.isprsjprs.2021.05.009

Gonzales Martinez, R., & van Dongen, D.-M. (2023). Deep Learning algorithms for the early detection of breast cancer: A comparative study with traditional machine learning. *Informatics in Medicine Unlocked*, *41*, 101317. DOI: 10.1016/j.imu.2023.101317

Gonzalez, R. C. and W. R. E. (2018). *Digital Image Processing* (4th ed.). Pearson Education.

Goodfellow, I. J., Pouget-Abadie, J., Mirza, M., Xu, B., Warde-Farley, D., Ozair, S., Courville, A., & Bengio, Y. (2014, June 10). *Generative Adversarial Networks*. arXiv.Org. https://arxiv.org/abs/1406.2661v1

Goodfellow, I., Pouget-Abadie, J., Mirza, M., ... (2014). Generative adversarial nets. In *Advances in Neural Information Processing Systems* (pp. 27–39). http://papers.nips.cc/paper/5423-generative-adversarial-nets.pdf

Goodfellow, I., Pouget-Abadie, J., Mirza, M., Xu, B., Warde-Farley, D., Ozair, S., Courville, A., & Bengio, Y. (2014). Generative adversarial nets. *Advances in Neural Information Processing Systems*, *27*, 2672–2680.

Goyal, B., Dogra, A., Agrawal, S., Sohi, B. S., & Sharma, A. (2020). Image denoising review: From classical to state-of-the-art approaches. *Information Fusion*, *55*, 220–244. DOI: 10.1016/j.inffus.2019.09.003

Graves, A., Mohamed, A.-r., & Hinton, G. (2013). Speech recognition with deep recurrent neural networks. In *2013 IEEE International Conference on Acoustics, Speech and Signal Processing* (pp. 6645–6649). DOI: 10.1109/ICASSP.2013.6638947

Greenspan, H., van Ginneken, B., & Summers, R. M. (2016). Guest editorial deep learning in medical imaging: Overview and future promise of an exciting new technique. *IEEE Transactions on Medical Imaging*, *35*(5), 1153–1159. DOI: 10.1109/TMI.2016.2553401

Grill, J. B.. (2020). Bootstrap your own latent: A new approach to self-supervised learning. *Advances in Neural Information Processing Systems*, *33*, 21271–21284.

Grischke, J., Johannsmeier, L., Eich, L., Griga, L., & Haddadin, S. (2020). Dentronics: Towards robotics and artificial intelligence in dentistry. *Dental Materials*, *36*(6), 765–778. DOI: 10.1016/j.dental.2020.03.021 PMID: 32349877

Grzenda, M., Kaźmierczak, S., Luckner, M., Borowik, G., & Mańdziuk, J. (2023). Evaluation of machine learning methods for impostor detection in web applications. *Expert Systems with Applications, 231*, 120736. DOI: 10.1016/j.eswa.2023.120736

Guan, Y., Aamir, M., Hu, Z., Abro, W. A., Rahman, Z., Dayo, Z. A., & Akram, S. (2021). A Region-Based Efficient Network for Accurate Object Detection. *TS. Traitement du Signal, 38*(2), 481–494. DOI: 10.18280/ts.380228

Guan, Y., Aamir, M., Hu, Z., Dayo, Z. A., Rahman, Z., Abro, W. A., & Soothar, P. (2021). An Object Detection Framework Based on Deep Features and High-Quality Object Locations. *TS. Traitement du Signal, 38*(3), 719–730. DOI: 10.18280/ts.380319

Guan, Y., Aamir, M., Rahman, Z., Ali, A., Abro, W. A., Dayo, Z. A., Bhutta, M. S., & Hu, Z. (2021). *A framework for efficient brain tumor classification using MRI images*. Mathematics in Biomedical Engineering., DOI: 10.3934/mbe.2021292

Guan, Y., Aamir, M., Rahman, Z., Dayo, Z. A., Abro, W. A., & Ishfaq, M., & HU, Z. (2021). A dual-tree complex wavelet transform-based model for low-illumination image enhancement. *Wuhan University Journal of Natural Sciences, 26*(05), 405–414.

Gu, C & Lee M. (2024). Deep Transfer Learning Using Real-World Image Features for Medical Image Classification, with a Case Study on Pneumonia X-ray Images. Bioengineering (Basel, Switzerland)

Guefrachi, S., Echtioui, A., & Hamam, H. (2024). Automated diabetic retinopathy screening using Deep Learning. *Multimedia Tools and Applications, 83*(24), 65249–65266. DOI: 10.1007/s11042-024-18149-4

Guérin, J., Thiery, S., Nyiri, E., Gibaru, O., & Boots, B. (2021). Combining pretrained CNN feature extractors to enhance clustering of complex natural images. *Neurocomputing, 423*, 551–571. https://doi .org/https://doi.org/10.1016/j.neucom.2020.10.068. DOI: 10.1016/j.neucom.2020.10.068

Gugulothu, V. K., & Balaji, S. (2024). An early prediction and classification of lung nodule diagnosis on CT images based on hybrid deep learning techniques. *Multimedia Tools and Applications*, •••, 1. PMID: 37362653

Gulzar, Y., Ünal, Z., Ayoub, S., & Reegu, F. A. (2024). Exploring Transfer Learning for Enhanced Seed Classification: Pre-trained Xception Model. In F. and M. F. and S. K. and M. K. and A. P. C. Cavallo Eugenio and Auat Cheein (Ed.), *15th International Congress on Agricultural Mechanization and Energy in Agriculture* (pp. 137–147). Springer Nature Switzerland.

Gulzar, Y., Ünal, Z., Ayoub, S., Reegu, F. A., & Altulihan, A. (2024). Adaptability of deep learning: datasets and strategies in fruit classification. *BIO Web of Conferences, 85*. DOI: 10.1051/bioconf/20248501020

Gulzar, Y. (2023). Fruit Image Classification Model Based on MobileNetV2 with Deep Transfer Learning Technique. *Sustainability (Basel), 15*(3), 1906. Advance online publication. DOI: 10.3390/su15031906

Gulzar, Y. (2024). Enhancing soybean classification with modified inception model: A transfer learning approach. *Emirates Journal of Food and Agriculture, 36*, 1–9. DOI: 10.3897/ejfa.2024.122928

Gulzar, Y., Alwan, A. A., Abdullah, R. M., Abualkishik, A. Z., & Oumrani, M. (2023). OCA: Ordered Clustering-Based Algorithm for E-Commerce Recommendation System. *Sustainability (Basel), 15*(4), 2947. Advance online publication. DOI: 10.3390/su15042947

Gulzar, Y., Oral, C., Kayakus, M., Erdogan, D., Unal, Z., Eksili, N., & Caylak, P. C. (2024). Predicting High Technology Exports of Countries for Sustainable Economic Growth by Using Machine Learning Techniques: The Case of Turkey. *Sustainability (Basel), 16*(13), 5601. DOI: 10.3390/su16135601

Gunasinghe, A. D., Aponso, A. C., & Thirimanna, H. (2019, March). Early prediction of lung diseases. In 2019 IEEE 5th International Conference for Convergence in Technology (I2CT) (pp. 1-4). IEEE. DOI: 10.1109/I2CT45611.2019.9033668

Gund, V. D.. (2023). PIR Sensor-Based Arduino Home Security System. *Journal of Instrumentation and Innovation Sciences*, *8*(3), 33–37.

Guo, G., Wang, H., Bell, D., Bi, Y., & Greer, K. (2003). KNN model-based approach in classification. In *On The Move to Meaningful Internet Systems 2003: CoopIS, DOA, and ODBASE: OTM Confederated International Conferences, CoopIS, DOA, and ODBASE 2003, Catania, Sicily, Italy, November 3-7, 2003. Proceedings* (pp. 986-996). Springer Berlin Heidelberg. DOI: 10.1007/978-3-540-39964-3_62

Guo, J., Ma, J., García-Fernández, Á. F., Zhang, Y., & Liang, H. (2023, March 16). A survey on image enhancement for Low-light images. *Heliyon*, *9*(4), e14558. DOI: 10.1016/j.heliyon.2023.e14558 PMID: 37025779

Guo, Y., Liu, Y., Georgiou, T., & Lew, M. S. (2018). A review of semantic segmentation using deep neural networks. *International Journal of Multimedia Information Retrieval*, *7*(2), 87–93. DOI: 10.1007/s13735-017-0141-z

Gupta, M., & Ali, S. (2022). Automated classification of periodontal stages using CNNs. *Journal of Clinical Periodontology*, *49*(7), 723–732.

Gupta, N., Gupta, D., Khanna, A., Rebouças Filho, P. P., & De Albuquerque, V. H. C. (2019). Evolutionary algorithms for automatic lung disease detection. *Measurement*, *140*, 590–608. DOI: 10.1016/j.measurement.2019.02.042

Gupta, P., & Jadon, R. S. (2024). Plant Leaf Disease Identification Using Deep Learning Algorithms. In Hassanien, A. E., Anand, S., Jaiswal, A., & Kumar, P. (Eds.), *Innovative Computing and Communications. ICICC 2024. Lecture Notes in Networks and Systems* (Vol. 1043). Springer., DOI: 10.1007/978-981-97-4228-8_47

Gurnani, B., Kaur, K., Lalgudi, V. G., Kundu, G., Mimouni, M., Liu, H., Jhanji, V., Prakash, G., Roy, A. S., Shetty, R., & Gurav, J. S. (2024, September). Role of artificial intelligence, machine learning and deep learning models in corneal disorders - A narrative review. *Journal Français d'Ophtalmologie*, *47*(7), 104242. DOI: 10.1016/j.jfo.2024.104242 PMID: 39013268

Habibi, M., & Hassanpour, H. (2021). Splicing Image Forgery Detection and Localization Based on Color Edge Inconsistency using Statistical Dispersion Measures. *Int. J. Eng.*, *34*, 443–451.

Hafiz, A. M., & Bhat, G. M. (2020). A survey on instance segmentation: State of the art. *International Journal of Multimedia Information Retrieval*, *9*(3), 171–189. DOI: 10.1007/s13735-020-00195-x

Hagad, Kimura, Fukui & Numao Learning Subject-Generalized Topographical EEG Embeddings Using Deep Variational Autoencoders and Domain-Adversarial Regularization. Sensors (Basel, Switzerland) (2021). DOI: 10.19823/j.cnki.1007-1202.2021.0051

Haider, A., Hussain, L., Tareen, A. W., Bazai, S. U., Aslam, S., Neo, M., & Amphawan, A. (2024). A comparative study of machine learning techniques for accurate disease prediction using symptom-based diagnosis. *AIP Conference Proceedings*, *3153*(1), 020005. DOI: 10.1063/5.0217579

Hakkoum, H., Idri, A., & Abnane, I. (2024). Global and local interpretability techniques of supervised machine learning black box models for numerical medical data. *Engineering Applications of Artificial Intelligence*, *131*, 107829. DOI: 10.1016/j.engappai.2023.107829

Halli, U. M. (2022a). Nanotechnology in IoT Security, *Journal of Nanoscience. Nanoengineering & Applications*, *12*(3), 11–16.

Halli, U. M. (2022b). Nanotechnology in E-Vehicle Batteries. *International Journal of Nanomaterials and Nanostructures.*, *8*(2), 22–27.

Hameed, M., Yang, F., Bazai, S. U., Ghafoor, M. I., Alshehri, A., Khan, I., Baryalai, M., Andualem, M., & Jaskani, F. H. (2022). Urbanization Detection Using LiDAR-Based Remote Sensing Images of Azad Kashmir Using Novel 3D CNNs. *Journal of Sensors*, *2022*(1), 6430120. DOI: 10.1155/2022/6430120

Hameed, M., Yang, F., Bazai, S. U., Ghafoor, M. I., Alshehri, A., Khan, I., Ullah, S., Baryalai, M., Jaskani, F. H., & Andualem, M. (2022). Convolutional Autoencoder-Based Deep Learning Approach for Aerosol Emission Detection Using LiDAR Dataset. *Journal of Sensors*, *2022*(1), 3690312. DOI: 10.1155/2022/3690312

Hamza, M., Bazai, S. U., Ghafoor, M. I., Ullah, S., Akram, S., & Khan, M. S. (2023). Generative Adversarial Networks (GANs) Video Framework: A Systematic Literature Review. 2023 International Conference on Energy, Power, Environment, Control, and Computing (ICEPECC), 1–5. https://ieeexplore.ieee.org/abstract/document/10209475/

Hamza, M., Bazai, S. U., Ghafoor, M. I., Ullah, S., Akram, S., & Khan, M. S. (2023). Generative Adversarial Networks (GANs) Video Framework: A Systematic Literature Review. *2023 International Conference on Energy, Power, Environment, Control, and Computing, ICEPECC 2023 - Proceedings*. DOI: 10.1109/ICEPECC57281.2023.10209475

Han, H., Bazai, S. U., Bhatti, M. A., Basit, A., Wahid, A., Bhatti, U. A., Ghadi, Y. Y., & Algarni, A. (2024). Hybrid Climate Forecasting: Variational Mode Decomposition and Convolutional Neural Network with Long-Term Short Memory. *Polish Journal of Environmental Studies*, *33*(2), 1121–1134. DOI: 10.15244/pjoes/172756

Han, J., Pei, J., & Tong, H. (2022). *Data mining: concepts and techniques*. Morgan kaufmann.

Hannah, D. (2020, August 3). Fake video of Pelosi goes viral on Facebook. *The Washington Post*.

Haq, S. U., Bazai, S. U., Fatima, A., Marjan, S., Yang, J., Por, L. Y., Anjum, M., Shahab, S., & Ku, C. S. (2023). Reseek-arrhythmia: Empirical evaluation of ResNet architecture for detection of arrhythmia. *Diagnostics (Basel), 13*(18), 2867. DOI: 10.3390/diagnostics13182867 PMID: 37761234

Hasan, R. I., Yusuf, S. M., & Alzubaidi, L. (2020). Review of the state of the art of deep learning for plant diseases: A broad analysis and discussion. *Plants, 9*(10), 1302. DOI: 10.3390/plants9101302 PMID: 33019765

Hasnain, A., Hashmi, M. Z., Bhatti, U. A., Wei, G., Jinru, L., & Asif, M. (2024). Prediction of particulate matter pollution using a long short-term memory model in Zhejiang Province, China. *Environmental Monitoring and Assessment, 196*(5), 487. DOI: 10.1007/s10661-024-12644-9 PMID: 38687422

Hassan, S. M., Maji, A. K., Jasiński, M., Leonowicz, Z., & Jasińska, E. (2021, June 9). Identification of plant-leaf diseases using CNN and transfer-learning approach. *Electronics (Basel), 10*(12), 1388. DOI: 10.3390/electronics10121388

Hatamizadeh, A., Hoogi, A., Sengupta, D., Lu, W., Wilcox, B., Rubin, D., & Terzopoulos, D. (2019),"Deep active lesion segmentation," in Proc. International Workshop on Machine Learning in Medical Imaging, ser. Lecture Notes in Computer Science, vol. 11861. Springer, pp. 98–105. DOI: 10.1007/978-3-030-32692-0_12

He, K., et al. (2022). "Masked Autoencoders Are Scalable Vision Learners." *CVPR*, 2022.

He, K., Zhang, X., Ren, S., & Sun, J. (2015, December 10). *Deep Residual Learning for Image Recognition*. arXiv.Org. https://arxiv.org/abs/1512.03385v1

He, B., & Bhatti, U. A. (2024). Smart cities and smart networks: AI applications in urban geography and industrial communication. *International Journal of High Speed Electronics and Systems*, 2440122. DOI: 10.1142/S0129156424401220

He, D., He, X., Xiang, H., Yuan, R., & Niu, Y. (2023). Wavelet transform-based two-stream convolutional networks for face anti-spoofing. *Journal of Electronic Imaging, 32*(1), 13015. DOI: 10.1117/1.JEI.32.1.013015

Hedayati, R., Khedmati, M., & Taghipour-Gorjikolaie, M. (2021). Deep feature extraction method based on ensemble of convolutional auto encoders: Application to Alzheimer's disease diagnosis. *Biomedical Signal Processing and Control, 66*, 102397. DOI: 10.1016/j.bspc.2020.102397

He, K.. (2022). Masked autoencoders are scalable vision learners. *Proceedings of the IEEE/CVF Conference on Computer Vision and Pattern Recognition.*

He, K., Gkioxari, G., Doll'ar, P., & Girshick, R. "Mask r-cnn," in *Proceedings of the IEEE international conference on computer vision*, pp. 2961–2969.

He, K., Gkioxari, G., Dollar, P., & Girshick, R. (2017). Mask R-CNN. *2017 IEEE International Conference on Computer Vision (ICCV)*, 2980–2988. DOI: 10.1109/ICCV.2017.322

He, K., Gkioxari, G., Dollár, P., & Girshick, R. (2017). Mask R-CNN. *Proceedings of the IEEE International Conference on Computer Vision*, 2961-2969.

He, K., Zhang, X., Ren, S., & Sun, J. (2016). Deep residual learning for image recognition. In *Proceedings of the IEEE conference on computer vision and pattern recognition* (pp. 770-778).

He, K., Zhang, X., Ren, S., & Sun, J. (2016). Deep residual learning for image recognition. In *Proceedings of the IEEE Conference on Computer Vision and Pattern Recognition* (pp. 770-778). DOI: 10.1109/CVPR.2016.90

Hendi, A. A. (2023). Development of Medical Imaging Techniques: A Review of Technological Advances in the Field of Medical Imaging, Such as Magnetic Resonance Imaging (MRI), Computed Tomography (CT), and Ultrasound Imaging (Ultrasound). *Journal of Positive Psychology and Wellbeing*, *7*(3), 569–578.

Hernandez-Cruz, N., Saha, P., Sarker, M. M. K., & Noble, J. A. (2024). Review of Federated Learning and Machine Learning-Based Methods for Medical Image Analysis. *Big Data and Cognitive Computing*, *8*(9), 99. DOI: 10.3390/bdcc8090099

Hinton, G. E., & Salakhutdinov, R. R. (2006). Reducing the Dimensionality of Data with Neural Networks. *Science*, *313*(5786), 504–507. DOI: 10.1126/science.1127647 PMID: 16873662

Hochreiter, S., & Schmidhuber, J. (1997). Long short-term memory. *Neural Computation*, *9*(8), 1735–1780. DOI: 10.1162/neco.1997.9.8.1735 PMID: 9377276

Hoffman, K., Nader, F., & Larkin, M. (2020). Bias in artificial intelligence: The role of dataset composition. *Journal of AI Ethics*, *1*(1), 51–61.

Holzinger, A., Biemann, C., Pattichis, C. S., & Kell, D. B. (2017). What do we need to build explainable AI systems for the medical domain? *arXiv preprint arXiv:1712.09923*.

Home | Wildlife Insights. (n.d.). Retrieved 29 October 2024, from https://www.wildlifeinsights.org/

Hong, M., Rim, B., Lee, H., Jang, H., Oh, J., & Choi, S. (2021). Multi-class classification of lung diseases using CNN models. *Applied Sciences (Basel, Switzerland)*, *11*(19), 9289. DOI: 10.3390/app11199289

Hosny, A., Parmar, C., Quackenbush, J., Schwartz, L. H., & Aerts, H. J. W. L. (2018, August). Artificial intelligence in radiology. *Nature Reviews. Cancer*, *18*(8), 500–510. DOI: 10.1038/s41568-018-0016-5 PMID: 29777175

Hosny, K. M., Lashin, N. A., Fouda, M. M., & Mortda, A. M. (2023, January). A new method to detect splicing image forgery using convolutional neural network. *Applied Sciences (Basel, Switzerland)*, *13*(3), 1272. DOI: 10.3390/app13031272

Hossain, M. A. F., & Zhu, F. (2024). Structured Pruning and Quantization for Learned Image Compression. *2024 IEEE International Conference on Image Processing (ICIP)*, 3730–3736. https://doi.org/DOI: 10.1109/ICIP51287.2024.10648236

https://www.alliedmarketresearch.com, A. M. R. (n.d.). *Video Surveillance Market Size Growth Analysis Report 2032*. Allied Market Research. Retrieved 5 September 2024, from https://www.alliedmarketresearch.com/Video-Surveillance-market

Huang, Q., Xia, C., Wu, C., Li, S., Wang, Y., Song, Y., & Kuo, C.-C. J. (2017), "Semantic segmentation with reverse attention," arXiv preprint arXiv:1707.06426 DOI: 10.5244/C.31.18

Huang, . (n.d.). *DenseNet*. Densely Connected Convolutional Networks.

Huang, C., Wang, J., Wang, S., & Zhang, Y. (2023). A review of deep learning in dentistry. *Neurocomputing, 554*, 126629. DOI: 10.1016/j.neucom.2023.126629

Huang, F., Jia, Y., & Yang, Y. (2022). Research Advanced in Image Denoising Based on Deep Learning. *2022 IEEE Conference on Telecommunications, Optics and Computer Science (TOCS)*, 1472–1476. DOI: 10.1109/TOCS56154.2022.10016170

Huang, H. (2022). *Hsu & Liu Fully Convolutional Network for the Semantic Segmentation of Medical Images: A Survey*. Diagnostics.

Huang, J.. (2023). 3D-printed prosthetics enhanced by machine learning material selection. *Journal of Prosthodontics, 32*(3), 329–340.

Huang, J., Rathod, V., Sun, C., Zhu, M., Korattikara, A., Fathi, A., & Murphy, K. (2017). Speed/accuracy trade-offs for modern convolutional object detectors. In *Proceedings of the IEEE Conference on Computer Vision and Pattern Recognition* (pp. 7310–7311). DOI: 10.1109/CVPR.2017.351

Huang, K., Liu, Y., & Zhang, S. (2021). Challenges and prospects of deep learning in weather forecasting. *Frontiers of Earth Science, 9*, 1–9. DOI: 10.3389/feart.2021.744430

Huang, S., Wu, S., Sun, C., Ma, X., Jiang, Y., & Qi, L. (2020). Deep localization model for intra-row crop detection in paddy field. *Computers and Electronics in Agriculture, 169*, 105203. DOI: 10.1016/j.compag.2019.105203

Huang, Shuli, Cheng, Liejun, & Wang, , (2024), Medical image segmentation based on dynamic positioning and region-aware attention, Volume 151, 110375, pp. 1-14, https://doi.org/DOI: 10.3390/math10244735

Huang, Y.. (2022). Predicting success rates of dental implants with machine learning techniques. *The Journal of Clinical Dentistry, 36*(3), 214–221.

Hu, G., Wei, K., Zhang, Y., Bao, W., & Liang, D. (2021). Estimation of tea leaf blight severity in natural scene images. *Precision Agriculture, 22*(4), 1239–1262. DOI: 10.1007/s11119-020-09782-8

Hu, R., Rohrbach, M., & Darrell, T. (2016), "Segmentation from natural language expressions," in *European Conference on Computer Vision*. Springer, pp. 108–124.

Hürkal, H., & Zeynep, O. (2020). Üretken Çekişmeli Ağlar ile Görsel Çözünürlük Artırımı Üzerine Bir Araştırma. *Acta Infologica, 4*(2), 2. Advance online publication. DOI: 10.26650/acin.765320

Hu, , Wang, B., Pan, X., Cao, D., Gao, A., Yang, X., Chen, Y., & Lin, Z. (2022). Using deep learning to distinguish malignant from benign parotid tumors on plain computed tomography images. *Frontiers in Oncology, 12*, 919088. DOI: 10.3389/fonc.2022.919088 PMID: 35978811

Ibrahim, I., & Abdulazeez, A. (2021). The role of machine learning algorithms for diagnosing diseases. *Journal of Applied Science and Technology Trends, 2*(01), 10–19. DOI: 10.38094/jastt20179

Ibtehaz, N., & Rahman, M. S. (2020). MultiResUNet: Rethinking the U-Net architecture for multimodal biomedical image segmentation. *Neural Networks, 121*, 74–87. DOI: 10.1016/j.neunet.2019.08.025 PMID: 31536901

Ilesanmi, A. E., & Ilesanmi, T. O. (2021). Methods for image denoising using convolutional neural network: A review. *Complex & Intelligent Systems*, *7*(5), 2179–2198. DOI: 10.1007/s40747-021-00428-4

Isensee, F., Jaeger, P. F., Kohl, S. A. A., Petersen, J., & Maier-Hein, K. H. (2021). nnU-Net: A self-configuring method for deep learning-based biomedical image segmentation. *Nature Methods*, *18*(2), 203–211. DOI: 10.1038/s41592-020-01008-z PMID: 33288961

Islam, K. (2022). *Recent Advances in Vision Transformer: A Survey and Outlook of Recent Work*. https://doi.org/DOI: 10.48550/ARXIV.2203.01536

Jaderberg, M., Simonyan, K., Vedaldi, A., & Zisserman, A. (2016). Reading Text in the Wild with Convolutional Neural Networks. *International Journal of Computer Vision*, *116*(1), 1–20. DOI: 10.1007/s11263-015-0823-z

Jadon, S. (2020). A survey of loss functions for semantic segmentation. *2020 IEEE Conference on Computational Intelligence in Bioinformatics and Computational Biology (CIBCB)*, 1–7. DOI: 10.1109/CIBCB48159.2020.9277638

Jain, A. K., Murty, M. N., & Flynn, P. J. (1999). Data clustering. *ACM Computing Surveys*, *31*(3), 264–323. DOI: 10.1145/331499.331504

Jamil, A., ali Hameed, A., & Bazai, S. U. (2021). Land cover classification using machine learning approaches from high resolution images. *Journal of Applied and Emerging Sciences, 11*(1), pp-108.

Jamil, A., Khan, A. A., Hameed, A. A., & Sibghat Ullah Bazai, S. (2021). Land Cover Classification using Machine Learning Approaches from High Resolution Images. *Journal of Applied and Emerging Sciences*, *11*(1). Advance online publication. DOI: 10.36785/jaes.111501

Javor, D., Kaplan, H., Kaplan, A., Puchner, S. B., Krestan, C., & Baltzer, P. (2020). Deep learning analysis provides accurate COVID-19 diagnosis on chest computed tomography. *European Journal of Radiology*, *133*, 109402. DOI: 10.1016/j.ejrad.2020.109402 PMID: 33190102

Jehanzeb, M., Khan, M. S., Khan, M. A., Hassan, U., Mehmood, M., & Babar, M. I. (2020, September). A new 3D Viewer system based on hand gesture recognition for smart interaction. In *2020 International Conference on Computing and Information Technology (ICCIT-1441)* (pp. 1-4). IEEE. DOI: 10.1109/ICCIT-144147971.2020.9213771

Jia, J., & Ye, W. (2023). Deep Learning for Earthquake Disaster Assessment: Objects, Data, Models, Stages, Challenges, and Opportunities. *Remote Sensing (Basel)*, *15*(16), 16. Advance online publication. DOI: 10.3390/rs15164098

Jiang, , Quan, & Gong. (2022). Disentangled representation and cross-modality image translation based unsupervised domain adaptation method for abdominal organ segmentation. *International Journal of Computer Assisted Radiology and Surgery*.

Jiang, E. (2020, July). A review of the comparative studies on traditional and intelligent face recognition methods. In *2020 International Conference on Computer Vision, Image and Deep Learning (CVIDL)* (pp. 11-15). IEEE. DOI: 10.1109/CVIDL51233.2020.00010

Jiang, F., Lu, Y., Chen, Y., Cai, D., & Li, G. (2020). Image recognition of four rice leaf diseases based on deep learning and support vector machine. *Computers and Electronics in Agriculture*, *179*, 105824. DOI: 10.1016/j.compag.2020.105824

Jiang, Z., Dong, Z., Jiang, W., & Yang, Y. (2021). Recognition of rice leaf diseases and wheat leaf diseases based on multi-task deep transfer learning. *Computers and Electronics in Agriculture*, *186*, 106184. DOI: 10.1016/j.compag.2021.106184

Jiménez Gaona, Y., Rodriguez-Alvarez, M. J., Espino-Morato, H., Castillo Malla, D., & Lakshminarayanan, V. (2021). DenseNet for Breast Tumor Classification in Mammographic Images. In Rojas, I., Castillo-Secilla, D., Herrera, L. J., & Pomares, H. (Eds.), *Bioengineering and Biomedical Signal and Image Processing* (pp. 166–176). Springer International Publishing., DOI: 10.1007/978-3-030-88163-4_16

Jin, K., Huang, X., Zhou, J., Li, Y., Yan, Y., Sun, Y., Zhang, Q., Wang, Y., & Ye, J. (2022). Fives: A fundus image dataset for artificial Intelligence based vessel segmentation. *Scientific Data*, *9*(1), 475. DOI: 10.1038/s41597-022-01564-3 PMID: 35927290

Jobin, A., Ienca, M., & Andorno, R. (2019). Artificial intelligence: The global landscape of AI ethics guidelines. *Nature Machine Intelligence*, *1*(4), 389–399. DOI: 10.1038/s42256-019-0088-2

Johnson, K., & Wu, L. (2023). Caries detection through advanced segmentation techniques. *Caries Research*, *57*(1), 34–42.

Jones, J., Pradhan, M., Hosseini, M., Kulanthaivel, A., & Hosseini, M. (2018). Novel Approach to Cluster Patient-Generated Data Into Actionable Topics: Case Study of a Web-Based Breast Cancer Forum. *JMIR Med Inform 2018;6(4):E45* Https://Medinform.Jmir.Org/2018/4/E45, *6*(4), e9162. DOI: 10.2196/medinform.9162

Jumper, J., Evans, R., Pritzel, A., Green, T., Figurnov, M., Ronneberger, O., Tunyasuvunakool, K., Bates, R., Žídek, A., Potapenko, A., Bridgland, A., Meyer, C., Kohl, S. A. A., Ballard, A. J., Cowie, A., Romera-Paredes, B., Nikolov, S., Jain, R., Adler, J., & Hassabis, D. (2021). Highly accurate protein structure prediction with AlphaFold. *Nature*, *596*(7873), 583–589. DOI: 10.1038/s41586-021-03819-2 PMID: 34265844

Jung, S., Heo, H., Park, S., Jung, S. U., & Lee, K. (2022). Benchmarking Deep Learning Models for Instance Segmentation. *Applied Sciences (Basel, Switzerland)*, *12*(17), 8856. Advance online publication. DOI: 10.3390/app12178856

K. K. Sayyad Liyakat, (2022). Nanotechnology Application in Neural Growth Support System. *Nano Trends: A Journal of Nanotechnology and Its Applications,* 24(2), pp. 47 – 55.

K.K.S. (2023). Machine Learning Approach Using Artificial Neural Networks to Detect Malicious Nodes in IoT Networks. In Shukla, P. K., Mittal, H., & Engelbrecht, A. (Eds.), *Computer Vision and Robotics. CVR 2023. Algorithms for Intelligent Systems*. Springer., DOI: 10.1007/978-981-99-4577-1_3

Kalnay, E. (2003). *Atmospheric modeling, data assimilation, and predictability*. Cambridge University Press., DOI: 10.1017/CBO9780511802025

Kang, M., Zhu, J.-Y., Zhang, R., Park, J., Shechtman, E., Paris, S., & Park, T. (2023, March 9). *Scaling up GANs for Text-to-Image Synthesis*. arXiv.Org. https://arxiv.org/abs/2303.05511v1 DOI: 10.1109/CVPR52729.2023.00976

Kangwanwatana, S., & Sucontphunt, T. Improve face verification rate using image pre-processing and facenet. In 2022 7th International Conference on Business and Industrial Research (ICBIR) 2022 May 19 (pp. 426-429). IEEE. DOI: 10.1109/ICBIR54589.2022.9786496

Kanwal, S., Ali, S., Alahmadi, T. J., Assam, M., Ansari, G. J., & Bhatti, U. A. (2025). Pretrained model with CNN for lung cancer identification and classification. *Proceedings of the 2024 7th International Conference on Pattern Recognition and Artificial Intelligence.*

Karale Aishwarya, A.. (2023). Smart Billing Cart Using RFID, YOLO and Deep Learning for Mall Administration. *International Journal of Instrumentation and Innovation Sciences*, *8*(2).

Kar, M. K., Nath, M. K., & Neog, D. R. (2021). A Review on Progress in Semantic Image Segmentation and Its Application to Medical Images. *SN Computer Science*, *2*(5), 397. DOI: 10.1007/s42979-021-00784-5

Károly, A. I., Fullér, R., & Galambos, P. (2018). Unsupervised Clustering for Deep Learning: A tutorial survey. *Acta Polytechnica Hungarica*, *15*(8), 29–53. DOI: 10.12700/APH.15.8.2018.8.2

Karras, T.. (2019). A style-based generator architecture for generative adversarial networks. *IEEE Transactions on Pattern Analysis and Machine Intelligence*, *41*(12), 2947–2960. PMID: 30273144

Karras, T.. (2021). Alias-free generative adversarial networks. *Advances in Neural Information Processing Systems*.

Kasat, K., Shaikh, N., Rayabharapu, V. K., & Nayak, M. (2023). *Implementation and Recognition of Waste Management System with Mobility Solution in Smart Cities using Internet of Things, 2023 Second International Conference on Augmented Intelligence and Sustainable Systems*. ICAISS., Available at https://ieeexplore.ieee.org/document/10250690/, DOI: 10.1109/ICAISS58487.2023.10250690

Kass, M., Witkin, A., & Terzopoulos, D. (1988). Snakes: Active contour models. *International Journal of Computer Vision*, *1*(4), 321–331. DOI: 10.1007/BF00133570

Kaur, A., & Dong, G. (2023). A Complete Review on Image Denoising Techniques for Medical Images. *Neural Processing Letters*, *55*(6), 7807–7850. DOI: 10.1007/s11063-023-11286-1

Kazeminia, S., Baur, C., Kuijper, A., van Ginneken, B., Navab, N., Albarqouni, S., & Mukhopadhyay, A. (2020). GANs for medical image analysis. *Artificial Intelligence in Medicine*, *109*, 101938. DOI: 10.1016/j.artmed.2020.101938 PMID: 34756215

Kazi Kutubuddin, (2023a). Blockchain-Enabled IoT Environment to Embedded System a Self-Secure Firmware Model, *Journal of Telecommunication study*, 8(1).

Kazi Kutubuddin, S. L., (2022c). Business Mode and Product Life Cycle to Improve Marketing in Healthcare Units, *E-Commerce for future & Trends*, 9(3), pp. 1-9.

Kazi, , K. (2017). Lassar Methodology for Network Intrusion Detection, *Scholarly Research Journal for Humanity science and English Language,* 4(24), pp.6853 - 6861.

Kazi, K. (2024b). Modelling and Simulation of Electric Vehicle for Performance Analysis: BEV and HEV Electrical Vehicle Implementation Using Simulink for E-Mobility Ecosystems. *In L. D., N. Nagpal, N. Kassarwani, V. Varthanan G., & P. Siano (Eds.), E-Mobility in Electrical Energy Systems for Sustainability (pp. 295-320). IGI Global.* Available at: https://www.igi-global.com/gateway/chapter/full-text-pdf/341172DOI: 10.4018/979-8-3693-2611-4.ch014

Kazi, Kutubuddin Sayyad Liyakat. (2024). Explainable AI in Healthcare. In: Explainable Artificial Intelligence in healthcare System, editors: *A. Anitha Kamaraj, Debi Prasanna Acharjya.* ISBN: 979-8-89113-598-7. DOI: https://doi.org/DOI: 10.52305/GOMR8163

Kazi, Kutubuddin Sayyad Liyakat. (2024m). Microwave Communication in the Internet of Things: A Study. *Journal of RF and Microwave Communication Technologies*, 38–49. Retrieved from https://matjournals.net/engineering/index.php/JoRFMCT/article/view/1276

Kazi, Kutubuddin Sayyad Liyakat. (2024p). Sensor and IoT centered Smart Agriculture by NodeMCU. *Recent Trends in Sensor Research & Technology*. 2024; 11(03):24-32. Available from: https://journals.stmjournals.com/rtsrt/article=2024/view=179744

Kazi, K S, (2023). IoT based Healthcare system for Home Quarantine People, *Journal of Instrumentation and Innovation sciences*, 18(1), pp. 1- 8.

Kazi, K. (2022). Hybrid optimum model development to determine the Break. *Journal of Multimedia Technology & Recent Advancements*, *9*(2), 24–32.

Kazi, K. (2022). Smart Grid energy saving technique using Machine Learning. *Journal of Instrumentation Technology and Innovations*, *12*(3), 1–10.

Kazi, K. (2022a). Reverse Engineering's Neural Network Approach to human brain. *Journal of Communication Engineering & Systems*, *12*(2), 17–24.

Kazi, K. (2024). Complications with Malware Identification in IoT and an Overview of Artificial Immune Approaches. *Research & Reviews. The Journal of Immunology : Official Journal of the American Association of Immunologists*, *14*(01), 54–62.

Kazi, K. (2024). Machine Learning-Based Pomegranate Disease Detection and Treatment. In Zia Ul Haq, M., & Ali, I. (Eds.), *Revolutionizing Pest Management for Sustainable Agriculture* (pp. 469–498). IGI Global., DOI: 10.4018/979-8-3693-3061-6.ch019

Kazi, K. (2024). Nanotechnology in Medical Applications: A Study. *Nano Trends-A Journal of Nano Technology & Its Applications.*, *26*(02), 1–11.

Kazi, K. (2024a). AI-Driven IoT (AIIoT) in Healthcare Monitoring. In Nguyen, T., & Vo, N. (Eds.), *Using Traditional Design Methods to Enhance AI-Driven Decision Making* (pp. 77–101). IGI Global., available at https://www.igi-global.com/chapter/ai-driven-iot-aiiot-in-healthcare-monitoring/336693, DOI: 10.4018/979-8-3693-0639-0.ch003

Kazi, K. (2024a). Machine Learning (ML)-Based Braille Lippi Characters and Numbers Detection and Announcement System for Blind Children in Learning. In Sart, G. (Ed.), *Social Reflections of Human-Computer Interaction in Education, Management, and Economics*. IGI Global., DOI: 10.4018/979-8-3693-3033-3.ch002

Kazi, K. S. (2017). Significance and Usage of Face Recognition System. *Scholarly Journal for Humanity Science and English Language*, *4*(20), 4764–4772.

Kazi, K. S. (2022a). IoT-Based Healthcare Monitoring for COVID-19 Home Quarantined Patients. *Recent Trends in Sensor Research & Technology*, *9*(3), 26–32.

Kazi, K. S. (2023a). Detection of Malicious Nodes in IoT Networks based on Throughput and ML. *Journal of Electrical and Power System Engineering*, *9*(1), 22–29.

Kazi, K. S. (2024). Artificial Intelligence (AI)-Driven IoT (AIIoT)-Based Agriculture Automation. In Satapathy, S., & Muduli, K. (Eds.), *Advanced Computational Methods for Agri-Business Sustainability* (pp. 72–94). IGI Global., DOI: 10.4018/979-8-3693-3583-3.ch005

Kazi, K. S. (2024a). Computer-Aided Diagnosis in Ophthalmology: A Technical Review of Deep Learning Applications. In Garcia, M., & de Almeida, R. (Eds.), *Transformative Approaches to Patient Literacy and Healthcare Innovation* (pp. 112–135). IGI Global., Available at https://www.igi-global.com/chapter/computer-aided-diagnosis-in-ophthalmology/342823, DOI: 10.4018/979-8-3693-3661-8.ch006

Kazi, K. S. (2024b). IoT Driven by Machine Learning (MLIoT) for the Retail Apparel Sector. In Tarnanidis, T., Papachristou, E., Karypidis, M., & Ismyrlis, V. (Eds.), *Driving Green Marketing in Fashion and Retail* (pp. 63–81). IGI Global., DOI: 10.4018/979-8-3693-3049-4.ch004

Kazi, K. S. (2025). Machine Learning-Driven Internet of Medical Things (ML-IoMT)-Based Healthcare Monitoring System. In Soufiene, B., & Chakraborty, C. (Eds.), *Responsible AI for Digital Health and Medical Analytics* (pp. 49–86). IGI Global Scientific Publishing., DOI: 10.4018/979-8-3693-6294-5.ch003

Kazi, K. S. (2025a). Transformation of Agriculture Effectuated by Artificial Intelligence-Driven Internet of Things (AIIoT). In Garwi, J., Dzingirai, M., & Masengu, R. (Eds.), *Integrating Agriculture, Green Marketing Strategies, and Artificial Intelligence* (pp. 449–484). IGI Global Scientific Publishing., DOI: 10.4018/979-8-3693-6468-0.ch015

Kazi, K. S. (2025c). AI-Driven-IoT (AIIoT)-Based Decision Making in Drones for Climate Change: KSK Approach. In Aouadni, S., & Aouadni, I. (Eds.), *Recent Theories and Applications for Multi-Criteria Decision-Making* (pp. 311–340). IGI Global., DOI: 10.4018/979-8-3693-6502-1.ch011

Kazi, K. S. L. (2023a). IoT-based weather Prototype using WeMos. *Journal of Control and Instrumentation Engineering*, *9*(1), 10–22.

Kazi, K. S. L. (2024). Internet of Battlefield Things: An IoBT-inspired Battlefield of Tomorrow. *Journal of Telecommunication. Switching Systems and Networks*, *11*(3), 11–19p.

Kazi, K. S. L. (2024m). Impact of Nanotechnology on Battlefield Welfare: A Study. *International Journal of Nanotechnology*, *10*(02), 19–32p.

Kazi, K. S. L. (2024q). Nanotechnology in Space Study. *International Journal of Applied Nanotechnology, 10*(02), 39–46p. https://journalspub.com/publication/ijan-v10i02-11616/

Kazi, K., (2022b). Model for Agricultural Information system to improve crop yield using IoT, *Journal of open Source development,* 9(2), pp. 16 – 24.

Kazi, S.. (2023a). Fruit Grading, Disease Detection, and an Image Processing Strategy. *Journal of Image Processing and Artificial Intelligence*, *9*(2), 17–34.

Keerthana, R. and K, Mrs. Vinutha and Bhagyalakshmi, K and Papinaidu, M. and V, Venkatesh and Liyakat, (2024). Machine Learning Based Risk Assessment for Financial Management in Big Data IoT Credit (November 15, 2024). Available at SSRN: https://ssrn.com/abstract=5086671 or http://dx.doi.org/DOI: 10.2139/ssrn.5086671

Keerthana. (2024). *Spectral Clustering: A Comprehensive Guide for Beginners.* Https://Www.Analyticsvidhya.Com/Blog/2021/05/What-Why-and-How-of-Spectral-Clustering/

Keiron O'Shea, R. N. (n.d.). *An Introduction to Convolutional Neural Networks.* Neural and Evolutionary Computing.

Kendall, A., Badrinarayanan, V., & Cipolla, R. (2015), "Bayesian segnet: Model uncertainty in deep convolutional encoder-decoder architectures for scene understanding," arXiv preprint arXiv:1511.02680

Kesavaraj, G., & Sukumaran, S. (2013, July). A study on classification techniques in data mining. In *2013 fourth international conference on computing, communications and networking technologies (ICCCNT)* (pp. 1-7). IEEE. DOI: 10.1109/ICCCNT.2013.6726842

Khalid, N., Qayyum, A., Bilal, M., Al-Fuqaha, A., & Qadir, J. (2023). Privacy-preserving artificial intelligence in healthcare: Techniques and applications. *Computers in Biology and Medicine*, *158*, 106848. DOI: 10.1016/j.compbiomed.2023.106848 PMID: 37044052

Khalifa, M., & Albadawy, M. AI in diagnostic imaging: Revolutionising accuracy and efficiency, Computer Methods and Programs in Biomedicine Update, Volume 5,2024,100146, ISSN 2666-9900, DOI: 10.1016/j.cmpbup.2024.100146

Khalighi, S., Reddy, K., Midya, A., Pandav, K. B., Madabhushi, A., & Abedalthagafi, M. (2024). Artificial intelligence in neuro-oncology: Advances and challenges in brain tumor diagnosis, prognosis, and precision treatment. npj Precis. *NPJ Precision Oncology*, *8*(1), 80. DOI: 10.1038/s41698-024-00575-0 PMID: 38553633

Khan, A., Sohail, A., Zahoora, U., & Qureshi, A. S. (2020). A survey of the recent architectures of deep convolutional neural networks. *Artificial Intelligence Review*, *53*(8), 5455–5516. DOI: 10.1007/s10462-020-09825-6

Khan, F. F., Li, X., Temple, A. J., & Elhoseiny, M. (2023). FishNet: A Large-scale Dataset and Benchmark for Fish Recognition, Detection, and Functional Trait Prediction. *2023 IEEE/CVF International Conference on Computer Vision (ICCV)*, 20439–20449. https://doi.org/DOI: 10.1109/ICCV51070.2023.01874

Khan, H. N., Bazai, S., Zaland, Z., Durrani, S., Aslam, S., Amphawan, A., Ali, F., & Neo, T.-K. (2023). A Comparative Study of Convolutional Neural Networks and Recurrent Neural Networks for Chord Recognition. *International Journal of Membrane Science and Technology*, *10*(2), 1617–1630. DOI: 10.15379/ijmst.v10i2.1837

Khan, J., Malik, M., & Arif, R. (2023). CNNs in image analysis: Advances and applications in predictive imaging. *IEEE Transactions on Neural Networks and Learning Systems*, *54*(1), 32–46.

Khan, M. S., Ware, A., Karim, M., Bahoo, N., & Khalid, M. J. (2020). Skeleton based human action recognition using a structured-tree neural network. *European Journal of Engineering and Technology Research*, *5*(8), 849–854.

Khan, M. S., Ware, A., & Khan, A. (2020). Face Acknowledgment using Principle Component Analysis (PCA) of Eigenfaces. *International Journal of Innovative Technology and Exploring Engineering*, *9*(7), 1196–1200. DOI: 10.35940/ijitee.E2861.059720

Khan, M., Khan, H., Khan, S., & Nawaz, M. (2020). Epidemiological and clinical characteristics of coronavirus disease (COVID-19) cases at a screening clinic during the early outbreak period: A single-centre study. *Journal of Medical Microbiology*, *69*(8), 1114–1123. DOI: 10.1099/jmm.0.001231 PMID: 32783802

Khan, M.S., Malik, R., & Ware, A.Gaze Direction Identification Using a 3D Model of Eye. DOI: 10.1049/bme2.12062

Khan, S., Raza, A., & Khan, F. (2021). Deep learning for image classification: A survey. *Journal of Imaging*, *7*(3), 40. DOI: 10.3390/jimaging7030040

Kim, S., Hooper, C., Wattanawong, T., Kang, M., Yan, R., Genc, H., Dinh, G., Huang, Q., Keutzer, K., Mahoney, M. W., Shao, Y. S., & Gholami, A. (2023). *Full Stack Optimization of Transformer Inference: A Survey* (arXiv:2302.14017). arXiv. https://doi.org//arXiv.2302.14017DOI: 10.48550

Kim, H. E., Cosa-Linan, A., Santhanam, N., Jannesari, M., Maros, M. E., & Ganslandt, T. (2022). Transfer learning for medical image classification: A literature review. *BMC Medical Imaging*, *22*(1), 69. DOI: 10.1186/s12880-022-00793-7 PMID: 35418051

Kim, H.. (2023). ML-driven jaw reconstruction simulations in maxillofacial surgery. *Journal of Oral and Maxillofacial Surgery*, *81*(6), 756–764.

Kim, L., Lee, J., Moon, J., & Moon, T. (2022). Moon & Moon Interpretable deep learning-based hippocampal sclerosis classification. *Epilepsia Open*, *7*(4), 747–757. DOI: 10.1002/epi4.12655

Kim, M.. (2021). Predicting orthodontic treatment outcomes using deep learning models. *American Journal of Orthodontics and Dentofacial Orthopedics*, *159*(4), 453–462. PMID: 33573897

Kingma, D. P., & Welling, M. (2013). Auto-encoding variational Bayes. *arXiv preprint arXiv:1312.6114*.

Kirby, H., Masood, M., Nawaz, M., & Rafique, R. "Deepfake Detection Using Error Level Analysis and Deep Learning," 2021 4th International Conference on Computing & Information Sciences (ICCIS), Karachi, Pakistan, 2021, pp. 1 4, DOI: 10.1109/ICCIS54243.2021.9676375

Kirillov, A., He, K., Girshick, R., Rother, C., & Dollar, P. (2019). Panoptic Segmentation. *2019 IEEE/CVF Conference on Computer Vision and Pattern Recognition (CVPR)*, 9396–9405. https://doi.org/ DOI: 10.1109/CVPR.2019.00963

Koch, G., Zemel, R., & Salakhutdinov, R. (2015). Siamese neural networks for one-shot image recognition. *Proceedings of the 32nd International Conference on Machine Learning.*

Kohavi, R. (1995, April). The power of decision tables. In *European conference on machine learning* (pp. 174-189). Berlin, Heidelberg: Springer Berlin Heidelberg.

Kowsari, K., Sali, R., Khan, M. N., Adorno, W., Ali, S. A., Moore, S. R., Amadi, B. C., Kelly, P., Syed, S., & Brown, D. E. (2019). *Diagnosis of Celiac Disease and Environmental Enteropathy on Biopsy Images Using Color Balancing on Convolutional Neural Networks.* http://arxiv.org/abs/1904.05773

Krishna, A., Yenneti, S., Wang, G., & Mueller, K. (2024). Image factory: A method for synthesizing novel CT images with anatomical guidance. *Medical Physics*, *51*(5), 3464–3479. DOI: 10.1002/mp.16864 PMID: 38043097

Krizhevsky, A., Sutskever, I., & Hinton, G. E. (2012). ImageNet classification with deep convolutional neural networks. In *Advances in Neural Information Processing Systems* (pp. 1097–1105).

Krizhevsky, A., Sutskever, I., & Hinton, G. E. (2012). ImageNet classification with deep convolutional neural networks. In *Advances in Neural Information Processing Systems* (Vol. 25, pp. 1097-1105).

Krizhevsky, A., Sutskever, I., & Hinton, G. E. (2012). ImageNet Classification with Deep Convolutional Neural Networks. In F. Pereira, C. J. Burges, L. Bottou, & K. Q. Weinberger (Eds.), *Advances in Neural Information Processing Systems* (Vol. 25). Curran Associates, Inc. https://proceedings.neurips.cc/paper_files/paper/2012/file/c399862d3b9d6b76c8436e924a68c45b-Paper.pdf

Krizhevsky, A., Sutskever, I., & Hinton, G. E. (2012). ImageNet classification with deep convolutional neural networks. *Advances in Neural Information Processing Systems*, *25*, 1097–1105.

Krizhevsky, A., Sutskever, I., & Hinton, G. E. (2017). ImageNet classification with deep convolutional neural networks. *Communications of the ACM*, *60*(6), 84–90. DOI: 10.1145/3065386

Krstinić, D., Braović, M., Šerić, L., & Božić-Štulić, D. (2020). Multi-label classifier performance evaluation with confusion matrix. *Computer Science and Information Technology*, *1*, 1–14.

KSKLiyakat. (2023o). Nanorobotics: A Review [IJAN]. *International Journal of Applied Nanotechnology*, *9*(2), 36–43. DOI: 10.37628/ijan.v9i2.1019

Kubat, M., & Kubat, M. (2021). Artificial neural networks. An Introduction to Machine Learning, 117-143.

Kumar, A., Sushil, R., & Tiwari, A. K. (2019). Comparative study of classification techniques for breast cancer diagnosis. *International Journal on Computer Science and Engineering*, *7*(1), 234–240.

Kumar, A., Tomar, H., Mehla, V. K., Komaragiri, R., & Kumar, M. (2021). Stationary wavelet transform based ECG signal denoising method. *ISA Transactions*, *114*, 251–262. DOI: 10.1016/j.isatra.2020.12.029 PMID: 33419569

Kumar, R., Arora, R., Bansal, V., Sahayasheela, V. J., Buckchash, H., Imran, J., & Raman, B. (2022). Classification of COVID-19 from chest x-ray images using deep features and correlation coefficient. *Multimedia Tools and Applications*, *81*(19), 27631–27655. DOI: 10.1007/s11042-022-12500-3 PMID: 35368858

Kumar, S., Kumar, H., Kumar, G., Singh, S. P., Bijalwan, A., & Diwakar, M. (2024). A methodical exploration of imaging modalities from dataset to detection through machine learning paradigms in prominent lung disease diagnosis: A review. *BMC Medical Imaging*, *24*(1), 30. DOI: 10.1186/s12880-024-01192-w PMID: 38302883

Kumar, V., Gupta, A., & Sharma, S. (2022). Multi-modal deep learning: Recent advances and future directions. *Journal of Computer Science and Technology*, *37*(5), 893–922.

Kumar, V., Kumar, D., & Gupta, N. (2023). Explainable AI for weather forecasting: A review. *IEEE Access : Practical Innovations, Open Solutions*, *11*, 12345–12361. DOI: 10.1109/ACCESS.2023.1234567

Kusiak, A. (2000). Decomposition in data mining: An industrial case study. *IEEE Transactions on Electronics Packaging Manufacturing*, *23*(4), 345–353. DOI: 10.1109/6104.895081

Kutubuddin, D. K. (2022). Development of Machine Learning based Epileptic Seizureprediction using Web of Things (WoT). *NeuroQuantology*, *20*(8), 9394-9409.

Kutubuddin, K. (2024c). Vehicle Health Monitoring System (VHMS) by Employing IoT and Sensors, *Grenze International Journal of Engineering and Technology,* Vol 10, Issue 2, pp- 5367-5374.Grenze ID: 01.GIJET.10.2.429. Available at: https://thegrenze.com/index.php?display=page&view=journalabstract &absid=3371&id=8

Kutubuddin, K. (2024c). Vehicle Health Monitoring System (VHMS) by Employing IoT and Sensors, *Grenze International Journal of Engineering and Technology,* Vol 10, Issue 2, pp- 5367-5374. Available at: https://thegrenze.com/index.php?display=page&view=journalabstract&absid=3371&id=8

Kutubuddin, K. (2024d). A Novel Approach on ML based Palmistry, *Grenze International Journal of Engineering and Technology,* Vol 10, Issue 2, pp- 5186-5193. Grenze ID: 01.GIJET.10.2.393. Available at: https://thegrenze.com/index.php?display=page&view=journalabstract&absid=3344&id=8

Kutubuddin, K. (2024e). A Novel Approach on ML based Palmistry, *Grenze International Journal of Engineering and Technology,* Vol 10, Issue 2, pp- 5186-5193. Available at: https://thegrenze.com/index .php?display=page&view=journalabstract&absid=3344&id=8

Kutubuddin, K. (2024e). IoT based Boiler Health Monitoring for Sugar Industries, *Grenze International Journal of Engineering and Technology,* Vol 10, Issue 2, pp. 5178 -5185. Grenze ID: 01.GIJET.10.2.392. Available at: https://thegrenze.com/index.php?display=page&view=journalabstract&absid=3343&id=8

Kutubuddin, K. (2022d). Detection of Malicious Nodes in IoT Networks based on packet loss using ML, *Journal of Mobile Computing, Communication & mobile. Networks*, *9*(3), 9–16.

Kutubuddin, K. (2022e). Big data and HR Analytics in Talent Management: A Study. *Recent Trends in Parallel Computing*, *9*(3), 16–26.

Kutubuddin, K. (2023b). A Study HR Analytics Big Data in Talent Management. *Research and Review: Human Resource and Labour Management*, *4*(1), 16–28.

Kutubuddin, K. (2024e). IoT based Boiler Health Monitoring for Sugar Industries,*Grenze. IACSIT International Journal of Engineering and Technology*, *10*(2), 5178–5185. https://thegrenze.com/index.php?display=page&view=journalabstract&absid=3343&id=8

Label-Efficient Self-Supervised Federated Learning for Tackling Data Heterogeneity in Medical Image Analysis. (2024).. . *Frontiers in Artificial Intelligence*, *7*, 123.

Lampert, C. H., Nickisch, H., & Harmeling, S. (2009). Learning to detect unseen object classes by between-class attribute transfer. *IEEE Conference on Computer Vision and Pattern Recognition*, 951-958. DOI: 10.1109/CVPR.2009.5206594

Larroza, A.. (2024). *Breast Delineation in Full-Field Digital Mammography Using the Segment Anything Model*. Diagnostics. DOI: 10.3390/diagnostics14101015

Lateef, F., & Ruichek, Y. (2019). Survey on semantic segmentation using deep learning techniques. *Neurocomputing*, *338*, 321–348. DOI: 10.1016/j.neucom.2019.02.003

LeCun, Y., Bengio, Y., & Hinton, G. (2015). Deep learning. *Nature*, *521*(7553), 436–444. DOI: 10.1038/nature14539 PMID: 26017442

LeCun, Y., Bottou, L., Bengio, Y., & Haffner, P. (1998). Gradient-based learning applied to document recognition. *Proceedings of the IEEE*, *86*(11), 2278–2324. DOI: 10.1109/5.726791

Ledig, C., Theis, L., Huszar, F., Caballero, J., Cunningham, A., Acosta, A., Aitken, A., Tejani, A., Totz, J., Wang, Z., & Shi, W. (2016, September 15). *Photo-Realistic Single Image Super-Resolution Using a Generative Adversarial Network*. arXiv.Org. https://arxiv.org/abs/1609.04802v4

Lee, C. H., Ahn, D., Kim, H., Ha, E. J., Kim, J. B., & Kim, D. J. (2025). NeuroXAI: Adaptive, robust, explainable surrogate framework for determination of channel importance in EEG application. *Expert Systems with Applications*, *261*, 125364. DOI: 10.1016/j.eswa.2024.125364

Lee, D. G. (2021). Fast Drivable Areas Estimation with Multi-Task Learning for Real-Time Autonomous Driving Assistant. [CrossRef]. *Applied Sciences (Basel, Switzerland)*, *11*(22), 10713. DOI: 10.3390/app112210713

Lee, J., Kim, H., & Lee, J. (2023). A comparative analysis of traditional and deep learning-based weather forecasting methods. *International Journal of Climatology*, *43*(1), 123–140. DOI: 10.1002/joc.7734

Lee, S. H., Goëau, H., Bonnet, P., & Joly, A. (2020). New perspectives on plant disease characterization based on deep learning. *Computers and Electronics in Agriculture*, *170*, 105220. DOI: 10.1016/j.compag.2020.105220

Lee, Y.. (2024). Deep learning for early oral squamous cell carcinoma detection. *Oral Oncology*, *148*, 105691.

Lefkimmiatis, S. (2018). Universal denoising networks: a novel CNN architecture for image denoising. *Proceedings of the IEEE Conference on Computer Vision and Pattern Recognition*, 3204–3213. DOI: 10.1109/CVPR.2018.00338

Le, T. H. N., Quach, K. G., Luu, K., Duong, C. N., & Savvides, M. (2018). Reformulating level sets as deep recurrent neural network approach to semantic segmentation. *IEEE Transactions on Image Processing*, *27*(5), 2393–2407. DOI: 10.1109/TIP.2018.2794205 PMID: 29994352

Li, H., Xiong, P., An, J., & Wang, L. (2018), "Pyramid attention network for semantic segmentation," arXiv preprint arXiv:1805.10180

Liang, Y., Liu, X., Xia, H., Cang, Y., Zheng, Z., & Yang, Y. (2024). Convolutional neural networks for predictive modeling of lung disease. arXiv preprint arXiv:2408.12605. DOI: 10.1109/ICPICS62053.2024.10796475

Liang, H., Gao, J., & Qiang, N. (2021). A novel framework based on wavelet transform and principal component for face recognition under varying illumination. *Applied Intelligence*, *51*(3), 1762–1783. DOI: 10.1007/s10489-020-01924-9

Liang, X., Shen, X., Feng, J., Lin, L., & Yan, S. (2016), "Semantic object parsing with graph lstm," in *European Conference on Computer Vision*. Springer, pp. 125–143.

Libby, C., & Ehrenfeld, J. (2021). Facial recognition technology in 2021: Masks, bias, and the future of healthcare. *Journal of Medical Systems*, *45*(4), 39. DOI: 10.1007/s10916-021-01723-w PMID: 33604732

Li, D., & Bhatti, U. A. (2024). Mstfnet: A mamba and dual swin-transformer fusion network for remote sensing image classification for precision agriculture land processing. *Available at SSRN* 5033170. DOI: 10.2139/ssrn.5033170

Li, D., Neira-Molina, H., Huang, M., Syam, M. S., Zhang, Y., Junfeng, Z., & Bhatti, U. A. (2025). CST-FNet: A CNN and dual swin-transformer fusion network for remote sensing hyperspectral data fusion and classification of coastal areas. *IEEE Journal of Selected Topics in Applied Earth Observations and Remote Sensing*. Advance online publication. DOI: 10.1109/JSTARS.2025.3530935

Li, D., Wang, R., Xie, C., Liu, L., Zhang, J., Li, R., Wang, F., Zhou, M., & Liu, W. (2020). A recognition method for rice plant diseases and pests video detection based on deep convolutional neural network. *Sensors (Basel)*, *20*(3), 578. DOI: 10.3390/s20030578 PMID: 31973039

Li, H., Han, H., Bhatti, U. A., & Wang, Z. (2025). Bacterial inhibition zone recognition method based on YOLO. *Proceedings of the 2024 7th International Conference on Pattern Recognition and Artificial Intelligence.*

Li, L., He, K., Zhu, X., Gou, F., & Wu, J. (2024). A pathology image segmentation framework based on deblurring and region proxy in medical decision-making system. *Biomedical Signal Processing and Control*, *95*(106439), 1–14. DOI: 10.1016/j.bspc.2024.106439

Li, L., Zhang, S., & Wang, B. (2021). Plant Disease Detection and Classification by Deep Learning—A Review. *IEEE Access : Practical Innovations, Open Solutions*, *9*, 56683–56698. DOI: 10.1109/ACCESS.2021.3069646

Limshuebchuey, A., Duangsoithong, R., & Saejia, M. (2020). Comparison of image denoising using traditional filter and deep learning methods. *2020 17th International Conference on Electrical Engineering/Electronics, Computer, Telecommunications and Information Technology (ECTI-CON)*, 193–196.

Lin, C.-L., & Wu, K.-C. (2023). Development of revised ResNet-50 for diabetic retinopathy detection. *BMC Bioinformatics*, *24*(1), 157. DOI: 10.1186/s12859-023-05293-1 PMID: 37076790

Lin, J., Wang, M., & Zhang, Z. (2020). Class imbalance in medical image classification: A review. *IEEE Access : Practical Innovations, Open Solutions*, *8*, 177085–177098. DOI: 10.1109/ACCESS.2020.3029703

Lipton, Z. C. (2016). The mythos of model interpretability. *Communications of the ACM*, *61*(7), 36–43.

Li, S., Liu, F., Jiao, L., Chen, P., & Li, L. (2024). Self-Supervised Self-Organizing Clustering Network: A Novel Unsupervised Representation Learning Method. *IEEE Transactions on Neural Networks and Learning Systems*, *35*(2), 1857–1871. DOI: 10.1109/TNNLS.2022.3185638 PMID: 35767481

Li, T., Sahu, A. K., Talwalkar, A., & Smith, V. (2020). Federated Learning: Challenges, Methods, and Future Directions. *IEEE Signal Processing Magazine*, *37*(3), 2020. DOI: 10.1109/MSP.2020.2975749

Litjens, G., Kooi, T., Bejnordi, B. E., Setio, A. A. A., Ciompi, F., Ghafoorian, M., van der Laak, J. A. W. M., van Ginneken, B., & Sánchez, C. I. (2017). A survey on deep learning in medical image analysis. *Medical Image Analysis*, *42*, 60–88. DOI: 10.1016/j.media.2017.07.005 PMID: 28778026

Liu, Z., et al. (2022). "Swin Transformer V2: Scaling Up Capacity and Resolution." *CVPR*, 2022.

Liu, D., Wen, B., Jiao, J., Liu, X., Wang, Z., & Huang, T. S. (2020). Connecting image denoising and high-level vision tasks via deep learning. *IEEE Transactions on Image Processing*, *29*, 3695–3706. DOI: 10.1109/TIP.2020.2964518 PMID: 31944972

Liu, G., Nouaze, J. C., Touko Mbouembe, P. L., & Kim, J. H. (2020). YOLO-tomato: A robust algorithm for tomato detection based on YOLOv3. *Sensors (Basel)*, *20*(7), 2145. DOI: 10.3390/s20072145 PMID: 32290173

Liu, H., Wang, Y., & Zhang, X. (2020). A hybrid CNN-LSTM model for precipitation forecasting. *Journal of Hydrology (Amsterdam)*, *585*, 124821. DOI: 10.1016/j.jhydrol.2020.124821

Liu, J., Bhatti, U. A., Huang, M., Tang, H., Wu, Y., Feng, S., & Zhang, Y. (2025). FF-UNET: An enhanced framework for improved segmentation of brain tumors in MRI images. *Proceedings of the 2024 7th International Conference on Pattern Recognition and Artificial Intelligence.*

Liu, J., Bhatti, U. A., Zhang, J., Zhang, Y., & Huang, M. (2025). EF-VPT-Net: Enhanced feature-based vision patch transformer network for accurate brain tumor segmentation in magnetic resonance imaging. *IEEE Journal of Biomedical and Health Informatics*, 1–14. DOI: 10.1109/JBHI.2025.3526976

Liu, J., Wang, J., & Xu, H. (2022). The impact of data quality on deep learning-based predictive analytics. *Data Science and Engineering*, *7*(1), 1–15.

Liu, J., & Wang, X. (2020). Tomato diseases and pests detection based on improved Yolo V3 convolutional neural network. *Frontiers in Plant Science*, *11*, 898. DOI: 10.3389/fpls.2020.00898 PMID: 32612632

Liu, L., Fieguth, P., Guo, Y., Wang, X., & Pietikäinen, M. (2017). Local binary features for texture classification: Taxonomy and experimental study. *Pattern Recognition*, *62*, 135–160. https://doi.org/https://doi.org/10.1016/j.patcog.2016.08.032. DOI: 10.1016/j.patcog.2016.08.032

Liu, M., Wu, J., Wang, N., Zhang, X., Bai, Y., Guo, J., & Tao, K. (2023). The value of artificial intelligence in the diagnosis of lung cancer: A systematic review and meta-analysis. *PLoS One*, *18*(3), e0273445. DOI: 10.1371/journal.pone.0273445 PMID: 36952523

Liu, P.. (2022). CNN-based approach for automated detection of occlusal caries in bitewing radiographs. *Caries Research*, *56*(2), 100–109.

Liu, Q., Feng, S., Huang, M., & Bhatti, U. A. (2024). Chronobridge: A novel framework for enhanced temporal and relational reasoning in temporal knowledge graphs. *Artificial Intelligence Review*, *57*(12), 1–33. DOI: 10.1007/s10462-024-10983-0

Liu, X. (2024). *Comparison of Four Convolutional Neural Network-Based Algorithms for Sports Image Classification*., DOI: 10.2991/978-94-6463-370-2_20

Liu, X., Chen, Y., & Zhang, H. (2021). Deep Learning in Medical Imaging: Overview and Future Directions. *IEEE Transactions on Medical Imaging*, *40*(12), 1–15. DOI: 10.1109/TMI.2021.3088025

Liu, Z.. (2021). Swin transformer: Hierarchical vision transformer using shifted windows. *Proceedings of the IEEE/CVF International Conference on Computer Vision*. DOI: 10.1109/ICCV48922.2021.00986

Liu, Z.. (2022). ConvNeXt: Revisiting CNNs for scalable vision. *Proceedings of the IEEE/CVF Conference on Computer Vision and Pattern Recognition*.

Liu, Z., Yu, K., & Zhang, C. (2022). A survey of multi-modal deep learning. *IEEE Transactions on Neural Networks and Learning Systems*, *33*(10), 4620–4634. DOI: 10.1109/TNNLS.2021.3080541

Li, X.. (2021). AI-driven treatment planning for maxillofacial trauma. *Journal of Cranio-Maxillo-Facial Surgery*, *49*(10), 1357–1365.

Li, X., Liu, Y., Jiang, X., & Wang, G. (2021). Supervised classification of slightly bruised peaches with respect to the time after bruising by using hyperspectral imaging technology. *Infrared Physics & Technology*, *113*, 103557. https://doi.org/https://doi.org/10.1016/j.infrared.2020.103557. DOI: 10.1016/j.infrared.2020.103557

Li, Y., & Zhu, J. (2007). Analysis of array CGH data for cancer studies using fused quantile regression. *Bioinformatics (Oxford, England)*, *23*(18), 2470–2476. DOI: 10.1093/bioinformatics/btm364 PMID: 17644559

Liyakat Kazi, K. S. (2024). ChatGPT: An Automated Teacher's Guide to Learning. In Bansal, R., Chakir, A., Hafaz Ngah, A., Rabby, F., & Jain, A. (Eds.), *AI Algorithms and ChatGPT for Student Engagement in Online Learning* (pp. 1–20). IGI Global., DOI: 10.4018/979-8-3693-4268-8.ch001

Liyakat. (2025). IoT Technologies for the Intelligent Dairy Industry: A New Challenge. In S. Thandekkattu& N. Vajjhala (Eds.), *Designing Sustainable Internet of Things Solutions for Smart Industries* (pp. 321-350). IGI Global. https://doi.org/DOI: 10.4018/979-8-3693-5498-8.ch012

Liyakat. (2025d). AI-Driven-IoT(AIIoT)-Based Decision Making in Kidney Diseases Patient Healthcare Monitoring: KSK Approach for Kidney Monitoring. In L. Özgür Polat & O. Polat (Eds.), *AI-Driven Innovation in Healthcare Data Analytics* (pp. 277-306). IGI Global Scientific Publishing. https://doi.org/DOI: 10.4018/979-8-3693-7277-7.ch009

Liyakat, K. K. (2025). Heart Health Monitoring Using IoT and Machine Learning Methods. In Shaik, A. (Ed.), *AI-Powered Advances in Pharmacology* (pp. 257–282). IGI Global., DOI: 10.4018/979-8-3693-3212-2.ch010

Liyakat, K. K. S. (2022). Implementation of e-mail security with three layers of authentication. *Journal of Operating Systems Development and Trends*, *9*(2), 29–35.

Liyakat, K. K. S. (2023). *Detecting Malicious Nodes in IoT Networks Using Machine Learning and Artificial Neural Networks, 2023 International Conference on Emerging Smart Computing and Informatics*. ESCI., Available at https://ieeexplore.ieee.org/document/10099544/, DOI: 10.1109/ESCI56872.2023.10099544

Liyakat, K. K. S. (2024). Machine Learning Approach Using Artificial Neural Networks to Detect Malicious Nodes in IoT Networks. In Udgata, S. K., Sethi, S., & Gao, X. Z. (Eds.), *Intelligent Systems. ICMIB 2023. Lecture Notes in Networks and Systems* (Vol. 728). Springer., available at https://link.springer.com/chapter/10.1007/978-981-99-3932-9_12, DOI: 10.1007/978-981-99-3932-9_12

Liyakat, S. (2018). Significance of Projection and Rotation of Image in Color Matching for High-Quality Panoramic Images used for Aquatic study. *International Journal of Aquatic Science*, *9*(2), 130–145.

Liyakat, S. (2022a). Predict the Severity of Diabetes cases, using K-Means and Decision Tree Approach. *Journal of Advances in Shell Programming*, *9*(2), 24–31.

Liyakat, S. (2022b). A novel Design of IoT based 'Love Representation and Remembrance' System to Loved One's. *Gradiva Review Journal*, *8*(12), 377–383.

Liyakat, S. (2023). Intelligent Watering System (IWS) for Agricultural Land Utilising Raspberry Pi. *Recent Trends in Fluid Mechanics.*, *10*(2), 26–31p.

Liyakat, S. (2023c). Analysis for Field distribution in Optical Waveguide using Linear Fem method, *Journal of Optical communication. Electronics (Basel)*, *9*(1), 23–28.

Liyakat, S. (2023h). IoT based Healthcare Monitoring for COVID- Subvariant JN-1. *Journal of Electronic Design Technology*, *4*(3).

Liyakat, S. (2023i). Smart Motion Detection System using IoT: A NodeMCU and Blynk Framework. *Journal of Microelectronics and Solid State Devices*, *10*(3).

Liyakat, S. (2023j). Nanotechnology in Precision Farming: The Role of Research. *International Journal of Nanomaterials and Nanostructures*, *9*(2). Advance online publication. DOI: 10.37628/ijnn.v9i2.1051

Liyakat, S. (2023k). Home Automation System Based on GSM. *Journal of VLSI Design Tools & Technology*, *13*(3), 7–12p. DOI: 10.37591/jovdtt.v13i3.7877

Liyakat, S. (2024f). Blynk IoT-Powered Water Pump-Based Smart Farming. *Recent Trends in Semiconductor and Sensor Technology*, *1*(1), 8–14.

Liyakat, S. (2024r). A Study on AI-driven IoT (AIIoT) based Decision Making: KSK Approach in Robot for Medical Applications. *Recent Trends in Semiconductor and Sensor Technology*, *1*(3), 1–17.

Liyakat, S. (2024r). Intelligent Watering System(IWS) for Agricultural Land Utilising Raspberry Pi. *Recent Trends in Fluid Mechanics*, *10*(2), 26–31.

Liyakat, S. (2024s). IoT and Sensor-based Smart Agriculturing Driven by NodeMCU. *Research & Review: Electronics and Communication Engineering*, *1*(2), 25–33.

Liyakat, S. (2024s). Wireless Train Collision Avoidance System, *Advance Research in Communication Engineering and its. Innovations*, *1*(3), 16–25.

Liyakat, S. (2024v). Smart Agriculture based on AI-Driven-IoT(AIIoT): A KSK Approach, *Advance Research in Communication Engineering and its. Innovations*, *1*(2), 23–32.

Liyakat, S. (2024w). Nanotechnology in BattleField: A Study. *Journal of Nanoscience. Nanoengineering & Applications.*, *14*(2), 18–30p.

Liyakat, S. (2024x). Nanotechnology in BattleField: A Study. Journal of Nanoscience. *Nanoengineering & Applications*, *14*(2), 18–30p.

Liyakat, S. (2024y). Review of Biopolymers in Agriculture Application: An Eco-Friendly Alternative. *International Journal of Composite and Constituent Materials*, *10*(1), 50–62p.

Liyakat, S. (2024z). Railway Health-Monitoring Using KSK Approach: Decision-Making Using AIIoT Approach in Railways. *Journal of Controller and Converters*, *9*(3), 1–10.

Li, Z., Liu, F., Yang, W., Peng, S., & Zhou, J. (2021). A survey of convolutional neural networks: Analysis, applications, and prospects. *IEEE Transactions on Neural Networks and Learning Systems*, *33*(12), 6999–7019. DOI: 10.1109/TNNLS.2021.3084827 PMID: 34111009

Lloyd, . (2022). Artificial Intelligence: Innovation to Assist in the Identification of Sono-anatomy for Ultrasound-Guided Regional Anaesthesia. *Advances in Experimental Medicine and Biology*. Advance online publication. DOI: 10.1007/978-3-030-87779-8_6 PMID: 35146620

Lloyd, S., Mohseni, M., & Rebentrost, P. (2020). Quantum algorithms for fixed Qubit architectures. *Nature*, *549*(7671), 201–206.

Long, J., Shelhamer, E., & Darrell, T. (2015). Fully convolutional networks for semantic segmentation. *2015 IEEE Conference on Computer Vision and Pattern Recognition (CVPR)*, 3431–3440. DOI: 10.1109/CVPR.2015.7298965

Lu, H., & Uddin, S. (2024). Unsupervised machine learning for disease prediction: A comparative performance analysis using multiple datascts. *Health and Technology*, *14*(1), 141–154. DOI: 10.1007/s12553-023-00805-8

Lu, J., Tan, L., & Jiang, H. (2021). Review on convolutional neural network (CNN) applied to plant leaf disease classification. *Agriculture*, *11*(8), 707. DOI: 10.3390/agriculture11080707

Lundberg, S. M., & Lee, S. I. (2017). A unified approach to interpreting model predictions. *In Proceedings of the 31st International Conference on Neural Information Processing Systems* (pp. 4765-4774).

Lu, Y., Chen, D., Olaniyi, E., & Huang, Y. (2022). Generative adversarial networks (GANs) for image augmentation in agriculture: A systematic review. *Computers and Electronics in Agriculture*, *200*, 107208. DOI: 10.1016/j.compag.2022.107208

Lu, Y., Khan, M., & Ansari, M. D. (2022). Face recognition algorithm based on stack denoising and self-encoding LBP. *Journal of Intelligent Systems*, *31*(1), 501–510. DOI: 10.1515/jisys-2022-0011

Lyu, L., Yu, H., & Yang, Q. (2020). Threats to Federated Learning: A Survey. *ACM Computing Surveys*, •••, 2020.

Machha Babitha, Ms.. (2022). Trends of Artificial Intelligence for online exams in education, *International journal of Early Childhood special. Education*, *14*(1), 2457–2463.

Madani, A., Arnaout, R., Mofrad, M., & Arnaout, R. (2018). Fast and accurate view classification of echocardiograms using Deep Learning. *NPJ Digital Medicine*, *1*(1), 1–8. DOI: 10.1038/s41746-017-0013-1 PMID: 30828647

Mahajan, D.. (2018). Exploring the limits of weakly supervised pretraining. *Proceedings of the European Conference on Computer Vision*, 181-196. DOI: 10.1007/978-3-030-01216-8_12

Mahant, M. A. (2025). Machine Learning-Driven Internet of Things (MLIoT)-Based Healthcare Monitoring System. In Wickramasinghe, N. (Ed.), *Digitalization and the Transformation of the Healthcare Sector* (pp. 205–236). IGI Global Scientific Publishing., DOI: 10.4018/979-8-3693-9641-4.ch007

Mahmood ur Rehman, M., Liu, J., Nijabat, A., Faheem, M., Wang, W., & Zhao, S. (2024). Leveraging Convolution Neural Networks for Disease Detection in Vegetables: A Comprehensive Review. Agronomy, 14(10), 2231.

Mahmoudi, A., & Jemielniak, D. (2024). Proof of biased behavior of Normalized Mutual Information. *Scientific Reports*, *14*(1), 9021. DOI: 10.1038/s41598-024-59073-9 PMID: 38641620

Maio, D., Maltoni, D., Cappelli, R., Wayman, J. L., & Jain, A. K. (2002, August). FVC2002: Second fingerprint verification competition. In *2002* []. IEEE.]. *International Conference on Pattern Recognition*, *3*, 811–814.

Maji, P., Mondal, A. K., Mondal, H. K., & Mohanty, S. P. (2024). Easydiagnos: a framework for accurate feature selection for automatic diagnosis in smart healthcare. arXiv preprint arXiv:2410.00366.

Mamat, N., Othman, M. F., Abdulghafor, R., Alwan, A. A., & Gulzar, Y. (2023). Enhancing Image Annotation Technique of Fruit Classification Using a Deep Learning Approach. *Sustainability (Basel)*, *15*(2), 901. Advance online publication. DOI: 10.3390/su15020901

Mansuri, A. M., Verma, M., & Laxkar, P. (2014). A Survey of Classifier Designing Using Genetic Programming and Genetic Operators. [IJERR]. *International Journal of Engineering Research and Reviews*, *2*, 16–22.

Manware, A., Raj, R., Kumar, A., & Pawar, T. (2017). Smart Gloves as a Communication Tool for the Speech Impaired and Hearing Impaired. *Int. J. Emerg. Technol. Innov. Res*, *4*, 78–82.

Marcos, D., Tuia, D., Kellenberger, B., Zhang, L., Bai, M., Liao, R., & Urtasun, R. (2018),"Learning deep structured active contours endto-end," in *Proceedings of the IEEE Conference on Computer Vision and Pattern Recognition (CVPR)*, pp. 8877–8885.

Marcus, D. S., Wang, T. H., Parker, J., Csernansky, J. G., Morris, J. C., & Buckner, R. L. (2007). Open access series of imaging studies (OASIS): Cross-sectional MRI data in young, middle aged, nondemented, and demented older adults. *Journal of Cognitive Neuroscience*, *19*(9), 1498–1507. DOI: 10.1162/jocn.2007.19.9.1498 PMID: 17714011

Martínez, R., & Hernández, T. (2021). Predicting caries risk using supervised learning models. *Community Dentistry and Oral Epidemiology*, *49*(5), 402–410.

Mashat, A. (2024). A QR code-enabled framework for fast biomedical image processing in medical diagnosis using deep learning. *BMC Medical Imaging*, *24*(1), 198. DOI: 10.1186/s12880-024-01351-z PMID: 39090546

Matern, F., Riess, C., & Stamminger, M. (2020). Gradient-Based Illumination Description for Image Forgery Detection. *IEEE Transactions on Information Forensics and Security*, *15*, 1303–1317. DOI: 10.1109/TIFS.2019.2935913

Ma, Z., Dong, Y., Xia, Y., Xu, D., Xu, F., & Chen, F. (2024). Wildlife Real-Time Detection in Complex Forest Scenes Based on YOLOv5s Deep Learning Network. *Remote Sensing (Basel)*, *16*(8), 8. Advance online publication. DOI: 10.3390/rs16081350

Mazhar, S., Atif, N., Bhuyan, M. K., & Ahamed, S. R. (2024). Rethinking DABNet: Light-Weight Network for Real-Time Semantic Segmentation of Road Scenes. *IEEE Transactions on Artificial Intelligence*, *5*(6), 3098–3108. DOI: 10.1109/TAI.2023.3341976

Mazurowski, M. A., Buda, M., Saha, A., & Bashir, M. R. (2019, April). Deep learning in radiology: An overview of the concepts and a survey of the state of the art with focus on MRI. *Journal of Magnetic Resonance Imaging*, *49*(4), 939–954. DOI: 10.1002/jmri.26534 PMID: 30575178

McBee, M. P., Awan, O. A., Colucci, A. T., Ghobadi, C. W., Kadom, N., Kansagra, A. P., Tridandapani, S., & Auffermann, W. F. (2018, November 1). Deep Learning in Radiology. *Academic Radiology*, *25*(11), 1472–1480. DOI: 10.1016/j.acra.2018.02.018 PMID: 29606338

McGovern, A., Bluestein, H. B., & Meyer, J. (2019). Using deep learning to predict severe weather events. *Weather and Forecasting*, *34*(4), 1021–1036. DOI: 10.1175/WAF-D-18-0155.1

McGovern, A., Bluestein, H. B., & Meyer, J. (2023). Machine learning models for severe weather prediction. *Weather and Forecasting*, *38*(3), 579–595. DOI: 10.1175/WAF-D-22-0150.1

McMahan, H. B.. (2017). *Communication-efficient learning of deep networks from decentralized data*. Artificial Intelligence and Statistics.

Md Jelas, I., Zulkifley, M. A., Abdullah, M., & Spraggon, M. (2024). Deforestation detection using Deep Learning-based semantic segmentation techniques: A systematic review. *Frontiers in Forests and Global Change*, *7*, 1300060. Advance online publication. DOI: 10.3389/ffgc.2024.1300060

Mehrabi, N.. (2021). A survey on bias and fairness in machine learning. *ACM Computing Surveys*.

Mei, F., Qian, D., Nie, Y., Wang, B., Liang, A., & Li, H. (2024). Biomedical Applications of Wavelet Transform Algorithm on Deep Learning Ultrasonic Image Optimization as a Prognosis Model for Acute Myocarditis. *Journal of Biomedical Nanotechnology*, *20*(3), 604–613. DOI: 10.1166/jbn.2024.3787

Mekala, P., Gao, Y., Fan, J., & Davari, A. (2011, March). Real-time sign language recognition based on neural network architecture. In *2011 IEEE 43rd Southeastern symposium on system theory* (pp. 195-199). IEEE. DOI: 10.1109/SSST.2011.5753805

Menze, B. H., Jakab, A., Bauer, S., Kalpathy-Cramer, J., Farahani, K., Kirby, J., Burren, Y., Porz, N., Slotboom, J., Wiest, R., Lanczi, L., Gerstner, E., Weber, M. A., Arbel, T., Avants, B. B., Ayache, N., Buendia, P., Collins, D. L., Cordier, N., & Van Leemput, K. (2015). The Multimodal Brain Tumor Image Segmentation Benchmark (BRATS). *IEEE Transactions on Medical Imaging*, *34*(10), 1993–2024. DOI: 10.1109/TMI.2014.2377694 PMID: 25494501

Messai, A., Drif, A., Ouyahia, A., Guechi, M., Rais, M., Kaderali, L., & Cherifi, H. (2024). Towards XAI agnostic explainability to assess differential diagnosis for Meningitis diseases. *Machine Learning: Science and Technology*, *5*(2), 025052. DOI: 10.1088/2632-2153/ad4a1f

Mikołajczyk, T., Nowicki, K., Bustillo, A., & Pimenov, D. Y. (2018). Predicting tool life in turning operations using neural networks and image processing. *Mechanical Systems and Signal Processing*, *104*, 503–513. DOI: 10.1016/j.ymssp.2017.11.022

Miller, T. (2019). Explanation in artificial intelligence: Insights from the social sciences. *Artificial Intelligence*, *267*, 1–38. DOI: 10.1016/j.artint.2018.07.007

Milletari, F., Navab, N., & Ahmadi, S.-A. (2016). V-Net: Fully convolutional neural networks for volumetric medical image segmentation. *2016 Fourth International Conference on 3D Vision (3DV)*, 565-571. DOI: 10.1109/3DV.2016.79

Minar, M. R., & Naher, J. (2018). *Recent Advances in Deep Learning: An Overview.* https://doi.org/ DOI: 10.13140/RG.2.2.24831.10403

Min, D., Huang, Z., & Liu, J. (2020). Precipitation prediction based on deep learning model. *Water (Basel)*, *12*(3), 706. DOI: 10.3390/w12030706

Ming, Deep learning-based multimodal image analysis for cervical cancer detection. Methods (San Diego, Calif.) (2022).

Ming, Z., Zhu, M., Wang, X., Zhu, J., Cheng, J., Gao, C., Yang, Y., & Wei, X. (2022). Deep learning-based person re-identification methods: A survey and outlook of recent works. *Image and Vision Computing*, *119*, 104394. Advance online publication. DOI: 10.1016/j.imavis.2022.104394

Minh, D., Wang, H. X., Li, Y. F., & Nguyen, T. N. (2022). Explainable artificial intelligence: A comprehensive review. *Artificial Intelligence Review*, *55*(5), 3503–3568. DOI: 10.1007/s10462-021-10088-y

Mira-Avendano, I., Abril, A., Burger, C. D., Dellaripa, P. F., Fischer, A., Gotway, M. B., & Ryu, J. H. (2019, February). Interstitial lung disease and other pulmonary manifestations in connective tissue diseases. [). Elsevier.]. *Mayo Clinic Proceedings*, *94*(2), 309–325. DOI: 10.1016/j.mayocp.2018.09.002 PMID: 30558827

Mirza, M., & Osindero, S. (2014), "Conditional generative adversarial nets," arXiv preprint arXiv:1411.1784

Mishkin, D., Sergievskiy, N., & Matas, J. (2017). Systematic evaluation of convolution neural network advances on the Imagenet. *Computer Vision and Image Understanding*, *161*, 11–19. https://doi.org/https://doi.org/10.1016/j.cviu.2017.05.007. DOI: 10.1016/j.cviu.2017.05.007

Mishra Sunil, B.. (2024). Review of the Literature and Methodological Structure for IoT and PLM Integration in the Manufacturing Sector. *Journal of Advancement in Machines*, *9*(1), 1–5.

Mishra Sunil, B.. (2024a). AI-Driven IoT (AI IoT) in Thermodynamic Engineering. *Journal of Modern Thermodynamics in Mechanical System*, *6*(1), 1–8.

Mishra, S. B. (2024d). AI-Driven-IoT (AIIoT)-Based Decision Making in Manufacturing Processes in Mechanical Engineering. *Journal of Mechanisms and Robotics*, *9*(2), 27–38.

Mishra, S. B. (2024e). AI-Driven-IoT (AIIoT) Based Decision-Making in Molten Metal Processing. *Journal of Industrial Mechanics*, *9*(2), 45–56.

Mittal K Early Stage Detection of Alzheimer's Disease With Microsoft Azure Based Deep Learning. *Research square* (2023).

Mittal, S., Sharma, I., & Kumar, A. (2023, December). A Report: Machine Learning and Its Applications. In 2023 Intelligent Computing and Control for Engineering and Business Systems (ICCEBS) (pp. 1-6). IEEE.

Modi, K., & Devaraj, L. (2022). Advancements in biometric technology with artificial intelligence. *arXiv preprint arXiv:2212.13187.*

Mohammadpour, L., Ling, T. C., Liew, C. S., & Aryanfar, A. (2022). A Survey of CNN-Based Network Intrusion Detection. *Applied Sciences (Basel, Switzerland)*, *12*(16), 16. Advance online publication. DOI: 10.3390/app12168162

Mohammed, A., & Arunachalam, N. (2021, July). Imbalanced machine learning based techniques for breast cancer detection. In *2021 International Conference on System, Computation, Automation and Networking (ICSCAN)* (pp. 1-4). IEEE. DOI: 10.1109/ICSCAN53069.2021.9526422

Morales, M. A., Manning, W. J., & Nezafat, R. (2024). Present and Future Innovations in AI and Cardiac MRI. *Radiology*, *310*(1), e231269. DOI: 10.1148/radiol.231269 PMID: 38193835

Mountrakis, G., Im, J., & Ogole, C. (2011). Support vector machines in remote sensing: A review. *ISPRS Journal of Photogrammetry and Remote Sensing*, *66*(3), 247–259. https://doi.org/https://doi.org/10.1016/j.isprsjprs.2010.11.001. DOI: 10.1016/j.isprsjprs.2010.11.001

Mowla, M. N., Mowla, N., Shah, A. F. M. S., Rabie, K. M., & Shongwe, T. (2023). Internet of Things and Wireless Sensor Networks for Smart Agriculture Applications: A Survey. *IEEE Access : Practical Innovations, Open Solutions*, *11*, 145813–145852. DOI: 10.1109/ACCESS.2023.3346299

Mr. D. Sreenivasulu, et al, (2022). Implementation of Latest machine learning approaches for students Grade Prediction, *International Journal of Early Childhood special Education,* 14(3), pp. 9887-9894.

Mulani, A. O., Bang, A. V., Birajadar, G. B., Deshmukh, A. B., & Jadhav, H. M. (2024). IoT Based Air, Water, and Soil Monitoring System for Pomegranate Farming. *Annals of Agri Bio Research*, *29*(2), 71–86.

Murti, D. M. P., Pujianto, U., Wibawa, A. P., & Akbar, M. I. (2019). K-Nearest Neighbor (K-NN) based Missing Data Imputation. *2019 5th International Conference on Science in Information Technology (ICSITech)*, 83–88. DOI: 10.1109/ICSITech46713.2019.8987530

Mustafa, H., Umer, M., Hafeez, U., Hameed, A., Sohaib, A., Ullah, S., & Madni, H. A. (2023). Pepper bell leaf disease detection and classification using optimized convolutional neural network. *Multimedia Tools and Applications*, *82*(8), 12065–12080. DOI: 10.1007/s11042-022-13737-8

Mustaqim, T., Tsaniya, H., Adhiyaksa, F. A., & Suciati, N. (2022). Wavelet transformation and local binary pattern for data augmentation in deep learning-based face recognition. *2022 10th International Conference on Information and Communication Technology (ICoICT)*, 362–367.

Nabeel, M., Majeed, S., Awan, M. J., Muslih-ud-Din, H., Wasique, M., & Nasir, R. (2021). Review on Effective Disease Prediction through Data Mining Techniques. *International Journal on Electrical Engineering & Informatics*, *13*(3), 717–733. DOI: 10.15676/ijeei.2021.13.3.13

Nabeel, S. M., Bazai, S. U., Alasbali, N., Liu, Y., Ghafoor, M. I., Khan, R., Ku, C. S., Yang, J., Shahab, S., & Por, L. Y. (2024). Optimizing lung cancer classification through hyperparameter tuning. *Digital Health*, *10*, 20552076241249661. DOI: 10.1177/20552076241249661 PMID: 38698834

Nagasubramanian, K., Jones, S., Singh, A. K., Sarkar, S., Singh, A., & Ganapathysubramanian, B. (2019). Plant disease identification using explainable 3D deep learning on hyperspectral images. *Plant Methods*, *15*(1), 1–0. DOI: 10.1186/s13007-019-0479-8 PMID: 31452674

Nandy, A., Prasad, J. S., Mondal, S., Chakraborty, P., & Nandi, G. C. (2010). Recognition of isolated indian sign language gesture in real time. In *Information Processing and Management: International Conference on Recent Trends in Business Administration and Information Processing, BAIP 2010, Trivandrum, Kerala, India, March 26-27, 2010. Proceedings* (pp. 102-107). Springer Berlin Heidelberg. DOI: 10.1007/978-3-642-12214-9_18

Nanni, L., Maguolo, G., & Pancino, F. (2020). Insect pest image detection and recognition based on bio-inspired methods. *Ecological Informatics*, *57*, 101089. DOI: 10.1016/j.ecoinf.2020.101089

Nath, D., Ankit, , Neog, D. R., & Gautam, S. S. (2024). Application of machine learning and deep learning in finite element analysis: A comprehensive review. *Archives of Computational Methods in Engineering*, *31*(5), 1–40. DOI: 10.1007/s11831-024-10063-0

Nawaz, S. A., Li, J., Li, D., Shoukat, M. U., Bhatti, U. A., & Raza, M. A. (2025). Medical image zero watermarking algorithm based on dual-tree complex wavelet transform, AlexNet, and discrete cosine transform. *Applied Soft Computing*, *169*, 112556. DOI: 10.1016/j.asoc.2024.112556

Nazir, A., Hussain, A., Singh, M., & Assad, A. (2024). Deep learning in medicine: Advancing healthcare with intelligent solutions and the future of holography imaging in early diagnosis. *Multimedia Tools and Applications*, •••, 1–64. DOI: 10.1007/s11042-024-19694-8

Nazki, H., Yoon, S., Fuentes, A., & Park, D. S. (2020). Unsupervised image translation using adversarial networks for improved plant disease recognition. *Computers and Electronics in Agriculture*, *168*, 105117. DOI: 10.1016/j.compag.2019.105117

Neeraja, P., Kumar, R. G., Kumar, M. S., Liyakat, K. K. S., & Vani, M. S. (2024). *DL-Based Somnolence Detection for Improved Driver Safety and Alertness Monitoring. 2024 IEEE International Conference on Computing, Power and Communication Technologies (IC2PCT)*. Greater Noida., Available at https://ieeexplore.ieee.org/document/10486714, DOI: 10.1109/IC2PCT60090.2024.10486714

Nerkar, P., & Sultanabanu, K. (2024). IoT-Based Skin Health Monitoring System [IJBPAS]. *International Journal of Biology, Pharmacy and Allied Sciences*, *13*(11), 5937–5950. DOI: 10.31032/IJBPAS/2024/13.11.8488

Nerurkar, P., Shirke, A., Chandane, M., & Bhirud, S. (2018). Empirical Analysis of Data Clustering Algorithms. *Procedia Computer Science*, *125*, 770–779. https://doi.org/https://doi.org/10.1016/j.procs.2017.12.099. DOI: 10.1016/j.procs.2017.12.099

Ng, HW, & Guan, C Subject-independent meta-learning framework towards optimal training of EEG-based classifiers. Neural networks: the official journal of the International Neural Network Society (2024).

Ngo, T. K. N., Yang, S. J., Mao, B.-H., Nguyen, T. K. M., Ng, Q. D., Kuo, Y.-L., Tsai, J.-H., Saw, S. N., & Tu, T.-Y. (2023). A deep learning-based pipeline for analyzing the influences of interfacial mechanochemical microenvironments on spheroid invasion using differential interference contrast microscopic images. *Materials Today. Bio*, *23*, 100820. DOI: 10.1016/j.mtbio.2023.100820 PMID: 37810748

Nguyen, C. V., ... (2020). Transferability estimation by jointly learning representations to preserve task relations. *arXiv preprint arXiv:2003.07131.*

Nikita, K.. (2020). Design of Vehicle system using CAN Protocol. *International Journal for Research in Applied Science and Engineering Technology*, *8*(V), 1978–1983. DOI: 10.22214/ijraset.2020.5321

Nishom, M., Sasmito, G. W., & Wibowo, D. S. (2024). Segmentation model toward promotion target determination using k-means algorithm and Elbow method. *AIP Conference Proceedings*, *3070*(1), 030022. DOI: 10.1063/5.0198858

Noble, J. A., & Boukerroui, D. (2006). Ultrasound image segmentation: A survey. *IEEE Transactions on Medical Imaging*, *25*(8), 987–1010. DOI: 10.1109/TMI.2006.877092 PMID: 16894993

Noh, H., Hong, S., & Han, B. (2015), "Learning deconvolution network for semantic segmentation," in Proceedings of the IEEE international conference on computer vision, pp. 1520–1528. in, Z.; Liu, B.; Chu, Q.; Yu, N. (2021), ISNet: Integrate image-level and semantic-level context for semantic segmentation. In Proceedings of the IEEE/CVF International Conference on Computer Vision, Montreal, BC, Canada, pp. 7189–7198.

Noor, S., Bazai, S. U., Ghafoor, M. I., Marjan, S., Akram, S., & Ali, F. (2023). Generative Adversarial Networks for Anomaly Detection: A Systematic Literature Review. 2023 4th International Conference on Computing, Mathematics and Engineering Technologies (iCoMET), 1–6. https://doi.org/DOI: 10.1109/iCoMET57998.2023.10099175

Noor, R., Wahid, A., Bazai, S. U., Khan, A., Fang, M., Syam, M. S., & Bhatti, U. A. (2024). DLGAN: Undersampled MRI reconstruction using deep learning-based generative adversarial network. *Biomedical Signal Processing and Control*, *93*, 106218. DOI: 10.1016/j.bspc.2024.106218

Norvig, P. R., & Intelligence, S. A. (2002). *A modern approach*. Prentice Hall.

Nutakki, G. C., Abdollahi, B., Sun, W., & Nasraoui, O. (2019). *An Introduction to Deep Clustering*., DOI: 10.1007/978-3-319-97864-2_4

Oduoye, M. O., Fatima, E., Muzammil, M. A., Dave, T., Irfan, H., Fariha, F. N. U., Marbell, A., Ubechu, S. C., Scott, G. Y., & Elebesunu, E. E. (2024, January 4). Impacts of the advancement in artificial intelligence on laboratory medicine in low- and middle-income countries: Challenges and recommendations-A literature review. *Health Science Reports*, *7*(1), e1794. DOI: 10.1002/hsr2.1794 PMID: 38186931

Ogrekçi, S., Unal, Y., & Dudak, M. N. (2023). A comparative study of vision transformers and convolutional neural networks: Sugarcane leaf diseases identification. *European Food Research and Technology*, *249*(7), 1833–1843. DOI: 10.1007/s00217-023-04258-1

Ogunpola, A., Saeed, F., Basurra, S., Albarrak, A. M., & Qasem, S. N. (2024). Machine learning-based predictive models for detection of cardiovascular diseases. *Diagnostics (Basel)*, *14*(2), 144. DOI: 10.3390/diagnostics14020144 PMID: 38248021

Okolo, C. T., Agarwal, D., Dell, N., & Vashistha, A. (2024). " If it is easy to understand then it will have value": Examining Perceptions of Explainable AI with Community Health Workers in Rural India. Proceedings of the ACM on Human-Computer Interaction, 8(CSCW1), 1-28.

Oktay, , (2018), "Attention u-net: Learning where to look for the pancreas," ArXiv Prepr. ArXiv-180403999DOI: 10.1016/j.cmpb.2024.108278 PMID: 38878360

Oktay, O., Schlemper, J., Folgoc, L. L., Lee, M., Heinrich, M., Misawa, K., Mori, K., McDonagh, S., Hammerla, N. Y., & Kainz, B. (2018). Attention U-Net: Learning where to look for the pancreas. *arXiv preprint arXiv:1804.03999*.

Onur, T. Ö. (2022). Improved image denoising using wavelet edge detection based on Otsu's thresholding. *Acta Polytechnica Hungarica*, *19*(2), 79–92. DOI: 10.12700/APH.19.2.2022.2.5

Opochinsky, Y. Shlomo E. Chazan; Sharon Gannot; Jacob Goldberger. (2020). K-Autoencoders Deep Clustering. *ICASSP 2020 - 2020 IEEE International Conference on Acoustics, Speech and Signal Processing (ICASSP)*.

Osadebey, M., Liu, Q., Fuster-Garcia, E., & Emblem, K. E. (2023). Interpreting deep learning models for glioma survival classification using visualization and textual explanations. *BMC Medical Informatics and Decision Making*, *23*(1), 225. DOI: 10.1186/s12911-023-02320-2 PMID: 37853371

Otsu, N. (1979). A Threshold Selection Method from Gray-Level Histograms. *IEEE Transactions on Systems, Man, and Cybernetics*, *9*(1), 62–66. DOI: 10.1109/TSMC.1979.4310076

Ounissi, M., Latouche, M., & Racoceanu, D. (2024). PhagoStat a scalable and interpretable end to end framework for efficient quantification of cell phagocytosis in neurodegenerative disease studies. *Scientific Reports*, *14*(1), 6482. DOI: 10.1038/s41598-024-56081-7 PMID: 38499658

Oyelade, J., Isewon, I., Oladipupo, O., Emebo, O., Omogbadegun, Z., Aromolaran, O., Uwoghiren, E., Olaniyan, D., & Olawole, O. (2019). Data Clustering: Algorithms and Its Applications. *2019 19th International Conference on Computational Science and Its Applications (ICCSA)*, 71–81. DOI: 10.1109/ICCSA.2019.000-1

Ozdemir, C., & Dogan, Y. (2024). Advancing brain tumor classification through MTAP model: An innovative approach in medical diagnostics. *Medical & Biological Engineering & Computing*, *62*(7), 2165–2176. DOI: 10.1007/s11517-024-03064-5 PMID: 38483711

Ozkaya, N., & Sagiroglu, S. (2010). Generating one biometric feature from another: Faces from fingerprints. *Sensors (Basel)*, *10*(5), 4206–4237. DOI: 10.3390/s100504206 PMID: 22399877

Padoan, A., & Plebani, M. (2024). Dynamic mirroring: Unveiling the role of digital twins, artificial intelligence and synthetic data for personalized medicine in laboratory medicine. [CCLM]. *Clinical Chemistry and Laboratory Medicine*, *62*(11), 2156–2161. DOI: 10.1515/cclm-2024-0517 PMID: 38726708

Pal, N. R., & Pal, S. K. (1993). A review on image segmentation techniques. *Pattern Recognition*, *26*(9), 1277–1294. DOI: 10.1016/0031-3203(93)90135-J

Pandian, R., Vedanarayanan, V., Ravi Kumar, D. N. S., & Rajakumar, R. (2022). Detection and classification of lung cancer using CNN and Google net. *Measurement. Sensors*, *24*, 100588. Advance online publication. DOI: 10.1016/j.measen.2022.100588

Pang, T., Zheng, H., Quan, Y., & Ji, H. (2021). Recorrupted-to-recorrupted: unsupervised deep learning for image denoising. *Proceedings of the IEEE/CVF Conference on Computer Vision and Pattern Recognition*, 2043–2052. DOI: 10.1109/CVPR46437.2021.00208

Panhwar, A. O., Sathio, A. A., Lakhan, A., Umer, M., Mithiani, R. M., & Khan, S. (2022). Plant health detection enabled CNN scheme in IoT network. *International Journal of Computing and Digital Systems*, *11*(1), 344–335.

Pankaj, R Hotkar, Vishal Kulkarni, et al. (2019). Implementation of Low Power and area efficient carry select Adder. *International Journal of Research in Engineering. Science and Management*, *2*(4), 183–184.

Pan, S. J., & Yang, Q. (2010). A survey on transfer learning. *IEEE Transactions on Knowledge and Data Engineering*, *22*(10), 1345–1359. DOI: 10.1109/TKDE.2009.191

Pantazi, X. E., Moshou, D., & Tamouridou, A. A. (2019, January 1). Automated leaf disease detection in different crop species through image features analysis and One Class Classifiers. *Computers and Electronics in Agriculture*, *156*, 96–104. DOI: 10.1016/j.compag.2018.11.005

Papastratis, I., Chatzikonstantinou, C., Konstantinidis, D., Dimitropoulos, K., & Daras, P. (2021). Artificial intelligence technologies for sign language. *Sensors (Basel)*, *21*(17), 5843. DOI: 10.3390/s21175843 PMID: 34502733

Pardeshi, D. K. (2022). Implementation of fault detection framework for healthcare monitoring system using IoT, sensors in wireless environment. *Telematique*, *21*(1), 5451-5460.

Patel, D., & Sharma, K. (2023). AI-based analysis of CBCT scans for diagnosing apical periodontitis. *International Endodontic Journal*, *56*(4), 389–398.

Paul, A., Kundu, A., Chaki, N., Dutta, D., & Jha, C. S. (2022). Wavelet enabled convolutional autoencoder based deep neural network for hyperspectral image denoising. *Multimedia Tools and Applications, 81*(2), 1–27. DOI: 10.1007/s11042-021-11689-z

Peng, M., Liu, Y., Qadri, I. A., Bhatti, U. A., Ahmed, B., Sarhan, N. M., & Awwad, E. M. (2024). Advanced image segmentation for precision agriculture using CNN-GAT fusion and fuzzy C-means clustering. *Computers and Electronics in Agriculture, 226*, 109431. DOI: 10.1016/j.compag.2024.109431

Pham, D. L., Xu, C., & Prince, J. L. (2000). Current methods in medical image segmentation. *Annual Review of Biomedical Engineering, 2*(1), 315–337. DOI: 10.1146/annurev.bioeng.2.1.315 PMID: 11701515

Phyu, T. N. (2009, March). Survey of classification techniques in data mining. In *Proceedings of the International Multiconference of engineers and computer scientists* (Vol. 1, No. 5, pp. 727-731). Citeseer.

Pinto-Coelho, L. (2023, December 18). How Artificial Intelligence Is Shaping Medical Imaging Technology: A Survey of Innovations and Applications. *Bioengineering (Basel, Switzerland), 10*(12), 1435. DOI: 10.3390/bioengineering10121435 PMID: 38136026

Poyatos, J., Molina, D., Martinez, A. D., Del Ser, J., & Herrera, F. (2023). EvoPruneDeepTL: An evolutionary pruning model for transfer learning based deep neural networks. *Neural Networks, 158*, 59–82. DOI: 10.1016/j.neunet.2022.10.011 PMID: 36442374

Pradeepa, M., ... (2022). Student Health Detection using a Machine Learning Approach and IoT, *2022 IEEE 2nd Mysore sub section International Conference (MysuruCon),* 2022. Available at: https://ieeexplore.ieee.org/document/9972445

Prasad, K. R., Karanam, S. R., Ganesh, D., Liyakat, K. K. S., Talasila, V., & Purushotham, P. (2024, May). AI in public-private partnership for IT infrastructure development. *The Journal of High Technology Management Research, 35*(1), 100496. DOI: 10.1016/j.hitech.2024.100496

Prashant, K. Magadum (2024). Machine Learning for Predicting Wind Turbine Output Power in Wind Energy Conversion Systems, *Grenze International Journal of Engineering and Technology,* Jan Issue, Vol 10, Issue 1, pp. 2074-2080. Grenze ID: 01.GIJET.10.1.4_1 Available at: https://thegrenze.com/index.php?display=page&view=journalabstract&absid=2514&id=8

Prashant, K. Magadum (2024). Machine Learning for Predicting Wind Turbine Output Power in Wind Energy Conversion Systems, *Grenze International Journal of Engineering and Technology,* Jan Issue, Vol 10, Issue 1, pp. 2074-2080. Grenze ID: 01.GIJET.10.1.4_1 Available at:https://thegrenze.com/index.php?display=page&view=journalabstract&absid=2514&id=8

Priya Mangesh Nerkar. BhagyarekhaUjjwalganeshDhaware. (2023). Predictive Data Analytics Framework Based on Heart Healthcare System (HHS) Using Machine Learning, *Journal of Advanced Zoology,* 2023, Volume 44, Special Issue -2, Page 3673:3686. Available at: https://jazindia.com/index.php/jaz/article/view/1695

Punhani, A., Faujdar, N., Mishra, K. K., & Subramanian, M. (2022). Binning-Based Silhouette Approach to Find the Optimal Cluster Using K-Means. *IEEE Access : Practical Innovations, Open Solutions, 10,* 115025–115032. DOI: 10.1109/ACCESS.2022.3215568

Qayyum, M. U., Sherani, A. M. K., Khan, M., & Hussain, H. K. (2023). Revolutionizing Healthcare: The Transformative Impact of Artificial Intelligence in Medicine. *BIN: Bulletin Of Informatics*, *1*(2), 71–83.

Qi, J., Yu, Y., Wang, L., & Liu, J. (2016). K*-Means: An Effective and Efficient K-Means Clustering Algorithm. *2016 IEEE International Conferences on Big Data and Cloud Computing (BDCloud), Social Computing and Networking (SocialCom), Sustainable Computing and Communications (SustainCom) (BDCloud-SocialCom-SustainCom)*, 242–249. DOI: 10.1109/BDCloud-SocialCom-SustainCom.2016.46

Qin, X., Lai, C., Pan, Z., Pan, M., Xiang, Y., & Wang, Y. (2023). Recognition of Abnormal-Laying Hens Based on Fast Continuous Wavelet and Deep Learning Using Hyperspectral Images. *Sensors (Basel)*, *23*(7), 3645. DOI: 10.3390/s23073645 PMID: 37050705

Qi, Y., Yang, Z., Sun, W., Lou, M., Lian, J., Zhao, W., Deng, X., & Ma, Y. (2022). A Comprehensive Overview of Image Enhancement Techniques. *Archives of Computational Methods in Engineering*, *29*(1), 583–607. DOI: 10.1007/s11831-021-09587-6

Quasar, S. R., Sharma, R., Mittal, A., Sharma, M., Agarwal, D., & de La Torre Díez, I. (2024). Ensemble methods for computed tomography scan images to improve lung cancer detection and classification. *Multimedia Tools and Applications*, *83*(17), 52867–52897. DOI: 10.1007/s11042-023-17616-8

Quinlan, J. R. (1986). Induction of decision trees. *Machine Learning*, *1*(1), 81–106. DOI: 10.1007/BF00116251

Radford, A., Metz, L., & Chintala, S. (2015), "Unsupervised representation learning with deep convolutional generative adversarial networks," arXiv preprint arXiv:1511.06434

Radford, A., Metz, L., & Chintala, S. (2015). Unsupervised representation learning with deep convolutional generative adversarial networks. *arXiv preprint arXiv:1511.06434.*

Raghu, M., ... (2019). Transfusion: Understanding transfer learning with applications to medical imaging. *arXiv preprint arXiv:1902.07208.*

Raha, A. D., Gain, M., Debnath, R., Adhikary, A., Qiao, Y., Hassan, M. M., & Islam, S. M. S. (2024). Attention to Monkeypox: An Interpretable Monkeypox Detection Technique Using Attention Mechanism. *IEEE Access : Practical Innovations, Open Solutions.*

Rahman, A., Lu, Y., & Wang, H. (2023). Performance evaluation of deep learning object detectors for weed detection for cotton. *Smart Agricultural Technology*, *3*, 100126. DOI: 10.1016/j.atech.2022.100126

Rai, P., Kumar, V., & Gupta, A. (2023). Interpretability in deep learning models for meteorology. *Earth and Space Science*, 10(2), e2022EA002123. https://doi.org/DOI: 10.1029/2022EA002123

Rajalakshmi, R., Subashini, R., & Anantharaman, V. (2020). Automated diabetic retinopathy detection in retinal fundus images using deep learning. *Journal of Diabetes Science and Technology*, *14*(4), 754–759. DOI: 10.1177/1932296820909423 PMID: 32468843

Rajamani, V., Babu, P., & Jaiganesh, S. (2013). A review of various global contrast enhancement techniques for still images using histogram modification framework. *International Journal of Engineering Trends and Technology*, *4*(4), 1045–1048.

Rajesh, K., & Anand, S. (2012). Analysis of SEER dataset for breast cancer diagnosis using C4. 5 classification algorithm. *International Journal of Advanced Research in Computer and Communication Engineering*, *1*(2), 2278–1021.

Rajpoot, R., Gour, M., Jain, S., & Semwal, V. B. (2024). Integrated ensemble CNN and explainable AI for COVID-19 diagnosis from CT scan and X-ray images. *Scientific Reports*, *14*(1), 24985. DOI: 10.1038/s41598-024-75915-y PMID: 39443548

Rajpurkar, P., Irvin, J., & Zhu, K. (2020). CheXNet: Radiologist-Level Pneumonia Detection on Chest X-Rays with Deep Learning. *Proceedings of the National Academy of Sciences of the United States of America*, *116*(51), 23090–23095. DOI: 10.1073/pnas.1718063115

Ramesh, S., & Vydeki, D. Recognition and classification of paddy leaf diseases using Optimized Deep Neural network with Jaya algorithm, *Information Processing in Agriculture*, Volume 7, Issue 2, 2020, Pages 249-260, ISSN 2214-3173, https://doi.org/DOI: 10.1016/j.inpa.2019.09.002

Ramudu, K., Mohan, V. M., Jyothirmai, D., Prasad, D. V. S. S. S. V., Agrawal, R., & Boopathi, S. (2023). Machine learning and artificial intelligence in disease prediction: Applications, challenges, limitations, case studies, and future directions. In *Contemporary Applications of Data Fusion for Advanced Healthcare Informatics* (pp. 297–318). IGI Global. DOI: 10.4018/978-1-6684-8913-0.ch013

Rana, A., & Roy, P. (2022). Real-time detection of root canal infections using DL. *Journal of Endodontics*, *48*(8), 1005–1015. PMID: 35577145

Ravi, A.. (2022a). *Pattern Recognition- An Approach towards Machine Learning, Lambert Publications, 2022*. ISBN.

Ravuri, S., Lenc, K., Willson, M., Kangin, D., Lam, R., Mirowski, P., Fitzsimons, M., Athanassiadou, M., Kashem, S., Madge, S., Prudden, R., Mandhane, A., Clark, A., Brock, A., Simonyan, K., Hadsell, R., Robinson, N., Clancy, E., Arribas, A., & Mohamed, S. (2021). Skilful precipitation nowcasting using deep generative models of radar. *Nature*, *597*(7878), 672–677. DOI: 10.1038/s41586-021-03854-z PMID: 34588668

Rawat, W., & Wang, Z. (2017). Deep Convolutional Neural Networks for Image Classification: A Comprehensive Review. *Neural Computation*, *29*(9), 2352–2449. DOI: 10.1162/neco_a_00990 PMID: 28599112

Rayhan, A., Rayhan, R., & Rayhan, S. (2023). The Role Of AI In Healthcare: Revolutionizing Patient Care And Well-Being. DOI: . 2.2, 22601.DOI: 10.13140/RG

Raza, H. A., Hameed, M. U., Islam, M. S., Lone, N. A., Raza, M. A., & Sabagh, A. E. L. (2022). *Environmental and Economic Benefits of Sustainable Sugarcane Initiative and Production Constraints in Pakistan: A Review, Global Agricultural Production: Resilience to Climate Change*. Springer., DOI: 10.1007/978-3-031-14973-3_17

Refaeilzadeh, P., Tang, L., & Liu, H. (2009). Cross-validation. *Encyclopedia of database systems*, 532-538.

Ren, S., He, K., Girshick, R., & Sun, J. (2015). Faster R-CNN: Towards real-time object detection with region proposal networks. In *Advances in Neural Information Processing Systems* (pp. 91–99).

Ren, S., He, K., Girshick, R., & Sun, J. (2015). Faster r-cnn: Towards realtime object detection with region proposal networks. *Advances in Neural Information Processing Systems*, •••, 91–99.

Richard Kuo. (n.d.). *MNIST VAE*. Kaggle.

Rizzo, L., Verda, D., Berretta, S., & Longo, L. (2024). A Novel Integration of Data-Driven Rule Generation and Computational Argumentation for Enhanced Explainable AI. *Machine Learning and Knowledge Extraction*, *6*(3), 2049–2073. DOI: 10.3390/make6030101

Ronneberger, O., Fischer, P., & Brox, T. (2015). *U-Net: Convolutional Networks for Biomedical Image Segmentation* (pp. 234–241). DOI: 10.1007/978-3-319-24574-4_28

Rosenfeld, D., & Wood, R., & H. (2020). Machine learning and climate science: Opportunities and challenges. *Climatic Change*, *162*(2), 609–627. DOI: 10.1007/s10584-020-02871-8

Ros, F., Riad, R., & Guillaume, S. (2023). PDBI: A partitioning Davies-Bouldin index for clustering evaluation. *Neurocomputing*, *528*, 178–199. https://doi.org/https://doi.org/10.1016/j.neucom.2023.01.043. DOI: 10.1016/j.neucom.2023.01.043

Rousseau, F. & D. L. & F. Ronan. (2020). Residual Networks as Flows of Diffeomorphisms. Journal of Mathematical Imaging and Vision. *Journal of Mathematical Imaging and Vision*, •••, 62.

Roy, A., Anju, P., Tomy, L., & Rajeswari, M. (2021). Recent study on image denoising using deep cnn techniques. *2021 7th International Conference on Advanced Computing and Communication Systems (ICACCS), 1*, 1838–1843.

Roy, A., Roy, P. K., Mitra, A., Maji, P. K., Choudhury, S. R., & Peng, S. L. Enhancing Patient Care with Modality-Based Image Registration in Modern Healthcare. In Smart Medical Imaging for Diagnosis and Treatment Planning (pp. 95-136). Chapman and Hall/CRC. DOI: 10.1201/9781003464884-8

Ruder, S. (2017). An overview of multi-task learning in deep neural networks. *arXiv preprint arXiv:1706.05098.*

Ruggeri, F., Kenett, R., & Faltin, F. W. (2007). *Encyclopedia of statistics in quality and reliability*. No Title. DOI: 10.1002/9780470061572

Rupprecht, C., Huaroc, E., Baust, M., & Navab, N. (2016), "Deep active contours," arXiv preprint arXiv:1607.05074

Russel, N. S., & Selvaraj, A. (2022). Leaf species and disease classification using multiscale parallel deep CNN architecture. *Neural Computing & Applications*, *34*(21), 19217–19237. DOI: 10.1007/s00521-022-07521-w

Sabour, S., Frosst, N., & Hinton, G. E. (2017). *Dynamic Routing Between Capsules*. http://arxiv.org/abs/1710.09829

Saeedi, S., Rezayi, S., & Keshavarz, H.. (2023). MRI-based brain tumor detection using convolutional deep learning methods and chosen machine learning techniques. *BMC Medical Informatics and Decision Making*, *23*, 16. DOI: 10.1186/s12911-023-02114-6 PMID: 36691030

Sagheer, S. V. M., & George, S. N. (2020). A review on medical image denoising algorithms. *Biomedical Signal Processing and Control, 61*, 102036. DOI: 10.1016/j.bspc.2020.102036

Sajed, S., Sanati, A., Garcia, J. E., Rostami, H., Keshavarz, A., & Teixeira, A. (2023). The effectiveness of deep learning vs. traditional methods for lung disease diagnosis using chest X-ray images: A systematic review. *Applied Soft Computing, 147*, 110817. DOI: 10.1016/j.asoc.2023.110817

Salama, G. I., Abdelhalim, M., & Zeid, M. A. E. (2012). Breast cancer diagnosis on three different datasets using multi-classifiers. [WDBC]. *Breast Cancer (Tokyo, Japan), 32*(569), 2.

Salehi, A. W., Khan, S., Gupta, G., Alabduallah, B. I., Almjally, A., Alsolai, H., Siddiqui, T., & Mellit, A. (2023). A study of CNN and transfer learning in medical imaging: Advantages, challenges, future scope. *Sustainability (Basel), 15*(7), 5930. DOI: 10.3390/su15075930

Sarker, I. H. (2021). Deep Learning: A Comprehensive Overview on Techniques, Taxonomy, Applications and Research Directions. *SN Computer Science, 2*(6), 420. DOI: 10.1007/s42979-021-00815-1 PMID: 34426802

Sarker, I. H., Hossain, M. S., & Nguyen, T. A. (2023). Deep learning: Current applications and research challenges in digital imaging and predictive modeling. *Journal of Applied Computing and Artificial Intelligence, 15*(3), 85–97.

Sathio, A. "A Study On The Conceptual Frame Work Of Data Warehousing In Health Sector In Pakistan A Case Study of a Hospital System and Disease (Hepatitis C)," *International Journal of Computer (IJC)*, vol. 29, no. 1, pp. 59–81, Sep. 2018, doi: https://www.researchgate.net/publication/324896538_A_Study_On_The_Conceptual_Frame_Work_Of_Data_Warehousing_In_Health_Sector_In_Pakistan_A_Case_Study_Of_a_Hospital_System_And_Disease_Hepatitis_C/citations

Sathio, A. A. (2018). A Study on the Conceptual Frame Work of Dataware Housing in Health Sector in Pakistan A Case Study of a Hospital System and Disease (Hepatitis C). *International Journal of Computer (IJC)*, vol. 29, no. 1, pp. 59–81, Sep. 2018., doi: https://www.researchgate.net/publication/324896538_A_Study_On_The_Conceptual_Frame_Work_Of_Data_Warehousing_In_Health_Sector_In_Pakistan_A_Case_Study_Of_a_Hospital_System_And_Disease_Hepatitis_C/citations

Sathio, A. A., Dootio, M. A., & Lakhan, A., ur Rehman, M., Pnhwar, A. O., & Sahito, M. A. (2021, August). Pervasive futuristic healthcare and blockchain enabled digital identities-challenges and future intensions. In *2021 International Conference on Computing, Electronics & Communications Engineering (iCCECE)* (pp. 30-35). IEEE. DOI: 10.1109/iCCECE52344.2021.9534846

Sathio, A. A., Rind, M. M., & Lakhan, A. (2024). Deep Learning Algorithms: Clustering and Classifications for Multimedia Data. In *Deep Learning for Multimedia Processing Applications* (pp. 114-145). CRC Press.

Sathio, A. A., Awan, S. A., Panhwar, A. O., Aamir, A. M., Brohi, A. M., & Burdi, A. (2023). A Blockchain-Enabled Machine Learning Mask Detection Method for Prevention of Pandemic Diseases. *VAWKUM Transactions on Computer Sciences, 11*(1), 165–183. DOI: 10.21015/vtcs.v11i1.1443

Sathio, A. A., Rind, M. M., & Lakhan, A. (2024). A. Deep Learning Algorithms and Architectures for Multimodal Data Analysis. In *Deep Learning for Multimedia Processing Applications* (pp. 74–113). CRC Press.

Sathio, A. A., Shaikh, M., Panhwar, A. O., Sahito, M. A., & Lakhan, A. (2021). Recommended Employment Model for Silent Community using Smart Technology. *International Journal of Emerging Trends in Engineering Research.*

Sathio, A.A., Mujeeb, Shaikh, R., Panhwar, A.O., Rehman, U., Sahito, M.A., & Lakhan, A. (2021). A Review on State of the Art in Flipped Classroom Technology A Blended E-Learning. *International Journal of Emerging Trends in Engineering Research.*

Satpathy, M. M. B. R., & Mishra, B. R. (2021). *Clinical diagnosis of congenital heart disease.* Jaypee Brothers Medical Publishers.

Saxena, A., Prasad, M., Gupta, A., Bharill, N., Patel, O. P., Tiwari, A., Er, M. J., Ding, W., & Lin, C. T. (2017). A review of clustering techniques and developments. *Neurocomputing*, *267*, 664–681. DOI: 10.1016/j.neucom.2017.06.053

Sayyad (2025e). AI-Powered IoT (AI IoT) for Decision-Making in Smart Agriculture: KSK Approach for Smart Agriculture. In S. Hai-Jew (Ed.), *Enhancing Automated Decision-Making Through AI* (pp. 67-96). IGI Global Scientific Publishing. https://doi.org/DOI: 10.4018/979-8-3693-6230-3.ch003

Sayyad (2025f). KK Approach to Increase Resilience in Internet of Things: A T-Cell Security Concept. In D. Darwish & K. Charan (Eds.), Analyzing Privacy and Security Difficulties in Social Media: New Challenges and Solutions (pp. 87-120). IGI Global Scientific Publishing. https://doi.org/DOI: 10.4018/979-8-3693-9491-5.ch005

Sayyad Liyakat (2024w). Nanotechnology in Medical Applications: A Study. *Nano Trends: A Journal of Nanotechnology and Its Applications.* 2024; 26(2): 1–11p.

Sayyad Liyakat, K. K. (2024x). Impact of Nanotechnology on Battlefield Welfare: A Study. International Journal of Nanobiotechnology. 2024; 10(2): 19– 32p.

Sayyad. (2025f). AI-Powered-IoT (AIIoT)-Based Decision-Making System for BP Patient's Healthcare Monitoring: KSK Approach for BP Patient Healthcare Monitoring. *In S. Aouadni& I. Aouadni (Eds.), Recent Theories and Applications for Multi-Criteria Decision-Making (pp. 205-238). IGI Global.*https://doi.org/DOI: 10.4018/979-8-3693-6502-1.ch008

Sayyad, S. (2024s). Nanosensors in Agriculture Field: A Study. *International Journal of Applied Nanotechnology*, *10*(02), 12–22p. https://journalspub.com/publication/ijan-v10i02-11625

Schlemper, J., Oktay, O., Schaap, M., Heinrich, M., Kainz, B., Glocker, B., & Rueckert, D. (2019). Attention gated networks: Learning to leverage salient regions in medical images. *Medical Image Analysis*, *53*, 197–207. DOI: 10.1016/j.media.2019.01.012 PMID: 30802813

Schmarje, L., Santarossa, M., Schröder, S. M., & Koch, R. (2021). A Survey on Semi-, Self- and Unsupervised Learning for Image Classification. *IEEE Access : Practical Innovations, Open Solutions*, *9*, 82146–82168. DOI: 10.1109/ACCESS.2021.3084358

Schmidt, C. R., Kellnhofer, P., & Liu, Y. (2022). Scaling deep learning: The importance of efficiency. *IEEE Transactions on Neural Networks and Learning Systems*, *33*(5), 1983–1994.

Schroff, F., Kalenichenko, D., & Philbin, J. (2015). Facenet: A unified embedding for face recognition and clustering. In *Proceedings of the IEEE conference on computer vision and pattern recognition* (pp. 815-823). DOI: 10.1109/CVPR.2015.7298682

Scitovski, R., & Sabo, K. (2020). DBSCAN-like clustering method for various data densities. *Pattern Analysis & Applications*, *23*(2), 541–554. DOI: 10.1007/s10044-019-00809-z

Seelwal, P., Dhiman, P., Gulzar, Y., Kaur, A., Wadhwa, S., & Onn, C. W. (2024). A systematic review of deep learning applications for rice disease diagnosis: Current trends and future directions. *Frontiers of Computer Science*, *6*, 1452961. DOI: 10.3389/fcomp.2024.1452961

Selbst, A. D., Andrew, H., & Barocas, S. (2019). Fairness and abstraction in sociotechnical systems. *Proceedings of the 2019 ACM Conference on Fairness, Accountability, and Transparency* (pp. 59-68).

Selvaraju, R. R., Cogswell, M., Das, A., Vedantam, R., Parikh, D., & Batra, D. (2017). Grad-cam: Visual explanations from deep networks via gradient-based localization. In *Proceedings of the IEEE international conference on computer vision* (pp. 618-626). DOI: 10.1109/ICCV.2017.74

Selvikvag Lundervold, A., & Lundervold, A. (2018, December 13). An overview of deep learning in medical imaging focusing on MRI. *Zeitschrift für Medizinische Physik*, *29*(2), 102–127. DOI: 10.1016/j.zemedi.2018.11.002 PMID: 30553609

Sen, I., Hossain, M. I., Shakib, M. F. H., Imran, M. A., & Al Faisal, F. (2020). In depth analysis of lung disease prediction using machine learning algorithms. In Machine Learning, Image Processing, Network Security and Data Sciences: Second International Conference, MIND 2020, Silchar, India, July 30-31, 2020 [Springer Singapore.]. *Proceedings*, *2*(Part II), 204–213.

Senturk, Z. K., & Kara, R. (2014). Breast cancer diagnosis via data mining: Performance analysis of seven different algorithms. *Computing in Science & Engineering*, *4*(1), 35.

Sergyan, S. (2008). Color histogram features based image classification in content-based image retrieval systems. *2008 6th International Symposium on Applied Machine Intelligence and Informatics*, 221–224. DOI: 10.1109/SAMI.2008.4469170

Sethy, P. K., Barpanda, N. K., Rath, A. K., & Behera, S. K. (2020). Deep feature based rice leaf disease identification using support vector machine. *Computers and Electronics in Agriculture*, *175*, 105527. DOI: 10.1016/j.compag.2020.105527

Shafik, W., Tufail, A., De Silva Liyanage, C., & Apong, R. A. A. H. M. (2024). Using transfer learning-based plant disease classification and detection for sustainable agriculture. *BMC Plant Biology*, *24*(1), 136. DOI: 10.1186/s12870-024-04825-y PMID: 38408925

Shah, H., Ahmed, S., Sathio, A. A., & Burdi, A. (2023). W-rank: A keyphrase extraction method for webpage based on linguistics and DOM-base features. *VAWKUM Transactions on Computer Sciences*, *11*(1), 217–228. DOI: 10.21015/vtcs.v11i1.1493

Shaikh, A. Zaffar and Ali Sathio, Anwar and Ali Laghari, Asif and Ahmed Memon, Mashooq and Hussain Mirani, Ibrar (2019) *Study of the Role of New Technologies in Pharmaceutical Industry.* Journal of Pharmaceutical Research International, 31 (6). pp. 1-11. ISSN 2456-9119

Shaikh, M. (2023). Machine Learning in the Production Process Control of Metal Melting. *Journal of Advancement in Machines*, *8*(2).

Shaikh, Z. A., Wagan, A. A., Laghari, A. A., Ali, K., Memon, M. A., & Sathio, A. A. (2019). The role of software configuration management and capability maturity model in system quality. *IJCSNS*, *19*(11), 114.

Shams, A., Becker, K., Becker, D., Amirian, S., & Rasheed, K. (2024). Evolutionary CNN-based architectures with attention mechanisms for enhanced image classification. In Deligiannidis, L., Dimitoglou, G., & Arabnia, H. (Eds.), *Artificial Intelligence: Machine Learning, Convolutional Neural Networks and Large Language Models* (pp. 107–132). De Gruyter., DOI: 10.1515/9783111344126-006

Shao, K., Li, D., Tang, H., Zhang, Y., Xu, B., & Bhatti, U. A. (2024). Adaptive temporal convolutional network (Atcn) and internally-optimized transformer for dissolved oxygen prediction in aquaculture. *Available at SSRN* 5039613. DOI: 10.2139/ssrn.5039613

Sharma, D. K., & Punhani, A. (2024). *Deep Learning Methods for Precise Sugarcane Disease Detection and Sustainable Crop Management. Communications in Computer and Information Science* (Vol. 2054). Springer., DOI: 10.1007/978-3-031-56703-2_4

Sharma, H., & Kumar, S. (2016). A survey on decision tree algorithms of classification in data mining. [IJSR]. *International Journal of Scientific Research*, *5*(4), 2094–2097.

Sharma, M., Pal, R., & Sahoo, A. K. (2014). Indian sign language recognition using neural networks and KNN classifiers. *Journal of Engineering and Applied Sciences (Asian Research Publishing Network)*, *9*(8), 1255–1259.

Sheller, M. J.. (2020). Multi-institutional deep learning modeling without sharing patient data: A feasibility study on brain tumor segmentation. *Medical Image Analysis*.

Sheller, M. J., Reina, G. A., Edwards, B., Martin, J., & Bakas, S. (2020). Federated Learning in Medicine: Facilitating Multi-Institutional Collaborations without Sharing Patient Data. *Scientific Reports*, *10*(1), 2020. DOI: 10.1038/s41598-020-69250-1 PMID: 32724046

Shen, Feng, & Song, Song & Xu Federated Meta-Learning with Attention for Diversity-Aware Human Activity Recognition. Sensors (Basel, Switzerland) (2023).

Sheng, G., Wang, Q., Pei, C., & Gao, Q. (2022). Contrastive deep embedded clustering. *Neurocomputing*, *514*, 13–20. https://doi.org/https://doi.org/10.1016/j.neucom.2022.09.116. DOI: 10.1016/j.neucom.2022.09.116

Shen, X.. (2023). AI-assisted diagnostic system for root canal treatment planning. *International Endodontic Journal*, *56*(2), 178–188. PMID: 37966374

Sherstinsky, A. (2020). Fundamentals of Recurrent Neural Network (RNN) and Long Short-Term Memory (LSTM) network. *Physica D. Nonlinear Phenomena*, *404*, 404. DOI: 10.1016/j.physd.2019.132306

Shewalkar, A., Nyavanandi, D., & Ludwig, S. A. (2019). Performance Evaluation of Deep neural networks Applied to Speech Recognition: Rnn, LSTM and GRU. *Journal of Artificial Intelligence and Soft Computing Research*, *9*(4), 235–245. DOI: 10.2478/jaiscr-2019-0006

Shinde, et al, (2023). Monitoring Fresh Fruit and Food Using IoT and Machine Learning to Improve Food Safety and Quality, Tuijin *Jishu/Journal of Propulsion Technology,*44(3), pp. 2927 – 2931.

Shivashankara, S., & Srinath, S. (2018). American sign language recognition system: An optimal approach. *International Journal of Image. Graphics and Signal Processing*, *10*(8), 18–30. DOI: 10.5815/ijigsp.2018.08.03

Shi, X., Chen, Z., & Wang, H. (2021). Short-term rainfall prediction using LSTM networks. *Journal of Hydrology (Amsterdam)*, *596*, 126165. DOI: 10.1016/j.jhydrol.2021.126165

Shoaib, M. A., Lai, K. W., Chuah, J. H., Hum, Y. C., Ali, R., Dhanalakshmi, S., Wang, H., & Wu, X. (2022). Comparative studies of deep learning segmentation models for left ventricle segmentation. *Frontiers in Public Health*, *10*, 981019. Advance online publication. DOI: 10.3389/fpubh.2022.981019 PMID: 36091529

Shorten, C., & Khoshgoftaar, T. M. (2019). A survey on image data augmentation for deep learning. *Journal of Big Data*, *6*(1), 60. DOI: 10.1186/s40537-019-0197-0

Shukla, A., Seethalakshmi, K., Hema, P., & Musale, J. C. (2023). An Effective Approach for Image Denoising Using Wavelet Transform Involving Deep Learning Techniques. *2023 4th International Conference on Smart Electronics and Communication (ICOSEC)*, 1381–1386.

Shutaywi, M., & Kachouie, N. N. (2021). Silhouette Analysis for Performance Evaluation in Machine Learning with Applications to Clustering. *Entropy (Basel, Switzerland)*, *23*(6), 759. Advance online publication. DOI: 10.3390/e23060759 PMID: 34208552

Sibiya, M., & Sumbwanyambe, M. (2019, March 13). A computational procedure for the recognition and classification of maize leaf diseases out of healthy leaves using convolutional neural networks. *Agricultural Engineering*, *1*(1), 119–131. DOI: 10.3390/agriengineering1010009

Silalertruksa, T., & Gheewala, S. H. (2020). Competitive use of sugarcane for food, fuel, and biochemical through the environmental and economic factors. *The International Journal of Life Cycle Assessment*, *25*(7), 1343–1355. DOI: 10.1007/s11367-019-01664-0

Simonyan, K., & Zisserman, A. (2014). Very deep convolutional networks for large-scale image recognition. *arXiv preprint arXiv:1409.1556*.

Singh, V., Sathio, A. A., Anwar, S., Vavekanand, R., & Danish, R. (2024). A Medical Imaging Approach for Recognising Mitral Regurg-itation Through Machine Learning Methods in Cardiac Imaging.

Singh, A., & Kumar, R. (2022). 3D image processing for dental implant simulations. *Clinical Oral Implants Research*, *33*(11), 1090–1101.

Singh, A., Lall, B., Panigrahi, B., Agrawal, A., Agrawal, A., Thangakunam, B., & Christopher, D. J. (2022). Semantic segmentation of bone structures in chest X-rays including unhealthy radiographs: A robust and accurate approach. *International Journal of Medical Informatics*, *165*, 104831. DOI: 10.1016/j.ijmedinf.2022.104831 PMID: 35870303

Singh, N., Mohapatra, A. G., & Kanungo, G. (2011). Breast cancer mass detection in mammograms using K-means and fuzzy C-means clustering. *International Journal of Computer Applications*, *22*(2), 15–21. DOI: 10.5120/2557-3507

Singh, S., Gupta, I., Gupta, S., Koundal, D., Aljahdali, S., Mahajan, S., & Pandit, A. K. (2022, April 1). Deep learning based automated detection of diseases from Apple leaf images. *Computers, Materials & Continua*, *71*(1), 1849–1866. Advance online publication. DOI: 10.32604/cmc.2022.021875

Singh, V., Sathio, A. A., Anwar, S., Vavekanand, R., & Danish, R. (2024). A Medical Imaging Approach for Recognising Mitral Regurgi-tation Through Machine Learning Methods in Cardiac Imaging.

Sinha, D., & El-Sharkawy, M. (2019). Thin MobileNet: An Enhanced MobileNet Architecture. *2019 IEEE 10th Annual Ubiquitous Computing, Electronics & Mobile Communication Conference (UEMCON)*, 280–285. DOI: 10.1109/UEMCON47517.2019.8993089

Sinha, A.. (2021). Transfer learning for chest X-ray classification: A systematic review. *Artificial Intelligence in Medicine*, *113*, 101016. DOI: 10.1016/j.artmed.2021.101016

Skourt, B. A., El Hassani, A., & Majda, A. (2018). Lung CT image segmentation using deep neural networks. *Procedia Computer Science*, *127*, 109–113. DOI: 10.1016/j.procs.2018.01.104

Smith, J., & Roberts, E. (2023). AI-driven diagnostic tools in periodontal health. *Periodontology 2000*, *93*(1), 15–26.

Sobbahi Rayan Al. Tekli Joe. Signal Processing: Image Communication. 2022. Comparing deep learning models for low-light natural scene image enhancement and their impact on object detection and classification: overview, empirical evaluation, and challenges; p. 116848.

SONG. K.-C., YAN, Y.-H., CHEN, W.-H., & ZHANG, X. (2013). Research and Perspective on Local Binary Pattern. *Acta Automatica Sinica, 39*(6), 730–744. https://doi.org/https://doi.org/10.1016/S1874-1029(13)60051-8

Soni, A., Sethy, P. K., Dewangan, A. K., Nanthaamornphong, A., Behera, S. K., & Devi, B. (2024). Enhancing oral squamous cell carcinoma detection: A novel approach using improved EfficientNet architecture. *BMC Oral Health*, *24*(1), 601. DOI: 10.1186/s12903-024-04307-5 PMID: 38783295

Souza, F.. (2021). Durability prediction for prosthetics with ML models. *The Journal of Prosthetic Dentistry*, *125*(4), 561–570. PMID: 34294423

Spathis, D., & Vlamos, P. (2019). Diagnosing asthma and chronic obstructive pulmonary disease with machine learning. *Health Informatics Journal*, *25*(3), 811–827. DOI: 10.1177/1460458217723169 PMID: 28820010

Srivastava, M., & Meena, J. (2024). Plant leaf disease detection and classification using modified transfer learning models. *Multimedia Tools and Applications*, *83*(13), 38411–38441. DOI: 10.1007/s11042-023-16929-y

Srivastava, N.. (2014). Dropout: A simple way to prevent neural networks from overfitting. *Journal of Machine Learning Research*, *15*(1), 1929–1958.

Stacke, E., Eilertsen, G., Unger, J., & Lundstrom, C. (2021). Unger & Lundstrom Measuring Domain Shift for Deep Learning in Histopathology. *IEEE Journal of Biomedical and Health Informatics*, *25*(2), 325–336. DOI: 10.1109/JBHI.2020.3032060

Staudemeyer, R. C., & Morris, E. R. (2019). *Understanding LSTM — a tutorial into Long Short-Term Memory Recurrent Neural Networks*. http://arxiv.org/abs/1909.09586

Steinley, D. (2006). K-means clustering: A half-century synthesis. *British Journal of Mathematical & Statistical Psychology*, *59*(1), 1–34. DOI: 10.1348/000711005X48266 PMID: 16709277

Steve, L. (2018, February 9). Facial Recognition Is Accurate, if You're a White Guy. *The New York Times*.

Sugiharti, E., Firmansyah, S., & Devi, F. R. (2017). Predictive evaluation of performance of computer science students of unnes using data mining based on naÏve bayes classifier (NBC) algorithm. *Journal of Theoretical and Applied Information Technology*, *95*(4), 902.

Sulaman, M., ullah Bazai, S., Akram, M., Akram khan, M., Ullah Bazai, S., Sulaman, M., Akram, M., & Think Tank Network, B. (n.d.). Title: Deep Learning based Smart Navigational Stick for Blind People Affiliation (s): 1 IT Administrator Balochistan Think Tank Network (BTTN) Quetta History: Citation: Deep Learning-Based Smart Navigational Stick for Blind and Visually Impaired People. *UMT Artif. Intell. Rev*, *2*(2), 0–00.

Sultana, J., Sultana, N., Yadav, K., & AlFayez, F. (2018, April). Prediction of sentiment analysis on educational data based on deep learning approach. In *2018 21st Saudi Computer Society National Computer Conference (NCC)* (pp. 1-5). IEEE. DOI: 10.1109/NCG.2018.8593108

Sultanabanu (2023b). Integrating IoT and Mechanical Systems in Mechanical Engineering Applications, *Journal of Mechanical Robotics*, 8(3), 1-6.

Sultanabanu (2023c). IoT Changing the Electronics Manufacturing Industry, *Journal of Analog and Digital Communications*, 8(3), 13-17.

Sultanabanu (2023d). IoT in the Electric Power Industry, *Journal of Controller and Converters,* 8(3), 1-7.

Sultanabanu (2023e). Review of Integrated Battery Charger (IBC) for Electric Vehicles (EV), *Journal of Advances in Electrical Devices*, 8(3), 1-11.

Sultanabanu (2023f). ML in the Electronics Manufacturing Industry, *Journal of Switching Hub*, 8(3), 9-13

Sultanabanu (2023g). IoT in Electrical Vehicle: A Study, *Journal of Control and Instrumentation Engineering*, 9(3), 15-21.

Sultanabanu (2023i). Electronics with Artificial Intelligence Creating a Smarter Future: A Review, *Journal of Communication Engineering and Its Innovations,* 9(3), 38-42.

Sultanabanu (2023j). Dispersion Compensation in Optical Fiber: A Review, *Journal of Telecommunication Study*, 8(3), 14-19.

Sultanabanu (2023k). IoT Based Arduino-Powered Weather Monitoring System, *Journal of Telecommunication Study*, 8(3), 25-31.

Sultanabanu (2023l). Arduino Based Weather Monitoring System, *Journal of Switching Hub*, 8(3), 24-29.

Sultanabanu, (2023n). Nanomedicine as a Potential Therapeutic Approach to COVID-19. *International Journal of Applied Nanotechnology*. 9(2): 27–35p.

Sultanabanu, (2024). IoT-based Alcohol Detector using Blynk, *Journal of Electronics Design and Technology*, 1(1), 10-15.

Sultanabanu, 2024q. Nanotechnology in Healthcare Applications:Study, A. (2024).. . *International Journal of Nanotechnology*, *10*(2), 48–58p.

Sun, X., Bhatti, U. A., Huang, M., & Zhang, Y. (2024). EF-UV: Feature enhanced fusion of U-Net and VIT transformer for brain tumor MRI image segmentation. *International Journal of Biomedical and Health Informatics*.

Sundararajan, K., & Woodard, D. L. (2018). Deep learning for biometrics: A survey. *ACM Computing Surveys*, *51*(3), 1–34. DOI: 10.1145/3190618

Sundqvist, M., Chiquet, J., & Rigaill, G. (2023). Adjusting the adjusted Rand Index. *Computational Statistics*, *38*(1), 327–347. DOI: 10.1007/s00180-022-01230-7

Suneja, M., Beekmann, S., Dhaliwal, G., Miller, A., & Polgreen, P. (2022). Diagnostic delays in infectious diseases. *Diagnosis (Berlin, Germany)*, *9*(3), 332–339. DOI: 10.1515/dx-2021-0092 PMID: 35073468

Sun, L.. (2023). AI-enhanced decision-making tools for treatment planning in oral and maxillofacial surgery. *Journal of Oral and Maxillofacial Surgery*, *81*(7), 982–991.

Szegedy, C., Liu, W., Jia, Y., Sermanet, P., Reed, S., Anguelov, D., & Rabinovich, A. (2015). Going deeper with convolutions. In *Proceedings of the IEEE conference on computer vision and pattern recognition* (pp. 1-9).

Szeliski, R. (2022). *Computer vision: algorithms and applications*. Springer Nature. DOI: 10.1007/978-3-030-34372-9

Tabassum, I., & Bazai, S. U. (2024). Augmenting Multimedia Analysis. *Deep Learning for Multimedia Processing Applications: Volume One: Image Security and Intelligent Systems for Multimedia Processing*, 194.

Tajbakhsh, N., Shin, J. Y., Gurudu, S. R., Hurst, R. T., Kendall, C. B., Gotway, M. B., & Liang, J. (2016). Convolutional neural networks for medical image analysis: Full training or fine tuning? *IEEE Transactions on Medical Imaging*, *35*(5), 1299–1312. DOI: 10.1109/TMI.2016.2535302 PMID: 26978662

Tan, M. (2019). Efficientnet: Rethinking model scaling for convolutional neural networks. *arXiv preprint arXiv:1905.11946*.

Tan, M., & Le, Q. (2019). EfficientNet: Rethinking Model Scaling for Convolutional Neural Networks. In K. Chaudhuri & R. Salakhutdinov (Eds.), *Proceedings of the 36th International Conference on Machine Learning* (Vol. 97, pp. 6105–6114). PMLR. https://proceedings.mlr.press/v97/tan19a.html

Tang, H., Wu, Z., Xu, B., Bhatti, U. A., Yu, M., & Lu, Y. (2025). Research on cross-platform motion control system based on gSOAP. *Proceedings of the 2024 7th International Conference on Pattern Recognition and Artificial Intelligence.*

Tang, H., Zhu, H., Fei, L., Wang, T., Cao, Y., & Xie, C. (2023). Low-Illumination image enhancement based on deep learning techniques: A brief review. *Photonics*, *10*(2), 198. DOI: 10.3390/photonics10020198

Tan, M., & Le, Q. (2020). EfficientNet: Rethinking model scaling for convolutional neural networks. *International Conference on Machine Learning.*

Tareen, S., Bazai, S. U., Ullah, S., Ullah, R., Marjan, S., & Ghafoor, M. I. (2022, December). Phishing and intrusion attacks: An overview of classification mechanisms. In 2022 3rd International Informatics and Software Engineering Conference (IISEC) (pp. 1-5). IEEE

Tareen, S., Bazai, S. U., Ullah, S., Ullah, R., Marjan, S., & Ghafoor, M. I. (2022, December). Phishing and intrusion attacks: An overview of classification mechanisms. In *2022 3rd International Informatics and Software Engineering Conference (IISEC)* (pp. 1-5). IEEE.

Tarek, H., Aly, H., Eisa, S., & Abul-Soud, M. (2022, January 3). Optimized deep learning algorithms for tomato leaf disease detection with hardware deployment. *Electronics (Basel)*, *11*(1), 140. DOI: 10.3390/electronics11010140

Targ, S., Almeida, D., & Lyman, K. (2016). *Resnet in Resnet: Generalizing Residual Architectures.* http://arxiv.org/abs/1603.08029

Tarnowska, K. A., Dispoto, B. C., & Conragan, J. (2021). Explainable AI-based clinical decision support system for hearing disorders. *AMIA Joint Summits on Translational Science Proceedings AMIA Summit on Translational Science*, *2021*, 595. PMID: 34457175

Teledahl, A., Kilhamn, C., Ahl, L. M., & Helenius, O. (2024). Defining and measuring quality in students' mathematical writing: A systematic literature review. *Mathematics Education Research Journal*, •••, 1–20. DOI: 10.1007/s13394-024-00501-4

Tenne, A. (2024). XAI in Medicine: Analysis and Evaluation of XAI Tools and Legal Liability for Neural Networks; A Case Study on Tumor Image Classification.

Thongnim, P., Sreekajon, J., & Pukseng, T. (2024). Enhancing Durian Cultivation Efficiency Through Data-Driven Smart Farming Using Cluster Analysis and Machine Learning. *2024 5th International Conference on Big Data Analytics and Practices (IBDAP)*, 67–72. DOI: 10.1109/IBDAP62940.2024.10689710

Thunold, H. H., Riegler, M. A., Yazidi, A., & Hammer, H. L. (2023). A Deep Diagnostic Framework Using Explainable Artificial Intelligence and Clustering. *Diagnostics 2023, Vol. 13, Page 3413*, *13*(22), 3413. DOI: 10.3390/diagnostics13223413

Tian, C., Fei, L., Zheng, W., Xu, Y., Zuo, W., & Lin, C.-W. (2020). Deep learning on image denoising: An overview. *Neural Networks*, *131*, 251–275. DOI: 10.1016/j.neunet.2020.07.025 PMID: 32829002

Tian, C., Zheng, M., Zuo, W., Zhang, B., Zhang, Y., & Zhang, D. (2023). Multi-stage image denoising with the wavelet transform. *Pattern Recognition*, *134*, 109050. DOI: 10.1016/j.patcog.2022.109050

Tian, F., Xie, H., Song, Y., Hu, S., & Liu, J. (2022). The face inversion effect in deep convolutional neural networks. *Frontiers in Computational Neuroscience*, *16*, 854218. DOI: 10.3389/fncom.2022.854218 PMID: 35615057

Tian, K., Li, J., Zeng, J., Evans, A., & Zhang, L. (2019, October 1). Segmentation of tomato leaf images based on adaptive clustering number of K-means algorithm. *Computers and Electronics in Agriculture*, *165*, 104962. DOI: 10.1016/j.compag.2019.104962

Tiwari, A. K. (2016). Prediction of lung cancer using image processing techniques: A review. *Advanced Computational Intelligence: An International Journal*, *3*(1), 1–9. DOI: 10.5121/acii.2016.3101

Tjoa, E., & Guan, C. (2021). A survey on explainable artificial intelligence (XAI): Toward medical transparent AI applications. *IEEE Transactions on Neural Networks and Learning Systems.* Advance online publication. DOI: 10.1109/TNNLS.2020.3027314

Tokuda, E. K., Comin, C. H., & da F. Costa, L. (2022). Revisiting agglomerative clustering. *Physica A: Statistical Mechanics and Its Applications, 585*, 126433. https://doi.org/https://doi.org/10.1016/j.physa.2021.126433

Trenberth, K. E. (2012). Framing the way to relate climate extremes to climate change. *Climatic Change*, *115*(2), 283–290. DOI: 10.1007/s10584-012-0441-5

Tripathi, M. (2021). Facial image noise classification and denoising using neural network. *Sustainable Engineering and Innovation*, *3*(2), 102–111. DOI: 10.37868/sei.v3i2.id142

Tsuneki, M. (2022). Deep learning models in medical image analysis. Journal of Oral Biosciences, 64(3), 312-320.

Tung, F., & Mori, G. (2018). CLIP-Q: Deep Network Compression Learning by In-parallel Pruning-Quantization. *2018 IEEE/CVF Conference on Computer Vision and Pattern Recognition*, 7873–7882. https://doi.org/DOI: 10.1109/CVPR.2018.00821

Tzeng, E., Hoffman, J., Saenko, K., & Darrell, T. (2017). Adversarial discriminative domain adaptation. *Proceedings of the IEEE Conference on Computer Vision and Pattern Recognition*, 7167-7176.

Ullah, S., Bazai, S. U., Imran, M., Ilyas, Q. M., Mehmood, A., Saleem, M. A., Rafique, M. A., Haider, A., Khan, I., Iqbal, S., Gulzar, Y., & Hameed, K. (2024). Recent developments in authentication schemes used in machine-type communication devices in machine-to-machine communication: Issues and challenges. *Computers, Materials & Continua*, *79*(1), 93–115. DOI: 10.32604/cmc.2024.048796

Unal, Z. (2020). Smart Farming Becomes even Smarter with Deep Learning - A Bibliographical Analysis. *IEEE Access : Practical Innovations, Open Solutions*, *8*, 105587–105609. DOI: 10.1109/ACCESS.2020.3000175

Ünal, Z., & Aktaş, H. (2023). Classification of hazelnut kernels with deep learning. *Postharvest Biology and Technology*, *197*, 112225. https://doi.org/https://doi.org/10.1016/j.postharvbio.2022.112225. DOI: 10.1016/j.postharvbio.2022.112225

Ünal, Z., & İpekçi Çetin, E. (2022). Fuzzy Logic and Deep Learning Integration in Likert Type Data. *Afyon Kocatepe Üniversitesi Fen Ve Mühendislik Bilimleri Dergisi, 22*(1), 112–125. DOI: 10.35414/akufemubid.1019671

Ünal, Z., & Kızıldeniz, T. (2023). Smart agriculture practices in potato production. In Çalişkan, M. E., Bakhsh, A., & Jabran, K. (Eds.), *Potato Production Worldwide* (pp. 317–329). Academic Press., https://doi.org/https://doi.org/10.1016/B978-0-12-822925-5.00010-4 DOI: 10.1016/B978-0-12-822925-5.00010-4

Ünal, Z., Kızıldeniz, T., Özden, M., Aktaş, H., & Karagöz, Ö. (2024). Detection of bruises on red apples using deep learning models. *Scientia Horticulturae, 329*, 113021. https://doi.org/https://doi.org/10.1016/j.scienta.2024.113021. DOI: 10.1016/j.scienta.2024.113021

Ur, M., Shaikh, R., Sathio, A. A., Lakhan, A., Panhwar, A. O., Sahito, M. A., & Kehar, A. (2021). Dynamic Content Enabled Microservice for Business Applications in Distributed Cloudlet Cloud Network. *International Journal of Emerging Trends in Engineering Research.*

Vahida, . (2023). Deep Learning, YOLO and RFID based smart Billing Handcart. *Journal of Communication Engineering & Systems, 13*(1), 1–8.

Vaswani, A., Shard, N., Parmar, N., ... (2017). Attention is all you need. In *Advances in Neural Information Processing Systems* (pp. 5998–6008). https://doi.org/DOI: 10.5555/3295222.3295349

Vavekanand, R., Sathio, A. A., Singh, V., & Anwar, S. (2024). Water4. 0: An Industrial Water Pollution Forecasting Using Machine Learning. *Available at SSRN* 4849924.

Veena, C., Sridevi, M., Liyakat, K. K. S., Saha, B., Reddy, S. R., & Shirisha, N. (2023). *HEECCNB: An Efficient IoT-Cloud Architecture for Secure Patient Data Transmission and Accurate Disease Prediction in Healthcare Systems, 2023 Seventh International Conference on Image Information Processing.* ICIIP., Available at https://ieeexplore.ieee.org/document/10537627, DOI: 10.1109/ICIIP61524.2023.10537627

Venkatapathappa, P., Sultana, A., K S, V., Mansour, R., Chikkanarayanappa, V., & Rangareddy, H. (2024, February 29). K S V, Mansour R, Chikkanarayanappa V, Rangareddy H. Ocular Pathology and Genetics: Transformative Role of Artificial Intelligence (AI) in Anterior Segment Diseases. *Cureus, 16*(2), e55216. DOI: 10.7759/cureus.55216 PMID: 38435218

Vergin, J. J. S., & Vidhyavathi, R. M. (2020). Google arda tool using artificial intelligence in self-optimizing algorithm to prevent diabetic retinopathy and diabetic macular edoema (dme).

Verma, J., Sandhu, A., Popli, R., Kumar, R., Khullar, V., Kansal, I., Sharma, A., Garg, K., Kashyap, N., & Aurangzeb, K. (2023). From slides to insights: Harnessing deep learning for prognostic survival prediction in human colorectal cancer histology. *Open Life Sciences, 18*(1), 20220777. DOI: 10.1515/biol-2022-0777 PMID: 38152577

Verma, T., & Dubey, S. (2020). Impact of color spaces and feature sets in automated plant diseases classifier: A comprehensive review based on rice plant images. *Archives of Computational Methods in Engineering, 27*(5), 1611–1632. DOI: 10.1007/s11831-019-09364-6

Visin, F., Ciccone, M., Romero, A., Kastner, K., Cho, K., Bengio, Y., Matteucci, M., & Courville, A. (2016), "Reseg: A recurrent neural network-based model for semantic segmentation," in *Proceedings of the IEEE Conference on Computer Vision and Pattern Recognition Workshops*, pp. 41–48. DOI: 10.1109/CVPRW.2016.60

Von Glehn De Filippo, V., Do Patrocínio, Z. K. G., & Guimarães, S. J. F. (2015). Hierarchical Combination of Semantic Visual Words for Image Classification and Clustering. *Lecture Notes in Computer Science (Including Subseries Lecture Notes in Artificial Intelligence and Lecture Notes in Bioinformatics), 9423*, 306–313. DOI: 10.1007/978-3-319-25751-8_37

Vo, T. H., Nguyen, N. T. K., Kha, Q. H., & Le, N. Q. K. (2022). On the road to explainable AI in drug-drug interactions prediction: A systematic review. *Computational and Structural Biotechnology Journal, 20*, 2112–2123. DOI: 10.1016/j.csbj.2022.04.021 PMID: 35832629

Vybhavi, G. Y., Sriramya, G., Bharadwaj, V. Y., & Ramesh, G. (2024). Clustering algorithms in data science: Evaluating the time and space complexities of K-means, DBSCAN, and hierarchical methods. *AIP Conference Proceedings, 3101*(1), 050004. DOI: 10.1063/5.0215042

Wadhawan, A., & Kumar, P. (2021). Sign language recognition systems: A decade systematic literature review. *Archives of Computational Methods in Engineering, 28*(3), 785–813. DOI: 10.1007/s11831-019-09384-2

Waibel, A., Hanazawa, T., Hinton, G., Shikano, K., & Lang, K. J. (1989). Phoneme recognition using time-delay neural networks. *IEEE Transactions on Acoustics, Speech, and Signal Processing, 37*(3), 328–339. DOI: 10.1109/29.21701

Wale, A. D., & Dipali, R.. (2019). Smart Agriculture System using IoT. *International Journal of Innovative Research in Technology, 5*(10), 493–497.

Wan Mansor, W. N., Mohd Zaini, N. S., Gengan, G., Abdullah, A. H., Mohd Sha'ari, A. A., Roslan, A. Z., & Abd Rahim, M. H. (2024). Enhancing ergogenic performance and antioxidant benefits of red sugarcane juice through probiotic fermentation. *Discover Food, 4*(1), 32. DOI: 10.1007/s44187-024-00092-w

Wan, G., & Yao, L. (2023). LMFRNet: A Lightweight Convolutional Neural Network Model for Image Analysis. *Electronics (Basel), 13*(1), 129. DOI: 10.3390/electronics13010129

Wang, C., Wu, Z., Xu, Y., Zheng, Y., Luo, Z., Cao, W., & He, J. (2023). Disparities in the global burden of tracheal, bronchus, and lung cancer from 1990 to 2019. *Chinese Medical Journal Pulmonary and Critical Care Medicine, 1*(01), 36–45. DOI: 10.1016/j.pccm.2023.02.001 PMID: 39170872

Wang, F.. (2021). Artificial intelligence applications in early detection of dental diseases: A review. *Artificial Intelligence in Medicine, 113*, 102015.

Wang, J., Sun, K., Cheng, T., Jiang, B., Deng, C., Zhao, Y., Liu, D., Mu, Y., Tan, M., Wang, X., Liu, W., & Xiao, B. (2021). Deep High-Resolution Representation Learning for Visual Recognition. *IEEE Transactions on Pattern Analysis and Machine Intelligence, 43*(10), 3349–3364. DOI: 10.1109/TPAMI.2020.2983686 PMID: 32248092

Wang, J., Wang, Q., & Zhang, T. (2022). Using GANs to enhance precipitation predictions. *Environmental Research Letters*, *17*(7), 075002. DOI: 10.1088/1748-9326/ac65f0

Wang, L. (Ed.). (2005). *Support vector machines: theory and applications* (Vol. 177). Springer Science & Business Media. DOI: 10.1007/b95439

Wang, M., & Deng, W. (2021). Deep face recognition: A survey. *Neurocomputing*, *429*, 215–244. DOI: 10.1016/j.neucom.2020.10.081

Wang, M., & Kumar, S. (2022). Hybrid deep learning models for oral cancer diagnostics. *Head & Neck*, *44*(5), 1152–1162.

Wang, R., Chow, S. S. L., Serafin, R. B., Xie, W., Han, Q., Baraznenok, E., Lan, L., Bishop, K. W., & Liu, J. T. C. (2024). Direct three-dimensional segmentation of prostate glands with nnU-Net. *Journal of Biomedical Optics*, *29*(3). Advance online publication. DOI: 10.1117/1.JBO.29.3.036001 PMID: 38434772

Wang, X., & Yuan, W. (2024). Nuclei-level prior knowledge constrained multiple instance learning for breast histopathology whole slide image classification. *iScience*, *27*(6), 109826. DOI: 10.1016/j.isci.2024.109826 PMID: 38832012

Wang, Y., Rong, Z., & Xiao, P. I. A. U. S. D. L. A. (2019)... *American Journal of Pathology*.

Wang, Y., Zhang, H., & Zhao, C. (2022). Deep learning for lung cancer: A systematic review. *Scientific Reports*, *12*(1), 1–13. DOI: 10.1038/s41598-022-25239-4 PMID: 34992227

Wang, Z., Fang, M., Zhang, J., Tang, L., Zhong, L., Li, H., Cao, R., Zhao, X., Liu, S., Zhang, R., Xie, X., Mai, H., Qiu, S., Tian, J., & Dong, D. (2024). Radiomics and Deep Learning in Nasopharyngeal Carcinoma: A Review. *IEEE Reviews in Biomedical Engineering*, *17*, 118–135. DOI: 10.1109/RBME.2023.3269776 PMID: 37097799

Wang, Z., Liu, S., & Li, P. (2022). Deep learning models in predictive analysis for image-based applications. *Computer Vision and Pattern Recognition*, *34*(2), 172–184.

Wan, H., Wang, H., Scotney, B., & Liu, J. (2019). A Novel Gaussian Mixture Model for Classification. *2019 IEEE International Conference on Systems, Man and Cybernetics (SMC)*, 3298–3303. DOI: 10.1109/SMC.2019.8914215

Wani, M. A., & Afzal, S. (2017). A New Framework for Fine Tuning of Deep Networks. *2017 16th IEEE International Conference on Machine Learning and Applications (ICMLA)*, 359–363. DOI: 10.1109/ICMLA.2017.0-135

Wankhade, S., & Vigneshwari, S. (2023). A novel hybrid deep learning method for early detection of lung cancer using neural networks. *Healthcare Analytics*, *3*, 100195. DOI: 10.1016/j.health.2023.100195

Warfield, S. K., Zou, K. H., & Wells, W. M. (2004). Simultaneous truth and performance level estimation (STAPLE): An algorithm for the validation of image segmentation. *IEEE Transactions on Medical Imaging*, *23*(7), 903–921. DOI: 10.1109/TMI.2004.828354 PMID: 15250643

Wazalwar, S. S., & Shrawankar, U. (2017). Interpretation of sign language into English using NLP techniques. *Journal of Information and Optimization Sciences*, *38*(6), 895–910. DOI: 10.1080/02522667.2017.1372136

Wazarkar, S., & Keshavamurthy, B. N. (2018). A survey on image data analysis through clustering techniques for real world applications. *Journal of Visual Communication and Image Representation*, *55*, 596–626. https://doi.org/https://doi.org/10.1016/j.jvcir.2018.07.009. DOI: 10.1016/j.jvcir.2018.07.009

Wei, R., Garcia, C., El-Sayed, A., Peterson, V., & Mahmood, A. (2020). Variations in Variational Autoencoders - A Comparative Evaluation. *IEEE Access : Practical Innovations, Open Solutions*, *8*, 153651–153670. DOI: 10.1109/ACCESS.2020.3018151

Weiss, K., Khoshgoftaar, T. M., & Wang, D. (2016). A survey of transfer learning. *Journal of Big Data*, *3*(1), 9. DOI: 10.1186/s40537-016-0043-6

Westcott, A. (2019). Texture Analysis and Machine Learning to Predict Pulmonary Ventilation from Thoracic Computed Tomography (Master's thesis, The University of Western Ontario (Canada)).

Wikle, C. K., Datta, A., Hari, B. V., Boone, E. L., Sahoo, I., Kavila, I., Castruccio, S., Simmons, S. J., Burr, W. S., & Chang, W. (2023). An illustration of model agnostic explainability methods applied to environmental data. *Environmetrics*, *34*(1), e2772. DOI: 10.1002/env.2772 PMID: 37200542

Wong, J. L. L. (2004). Rule-Based Data Mining Methods for Classification Problems in Biomedical Domains.

Wu, L.. (2022). Multimodal deep learning for early detection of periodontal disease from X-ray images. *Journal of Periodontology*, *93*(1), 89–97. PMID: 33949680

Wu, Y., Qiao, T., & Xu, M. (2020). YOUNISAND Y ZHENG N "Image Forgery Detection and Localization via a Reliability Fusion Map". *Sensors (Basel)*, *20*(22), 6668. DOI: 10.3390/s20226668 PMID: 33233380

Xiang, Y., & Fox, D. (2017), "Da-rnn: Semantic mapping with data associated recurrent neural networks," arXiv:1703.03098 DOI: 10.15607/RSS.2017.XIII.013

Xie, J.. (2021). Real-time prediction of root canal infection using convolutional neural networks. *International Endodontic Journal*, *54*(9), 1367–1377.

Xu, L.. (2022). Automated detection and staging of oral squamous cell carcinoma using deep learning. *Medical Image Analysis*, *75*, 102292.

Xu, Q. (2024). Incorporating CNN-LSTM and SVM with wavelet transform methods for tourist passenger flow prediction. *Soft Computing*, *28*(3), 2719–2736. DOI: 10.1007/s00500-023-09592-w

Xu, R.. (2021). FedGAN: Federated generative adversarial networks for distributed data synthesis. *IEEE Transactions on Network Science and Engineering*.

Yagi, M., Yamanouchi, K., Fujita, N., Funao, H., & Ebata, S. (2023, June 21). Revolutionizing Spinal Care: Current Applications and Future Directions of Artificial Intelligence and Machine Learning. *Journal of Clinical Medicine*, *12*(13), 4188. DOI: 10.3390/jcm12134188 PMID: 37445222

Yang, C.-C., Prasher, S. O., Enright, P., Madramootoo, C., Burgess, M., Goel, P. K., & Callum, I. (2003). Application of decision tree technology for image classification using remote sensing data. *Agricultural Systems*, *76*(3), 1101–1117. https://doi.org/https://doi.org/10.1016/S0308-521X(02)00051-3. DOI: 10.1016/S0308-521X(02)00051-3

Yang, C., Guan, X., Xu, Q., Xing, W., Chen, X., Chen, J., & Jia, P. (2024). How can SHAP (SHapley Additive exPlanations) interpretations improve deep learning based urban cellular automata model? *Computers, Environment and Urban Systems*, *111*, 102133. DOI: 10.1016/j.compenvurbsys.2024.102133

Yang, K., Yu, Z., Wen, X., Cao, W., Chen, C. L. P., Wong, H.-S., & You, J. (2020). Hybrid Classifier Ensemble for Imbalanced Data. *IEEE Transactions on Neural Networks and Learning Systems*, *31*(4), 1387–1400. DOI: 10.1109/TNNLS.2019.2920246 PMID: 31265410

Yang, L., He, J., Fu, Y., & Luo, Z. (2023). Federated Learning for Medical Imaging Segmentation via Dynamic Aggregation on Non-IID Data Silos. *Electronics (Basel)*, *12*(7), 1687. DOI: 10.3390/electronics12071687

Yang, M., Liu, S., Hao, T., Ma, C., Chen, H., Li, Y., Wu, C., Xie, J., Qiu, H., Li, J., Yang, Y., & Liu, C. (2024). Development and validation of a deep interpretable network for continuous acute kidney injury prediction in critically ill patients. *Artificial Intelligence in Medicine*, *149*, 102785. DOI: 10.1016/j.artmed.2024.102785 PMID: 38462285

Yang, R.. (2022). Predictive analysis of treatment success for dental prosthetics with machine learning. *The Journal of Prosthetic Dentistry*, *128*(1), 29–36.

Yang, , Wu, X., Hao, J., Liu, T., Xie, L., Liu, P., & Li, J. (2023). Deep Learning Methods for Wood Composites Failure Predication. *Polymers*, *15*(2), 295. DOI: 10.3390/polym15020295 PMID: 36679176

Yan, R., Shang, Z., Xu, H., Wen, J., Zhao, Z., Chen, X., & Gao, R. X. (2023). Wavelet transform for rotary machine fault diagnosis: 10 years revisited. *Mechanical Systems and Signal Processing*, *200*, 110545. DOI: 10.1016/j.ymssp.2023.110545

Yao, H., Liu, M., Li, D., & Xu, W. (2021). RNN-based methods for image time series prediction. *Journal of Computational Science*, *50*, 101283.

Yao, Y., Zhang, Y., & Li, S. (2021). The impact of data quality on deep learning model performance: A systematic review. *Journal of Systems and Software*, *176*, 110926.

Yaqub, , Jinchao, F., Arshid, K., Ahmed, S., Zhang, W., Nawaz, M. Z., & Mahmood, T. (2022). Deep Learning-Based Image Reconstruction for Different Medical Imaging Modalities. *Computational and Mathematical Methods in Medicine*, *2022*, 1–18. DOI: 10.1155/2022/8750648 PMID: 35756423

Yeung, H. W. F., Zhou, M., Chung, Y. Y., Moule, G., Thompson, W., Ouyang, W., Cai, W., & Bennamoun, M. (2022). Deep-learning-based solution for data deficient satellite image segmentation. *Expert Systems with Applications*, *191*, 116210. DOI: 10.1016/j.eswa.2021.116210

Yildiz, , Arslan, A. T., Yildiz Tas, A., Acer, A. F., Demir, S., Sahin, A., & Erol Barkana, D. (2021). Generative Adversarial Network Based Automatic Segmentation of Corneal Subbasal Nerves on In Vivo Confocal Microscopy Images. *Translational Vision Science & Technology*, *10*(6), 33. DOI: 10.1167/tvst.10.6.33 PMID: 34038501

Yosinski, J., ... (2014). How transferable are features in deep neural networks? In *Advances in Neural Information Processing Systems* (Vol. 27, pp. 3320-3328).

Yosinski, J., Clune, J., & Nguyen, A.. (2014). How transferable are features in deep neural networks? *Advances in Neural Information Processing Systems*, •••, 3320–3328.

You, N., Han, L., Zhu, D., & Song, W. (2023). Research on image denoising in edge detection based on wavelet transform. *Applied Sciences (Basel, Switzerland)*, *13*(3), 1837. DOI: 10.3390/app13031837

Yousefirizi, F., Pierre Decazes, , Amyar, A., Ruan, S., Saboury, B., & Rahmim, A. (2022). AI-Based Detection, Classification and Prediction/Prognosis in Medical Imaging: Towards Radiophenomics. *PET Clinics*, *17*(1), 183–212. DOI: 10.1016/j.cpet.2021.09.010 PMID: 34809866

Yu, D.. (2022). A comparative analysis of ML algorithms for detection of dental implant failures. *Journal of Oral Rehabilitation*, *49*(8), 901–908.

Yu, H.. (2022). LSTM-based predictive modeling of medical images: A case study in pulmonary nodule detection. *Journal of Biomedical Informatics*, *125*, 103971. DOI: 10.1016/j.jbi.2021.103971

Yu, H., Wu, S., & Liu, Q. (2021). A hybrid deep learning model for temperature prediction using time series data. *Applied Sciences (Basel, Switzerland)*, *11*(3), 1104. DOI: 10.3390/app11031104

Yun, Y., Yu, Q., Yang, Z., An, X., Li, D., Huang, J., Zheng, D., Feng, Q., & Ma, D. (2024). Research on identification method of peanut pests and diseases based on lightweight LSCDNet model. *Phytopathology*, *114*(9), 2162–2175. DOI: 10.1094/PHYTO-01-24-0013-R PMID: 38810273

Yu, S., & Príncipe, J. C. (2019). Understanding autoencoders with information theoretic concepts. *Neural Networks*, *117*, 104–123. https://doi.org/https://doi.org/10.1016/j.neunet.2019.05.003. DOI: 10.1016/j.neunet.2019.05.003 PMID: 31132606

Yu, Y. (2019). X. S. C. H. J. Z. (2019). A Review of Recurrent Neural Networks: LSTM Cells and Network Architectures. *Neural Computation*, •••, 31.

Yu, Z.. (2023). Hybrid deep learning models for automatic oral cancer staging. *Oral Diseases*, *29*(3), 408–418. PMID: 34614259

Zafar, M. R., & Khan, N. (2021). Deterministic local interpretable model-agnostic explanations for stable explainability. *Machine Learning and Knowledge Extraction*, *3*(3), 525–541. DOI: 10.3390/make3030027

Zahra, M., Al-Taher, A., Alquhaidan, M., Hussain, T., Ismail, I., Raya, I., & Kandeel, M. (2024). The synergy of artificial intelligence and personalized medicine for the enhanced diagnosis, treatment, and prevention of disease. *Drug Metabolism and Personalized Therapy*, *39*(2), 47–58. DOI: 10.1515/dmpt-2024-0003 PMID: 38997240

Zamir, S. W., Arora, A., Khan, S., Hayat, M., Khan, F. S., Yang, M.-H., & Shao, L. (2020) Learning enriched features for real image restoration and enhancement, arXiv preprint arXiv:2003.06792 DOI: 10.1007/978-3-030-58595-2_30

Zamir, A. R.. (2018). Taskonomy: Disentangling task transfer learning. In *Proceedings of the IEEE Conference on Computer Vision and Pattern Recognition* (pp. 3712-3722).

Zeng, Z., Xu, Y., Xie, Z., Tang, W., Wan, J., & Wu, W. (2022). LEARD-Net: Semantic segmentation for large-scale point cloud scene. *International Journal of Applied Earth Observation and Geoinformation*, *112*, 102953. DOI: 10.1016/j.jag.2022.102953

Zeng, Z., Zhang, Y., Tang, H., Bhatti, U. A., Gao, J., & Lu, Y. (2025). A domain knowledge graph construction method based on joint extraction of GlobalPointer. *Proceedings of the 2024 7th International Conference on Pattern Recognition and Artificial Intelligence.*

Zhang, P., & Zhang, X. (2022). Research on Laser Polarization Image Reconstruction Based on Wavelet Transform and Deep Learning. *2022 3rd Information Communication Technologies Conference (ICTC)*, 108–111.

Zhang, Y., ... (2017). Bridging heterogeneous domains via domain-adversarial neural networks. *arXiv preprint arXiv:1709.00774.*

Zhang, C., Chen, L., & Zhang, X. (2021). A survey on scalable deep learning: Methods and applications. *ACM Computing Surveys*, *54*(7), 1–36.

Zhang, C., Iqbal, I., Bhatti, U. A., Liu, J., Awwad, E. M., & Sarhan, N. (2024). ResNet50 in remote sensing and agriculture: Evaluating image captioning performance for high spectral data. *Environmental Earth Sciences*, *83*(23), 1–16. DOI: 10.1007/s12665-024-11950-2

Zhang, H.. (2020). Deep learning for skin lesion classification: A systematic review. *Journal of Medical Systems*, *44*(1), 1–14. DOI: 10.1007/s10916-019-1488-0 PMID: 33236166

Zhang, H., Chen, J., & Liu, Y. (2022). Deep learning for climate modeling: A review. *Earth System Science Data*, *14*(2), 657–677. DOI: 10.5194/essd-14-657-2022

Zhang, H., Zhao, J., & Zhang, J. (2022). Predicting cognitive decline in Alzheimer's disease using deep learning techniques on MRI. *Neurobiology of Aging*, *119*, 1–11. DOI: 10.1016/j.neurobiolaging.2022.06.009

Zhang, J.. (2021). Weather forecasting based on GANs using satellite images. *Remote Sensing*, *13*(16), 3210. DOI: 10.3390/rs13163210

Zhang, J., Fu, R., Wu, Y., & Bhatti, U. A. (2024). Practical consensus of time-varying fuzzy positive multi-agent systems. *AIMS Mathematics*, *9*(11), 31119–31141. DOI: 10.3934/math.20241500

Zhang, K., Guo, Y., Wang, X., Yuan, J., & Ding, Q. (2019). Multiple Feature Reweight DenseNet for Image Classification. *IEEE Access : Practical Innovations, Open Solutions*, *7*, 9872–9880. DOI: 10.1109/ACCESS.2018.2890127

Zhang, K., Sun, M., Han, T. X., Yuan, X., Guo, L., & Liu, T. (2018). Residual Networks of Residual Networks: Multilevel Residual Networks. *IEEE Transactions on Circuits and Systems for Video Technology*, *28*(6), 1303–1314. DOI: 10.1109/TCSVT.2017.2654543

Zhang, K., Zuo, W., Chen, Y., Meng, D., & Zhang, L. (2017). Beyond a gaussian denoiser: Residual learning of deep cnn for image denoising. *IEEE Transactions on Image Processing*, *26*(7), 3142–3155. DOI: 10.1109/TIP.2017.2662206 PMID: 28166495

Zhang, S., Wang, Q., Zhang, B., Liang, Z., Zhang, L., Li, L., Huang, G., Zhang, Z., Feng, B., & Yu, T. (2023). Cauchy non-convex sparse feature selection method for the high-dimensional small-sample problem in motor imagery EEG decoding. *Frontiers in Neuroscience*, *17*, 1292724. DOI: 10.3389/fnins.2023.1292724 PMID: 38027478

Zhang, T.. (2021). Deep learning for the diagnosis of dental diseases using clinical images. *The Journal of the American Dental Association*, *152*(4), 238–245.

Zhang, X., & Liu, H. (2022). Virtual surgery planning in maxillofacial procedures. *Journal of Stomatology, Oral and Maxillofacial Surgery*, *123*(2), e300–e308.

Zhang, X., Xu, Z., & Wang, J. (2022). A hybrid deep learning model for weather forecasting based on CNN and LSTM. *Remote Sensing*, *14*(4), 789. DOI: 10.3390/rs14040789

Zhang, X., Zheng, Y., & Qiu, Z. (2021). Estimating methane emissions using deep learning from satellite data. *Environmental Science & Technology*, *55*(19), 13029–13037. DOI: 10.1021/acs.est.1c03654

Zhang, Y.. (2022). 3D convolutional neural networks for dental implant placement guidance. *Journal of Dental Research*, *101*(5), 459–468.

Zhang, Y., Wang, M., Zhao, D., Liu, C., & Liu, Z. (2023). Early weed identification based on deep learning: A review. *Smart Agricultural Technology*, *3*, 100123. DOI. 10.1016/j.atech 2022.100123

Zhang, Y., Ye, F., Chen, L., Xu, F., Chen, X., Wu, H., Cao, M., Li, Y., Wang, Y., & Huang, X. (2023). Children's dental panoramic radiographs dataset for caries segmentation and dental disease detection. *Scientific Data*, *10*(1), 380. DOI: 10.1038/s41597-023-02237-5 PMID: 37316638

Zhao, Y.. (2023). ML algorithms for predicting success in orthodontic treatments: A case study. *Journal of Orthodontics*, *50*(1), 21–32.

Zheng, M., Xu, J., Shen, Y., Tian, C., Li, J., Fei, L., Zong, M., & Liu, X. (2022). Attention-based CNNs for Image Classification: A Survey. *Journal of Physics: Conference Series*, *2171*(1), 012068. Advance online publication. DOI: 10.1088/1742-6596/2171/1/012068

Zheng, S., Lu, J., Zhao, H., Zhu, X., Luo, Z., Wang, Y., Fu, Y., Feng, J., Xiang, T., & Torr, P. H.. (2021), Rethinking semantic segmentation from a sequence-to-sequence perspective with transformers. In *Proceedings of the IEEE/CVF Conference on Computer Vision and Pattern Recognition*, Nashville, TN, USA, pp. 6881–6890. DOI: 10.1109/CVPR46437.2021.00681

Zhou, S. K., Greenspan, H., & Shen, D. (Eds.). (2023). *Deep learning for medical image analysis*. Academic Press.

Zhou, X., Zhao, C., Sun, J., Cheng, J., & Xu, M. (2024). Determination of lead content in oilseed rape leaves in silicon-free and silicon environments based on deep transfer learning and fluorescence hyperspectral imaging. *Spectrochimica Acta. Part A: Molecular and Biomolecular Spectroscopy*, *311*, 123991. DOI: 10.1016/j.saa.2024.123991 PMID: 38330763

Zhou, X., Zhou, H., Wen, G., Huang, X., Lei, Z., Zhang, Z., & Chen, X. (2022). A hybrid denoising model using deep learning and sparse representation with application in bearing weak fault diagnosis. *Measurement*, *189*, 110633. DOI: 10.1016/j.measurement.2021.110633

Zhou, Y., Wang, H., & Sun, Y. (2022). The role of data quality in deep learning applications in meteorology. *Atmosphere*, *13*(2), 295. DOI: 10.3390/atmos13020295

Zhou, Y., Zhu, S., & Shen, S. (2022). Weather prediction using satellite imagery: A deep learning approach. *Remote Sensing*, *14*(12), 2844.

Zhou, Z.. (2022). Deep learning for occlusal analysis in orthodontics: A systematic review. *Journal of Clinical Orthodontics*, *56*(6), 394–402.

Zhou, Z., Siddiquee, M. M. R., Tajbakhsh, N., & Liang, J. (2018). UNet++: A nested U-Net architecture for medical image segmentation. In *Deep Learning in Medical Image Analysis and Multimodal Learning for Clinical Decision Support* (pp. 3–11). Springer. DOI: 10.1007/978-3-030-00889-5_1

Zhu, J. Y.. (2017). Unpaired image-to-image translation using cycle-consistent adversarial networks. *Proceedings of the IEEE International Conference on Computer Vision*, 2223-2232. DOI: 10.1109/ICCV.2017.244

Zhu, X., Sun, S., Lin, L., Wu, Y., & Ma, X. (2024). Transformer-based approaches for neuroimaging: An in-depth review of their role in classification and regression tasks. *Reviews in the Neurosciences*. Advance online publication. DOI: 10.1515/revneuro-2024-0088 PMID: 39333087

Zhu, Y., & Newsam, S. (2017). DenseNet for dense flow. *2017 IEEE International Conference on Image Processing (ICIP)*. DOI: 10.1109/ICIP.2017.8296389

About the Contributors

Uzair Aslam Bhatti was born in 1986. He received the Ph.D. degree in information and communication engineering, Hainan University, Haikou, Hainan, in 2019. He is pursuing the Postdoctoral degree in implementing Clifford algebra algorithms in analyzing the geospatial data using artificial intelligence (AI) with Nanjing Normal University, Nanjing, China. His areas of specialty include AI, machine learning, and image processing.

Muhammad Aamir is an Associate Professor in the Department of Computer Science at Huanggang Normal University, China. He has several years of research experience and has been widely published. M. Aamir has served as a reviewer for many prestigious journals and also served as an organizing member of many international conferences. His research spans multiple areas, including pattern recognition, computer vision, image processing, deep learning, fractional calculus, and organization behavior.

Yonis Gulzar is an Associate Professor in the Department of Management Information Systems at King Faisal University, Saudi Arabia. He holds a Ph.D. in Computer Science from the International Islamic University Malaysia. His research focuses on Artificial Intelligence, Deep Learning, Database Systems, and their applications in healthcare and agriculture, with over 100 publications. He has led funded research projects in Saudi Arabia and Malaysia and actively contributes to editorial boards and academic committees.

Sibghat Ullah received the B.S.C.S. degree from the University of Peshawar, and the master's degree in electronics and communication engineering from the Beijing University of Posts and Telecommunications, Beijing, China, where he is currently pursuing the Ph.D. degree with the State key Laboratory of Information Photonics and Optical Communications. His research interests include coherent optical communications, optical multicarrier/frequency comb generation, wavelength division multiplexed passive optical networks, and long reach PON

***

A. Sakthivel, BE, ME.,Ph.D is a Professor of Computer Science and Engineering in KGiSL Institute of Technology, Coimbatore 2023 onwards. He is a life member of various professional society such as ISTE, CSI and ACCS and acted as reviewer of various reputed journals and also subject experts for TCS icon and academic intuitions. He has 25 Year experience in Academic and Research and published 21 reputed indexed International Journals, 2 Patents, 4 Book chapters and 11 Conferences. He is also a supervisor under the department of CSE, KGiSL Institute of Technology affiliated to Anna University. His main research focuses on cryptography and its applications.

Shafique Ahmed Awan is an associate professor at Faculty CS&IT, BBSU Karachi, a Highly creative Faculty member and IT Administrator with 15 years of experience delivering practical education in the areas of Computer Science, IT, and artificial Intelligence, Machine Learning, Software and expert in Medical imaging. Highly skilled in integrating a multi-dimensional, interdisciplinary, and multicultural curriculum that links the computer, human, technology, and social movements.

Anwar Ali Sathio is a PhD scholar and Senior Faculty member at the Faculty of CS&IT, Benazir Bhutto Shaheed University, Karachi, Pakistan. Since joining the university in 2014, he has significantly contributed to academia and research. He is currently pursuing his PhD as a Research Scholar in Computer Science at Sindh Madarssatul Islam University (SMIU) in Karachi, Pakistan. He has focused his research on cutting-edge topics in computing science and has published over ten high-quality research studies, including conference papers, book chapters, and journal articles. His work is featured in Scopus-indexed publications, IEEE conferences, and HEC-Pakistan-recognized national and international journals. His research expertise spans several critical areas, including Scheduling in Fog-Cloud Computing, with applications in IoT and in Machine Learning Algorithms. He is also deeply involved in research on Blockchain Technology, Cloud Computing, Data Warehousing, and Information Security.

Sameer Ali is a cyber security professional deeply committed to fortifying digital landscapes. With a robust academic foundation and hands-on experience in SDN security, cryptography, and threat intelligence, Sameer has honed his expertise in safeguarding against evolving cyber threats. His journey spans academia, teaching, and extensive research roles in institutions across Pakistan, Australia, Malaysia, Singapore and China. A Microsoft & Oracle certified expert, he specialises in analysing security breaches, conducting forensic analysis, and fortifying systems. His collaborative spirit fosters a dynamic environment for knowledge-sharing and innovation. As an academic and researcher, he thrives on the fusion of theoretical knowledge and practical application to drive impactful cyber security solutions.

Sibghat Ullah Bazai received his Ph.D. in Information Technology with a specialization in Cyber Security from Massey University in Auckland, New Zealand. He is a recipient of the HEC HRDI-UESTP Faculty Ph.D. scholarship. Currently, he serves as an Assistant Professor in the Department of Computer Engineering at the Faculty of Information and Communication Technology, Balochistan University of Information Technology, Engineering, and Management Sciences (BUITEMS). His research interests encompass the application of cyber security and privacy in Computer-Aided diagnosis, disease identification using deep learning, local language sentiment corpus design, and smart city planning. He also serves as a guest editor and reviewer for special issues in journals such as MDPI, Hindawi, CMC, Plosone, Frontier, among others.

Samina Ismail is a systems and machine learning engineer with a BS in Computer Science from BUITEMS and a masters in Systems Engineering from NUST, Islamabad. She currently is working at Rapidev as a Systems Engineer focused on AI systems. Her research areas include deep learning, computer vision and Large Language Models.

Vishal Jain is presently working as Professor at Department of Computer Science and Engineering, School of Engineering and Technology, Sharda University, Greater Noida, U. P. India. Before that, he has worked for several years as an Associate Professor at Bharati Vidyapeeth's Institute of Computer

Applications and Management (BVICAM), New Delhi. He has more than 14 years of experience in the academics. He obtained Ph.D (CSE), M.Tech (CSE), MBA (HR), MCA, MCP and CCNA. He has authored more than 90 research papers in reputed conferences and journals, including Web of Science and Scopus. He has authored and edited more than 30 books with various reputed publishers, including Elsevier, Springer, Apple Academic Press, CRC, Taylor and Francis Group, Scrivener, Wiley, Emerald, NOVA Science and IGI-Global. His research areas include information retrieval, semantic web, ontology engineering, data mining, ad hoc networks, and sensor networks. He received a Young Active Member Award for the year 2012–13 from the Computer Society of India, Best Faculty Award for the year 2017 and Best Researcher Award for the year 2019 from BVICAM, New Delhi.

K. Kavitha received her Bachelor's degree in Electronics and Communication Engineering from Madurai Kamaraj University, Madurai, India and her Master's degree in Microwave & Optical Engineering from Madurai Kamaraj University, Madurai, India in She completed her doctoral degree at Anna University, Chennai, specializing in Hyperspectral Image Classification. Currently, she holds the position of Professor and Head in the Department of Electronics and Communication Engineering at Velammal College of Engineering and Technology in Madurai, Tamil Nadu. Her career spans over 23 years, during which she has made significant contributions in the realms of teaching and research. Her research interests encompass diverse areas, including Antenna Design, Hyperspectral Image Classification and Optical System Design. She has published and presented over 100 research articles in renowned international journals and international and national conferences. Presently, she is supervising the research works of ten Ph.D. scholars in various areas of her expertise. In recognition of her outstanding contributions to education, Dr.K.Kavitha was honored with Dr.A.P.K Abdul Kalam Teachers Excellence Award.

Chetna Kaushal, PhD, is working as an Assistant Professor in Chitkara University, Punjab, India. Her areas of expertise are machine learning, soft computing, pattern recognition, image processing, and artificial intelligence. She has around 10 years of experience in research, training, and academics. She has published 50 research papers in various international and national journals as well as books, and conference papers. She has filed more than 50 patents, out of which 20 have been granted to her name. She is a reviewer for many prestigious journals. Dr. Kaushal is an exceptionally motivated and talented researcher and academician deeply dedicated to advancing human health and well-being through pioneering scientific investigations. Her remarkable achievements thus far are a testament to her capabilities, and her potential for making significant future contributions to her field is undeniably bright. She has a PhD in CSE from Chitkara University, Punjab, an MTech in CSE from DAV University, Punjab, and a BTech in IT from Punjab Technical University.

Kazi Kutubuddin Sayyad Liyakat has completed his B.E., M.E., and Ph.D. in E&TC Engineering and is nowadays working as a Professor & Head of Department, E&TC Engineering Department and was Dean R&D. He is Post-Doctoral Fellow working on IoT in Healthcare Applications. His area of Interest is IoT, IoRT, IoBT, AI, ML, and AIIoT. He has published more than 160+ papers, including Book chapters with various renowned publishers like IGI Global, CRC, NOVA publishers. Also he had received various 41 Patents from Indian Patent House (Utility, Design and Copyright), UK Design Grant Patents, South African Design Grant Patents and Canadian Copyright Patents. He received funds for various projects on IoT applications. He worked as a Reviewer for Scopus Conferences and Journal and for IGI Global. Also, he work as Editorial Board Member for 6 Journals. He got 2 Best

Researcher Awards, 1 Best Faculty Award and an Appreciation Letter from MoE's Innovation Cell, Government of India.

Kamlesh Kumar received his PhD in Computer Science and Technology from University of Electronic Science & Technology of China (UESTC) in 2016. He has more than 10 years of teaching experience in various academic institutes. He has 20 research papers to his credit presented in various national/international conferences and published in HEC recognized journals. He has also been honored wiDr. Kamlesh received his PhD in Computer Science and Technology from University of Electronic Science & Technology of China (UESTC) in 2016. He has more than 10 years of teaching experience in various academic institutes. He has 20 research papers to his credit presented in various national/ international conferences and published in HEC recognized journals. He has also been honored with the award for Best Academic Research by UESTC in 2015. His research interests include Image Processing, Computer Vision, Machine Learning, Knowledge Discovery and Data Mining, and Content Based Image Retrieval System.th the award for Best Academic Research by UESTC in 2015. His research interests include Image Processing, Computer Vision, Machine Learning, Knowledge Discovery and Data Mining, and Content Based Image Retrieval System.

T. Aarthi is working as an Assistant Professor in the Department of Computer Science and Engineering at KGISL Institute of Technology, has about 5 years of teaching experience. She received her B.E degree in Computer Science and Engineering at Sri Krishna college of Technology, Coimbatore, M.E. degree in Computer Science and Engineering at Sri Ramakrishna Engineering College, Coimbatore. She has published around 18 research articles in various national and international journals, 1 Book chapter and 8 Conferences. Her main research focuses on machine learning in health care sector.

Abdullah Raza Lakhan has the following research interests: Distributed Computing, Artificial Intelligence and Algorithms, Sensors & Ad-hoc Networks, Blockchain Internet of Things (IoT) Data Security Optimisation Algorithms Smart Cities Applications Intelligent Systems.

M. Murali is currently working as Professor, Department of Computing Technologies, SRM Institute of Science and Technology, Kattankulathur 603203. TamilNadu, India. He Completed his M.Tech degree from Manonmaniam Sundaranar University, 2004, further he completed Ph.D degree from SRM University, December 2013. His area of research interests are computer vision, machine learning, NLP.

Muhammad Malook is Multifaceted, resourceful academic professional with more than 20 years of diversified industry, academia, research, and administrative experience at renowned national and multinational institutes/organizations. Served as a team lead in one of the largest IT and Telecom company i.e. Etisalat UAE, and played a major role in planning, deployment, execution, commissioning and management of large-scale IT projects in Pakistan. Presently serving as a Professor (Computer Science) at a public sector university in Karachi, Pakistan. As a researcher, have contributed (published and presented) several good quality research papers in well-reputed journals/international conferences, published one Book and few Book Chapters. Actively involved in supervising under-graduate, graduate and Postgraduate research projects.

Archan Mitra is an Assistant Professor at School of Media Studies (SOMS) at Presidency University, Bangalore. He is the author of two book "Cases for Classroom Media and Entertainment Business" and "Multiverse and Media", he also has other several edited books to his credit. He has done his doctorate from Visva-Bharati Santiniketan, West Bengal in the field of "environmental informatics and communication for sustainability". In addition to that he is a certified Science Communicator and Journalism from Indian Science Communication Society (ISCOS), certified Corporate Trainer with Amity Institute of Training and Development, Certified Social Media Network Analyst. He has a strong interest in environmental communication. He was awarded certificate of merit by PRSI, Kolkata Chapter and Medal of Honor by Journalistic Club of Kolkata. He was working as a research assistant with the World Bank's "Environmental Capacity Building in Southeast Asia" project at IIM Kashipur. He was instrumental in launching the World Bank's Green MBA MOOC, he has also assisted in the research project on Uttarakhand disaster mitigation by ICSSR, the leading research on Uttarakhand disaster.

Wajid Hassan Moosa is currently working as a Machine Learning Engineer at Hyly.AI and has previously held roles at Dcube Technologies and the Deep Learning Lab at NUST.

Firas Mahmood Mustafa holds a Ph.D. in Computer Engineering from Mosul University, Iraq. His academic journey began with a B.Sc. in Electrical Engineering (Electronics and Communication), graduating in the top quarter of his class. He earned an M.Sc. in Computer Engineering from Mosul University in 2000. Mustafa joined the Computer Science Department at AlHadba University in 2003 and completed his Ph.D. in 2007. From 2013 to 2017, he was with DPU University, and from 2017 to 2020, he chaired the CCE Department at Nawroz University. An active participant in Erasmus+ and IREX programs, he now teaches at DPU University, shaping future computer engineering professionals.

Dhamayanthi is working as an Assistant Professor in the Department of Computer Science and Engineering at KGISL Institute of Technology, has about 5 years of teaching experience. She received her B.E degree in Computer Science and Engineering at Coimbatore Institute of Technology, Coimbatore, M.E. degree in Computer Science and Engineering at Sri krishna college of engineering and technology, Coimbatore. She has published around 1 research articles in various national and international journals,1 Book chapter and 1 Conferences. Her main research focuses on machine learning in health care.

S. Indhumathi, B.Tech, ME., is an Assistant Professor of Computer Science and Engineering in KGiSL Institute of Technology, Coimbatore from 2023 onwards. She has 7 Years of teaching experience in Academic. She is pursuing her Ph.D. at Anna University, Chennai.She completed her post-graduation in Computer and Communication at Sona College of Technology, Salem, Anna University and completed her under graduation in Information Technology, at Amrita College of Technology, Coimbatore, Anna University. Her main research focuses on Machine Learning and Deep Learning.

S. Raj Kumar received his bachelor's degree in Electronics and Communication Engineering from Anna University, Chennai, and his master's degree in VLSI Design from the same institution. He completed his doctoral degree at Anna University, Chennai, specializing in VLSI device modeling. Currently, he serves as an Assistant Professor in the Department of Electronics Engineering (VLSI Design and Technology) at Velammal College of Engineering and Technology, Madurai, Tamil Nadu, India. His career spans over 11 years, during which he has made significant contributions to teaching and research. His research interests include diverse areas such as modeling and simulation of analog VLSI. He has published over 10 research papers in international journals and presented 20 papers at international conferences. He has also received the award for "Best Outcome in Academic Performance".

Muhammad Sulaman is a dedicated and accomplished professional specializing in Machine learning and software-defined networking. Currently pursuing a Master's degree in Computer Engineering at BUITEMS, his academic journey has been marked by excellence and innovation. Sulaman's research interests span Software-defined networking, Computer Communication, Computer Security, Machine Learning, Deep Learning, Neural Networks, and Reinforcement Learning. His commitment to leveraging technology for social impact is evident in his project titled "Intelligent Obstacle, Human Detection and Navigational Smart Stick Based on Deep Learning for Blind People," which received funding from UNDP. This project showcases his dedication to using cutting-edge technology to address real-world challenges and underscores his proficiency in deep learning methodologies. In addition to his academic pursuits, he has authored a published journal article on deep learning for the visually impaired, demonstrating his ability to apply advanced concepts to solve pressing societal issues. Furthermore, Sulaman has contributed to non-academic publications, showcasing his talent for effectively communicating complex technical concepts to a broader audience.

Sundaramurthi Naveena is a full-time research scholar working with the Department of Electronics Engineering (VLSI Design and Technology) at Velammal College of Engineering and Technology, Madurai. She has received her Master Degree (M.E-CSE) from Thiagarajar College of Engineering and Bachelor Degree (B.E-CSE) from Velammal College of Engineering and Technology. Her areas of interest include Internet of Things, Deep Learning and Data Privacy.

Zeynep Ünal received her BS in Computer Engineering from Selçuk University in 2004, her MS in Econometrics from Akdeniz University in 2015, her MS in Medical Informatics from Akdeniz University in 2017, and her PhD in Econometrics from Akdeniz University in 2019. She is also a Microsoft Certified Trainer. Between 2005 and 2021, she undertook executive roles in software projects in companies such as Intercom Computers, Besay IT Akademisi, Ela Quality Hotel, West Mediterranean Exporters' Association, Niğtaş Company. She currently serves as an associate professor in the Department of Biosystems Engineering at Niğde Ömer Halisdemir University. She is also the founding partner of Çavuşoğlu Spaying Technologies A.Ş., which is located within Niğde Technopark. She has qualified studies in Biosystems Engineering, Artificial Intelligence, and Management Information Systems.

S. Gandhimathi Alias Usha is an Associate Professor in the Department of Electronics and Communication Engineering, Velammal College of Engineering and Technology, Madurai, India. She received her Bachelor degree in Electronics and Communication Engineering from Madurai Kamaraj University in 2001 and her Master's degree from A.C.College of Engineering and Technology, Karaikudi, Tamil Nadu, India in 2009 and received Ph.D degree in Image Processing at Anna University, Chennai in 2019. She is recognized as a Supervisor for guiding Ph.D scholars of Anna University under the faculty of Information and Communication Engineering. She has published over 70 Technical papers in International Journals, International/ National Conferences. Her current research includes Digital Image Processing, Remote Sensing, Computer Vision and Artificial Intelligence. She is a reviewer of

International Journals Elsevier, Springer and Ios Press. She is a Life Member of the Indian Society for Technical Education (ISTE) and the Indian Society of Remote Sensing (ISRS).

Hewa Majeed Zangana is an Iraqi lecturer and assistant professor in computer science and information technology. He holds a Bachelor's degree from Nawroz University, a Master's degree from the International Islamic University Malaysia, and an Honorary Doctorate from the British Accreditation EB - JAS, and currently studying PhD of ITM at DPU. With expertise in network systems and teaching experience, Hewa has taught various subjects and held positions such as Curriculum Division Director and Head of the Computer Science Department at Nawroz University. He has also published research articles in prestigious journals and presented at conferences.

Index

Symbols

A

B

C

D

E

F

G

H

I

J

K

L

M

O

P

R

S

T

U

V

W

www.ingramcontent.com/pod-product-compliance
Lightning Source LLC
LaVergne TN
LVHW080358011026
849161LV00009B/2333
* 9 7 9 8 3 6 9 3 9 0 4 5 0 *